WE MAY DOMINATE THE WORLD

*Celebrating Li Li + Michael —
a power couple who will
dominate the world!*

WE MAY
DOMINATE
THE WORLD

*Ambition, Anxiety, and
the Rise of the American Colossus*

Sean Mirski

SEAN A. MIRSKI

PUBLICAFFAIRS
New York

PublicAffairs
Hachette Book Group
1290 Avenue of the Americas, New York, NY 10104
www.publicaffairsbooks.com
@Public_Affairs

Printed in the United States of America

First Edition: June 2023

Published by PublicAffairs, an imprint of Perseus Books, LLC, a subsidiary of
Hachette Book Group, Inc. The PublicAffairs name and logo is a trademark
of the Hachette Book Group.

The Hachette Speakers Bureau provides a wide range of authors for speaking events.
To find out more, go to hachettespeakersbureau.com or email
HachetteSpeakers@hbgusa.com.

PublicAffairs books may be purchased in bulk for business, educational, or promotional
use. For more information, please contact your local bookseller or the Hachette Book
Group Special Markets Department at special.markets@hbgusa.com.

The publisher is not responsible for websites (or their content) that are not owned by
the publisher.

Book image of First Assistant Secretary of State Francis M. Huntington Wilson courtesy
of the Ursinus College Library Special Collections. Other book images courtesy of the
collections of the U.S. Government, including those of the Library of Congress, the
National Archives and Records Administration, the National Archives at College Park,
and the U.S. Naval History and Heritage Command.

Print book interior design by Jeff Williams.

Library of Congress Cataloging-in-Publication Data has been applied for.

ISBNs: 9781541758438 (hardcover), 9781541758469 (ebook)

LSC-C

Printing 1, 2023

FOR MY MOTHER,
WHO MADE EVERYTHING POSSIBLE.

CONTENTS

viii   Contents

I see no reason why the present administration should not go down as the turning point in our history—as the moment when we won the great prize. I do deeply believe that we may dominate the world, as no nation has dominated it in recent times. . . . For the first time in my life I feel that for us is the earth and the fulness thereof.

—Brook Adams to Henry Cabot Lodge, October 26, 1901[1]

Time was not passing . . . it was turning in a circle.

—Gabriel García Márquez,
One Hundred Years of Solitude[2]

INTRODUCTION

On July 28, 1915, Rear Admiral William B. Caperton stood on the quarterdeck of the USS *Washington* with a pair of binoculars at his eyes and several questions running through his head. A slender man with a weathered face, a silver mustache, and a penchant for decisive action, Caperton was the recently appointed commander of the U.S. Navy Atlantic Fleet's Cruiser Squadron. He had been stationed in Haiti's waters off and on since January, and in that time he had seen many oddities in the war-torn country. Still, this was different. Caperton could not make out exactly what was happening onshore in Port-au-Prince, but through his glasses, it almost appeared as if the Haitians were parading through the capital.[1]

A parade was one of the last things the admiral had been expecting. For a month, Caperton and the *Washington* had been patrolling up north, monitoring a flailing insurrection in Cap-Haïtien as well as the French forces lurking nearby. By late July the situation had settled down, and things were quiet enough that the U.S. chief of naval operations could cable Caperton complacently about the end of the Haitian troubles. But this peace had been rudely interrupted the previous morning when frantic reports had begun reaching Caperton about fighting in Port-au-Prince and—more ominously—approaching European warships. Filled with "a natural apprehension," the admiral had decided to steam south immediately.[2]

Caperton hoped to arrive in Port-au-Prince before widespread violence broke out, and he must have been greatly relieved to see only a seemingly innocuous procession winding through the capital's streets. Little did the admiral know that his arrival, far from stabilizing the volatile situation, had effectively sentenced the president of Haiti to death—and the United States to yet another in a long series of interventions in the affairs of its neighbors.

What was about to happen was one small part of a much, much larger story—a century-long and often violent game of keep-away, in which a rising United States had sought to prevent unstable parts of the Western Hemisphere from falling into the hands of its great-power rivals. Events in Haiti would soon remind the world just how seriously the United States took that objective.

—

LIKE MOST TINPOT dictators, Vilbrun Guillaume Sam was constantly afraid. He had seized Haiti's presidency less than five months earlier, the latest in a line of short-lived revolutionary leaders. In the previous seven years, Haiti had churned through seven presidents—five deposed, one poisoned, and the last blown up in the National Palace with his family. Sam desperately wanted to end this wave of revolutions and bring lasting peace and stability to his troubled country. But in Haiti, heads would roll almost as soon as they were crowned, and the new president knew that it wouldn't be long before it was his turn.[3]

Sure enough, only a few months into his term, another revolution had begun brewing in the north. If Sam had followed his predecessors' example, he would have started packing his bags. But Sam's dreams had long since outpaced his instinct for self-preservation. He declared martial law and took his political opponents in Port-au-Prince hostage, including many members of the traditionally inviolable upper class. "Such a disgrace!" clucked one appalled observer. "Even [the prisoners] could hardly believe that Sam meant it seriously."[4]

Sam was quite serious, and it sealed his doom. On July 27, 1915, an early-morning uprising in the capital forced Sam to flee the presidential palace and seek sanctuary in the French Legation. Earlier, however, Sam had ordered the prison commandant to kill every one of the hostages if revolutionaries ever drove him from the palace. Following Sam's flight, his order was executed with grim efficiency, and the walls of the capital prison were soon stained with the blood of some 167 detainees, including two former presidents.[5]

Such unprecedented barbarity broke every rule of Haiti's informal revolutionary system, and Port-au-Prince exploded in rage. Over the next day, the besieged French Legation beat back several attempts by angry mobs to seize the president cowering inside. With the situation spiraling out of control, the American chargé d'affaires called for help.

"French Minister and British Chargé d'Affairs have telegraphed for ships," he cabled. "Situation very grave." Suitably alarmed, Caperton and the *Washington* set course for Port-au-Prince.[6]

—

CAPERTON'S TIMING COULD hardly have been worse. Black smoke pouring from its stacks, the *Washington* hove into view of the Haitian capital just as a funeral for several of Sam's slain victims was ending. Convinced that the Americans would soon escort Sam to exile, many of the recently bereaved concluded that this was their last opportunity to exact revenge on the murderous president.[7]

Some seventy-five young Haitian men poured over the French Legation's walls and stormed the building. Before anyone could do anything, they had grabbed the terrified President Sam, pulled him out of the house, and dragged him along the long cobblestone driveway to the locked gates. Outside, an angry crowd seethed. Sam, begging for his life, was thrown over the iron gates to the feeding frenzy below, and with a furious howl, the mob tore the president apart. Sam's head and limbs were impaled onto poles and marched around the city, his torso trailing behind.[8]

Offshore, Caperton stood on the *Washington*'s quarterdeck and watched the macabre parade through his binoculars, too far away to know what to make of it. But after his ship anchored and he learned that this was no celebration, the commander sprang into action. Since violating a legation was a severe international offense, Caperton immediately understood it was "necessary for us to land or permit Europeans to do so." Tactical reasons counseled in favor of holding back. Nightfall was imminent, and it would be dangerous to send Americans ashore into the twilight of a strange and hostile city. But Caperton concluded that "reasons of policy greatly outweighed those of tactics," and the admiral decided to land at once to leave "as little excuse as possible for the French to disembark."[9]

With the *Washington*'s guns trained on the city, Caperton beached a small company of marines and bluejackets early in the evening. As dusk fell, they fanned out over the darkening city. From the bay, one marine sergeant later recalled, Port-au-Prince appeared "a beautiful romantic prospect," a "city of past ages whose glory had survived all modern ugliness." But once inside the capital, he felt instead that he "had been delivered into a land of evil enchantment." Days after the initial landing, American forces were marching "through walls of human silence and dead-eyed stares." They would occupy Haiti for the next nineteen years.[10]

With Remarkable Regularity

For Haitians, the American occupation was a tragedy. For Americans, it was merely a statistic. Over the late nineteenth and early twentieth centuries, the United States went on a regional rampage of staggering scope and scale. There were coups and countercoups, protectorates and annexations. Invasions were followed by occupations, and occupations by insurgencies and counterinsurgencies. Foreign capitals grew used to American marines policing their streets and American warships patrolling their waters. American policy became practically synonymous with intervention, the use or threat of force to coerce a state into exercising its sovereign functions in a particular way. Even where it did not intervene outright, Washington imposed its will through tools like loans, customs receiverships, embedded financial advisors, and the threat of diplomatic nonrecognition. Elsewhere, American diplomats simply made suggestions, knowing full well their advice would often be treated as law.

So by the time the marines fanned out over Port-au-Prince's darkening streets, Washington had already intervened in the affairs of Cuba (1898–1901, 1906–1909, 1912), Panama (1903, 1908), the Dominican Republic (1905, 1912, 1914), Nicaragua (1909, 1910, 1912), Honduras (1911), and Mexico (1914), to name only the most prominent interventions. Soon, the United States would also be intervening in the Dominican Republic (1916), Mexico (1916), the Danish West Indies (1917), Cuba (1917, 1933), Panama (1918), Honduras (1924), and Nicaragua (1927). By 1940, this interventionist record had become so glaring that the U.S. Marine Corps began its *Small Wars Manual* with the observation that "in spite of the varying trend of the foreign policy of succeeding administrations, this Government has interposed or intervened in the affairs of other states with remarkable regularity." Somewhat unnecessarily, the *Manual* then hazarded: "It may be anticipated that the same general procedure will be followed in the future."[11]

Against that history, what made the Haitian intervention remarkable is just how unremarkable it was.

———

STATES HAVE, OF course, been intervening in their neighbors' affairs since time immemorial. But these particular interventions stand out because of how much they foreshadowed the future of American foreign policy. Before American soldiers ever stormed the beaches of Normandy, they were landing in the surf of the Dominican Republic. Before the

Major U.S. Interventions in the Caribbean Region, 1860–1945

United States ever engaged in nuclear brinksmanship over Cuba, it was going toe to toe with European forces in Mexico and Venezuela. And before the nation ever became mired in the "forever wars" of Vietnam and Afghanistan, it was slogging through counterinsurgencies in Haiti, Nicaragua, and elsewhere. In short, before the United States ever turned into a global power, it became a regional one.

The parallels are no coincidence. By the end of its interventionist streak, the United States had accomplished something remarkable and, in the modern era, unprecedented, something that would allow it to claim the mantle of world power like no other nation before it. It had become a regional hegemon.[12]

Only a few countries are considered "great powers," those states that can hold their own in a war against any other state. But above even the great powers are what political scientists call "regional hegemons," those great powers that have grown so overwhelmingly strong that no other state, anywhere in the world, can put up a serious fight against them in their own region. In essence, a state becomes a regional hegemon only after it has eliminated or neutralized every other great power in its neighborhood.[13]

Such supremacy renders a state practically invulnerable, and strategists accordingly consider regional hegemony the holy grail of international power politics. Much like the search for the grail, however, pursuing this kind of power is a quest fraught with danger and moral compromise. Over the centuries, great powers like Napoleonic France, Imperial Japan, and Nazi Germany have all made runs at regional hegemony. But in the modern era, no state has ever managed to achieve it—no state, that is, except the United States.[14]

Perhaps no inflection point has been as critical to the republic's trajectory. Securing regional hegemony came at great cost, both to the United States and to those whom it encountered and often subdued. But it also freed the United States to leave the hemisphere behind and to become a global superpower invested in the security and stability of the world at large. Without enemies at its gates, the United States could venture further afield. And so it did. For better or worse, the results have been far-reaching, ranging from involvement in dozens of foreign conflicts to the creation of an international order that endures to this day.

Surprisingly, however, the story of the United States's rise to regional hegemony has not received anywhere near the attention it deserves. Most Americans take their country's unassailable position for granted, having lived with its effects all their lives. They likewise ignore the trail of broken states and mangled nations the United States left behind on its way to the top. Few know the full story of how the United States consolidated hegemony over the Western Hemisphere; fewer still dwell on why it did so.

Contemporary historians also often gloss over this missing chapter of American foreign policy, and even those who don't have tended to explain it away—with important exceptions—as an anachronism limited to a particular time and place.

Recently, some historians have begun revisiting this missing chapter from a new perspective. Concentrating on its consequences, these scholars have continued revising the sometimes too-sunny view of how the republic's interventions affected both itself and those it interacted with. Simultaneously, these scholars have embraced comparative and transnational research to bring to light the stories of marginalized groups—including indigenous peoples, women, and minorities—and to expose some of the ugly prejudices, ignorance, and greed that often characterized American involvement on the ground.[15]

Commendable and long overdue as this new research is, it remains incomplete. As important as it surely is to understand the effects and course of American interventionism, it's also important to understand what led senior officials in Washington to decide—again and again—to threaten or use force against their neighbors in the first place. By understanding the former, policymakers can better appreciate and redress historical injustices; by understanding the latter, policymakers can hopefully prevent new injustices from arising at all.

Dangerous to Our Peace and Safety

We May Dominate the World tells the story of a century of American statesmen, the constraints they faced, and the choices they made that together powered the United States to the pinnacle of international relations while leaving behind a string of shattered peoples and principles. From 1860 to 1945, the United States found itself intervening time and again in its neighbors' affairs primarily for one overriding and paradoxically defensive reason—to forestall the threat of intervention by hostile great powers.[16]

Concerns about hostile powers have, of course, been driving American foreign policy since the republic's founding. American leaders understood then that the greatest threat to their country's security came from Europe's great powers, the only nation-states with the economic, political, and military might to seriously harm the young republic. Geography, however, had blessed the United States with one major advantage: distance. Europe was far away, and its colonies could never compete in importance with its metropoles. Thomas Jefferson thus prayed that Europe's internal squabbles would keep the continent's bayonets at home, allowing "the new world [to] fatten on the follies of the old." George Washington crystallized the country's resulting grand strategy in his famous Farewell Address, in which he urged the United States to maintain "as little political connection as possible" with European powers while taking advantage of its "detached and distant situation" to grow stronger.[17]

Opportunistic isolation was the essence of Washington's counsel, and early American statesmen practiced it as best they could. By following the first president's guidance, the United States successfully drove Spain out of Florida and secured the vast territory of the Louisiana Purchase from a France distracted and impoverished by the Napoleonic Wars. But Washington's strategy also proved potentially unsustainable. Despite its best efforts, the United States was embroiled in costly conflicts with first France and then Great Britain. Even worse, the republic was rocked by a series of secession scares linked to foreign policy crises, including in the west and north. As long as Europe's great powers had major interests in the Western Hemisphere, it seemed like events on one side of the Atlantic would invariably provoke crises on the other.[18]

Emperor Napoleon Bonaparte, however, gave the United States an unparalleled strategic opening in 1807 when he marched his forces into the Iberian Peninsula and severed the ties that bound Spain and Portugal to their colonies on the far side of the ocean. Royalists and revolutionaries would battle across the Americas for the next decade and a half, but by the early 1820s, the tide had decisively shifted toward Latin American independence. Save for Canada and a handful of tiny European colonies in and around the Caribbean, the hemisphere was now essentially free.[19]

The collapse of the old colonial order—and the rise of new nations from its ashes—revolutionized American strategic thinking. Europe's great powers had always seemed like permanent fixtures of the Americas, but it was now possible to imagine a new world without them. If the United States could pull up the great powers' remaining stakes in the Western Hemisphere while preventing them from driving in new ones, then the United States would be able to rely on its oceanic moats for lasting security against the only real threat it faced. Jefferson was one of the first to appreciate what all of this meant for the United States and Latin America alike. "The object of both," he realized, "must be to exclude all European influence from this hemisphere."[20]

Jefferson's vision was intoxicating, but it had its challenges. Following Napoleon's final defeat, the three great monarchies of Europe—Russia, Austria, and Prussia—had banded together to form the Holy Alliance, a coalition dedicated to banishing the specter of republicanism and secularism from Europe. Once the Alliance had achieved that objective, American leaders feared, it might next try to recolonize the Latin American republics, whose weaknesses and divisions would make them easy targets. Americans grew even more concerned when Russia claimed a vast swath of Pacific waters as its exclusive preserve. All at once, Europe seemed set to roll back republicanism's gains in the New World.[21]

On December 2, 1823, President James Monroe responded with what would become known as the Monroe Doctrine. The United States would not interfere with Europe's "existing colonies or dependencies," he pledged to Congress, but Americans would consider it "dangerous to our peace and safety" if the Holy Alliance ever tried "to extend [its] system to any portion of this hemisphere." Accordingly, the United States would oppose any attempt to oppress or otherwise control the destinies of the new republics of the Western Hemisphere. "By the free and independent condition which they have assumed," Monroe proclaimed, "the American continents ... are henceforth not to be considered as subjects for future colonization by any European powers."[22]

The Monroe Doctrine was revolutionary. Taken to its logical conclusion, it promised the total expulsion of Europe's great powers from the Americas, and a complete political separation between the Old World and the New. Once finished, that project would presumably leave the United States as the only truly powerful state in the whole hemisphere—a regional hegemon, secure against the entire world.

But in 1823, that objective remained a distant dream. European leaders scoffed at Monroe's pretensions, and most powers considered it beneath their dignity to even respond to his Doctrine. The Holy Alliance never did send its fleets west, but that was mostly to avoid irritating Great Britain, not the United States. Russia, too, withdrew its claims for reasons other than Monroe's warning.[23]

For forty years, Washington did little to enforce the Monroe Doctrine despite regular violations by Europe's powers. Partly, that reflected the republic's weakness; what few resources the federal government had were consumed by internal matters, including western expansion. But Americans also failed to enforce the Doctrine because, like every other issue, it became bound up in the nation's sectional conflict. Shortly before Monroe's message, the debates over the Missouri Compromise had revealed the widening gulf between the North and the South over slavery. As the divide grew, each section championed a distinct foreign policy aimed primarily at keeping the other section in check. Determined to keep an eye on each other, the North and South turned inward, even as the threat from Europe began to mount.[24]

Only in the aftermath of the Civil War would the United States have the strength and focus to make good on the Monroe Doctrine's promise. It is there that the story of the republic's rise to regional hegemony—and this book—begins.

The Problem of Order

Over the next century, the United States would strive to achieve Monroe's vision in several different ways. But throughout this period, American policy was consistently shaped by one central, overarching challenge, what might be called "the problem of order." That problem reflected the fact that it would be dangerous for the United States to let strategically important areas of the world—including most of its neighborhood—fall prey to internal instability and weakness in the face of serious foreign threats.

Officials in Washington generally believed they could attain their ultimate objective of regional hegemony simply by waiting Europe's powers out, letting time, distance, and the natural course of events fray the continent's remaining links to the hemisphere while the United States continued to grow. But that plan would only work if the republic held the line in the meantime, preventing its European rivals from reversing their natural decline by acquiring new regional footholds or by significantly expanding their regional influence. For the sake of its own security, then, the United States recommitted itself at the end of the Civil War to defending not only its own shores, but also the shores of its neighbors.

Defending its neighbors was easier said than done, however, because those neighbors were often consumed by internal chaos. Since independence, many countries in the region had succumbed to dictators, civil wars, and foreign influence; others strained under the yoke of Europe's colonial legacy, the region's challenging geography, or invasions from nearby countries. Though not necessarily through any fault of their own, several of the United States's neighbors were extremely economically and politically unstable—failed or failing states, in today's terms.

Such instability complicated the United States's defense of the region. Instability can offer hostile foreign powers both the opportunity and the motivation to intervene: opportunity, because unstable states are internally divided and cannot effectively defend themselves; and motivation, because unstable states often fail to repay their debts or protect foreign property and persons, offering tailor-made justifications for foreign involvement. If left to fester, instability in the New World thus threatened to invite intervention by the Old.

Americans could perhaps have safely ignored the instability around them if they had been living in a more peaceful and enlightened time. But the end of the Civil War coincided with the start of the second Age of Imperialism in the 1870s, during which Eurasia's great powers aggressively expanded across the rest of the world. From the west coast of Africa to the islands of the Pacific, the powers scrambled to colonize what land they could while subjecting the remainder to their control, a vicious competition that eventually turned inward and helped lead to two devastating world wars. For Americans, this escalating imperial rivalry threatened to bring Europe's powers rushing back into the Western Hemisphere, and it turned the region's chronic instability from a minor annoyance into a major strategic liability.

Officials in Washington thus faced a serious problem, the problem of order, whenever one of their neighbors met three conditions: it was strategically important, it was threatened by foreign powers, and it was too unstable or otherwise weak to defend itself. Some of the United States's neighbors did not match that description. Canada, for instance, occupied a strategically important position as the republic's next-door neighbor, but throughout this period it presented few opportunities for European expansion and was primarily a vulnerability for the British Empire. But the problem of order unfortunately described much of the rest of the Western Hemisphere, especially in the Caribbean basin.[25]

Officials in Washington couldn't make their neighborhood less strategically important, and they couldn't usually control how much of a foreign threat it faced. But American officials thought they could do something about the problem of order's third prong: instability. If Americans could just stabilize and strengthen the weak states of the Western Hemisphere, the thinking went, they could remove tempting opportunities for European expansion and thereby safeguard their country's own security.

Less obvious was exactly how the United States should go about stabilizing and strengthening its weak neighbors. Several approaches were possible, ranging from hands-off measures like trade to more direct, invasive, and potentially coercive steps like protectorates, interventions, and annexations. Over the next century, American thinking on this issue would go through three phases.

From 1860 to 1898, the United States tried its first strategy. Europe's great powers had exploited American weakness and distraction during the Civil War to try to expand into the hemisphere, most notably in war-torn Mexico. In response to these near-misses, American leaders began trying to stabilize the region indirectly, through commercial and diplomatic engagement. By trading and staying on friendly terms with its neighbors, the United States hoped to strengthen them to the point where they could resist European incursions on their own. But where necessary, the United States would also lend a helping hand and confront Europe's powers directly; in extreme cases, it would even preempt foreign intervention through annexation.

European imperialism continued to surge, however, and from 1898 to 1918, the United States shifted to a second, more drastic approach.

After occupying Cuba during the Spanish-American War, Americans had the opportunity to directly meddle in the internal affairs of a nearby state in order to ensure its long-term stability. Once they did, there was no going back.

Over the next two decades, the United States launched wave after wave of increasingly invasive interventions against its neighbors. Washington wanted to exclude rival great powers from the region, but as its neighbors kept imploding, they continuously re-created power vacuums that encouraged foreign intervention. To stop that from happening, the United States began filling those vacuums with its own power. Over time, the defensive strategy of European exclusion turned into the reality of aggressive American expansion, as expansion proved the most effective and often the only way of excluding the country's European rivals.

Some in Washington welcomed this aggressive expansion, but most opposed it. Either way, however, the problem of order consistently channeled American foreign policy in a certain direction and made it difficult for policymakers to chart a different course. Of course, no decision to intervene was ever motivated exclusively by the problem. But while other factors were always relevant, they often played a distinctly secondary role. And even where other factors predominated, the problem of order still lurked in the background, continuously framing and limiting the choices that officials in Washington made.

Furthermore, the problem itself was self-perpetuating. Time and again, the United States would intervene to stabilize and strengthen its troubled neighbors; time and again, those interventions would miscarry, leading to greater instability that required new and more intrusive interventions. And even when the United States wasn't intervening, it was often destabilizing the region inadvertently, through the warping effects of its sheer size and rise alone. The result was a region gripped by ever-widening and ever-deepening power vacuums that kept drawing the United States further in as long as the foreign threat remained present.

From 1918 to 1945, the United States finally pulled back from this second strategy. By the end of World War I, the republic had found itself in an unsustainable position: having tipped from a great power into a full-blown regional hegemon, it no longer faced any meaningful foreign threat, but it was still enmeshed in a series of costly, inconclusive, and open-ended interventions across half the world. Americans decided they had had enough, and Washington drew back its regional military commitments while aspiring to a new, more neighborly strategy.

Once again, this new approach proved sustainable only in the short term. As long as the hemisphere faced no serious threat from abroad, the problem of order disappeared and the republic could live up to its ideals, ushering in a golden age in regional relations. But as soon as the great-power threat returned during the 1930s, so did the United States's ultimate willingness to intervene to preempt hostile foreign influence. Try as they might, officials in Washington could not escape the problem of order's basic logic. That logic would drag the country back into its expansionist ways, first at a regional level and then—as the Cold War heated up—on a global scale.

Full Circle

Today, the Western Hemisphere can sometimes seem like an afterthought in American policy. It can therefore be easy to dismiss the United States's history there as an artifact of its time, a relic with few lessons for the modern world. That would be a mistake.

Admiral Caperton and his colleagues would quickly recognize most of the challenges facing the United States today. They were used to revanchist great powers, ailing democratization efforts, and ominous war games. For them, there was nothing unusual about fleets jostling for supremacy, foreign occupations turning into quagmires, and the fates of entire empires being decided by banknotes and bullets. They lived in a time when the United States wrestled with failing states, counterinsurgency campaigns, and foreign assassinations. So do we.

The Western Hemisphere may have faded in geopolitical prominence, but the issues the United States confronted there a century ago remain startlingly contemporary. Today's American grand strategists remain as concerned as ever about the prospect of instability abroad and the national security threats that follow in its train. The United States first cut its teeth on that problem in its neighborhood, and modern American policymakers would do well to heed the lessons the country learned there at immense cost to itself and to others.

One of those lessons is an insight into what makes rising powers act the way they do. Historians often observe that rising powers tend to pursue aggressive and expansionist foreign policies on their way to the top. That is true, but what's less clear is *why*. One answer is the problem of order, which influences rising powers in a uniquely powerful way. Rising powers are especially likely to confront the three factors that create the problem; rising powers are also especially likely to have the capability to do something about it. The result is often aggression and expansion, as the United States learned firsthand.[26]

By understanding how the problem of order drove the United States's behavior, *We May Dominate the World* offers a window into the trajectory that other regional powers—including China, Russia, and Iran—may take in the coming decades. And the stakes could scarcely be higher. At a time when some claim that a declining United States is "destined for war" with a rising China, and when Russia's invasion of Ukraine has sparked fresh concerns about nuclear war, understanding the factors that led a rising United States to conduct a muscular foreign policy in its neighborhood can shed valuable light on how to prevent Armageddon in our own century.[27]

PART I
GUARDIAN

CHAPTER 1

WEAKNESS OFFERS TEMPTATION

The Civil War and Aftermath, 1860–1867

General Philip H. Sheridan sat motionless atop his horse as the summer sun beat down upon him. At his feet swirled the murky brown waters of the Rio Grande; just across it lay war-torn Mexico. Behind him, spread out all along the river, were thirty thousand soldiers in blue coats, veterans of the recently ended American Civil War.[1]

Sheridan and the North had won, but victory had not come cheaply. Seven hundred fifty thousand Americans were dead. Half a million more were wounded, including fifty thousand who had left limbs on battlefields and stacked beside surgeons' tents. By war's end, the North had lost more than 6 percent of its white male military-age population; in the South, it was over 13 percent. And less than a week after Confederate General Robert E. Lee raised the white flag, the nation had lost its president as well. By any metric, the Civil War had been the most brutal war the country had ever fought.[2]

Sheridan, however, had little time to dwell on the past; it was the wars of the future that concerned him. Only days after Sheridan had witnessed Lee's surrender at Appomattox, General Ulysses S. Grant had sent him deep into the recently subdued South on a mission so secret that Grant had refused to commit it to paper. Even in the midst of the Civil War, Grant had been watching events south of the border, including a civil war being fought in parallel in Mexico. Mexico was no stranger to domestic turmoil, but this was different: Mexicans were fighting not only each other, but also the French Empire. France had exploited the distractions of the American Civil War to invade Mexico with overwhelming force, and now the country was occupied territory, its republic reduced to ruins and a puppet emperor seated on the throne of Montezuma.[3]

Grant and Sheridan believed that France's occupation of Mexico was the last act in the drama the South had started with its rebellion. One of Europe's great powers was directly threatening the heart of American national security. Until the French were expelled from Mexico, Grant had told Sheridan, "our success in putting down secession would never be complete."[4]

Sheridan's eyes flicked over the Rio Grande, but his mind was focused on the pockmarked territory beyond it. Only two months after the end of the Civil War, Sheridan and the Union army were once again preparing to go to war.

The Gathering of the Vultures

Sheridan's mission—and the astounding willingness of many Americans to go to war with one of Europe's great powers months after the end of the most devastating conflict in American history—would become a defining moment in American foreign policy. Over the next century, the episode would come to symbolize just how far the country was willing to go to protect its neighborhood. Even more significant, however, were the events that had led up to Sheridan's mission, which would remind officials in Washington of what they saw as a harsh and enduring truth: Europe's great powers had not reconciled themselves to the United States's rise, and they would take advantage of any weakness—on the part of either the United States or its neighbors—if given the chance.

Europe's largely monarchical powers had always distrusted the virulent republicanism of the United States, but by the late 1840s they had come to fear its growing material power too. Earlier that decade, the republic had annexed Texas and then swallowed an additional five hundred thousand square miles from its southern neighbor after a stunning victory in the Mexican-American War. In 1855, a French diplomat concluded that what remained of Mexico would soon disappear down the gullet of its land-hungry neighbor. "Mexico has become the avowed object of the conquering ambition of the United States," he warned. "If it finishes by falling into their hands, it would be difficult to arrest the march of their domination in the New World."[5]

Europe's powers were also unsettled by other aspects of the republic's self-assigned manifest destiny. In the 1850s, Americans known as "filibusters" had launched waves of private military expeditions against their southern neighbors, seeking to liberate European colonies, spread slavery, and gain gold and glory. Sometimes Washington supported the filibusters, but even when it did not, it messed with European imperial interests in other ways, like blunting Great Britain's influence in Central America or threatening to seize Cuba from Spain. It became conventional wisdom in Europe's capitals that a rising United States had to be stopped—and soon.[6]

So it was a welcome development when Americans began tearing themselves apart over the issue of slavery. With the republic divided and distracted, Europe's powers could recalibrate the balance of power in the New World as they saw fit. It was not long before they seized the opportunity.

———

SPAIN STRUCK FIRST. Spanish politicians still pined for the glory days of the Spanish Empire, even as they feared that the United States might take away what few Caribbean colonies Madrid had left. Over the 1850s, this concern led Spain to start intriguing in the Dominican Republic, a nation strategically sandwiched between Cuba and Puerto Rico on the island of Hispaniola. Conveniently enough, Dominican leaders were simultaneously searching for a foreign power to protect them from their neighbor Haiti's repeated invasions. It seemed like a match made in heaven: Spain would restore control over its former colony, securing its flanks and burnishing its prestige, and in exchange the Dominican Republic would gain lasting security.[7]

The South's secession gave both sides the opening they needed to consummate the deal. On March 18, 1861, the Dominican president announced that the island nation was ready to be reannexed by Spain; two months later, after the Civil War had begun, Queen Isabel II officially accepted the offer and reincorporated the Dominican Republic by royal decree.[8]

One panicked American newspaper headlined "The Gathering of the Vultures." "Our domestic dissensions are producing their natural fruits," agreed the *New York Times*. "We are just beginning to suffer the penalties of being a weak and despised Power." Barring "decisive measures," the paper predicted gloomily, "we may speedily look for the advent of fresh fleets from Europe—and the intervention of other Powers in the affairs of this Continent."[9]

IMPERIAL FRANCE WAS the next power to exploit the United States and its neighbors' weakness.

Charles Louis Napoléon Bonaparte had been fascinated by Latin America long before he was crowned Emperor Napoleon III. He dreamed of reshaping the hemisphere in accordance with a "Grand Design for the Americas," which would see France leading a regional confederation of monarchies. The Grand Design was a breathtakingly ambitious scheme, one worthy, he hoped, of the Bonaparte name. But Napoleon III also justified it in the cold language of balance-of-power politics. He explained to one subordinate that if Americans "should take possession of the whole of the Gulf of Mexico, thence command the Antilles as well as South America," they would dictate terms to Europe as "the only dispenser of the products of the New World."[10]

Napoleon III believed that Mexico had both made such a catastrophe possible and also become the key to preventing it. Since independence,

Emperor Napoleon III of France: "A pallid face, its bony emaciated angles thrown into bold relief by the shaded lamps, a nose large and long, moustaches, a curled lock of hair above a narrow forehead, eyes small and dull, and with a timid and uneasy manner."

Mexico had been plagued by nearly constant civil war and revolution. By one count, the country had endured thirty-six governments and seventy-three presidents in less than forty years. Most recently, the country's two political factions—the Liberals and the Conservatives—had fought the especially bloody *La Guerra de Reforma*, or War of Reform. Liberals wanted to modernize their nation along Enlightenment-era lines, whereas Conservatives sought a dominant—some would say domineering—role for the institutions and privileges of precolonial Mexico. The Liberals had won the war but not the argument, and Mexico was left less prepared than ever to withstand outside influences.[11]

Napoleon III thought that Mexico's weakness gave him an unprecedented opportunity to implement his Grand Design and thereby stop the United States. Europe, he believed, had a "common interest ... in seeing Mexico pacified and endowed with a stable"—that is, monarchic— "government." Not only would a monarchized Mexico offer commercial advantages, but it would also "form an impassable barrier to the encroachments of North America." Once "regenerated" as a monarchy, moreover, Mexico would become a beachhead for the gradual regeneration of its neighbors, until the entire hemisphere was once again made safe for monarchy.[12]

The French emperor had hesitated to realize this plan during the 1850s because, as he told the British, he did not want to risk a "falling out with the United States." By late 1861, though, he knew that the Civil War had "made it impossible for the United States to interfere." So when a Mexican monarchist informed the French emperor that a military expedition was now feasible, Napoleon III finished his cigarette and cautiously agreed. "If [Mexico] declares that it desires to organize itself with the support of the European powers, I will lend a hand," he said. "For the rest, as you justly say, the state of affairs in the United States is very propitious."[13]

Equally propitious was the pretext for intervention that Mexico had provided. During the War of Reform, a succession of Mexican presidents had raided the treasury and, after it was bankrupted, turned to foreign loans for support. The war had also racked up individual claims against the Mexican government as bands of guerrillas and highwaymen took the property—and often the lives—of those foreigners unlucky enough to fall under their control. By 1861, Mexico allegedly owed more than $80 million to European creditors. With no way to pay off that sum, the new Liberal president, Pablo Benito Juárez, declared a two-year moratorium on Mexico's debt repayments.[14]

Napoleon III was overjoyed. Juárez's moratorium gave him (and Europe) the "legitimate motive for interference" that he had been waiting for. It was scandalous, really, that Mexico would repudiate its debts unilaterally, and the French emperor successfully persuaded British and Spanish leaders that the upstart nation needed some imperial discipline. On October 31, 1861, the three powers agreed to dispatch a joint military expedition to force Juárez's government to pay the money it owed and to better protect their subjects. Over the winter of 1861–1862, the three powers overran the Mexican port city of Veracruz with almost fourteen thousand soldiers.[15]

Great Britain and Spain soon resolved their claims and withdrew their forces, but Napoleon III was far from done. French forces advanced toward Mexico City, and after being reinforced by tens of thousands of veterans, they defeated Juárez's army, forced the Mexican president to flee north, and took the capital in early summer 1863. Over the next year, the French rolled over the devastated country like a tidal wave, sweeping up city after city. From the sidelines, Europe's other great powers cheered France's invasion and the challenge it posed to the United States. British Prime Minister Lord Palmerston said he could not imagine a "more advantageous" arrangement than the Confederacy winning the Civil War and Mexico simultaneously turning into "a prosperous monarchy." British statesman Lord Clarendon agreed, snickering at the thought of Napoleon III "cocking up his leg against [the United States's] Monroe Doctrine which ought long ago to have been *arrosé* [watered] in that manner."[16]

By 1864, Napoleon III was ready to crown his conquest of Mexico with the final touch—a foreign-born emperor who would nominally rule an independent Mexico, but who would really be bound to the French emperor's wishes. For Napoleon III, there were few better candidates for this role than Austrian Archduke Ferdinand Maximilian von Habsburg.

Charming, amiable, and kind, Maximilian was a true romantic. Born in 1832, he had stagnated in his older brother Franz Joseph's shadow, especially after Franz Joseph became emperor of Austria. Seeking an outlet, Maximilian traveled widely, first within Italy, then elsewhere in Europe, and eventually all the way to Brazil. It was there, on "the sun-lit wave-washed shore of the new continent," that the restless archduke got his first taste of what the New World could offer: "an admirable asylum," he confided to his journal, the chance "to break with the stormy past and to work [one's] way to a blameless future."[17]

<u>Emperor Maximilian I of Mexico</u>: "What a lot of cannon-shots it will take to set up an emperor in Mexico, and what a lot to maintain him there!"

Napoleon III had the power to turn these escapist fantasies into reality. He fired the young Habsburg's imagination with the demands of ancestral honor and visions of a rising empire across the sea. No responsibility could "produce greater results" than ruling Mexico, the French emperor promised, "for it is a question of rescuing a whole continent from anarchy and misery" and "raising the monarchist flag … in the face of dangerous Utopias and bloody disorders." It was an illusion Maximilian could not refuse.[18]

In March 1864, the archduke negotiated the terms of France's future support for his new empire. Napoleon III pledged to keep twenty thousand French troops in Mexico through 1867 and eight thousand foreign legionnaires for six years thereafter. Additionally, Napoleon III would help fund the beginning of Maximilian's reign. Beholden to French troops and money, Maximilian would effectively be a puppet emperor. If that bothered the archduke, however, he gave no sign.[19]

On June 12, 1864, to the celebratory boom of bells and cannons, Maximilian triumphantly entered Mexico City in a gilded coach led by four splendidly decorated white horses. Roars of "*¡Viva el Emperador!*" greeted him from the crowds thronging his path, many of whom had turned out at the strong "suggestion" of French troops. As he surveyed his new subjects, Emperor Maximilian I of Mexico felt his heart thrill. At last, he was home.[20]

—

MAXIMILIAN'S CORONATION STRUCK many Americans as just the beginning of Europe's return to the hemisphere. If Europe's powers could impose a monarchy on Mexico, the *New York Times* had opined, they would surely "repeat the operation in the other Spanish-American Republics." After all, why not? "Those Republics have been all offenders, in the same way, if not to the same extent, as their more Northern sister; like her, they are debtors to European capitalists; like her, they are turbulent and anarchical. Hence there will be just as valid ground for intervention in their case, as in Mexico." If Europe's past conduct had proven anything, it was that Europe's great powers were unlikely to stop of their own volition. "Ambition grows by what it feeds on," the *Times* warned darkly.[21]

The Very Most Glorious Original

Combatting these European ambitions was the unenviable job of William Henry Seward, who had become the new American secretary of state on March 6, 1861.

Just turning sixty, Seward could easily have passed for a disheveled scarecrow rather than an elder statesman. One observer commented on "his big nose and his wire hair and grizzly eyebrows and miserable dress"; another thought Seward's head resembled "a straw sack in shape and color." Despite his age and appearance, however, Seward still had a restless "school-boy elasticity" about him. Henry Adams, one of the age's sharpest political commentators, laughed at how "hopelessly lawless" Seward could be in social situations—snorting, belching, sprawling across chairs, and patting ladies on the head whenever the mood struck him. Seward often kept "all the talking to himself," but listeners usually failed to notice, for the garrulous secretary rolled out "grand, broad ideas" so effortlessly he could "inspire a cow with statesmanship." All in all, Adams decided, Seward was "the very most glorious original."[22]

Seward's appointment as secretary of state had been a bittersweet moment for the New Yorker. He had spent his entire adult life striving for the presidency, rising to become a preeminent voice against slavery as well as the undisputed leader of the new Republican party. Going into the 1860 nominating convention, Seward was the surefire nominee. At the last minute, however, the nomination had been yanked out of his hands and awarded to some political unknown born in the backwoods

<u>Secretary of State William Henry Seward</u>: "A subtle, quick man,
rejoicing in power, given to perorate and to oracular utterances,
fond of badinage, bursting with the importance of state mysteries."

and distinguished primarily by his almost total lack of distinction. Anyone would have been crushed, but for someone of Seward's ambition and
accomplishment, it was an especially devastating blow.[23]

Seward initially envisioned himself as the power behind the new
throne; whoever this Abraham Lincoln was, he would surely be putty in
the secretary's dexterous grip. In time, however, Seward's wounded ego
gave way to admiration for his new boss, and the two formed a partnership that would steer the nation through civil war and international peril
alike.[24]

———

SECRETARY SEWARD CRAFTED the Union's foreign policy during the
Civil War with two constraints in mind. First, the Union could not allow Europe to flout the Monroe Doctrine by permanently expanding
its military presence in the New World. Even more importantly, however, the Union also had to win its war against the Confederacy, which
meant preventing foreign powers from getting involved in the conflict.
These often-competing constraints drove Seward to try several different
solutions to Europe's schemes in the hemisphere.

First, he tried to drive Europe back with menacing diplomatic notes and even threats of war. But these warnings were never realistic, and as the republic descended into civil war, Europe's powers began ignoring Seward's warnings.[25]

Seward next tried to combat Europe's interest in Mexico through an intergovernmental loan that Juárez could use to satisfy his country's seething creditors and thereby eliminate any pretense for further intervention. Such a loan was unprecedented; never before had the United States loaned money directly to a foreign government, and critics like the attorney general fulminated against the folly of aiding "the crippled and insane nations round us" when "we are ourselves torn by civil dissensions." But Mexico was too important a battleground to cede to Europe, and Lincoln ultimately agreed to roll the dice on Seward's loan plan.[26]

Their luck ran out in the Senate, however. At a time when the Union was pinching pennies for the widening war effort, senators were in no mood to consider large cash outlays, even ones of "momentous interest to the two Governments" involved. They shot down Seward's proposed loan, twenty-eight to eight.[27]

Seward looked for other ways to rescue the hemisphere from European plots, but he found himself increasingly hamstrung by the Civil War's course. The Confederacy was stonewalling the Union's armies, and the volleys of even one conflict threatened to overwhelm the North. Given the precarious military situation, Seward realized that his first priority had to be preventing Europe's great powers from recognizing the Confederacy or, worse, allying with it against the Union.[28]

Seward was playing a dangerous game. Deliverance lay in walking the thin line between being belligerent enough to scare Europe away from recognition or an alliance with the South, but not being so belligerent as to actually provoke a conflict. Balancing those two imperatives became the touchstone of the Union's foreign relations for the rest of the war, and Seward soon proved himself a master.[29]

This balancing act, however, left little room for picking a fight with European powers elsewhere in the hemisphere. Even helping Latin Americans resist foreign encroachment was dangerous, as it could become a precedent for foreign aid to the Confederacy. Before the United States could do anything for the hemisphere, it had to put its own house in order.[30]

Seward therefore settled on a foreign policy later dubbed "masterly inactivity." The secretary would concede as little as possible to the covetous grasp of the European powers. At the same time, however, Seward would do little to oppose them directly as long as the Civil War raged. Instead, Washington would simply lie low, biding its time, waiting until someday it was powerful enough to act.[31]

———

SEWARD BELIEVED THAT day would not arrive until "time and events" had cured the United States's "suicidal division." Other Americans were less patient, however, and the secretary of state's policy of masterly in-activity became harder to sustain as the tide of public opinion turned steadily against Europe's intrusions.[32]

Seward responded acidly in 1864 when one of his diplomats dared question his wait-and-see policy. "I regret that you think my course towards the French Government is too conciliatory and courteous," the secretary noted sarcastically, but it was hardly "the most suitable time ... for offering idle menaces to the Emperor of France." Confederate forces were still in the field; until they were beaten, little else mattered. In the meantime, Seward snapped, he had "compromised nothing, surren-dered nothing, and [did] not propose to surrender anything." "Why," he pressed, "should we gasconade about Mexico when we are in a struggle for our own life?"[33]

Seward's in-house critics, however, were the least of his problems. Despite the war, Americans were flocking to new political clubs ded-icated to defending the Monroe Doctrine and expelling the French from Mexico. France's actions had excited "a popular impulse which is as strong as it is universal," Seward admitted, and "I am now appealed to, to declare war, to drive the French out of Mexico." Sometimes he dreamed of agreeing. "The Union is a serpent of thirty-five long joints," he told his wife wearily. "One-third are trying to disengage themselves, and the other two-thirds languish of the pain. How I wish for the power to compel them to reunite, so as to be able to coil and spring in their own defense."[34]

On April 4, 1864, the House of Representatives heeded popular opinion and unanimously passed a resolution denouncing "any monar-chical Government erected on the ruins of any republican Government in America under the auspices of any European Power." Seward's al-lies buried the resolution in the Senate, but the damage was done. On an American diplomat's next visit to the Tuileries, the French foreign minister demanded: "Do you bring us peace, or bring us war?" At that moment, the answer was still peace, but the disjointed American serpent was getting closer and closer to a striking position.[35]

On April 9, 1865, General Grant accepted Confederate General Lee's surrender at Appomattox. The next day, Grant took a special train back to his headquarters at City Point, arriving early the following morning. Everyone else was celebrating or sleeping, and Grant himself should have been thrilled to have finally accomplished what he had spent years striving for. Instead, he was restless; he knew the Union still had other unfinished business. So in his dimly lit office, the victorious commanding general of the U.S. Army suddenly paused and looked up at his yawning staff. "Now for Mexico," he announced.[36]

Our Faces Turned Towards the City of Mexico

For four long years, Americans had gritted their teeth as Europe's powers flouted the Monroe Doctrine. But by mid-April 1865, the strategic balance had seesawed, and officials at the highest levels of government began debating how the United States should revenge itself on those who had exploited its weakness.

Some European powers didn't wait around to see what Washington might do. Spain's attempt to reannex the Dominican Republic had devolved into a bloody and expensive counterinsurgency. Facing a massive deficit, 7,500 dead troops, and a resurgent United States, Spain unilaterally decided to vacate the island only weeks after Lee's surrender.[37]

Mexico was another matter, and Napoleon III showed few signs of wanting to leave. But Washington was now in a much stronger bargaining position. Most obviously, Lee's surrender had sealed the Confederacy's fate, freeing up hundreds of thousands of Union veterans for new undertakings. But there were also changes in leadership. Five days after Appomattox, John Wilkes Booth had shot Lincoln in the head while one of Booth's confederates attacked Seward with a Bowie knife. Both men had opposed escalating the conflict with Europe, but with Lincoln dead, Seward struggling to survive, and the Civil War over, the path was now clear for a more aggressive course.[38]

General Grant took full advantage of the opportunity. He had objected to marching into Mexico while the Confederacy remained a going concern. But he had always regarded the French occupation "as a direct act of war against the United States," and he had supposed that Americans "would treat it as such when their hands were free to strike." In his view, that moment had arrived. He wanted to demand Maximilian's abdication and Napoleon III's withdrawal from Mexico. If either refused—as seemed likely—then the United States would invade.[39]

On May 17, 1865, Grant set his plan in motion. He assigned General Philip H. Sheridan to command west of the Mississippi. Ostensibly, Sheridan was to subdue the Confederate rump; in reality, Grant explained, Sheridan was being sent south to compel the French "to quit the territory of our sister republic."[40]

At first glance, Sheridan seemed an odd choice for the mission. He was, one observer noted, "a stumpy, quadrangular little man, with a forehead of no promise and hair so short that it looks like a coat of black paint." But by the time Sheridan stood with Grant at Appomattox, he was the fourth-ranking officer in the Union army and a living legend. Outside of battle, Sheridan could be withdrawn and sphinxlike. But "with the first smell of powder," a change came over him; "he became a blazing meteor, a pillar of fire," one war correspondent recalled. "Little Phil" would gallop along the front with demonic energy, spurring men on with a steady stream of curses from his foaming mouth. As bullets flew, he "was more than magnetic," another war correspondent marveled; "he was electric." Grant agreed. "As a soldier, as a commander," he assessed, "there is no man living greater than Sheridan."[41]

Sheridan took to his new assignment with characteristic pit-bull enthusiasm. He informed Grant's chief of staff in early June that he planned

General Philip Sheridan: "Sheridan is like Grant, a persevering terrier dog [who] won't be shaken off."

to move "a strong force" of more than fifty thousand soldiers into Texas, stationing thirty thousand of them along the Rio Grande. "This may seem like the employment of a large force to you," Sheridan shrugged, "but it is always best to go strong-handed." By concentrating in Texas, Sheridan planned to build "an army strong enough to move against the invaders of Mexico if occasion demanded." Exemplifying the best of military humor, his force would be called the "Army of Observation."[42]

Sheridan's arrival turned the Rio Grande into a powder keg. In response to the American buildup, Maximilian reinforced the border city of Matamoros with thousands of French soldiers, led by officers who were (in Sheridan's view) "very saucy and insulting." But rather than trying to defuse the situation, Sheridan hoped to spark an explosion. "Affairs on the Rio Grande frontier are getting beautifully mixed up," he crowed. He encouraged his subordinates to "annoy the French authorities as much as you can," explaining that their "assistance to the rebels is and has been infamous."[43]

On June 29, 1865—less than three months after the end of the most devastating war in American history—Sheridan was panting for permission to let slip the dogs of war. "There is no use to beat around the bush in this Mexican matter," he wrote Grant, arguing that "the advent of Maximilian was a portion of the rebellion and his fall should belong to its history." With his cavalry columns in "magnificent trim," Sheridan hoped to soon "have the pleasure of crossing the Rio Grande with them with our faces turned towards the city of Mexico."[44]

—

GRANT, TOO, WAS itching to cross the border. On July 12, 1865, he passed Sheridan's call for war on to the new president, Andrew Johnson, saying, "Sheridan here expresses exactly the sentiments which I believe in, and have often expressed."[45]

Johnson, however, was conflicted, and he decided to present the letter to his cabinet two days later for debate.[46]

Sheridan's letter hit the cabinet like a bombshell. Grant had successfully snuck Sheridan and his army down to the border while Seward was still convalescing from the attempted assassination, but by mid-June the secretary was tottering back into cabinet meetings and expressing his "emphatic ... opposition" to Grant's call for more "decisive measures" against Maximilian. If Washington demanded that Napoleon III withdraw, Seward argued, it would only "wound French pride and produce a war." Instead, the secretary thought Americans should wait for Maximilian's empire to collapse under its own weight.[47]

Seward was thus "astounded" by Sheridan's letter, and he took to the ramparts immediately. "If we got in [a] war and drove out the French," he warned crossly, "we could not get out ourselves." The treasury secretary agreed, adding that nation and purse were both exhausted. The interior and navy secretaries backed Seward as well, but other cabinet members—as well as much of the army—supported Grant and Sheridan.[48]

Johnson remained torn. In 1864, he had campaigned on this very issue, promising one roaring crowd that Union soldiers could use "Mexico [as] a sort of recreation" after putting down the rebellion. "The French concern," Johnson had blustered, "would quickly be wiped out." One year and one significant political promotion later, however, Johnson was having second thoughts.[49]

Grant, however, was not deterred, and he presented a compromise plan. General John M. Schofield, another Union war hero, could resign his commission and lead Union troops into Mexico. Officially, Schofield would fight Maximilian as a private citizen—albeit one leading thousands of other Union veterans, all ostensibly on leaves of absence, and all armed out of the Union's postwar surplus.[50]

Johnson was intrigued by Grant's compromise plan and put it to the cabinet. This time, Seward was decisively outmaneuvered, and on July 18, 1865, the cabinet sent the plan to the secretary of war "to be worked out as he might see fit." Grant left the capital for an eleven-week tour of the country, confident that the United States was irrevocably headed for war against France.[51]

———

SEWARD, HOWEVER, WAS not ready to give up. Once Grant left Washington, the secretary invited Schofield on a one-week outing to Cape May. Away from Grant's influence, the guileless general was easy pickings. Seward persuaded Schofield to postpone his foray into Mexico and instead go on a special diplomatic mission to Paris. "I want you to get your legs under Napoleon's mahogany," Seward urged, "and tell him he must get out of Mexico."[52]

Schofield's diplomatic "mission" was a stalling tactic, designed (as Seward later confessed) to "squelch [Grant's] wild scheme." Seward delayed Schofield's departure until late fall, and then he organized a stream of distracting soirées once the general arrived in Paris to keep him just out of range of Napoleon's mahogany.[53]

With Schofield safely preoccupied, Seward worked on the president, arguing behind closed doors for diplomacy over military action. Johnson began losing interest in Grant's plan, and by the time Grant finished his tour of the country in early October, the Schofield expedition was dead in the water.[54]

Grant and Sheridan were furious. But in their eyes, the debate was far from over.

Dangers of Collision

Seward had deprived Sheridan of a hot war, but the secretary could not stop him from starting a cold one. Grant had given Sheridan a long leash and Sheridan, as expected, strained his authority even further. He believed the government of Maximilian, "the imperial buccaneer," was "a farce" that could be toppled by Juárez and his hardscrabble rebel forces with a little help from their northern neighbor. "For it is not their quarrel alone but ours too," Sheridan wrote a friend. "Not their safety but ours also in time to come." Far from the capital's prying eyes, Little Phil thus launched one of the biggest, most audacious, and most unauthorized covert wars in American history.[55]

Sheridan, a former bookkeeper, began losing track of his army's supplies. His men would leave large piles of guns unguarded near Juarista camps, only to find them missing the next morning. Munitions were listed as destroyed, but no one could quite remember if they had been. Sheridan later admitted that thirty thousand muskets from the Baton Rouge arsenal alone made their way into Juarista hands.[56]

Despite being called the Army of Observation, Sheridan's troops meanwhile proved blind to the flow of men and supplies across the Rio Grande. Juaristas crossed the border regularly to escape their imperialist pursuers. Union soldiers, in turn, chased adventure and the Monroe Doctrine into Mexico. Many joined Juárez's forces; others just drunkenly raided the camps of Maximilian's troops. But the border was only selectively permeable, as Sheridan bottled up Juárez's political rivals and anti-Juarista Confederates inside the United States.[57]

Sheridan further strained Maximilian's nerves by rattling his saber up and down the border. He ostentatiously reviewed troops, positioned a pontoon bridge in Brownsville, Texas, and inquired loudly about "the quantity of forage we could depend upon getting in Mexico." Sheridan also communicated with Juárez, "taking care not to do this in the dark." "Like wildfire," Sheridan later remembered, word spread that the squat general would shortly cross the border.[58]

Such rumors helped reverse the conflict's momentum. Imperialist forces had been spread thin in Mexico even at the occupation's height, with approximately sixty thousand French and allied Mexican troops garrisoning a territory almost three times the size of France. Once the Army of Observation appeared on the border, however, Napoleon III had to concentrate the scattered French forces to parry a possible attack from the United States. As French detachments evacuated lightly held towns across the north, vengeful Juaristas replaced them, celebrating their newfound control with public executions of imperial supporters. Once it became clear that the Mexican Empire could not protect its own, Mexicans began rallying to Juárez's banner and defecting from the imperial army en masse.[59]

———

SHERIDAN FUSSED ABOUT needing "the patience of Job to abide the slow and poky methods of our State Department," but Seward was taking a harder line with France too.[60]

Seward began firing warning shots across the Atlantic in September 1865. In messages to Paris, he acknowledged how the Civil War had distracted Washington from tending to its neighborhood. But now Americans were turning back to foreign policy, and chief among their concerns was going to be how Napoleon III's "injurious and menacing" actions in Mexico had thrust Franco-American relations into "imminent jeopardy." Seward therefore repeatedly advised France to withdraw from Mexico.[61]

Seward also repurposed Sheridan's belligerence to great effect, sending snippets from the general's fiery reports to the Tuileries as a reminder of the combustible "condition of irritability existing on that remote frontier." As long as French troops stayed in place, Seward warned darkly, there existed serious "dangers of collision."[62]

Other factors reinforced Seward's mafioso warnings. Since Appomattox, Maximilian's position had deteriorated dramatically. Imperialist forces nominally controlled three-quarters of the country, but Mexicans seemed loyal to the Empire only within range of French guns. Guerrillas appeared on the horizon more frequently, armed to the teeth with state-of-the-art weapons from Sheridan's stockpiles. Maximilian, meanwhile, had done little to consolidate either his position on the throne or his empire's tottering finances, instead remaining addicted to French loans in increasingly short supply. Napoleon III also worried about the deteriorating situation in Europe, where he confronted criticism of his Mexican policy at home and a rising Prussia next door.[63]

France put out diplomatic feelers in late 1865 to see if Washington might consider recognizing Maximilian's government in exchange for France's withdrawal. Seward flatly refused. Instead, he had a fierce critic of the French expedition appointed minister to Juárez's government—a move that, Seward cheerfully learned, had scared the French representative in Washington "out of his wits."[64]

━━

FOR MONTHS, MAXIMILIAN had refused to even contemplate the possibility that the French might abandon him. His regime depended almost entirely on foreign support, and Napoleon III had given his word that France would provide it. Even so, Maximilian knew his empire was in trouble. "I tell Your Majesty frankly," he wrote nervously to Napoleon III in the waning days of 1865, "this situation is difficult for me."[65]

But Napoleon III had already made his decision. On January 15, 1866, he wrote Maximilian that despite his previous promises, "all the difficulties caused me by the Mexican question" had forced him "to fix a definitive limit to the French occupation." Struggling to put a positive spin on the betrayal, Napoleon III added feebly that "the departure of our troops may be a temporary weakness, but it will have the advantage of removing all pretext for intervention on the part of the United States."[66]

Cold comfort, thought Maximilian, who would undoubtedly have preferred facing down American forces with France's help than confronting the Juaristas alone. The young emperor put on a brave face in his response, but he and his wife were shaken. The French minister reported that their position "is sad and painful beyond anything they expected. They are desperate and frightened."[67]

More heartache was to come. Napoleon III officially informed Washington in April 1866 that French troops would withdraw from Mexico in three detachments, beginning that November and ending the following year. Seward demanded a speedier withdrawal, and he would soon get it. Meanwhile, Maximilian begged his older brother, the Austrian emperor, to send fresh forces to replace the departing French. At first Franz Joseph agreed. But when Seward caught wind of the scheme and threatened war, Vienna backed down. Maximilian was to have no friends abroad, not even his own brother.[68]

As 1866 wore on, Sheridan continued to grouse about Seward's "butt-headedness," and Seward continued to fret about Little Phil's belligerence. But despite their mutual antipathy, the two men had caught

Maximilian's empire in a vise. Abroad, Seward was systematically isolating Maximilian from his European patrons, cutting the strings that connected the puppet emperor to his masters. Meanwhile, Sheridan was doing everything in his power on the American side of the border—and sometimes on the Mexican side—so that when Maximilian's isolation was complete, the Juaristas would obliterate him and everything he stood for.[69]

I Have Always Wanted to Die on Just Such a Day

In early 1862, a Spanish politician had predicted gloomily that a Mexican "monarchy under a European prince, if not guaranteed by Europe, would not last a year." That proved too optimistic.[70]

Even before French forces withdrew, Maximilian's empire was going under. For years, his forces had barely fought off guerrilla attacks, but in June 1866, the imperialists lost a set-piece battle in the hills of Santa Gertrudis near the port city of Matamoros. The Juaristas cut the similarly sized imperialist forces to shreds with their new American carbines and repeating rifles; critically, too, almost one-fourth of the Juarista forces were *norteamericanos* Sheridan had allowed to slip over the border.[71]

Defeat at Santa Gertrudis set off a chain reaction. Surrounded by rebel armies, imperialist forces were forced to abandon Matamoros. Losing the port meant losing its lucrative customs receipts, which were desperately needed to keep Maximilian's dwindling military in the field. One month later, the French also withdrew from the ports of Monterrey and Tampico. Reports of new losses began to pour into Mexico City daily as the Juaristas tore chunk after chunk out of Maximilian's disintegrating empire.[72]

Over the autumn of 1866, Maximilian considered abdicating and joining his wife in Europe. But at the end of the year, he declared himself ready to "shed the last drop of his blood in defense of his dear country." The French were incredulous. "From the moment that the United States boldly pronounced their *veto* against the imperial system, your throne was nothing but a bubble," the marshal of France's forces in Mexico scolded in vain.[73]

On February 5, 1867, the last column of French troops slunk out of Mexico City under the cover of darkness. Maximilian watched them leave from behind a curtain in the National Palace. "At last," he breathed, "I'm free."[74]

FOREVER TRUE TO his romantic image of what an emperor should be, Maximilian sought to reverse his fading fortunes by taking the field at the head of his remaining troops. He led them to Querétaro—a picturesque town notable for the surrounding high hills that made it especially vulnerable to enemy encirclement—and was soon cornered by Juárez's forces. In the ensuing siege, Maximilian seemed indifferent to death's shadow, rushing back and forth along the front in full view of his enemies and their belching cannons. On May 15, 1867, one of Maximilian's officers finally betrayed the city into Juarista hands. Maximilian was captured, imprisoned, and sentenced to death for treason.[75]

Even until the very end, the European nobility could not quite believe that Juárez would actually execute one of their own. Seward was also cavalier. On June 17, he assured the Austrian minister at a dinner party that the emperor's life was "quite as safe as yours and mine."[76]

Two days later, just shy of his thirty-fifth birthday, Maximilian was led out of his cell into a crisp and cloudless morning. Pausing, he looked around and said happily, "What a glorious day! I have always wanted to die on just such a day."[77]

In the hills outside Querétaro, a fifteen-man firing squad checked their weapons as the emperor and two of his generals took their assigned spots. "*¡Viva México!*" cried out the Austrian Habsburg. "*¡Viva la Independencia!*"[78]

Orders were barked, rifles raised, and then, with an earsplitting crack, Maximilian's Mexican Empire ended.[79]

A Common and Indispensable Interest

Two years later, Seward and some other Americans picked their way through the rocks and cacti littering the path up a Mexican hillside. It was getting dark, and they had to tread carefully in the dying light. Their shadows stretched out behind them toward the farmers they had just passed, still hard at work in fields that had recently seen screaming shells and muddied armies smashing against each other. Seward's party caught the farmers' attention only for a moment; many stranger sights had already passed through Querétaro.[80]

Soon the Americans arrived at their destination, a small clearing. It was marked only by a mound of jumbled stones topped with three black wooden crosses—a makeshift memorial to the last moments of Maximilian's Mexican Empire.[81]

Seward had retired earlier that year after serving longer than any previous secretary of state. But the sixty-eight-year-old remained as restless as ever, and he had leaped at the chance to visit Mexico to trace the rise and fall of Maximilian's tumultuous reign. Fragments of the recent conflict fascinated him, and Seward had pursued them throughout his three-month tour—in ruins, eyewitnesses, and battlefields so recently won that cannon smoke still seemed to hang over them. In Mexico's National Palace, Seward had stumbled into storerooms packed with paintings, royal busts, monogrammed silverware, fading costumes and uniforms, and every other conceivable type of imperial bagatelle—all the flotsam and jetsam that had floated up from the wreckage of empire, flung into massive, haphazard piles and laid to rest in a tomb of dust.[82]

Nothing, however, symbolized Maximilian's fall quite like three crosses on a hill near Querétaro, the only commemoration Juárez would permit of the spot where the puppet emperor and his senior officers had been executed.

Seward left posterity no account of his thoughts that evening. But it is hard to imagine he didn't feel, if only for a moment, a chill run down his spine. Combined with events elsewhere in the hemisphere, the rise and fall of Napoleon III's Mexican Empire had taught him and his fellow Americans three harsh lessons that they would not soon forget.

First, Americans had belatedly rediscovered the European threat to the hemisphere. It was now clear that Europe's great powers had not reconciled themselves either to the United States's rise or to their assigned place in the region; they had also proven that they would do something about it if they could.

France's occupation of Mexico was the most obvious example, and it had dramatically underscored the stakes behind the Monroe Doctrine. If Napoleon III had succeeded in standing up Maximilian's empire, the United States would have confronted a European puppet state right on its borders. During the Civil War, that could have been fatal; the French emperor strongly favored the South, and he likely would have calculated that sustaining the Confederacy across the border with arms and military materiel would have been the best way to protect his embryonic empire in Mexico while keeping the United States divided. In the worst-case scenario, France might even have intervened on the Confederacy's side.[83]

But the real long-term danger from the French intervention lay in the ways in which Maximilian's empire would have expanded European interests in the hemisphere—interests often diametrically opposed to those of the United States. Some of Europe's great powers, for example, would have used Mexico to check American growth and prosperity. Others would have used Mexico as a pawn in their ideological contests. Indeed, before Maximilian's death, he and Napoleon III had already set in motion plans to reorder the rest of Latin America along monarchical lines. Maximilian's empire would also have inevitably drawn Americans into the bloody vortex of European power politics. For centuries, the great powers had settled their scores through wars on other continents, and nothing would have attracted European rivalries to American shores quite like a vast French protectorate headed by a former Habsburg archduke.[84]

Of course, none of these dire scenarios came to pass. Napoleon III bungled much of his Mexican campaign, and even absent American pressure, he and Maximilian likely could not have mustered the personnel and resources needed to repress Mexican nationalism over the long term.

Still, it was enough of a close call that one of the Civil War's legacies was a new, nationwide commitment to the Monroe Doctrine. Europe's onslaught had persuaded most Americans that ejecting the great powers from the hemisphere was crucial, and that keeping them out was even more so. Even during the war, *Harper's Weekly* had called the Doctrine "a fixed principle of American political faith," while another pamphlet had described it as "an axiomatic truth." Europeans might pooh-pooh Monroe's wisdom, one Russian official warned, but in the United States, "the latest generation imbibes it with its mother's milk."[85]

Second, Seward and other Americans had also drawn a second lesson from Maximilian's empire: that they could not afford to simply cross their arms and wait for the next European threat to materialize. If Europe's powers decided to wade across the Atlantic again, it would be taxing, even debilitating, for the United States to hurl them back. Plus, as the Civil War had shown, Americans couldn't always count on their being able to meet danger when it came calling. And that was even assuming Americans would recognize the threat in time, an uncertain proposition when the line between lawful interventions and dangerous power grabs remained so blurry. For better or worse, Americans could not bar European interventions in the region entirely; during this time, great powers regularly used force to protect their citizens' rights abroad (including property rights), and international law sanctioned the practice. Even the United States regularly landed troops in Latin America and elsewhere to keep its nationals safe when violence broke out. On their own, such landings seemed harmless: they were short, small, and not aimed at usurping a local state's sovereign authority. But the problem was that European powers could easily use such incursions for more nefarious ends—as France had done—and it was often hard to tell where the murky line between lawful interventions and perilous power grabs lay until it was too late.[86]

Of course, a serious incursion from Europe was unlikely at any given moment. But its long-run probability and dire consequences meant that Washington could not afford to be complacent; the United States had to start thinking about how to proactively stop European interventions from ever getting off the ground.

Finally, Americans had learned an important lesson about weakness. Seward summed that lesson up when he reflected on how Europe's capitals sized up the United States. Each power's attitude, Seward observed coldly, would "depend much more on her estimate of our power than on any moral considerations." Tragic as that was, "it could not happen otherwise, for nations are human and weakness offers temptations which the strong cannot reasonably be expected to resist."[87]

Seward was talking about the temptations offered by not only his own nation's weakness, but also that of its neighbors. If Americans had learned anything during the Civil War, it was that the weakness of their neighbors had practically invited foreign interventions by offering Europe's powers both the means and the motivation to intervene.[88]

Mexico provided a good example. For years, civil war and revolution had decimated Mexico's military strength, wiped out its fiscal system, and left it drowning in debt. Meanwhile, foreign states had racked up hundreds of monetary claims against Mexico stemming from the abuse their citizens and property endured.

Seward worried as early as April 1861 that this "condition of anarchy ... must necessarily operate as a seduction to those who are conspiring ... to seek strength and aggrandizement for themselves by conquests." Seward was thinking primarily of the Confederacy, but he knew that Mexico's disorder could attract "other governments" as well. He therefore advised "that the surest guaranty of [Mexico's] safety against such aggressions is to be found in a permanent restoration of the authority of that government."[89]

But it was too late. Juárez declared a two-year debt moratorium, Europe's creditors snapped, and Napoleon III had his long-awaited opportunity. Even British and Spanish leaders were itching to attack, both to collect claims owed and to remind Mexico City of the need to protect their subjects. Once they hit the beaches of Veracruz, the three powers took quick advantage of Mexico's weakness to get what they wanted. They were technologically superior, but it also helped that Mexicans were drained from years of fighting and that a portion of them—the monarchists—cooperated with the intervening powers. Even on its own, France steamrolled Mexican forces for most of the war and managed to occupy three-quarters of the country with only forty thousand soldiers.[90]

If it wasn't quite on the level of Hernando Cortés's conquest centuries earlier, it came close, and it underscored how easily weakness could encourage and facilitate foreign aggression.

━━

COMBINING THESE THREE lessons, Seward and other Americans began drawing one overarching conclusion that the secretary thought "even the dullest observer" could grasp: that "peace, order, and constitutional authority in each and all of the several republics of this continent are not exclusively an interest of any one or more of them, but a common and indispensable interest of them all." Instability anywhere concerned everyone; it was the chink in the armor that left the whole hemisphere open to serious blows. As long as the region remained unstable and weak, it would be extraordinarily difficult, if not impossible, for the United States to keep European influence perpetually in check.[91]

Officials in postwar Washington thus concluded that, for the sake of its own security, the United States needed to help stabilize and strengthen its neighbors. That objective, and the problem of order that prompted it, would take center stage in American foreign policy for the next century.

CHAPTER 2

IN DIVISION THERE IS WEAKNESS

A New Hemispheric Strategy, 1867–1893

James G. Blaine was dying in the summer of 1892, though many refused to believe it. The two-time secretary of state was a notorious hypochondriac, and he had pleaded ill health in service of political ends before. Even his boss, President Benjamin Harrison, was incredulous, suspecting that Blaine was using doctor's notes to paper over plans to steal the Republican presidential nomination. But this time, it was no act. The weakness, the spells of dizziness, the sudden collapses—it was all genuine, and in less than eight months, the most famous politico of the Gilded Age would be dead.[1]

Blaine's passing would mark the end of a boisterous career. "Blaine of Maine" had worked as a journalist during his twenties, earning a reputation as an intelligent and dogged advocate of the Republican cause. In 1863, he brought his acid quill to the U.S. House of Representatives, where he exchanged it for the Speaker's gavel six years later. It was not long before he had become the most powerful Republican politician since Abraham Lincoln.[2]

Even in an era known for it, Blaine stood out for his rabid partisanship. He had come to political maturity during the Civil War, and he would never lose his keen sense that Democrats and power did not mix. Fellow Republicans christened Blaine "the Plumed Knight" for his tendency to charge lance-first into partisan fights. Yet Blaine was an equally enthusiastic warrior in his own party's intramural jousts. When his friend James A. Garfield was elected president in 1880, the new secretary of state advised the president-elect to purge a rival Republican faction by having "their throats cut with a feather."[3]

Such a man elicited strong reactions. Blaine was earnest in his passions—"when I want a thing, I want it dreadfully," he confessed—and that authenticity combined with personal charm, hypnotic oratory, and an unbelievable memory to win Maine's "magnetic man" the unquestioning allegiance of millions. But magnets also repel, and Blaine was despised by many who saw him as the epitome of Gilded Age excess. Allegations of corruption, never proven, stalked him throughout his career, and the subject became as polarized as the man. Blaine was also a relentless political provocateur, and it drove fellow politicians up the wall. Shortly after Blaine moved from the House to the Senate, one of his new colleagues complained, "We had peace and good order in this body before he was transplanted from the other side of the Capitol!"[4]

Yet peace and good order were ironically at the heart of what Blaine wanted his foreign policy to stand for. In the 1880s, he developed a new regional strategy focused on uniting the Americas in the interest of keeping Europe's powers out. Known as Pan-Americanism, Blaine's approach symbolized what the republic wanted its relations with the rest of the region to look like: peaceful and orderly, respectful and prosperous, perhaps with the United States first among equals, but never violently dominating its neighbors. For many years, however, Blaine's vision would remain just that: a vision hanging enticingly on the horizon, guiding him and other statesmen but somehow never quite coming within their grasp. Swamped by exigencies and emergencies, Pan-Americanism would instead remain an ideal whose realization remained frustrated by the rising threat from Europe.

Your Navy and Your Manners

On March 7, 1881, Blaine became President Garfield's secretary of state in a world that seemed to be growing more and more dangerous. In the decade and a half following the Civil War, the United States had mostly enjoyed geopolitical peace and quiet as its great-power rivals fixated on problems in Europe, above all Chancellor Otto von Bismarck's efforts to forge a powerful new German nation-state out of iron and blood. By the early 1880s, however, Germany had consolidated its rise, setting off a new and increasingly ominous struggle among Europe's great powers for control and preeminence.[5]

For the most part, this competition did not take place directly on the continent. Instead, Europe's powers began using new industrial technologies to conquer, colonize, and administer areas of the world previously thought untouchable. The result was a second Age of Imperialism that rivaled even the first of Christopher Columbus and the conquistadors. Between 1870 and 1900, Great Britain, France, and Germany alone added over nine million square miles to their imperial portfolios, an area more than double the size of Europe itself. Africa was sliced apart along with much of Asia and the Middle East, and even those few nations lucky enough to escape outright colonization often fell under tacit European control. By World War I, colonial powers would occupy or control a staggering 84.4 percent of the earth's landmass.[6]

Sinister enough on its own, Europe's colonial scramble alarmed Americans in particular because Latin America appeared to be next. Europe's great powers were investing in the hemisphere at unprecedented rates, and they could easily turn those economic stakes into political wedges, as they had so often done elsewhere. Great Britain was a recurring bogeyman; suspicious American diplomats feared it might soon cash in on its enormous commercial influence. Germany, a latecomer to the game of empire, loomed as another avaricious power, and warnings abounded about its designs on the territories of Haiti, Nicaragua, El Salvador, and the Dominican Republic. Even Napoleon III's ghost returned to haunt the continent when a French company began digging a canal in Panama. Some days, it seemed like every diplomatic pouch that arrived at the State Department's door brought rumors of new European plots to invade the hemisphere.[7]

On all sides of the political aisle, Americans sounded the alarm. Republican Representative John A. Kasson of Iowa, who would spend much of his career representing the United States in Europe, warned that "covetous eyes are cast on outlying islands and continental coasts of Central and South America," a situation made all the more dangerous because the instability of the United States's neighbors "has invited ... the acquisitive passions of several European governments." Samuel J. Tilden, the Democrats' presidential nominee in 1876, agreed. He wrote glumly that "it is impossible to foresee, in the recent scramble of the European powers for the acquisition of colonies, how soon an occasion may arise for our putting in practice the Monroe Doctrine."[8]

EUROPE'S IMPERIALIST EXPLOSION would have frightened Americans less if they had felt prepared to meet it. But when they looked for reassurance to their military—especially their navy—they found it in a distressing state of neglect.

In 1865, Americans had boasted one of the world's most formidable military machines. But peace brought demobilization, and Congress shrunk the one-million-man-plus Civil War army down to a piddling twenty-eight thousand soldiers, most of whom deployed to the Western Plains to fight Native American tribes with Sheridan. Equally dramatic reductions occurred on the water, where Congress retired much of the Union's seven-hundred-ship navy. By 1870, only two hundred ships remained, most obsolete or out of commission.[9]

Over the next decade, the navy continued to deteriorate. Policymakers had little time and less money to spend on naval affairs, and legend has it that one new navy secretary, upon boarding a ship for the very first time, exclaimed, "I'll be blessed! Why, the durned thing's hollow!" Both the country's navy and its commercial fleet reached dangerously depleted levels, and what few ships remained afloat could neither catch their probable targets nor outrun their probable pursuers. By the early 1880s, the republic had fewer than fifty ships that could fire their guns safely, and even those vessels were packing popguns and peashooters compared to the artillery on European warships.[10]

Critics took notice. In 1881, the *Buffalo Daily Courier* chastised the state of "what is by courtesy called a navy." Others were less well-mannered. Civilians and military men alike disparaged the navy as "useless rubbish," "an alphabet of floating wash-tubs," "a heterogeneous collection of naval trash," "an impotent parody of naval force," and even "a sort of marine Falstaffian burlesque." Scarcely worth dignifying "by the name of a 'fleet,'" the navy menaced itself more than any potential enemy. Even Oscar Wilde got in on the joke. When Virginia guessed that the Canterville Ghost might not enjoy visiting the United States because the nation lacked either ruins or curiosities, the Ghost was astounded. "No ruins! No curiosities! You have your navy and your manners."[11]

The Aid of a Common Friend

Convinced that Europe's great powers were again gunning for the hemisphere, and that neither the republic's navy nor its manners could stop them, Secretary Blaine came into office in 1881 ready to chart a new course. Safeguarding the region, however, was easier said than done, and Blaine worried that his predecessors' policies were not enough. Something new, something bolder, was needed, and Blaine thought he had

Secretary of State James G. Blaine: "There has probably never been a man in our history upon whom so few people looked with indifference. He was born to be loved or hated."

the answer: Pan-Americanism, a two-part strategy in which the United States would first mediate and resolve the region's disputes, and then engineer close commercial relations that would eventually culminate in an exclusive hemispheric trading bloc.

Even more than his predecessors, Blaine understood how weak neighbors threatened American security. He had been a freshman representative when Seward and Sheridan were battling Maximilian, and the close calls of those days had made a lasting impression. Blaine believed "a Foreign Empire in Mexico would have been fatal to all that the United States cherished," and like Seward, he had instantly grasped how France's aggressions sprang from Mexico's weakness. Blaine observed later that "our popular maxim, that 'In union there is strength,' finds its counterpart in the equally manifest truth that, 'In division there is weakness.'" Even now, Blaine worried that such divisive weakness was hobbling Latin Americans in their efforts to beat back "the tendencies which operate from without to influence [their] internal affairs."[12]

Unfortunately, the problem was only getting worse. Latin American states had mostly kept their hands to themselves during the previous decade, but that self-control was fast fading. By 1881, border disputes were brewing between Mexico and Guatemala, Costa Rica and Colombia, and Chile and Argentina, while only two years earlier, Chile, Bolivia, and Peru had begun the sanguinary War of the Pacific.[13]

Blaine feared that any blood spilled in these fratricidal conflicts could touch off a European feeding frenzy. Civil wars in the region already made European interventions too easy, but inter-state wars were even worse. By destabilizing multiple countries simultaneously, they could bring "political anarchy and social disorder ... to the conquered, and evils scarcely less serious to the conqueror." Europe's powers could nose into the resulting power vacuums, including by acting as mediators and thereby gaining "enhanced influence and numberless advantages." Even territorial disputes scared Blaine, for they risked the weaker state shopping around Europe for protection. Whatever the particulars, Blaine suspected that these various disputes would always lead to the same result: "an unlimited increase of European and monarchical influence on this continent."[14]

Blaine did not think this problem of order would be solved by either of his predecessors' approaches. One approach—annexation—had been epitomized by Secretary of State William Henry Seward. For Seward, territorial expansion had been more than a vanity project; it was a national security imperative that would cleanse the hemisphere of the nation's rivals while eliminating opportunities for their return. One of his greatest accomplishments—the purchase of Alaska from Russia—had expressly been framed in those terms, but his territorial wish list had also extended to the hemisphere's unruly independent nations. Consensual annexation, he had reasoned, would be a win-win: by rescuing his country's neighbors from "chronic revolution and anarchy," as well as the "foreign possession or control" that often followed in its train, it would benefit both the region and the United States.[15]

Seward and other annexationists, however, had never managed to win the rest of the nation over to their program. Partly, that was because national attention had remained focused, as Seward sadly observed, "upon the domestic questions which have grown out of the late civil war." It was also partly because racism had made and would continue to make annexation unpalatable. Congressmen could stomach incorporating Alaska because they mistakenly believed it was an empty icebox, but annexing tropical places—and thus "tropical people"—was a different story. In combination, these anti-expansionist currents had helped scuttle several of Seward's annexationist projects, as well as President Ulysses S. Grant's misguided attempt to annex the Dominican Republic. By the early 1870s, most observers had pronounced the annexationist project dead, and Blaine was not eager to resurrect it. In any event, annexationism didn't offer much of a solution to the sort of inter-state conflicts now ripping through the region.[16]

Seward's successors, Hamilton Fish and William M. Evarts, had championed a second approach to keeping Europe out of the hemisphere. Like Seward, they had eyed instability in the region with unease, recognizing the temptations that weakness could offer foreign great powers. But rather than annexation, they had hoped to remedy this instability through trade and investment. Early in his tenure, Fish had observed that Latin American states were often stuck in a vicious trap: political instability sapped their economic growth, but without that economic growth, these states could never escape their political instability. Fish thought that the United States could interrupt this cycle of instability and help shift it into reverse by expanding commercial ties with the region. Properly encouraged, American capital and revenue would pour in, strengthening Latin America's governments, displacing rapacious Europeans, and stabilizing the region's politics and economies. That, in turn, would lead to closer commercial ties. On and on it would go—an ever-accelerating cycle of mutual stability and profitability.[17]

Blaine, however, doubted that commercial ties alone could fix the problem of order that the hemisphere faced. Blaine appreciated the stabilizing effects of commerce, but he thought that Fish and Evarts had been putting the cart before the horse by waiting for those ties to develop naturally. "Peace is essential to commerce," Blaine argued, and as long as the region remained politically divided, "it would be idle to attempt the development and enlargement of our trade." Only once Latin America had resolved its conflicts and become a real community could the United States take the next step of weaving the regional trade relations that Blaine, Fish, and Evarts all desired.[18]

Blaine accordingly devised a new approach to the region centered on Washington helping Latin America resolve its political conflicts. "Nations, like individuals, often require the aid of a common friend to restore relations of amity," and he could imagine no better friend to all Latin America than the United States. It was thus natural, he thought, for his country to tender its "amicable counsel." And by actively superintending its neighbors' quarrels, the United States could promote the regional unity that was so indispensable to keeping meddlesome Europeans out.[19]

In the meantime, Blaine would take a harder line against Europe. Over the previous decade, the State Department had begun policing European movements in the hemisphere with newfound doggedness, but Blaine would take this scrutiny to the next level. He was especially alarmed by the French canal company digging away in Panama, and he was determined to reassert the republic's "rightful and long-established claim to priority on the American continent" vis-à-vis Europe. Part of that reassertion would come in the form of prickly diplomatic circulars, but part of it would be grounded in military power. To that end, Blaine planned to scour the region for naval bases and coaling stations to be used in a program of hemispheric defense.[20]

On one level, Blaine's new approach to American regional policy seemed modest, even boring: he was hardly the first to try reinforcing the Monroe Doctrine through diplomacy. But Blaine's vision rose above its specifics by reconceptualizing his country's role in a fundamental way. For decades, Americans had stayed aloof from regional politics. Blaine wanted to end that isolation and engineer a new "American system" with the United States as its beating political heart. Henceforth, the republic would assume a leading role in hemispheric relations—not only passively relying on the region's natural suspicions of Europe, but actively cultivating Pan-American solidarity; not only binding the region's wounds, but managing and even restructuring its relationships from the ground up.[21]

BLAINE DIDN'T HAVE much time to implement this new strategy. On July 2, 1881, a disgruntled office seeker shot President Garfield in the capital's train station; on September 19, barely six months into office, Garfield succumbed to his injuries.[22]

Garfield's death left Blaine's policies and career in shambles. Europe's powers had not yet encroached on the Americas, but the region was more disorderly than ever. In his first few months in office, Blaine had tried mediating some of the hemisphere's ongoing conflicts, but his efforts had proved unsuccessful; worse, they had spawned rumors of corruption that ran all the way to the top. Such gossip was deadly for the Department's diplomatic initiatives, and also for Blaine, whose political future depended on escaping the cries of sleaze that had persistently dogged his career.[23]

Blaine submitted his resignation, knowing the new president, Chester A. Arthur, would want his own man in the job. Arthur graciously insisted that Blaine stay on until the new Congress met in December 1881, but Blaine's days were numbered and he knew it. He had only months to salvage his policies and his reputation.[24]

His solution was characteristically bold and imaginative—a Pan-American Peace Conference. Blaine was already tiring of "friendly intervention here and there"; he wanted something more comprehensive. He decided the answer was to convene all the free states of the hemisphere, establish a formal system of arbitration, and thereby make future wars on the continent impossible. In so doing, the Conference would erase "the extremest danger" Blaine saw confronting "the political institutions, the peaceful progress, and the liberal civilization of all America." It was also the sort of daring gesture that could revive Blaine's reputation as a statesman.[25]

Blaine did not have time to convene the Conference himself, but he thought he could lock it into the agenda of the new administration. After convincing Arthur of the Conference's merits, and with only a few weeks left on the job, Blaine ordered invitations sent to all the free capitals of the New World.[26]

Blaine had served as secretary of state for only nine and a half months, and for most of that time he was either incapacitated by Garfield's faltering health or a lame duck in Arthur's new administration. But in his limited tenure, Blaine had devised a coherent strategy to seal the hemisphere's most egregious fault lines, culminating in his plan for a Pan-American Conference. Mistakes, as they say, had been made, but Blaine left office with a spring in his step, confident that time would prove the wisdom of his policies.[27]

Snap and Vitality

Blaine would be out of power for the next seven years. During that time, his policies would be repeatedly reversed, ridiculed, and denounced. He would be pilloried in the press as "Jingo Jim," investigated by congressional committees, and abandoned by members of his own party. Yet by the time he took back the State Department in 1889, he had been vindicated. In the interim, his successors had lurched backward, forward, and sideways, but overall they had followed the course he had marked out. Gone were the days when the United States would rely passively on natural commercial ties for protection. Given the rising threat from Europe, the republic would instead take a more active role in shielding its neighbors from external interference.

Blaine had counted on President Arthur's approval of the Pan-American Conference to defend him from criticism once he left office, but he underestimated the lengths to which his political opponents would go. Blaine's Republican rivals hated him almost as much as the Democrats, and his successor as secretary, Frederick T. Frelinghuysen, was no exception. The new secretary decided that much of Blaine's diplomacy was incurably blighted, and shortly after entering office he began pulling the plug on Blaine's hemispheric initiatives, including the Pan-American Conference.[28]

At first, Blaine endured these reversals with what his wife called "the patient dignity of perfect silence." Alas, neither patience nor silence were Blaine's strong suits, and he quickly abandoned both. Pro-Blaine newspapers began carrying a blitz of interviews and letters in which Blaine vigorously defended his policies.[29]

Blaine justified his attempts to mediate regional conflicts using the logic of preemption. "The United States cannot play between nations the part of dog in the manger," he warned. "Our own Government cannot take the ground that it will not offer friendly intervention to settle troubles between American countries, unless, at the same time, it freely concedes to European governments the right of such intervention, and thus consents to a practical destruction of the Monroe Doctrine." In effect, Blaine argued, Americans could stop Europe's great powers from inserting themselves into the hemisphere's disputes only by getting there first.[30]

Few seemed persuaded by these arguments, and over the next several months, the Republican Party turned into a circular firing squad. In March 1882, the fight peaked when the Republican-controlled House Committee on Foreign Affairs launched an investigation into the allegations of corruption swirling around the State Department's diplomacy. Blaine was ostensibly outside the inquiry's scope, but everyone understood he was the true target.[31]

Characteristically, Blaine met the challenge head-on, appearing in person before the committee to testify. Over three days, he ran circles around infuriated congressmen, turning the hearings into a circus of which he was the undisputed ringleader. "You have not lost a tittle of your snap and vitality," one former senator congratulated him. In the end, the Committee declared unhappily that it had found no evidence of wrongdoing by any officer of the United States.[32]

For everyone but the Democrats, it had been a disastrous fight. Blaine had dodged all mortal blows, but the intraparty fracas had left him dirtied and smeared once again with allegations of corruption. Secretary of State Frelinghuysen and the rest of Arthur's administration had not fared much better, distancing themselves from Blaine's policies at the cost of party unity. By the time the dust settled, only one thing seemed certain: Blaine's policies were, like the man himself, politically radioactive.[33]

For all their criticism, however, Frelinghuysen and Arthur would ultimately follow in Blaine's footsteps to a remarkable degree. Both saw a rising threat across the Atlantic, and both shared Blaine's commitment to combating it proactively. All that changed was the emphasis. Whereas Blaine had focused his energies on the first part of his hemispheric strategy (diplomatic engagement), Frelinghuysen and Arthur chose to prioritize the second (commercial ties) while strengthening the country's ultimate backstop, the U.S. Navy.[34]

Frelinghuysen believed the Monroe Doctrine was premised on "the common interests of the states of North and South America," and that those common interests sprang "from unity of commercial interests." The key to "excluding foreign political influence" was correspondingly straightforward: the United States needed to bind the hemisphere together commercially.[35]

Like Blaine, however, Frelinghuysen concluded that those commercial ties were not flowering quickly enough on their own. Frelinghuysen sought to accelerate the process by negotiating trade reciprocity treaties with six states and colonies around the Caribbean basin that would spur trade by mutually reducing tariffs. Frelinghuysen also persuaded Congress to fund a special commission on Latin American trade. "At no time since the foundation of this Government," Frelinghuysen told the commissioners, "has there been a deeper conviction of the advisability of knitting closely the relations of the United States to the large family of independent nations which has grown up on the American continent."[36]

Commercial carrots were well and good, but the administration wagered they would mean little if the United States could not also hold Europe at bay with a strong navy. Garfield had already begun reforming the fleet, but it was only under Arthur that the effort picked up steam. In 1883, Congress authorized the construction of the White Squadron, three steel-plated cruisers and one dispatch boat. It was a modest start, but it would become the nucleus around which the rest of the "New Navy" would grow over the next two decades.[37]

In 1884, Blaine burst back onto the political scene when, after many previous failed attempts, he finally convinced the Republican Party to nominate him for president.[38]

If Blaine was hoping for a substantive election season, he was to be disappointed. He and his opponent, Grover Cleveland, became mutual victims of one of the dirtiest campaigns in American electoral history.

Blaine tried to highlight serious substantive issues, but few cared. Not for the last time, substance was sidelined by a public that craved sex and sleaze; voters were less interested in Pan-American peace than in Blaine's alleged graft and Cleveland's child out of marriage. On Election Day, Blaine's fanatic personal following came up just short. Only 1,149 more votes in New York—out of more than a million cast in the state— would have made him president.[39]

Cleveland's election did not bode well for Blaine's regional policies. Cleveland was the first Democrat elected president in almost three de-cades, and there was little love lost between him and Republicans, especially Blaine. But as with Frelinghuysen's "reversal" of Blaine's policies, Cleve-land's outward rejection of Republican orthodoxy masked an underlying continuity in vision and policies.[40]

Nothing proved the point like trade. On entering office, Cleveland strangled Frelinghuysen's regional reciprocity treaties in the crib. But the new president did not oppose using trade ties to advance national security objectives. Instead, Cleveland opposed the high tariff wall that surrounded the entire American economy, and he wanted to blast the trumpet of free trade to bring it down Jericho style. The problem with Frelinghuysen's reciprocity treaties was not that they had gone too far, but that they had not gone far enough—rather than the half measure of reciprocity covering a few goods with a few countries, Cleveland sought total reform.[41]

Cleveland also continued building up the New Navy despite some initial doubts. By the end of his administration, Congress had appropri-ated the funding for an additional thirty ships, including six protected cruisers, one armored cruiser, and two second-class battleships.[42]

Cleveland even grudgingly accepted the idea of a Pan-American Conference. Ever since Blaine had proposed it in 1881, the idea had resonated with politicians of both parties. Even Frelinghuysen—who had canceled invitations to the original conference—eventually changed his mind. Cleveland himself never got excited about the project, but he decided not to fight the rising tide when Congress (including a Demo-cratic House) passed a bill in 1888 calling for a Conference. Cleveland signed the bill and sent out invitations in mid-July.[43]

Blaine's Pan-American Conference would—almost eight years af-ter he had proposed it—finally happen. But the Conference would not actually begin until late 1889, at which point Cleveland would already be out of office. It would instead fall to Benjamin Harrison's incoming secretary of state to pilot the proceedings, and by a queer twist of fate, that secretary would be none other than Blaine himself.[44]

We Must Win Their Confidence By Deserving It

Much had changed in the previous seven-plus years. Several regional conflicts had fizzled out, and in early 1889, the French company digging a canal in Panama had collapsed into bankruptcy. No longer did the hemisphere seem to teeter on the brink of a war of all against all as it had when Blaine was last in charge.[45]

Yet the more things changed, the more they stayed the same. Blaine was older and more patient, but no less committed to his hemispheric vision. He would use his second stint as secretary of state to vindicate the central idea of his first—that to combat the rising European threat, Washington needed to restore order in the region through diplomacy and trade. The next four years would stand at once as a monument to his success in implementing that vision and a testament to its ultimate failure.

====

PRESIDENT BENJAMIN HARRISON had confided to Blaine before inauguration that he was "especially interested" in improving relations with Latin America, and that "we must win their confidence by deserving it." At first, Harrison made good on that pronouncement by earnestly supporting Blaine's two biggest priorities: hosting the Pan-American Conference and strengthening regional trade ties.[46]

Since the Garfield days, the Pan-American Conference's agenda had grown mightily to include not just political questions but also commercial affairs. For Blaine, though, the Conference's heart remained what it had always been—establishing a regional system of arbitration, all so that war could be banished from the hemisphere along with the resulting opportunities for European expansion.[47]

Blaine was to be disappointed. The State Department successfully persuaded delegates from seventeen Latin American countries to assemble in Washington in late 1889 for the First International Conference of American States. But the Department had not quelled its neighbors' suspicions that, as the Mexican representative put it, Washington aimed "to secure the political and commercial ascendancy of the United States on this continent." Blaine did his best to address these concerns through a friendly and conciliatory approach, but he was constantly confronted by strident opposition from several delegations.[48]

Stirred by this resistance, the Conference achieved little. The delegates established the International Union of American Republics, which would one day evolve into the Organization of American States but for now only shared commercial information among its members. Otherwise, the Conference watered down Blaine's grand visions and bold policies into the pulp of nonbinding resolutions.[49]

Few areas demonstrated the Conference's failure more clearly than arbitration. Recalling Blaine's first term as secretary, some Latin American delegates expressed fears that Washington might use any arbitration treaty as an excuse to butt into their affairs. The Conference accordingly produced only a report on arbitration, as well as a milquetoast treaty signed by seven delegations, none of whose states would ever ratify it.[50]

Only in retrospect would the irony become obvious. Latin Americans feared American primacy and thought they could resist it by diluting Blaine's Conference to the point of irrelevance. But they failed to appreciate the security concerns driving his effort, and the fact that if those anxieties were not addressed by the region, the United States might reach for more unilateral measures next.

—

ONCE THE CONFERENCE ended, Blaine turned to the second half of his regional strategy—stronger regional commercial relations. Blaine had originally wanted a regional customs union, but after the Conference buried that proposal, he decided to negotiate a series of reciprocity agreements instead.[51]

Following another vicious intraparty fight, Blaine persuaded a Republican Congress to grant the Executive Branch unilateral authority to impose duties on any country that refused to extend reciprocity to the United States. From Blaine's perspective, this arrangement was ideal because it allowed him to enact reciprocity agreements without needing to go to the temperamental Senate for approval.[52]

Blaine parlayed his new authority into a blitz of bilateral trade negotiations. He signed his first reciprocity agreement with Brazil, hoping to use trade ties to support and stabilize the country's new democratic regime and thereby avert a rumored European plan to restore a recently deposed emperor. By early 1892, the State Department had also struck reciprocity agreements with Spain (for Cuba and Puerto Rico), the Dominican Republic, Great Britain (the British West Indies), and four out of the five states of Central America.[53]

For the moment, it was an impressive accomplishment. Blaine's predecessor Frelinghuysen had only ever managed to negotiate a handful of regional reciprocity treaties, only one of which was implemented. By contrast, Blaine had enacted eight of them in a little over a year.[54]

The Danger to the United States

Signs that Blaine's successes and vision might not outlast him, however, began appearing even before he left office. In 1881, he had masterminded a regional strategy that some considered too spirited; a decade later, his strategy no longer seemed muscular enough.

Blaine first departed from his pacifist principles in Haiti. In 1891, Haiti was in the midst of civil war, and rumors were rife that one side wanted to buy France's support by leasing it one of Haiti's harbors. Blaine sprang into action and backed the opposing faction. But when his favored side won and reneged on its promises to lease the harbor to the United States, Blaine sent gunboats to get what he was owed. Blaine was bluffing, and when Port-au-Prince refused to negotiate, Washington ignored the advice of its naval officers and refused to use force against the island. But the threat alone did not bode well for the resilience of Blaine's regional vision.[55]

That vision took another hit in the aftermath of a civil war that broke out in Chile in January 1891. As always, Blaine was alert to the threat posed by instability; one administration mouthpiece warned that "the danger to the United States in these crises arises from the disposition of Europeans to interfere." American diplomats watched the conflict with wary eyes but stayed neutral, even though they clearly sympathized with the losing side.[56]

Chile's government had long mistrusted the *norteamericanos*, and when the war ended, the new regime was doubly hostile to a country it believed had aided its recent enemies. American leaders, in turn, were equally antagonistic because they believed the victorious forces had enjoyed British backing.[57]

On October 16, 1891, the powder keg exploded when a bar fight erupted in Valparaiso between Chileans and some uniformed sailors on shore leave from the USS *Baltimore*. By the end of the ensuing riot, eighteen American sailors were injured, one mortally; another lay dead. Washington demanded answers and an apology, especially after its sailors reported being bayoneted by Chilean policemen. Santiago was defiant, and hotheadedness on both sides escalated the crisis to the verge of war.[58]

Blaine urged conciliation and patience. But Harrison would not be mollified. Only after Chile—belatedly regaining its instinct for self-preservation—capitulated to the American president's demands did Blaine steer the imbroglio to a peaceful conclusion.[59]

Latin America could be a dangerous place, and Americans regularly met tragic ends there without dragging the United States to the brink of war. What made the *Baltimore* Affair different was the implicit threat to the Monroe Doctrine. Only a month before the riot, the American minister had attributed much of the "bitter feeling against the United States" to "the English element"; similar reports came from American naval officers. It was natural under these circumstances for the sailors' deaths to take on ominous undertones. Spurred by fears of foreign imperialism, the United States was becoming increasingly sensitive to perceived outrages against its flag.[60]

The *Baltimore* Affair augured ill for Blaine's regional strategy. Blaine had dedicated his two stints as secretary to spreading peace in the Western Hemisphere. If his approach had been working, perhaps Harrison would have been conciliatory. But as far as the administration could tell, Chile had instead taken another step into the European sphere of influence. Blaine's strategy had encountered its first direct challenge, and Harrison had dropped its core prescription without a second thought.[61]

———

PERHAPS THE *BALTIMORE* Affair would have unfolded differently had Blaine been operating at full capacity. But in the crucial first weeks of the crisis, he was recuperating away from the capital after a collapse. Even when he returned, Blaine was weak and worn out. Sometimes, he worked his ill health to his advantage; he broke up one belligerent cabinet meeting, for example, by feigning dizziness. But such ruses could not make up for the fact that Blaine was truly dying.[62]

In May 1892, he suddenly left the room midway through a cabinet meeting. When the war secretary followed him out, he discovered Blaine near collapse. One month later, the secretary resigned his post. Some thought the timing suspicious; the Republican nominating convention would open three days later, and the quadrennial boom in Blaine's favor was again underway. But his enemies need not have worried. Blaine was done with politics. He would slowly waste away before finally dying in his bed on January 27, 1893.[63]

His two stints as secretary of state had bookended a transitional period in American foreign policy, during which Washington had finally begun investing seriously in the Monroe Doctrine's defense. That investment took different forms in different places: militarily, in the New Navy; politically, in Pan-American cooperation, including mediation and regional arbitration; and economically, in a web of reciprocity treaties and hopes of a customs union. Not every aspect of that strategy found favor in every administration of the 1880s. But there was an enduring shift in the seriousness with which American leaders took the European threat, and Blaine led much of the initial charge.

For all of his successes, however—and many were remarkable—Blaine never got his policies to stick. Some failed because of inept implementation. Others fell prey to domestic politics, like his reciprocity treaties, which Democrats killed in 1894 after reclaiming Congress. Still others were foiled by hemispheric politics coupled with Blaine's inability to reconcile the forces working against his vision of institutionalized Pan-Americanism.[64]

Such obstacles, however, were particular to the moment, and in theory they could have been overcome by later statesmen. That they weren't speaks to what ultimately doomed Blaine's vision: the very momentum he had anticipated and exploited in 1881. Blaine's hemispheric vision decayed after his death not because Blaine failed to persuade others of its merits—he was, after all, the magnetic man—but because it increasingly seemed obsolete. As Americans became convinced that Europe's great powers were turning the hemisphere into their latest hunting grounds, it seemed quaint to talk about arbitration or reciprocity, much as it had seemed quaint in 1881 to talk about naturally expanding commercial ties.

Sidelined and increasingly ill, Blaine could not keep up with the mounting threat from Europe during his final months in office. He had been monitoring an escalating boundary dispute between Venezuela and Great Britain, and in late 1891, he wrote he would soon "take an advanced and decisive step" to support Caracas. But he never did. Blaine also worried about Hawai'i, which he feared was tilting irrevocably into the orbit of foreign powers. Once again, however, he did little to resolve the issue. Both problems were instead slopped onto the plate of his successors, where they would explode into two of the defining crises of the 1890s and mark the start of a new and far more assertive phase of American regional policy.[65]

CHAPTER 3

ALL THE WASTE PLACES OF THE EARTH

The First Venezuela Crisis, 1894–1895

O ut of the South American jungle came a dire warning. For decades, Venezuela had found itself at odds with one of the British Empire's colonies over a small patch of wilderness near the mouth of the Orinoco River. Now the boundary dispute was reaching its boiling point—or at least so claimed a pamphlet that began circulating inside the United States in late 1894. British forces were marching into the disputed territory, the pamphlet reported breathlessly, and unless the United States forced Great Britain to arbitrate, "the persistent aggressions of the stronger power" would lead to "the dismemberment of one of the Spanish American republics." The Monroe Doctrine was once again under siege.[1]

Such doom-and-gloom pamphlets were a fixture of *fin de siècle* political life in the United States, and at first glance there was little reason to believe that this one would break into the public consciousness. The pamphlet had a suitably provocative title—*British Aggressions in Venezuela, or the Monroe Doctrine on Trial*—but its pages wallowed in dry, technical arguments about the law of nations.

Nor did *British Aggressions* have a particularly reputable author. William Lindsay Scruggs had until recently been a second-rate American diplomat. But he had met his downfall in Caracas after pressing some private citizens' claims against the Venezuelan government. Accused of stealing part of the resulting settlement, Scruggs had unwisely defended himself by explaining he had used the missing money to bribe the president of Venezuela. Flabbergasted, the State Department forced Scruggs's resignation in late 1892.[2]

But apparently the Venezuelans did not mind being bribed very much, for only a year later they signed up Scruggs as a propagandist. It was the hire of a lifetime. After publishing *British Aggressions*, Scruggs set to work explaining to politicians and the American public alike why they should care about this hitherto obscure dispute. By spring 1895, Scruggs had convinced officials at the highest levels of the American government that, as the subtitle of his pamphlet promised, the Monroe Doctrine was undergoing its ultimate trial.[3]

Scruggs's propaganda, however, would end up being too successful for Venezuela's own good. It would not only trigger the most serious diplomatic crisis over the Doctrine since Seward's time, but also provoke a newly assertive interpretation of American rights. Like the fisherman who sets too ambitious a bait, Venezuela would come to rue the day it hooked the United States.[4]

The Grab Game

Scruggs and his pamphlet surfaced with impeccable timing. Europe's great powers had, after decades of jockeying, almost finished colonizing Africa. In the previous few years alone, Germany had settled the boundaries of Kamerun, France had established or organized colonies in Guinea, the Côte d'Ivoire, and the Dahomey while starting to conquer Madagascar, and the British had occupied Matabeleland, proclaimed the East African Protectorate, and annexed Pondoland and British Bechuanaland into their Cape Colony. In Asia, the story was much the same; France, for example, had just turned Laos into a protectorate.[5]

Strange and foreign as these developments must have seemed, Americans could not mistake their meaning: European colonialism was voracious, it was insatiable, and it was running low on rations in its half of the world. By the mid-1890s, Americans thus became convinced that their hemisphere was next on the menu, a crisis mentality that seemed amply confirmed by a streak of European interventions nearby.[6]

One of the first warnings came from Brazil. In September 1893, Brazil's navy revolted and began blockading Rio de Janeiro. Rumors flew that the rebels intended to overthrow the fledgling republican government and restore a recently deposed monarchy. Soon, authoritative sources reported that Great Britain and Germany were secretly supplying the rebels.[7]

In response, Washington dispatched the most powerful fleet it had ever assembled with orders to break the rebel blockade. When one of the rebel admirals decided to test the Americans' resolve by firing a blank shell over the bow of an American merchantman, the American navy responded by sending a real shell within six feet of the rebel ship. The rebels backed down, and within a few weeks the rebellion was collapsing.[8]

No sooner had the grateful Brazilian government begun erecting a monument to President Monroe, however, than his Doctrine came under threat farther north. In early 1894, Nicaragua tried to assert control over an indigenous reservation within its borders that had long been a British protectorate. Great Britain and the United States raced warships to the scene, but the American vessel sank on its way there—the New Navy was apparently still a work in progress—and, after landing unopposed, British forces pushed the Nicaraguan troops back. Washington protested strongly, and in July it took the opportunity presented by a revolution to send another ship. This one made it successfully, and the United States kept the British at bay long enough for Nicaragua to successfully incorporate the reservation.[9]

Great Britain, however, was not quite done. It demanded reparations for its consul's mistreatment during the incident. When Nicaragua refused to pay, British marines seized and occupied the port of Corinto on April 27, 1895. One week later, Managua caved and settled the claim, and the British withdrew.[10]

European gunboat diplomacy almost claimed another victim around the same time in the Dominican Republic. In February 1895, France sent a warship there to demand reparations for the death of a French citizen. A French attack was averted only when three American warships arrived, supposedly for gun practice.[11]

Europe's attention then swiveled back south. In May 1895, armed clashes broke out between Brazil and French Guiana over more than 150,000 square miles of gold-filled territory. Only two months later, the British occupied Trinidad, a small island also claimed by Brazil. Both disputes would be settled peacefully, but at that moment, they seemed suspiciously similar to the kinds of pretextual incidents and provocations the great powers had long used to justify what one State Department official called "the grab game."[12]

Leery Americans blamed the wave of European incursions on many causes. Some thought the fault lay with the future isthmian canal, which one day would redirect trade routes through the Caribbean and was thus now attracting the attention of the great powers. Others argued that rising great-power interest reflected a sort of colonial *lebensraum*: Europeans were simply running out of other places to colonize. Finally, most Americans agreed that European interventions were stoked by the weakness of the United States's neighbors. In 1891, the secretary of the navy reported on Europe's "systematic effort to take advantage of the disturbed conditions now prevailing in many of the [region's] smaller states." Left unchecked, he warned, Europe's "aggressive energy" would lead first to "commercial supremacy" and ultimately to "territorial control."[13]

AGAINST THIS BACKDROP, Venezuela's dispute with Great Britain took on sinister meanings. Venezuela had struggled since independence to define its eastern border with the neighboring colony of British Guiana. Caracas desperately wanted to settle the dispute through arbitration, but from its perspective, London was refusing to compromise. Worse, British claims seemingly grew larger every year as British settlers flocked farther and farther into the jungle. When gold had been found in the disputed area—including, at 509 ounces, the largest nugget ever discovered—the dispute had turned even more intractable.[14]

Caracas had little direct leverage over London, so Venezuelans had tried to convince the regional heavyweight, the United States, to champion their cause. But the United States, despite decades of interest, could not seem to get London to budge. Great Britain repeatedly said it was happy to arbitrate, but only if Venezuela conceded an unacceptably

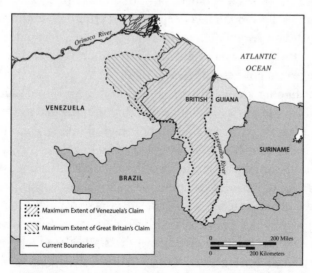

The Venezuela-British Guiana Border Dispute

large portion of British claims up front. There the matter had rested until Scruggs came onto the scene.[15]

Peaceably If We Can, Forcibly If We Must

Europe's streak of incursions convinced many Americans that it was past time to bare their teeth and leap to the hemisphere's defense. Secretary of State James Blaine had offered Pan-Americanism, in both its commercial and diplomatic flavors, as the solution to the problem of European imperialism. But many of his ideas had never bridged the gap between rhetoric and reality. Congress had been unable to get its act together and subsidize merchant shipping, reach a consensus on tariffs, or dig a transisthmian canal, and Latin Americans would not agree to a customs union or other forms of integration. Even if Blaine's vision had borne more fruit, however, it appeared powerless against Europe's colonialist juggernaut in the short term.[16]

Confrontation of some sort seemed increasingly necessary, and the environment was ripe for firebrands, alarmists, and propagandists. Ex-diplomat and now–Venezuelan propagandist Scruggs would take advantage, but he was not alone. Henry Cabot Lodge, the junior Republican senator from Massachusetts, was also deeply invested in the Monroe Doctrine's defense, and together the two men would send the nation's pulse racing.

—

LODGE WAS THE scion of one of Boston's first families. Like many Boston Brahmins, his blood ran a deep shade of crimson—Harvard for college, Harvard for law school, and Harvard again for a doctorate in history, one of the first three ever awarded in the country. Harvard, too, helped steer Lodge into politics in the early 1880s.[17]

Campaigning among the unwashed masses was not "Lah-de-dah" Lodge's forte. He was, one friend remarked, "unmitigated Boston"—heir to a centuries-old patrician tradition of "high thinking, dauntless intolerance, bleak bad manners, suppression of feeling, [and] tenacity in its stern beliefs." Among intimates, Lodge could be charming, witty, and well read, but to outsiders he appeared cold, sarcastic, and judgmental. He also could not orate to save his life; he rasped in a high-pitched voice that reminded some listeners of bedsheets being torn. Even Lodge's personal appearance—his thin lips, dapper dress, trim Van Dyke beard, and tall, stiff-necked bearing—bespoke his aristocratic origins.[18]

<u>Senator Henry Cabot Lodge</u>: "He has a trick, even among his friends, of so putting things as to excite, when you do not agree with him, instinctive resentment.... He gives stimulants when wiser practice would prefer sedatives."

Despite these hindrances, Lodge was elected to the House in 1887 and then the Senate in 1893, where he would lead the Republican caucus for over thirty years. He owed his political success to his energy, family wealth, and single-mindedness, as well as to his friends, who were few in number but great in influence. Lodge also benefited from his serrated brilliance, which multiplied his enemies endlessly but also made him a force to be reckoned with.[19]

One of Lodge's chief concerns as a politician was the pitiless nature of world politics. "The tendency of modern times is toward consolidation," Lodge observed, and Europe's great powers were rapidly swallowing up not only "all the waste places of the earth" but also "all that were weakly held." Colonialism per se did not bother him; after all, he boasted, "we have a record of conquest, colonization, and territorial expansion unequalled by any people in the nineteenth century." But those days were mostly behind the rounded-out republic. Less so for Europe; in Lodge's eyes, the European "land-hunger which had led to the partition of Africa was not likely to be satisfied while anything else remained undevoured." And Latin America was particularly ripe for the eating. Europe surely found "very tempting" the region's "many weak governments" and "almost endless quantities of rich and unoccupied land."[20]

Lodge accordingly favored an extremely nationalistic but ultimately defensive foreign policy. In the short term, that meant modernizing the navy, aggressively combatting European incursions, and expanding American influence over a handful of outposts necessary to guard the hemisphere. In the longer run, Lodge subscribed proudly to the benchmark principle that "there is to be no more Europe in America." "I do not think anything in our foreign relations is so important," he declared, "as the absolute maintenance of the principle which excludes Europe from America."[21]

———

SHORTLY AFTER MEETING Scruggs in early 1895, Lodge began raising the alarm about British aggressions in Venezuela. Once, Mexico had been the front line; now, Lodge argued, it was Venezuela's turn. If Great Britain took Venezuelan territory, "there is nothing to prevent her taking the whole of Venezuela or any other South American state. If Great Britain can do this with impunity, France and Germany will do it also." Once the Venezuelan domino tumbled, the rest of the hemisphere would fall alongside it. Only one option remained, the senator insisted: a sequel to the French expulsion from Mexico. "The supremacy of the Monroe doctrine should be established and at once—peaceably if we can, forcibly if we must."[22]

Scruggs added fuel to Lodge's public fire. Unlike Venezuela's other representatives in Washington, Scruggs was a creature of the American capital and knew his way around its inner sanctums. In January and February 1895, he masterminded the passage of a congressional resolution recommending arbitration of the dispute. He also arranged private meetings, ghostwrote favorable speeches and reports, and even buttonholed the president twice. All the while, Scruggs continued to circulate his pamphlet far and wide, sending it to congressmen, cabinet members, state officials, public libraries, and newspapers and magazines across the country. In late April, Scruggs's campaign received a boost when the British occupied the Nicaraguan port of Corinto. Scruggs seized on the incident to fan American apprehensions, helpfully issuing a new edition of his now-famous pamphlet.[23]

It wasn't long before anxiety over the dispute reached fever pitch. For Lodge and other red-blooded Americans, however, recently re-elected President Grover Cleveland remained unaccountably missing in action. "Under the present Administration our foreign policy has been everywhere a policy of retreat and surrender," thundered Lodge. Editorial pages nationwide agreed.[24]

In June 1895, Lodge leveled an ultimatum. If Cleveland had not enforced the Monroe Doctrine by December, the new Congress would have to do it for him.[25]

Words the Equivalent of Blows

Cleveland did not need much prompting. Even before Lodge's threats, the president already appreciated the dangers of British bullying, and he had decided to send a dispatch to London demanding that Great Britain arbitrate the dispute.[26]

Cleveland asked his new secretary of state, Richard Olney, to draft the text. Olney had joined the cabinet two years earlier as attorney general. Superhuman amounts of energy and drive made him the wonder of lesser men but also isolated him from his colleagues. "A cold sparkle, as of frost, not of fire, goes with Olney," reported one journalist. "He is clear, frigid, wintry and has no sympathies." He was also imperious. Obstacles were not to be reasoned or negotiated with; they were to be crushed underfoot. Olney would resolve disputes equitably, but on his terms, after squeezing complete and unconditional surrender from his adversaries.[27]

Secretary of State Richard Olney: "A man gem, as I have said; no influence, corrodes, no fires melt; under all pressures, through all conditions, Olney is immutable."

Olney had been reading up on the Venezuelan dispute even before becoming secretary of state, and once the affair officially became part of his portfolio, he redoubled his efforts. He devoured Scruggs's pamphlet, decades' worth of diplomatic correspondence, and every relevant State Department file. Slowly, the contours of a draft dispatch began to emerge.[28]

Olney's studies convinced him that, as Lodge had said, Europe's great powers were once again on the prowl. Stopping this and future incursions would take more than an occasional diplomatic note from Washington. "In English eyes the United States was … so completely a negligible quantity," Olney complained, that "only words the equivalent of blows would be really effective." His draft grew sharper.[29]

On July 2, Olney dropped the finished draft off at the Cape Cod estate where Cleveland was summering. He then retired nearby to anxiously await the president's review.[30]

Cleveland's reaction arrived five days later. "I read your deliverance on Venezuelan affairs," the president told him. "Its [sic] the best thing of the kind I have ever read and it leads to a conclusion that one cannot escape if he tries—that is if there is anything of the Monroe Doctrine at all." Cleveland had "some suggestions to make"—"I always have"—but they were generally "not of much account," just "a little more softened verbiage here and there." For the next two weeks, the president and his triumphant secretary worked the details out. On July 20, 1895, the dispatch was ready, and Olney ordered it sent to the Court of St. James.[31]

―――

OLNEY'S DISPATCH WOULD become known as the "twenty-inch gun," a reference to both its prodigious length (over eleven thousand words) and the force with which it hit London.[32]

Olney started out gently enough. He summarized the dispute, highlighted "the continuous growth of the undefined British claim," and contrasted Venezuela's interest in settling the boundary with Great Britain's steadfast refusal to do so.[33]

Olney then came to the crux of the issue—the Monroe Doctrine. In 1823, President Monroe had declared Latin America off limits to Europe's scheming powers, and since then the Doctrine had retained its "great import to the safety and welfare of the United States." For good reason, Olney argued. "To-day," he rhapsodized, "the United States is practically sovereign on this continent, and its fiat is law upon the subjects to which it confines its interposition." Such superiority did not come from the republic's "high character" or "wisdom and justice," much less any "friendship or good will felt for it." Instead, Olney explained, the country was "master of the situation and practically invulnerable" only because of its "infinite resources [and] isolated position."[34]

Such blessed security depended on the Monroe Doctrine's continuing integrity. If the Doctrine should crack, "the struggle now going on for the acquisition of Africa might be transferred to South America," with a continent-wide partition as "the ultimate result." "How a greater calamity than this could overtake us," Olney brooded, "is difficult to see." "Our only real rivals in peace as well as enemies in war would be found located at our very doors," and in response Americans would need to arm themselves "to the teeth," raise "huge warlike establishments," and divert their energies away from productive pursuits.[35]

Olney observed that Great Britain had insisted it meant no harm in Venezuela, but its promises were worth little. Americans still remembered bitterly how, during the Civil War, France had "set up a monarchy in the adjoining state of Mexico." If Europe's powers had "held important South American possessions to work from and to benefit, the temptation to destroy the predominance of the Great Republic in this hemisphere by furthering its dismemberment might have been irresistible."[36]

So no, Olney boomed, Washington would not stand idly by as Europe crept into the Americas. It did not matter that Great Britain was allegedly appropriating Venezuelan territory by moving the border of an old colony rather than planting a new one. Either way, the British would be colonizing new acres; either way, they would be expanding political control. Olney did not know whether this land theft was actually occurring, but the Monroe Doctrine would be "simply illusory" if Washington could not find out.[37]

Blaine had previously insisted that Europe not arbitrate border disputes among the region's republics. Now, Olney claimed, Europe could not unilaterally decide border disputes *with* the region's republics either. He therefore demanded that Great Britain submit its boundary dispute with Venezuela to international arbitration—or else.[38]

OLNEY AND CLEVELAND hoped to receive the British response to this blunderbuss by early December 1895, when the president would send his annual message to the new Congress. But the days turned into weeks, the weeks into months. Meanwhile, the American press seethed. "England never sleeps, never rests," the *Atlanta Constitution* groused. "If we do not wake up very soon England will have all of Central and South America under her control." In mid-October, reports surfaced that

London wanted reparations from Venezuela for arresting British citizens in disputed territory. If Caracas did not pay up, the British threatened to collect payment through "other means." "What is the limit of tolerance?" the *New York Times* cried.[39]

Olney anxiously followed up with Whitehall twice and was assured he would get an answer in time for Cleveland's annual message. But early December came and went. On December 2, Cleveland lamely informed Congress that Great Britain's answer was still "expected shortly." The next day, a chaplain led Congress in a rather pointed prayer: "Heavenly Father, let peace reign throughout our borders. Yet may we be quick to resent anything like an insult to this our nation."[40]

Great Britain's response finally arrived a few days later. It turned out that Prime Minister Lord Salisbury had somehow miscalculated when Cleveland's message to Congress was due. But it hardly mattered; Salisbury's poor timing only heaped insult on top of injury.[41]

Salisbury's response to Olney's message was a dismissive yawn. Sidestepping the Monroe Doctrine's validity, he denied its relevance to the Venezuelan dispute. Furthermore, he dismissed Olney's claim that Washington could force European states to arbitrate every regional border dispute. Such a prerogative came dangerously close in Salisbury's view to announcing a regional protectorate, which would impose "upon the United States the duty of answering for the conduct of these States, and consequently the responsibility of controlling it." Since Washington had not taken that step, Salisbury thought it should butt out.[42]

Cleveland and Olney were livid. Neither had expected a negative response, much less one so snide. Salisbury had, the president later complained, treated the Monroe Doctrine as "a mere plaything."[43]

On December 17, 1895, Cleveland fired back in a special message to Congress. Salisbury's response was "deeply disappointing," the president revealed, and had tacitly rejected a doctrine "essential to the integrity of our free institutions." Cleveland explained that "while it is a grievous thing to contemplate the two great English-speaking peoples of the world as being otherwise than friendly competitors in the onward march of civilization," there was only one option left—Americans needed to send their own commission to those distant wilds to decide "the true divisional line" between Venezuela and Great Britain. Washington would then be obliged to defend that line "by every means in its power." "In making these recommendations," the president finished darkly, "I am fully alive to the responsibility incurred, and keenly realize all the consequences that may follow."[44]

Everyone understood what Cleveland meant. For the first time in decades, the United States was threatening war over the Monroe Doctrine.

━━

CLEVELAND HAD EXPECTED his stand to resonate, but he could hardly have imagined just how fierce and wild the response would be. Congress pushed partisan rivalries aside and approved the funds for the president's proposed boundary commission unanimously and almost instantly. Lodge, until now the president's chief antagonist, applauded the "universal determination to be entirely firm and sustain the President." One poll of state governors similarly showed that twenty-six of twenty-eight endorsed Cleveland's stance unconditionally. On the eve of a presidential election year, Republicans were tripping over themselves to applaud a Democratic president.[45]

Cleveland was also overwhelmed by public support. Letters and resolutions hailing the president's position poured in, and everyone from Civil War veterans to the Irish National Alliance offered their aid if war began. "Let but a drum tap be heard from the White House grounds," bellowed the *Washington Post*, and "the whole surface of the earth will bristle with moving regiments, the sheen of whose bayonets will pale the stars. Now, let perfidious Albion tremble and the commission get to work! We rest upon our arms."[46]

Pettifogging

Across the Atlantic, jaws dropped. Had the Americans lost their bloody minds? British diplomats were used to a little unkindness from their former colony, but this was ridiculous. Salisbury could not comprehend war over a dispute in which the United States had "no apparent practical concern." The *London Times* likewise described the British mood as "incredulous bewilderment."[47]

Before the British could fully wrap their minds around Cleveland's threat, they were distracted by affairs elsewhere in their empire. On January 3, 1896, the German Kaiser publicly congratulated the president of the South African Republic for fending off a raid by British irregulars. By revealing German support for the Afrikaners, the Kaiser's telegram reinforced Great Britain's mounting sense of isolation. At a time when London felt at odds with most of Europe's great powers, it suddenly became imprudent to alienate the United States as well.[48]

Conciliation was further hastened by rising dissent within the United States. Cleveland's special message had elicited almost uniform support at first, but second thoughts soon emerged from businessmen, academics, and the clergy. Arguments in favor of peace were further reinforced by a short-lived stock market crash three days after Cleveland's message. The ticker tape eloquently said all that needed to be said about the ties binding the two countries together.[49]

Cleveland and Olney were annoyed at those cowardly Americans whose patriotism "traverses exclusively the pocket nerve," but in truth neither man had ever thought war likely. Quarrelsome language aside, Cleveland had called for a fact-finding commission precisely to buy time for negotiations.[50]

Olney opened back-channel talks with the British in January 1896 and, after finding them in a conciliatory mood, moved the negotiations to Washington. Olney did not enjoy painstaking diplomatic work very much, calling it "a sort of pettifogging which accomplishes nothing." But he had a knack for it. Over the course of the year, Olney pummeled the British into capitulating to almost every American demand.[51]

On November 12, 1896, Great Britain agreed to arbitrate the boundary line fully, though with a thumb on the scale for any areas with British settlements greater than fifty years old. Shortly thereafter, Venezuela accepted the terms as well.[52]

In October 1899, the arbitral tribunal announced its decision—Venezuela would receive the mouth of the Orinoco River and five thousand square miles in the interior; the rest was Great Britain's. Like all good compromises, it left both sides at a loss. Venezuela had received nowhere near its maximum claims, but Great Britain would surrender territory it had sworn never to arbitrate.[53]

Few Americans even noticed by that point, however. They had long since won the only victory that mattered. They had invoked the Monroe Doctrine against the greatest of Europe's great powers, and that power had—meekly, supinely, submissively—backed down.[54]

No Just Occasion for Foreign Interference

Some historians have taken the Venezuelan crisis as a barometer of rising jingoism in the United States. Certainly, there is no denying that the national conversation was often crudely chauvinistic, nor that Cleveland's message and Olney's twenty-inch gun practically swaggered off the page. But was this the rhetoric of a proud and self-confident nation, or did it come instead from a place of deep insecurity? Lodge and other politicians were happy to toss red meat to their constituents, but the public's appetite sprang more from pangs of anxiety than any hunger for glory. Secretary Blaine's strategy of Pan-Americanism no longer seemed sufficient to keep Europe at an ocean's distance, and Scruggs's warning had handed Americans a concrete battlefield on which to face off against the intangible fears that had been haunting them for over a decade.[55]

Jingo impulses also didn't move the administration. Olney later conceded that his dispatch's word choice had been "of the bumptious order." But he defended that bombastic approach as the only way to blast Great Britain out of its smug stupor. On that count, he succeeded brilliantly. However clumsy and sophomoric Olney's dispatch, a dispute that had festered for decades was all but resolved in a year.[56]

Cleveland was also no jingo. Shortly after he sent his special message to Congress, he wrote how he had known the Monroe Doctrine "to be troublesome" and that he was "quite willing, if possible within the limits of inflexible duty, to escape its serious contemplation." But duty did not permit him that reprieve. And while he knew that his policy would be popular domestically, he was not a man who played to the crowds. First and foremost, he and his administration acted aggressively because they felt the safety of their country demanded it. If anything, Cleveland hoped to snuff out jingoism by removing its ultimate cause—European interventions in the hemisphere.[57]

══

SURPRISINGLY, ONE OF the crisis's lasting effects would be a new warmth in Anglo-American relations. Cleveland and Olney's words had brought the two countries face-to-face with war, and neither liked what it saw. One British leader deplored a conflict with their American cousins as carrying "the unnatural horror of a civil war." Such sentiments were common, and they reflected a growing cultural kinship as well as a changing strategic landscape. For too long, the United States had split the hemisphere with its former colonial master—a condominium destined for trouble. By backing down in Venezuela, the British had bugled the start of their retreat from the New World and opened the door to a lasting rapprochement.[58]

Caracas, by contrast, was a victim of its own success. Once it lured the United States into the dispute, it was shut out of Olney's negotiations with London and lost all control of the crisis's resolution. More than Venezuelan vanity was wounded; Caracas believed that Olney had bargained away some of its best arguments. Indeed, Venezuelans were so incensed by the final agreement that their government, fearing revolution, ordered its citizens to turn in their arms.[59]

Some of this ill will was avoidable. Olney could have looped Scruggs into negotiations while maintaining overall control, and he also could have toned down language in his original dispatch that was guaranteed to rub the United States's neighbors the wrong way. Olney foolishly never considered how blustering about the United States being "practically sovereign on this continent" might sound to the continent's other occupants.[60]

Substantively, however, the secretary of state had little choice but to insist on control over negotiations with Great Britain. Washington had gone to the brink of great-power war on Venezuela's behalf, and it could not afford to let Caracas pull it over the edge. "What a suggestion it is that the issues of peace or war between the two Trustees of Civilization— the U.S. and Great Britain—should in any degree be made to depend upon the decision or conduct of such a menagerie as a *Venezuelan* Government," the American ambassador in London told Cleveland snidely. "For the U.S. to place in the control of such a set of men the virtual control of peace and war with European Powers would be simple madness." Condescension aside, he had a point. Since the United States would bear the brunt of any conflict, it needed to control which risks it was running, and that meant keeping Venezuela on a tight leash.[61]

Sound as it was, that logic nonetheless pointed toward some uncomfortable broader truths. If Americans wanted to regulate the behavior of Europe's powers in the hemisphere, then they would need to regulate the behavior of their neighbors as well. And the more vigorously the Monroe Doctrine needed defense, the more vigorously the region itself would need to be managed. Otherwise, Washington would constantly be gambling on its unruly region not provoking Europe's great powers beyond the limits of their tolerance.

Several contemporaries started to see what all this might imply. One British journalist argued that Great Britain had, by agreeing to arbitrate the boundary dispute, essentially admitted "the political hegemony of the United States in the two Americas." But in exchange the United States had assumed momentous responsibilities. By asserting "a claim to be the general protector and arbiter of the American continent," it had made itself answerable for that continent's conduct and responsible for "regulat[ing] the affairs of a whole quarter of the habitable globe." Such a feat, the journalist noted with equal parts awe and dread, had not been attempted since the Roman Empire.[62]

Others also saw what was coming. Salisbury himself hinted in his dismissive response to Olney's dispatch that the United States could not simultaneously claim an interest in the whole hemisphere while also refusing to assume responsibility for the hemisphere's behavior. Now that the United States had successfully asserted its interest, the equation needed to be balanced. Some Americans agreed; an editorial in the *Philadelphia Press* suggested that having "accepted the risk of war in [the region's] defense, the United States is bound to see that the countries it protects and safeguards give no just occasion for foreign interference."[63]

Olney himself spied many of the same unsettling implications flowing from his country's newfound belligerence. So even as his dispatch unveiled a new and far bolder Monroe Doctrine, the secretary tried to install guardrails to limit its future abuse. The Doctrine, he emphasized, "does not establish any general protectorate by the United States over other American states. It does not relieve any American state from its obligations as fixed by international law nor prevent any European power directly interested from enforcing such obligations or from inflicting merited punishment for the breach of them. It does not contemplate any interference in the internal affairs of any American state or in the relations between it and other American states. It does not justify any attempt on our part to change the established form of government of any American state." Olney later maintained that, far from "enlarg[ing] the Monroe Doctrine," the Cleveland administration had actually "confined its application within narrower limits than had ever been fixed."[64]

Olney's laundry list of what the Monroe Doctrine supposedly did not allow or do could easily be mistaken for a preview of the next thirty years of American foreign policy. That was no accident. Olney and Cleveland had adopted an attitude that would become all too familiar to later statesmen—that, yes, the exigencies and emergencies of the current crisis might require an unprecedented step forward, but surely *this* step would be the last. By articulating the Doctrine's limits, Olney and Cleveland thought they could set a ceiling on future administrations' belligerence. But when their efforts failed to solve the European problem, it was only natural that the ceiling turned into a floor, becoming the starting point for their successors.

Soon the region would know exactly what it meant for the United States to be practically sovereign on its continent, its resources infinite and its fiat law. And one of the first nations to learn would be Hawai'i.

CHAPTER 4

A JEHAD TO WHICH ALL THE FAITHFUL MUST GIVE HEED

The Annexation of Hawai'i, 1893–1898

On Saturday morning, January 14, 1893, in the Blue Room of 'Io-lani Palace, Queen Lydia Kamaka'eha Dominis Lili'uokalani in-formed her stunned cabinet that she planned to overthrow Hawai'i's constitution.[1]

Generous, dignified, and tenacious, Lili'uokalani cared deeply about her people. She had inherited the throne two years earlier from her brother, King David Kalākaua, along with a forcibly imposed "Bayonet Constitution" that had shackled the traditional prerogatives of the Ha-waiian monarchy. Lili'uokalani now wanted her cabinet's help setting herself and her people free.[2]

One of her flabbergasted ministers excused himself. He hurried downtown and burst into the Honolulu law office of his old school-mate. "Lorrin," he panted, "we've been having a hell of a time up at the Palace."[3]

Lorrin A. Thurston was not a palace functionary, but he was no stranger to palace intrigue, either. The grandson of an American mis-sionary family, Thurston was drawn to more worldly affairs like law and business. The profession that best suited him, however, was revolution. Shrewd and ruthless, the young firebrand had clashed with the Hawai-ian monarchy repeatedly, and it was his Bayonet Constitution the Queen was now trying to replace.[4]

Thurston had suspected Lili'uokalani might try something like this, and he was prepared—itching, even—for one last showdown. He roused the dormant Honolulu Rifles, a paramilitary group whose bayonets had lent the current constitution its name, and activated a subterranean network of mostly white, rich allies across the island. By late afternoon, Thurston was ready to do what he did best. He fiercely denounced the Queen's behavior at a gathering of associates and, with dramatic flair, called for a Jacobinesque "Committee of Safety" to depose her, establish a provisional government, and apply to the United States for annexation.[5]

On paper, the Committee's chances seemed middling. It could count on a couple hundred self-armed volunteers. By contrast, the Queen commanded all government buildings, including the barracks and police station, along with five hundred armed men, a dozen cannons, and two Gatling guns. If it came down to firepower, the royalists were sure to win.[6]

The Committee of Safety, however, had a secret weapon. As night fell, Thurston and two compatriots stole through the darkness to the door of John L. Stevens, the aging American minister to Hawai'i.[7]

If Stevens had done his job that evening, he would have expelled Thurston's party the second he realized what they were up to. Stevens was accredited to Lili'uokalani's government and not supposed to dabble in Hawaiian politics, much less commit outright treason. But Stevens had long since given up on Hawai'i's monarchy, whose slow and venal disintegration was, in his eyes, allowing foreign powers to sink their teeth into the islands. On that night, he ignored diplomatic protocol and helped his guests plot their next move.[8]

On Monday morning, January 16, citing "general alarm and terror," the Committee of Safety formally asked Stevens to land soldiers from the nearby USS *Boston*. By late afternoon, 164 American sailors and marines were rowing toward shore.[9]

Ordered to remain neutral, the *Boston*'s landing party had only one objective—to protect American property and persons if violence broke out. But Lili'uokalani didn't know that; Stevens had intentionally kept her in the dark, and she naturally assumed the worst about the force's purpose. With the odds seemingly mounting against her, the intimidated Queen did little to stop the gathering revolutionary storm.[10]

Shortly after 2 p.m. the next day, Thurston's rebels struck. They first occupied the unguarded seat of the legislature and cabinet ministries. They then proclaimed the end of the monarchy and the start of a provisional government. Stevens precipitately recognized their regime by four o'clock, and at six o'clock, Lili'uokalani surrendered. In just under four hours, Thurston and his co-conspirators had snuffed out the historic Hawaiian kingdom.[11]

Cleverly, though, Lili'uokalani had chosen not to surrender to the new Provisional Government. She had instead formally capitulated "to the superior force of the United States." Lili'uokalani had thus yielded her authority only temporarily—"until such time as the Government of the United States shall ... undo the action of its representative and reinstate me."[12]

Lili'uokalani's conditional surrender set off a race to the White House. On Thursday, Thurston left the islands aboard a chartered steamer, a delegation by his side and an offer of annexation in his hands. Close behind were the Queen's lawyers, ready to plead her case to the American people and their government.[13]

On paper, Thurston's chances again seemed middling. It would be a major departure for the United States to annex Hawai'i, one that ran counter to its republican principles, its racial prejudices, and its tradition of near-exclusive continental expansion.

Once again, however, Thurston had a secret weapon—the problem of order. Hawai'i had long been valuable, vulnerable, and envied by foreign powers. Over the coming years, these three factors would become ever more salient as Hawai'i's new, rickety government locked horns with a hostile great power. By 1897, most American policymakers had concluded that Thurston was right: if they wanted to prevent Hawai'i from falling under foreign control, annexation was their only option.

Key to the Pacific

Since the 1870s, the United States had found its Hawaiian policy shaped by three tightening constraints. First, Hawai'i was strategically vital. Second, Hawai'i was endangered, circled by avaricious powers sure to snap it up at the first opportunity. And third, Hawai'i was internally divided, fractured along economic, political, and racial lines. Together, these three constraints had plunged the United States further and further into the islands' tumultuous politics.

———

CAPTAIN ALFRED THAYER Mahan was not the first to explain why the United States couldn't allow a rival power to take control of the

<u>Captain Alfred Thayer Mahan</u>: "When he speaks the millennium fades and this stern, severe, actual world appears."

Hawaiian islands, but as the world's preeminent naval strategist, he was certainly the most influential.[14]

Mahan was born in 1840 on the grounds of West Point to one of the military school's most revered professors, but he decided to trade his father's landlubbing ways for a career in the U.S. Navy. It proved a huge mistake. Smart, sensitive, and neurotic, Mahan learned he had a mortal fear of the ocean matched only by his boredom of sea duty's "dead grind."[15]

Sea duty did offer this second-rate sailor one advantage, though: the time to read, to write, and above all to study the worlds he was traveling through. Mahan was frightened by much of what he saw. "All around us now is strife," he observed; "everywhere nation is arrayed against nation." Europe's great powers were swarming over the rest of the world, and Mahan repeatedly witnessed how their struggles were "drawing nearer to ourselves." His duties took him off Mexico's coast, as Sheridan fought his proxy war against Maximilian; across the isthmus, where a French company excavated a canal; and throughout Central and South America, where hovering imperial powers were attracted to the opportunities presented by "wretchedly disturbed social conditions."[16]

Mahan was initially repelled by Europe's muscular navalism. "I dread outlying colonies or interests," he avowed as late as 1884. "To me the very suspicion of an imperial policy is hateful; the mixing our politics with those of Latin republics especially." But these reservations did not survive Mahan's extended service in the region, which convinced him that only more forceful policies would resolve the threats posed by "un-settled political conditions" in areas of the hemisphere that were of "great military or commercial importance."[17]

Coincidentally, just as Mahan was brooding on these ideas in "the obscurity and let alonedness of the South American ports," he was in-vited to lecture on naval history and tactics at the newly established Na-val War College. Jumping at the opportunity, Mahan shut himself away in the library of the English Club in Lima and began formulating a theory of sea power.[18]

Mahan's theory was deceptively simple. States grow powerful off maritime trade, but that trade requires a strong navy to protect it. Only a strong navy can, by concentrating at the decisive point, defeat an enemy fleet and thereafter exert control over the sea. It followed that the United States should boost its commerce by excavating an isthmian canal; it should also build a battleship navy and obtain any outlying positions necessary to defend either its home waters or the future canal.[19]

Few of Mahan's ideas were original, but no one had organized, substantiated, and articulated them as forcefully and clearly. So when Mahan published *The Influence of Sea Power upon History, 1660–1783* in 1890, the tome felt both familiar and revolutionary. Domesti-cally, his scholarship gave direction and purpose to his country's New Navy just as it was steaming from the dockyards. Abroad, his works anointed the mild, middle-aged officer the high prophet of navalism. "The London *Times* has been calling me Copernicus again," he beamed in 1894.[20]

One of Mahan's favorite subjects was Hawai'i. Geographically speaking, Mahan observed, Hawai'i was defined by its isolation. If one drew a circle around Honolulu with a radius of 2,200 miles—roughly the distance to San Francisco—that circle would sweep in approximately a twelfth of the globe's surface. Such a vast expanse would, anywhere else, encompass dozens of states, nations, and civilizations. But in the dark waters of the northern Pacific, Hawai'i sits practically alone.[21]

Geographical remoteness ensured geopolitical centrality in an age when merchantmen and navies alike depended on coal for fuel. Coal was "the food of the ship," Mahan explained; without it, "the modern mon-sters of the deep die of inanition." Seeing as Hawai'i was the only place to take on coal for thousands of miles, it had unique importance—it was the only gas station in the middle of a vast and empty desert.[22]

Control of Hawai'i thus offered control of the northern Pacific. Ha-wai'i could be used as a base to attack enemy shipping or defend one's own; it could even become a launching pad for invasions. Once acquired by a great power, moreover, the islands could be made virtually impregnable. Any enemy would arrive at the islands exhausted and low on fuel, unprepared to face a fresh, well-maintained, and well-fueled fleet operating out of the inimitable Pearl Harbor.[23]

National security did not require the United States to control Hawai'i itself. As long as the republic kept Hawai'i from other powers, the West Coast would remain practically invulnerable. "Shut out from the [Hawaiian] Islands," Mahan calculated, "an enemy is thrown back for supplies of fuel to distances of thirty-five hundred or four thousand miles … an impediment to sustained maritime operations well-nigh prohibitive."[24]

Other experts largely concurred with Mahan's assessment of Hawai'i's importance to American security. "It may safely be said," one commodore summed up, "that on our globe there are no islands whose strategic position, with regard to the area commanded, equals that of Hawaii."[25]

HAWAI'I'S COMMANDING POSITION made it valuable to others too, and its history abounded with expressions of hostile foreign interest.

At one time or another, Russian, French, German, and British agents had all seized the islands, in whole or in part, on behalf of the empires they represented. In the 1840s, Washington had responded to some of these scares by effectively extending the Monroe Doctrine to Hawai'i. Great Britain and France subsequently renounced their territorial ambitions, at least publicly, but both nations quickly violated their pledges, and signs of British interest remained especially strong. One could not walk far down the streets of Honolulu in the 1880s and 1890s without seeing British diplomats huddling with the Hawaiian monarch's courtiers, storefronts hawking London's latest wares, or the Union Jack snapping in the wind over warships in the harbor.[26]

Americans also worried about Hawai'i because of red flags that were popping up in the seas around it. Years earlier, the United States had gotten tangled up in the Samoas, an island chain roughly 2,300 miles southwest of Hawai'i. In 1885, Germany went on a sudden tear through the archipelago, landing troops, seizing territory, stoking rebellion, deposing native rulers, and generally making an imperialist nuisance of itself. Officials in Washington were shocked, and although they forced Berlin to back off, it took a war scare, years of pressure, and an eventual agreement to a three-way protectorate with Germany and Great Britain.

Mahan thought the episode was "eminently suggestive of European ambitions" in places like Hawai'i.[27]

Senator Henry Cabot Lodge likewise agonized over the alarming rate at which great powers were pinching Pacific islands. He claimed in one Senate speech that Great Britain had already taken dozens, including the Gilbert, Ellice, Enderbury, and Union chains, along with the Kingman, Fanning, Washington, Palmyra, Christmas, Jarvis, Malden, Starbuck, Dudosa, Penryhn, Vostok, Flint, and Caroline islands. And that was just in 1888. A year later, Lodge observed, the British were right back at it, pocketing the Ruie, Suwaroff, and Coral islands. In 1891, London added only one island to its growing collection (Johnston), but that annexation particularly concerned Lodge because Hawai'i claimed the atoll too. No man is an island, but at the rate London was going, no man could *have* an island unless he happened to be British.[28]

Lodge made a related point even more graphically. Midway through another speech, aides brought in an enormous world map peppered with dozens of bright red Maltese crosses. These, Lodge explained with a flourish, marked the locations of British naval stations. The crosses practically surrounded the United States; off its east and southern coasts lay six alone. Lodge walked his audience through three others—the Falkland Islands, Vancouver, and the Fiji Islands—and then gestured toward the "great triangle" they formed. "In the center of that triangle," he announced, "where I am now pointing, lie the [Hawaiian] Islands. They are the key [to] the Pacific." Lodge noted with satisfaction that there was no red Maltese cross there—yet. But he had no doubt the British wanted to rectify that oversight at the earliest opportunity.[29]

—

FOREIGN THREATS MIGHT have unsettled Lodge, Mahan, and other American strategists less if Hawai'i had been better prepared to meet them. But against the might of empires, the little island chain boasted neither an army nor a navy. It was, militarily speaking, defenseless.[30]

Even worse, the Kingdom of Hawai'i seemed to be disintegrating in real time. Since their "discovery" by Europeans in 1778, the Hawaiian Islands had become a convenient stopping point for whalers, merchants, and sailors plying the waters of the Pacific. Contact with the outside world and its diseases, however, had proved devastating for Native Hawaiians. In 1778, they had numbered approximately 300,000; by 1820, roughly half had perished, and by 1890, there would be a scant 34,436 left. Not only did this demographic death spiral devastate Hawai'i's society, economy, and culture, but it also threatened to extinguish the royal bloodline. And as the Native Hawaiians' ranks continued to thin, the kingdom's ability to maintain its independence appeared ever more tenuous.[31]

In the early 1870s, Secretary of State Hamilton Fish and other American policymakers began grappling with this mounting problem. Fish generally opposed closer political ties with the islands—or, God forbid, annexation—but he worried that the United States might not have a choice. Hawai'i was "an outpost fronting and commanding the whole of our possessions on the Pacific Ocean," he brooded, and the kingdom's "evident tendency to decay and dissolution force[s] upon us the earnest consideration of its future—possibly its near future."[32]

Sure enough, the situation came to a head in 1874. Hawai'i's new ruler, King Kalākaua, visited the United States to lobby for a reciprocity treaty that would lift barriers to trade between the two countries— especially the American import tax on sugar—and thereby stabilize Hawai'i's flagging economy. Economically, the treaty would benefit Hawai'i far more than it would the United States. But Fish feared that if Washington did not take the deal, Kalākaua would try his luck in London next. Fish therefore agreed to economic reciprocity in exchange for the kingdom promising never to lease or otherwise alienate any part of its territory to other foreign powers. From Fish's perspective, the final arrangement seemed like a clear win for American national security: it would enrich Hawai'i, alleviate its demographic stresses, tie it to its eastern neighbor, and keep it out of the grasp of foreign powers.[33]

Far from stabilizing Hawai'i, however, the treaty made it weaker and more vulnerable. The problem was not that reciprocity didn't work, but that it worked too well. Hawai'i's sugar exports soared from 26 million pounds in 1876 to almost 331 million pounds in 1893—a nearly 1,300 percent jump in less than twenty years. Even as Hawai'i prospered, however, the sugar boom saddled the islands' already wobbly political order with three significant new stressors.[34]

The first related to labor. Sugar production requires tremendous amounts of backbreaking work, and with the native population unable to fill the demand, Hawai'i's sugar barons began importing tens of thousands of workers from Asia. But the influx of cheap foreign labor created new problems: it depressed the wages of local laborers, scrambled the islands' demographics, and gave foreign powers a direct stake in Hawaiian affairs.[35]

Capital problems worsened matters. Sugar production was incredibly capital intensive; even a small plantation cost approximately

$25,000, and a midsized one ran closer to $500,000. Native Hawaiians didn't have that kind of cash, but some foreigners—especially wealthy white Americans—did. So on the same day that news of the reciprocity treaty's passage arrived from the mainland, the first aspiring sugar mogul did too. By 1882, Hawai'i was home to thirty-eight new plantations.[36]

On its own, that development need not have been destabilizing; some reciprocity advocates had hoped for just such an infusion of American capital to stabilize Hawai'i's economy. But the gains from Hawai'i's increasing prosperity were not distributed evenly. Riches flowed to sugar planters and the small coterie of predominantly white lawyers, bankers, and traders who supported them, while Native Hawaiians and immigrant laborers were left mostly empty-handed.[37]

Sugar also aggravated a third problem: economic dependence. Small island chains will always struggle to maintain diversified and autarkic economies, but the sugar supernova turned Hawai'i into a single-crop economy exporting to a single market. By 1895, sugar captured over 94 percent of Hawai'i's total exports by value, and the United States bought a staggering 99.04 percent of the islands' total exports.[38]

Over time, these three stressors helped produce precisely the political "dissolution" that Fish and others so dreaded. Sugar divided islanders into two increasingly hostile camps—a small minority of wealthy whites who wanted greater political control, and an ever-dwindling majority of royalists, mostly Native Hawaiians, who felt their culture and country slipping away from them.[39]

Soon the two camps exploded into open conflict. In 1887, Lorrin Thurston organized a secret society, the Hawaiian League, "to protect the white community" and "secure efficient, decent and honest government." On June 30, the League unleashed its paramilitary arm, the Honolulu Rifles, and demanded that King Kalākaua sign a new constitution enfranchising white foreigners, curbing Native Hawaiians' voting power, and reducing the monarch to a ceremonial figurehead. Fearing revolution, Kalākaua buckled after a tense few days and signed the Bayonet Constitution.[40]

Little was resolved. Even though Thurston and his League had designed the Bayonet Constitution to entrench white rule, it mostly militarized island politics and further embittered their opponents, including future Queen Lili'uokalani. Her brother Kalākaua kept pushing back against white control, and the new white-led cabinet fended off numerous plots and rebellions by angry Native Hawaiians. It seemed to many like the Hawaiian Kingdom was increasingly verging on civil war.[41]

Time and Tide

In early 1889, Secretary of State James G. Blaine tried to address the islands' deteriorating situation with Henry A. P. Carter, Hawai'i's energetic minister in Washington. Each man wanted something from the other: Carter had approached Blaine to ask for help making reciprocity permanent, as Honolulu had grown tired of the uncertainty caused by the treaty's term limits, while Blaine wanted to prevent Hawai'i's turbulent politics from attracting unwanted foreign attention. Carter expertly stoked that fear, observing that reciprocity's end would alienate "our feelings for the United States" and possibly lead the islands to look for protection elsewhere.[42]

Carter and Blaine accordingly struck a deal. The United States would extend complete and permanent reciprocity to the islands and even match any subsidies given to domestic sugar growers. Washington would also expressly guarantee Hawai'i's independence. But in exchange, Hawai'i would become an American protectorate. Washington could veto any treaty the kingdom wanted to sign, as well as land military forces whenever necessary to suppress "domestic disturbances." Never before had Washington sought so much formal control over another state's internal affairs.[43]

Some suspected that Blaine wanted to use the protectorate as a Trojan horse for annexation. But that got it exactly backward. Blaine did expect the native kingdom to crumble, and he wanted his country picking up the pieces when that happened. Rather than push for immediate annexation, however, Blaine sought to postpone the day of reckoning as long as safely possible. A protectorate would make it harder for anyone else to capture the Hawaiian flag, buying the islands time before Washington needed to grasp their falling colors. It was a bitter bargain for the kingdom, to be sure—independence at the cost of sovereignty. But a protectorate was nonetheless designed to extend independent Hawai'i's lease on life.[44]

For better or worse, though, Hawai'i declined to ratify the treaty. It could not stomach a protectorate, not even for permanent reciprocity.[45]

▬

ONE YEAR LATER, Hawaiians saw their fears about reciprocity's shaky footing borne out in spectacular fashion. In 1890, Congress eliminated duties on all sugar imports, rendering Hawai'i's reciprocity deal worthless. Worse, Congress subsidized American sugar producers to the tune of two cents per pound, disadvantaging all foreign sugar, including

Hawai'i's. The result was economic disaster. Sugar prices nose-dived 40 percent, wages dropped, unemployment surged, and Hawai'i entered a depression.[46]

Depression opened the door to revolution. Some sugar planters began seeing annexation as a way to access the American market permanently. More broadly, many whites concluded that Thurston was right, and that the monarchy could no longer provide the stable leadership they craved.[47]

John L. Stevens, the American minister to Hawai'i, was meanwhile growing increasingly concerned that foreign powers were fishing in these troubled waters. From his perch in Honolulu, the minister sent progressively more dire reports to Washington. He referred incessantly to "powerful agencies," "the ultra English," and other "foreign political interests," all plotting the "embarrassment and injury of the United States." His paranoia echoed similar squawks from American naval commanders posted in the area.[48]

Soon Stevens escalated his recommendations and declared that the islands' "feverish" political situation had led him to see the light. "Annexation must be the future remedy," he pleaded, "or else Great Britain will be furnished with circumstances and opportunity to get a hold on these islands." He urged Washington to move quickly, for "time and tide wait neither for men nor nations."[49]

Stevens's warnings hit home. "There is a good deal of mischief brewing in those Islands!" exclaimed Blaine. President Benjamin Harrison concurred, responding that he felt "sure that American interests there are in jeopardy; but just how far we can go and what action we can take to thwart the schemes of those who are seeking to bring the islands under the control of European powers I do not yet see."[50]

By mid-1891, Blaine had given up on his protectorate plan. He confided to Harrison that if the opportunity arose, he would endorse annexation.[51]

That opportunity was closer than he imagined. Earlier that year, Kalākaua had passed away and his sister Lili'uokalani had ascended to the throne. Stevens frantically reported a month later that the new queen had fallen under bad influences and possessed "extreme notions of sovereign authority." It would not be long before she would act on those notions, and before Stevens would help Thurston's Committee of Safety overthrow her.[52]

Queen Lydia Kamakaʻeha Dominis Liliʻuokalani: "I have pursued the path of peace and diplomatic discussion, and not that of internal strife."

Not Much of an Annexationist

On February 3, 1893, Thurston and the other representatives of Hawaiʻi's new Provisional Government arrived in Washington, ready to beg for annexation. Thurston's overthrow of Liliʻuokalani was complete, but his troubles with the United States were just beginning.[53]

Stevens had far exceeded his official instructions when he had aided Thurston's revolution, and it was an open question whether his superiors would back him up. By his own admission, Harrison was "not much of an annexationist," though he did make an exception for "naval stations and points of influence." Harrison was also a lame-duck president, with barely a month left in office. It would be rather unseemly for him to ram an annexation treaty through Congress in that time.[54]

For Harrison, however, annexation was a no-brainer, largely because of the foreign dangers on the horizon. Like his predecessors, the president had previously promoted Hawaiʻi's independence. But, as he later explained, that independence rested on two foundations: "guaranties for the protection of life and property," and, even more critically, "a stability and strength that gave adequate security against the domination of any other power." The revolution had cracked those foundations, and Harrison concluded that he needed to move fast before the ground gave way completely.[55]

Secretary of State John W. Foster framed annexation in similar terms. Calling the situation "very critical," he later wrote that "if the islands did not soon become American territory, they would inevitably pass under the control of Great Britain or Japan."[56]

On Valentine's Day, 1893, a treaty of annexation was signed, and the next day Harrison submitted it to the Senate in a sealed envelope. He promised in his accompanying message that Washington had not promoted the monarchy's overthrow in any way. Instead, Queen Liliʻuokalani had instituted "a reactionary and revolutionary policy" that endangered not only American interests but also foreign ones. Given her government's collapse, "only two courses are now open—one the establishment of a protectorate by the United States, and the other annexation full and complete." He had chosen the latter, believing that annexation would better ensure "that none of the other great powers shall secure the islands."[57]

After receiving the president's message, the Senate solemnly cleared the public galleries, locked and barred the doors, and began debating the treaty.[58]

—

FOR HALF A moment, the treaty seemed like a sure thing. But many senators, not privy to the dispatches from Honolulu, concluded that there were too many unanswered questions, too many ugly rumors, to rush into annexation. Slamming Harrison's "hot haste" and "snap-shot diplomacy," the New York World called for "at least as much deliberation as is usually given to the hiring of a Harlem flat or the selection of a suit of clothes." Anti-annexationists also argued there was no imminent threat or need to hurry because—in a deliberate attempt to avoid provoking American annexation—Great Britain had failed to object to the treaty.[59]

Finally, in late February, president-elect Grover Cleveland made clear that he wanted the Senate to wait. Democrats dutifully thrust Harrison's annexation treaty into congressional limbo, leaving its fate to be decided by the incoming administration.[60]

A Virtual Protectorate

No foreign policy problem would dog Cleveland's second term quite like Hawaiʻi. One of the era's foremost anti-imperialists, the president trembled at the injustice of Liliʻuokalani's ouster. But while he could pause Hawaiʻi's annexation, he could neither restore the Queen to power nor avoid supporting the men who had overthrown her. For all his outrage, Cleveland remained caught in a basic dilemma—Hawaiʻi was too toxic to be embraced, but too important to be set free.

Cleveland was not initially opposed to annexing Hawai'i. He had fought for reciprocity during his first term, and he knew that Hawai'i was effectively the last island standing after Europe's colonialist binge in the Pacific. But Cleveland also had a streak of gallantry, and his chivalrous soul rebelled at the possibility that American bayonets had pried Lili'uokalani off her throne.[61]

On entering office, the president accordingly cloaked Georgia Democrat James H. Blount with "paramount" authority and dispatched him to the islands to learn more about Lili'uokalani's overthrow. In the meantime, the State Department met with the British, Japanese, and Russian representatives in Washington to ensure that their governments did not seize Hawai'i in the interim.[62]

In July 1893, "Paramount Blount" submitted the results of his investigation. It was not a happy story. Blount flayed Stevens for aiding the white revolutionaries and concluded that, but for American interference, Lili'uokalani would still be queen. Blount also demolished the idea that most islanders wanted to join the Union. "The undoubted sentiment of the people is for the Queen, against the Provisional Government and against annexation," he reported. Any fair vote, he estimated, would be "at least two to one" against annexation.[63]

Scandalized, Cleveland immediately ruled annexation out of the question. But that was not enough. He determined that Lili'uokalani's ouster was "a substantial wrong" in need of immediate repair, and he accordingly decided to restore the Queen to power through a comically idealistic plan. It required Hawai'i's new leaders to voluntarily step down, but when the American minister asked them to do so, they naturally refused. They would respect Cleveland's decision to shelve annexation, they explained, though declining "to regard it as the last word." As far as restoring the Queen, Hawai'i's leaders were offended Cleveland would even ask. Demonstrating either a blinding lack of self-awareness or an appallingly black sense of humor, they scolded the United States for trying "to interfere in our domestic affairs." Finally, to ensure the episode lost none of its surreal quality, the Provisional Government meanwhile began arming its supporters, sandbagging public buildings, and issuing shoot-to-kill orders—just in case it needed to defend itself against an armed attack from the country it hoped would soon annex it.[64]

———

CLEVELAND HAD LITTLE time to appreciate this debacle. Even as his restoration plan fizzled, newspapers crucified it. "The sentiments which [the president] professes might apply in Utopia," rebuked the *New York*

World. "They are not applicable to the affairs of nations." Out of ideas, options, and patience, Cleveland asked Congress for help.[65]

Salvation can be found anywhere, but nowhere are the odds longer than the halls of Congress. Cleveland had second-guessed his predecessor's judgment when he repudiated Harrison's annexation treaty. By lobbing the Hawaiian ball back to Congress, he gave his Republican opponents a chance to hit back. They did not disappoint.

Once, a spirit of bipartisanship had pervaded American policy toward Hawai'i, but no more—Cleveland's moralizing had killed it. Follow-on casualties included civility and truth, as both sides demonized their opponents and subordinated facts to factionalism in a no-holds-barred legislative melee.[66]

Lodge was especially quick to reprise his role as Cleveland's greatest congressional antagonist. The president had concerned himself with myopic questions of morality, but to Lodge "the main thing" was Hawai'i's unrivaled "military and strategic importance." The Massachusetts senator had "no desire to see this country enter on an unlimited career of acquisition of colonial possessions," which he dismissed as unnecessary and unprincipled. But he protested the administration's refusal to reinforce "the necessary outworks" of "the citadel of our greatness here on this continent."[67]

Just about the only common ground among the brawling legislators was that, whatever happened, no foreign power could be permitted to take the islands. By overwhelming margins, both the Senate and the House passed "hands-off" resolutions condemning foreign intervention. Cleveland meanwhile dispatched the USS *Philadelphia* with orders to sniff out attempts by "any foreign power to interfere in the political affairs of the Hawaiian Islands."[68]

Eventually, an uneasy truce emerged. Cleveland would neither annex Hawai'i nor restore the Queen; instead, he would uphold the status quo. Diplomatically, that meant recognizing the white revolutionaries' newly established "Republic of Hawaii." Militarily, it meant stationing naval forces offshore and turning Hawai'i into what the *Philadelphia*'s flagship officer candidly called a "virtual protectorate."[69]

———

CLEVELAND'S SENSE OF justice, however, led him to try to break out of this box one last time. Hawaiian royalists had complained that the constant presence of American warships in Honolulu offered moral support to the white oligarchy. In response, the Cleveland administration withdrew the *Philadelphia* in mid-1894 without sending a substitute. Hawai'i was, for the first time in a long time, on its own.[70]

Sensing an opportunity, Hawaiian royalists launched a counterrevolution in January 1895. But details of the plot leaked, and after a short firefight on Waikiki Beach, the white oligarchy squelched the insurrection and imprisoned Queen Lili'uokalani.[71]

Cleveland had meanwhile rushed the *Philadelphia* back to the islands amid rumors of British involvement in the disorder. But the *Philadelphia* arrived a little too late to affect the counterrevolution, and much too late to save Cleveland from another round of congressional censure. Only days before the uprising, Lodge had predicted that the absence of American naval vessels in Hawai'i would throw "the door wide open to an attempt at a counter revolution." Fully vindicated, Lodge led congressional forces in a spirited and now bipartisan wave of attacks on the administration.[72]

Chastened by Congress and experience, the president finally learned his lesson. From here on out, the islands would remain under the close watch of at least one vessel of the U.S. Navy.[73]

Cleveland had been given a choice: defend American security interests in the islands, or leave Hawai'i alone to determine its own destiny. Cleveland had no interest in promoting annexation or extending American influence further. But because he, like his detractors, feared foreign control of the islands, he was forced to permanently station a warship there even though doing so propped up a regime he despised.

The Least Dangerous Experiment

Cleveland's virtual protectorate might have worked indefinitely had the British Empire been the only perceived threat to Hawai'i's independence. But a new threat was taking shape, and this time, it could not be sidestepped by shuffling warships around the Pacific. Japan was rising, and it increasingly seemed like the only way the United States could prevent Hawai'i from falling into Tokyo's hands was by grabbing it first.[74]

Japan had not figured much in early American debates over Hawai'i because it seemed like a second-rank state, far more likely to be victimized by Europe's powers than to do any victimizing of its own. But by the 1890s, the balance of power had shifted. Japan had ruthlessly modernized, and in 1895, it clobbered China in the Sino-Japanese War. Despite its new great-power stripes, however, Tokyo still felt it had more to prove, and it was particularly sensitive to slights against its honor.[75]

Such slights came regularly from little Hawai'i, mainly over immigration. In 1886, Honolulu had sought to slake the sugar tycoons' insatiable labor demands by signing an immigration treaty with Tokyo. The treaty immediately had an effect: in 1884, a mere 116 Japanese had called Hawai'i home; six years later, there were 12,360. Japanese immigration received another boost in 1894 when Tokyo privatized the flow of laborers, which went from a preapproved, state-regulated stream to an uncontrolled—and uncontrollable—torrent.[76]

Soon the problem's full scope became apparent. In 1896, Hawai'i's sexennial census revealed that since 1890, the Japanese population had doubled to 24,407, out of a total island population of 109,020. The Japanese were now the second-largest ethnic group on the islands, behind only the Native Hawaiians, who continued their seemingly inexorable slide. But those figures, shocking as they were, understated the white oligarchy's predicament. The Japanese were now, bar none, the largest group of voting-age males—numbering approximately 18,000, compared to 13,000 Native Hawaiians and only 8,000 whites.[77]

Combined with Japan's touchy pride, this development had serious political implications. More and more, Tokyo was demanding the same voting rights for Japanese residents in Hawai'i as for resident white foreigners. Granting suffrage to Japanese residents, however, was the one thing the white oligarchy would not do; if the Japanese received the right to vote, they would control the island's government.[78]

Events reached the crisis point in early 1897 when Hawai'i started turning away boatloads of prospective Japanese laborers who had not complied with its immigration laws. Honolulu anticipated pushback, but hell hath no fury like a great power scorned. Japan was incandescent at its nationals' shabby treatment, and in an uproar dispatched a man-of-war to the islands.[79]

———

JUST THEN, WASHINGTON was enduring its quadrennial changing of the guard. Republicans had enjoyed a banner election year, retaining Congress and retaking the White House. Now they had to decide what to do with all that new power.[80]

Hawai'i did not top the party's priority list. Republicans generally favored annexation, but there was no consensus, and their electoral platform had merely proclaimed that the United States should control—not annex—the islands. Economic issues had dominated the election—1896 was the year of William Jennings Bryan, the populist revolt, and the

"Cross of Gold"—and president-elect William McKinley came into office focused on bread-and-butter issues, including his favorite topic, tariff reform. He showed little interest in Hawai'i and reassured one prominent anti-annexationist he was not "scheming" to get the islands. Chest swelling with emotion, the chief executive pledged, "You may be sure there will be no jingo nonsense under my Administration."[81]

Still, his administration was peppered with officials and advisors who were alive to the brewing crisis with Japan and favored annexation as the solution. Mahan, for one, warned a senior official in the Navy Department that a "very real present danger of war" hung over the islands. "Do nothing unrighteous," he counseled, "but as regards the problem, take them first and solve afterwards."[82]

The administration accordingly took certain precautions. By late spring 1897, the Navy Department had stationed four warships in Hawai'i and begun drawing up two separate war plans against Japan. McKinley also instructed the assistant secretary of state to secretly draft a treaty of annexation. Since the treaty was for emergency purposes only, the president told no one else about it—not the public, not Hawai'i's representatives, not even his own secretary of state.[83]

———

ON THE MORNING of May 5, 1897, Japan's answer to Hawai'i's impertinence arrived. From Honolulu's waterfront, one could see the hulking, three-hundred-foot silhouette of the *Naniwa* steaming slowly through the harbor's emerald water. The *Naniwa* was a warship, and not just any warship. It was the pride of the Japanese Imperial Navy, a veteran of the recent Sino-Japanese War, its hull still scarred by pockmarks from Chinese shells. By dispatching one of the most powerful ships in its fleet, Tokyo had sent the Republic of Hawai'i an unmistakable message. This was not a courtesy call.[84]

On board, the *Naniwa* carried a letter protesting Hawai'i's rejection of Japanese immigrants. But that was not all. Even though the dispute was supposedly about only the spurned laborers, Tokyo also demanded that Hawai'i vindicate a bevy of rights for Japanese residents already on the islands—including the right to vote.[85]

Hawai'i's leaders refused. Such intransigence in turn enraged Shimamura Hisashi, the Japanese minister. When a local paper asked him to comment, Shimamura spat on the Hawaiian response. "My Government tells me to get a reasonable excuse for the action taken. I cannot find it in this," he stormed, waving the Hawaiian reply. Barring some agreement, "the only tribunal" for such disputes was "the strong arm and the strong vessels." "If I withdraw," Shimamura added darkly, "you know what follows."[86]

What was about to happen seemed obvious to anyone schooled in the fine art of gunboat diplomacy. Hawai'i, not wanting to lose face and confident in its own righteousness, would ignore Shimamura's threat. Japan, rebuffed, would break off diplomatic relations, train the *Naniwa's* ten-inch guns on downtown Honolulu, and give the government one last chance to surrender. When Hawai'i stayed stubborn—as it likely would—the *Naniwa* would open fire.[87]

Washington could stomach that outcome elsewhere, but not in Hawai'i, and not at Japan's hands. If the United States stayed out of it, the defenseless islands could hold out for a few hours at most. Best case, Tokyo would exact voting rights for its subjects from the prostrated Hawaiian government. Worst case, Japan's attack would incite its thousands of subjects to rise up and seize power. Either way, the result would be Japanese domination.[88]

Good options seemed scarce. Washington would get nowhere asking the proud Republic of Hawai'i to fold; regardless, conceding would just expand Japan's influence and whet its appetite. Conversely, if Washington intervened, it would run the risk of war, in which Japan would initially have the upper hand.[89]

Signing a treaty of annexation offered a possible way out. It would send a clear warning to Japan without directly challenging its honor. McKinley had previously been unsure about annexation, but it now struck him like "the least dangerous experiment." On June 16, 1897, shortly after being sprung on Hawai'i's surprised representatives, a treaty of annexation was signed and submitted to the Senate.[90]

Secret orders were meanwhile cabled to the American flagship in Honolulu. "Watch carefully the situation," they instructed. "If Japanese openly resort to force, such as military occupation or the seizure of public buildings, confer with Minister and authorities, land a suitable force, and announce officially provisional assumption of protectorate." Everyone knew that if it came to that, war was probably inevitable.[91]

———

JAPAN'S DIPLOMATS WERE also considering military action. Japan's minister to Washington, Hoshi Toru, secretly cabled Tokyo the day after the treaty's signature with a startling recommendation. The only way for Japan to stop American annexation, Hoshi urged, was to immediately launch a surprise attack on Hawai'i.[92]

If Tokyo had accepted Hoshi's recommendation, it would have meant war. American forces in Hawai'i had standing instructions to land and declare a protectorate in the face of a Japanese assault. In the resulting confusion, it is hard to imagine that the soldiers of the two nations—one with orders to attack Hawai'i, the other with orders to defend it—would not have exchanged fire. Japanese leaders, however, balked at Hoshi's recommendation. Despite sharing his outrage, Tokyo wanted Hoshi to protest annexation using "as strong a language as is permissible" but "without running the risk of war." The date which would live in infamy was postponed for another forty-four years and five months.[93]

Japan's protest nevertheless unnerved Washington. Tokyo had not objected to annexation in 1893, and its newfound complaint underscored how dangerous the situation had grown. In response, Washington affirmed its earlier orders, put its naval forces on high alert, and sent warships scouting for strategic locations to seize if war broke out. The administration then signaled its resolve by leaking its military preparations.[94]

Such moves had their intended effect. Tokyo deescalated the immigration crisis and in mid-September recalled the *Naniwa*. In December, Tokyo withdrew its protest against the annexation treaty altogether, hoping that it would instead perish in that traditional graveyard of treaties, the U.S. Senate.[95]

———

SINCE HIS HAND had been unexpectedly forced, McKinley had not laid any groundwork for the annexation treaty in the Senate. Congress was still plumbing the eternally engrossing mysteries of the nation's tariff schedule, and it couldn't realistically take Hawai'i up until it reconvened in December 1897.[96]

For the administration, however, there was no going back. If annexation were not consummated—and soon—its deterrent value would vanish, leaving the islands more exposed than before. One senator gave the islands as little as ten weeks in that scenario. Every day the United States waited, it risked violence breaking out, jeopardizing foreign interests and inviting foreign intervention. One commentator likened Hawai'i to "a derelict flying a flag of distress in mid-ocean," its white-led minority government "liable to overthrow at any time from internal causes, or from dangerous complications growing out of the preponderance of aliens."[97]

Even Japan's waning assertiveness did not change things much. McKinley had defused the immediate crisis but believed that "matters are still in a very dangerous position." Hawai'i remained home to at least twenty-five thousand thoroughly disenfranchised Japanese subjects, and Japan was still "doubtless awaiting her opportunity." Even though the powder had stayed dry so far, Hawaiian independence could not last much longer in the middle of that combustible mix.[98]

So despite his earlier indifference, McKinley threw himself into the annexationist cause over the fall and winter of 1897. Upon learning that a certain senator might not support annexation, the president became distraught. "Well, I don't know what I shall do. We cannot let those Islands go to Japan. Japan has her eye on them. Her people are crowding in there.... If something be not done, there will be before long another Revolution, and Japan will get control." Behind the scenes, Lodge, Mahan, and others worked to stress the same danger to anyone who would listen.[99]

Originally, the administration had hoped to push the treaty through the Senate. But securing the necessary two-thirds vote there proved challenging, and when events in Cuba sent the nation hurtling toward war with Spain, McKinley decided on an alternative course: annexation by joint resolution, which would require only a majority of both houses of Congress.[100]

On June 15, 1898, the House passed a joint resolution annexing Hawai'i, 209 to 91. On July 6, the Senate followed suit, 42 to 21. (Counting the votes of paired and absent senators, the bill would have passed 56 to 32.) McKinley signed it into law the following day.[101]

The Cry of the Strong

On August 12, 1898, in front of the ornate and imposing facade of the former queen's palace, the United States annexed the Hawaiian Islands. For the occasion, the Navy Department landed four companies of infantry and two sections of artillery—over three hundred marines and bluejackets in total. They were met at the wharf by a Hawaiian National Guard escort, and together the crisply attired troops marched through the palm-lined streets to the central square where the ceremony would take place.[102]

It was a simple affair, with little show or even decoration beyond some red, white, and blue bunting wrapped around a dais. A prayer, some speeches, and then it was time. The Hawaiian band struck up "Hawai'i Pono'ī," the national anthem composed by Lili'uokalani's brother, as the Hawaiian flag was hauled down. Fifteen seconds after high noon, the flag of the United States replaced it; now "The Star-Spangled Banner" was playing. Mixed in with the music were thunderclaps from the harbor, where a twenty-one-gun salute reminded onlookers of the two American warships anchored nearby.[103]

Lili'uokalani was absent. So, for that matter, was almost every other Native Hawaiian. Some, including band members and the National Guard, had been forced to attend. But even the conscripts could not be made to smile, or to lift teary eyes when the stars and stripes were raised. Clad in black, Lili'uokalani's niece grieved to a reporter. "It was bad enough to lose the throne, but infinitely worse to have the flag go down. I would have given anything I possess to have prevented it."[104]

On the Senate floor, Senator Richard F. Pettigrew of South Dakota had excoriated those who dared defend Hawai'i's annexation with the slogan "manifest destiny." He knew better. "Manifest destiny has been the murderer of men," he sputtered. "It has committed more crimes, done more to oppress and wrong the inhabitants of the world than any other attribute to which mankind has fallen heir." The truth seemed obvious: "Manifest destiny is simply the cry of the strong in justification of their plunder of the weak."[105]

Senator Samuel D. McEnery of Louisiana was more concise. He simply denounced Hawai'i's annexation as "a piece of unblushing larceny."[106]

———

So IT WAS, at least from the perspective of most Native Hawaiians. Well before the final vote, they submitted a 556-page petition opposing annexation. It had collected an incredible 21,269 signatures—over half the total native population—in just six months.[107]

What happened? Where were the United States's vaunted principles, its hatred of colonies and colonizers, its commitment to sovereignty and self-determination, when they mattered most?

Since 1898, the story of how the islands were annexed has evolved from a triumph to a tragedy, and from a tragedy to a crime. Hawai'i had been stolen, and it was easy, even natural, to attribute felonious intent to those who had taken it. Soon the conspirators were uncovered— American imperialists, the expansionists of 1898, with an assist from advance men like Blaine and Harrison. Capping a premeditated plan stretching back decades, these architects of empire allegedly exploited a burst of jingoism during the Spanish-American War to annex the islands for glory, or for greed, or for white supremacy, or maybe just for an especially nice naval harbor.[108]

The truth is more complex. To start, Lili'uokalani's overthrow was not the result of a conspiracy hatched in Washington. Stevens actively aided the white revolutionaries, but there is little evidence he was directed to do so by Blaine or Harrison. Rather, Stevens acted out of a genuine belief that the islands were drifting into the hands of foreign powers. That same concern drove Harrison to sign a treaty of annexation, Cleveland to establish a virtual protectorate, and McKinley to finally take possession.[109]

Central to the policies of all three administrations was the problem of order. Hawai'i was too weak to keep great powers out, but too important to be allowed to fall under their sway. It was a problem born of Hawai'i's demographic decline, but it quickly metastasized into the islands' economy, society, and politics, especially under the stimulant of reciprocity. As Hawai'i's condition deteriorated, Washington waged a losing battle to keep the islands afloat—first through warnings and trade, then through warships and protectorates.[110]

By 1898, annexation appeared to many policymakers as not just the best solution but the only one. If demographics were destiny, then Hawai'i was destined to be a Japanese colony. Tokyo had made clear it would defend its growing interests there, and the islands had already gone through several near-misses. Many Americans believed, as the Senate Foreign Relations Committee concluded, "that the United States must act NOW." Citing Mahan extensively, the Committee spelled out the "*chief reason*" for annexation: "*to secure a vantage ground for the protection of what the United States already owns*. It is not primarily to secure new territory, promote shipping, and increase commerce, but as a measure of precaution to prevent the acquisition by a foreign ... power of an acknowledged military stronghold." Put differently, annexation was "only incidental to the policy of exclusion," an unavoidable by-product of what the Monroe Doctrine demanded. "And when the Monroe Doctrine is preached," observed one British newspaper tartly, "it is a jehad to which all the faithful must give heed."[111]

Other options seemed futile. The alternative bandied about by anti-annexationists—continuing Cleveland's virtual protectorate—appeared ineffective and dangerous. A protectorate could not protect the islands against internal influences, and it would impose, as the Senate Foreign Relations Committee observed, "responsibility without power to control." For a case in point, Americans needed to look no further than the serious complications with Japan that had arisen out of Hawaiian immigration policies in mid-1897.[112]

Given the seeming lack of alternatives, it is unsurprising that Native Hawaiians' protests didn't bulk large in the minds of annexationists. Some annexationists claimed that Native Hawaiians favored annexation, though whether anyone really believed that is doubtful. (Senator George Frisbie Hoar of Massachusetts, for instance, reassured his colleagues in July 1898 that Native Hawaiians "neither know nor care" about annexation. Evidently he had forgotten about their 556-page petition, presented to the Senate the previous December by none other than Hoar himself.) Other annexationists simply did not care; Native Hawaiians were brown, the regime was white, and that was all they needed to know. Still others discounted native opinion because caring about it seemed myopic—after all, the native islanders were going extinct, tragic (and thankfully mistaken) as that was. But the most powerful argument for ignoring native opinion was simply that it did not matter in light of the Japanese threat. "It is no longer a question of whether Hawaii shall be controlled by the Native Hawaiian or by some foreign people," assessed the Senate Foreign Relations Committee. "The question is, What foreign people shall control Hawaii?"[113]

For most Americans, the answer was obvious, and it was sufficiently compelling to broaden the annexationist coalition to many who saw themselves as stark opponents of imperialism in all its shades. Democratic Representative Francis G. Newlands of Nevada, for example, introduced the joint resolution that ultimately annexed Hawai'i even as he blasted the thought of annexing the Philippines during the Spanish-American War. "The Philippines mean conquest; Hawaii means defense," he explained. "Can we permit [Hawai'i], through the action of existing internal forces, to drift under the control of Japan … ?"[114]

Senator Hoar had a similar story. He would emerge as a leading anti-imperialist, the Republican who boldly subordinated party to principle. Yet he, too, supported Hawai'i's annexation. In an emotional speech, Hoar confessed it was the hardest issue he had encountered in almost half a century of public service. He had "hesitated and doubted and considered and reconsidered." But he ultimately concluded that "if we do not prevent it," Hawai'i would fall "prey to Japan."[115]

In the end, what separated annexationists from their opponents was less principle than perception and partisanship. Hoar observed near the end of the Senate debate that not a single anti-annexationist had actually questioned the need to keep Hawai'i out of foreign hands. All that distinguished the two sides was whether they thought that objective required annexation, an assessment that reflected threat perceptions filtered through a partisan lens.[116]

If the Japanese threat had not arisen, the United States would likely have annexed the islands at some point anyway. Hawai'i was simply too important, too weak, and too imperiled to be left alone forever. But the threat from Tokyo moved the timetable up, and the United States took the islands so Japan could not.

———

OF COURSE, MOST annexationists favored taking the islands for a variety of non-defensive reasons too. But though the verdict can never be conclusive, there are important hints in the record that other motives were relatively less important to the final result than the perceived threat from Japan and other great powers.

For example, Hawai'i's annexation is often wrongly conflated with the frenzy of the Spanish-American War. But McKinley had all the votes for annexation by joint resolution long before the war ever broke out, and he had not pursued that option only to avoid an intraparty fight with the powerful, anti-annexationist Republican Speaker of the House. The Spanish-American War provided a convenient narrative in favor of annexation, but it did not ultimately affect the outcome either way.[117]

Nor was Hawai'i taken primarily to boost American commerce. By 1898, Hawai'i had tied its economy so closely to the mainland that annexation offered few new commercial opportunities. Americans also did not need to own Hawai'i to promote their trade with East Asia, as the islands already extended every conceivable privilege to American merchants crossing the Pacific. From a commercial standpoint, the sole benefit to annexing Hawai'i was defensive—to protect against some other power using the islands to interfere with American trade in the future.[118]

Racism also played a counterintuitive role in Hawai'i's annexation. It certainly contributed to annexation insofar as white American policymakers sympathized more with pro-annexationist whites on the island than anti-annexationist Native Hawaiians. It likely also helped annexationists exaggerate the extent of the islands' demographic decline, though that problem was real enough. Finally, annexationists also made the Japanese threat more salient by drawing on the racist "yellow peril" narrative. On balance, however, racism hindered Hawai'i's annexation. Few white Americans wanted to welcome so many non-whites into the Union, and anti-annexationists preyed on those prejudices relentlessly. They dismissed Hawai'i as a "country of dusky ex-cannibals" and denigrated its vibrant ethnic mix as "this variegated agglomeration of the fag-ends of humanity." "How can we endure our shame," wailed one representative, "when a Chinese Senator from Hawaii ... shall rise from his curule chair and in pigeon English proceed to chop logic with George Frisbie Hoar or Henry Cabot Lodge? O tempora! O mores!"[119]

Finally, the United States did not annex Hawai'i to build a naval base. American strategists had admittedly hankered after Pearl Harbor for years and even acquired rights to use it in 1887. Once annexation occurred, they finally had their chance to build a permanent facility—and nothing happened. Congress mostly sat on its hands until 1908, at which point it belatedly authorized the construction of a station. It beggars belief that the United States annexed the islands to build a naval base but then waited another *decade* to authorize it. Owning the harbor mattered, to be sure, but mostly to keep other powers from bagging it.[120]

—

SINCE THE CIVIL War, the United States had faced relatively few hard choices between its principles and its sense of security. Both imperatives had required booting the French out of Mexico in 1865, and both had supported Washington's efforts to strengthen the hemisphere through trade and diplomacy. But as Eurasia's great powers loomed ever larger, the decisions had become harder, the trade-offs more vivid. In Hawai'i, for the first time, the United States had confronted a clear choice between its principles and its security. Not for the last time, it had subordinated the former to the latter.

Some saw it as a one-off decision rooted in Hawai'i's unique strategic importance. Mahan was ultimately correct: "unrighteous" or not, Hawai'i's annexation safeguarded the republic's rise by pushing back its defensive perimeter and clinching command of the northern Pacific. Partly as a result, Americans would not face serious threats from Asia for many years; when they finally did, control of the islands helped spare the mainland from attack and allowed the United States to punch back hard and fast. It is impossible to know exactly how World War II would have gone absent Hawai'i's annexation, but the United States would surely have spent far more blood and treasure. Over twelve thousand service members lost their lives taking Okinawa; one can only guess how many more would have died storming the shores of O'ahu.[121]

Elsewhere, Washington still held fast to its principles despite its neighbors' volatility. So when Haitians floated the possibility of an American protectorate in 1897 in response to a German intervention, the McKinley administration was aghast. "Obviously out of the question," it harrumphed—a violation of the republic's "true policies," which had "never" contemplated either "colonial dependenc[ies]" or "protectorates over our neighbors."[122]

By 1900, however, the United States would also annex the Philippines, Puerto Rico, and Guam, to name only the most prominent territories seized. That colonizing frenzy would be short-lived, but its involvement in the internal affairs of other states would not. Over the next two decades, the United States would start intervening left and right across the hemisphere in an increasingly bloody attempt to stabilize and strengthen its neighbors once and for all.

PART II
GREAT POWER

CHAPTER 5

THE CONQUEST OF THE UNITED STATES BY SPAIN

The Spanish-American War and Aftermath, 1898–1902

On the eve of the twentieth century, the United States had nearly everything it needed to be a great power. Since the Civil War, it had quadrupled the size of its economy, increased its exports of crude materials and food by more than 2,400 percent, and multiplied its exports of manufactured goods by almost 1,300 percent. It was simultaneously the world's breadbasket, workshop, and research lab. Demographically, too, the nation was surging: in just two decades, its population had jumped by 50 percent to almost seventy-five million, second only to Russia. By 1898, the country even had a halfway decent navy. Observing the trend lines, steel baron Andrew Carnegie rubbed his hands together in satisfaction. "The old nations of the earth creep on at a snail's pace," he scoffed. "The Republic thunders past with the rush of the express."[1]

One thing was still missing, however. In the hazy world of international politics, it is nearly impossible for states to judge each other's strength and mettle merely on paper. Great powers are thus almost always forged in the crucible of war.[2]

So it was with the United States. In 1898, Americans went to war with Spain to liberate Cuba, stunning not only European observers but also themselves with the speed, scope, and scale of their victory. By consensus, the republic had suddenly become the newest member of the great-power club.[3]

Somewhere along the way, however, Americans overshot the target. They had launched a war against Old World cruelty and colonialism that ended, to the surprise of many, with the United States acquiring colonies and protectorates of its own.

Critics could not understand how or why their nation had "pucked up its ancient soul at the first touch of temptation," entering upon a "mad career of empire in distant seas." But though the United States had undoubtedly opened a new chapter in its foreign policy, it was still the same old story. Equally sure of its virtues and others' vices, the republic had once again expanded its influence abroad in order to preempt other great powers from expanding theirs. And while the results backfired just enough to make further territorial extension nearly impossible, the war's aftermath also represented a turning point for the Western Hemisphere. Henceforth, the United States would be stabilizing its backyard with new, far more invasive instruments.[4]

Pure Act

On October 27, 1858, Theodore Roosevelt Jr. was born into a well-to-do family but an unwell body. He suffered from crippling attacks of asthma, many so bad they threatened to kill him. Some of Roosevelt's earliest memories were, as "a very small person," waking up in bed, frantically gasping for breath. In those moments, when the darkness itself seemed to be suffocating him, relief would arrive in the strong arms of his father. The elder Roosevelt would grab little "Teedie" and pace the room with him, his hold firm, his footsteps steady, calming the heaving child until his gasps had slowed to a gentle wheezing.[5]

Every cure was attempted, from bitter coffee to nicotine poisoning. But Teedie continued to struggle with life's most basic process. Eventually Roosevelt's father realized what was needed. "Theodore, you have the mind but you have not the body, and without the help of the body the mind cannot go as far as it should. You must *make* your body." The eleven-year-old looked up, pondered his father's advice, and then bared the large teeth that would one day become famous. "*I'll make my body,*" Teedie swore.[6]

Roosevelt kept that promise, starting a strenuous program of bars, swings, and weights that quickly evolved into feats of rowing, riding, and mountaineering. After two "boys of rougher antecedents" manhandled him on a stagecoach, the youngster extended his physical regimen to the martial arts; he would not be "a foreordained and predestined victim" if he could help it. So when a physician warned him at age twenty-one that he had a weak heart and the choice of either a sedentary lifestyle or an early grave, Roosevelt responded the only way he knew how: "Doctor, I'm going to do all the things you tell me not to do. If I've got to live the sort of life you have described, I don't care how short it is." He scaled the Matterhorn the next year. Nothing, not even his own body, was going to stand in Roosevelt's way.[7]

━━

GROWING UP, ROOSEVELT had loved studying the natural world. He had converted his childhood homes into witches' cauldrons, filling them to the brim with writhing bats, frogs, and snakes, all to the chagrin of the domestic staff. But in college he found himself drawn away from science and toward the even more spellbinding world of politics. After graduating from Harvard, Roosevelt began a double life: unenthusiastic law student by day, he spent his nights pressing flesh in the grubby confines of Morton Hall, the headquarters of New York's Twenty-First District Republican Association. Something about the dandified Ivy Leaguer grabbed the attention of local party leaders, and shortly after his twenty-third birthday, Roosevelt was elected to the state assembly.[8]

Going into professional politics was risky. Roosevelt had wealth, his family name, limitless energy, and a near-photographic memory. But he did not exactly look the part. Even to his friends he appeared "a bundle of eccentricities," pairing pompous fashion sense with oversized teeth, goofy spectacles, and strange mannerisms. He was not much of an orator, either; like a broken carburetor, he stuttered, sputtered, and emitted what his mother unkindly called a "sharp, ungreased squeak." Furthermore, Roosevelt labored under the distinct political disadvantage of being principled.[9]

Each of those weaknesses, however, was repurposed to his ultimate advantage. New Yorkers had tired of Tammany Hall's graft, allowing Roosevelt to make his political bones as a reformer. Central to that project was the press, and Roosevelt learned in Albany how to woo journalists with his colorful personality and natural combativeness. (Good copy came naturally from a man willing to menace his fellow legislators with a broken chair leg.) Roosevelt also refined his oratorical oddities until he became a distinctive and sought-after stump speaker.[10]

Two decades later, Roosevelt reminisced about how he "rose like a rocket"—blasting off from state assemblyman and flying through

Assistant Secretary of the Navy Theodore Roosevelt: "He shouts at the top of his voice, and wanders all over creation.... His forte is his push. He lacks the serenity of discussion."

the Civil Service Commission before finally landing in the New York City Police Commission. All the while he cranked out a series of well-received books and articles. No subject was too obscure to escape his scrutiny, and he sounded off on naval history, ranching, political biography, big-game hunting, municipal corruption, and the Australian ballot. His social circle widened, and he became intimate with power players like Alfred Thayer Mahan. "I have had rather too much of dinners lately," he complained to his sister in 1895 after overeating himself at "a perfect string of them." "Still, I have enjoyed them greatly, for here I meet just the people I care to. It is so pleasant to deal with big interests, and big men."[11]

No one better typified the age of Edison and Tesla. Roosevelt was "a many-sided man," reported one friend, "and every side was like an electric battery." Another described how "he bombards you with ever-flowing electrons of his energy," setting your "nerves tingling and [your] skin aglow." Henry Adams observed that more than anyone else, Roosevelt demonstrated that "singular primitive quality that belongs to ultimate matter—the quality that mediæval theology assigned to God." Roosevelt, he explained, "was pure act."[12]

———

OF ALL THE "big men" Roosevelt befriended, none became as close as Senator Henry Cabot Lodge. The two were brought together by James G. Blaine, whose doomed 1884 presidential campaign forced the young reformers to choose between their party and strict fidelity to their reformist principles. Both chose to support Blaine, but the decision cost them socially; ostracized by the communities they had once called home, they found solace in each other.[13]

Everyone agreed they made an odd couple—Roosevelt with his boisterous, childlike energy, Lodge with his cold, aristocratic bearing. "Theodore! Theodore! If you knew how ridiculous you look on top of that tree, you would come down at once," the senator once pled as his two-hundred-pound friend tried to traverse a creek via forest canopy. Different temperaments aside, though, the two saw the world similarly enough to form one of the most tight-knit friendships in American political history.[14]

One of their common interests was reforming the U.S. Navy, and by 1896 their passion for the subject had earned them a reputation as "those jingling jingoes." Roosevelt, however, wanted to do more than jingle; he envied his friend's perch in the Senate and wanted a comparable opportunity to advocate for bigger and better battleships. Lodge soon found it. He traveled at the close of the year to Canton, Ohio, where he and others begged president-elect William McKinley to appoint Roosevelt his assistant secretary of the navy.[15]

There was just one problem. "I want peace," the president-elect advised, "and I am told that your friend Theodore ... is always getting into rows with everybody." McKinley also feared, reasonably enough, that Roosevelt might barge into office with "preconceived plans which he would wish to drive through the moment he got in." Lodge promised, none too convincingly, that McKinley "need not give himself the slightest uneasiness on that score." Roosevelt, too, pledged to be on his best behavior.[16]

On April 6, 1897, months of carefully directed pressure bore fruit. After learning of his appointment, Roosevelt telegraphed Lodge the fateful and happy news: "Sinbad has evidently landed the old man of the sea."[17]

Blessed Be the Torch

During the Civil War, when Roosevelt was still just "a little shaver," his mother had spoken endlessly "about ships, ships, ships and fighting of ships, till they sank into the depths of my soul." As assistant secretary of the navy, Roosevelt wanted to make those stories come alive again, this time in Cuba.[18]

Cuba had long held a special place in the heart of every Spaniard, both for its riches and for its steadfast loyalty during the Latin American independence movements of the 1810s and 1820s. But by midcentury, the Ever-Faithful Isle was reconsidering its allegiances, and it finally re-volted in 1868.[19]

Spain extinguished the rebellion after ten long years, but little was resolved. Too many revolutionaries remained unrepentant and at large, including poet José Martí and General Máximo Gómez. While Madrid exhausted itself smothering other smaller rebellions over the next two decades, these leaders prepared one final push for independence.[20]

Conditions were favorable by 1895. The island was floundering through an economic depression inadvertently caused, as in Hawai'i, by American tariff policies. Cuba had reoriented its sugar industry north in response to the "free sugar" policies of the 1890 McKinley Tariff Act. When the Act was repealed four years later, it sent Cuba's economy into a tailspin. Martí had meanwhile organized the Cuban *emigré* community into a tight-knit revolutionary network. With Cuba ripe for rebellion, he decided it was time to strike.[21]

In early 1895, the Cuban War of Independence began. Martí was killed shortly after returning to the island, but the war continued under Gómez's leadership.[22]

Gómez planned to exhaust Spain until it retired from the island. To do that, the rebel armies needed to destroy Cuba's economy. Gómez's motto was accordingly simple: "Blessed be the torch." Cuba's revolution-aries burned and slashed their way across the length of the island, leaving it a smoking hellscape. Gómez also attacked Spanish troops, though he quipped that he had largely delegated their destruction to his three best generals, "June, July, and August"—the rainy season, when yellow fever rampaged through Spanish ranks.[23]

Cuba's revolutionaries did not generally want American interven-tion. "Once the United States is in Cuba," Martí had wondered, "who will get it out?" Instead, the revolutionaries sought American funds, sup-plies, and recognition, forming a "Junta" in New York to head the effort. As the war took off, the Junta publicized the Cuban cause, churning out rolls of pro-independence material that was then spoon-fed to newspa-pers across the country. The Junta also worked the back rooms of Wash-ington until "*Cuba libre*" was on every politician's tongue.[24]

Cuban efforts to win American sympathy were further stoked by Spanish brutality. In early 1896, General Valeriano Weyler y Nicolau took command of Spain's faltering war effort. Weyler herded Cuba's peasants into concentration camps, where at least a third of them died from starvation and disease. He then ordered the destruction of Cuba's countryside. American newspapers condemned Weyler's *reconcentrado* policy, dubbed him a "human hyena," and called for action. "Blood on the roadsides, blood in the fields, blood on the doorsteps, blood, blood, blood!" screeched the *New York World.* "Is there no nation wise enough, brave enough and strong enough to restore peace in this blood-smitten land?"[25]

Spanish atrocities were particularly galling because the Spanish seemed like outsiders. It was one thing for Latin Americans to suffer under their own rulers, but it seemed dangerously passé for the Old World to be their tormentor. Gómez played on this intuition, arguing to President Grover Cleveland that the Monroe Doctrine could not possibly "protect American territory and at the same time surrender its unarmed inhabitants to the cruelty of a ferocious and despotic European power." Congressman Roger Q. Mills of Texas went further. The Monroe Doctrine, he argued, had prevented other powers from rescuing the Cubans. Americans therefore had a moral responsibility to act. "We stand guard over Spain," Mills commented bitterly, as "she tears Cuba limb from limb, while the victim is crying to us to deliver her from the jaws of the monster."[26]

By 1897 Cuba was trapped in a gory stalemate. Gómez ran most of the countryside, Weyler controlled the main cities, and Cubans suffered regardless of where they found themselves. Spain could not win; the rebels would sooner destroy the island than surrender. But they still had a long fight ahead of them: without a navy, they could not stop Spanish reinforcements; without artillery, they could not seize Cuba's cities.[27]

To Americans, the situation appeared unsustainable. Something had to be done.

———

SHORTLY AFTER BECOMING assistant navy secretary, Roosevelt decided the United States should intervene in Cuba. He condemned the conflict's "unspeakable horror, degradation, and misery." He also thought that war—any war—would be good for Americans. "The trouble with our nation," he noted sourly, "is that we incline to fall into mere animal sloth and ease, and tend to venture too little instead of too much." In his eyes, bashing Spain's head in would be just the sort of character-building exercise the nation needed. "No triumph of peace," he trilled, "is quite so great as the supreme triumphs of war."[28]

Even more important, though, were the strategic implications of intervention. Roosevelt had entered office swearing up and down that he had "no preconceived policy of any kind," but that was far from true. "I should myself like to shape our foreign policy," he confessed to a friend, "with the purpose ultimately of driving off this continent every European power." Given that paramount objective, he told another, he would "take every opportunity to oust each European power in turn."[29]

Cuba seemed like the logical place to start. It was the hemisphere's last major European possession, and besides Hawai'i, it loomed in April 1897 as the most foreboding cloud on the strategic horizon. Clearing the island of Spain would not only advance Roosevelt's paramount goal of freeing "America from European dominion," but it would also head off bigger trouble. Spain was too addled to threaten the United States itself, but its very weakness unsettled Roosevelt. If Madrid could not beat back a handful of machete-waving revolutionaries, how could it stop some "strong European power" from supplanting it on the island? "Until we definitely turn Spain out," Roosevelt argued, "we will always be menaced by trouble there."[30]

Others shared these concerns. Former Secretary of State Richard Olney had worried that if Spain could not prevail, it would put Cuba on "the market for sale to the highest bidder." Lodge, too, fretted that Spain might turn Cuba over to another power, and the Senate Foreign Relations Committee likewise warned darkly that "conditions" there menaced the United States by making "European intervention ... possible."[31]

Few policymakers had any designs on the island itself. Roosevelt opposed "a land-grabbing war," and he revealed to his sister that he was "a quietly rampant 'Cuba Libre' man." Like Lodge and others, Roosevelt suspected that Cubans would botch the job of self-government, but like them he wanted to give Cubans a shot at independence anyway. Above all, he "most emphatically oppose[d]" forcible annexation.[32]

This Means War

Secretary of the Navy John D. Long was, in Roosevelt's estimation, "a perfect dear." He was also no match for his willful subordinate. The secretary much preferred gardening in New England and writing books of poetry (titled, for example, *Bites of a Cherry*) to managing his department. That suited his assistant secretary just fine.[33]

Over the summer of 1897, Roosevelt gently shooed his boss away from the heat of Washington to the cool purgatory of rural Massachusetts. Once Long was planted wrist-deep in soil, Roosevelt became, as he gleefully announced, the acting "hot-weather Secretary." "At last! This time I am in sole command, and your request goes through," he chirped to one correspondent. "I am having immense fun running the Navy," he warbled to another. He manically sent orders left and right to help get the Department shipshape for the war he prayed was coming. Long was content to let him work, knowing that the younger man's drive would generally steer the navy in the right direction.[34]

Even as Roosevelt prepared the navy for war, however, the supreme triumphs he dreamed of seemed ever more distant. Early in August 1897, an anarchist assassinated the archconservative Spanish prime minister. Madrid's new government offered Washington serious concessions in Cuba, including the recall of General Weyler, the end of the *reconcentrado* policy, and the start of a new autonomy program. McKinley duly asked Congress that December to give Spain time to implement its reforms.[35]

One month was all it took to shatter the president's illusions. On January 12, 1898, Weyler's sympathizers rioted in Havana against Spain's new autonomy program. No American was hurt, but the rampage shook the administration's confidence in Madrid's ability to implement its promised reforms. Soon Madrid's willingness also came into question. On February 9, William Randolph Hearst's *New York Journal* published a stolen letter in which the Spanish ambassador privately called McKinley "weak," "a would-be politician." But the real bombshell detonated five paragraphs later, when the ambassador advised Madrid to adopt certain policies "only for effect." Trust in Spanish sincerity was irreparably damaged.[36]

One last time bomb was still ticking away. Early in the new year, McKinley had learned of a large German war fleet roaming the Caribbean. Fearful that the Kaiser might exploit Spain's troubles, the president dispatched a battleship to keep an eye on things in Havana Harbor. Not everyone approved—one advisor compared it to "waving a match in an oil-well for fun"—but things seemed to be going well enough right up until 9:40 p.m. on February 15. At that moment, an explosion snapped the spine of the USS *Maine*, killed 266 men, and ripped apart what remained of the president's peace policy.[37]

———

"THIS MEANS WAR," exclaimed Hearst, and he was right. "Remember the *Maine*, to hell with Spain!" roared a pugnacious press, public, and Congress, especially after a naval commission blamed the disaster on a mine. Returning to his favorite theme, Roosevelt demanded "the full measure of atonement which can only come by driving the Spaniard from the New World." One priest overstepped ecclesiastical boundaries and vowed to personally "make Spanish the prevailing language of hell!"[38]

More sober voices, too, joined the call for war. Senator Redfield Proctor of Vermont had gone to Cuba, he told his colleagues, convinced that the "picture had been overdrawn." He returned to paint horrors beyond human imagination. His firsthand account of the humanitarian disaster converted many others who had thus far distrusted the jingoism of the yellow press.[39]

McKinley was despondent. He could not sleep and jumped at every sound. "I have been through one war; I have seen the dead piled up," the veteran of Antietam's battlefields insisted. "I do not want to see another." Leaving one White House reception, McKinley sank into a crimson-brocade sofa and began sobbing uncontrollably. Secretary Long agonized about the "weariness and nervous strain" overloading his chief. "He has been robbed of sleep, overworked," Long recorded in his diary. He had never seen the president "more oppressed and careworn."[40]

Long was also feeling the pressure, not least because his excitable assistant secretary wouldn't shut up about the coming war. One Friday afternoon, Long left Roosevelt in charge with strict instructions to manage only "the routine of the office." Long then visited his osteopath, who plopped the tired secretary into an electric massage chair that gently vibrated his legs and stomach.[41]

He discovered the next day that while he had been getting jiggled, Roosevelt had nearly caused "more of an explosion than happened to the Maine": ordering supplies, moving ships around, even demanding that Congress pass legislation. Roosevelt had also ordered Commodore George Dewey—head of the Asiatic Squadron, thanks to Roosevelt's help the previous year—to concentrate at Hong Kong, "keep full of coal," and, if war broke out, attack the Spanish squadron in Manila. Long rankled at his subordinate's disrespect, but the younger man's orders were mostly routine and in line with long-standing department policy, so Long generally let them stand.[42]

By early April, the pressure for war had become overwhelming. House Speaker Thomas Reed, when asked by a former governor to dissuade his combative colleagues, snorted. "Dissuade them! The Governor is too good. He might as well ask me to stand out in the middle of a Kansas waste and dissuade a cyclone. It can't be done." Congressmen now bayed almost uniformly for Spanish blood. If McKinley would not act, it increasingly seemed like Congress might act without him.[43]

Some think McKinley folded under the pressure; others argue he reluctantly decided on war himself. Both are likely true. McKinley could not ignore domestic pressures of this magnitude, but he also believed that Cuba's war had to end, and he no longer saw any possible negotiated settlement acceptable to both Cuba's rebels and Spain.[44]

On April 11, knowing it would mean war, McKinley asked Congress for authority to forcibly terminate the conflict in Cuba and "secure in the island the establishment of a stable government, capable of maintaining order." Congress soon obliged. But in a delicately negotiated amendment proposed by Senator Henry M. Teller of Colorado, Congress also underscored the country's honorable intentions: once the United States had pacified Cuba, Congress pledged to "leave the government and control of the island to its people."[45]

Madrid immediately broke off relations, and on April 25, Congress declared war as expected. A messenger braved the pouring rain to deliver the declaration to the White House, where McKinley was roused from a late-afternoon nap to receive it. Clad in a dressing gown and still in his bedroom, the groggy president blinked, signed the declaration, and formally began the Spanish-American War.[46]

A Gr-reat People

Four months later, Roosevelt and his Rough Riders returned triumphantly home from Cuba. They were met at the pier by cheering crowds and fawning reporters, all of whom wanted to see the heroes of the hour. "How are you, Colonel Roosevelt?" called out one. Roosevelt hollered back: "I am feeling disgracefully well!"[47]

He might well have been speaking for the nation. From coast to coast, flags waved higher than ever before as the country gloried in the end of what the colonel aptly called "a bully fight."[48]

On the water, the U.S. Navy had fought by the book—specifically Captain Mahan's classic, *The Influence of Sea Power upon History*. From beginning to end, naval leaders had prioritized hunting down and destroying the enemy's navy. This they did with spectacular efficiency.

Spain had two squadrons at the start of the war that the United States needed to disable—one based in the Philippines, the other in Spain. On May 1, Commodore Dewey and the Asiatic Squadron annihilated the first, destroying seven Spanish warships moored off Manila before lunchtime. Dewey's squadron suffered only one fatality, from heatstroke the night before. Two months later, the navy followed up Dewey's victory in Manila with another triumph off Cuba's coast. American warships had blockaded the second Spanish squadron inside the harbor of Santiago after it crossed the Atlantic; when the squadron

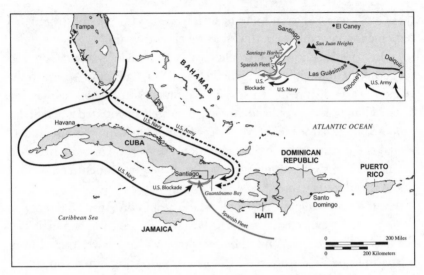

The Spanish-American War: The Caribbean Theater

made a run for it, the U.S. Navy gunned down the escaping ships one by one. Once again, there was only one American fatality.[49]

On land, the U.S. Army had a rougher go of it, but what it lacked in competence it more than made up for in luck and exuberance. In 1897, Roosevelt had predicted that the army would "drift into the war butt end foremost, and go at it in higgledy-piggledy fashion." That proved generous. After two months of logistical snarls, almost seventeen thousand soldiers blundered their way onto Cuban beaches a few miles southeast of Santiago. Excited to finally shoot some Spaniards, American soldiers raced into the jungle to see who could get ambushed first. On June 24, that dubious honor went to the Rough Riders and the 1st and 10th Cavalry, who romped through undergrowth and Mauser bullets to force a Spanish retreat at Las Guásimas. One week later came Roosevelt's famous "crowded hour," the first—and last—serious land battle of the war. Following a near-suicidal frontal assault, American forces dislodged Santiago's defenders from San Juan Hill and the other heights east of the city. Spanish forces surrendered soon afterward.[50]

"God takes care of drunken men, sailors, and the United States," the saying went, and nothing proved the point quite like the Spanish-American War. Oblivious to danger, the public had sprinted into the conflict as though it were a day at the fair, trusting that divine providence would see them through. By the time Spain surrendered, the nation's faith had been amply rewarded: despite the army's higgledy-pigglediness, the

<u>Soldiers Learn of Santiago's Surrender</u>: "It was a most happy-go-lucky expedition, run with real American optimism and readiness to take big chances, and with the spirit of a people who recklessly trust that it will come out all right in the end."

United States held not only Santiago and its environs, but also Manila, a third of Puerto Rico, and the island of Guam, all taken with minimal casualties.[51]

Americans could do no wrong; their enemies could do no right. Spain had been brought to its knees in record time, all for a selfless cause. Could any nation in history match either the greatness or the goodness of the American republic and its people? Some, like Mahan, tried to restrain their excitement. "The jocund youth of our peoples now passes away never to return," he wrote sternly; "the cares and anxieties of manhood's years henceforth are ours." But most Americans were delirious. "We have risen to be one of the great world powers," exclaimed Lodge.[52]

Mr. Dooley, a fictional Irish American barkeep who dispensed satirical wisdom in the weekly columns of the *Chicago Journal*, captured the ebullient mood. "We're a gr-reat people," observed his friend Mr. Hennessy. "We ar-re," agreed Mr. Dooley. "We ar-re that. An' th' best iv it is, we know we ar-re."[53]

———

ONLY TWO CLOUDS marred these otherwise dazzling military adventures. One was the Cuban rebels, who the prewar press had sold as dashing freedom fighters. Once American soldiers finally encountered these romanticized warriors, however, their disappointment could not have been keener. "They were the dirtiest, most slovenly looking lot of men I had ever seen," recalled one Rough Rider. Years of brutal campaigning had taken their toll. Each rebel was "infested with things that crawl and creep, often visibly, over his half-naked body," one soldier gagged.[54]

Cuban-American relations broke down instantly. Few Americans appreciated how much the rebels had tied down Spanish forces elsewhere on the island, and American biases sprang to the fore. One American lieutenant unloaded all his racist preconceptions when he opined that the Cuban rebel "is a treacherous, lying, cowardly, thieving, worthless, half-breed mongrel…He cannot be trusted like the Indian, will not work like a negro, and will not fight like a Spaniard." Others felt similarly. "Both officers and privates have the most lively contempt for the Cubans," observed a reporter. "They despise them."[55]

Cuban insurgents disappointed the Americans, but they were at least harmless compared to the scavengers that Dewey's military successes had attracted to the Philippines. Like sharks, Europe and Asia's great powers had scented the death throes of the sinking Spanish squadron and raced to the killing grounds, hoping to snag a piece of the exposed archipelago. Within days of Dewey's victory, Manila Bay was teeming with British, French, and Japanese warships.[56]

No nation, however, unnerved the Americans more than Germany. Germany had once seemed no more avaricious than the next European power, but now Americans were beginning to rethink that benign assessment. In the run-up to the war, Berlin had cautiously tried to organize a European coalition to support Spain against the United States. Germany then followed up this failed effort by amassing a five-ship fleet in Manila that outgunned even Dewey's forces and acted as if it owned the bay. Only after Dewey received reinforcements and threatened war did German behavior grudgingly improve.[57]

Germany's attitude would not soon be forgotten or forgiven. After Spain sued for peace, Dewey met with a French admiral who congratulated him on not making a single mistake since May. "Oh, yes, I have," Dewey ruefully corrected him. "I made one—I should have sunk that squadron over there," he said, pointing across the water at what remained of the German fleet.[58]

Pinchbeck Emperors and Pewter Kings

Going into the war, men like Lodge, Mahan, and Roosevelt had favored peace based on what the Massachusetts senator called "the large policy." They wanted to free Cuba, expel Spain from the hemisphere, and shore up the republic's strategic position, including by acquiring Puerto Rico. Expansionist in means, the large policy was nevertheless, as Mahan explained, "dominated by ... purely defensive ideas." It aimed to preemptively secure parts of the hemisphere "where it was increasingly evident that influences might be established dangerous to the United States."[59]

Even at its largest, however, the policy did not account for the Philippines. Since the islands were far outside the hemisphere, they did not rise above what Mahan styled the "mental horizon" of most prewar strategists. Mr. Dooley remarked that few even knew whether the Philippines "were islands or canned goods." Only Roosevelt gave their fate much thought, and he warned the State Department not to take them after the war because they were outside "our sphere."[60]

After Spain's surrender, however, the Philippines unexpectedly surfaced as the central question for end-of-war negotiations—should the United States take all, some, or none of the islands? Even for the large-policy men, the answer was unclear. Lodge quickly backed annexation, highlighting the islands' putative commercial and strategic value and declaring that "where the flag once goes up it must never come down." Mahan was not impressed. "I myself, though rather an expansionist, have not fully adjusted myself to the idea of taking them," he told Lodge. By mid-August the senator also had second thoughts about "the enormous difficulties of dealing with the Phillipines [*sic*]," and he decided that McKinley should instead trade most of the archipelago for Great Britain's Caribbean possessions. Fanciful though the scheme was, it reflected a return to the large policy's original focus on hemispheric defense.[61]

McKinley also didn't want to take the Philippines at first. By October, however, the president had reversed course. He explained his change of heart to different people in different ways at different times, often slanting his account to satisfy his immediate audience. (One popular though false myth has McKinley telling a Methodist delegation that the answer had come to him only after he "went down on my knees and prayed Almighty God for light and guidance.") But though the details differ, the basic story was always the same. Whatever the political, religious, or commercial benefits of annexation—and McKinley understood all three were doubtful—the president saw no other option.[62]

By destroying Spanish authority in the Philippines, the United States had opened a power vacuum that it could not easily let any other nation fill. Giving the islands back to Spain would be "cowardly and dishonorable," a betrayal of the war's humanitarian objectives, and bad politics besides—even the most ardent critic would, one senator joked, "as soon turn a redeemed soul over to the devil as give the Philippines back to Spain." McKinley thought conveying the islands to any other great power would be equally unacceptable; given the dangerously uncertain balance of power in Asia, "we should have a war on our hands in fifteen minutes."[63]

Nor could the United States grant the islands independence. McKinley believed that Emilio Aguinaldo y Famy, the twenty-nine-year-old leader of the islands' anti-Spanish insurgency, represented only his specific ethnic faction rather than all Filipinos. Anointing Aguinaldo leader of an independent Philippines could thus trigger a bloody civil war. McKinley also doubted the Filipinos' capacity for self-government, a racist assessment his advisors and most Americans shared. Creating a Filipino republic, the *New York Times* opined, would be like giving "a dynamite cartridge to a baby."[64]

Grave as those problems seemed, however, they paled in comparison to the troubling fact that an independent Philippines would not stay independent for long. East Asia was then the cockpit of imperial rivalries, with the great powers scavenging a prostrate China like carrion crows. Each of them was hunting for additional footholds in the region, and a free but weak Philippines would be too good to pass up. Great Britain made clear that if the United States did not annex the islands, London would do so to keep them away from Germany and Japan. Japan likewise feared German ambition and floated a joint protectorate with Washington to forestall Teutonic control. Concerns about Germany were fully warranted; Germany was just then secretly purchasing Spain's other Pacific possessions, and the American ambassador reported from Berlin that government-affiliated newspapers were pushing the Kaiser to exploit the expected "anarchy, confusion and insecurity under a 'Philippine Republic' … to secure a stronghold and centre of influence." Even Russia staked a position, opposing any control of the islands by Great Britain or Japan.[65]

Given the geopolitical state of play, McKinley concluded that any attempt to free the islands would fling "a golden apple of discord among the rival powers, no one of which could permit another to seize them unquestioned." The result would be "endless strife and bloodshed," a world war in which everyone would lose—the Filipinos, the great powers, the United States, and above all the "peace of the world."[66]

McKinley concluded annexation was less a choice than a necessity. On December 10, 1898, the United States therefore signed the Treaty of Paris with Spain, buying the Philippines for $20 million and annexing the islands of Puerto Rico and Guam.[67]

MCKINLEY NEVER REALLY made his peace with the decision. "If old Dewey had just sailed away when he smashed that Spanish fleet," the president once sighed, "what a lot of trouble he would have saved us." As so often happens in politics, however, a virtue was made of necessity. Yes, the United States was entering the business of colonialism. But it would not imitate the oppressive powers of the Old World; instead, it would magnanimously bring order and liberty to the benighted Filipinos, with their implied (if not yet fully formed) consent.[68]

The pitch was easy because in the war's intoxicating aftermath, most Americans truly believed in their own exceptionalism and superiority. America was good, its intentions pure. What else mattered? Lodge observed that he had entrusted his children's lives and liberty to the American people. "Am I to shrink from intrusting to that same people the fate and fortune of the inhabitants of the Philippine Islands?"[69]

Not everyone agreed, of course. Opponents of annexation had organized too late to save Hawai'i. But by the time McKinley submitted the Treaty of Paris to the Senate in January 1899, the self-described "anti-imperialists" had developed into a formidable political force ready to fight like mad against absorbing a distant archipelago peopled by dark-skinned foreigners.[70]

Over the fall and winter, the anti-imperialists clashed with the administration in one of the most heated and bitter political contests in American history. Republican Senator George Frisbie Hoar of Massachusetts led the anti-imperialists in the Senate, where he accused the administration of strutting "about in the cast-off clothing of pinchbeck emperors and pewter kings." His opponents gave as good as they got; Roosevelt would later dismiss leading anti-imperialists as "unhung traitors."[71]

Both sides fought dirty, but the administration gradually gained the upper hand. The final blow came two days before the scheduled vote on the treaty. Back in the Philippines, relations between the occupying American forces and Aguinaldo's Filipino rebels had remained tense but peaceful. On February 4, however, American and rebel patrols got into a firefight, touching off widespread fighting. McKinley was stunned when he heard the news. He at last said softly: "How foolish those people are. This means the ratification of the treaty." He was right; Americans rallied around the flag.[72]

Even so, it was a near-run thing. On February 6, 1899, the Senate approved the Treaty of Paris by a vote of only fifty-seven to twenty-seven. Just two switched votes could have prevented the republic from annexing the Philippines—and the new war that came with it.[73]

BY ANNEXING THE Philippines, the United States had fallen victim to one of history's classic blunders—it had gotten involved in a land war in Asia. For three years, the United States tried to stamp out Aguinaldo's insurgency in the kind of war that soldiers hate. The U.S. Army had been unprepared for conventional battles in Cuba, never mind a counterinsurgency in a jungled archipelago seven thousand miles away against a people it knew next to nothing about. The war was particularly thankless because the story seemed so familiar: a band of brave freedom fighters crusading for independence against a despotic foreign power. Only this wasn't 1776, and Americans weren't playing the part of the minutemen.[74]

Worse was yet to come. Confronted by a strange and brutal enemy in a dirty war they did not understand, many American soldiers lost both themselves and the values they had sworn to uphold. "No cruelty is too severe for these brainless monkeys," wrote one private. Americans at home were treated to sickening reports of looting, torture, and casual slaughter; one notorious tactic was the "water cure," a precursor to waterboarding that involved pouring dirty water through bamboo tubes into the throats of prisoners. One general responded to a massacre of American troops by ordering a whole island's interior turned into "a howling wilderness." "I want no prisoners," he instructed. "The more you kill and burn the better it will please me."[75]

Expansionists had resented the anti-imperialists' comparisons between the United States and the oppressive empires of the Old World. But as the Philippine-American War dragged on, the accounts of atrocities that trickled back became harder and harder to distinguish from the inhuman policies that had sparked the Spanish-American War in the first place.[76]

Americans handled the dissonance in different ways. Some, like the anti-imperialists, condemned unsparingly. "God damn the U.S. for its vile conduct in the Philippine Isles," stormed psychologist William James. Satirical character Mr. Dooley reported caustically on the countries' trade relations: "We import juke, hemp, cigar wrappers, sugar, an' fairy tales fr'm th' Ph'lippeens, an' export six-inch shells an' th' like." Americans were doing a brisk business, he said, and "'twud be a disgrace f'r to lave befure we've pounded these frindless an' ongrateful people into insinsibility."[77]

Others vacillated between disgust and disbelief, clinging to the smallest details as if the larger picture were too much to comprehend. Roosevelt admitted to one friend that while "our men have done well" in the Philippines, "there have been some blots on the record." But he blamed those lapses on the "violent and brutal language" used by superior officers; he was extremely upset, for instance, that a general had once spoken of "shooting n[—]s."[78]

The administration defended the campaign in public, arguing that any atrocities were one-off exceptions to the otherwise benign rule of the U.S. Army. Privately, however, the expansionists came to rue the day the Philippines was taken. "While I have never varied in my feeling that we had to hold the Philippines," wrote Roosevelt in 1901, "I have varied very much in my feelings whether we were to be considered fortunate or unfortunate in having to hold them." By 1907, Roosevelt had lost any vestige of doubt; he would be "glad to see the islands made independent." Only twenty-seven out of 138 congressmen polled that year still wanted them.[79]

On July 4, 1902, the Philippine-American War officially ended, though sporadic skirmishes would continue for decades. The United States had won, but at tremendous cost. It had bought the islands for $20 million; it had shelled out hundreds of millions more dollars, along with 4,234 American lives, to keep them. Such figures approached meaninglessness, however, compared to the burden borne by the Filipinos whom the United States had so charitably "civilized." At least 20,000 rebels were killed in action, and at least another 200,000 civilians died of war-related causes.[80]

Americans never came to terms with these costs. They were too overwhelming, too inexplicable, to be reconciled with the republic's image of itself. The memory of the war was instead embalmed inside layers of apathy and emotional fatigue, then buried in a quiet corner of the nation's history where it was unlikely to ever be disturbed.[81]

Try as they might, though, Americans could not rid themselves of the stench the war left behind. The United States had plowed into the Philippines with its head held high, supremely confident that moral purpose and divine destiny would see it safely through any challenge, even the formidable one of ruling a foreign people. But the country's colonial policies had turned to ashes in its mouth. Inertia would keep the United States in possession of the archipelago until 1946, but the nation was done with forcible colonial extension. "The American people have lost all interest in it," Lodge observed in 1903. Even he was not sad to see it go.[82]

Gunpowder in Hell

On the other side of the world, Secretary of War Elihu Root found himself in November 1900 on horseback, man and beast picking their way unsteadily through the Cuban hinterlands as they retraced the army's route to Santiago. Root stopped to pay his respects at Las Guásimas, where Secretary of State Hamilton Fish's grandson had been the first American killed by Spanish fire. But Root was less interested in Cuba's past than its future. He had come to learn how to reconcile the promise of *Cuba libre* with the precedent of Haiti and the other troubled countries of the hemisphere.[83]

Root had ended up trekking through Cuba somewhat unexpectedly. Back in July 1899, a telephone call had interrupted his summer vacation. "President [McKinley] directs me to say to you that he wishes you to take the position of Secretary of War," a smooth voice had announced. Root was flabbergasted. "Thank the President for me," he had responded firmly, "but say that it is quite absurd, I know nothing about war."[84]

Root was not exaggerating. His great-grandfather had commanded plucky colonials at the Battle of Concord, but his family's military service had ended with the War of 1812. Root himself had been born in rural Clinton, New York, on February 15, 1845. His father was a self-taught mathematics professor at nearby Hamilton College, and under "Cube" Root's tutelage, the younger Root seemed more likely to become a scholar than a soldier. He had graduated Hamilton as class valedictorian in 1864, then headed a year later to New York City to study law.[85]

Gotham had transformed Root from shy provincial to self-assured powerhouse. Shortly before graduating law school, he had declared confidently, "God means us to be ambitious." Eager to execute divine will, Root had vaulted up the legal establishment's *cursus honorum* and became an indispensable advisor to the country's most powerful individuals and corporations. Despite representing William "Boss" Tweed and the robber barons, however, Root had remained an idealist at heart. He had fought valiantly against municipal corruption and championed

<u>Secretary of War Elihu Root</u>: "About half the practice of a decent lawyer consists in telling would-be clients that they are damned fools and should stop."

the careers of other reformers, including a young man named Theodore Roosevelt.[86]

Stellar as it was, that career arc had not set Root up to be secretary of war. Nor was there some groundswell of support for his appointment. Conciliatory, able, and engaging, Root was popular enough. But few of his contemporaries ever felt like they really knew the man, who was self-contained enough to sometimes appear aloof. Root did not take half measures and he suffered no fools, two traits that did not always endear him to politicians. He was, in short, scarily competent, and when he smiled, even his friends noticed it was a "frank and murderous smile."[87]

On that July morning, however, Root's face had appeared more frank than murderous as he mulled over what he had just heard. McKinley "is not looking for any one who knows anything about war," the voice on the other end of the line had reassured him. "He has got to have a lawyer to direct the government of these Spanish islands, and you are the lawyer he wants."[88]

At that moment, Root had realized that "there was but one answer to make." He had accepted the president's offer and readied himself "to perform a lawyer's duty upon the call of the greatest of all our clients, the Government of our country."[89]

———

CUBA WAS, APART from the Philippines, the most important Spanish island waiting for the new secretary of war's direction. Madrid had transferred control of Cuba to the United States, and now Root was trying to figure out just what to do with it.[90]

Most Americans agreed that Cuba could not be granted independence immediately. Three years of total war had crisped the island to cinders, and withdrawing American troops rashly would have precipitated a serious humanitarian crisis. Cuba also lacked a universally recognized political authority, as Americans could not yet be sure the rebels represented all Cubans.[91]

Conditions were gradually improving, with signs that Cuba could soon stand on its own. Combined Cuban and American relief efforts had eased the prospect of famine and disease, and occupation officials were helping rebuild Cuba's infrastructure and institutions. With luck, the island would shortly start attracting the capital needed to resuscitate its economy. "When the people ask me what I mean by stable government," Military Governor Leonard Wood told the president, "I tell them money at six per cent."[92]

Even if all went well, however, the administration saw one continued obstacle to Cuban independence: Cubans themselves. Americans had once imagined their allies as gallant paladins. Not only had reality disappointed, but it had also caused many to rethink whether an independent Cuba was viable. Officials in Washington feared that Cubans were too illiterate and inexperienced to govern themselves; some also alleged complicating racial and environmental factors. "Self-government!" snorted the commander of the Santiago campaign. "Why, these people are no more fit for self-government than gunpowder is for hell."[93]

If Cuba was simply let go, American leaders feared it would quickly implode. Freeing Cuba, remarked the *Chicago Inter-Ocean*, would "deliver the island up to the fate of Hayti and [the Dominican Republic], with their thirty revolutions in the last thirty-three years." A *New York Times* correspondent expected "a reign of terror—[from] the machete and the torch, to insurrection and assassination." One senator agreed. Independence, he predicted, would snip the ribbon on "a picnic ... of throat cutting."[94]

Steering clear of that result became the administration's paramount objective. Root told one acquaintance that he would release Cuba only once he was sure it would avoid "the perpetual revolutions of Central America and the other West India Islands." McKinley also objected to "turning adrift any loosely framed commonwealth to face the vicissitudes which too often attend weaker States."[95]

Senior officials feared those vicissitudes for two reasons. First was a moral concern. Spanish outrages in Cuba had led to war, and it would be rather unseemly if the whole venture ended with the United States presiding over new atrocities. Second was the ever-present problem of order. If the United States abandoned the Cuban damsel to the distress of anarchy and civil war, there was no telling what kind of knights in shining armor might eventually start showing up—nor what kind of rapacious motives they might harbor.[96]

Germany elicited special concern. Root believed that Berlin had revealed through its actions in Manila and elsewhere that it was "a predatory government" ready to "pop up out of [no]where" and make Latin America its next meal. The secretary was especially concerned over the fate of the most important and simultaneously vulnerable island in the region. "Germany was nosing around all over trying to get a foothold," he later recalled. "We didn't propose to have her secure such a position in Cuba."[97]

———

Given the perils an independent Cuba posed, it was only natural that many Americans flirted with a tried-and-true solution: annexation. One of McKinley's advisors returned from the island looking "forward to the day when Cuba will be a State of the Union." In mid-1899, Roosevelt reported to Lodge (a recent convert himself) that McKinley was starting to favor taking the island. Even Senator Teller—who had lent his very name to the promise of *Cuba libre*—backtracked. Fearing "interference by some foreign power," he asked bluntly: "Who else can govern Cuba to-day but the United States?"[98]

Annexation, however, never really stood a chance. For one thing, there was Senator Teller's amendment, in which the United States had pledged in uncomfortably clear terms to "leave the government and control of the island to its people." Not for nothing had the U.S. Army stuffed a translation guide into haversacks bound for Cuba that included such helpful phrases as "We are your friends" and "We do not want Cuba." For the Americans to turn around and glibly say "*¡Estamos bromeando!*" would have been, to put it lightly, spectacularly bad form.[99]

Furthermore, it was plain that Cubans overwhelmingly wanted to govern themselves. Of course, local opposition had not always stopped the steamroller of American annexation, but each of the largest recent acquisitions—Hawai'i and the Philippines—had been spurred by the kind of clear and present danger not yet clear or present in Cuba.[100]

More than anything, however, it was the Filipino rebels who made forcible annexation of Cuba impossible. Every morning, Root scanned the headlines anxiously for news of "American troops firing on Cubans." As long as Americans occupied the island, he worried that "we were on the verge daily of the same sort of thing that happened to us in the Philippines." If another guerrilla war did break out, Root knew the consequences "would be too disastrous to contemplate."[101]

Few Americans doubted that Cuba would benefit from joining the Union—Lodge found it "amazing" that any Cuban thought otherwise—but that was a decision for Cubans to make on their own, after independence. In the meantime, Root would have to find some other way to stabilize the island.[102]

To Protect the Independence of Cuba

By the end of his trip to Cuba, Root thought he had his answer. On board a steamer in Santiago's harbor, he responded to one lunchtime toast with another: "I expect soon to see a free, self-governing republic in Cuba."[103]

Root, however, was raising his glass to a very specific sort of "free, self-governing republic." He had concluded based on his interviews, intuitions, and observations that the United States could not safely entrust Cubans with a full dose of sovereignty. Instead, Cuba needed statehood with safeguards, including a constitution, limited suffrage, and above all restrictions on how it could interact with the outside world.[104]

Just what Root had in mind became clear on February 9, 1901, in a long letter sent to Cuban Military Governor Leonard Wood. Citing almost a dozen American statesmen, the secretary reiterated that Washington had long had a "most vital interest" in Cuba's independence and "in preserving the people of that Island from the domination and control of any foreign power." But that was easier said than done; "a country so small as Cuba" could never fend off "the great powers of the world" through force alone. So Root had designed three primary safeguards to preserve Cuba's independence.[105]

First, Root wanted Cubans to swear not to agree to any treaty that might impair or interfere with their independence, including any treaty that would alienate any of their territory to a foreign power. He feared that a cash-strapped Cuban government might otherwise be tempted to sell or lease parts of the island in ways that would violate the Monroe Doctrine.[106]

Second, Root wanted Cubans to agree to live within their means. One of the leading causes of foreign intervention was the unfortunate regional habit of going on European-funded spending sprees and then failing to pay up when the bills came due. Root wanted to eliminate that risk entirely.[107]

Third, Root wanted Cubans to give the United States the right to intervene with armed force. Such a right would, most obviously, be used to defend the island against external attack. But it was also another answer to the problem of order. Cuba might someday descend into such chaos that it could not protect foreign lives or property. If the United States had the right to intervene, it could preempt any European intervention by stabilizing Cuba before things got out of hand. Root also wanted a right of intervention for its deterrent effect; by hanging over Havana's head like the proverbial Sword of Damocles, he thought, the right would ensure that Cubans governed wisely and took their international obligations seriously.[108]

Root's proposals took the United States into uncharted waters. The secretary had clearly been inspired by his country's old reciprocity treaties with Hawai'i, in which the archipelago had agreed not to alienate its territory to foreign powers. But Hawai'i had balked at going any further than that, bristling when Blaine asked for the right to land military forces. Root was not only resurrecting that right but also pioneering new rules that interfered with how Cuba could manage its finances.[109]

On top of that, Root was not planning to negotiate for these safeguards. His plan would instead be the kind of "enforcible advice [*sic*]" that "Great Britain might give to Egypt." In particular, he would insist that delegates to Cuba's ongoing Constitutional Convention incorporate his plan into their country's founding document.[110]

Root realized that this approach would run counter to the United States's previous promises about respecting Cuba's independence, but he feared that without these safeguards, both that independence and the United States would soon be in serious danger.[111]

POLITICS COMPLICATED ROOT'S task. Root had few illusions about how popular his plan was going to be among Cubans, and he hoped that Cuba's Constitutional Convention would take the initiative and adopt his plan as its own, knowing that the island might otherwise risk forfeiting American protection. But the Cuban delegates studiously ignored his plan, and Root fretted that by ceding the initiative, he was giving them the opportunity to flank him by allying with anti-administration forces in the U.S. Congress.[112]

So Root instead worked with Senator Orville H. Platt of Connecticut, chairman of the Committee on Cuban Relations, to introduce a revised version of his plan on the floor of Congress as an amendment to the annual Army Appropriations Bill.[113]

In its final form, the "Platt Amendment" had eight articles, four of which were especially important. Article I prohibited Cuba's government from entering into any treaty that would "impair or tend to impair the independence of Cuba," including any agreement that allowed a foreign power to obtain "lodgment in or control over any portion" of the island. Article II forbade Havana from taking on "any public debt" that "the ordinary revenues of the island" could not support. Article III gave the United States "the right to intervene for the preservation of Cuban independence" and "the maintenance of a government adequate for the protection of life, property, and individual liberty." Finally, Article VII gave Washington the means to carry out Article III, pledging that Havana "will sell or lease to the United States lands necessary for coaling or naval stations."[114]

On March 2, 1901, Congress passed the Platt Amendment with little debate and what Root cheerfully called the "most extraordinary unanimity." Strictly speaking, that was not true; it had been a party-line vote. But aside from token speeches, Democrats had essentially acquiesced, privately assuring the administration that they would offer no serious opposition. Even a leading anti-imperialist like Senator Hoar admitted sheepishly that he had the "uncommon pleasure" of finding the Platt Amendment "eminently wise and satisfactory."[115]

Getting Congress's buy-in protected Root's flank, but it also thrust his plan into the spotlight—where Cubans immediately made clear that they found the Amendment neither eminently wise nor satisfactory. They objected to the entire idea of it, and especially to the articles concerning intervention and naval bases. According to Wood, Cubans feared that Washington would use these provisions to interfere in Cuba's domestic affairs "for trifling reasons." To hear the "radical element" tell it, Wood griped, "intervention will take place at the whim of the officers occupying naval stations."[116]

Such concerns exasperated American policymakers. No doubt the Platt Amendment hobbled Cuba's external sovereignty, but the anxieties about Washington fiddling around in the island's *domestic* affairs seemed greatly overblown. Wood privately called them incorrect. Root agreed, scoffing at "the idea that the intervention described in the Platt Amendment is synonymous with intermeddling or interference with the affairs of a Cuban Government." Washington would intervene only "upon just grounds of actual failure or imminent danger" and always "to protect the independence of Cuba."[117]

Over the course of March 1901, Root faced off against the Cuban Constitutional Convention, which peevishly denied that it had the authority to incorporate the Amendment at all. Root dismissed this as "childish nonsense" and warned that if *this* Convention refused to act, Washington would simply convene another one. Every day the delegates did not agree to the Amendment, the secretary added darkly, they were risking "incalculable injury" to the island's future by predisposing Americans against the trade reciprocity that Cubans craved. Finally, the Platt Amendment itself established that the American occupation would end only once Cuba had inserted substantially all eight articles into its constitution. The Convention thus had the choice of either Cuba under the Platt Amendment or Cuba under the stars and stripes.[118]

Some of Root's firmness stemmed from an unpleasant reminder of the stakes. In late February, Wood had confirmed that the German and British consuls in Havana were quietly encouraging Cubans to resist American demands. Root testily informed the State Department of the consuls' behavior and asked the Department to ensure "either a change of conduct or a change of residence on their part."[119]

By mid-April, the Cuban Constitutional Convention was beginning to falter, and it dispatched a delegation to Washington to see if it could get any final concessions. Upon arrival, the delegation found only sweetness and light—sweetness in an endless array of banquets and cloying solicitude; light in six hours of illuminating conversations with Root. Over the course of the latter, the secretary repeated ad nauseam that the Amendment's "sole purpose" was to establish "precautions with respect to possible European complications." Article III, the intervention clause, was simply "the Monroe Doctrine, but with international force." It would deter European intrusions, and it would only ever be used to maintain "inviolate the independence of Cuba." Likewise, Root pledged that the naval bases of Article VII would "never give rise to intervention in the internal government of Cuba; they will only be utilized for defense against the foreigner." Platt chimed in as well, assuring the delegation that his Amendment had been "carefully drafted" to avoid interfering with Cuba's "independence or sovereignty."[120]

Such promises helped allay the Cuban delegates' suspicions, but they made one last stand after returning to Havana. By a vote of fifteen to fourteen, the Convention adopted the Platt Amendment but added what Wood called "explanatory remarks." Some were based on Root's confidential assurances, others on the delegates' own views. All, however, were intended to narrow the Amendment's scope.[121]

Root lost all patience the moment he read this "cloud of words." He had not minded formally clarifying that Articles III and VII were aimed exclusively at protecting Cuba's independence, but this latest obstinacy was too much. He closed ranks with Wood and fatefully insisted that the Convention accept the Amendment as written, with no clarifications whatsoever.[122]

On June 12, 1901, the delegates finally capitulated. By a vote of sixteen to eleven, they inserted the Platt Amendment into the new Cuban Constitution. Following national elections, the United States fulfilled its end of the bargain, and on May 20, 1902, the Republic of Cuba was born.[123]

An International Provision

Generations of historians have puzzled over the transformative power of the Spanish-American War. The United States launched a war of choice against colonialism and for *Cuba libre*. Months later, it was collecting colonies and squeezing Cuba into a protectorate. Such a dramatic reversal struck many, then and now, as more like the "conquest of the United States by Spain" than vice versa. Not only had the United States become a great power, it had also started acting like one.[124]

Some of this head-spinning turnaround reflected the flush of victory, which swelled the republic's self-confidence to dangerous levels. But that short-lived high tells only half the story. Long after victory's glow had faded, Americans were still stuck with a basic dilemma. By demolishing Spanish authority from Manila to Mayagüez, they had created a series of power vacuums. The United States could not allow rival great powers to fill those vacuums, but it doubted whether local authorities could do the job themselves.[125]

Officials in Washington tried solving that dilemma in two ways. First, they tried annexation, filling the gaps in the Philippines and elsewhere with American authority. But that solution went badly awry, provoking a bloody insurgency abroad and vehement criticism at home. The administration eventually prevailed in both theaters, but the slog was so draining that it effectively removed forcible annexation from the republic's foreign policy toolbox.

Cuba offered the opportunity to try something different. Root and others believed that the problem of order was less severe there, both because the island faced no immediate threat and because its people were perceived as relatively better suited for self-government. But grave dangers still lurked on the horizon, so rather than freeing Cuba entirely, the administration forced the Platt Amendment upon it.[126]

From one perspective, the Amendment was less intrusive than the annexationist alternative. But from another, it was a significant escalation from the historical baseline. Before the Spanish-American War, the United States had primarily protected its neighbors from the menace of European powers; afterward, it began protecting its neighbors primarily from themselves.

At the same time, it is easy to overstate just how intrusive the Platt Amendment was meant to be. Although it has since become synonymous with American imperialism, the Amendment was not originally intended to be a tool of domination. Germany had started sniffing around the Caribbean, and Root wanted to prevent Cuba from becoming its next prey. "You cannot understand the Platt Amendment," he later explained, "unless you know something about the character of Kaiser Wilhelm the Second." Root saw the Amendment as an "international provision," having "nothing to do with internal affairs" and mostly limiting Cuba's *external* relations. Even the high-debt prohibition was quintessentially foreign oriented, since Cuba could load up on dangerous levels of credit only with foreign lenders' help.[127]

There is little evidence that the framers of the Platt Amendment planned to use the right of intervention—or any other provision—to micromanage Cuba's domestic affairs. Root thought he had designed the Amendment to "be as little burdensome and annoying as possible," and he was genuinely dumbstruck by Cubans' fears to the contrary. "I think they really suspected," he wrote Platt in disbelief, "that under the provisions of the law was concealed a real purpose to make their independence merely nominal and really fictitious." Aside from his earlier support for suffrage restrictions, Root let Cubans draft the rest of their constitution with little interference. Senator Hoar, always on the lookout for imperialist shenanigans, also doubted it was "anybody's intention" to use the Amendment to meddle in "local commotions or disturbances," save for those "grave cases ... where other countries would interfere if we did not." Even Wood, who at times favored consensual annexation and once suggested that "there is, of course, little or no real independence left Cuba under the Platt Amendment," meant mostly that the United States had limited Cuba's ability to chart an independent course abroad. He, too, agreed with Root that the Amendment did not authorize regular interference in the island's domestic affairs.[128]

Some Americans nevertheless foresaw how the Amendment might have some unintended effects. "Suppose they have an election," Senator Joseph B. Foraker of Ohio told his colleagues moments before the final vote in Congress. By causing trouble, the losing party could force "an intervention of the United States to put the successful party out." Far from "having a restraining influence," Foraker warned, the Amendment might actually "invite intervention."[129]

Such predictions seemed theoretical in 1901, however. Congress passed the Amendment, and even Foraker voted in favor. Few anticipated just how prophetic his warnings would prove in a few short years.[130]

CHAPTER 6

THE HOMICIDAL CORRUPTIONISTS OF BOGOTÁ

The Panama Canal, 1903

"I f what is revolt composed?" asks Victor Hugo in *Les Misérables*. "Of nothing and of everything. Of an electricity disengaged, little by little, of a flame suddenly darting forth, of a wandering force, of a passing breath. This breath encounters heads which speak, brains which dream, souls which suffer ... and bears them away."[1]

Claptrap, thought another Frenchman. Philippe-Jean Bunau-Varilla was a man of science, with no time for Hugo's muddled mysticisms. Every inch of Bunau-Varilla's petite frame radiated righteous precision, from his flawless manners and stiff-necked posture to his expansive mustache, each end waxed to an imperious spike. The overall effect might have been laughable but for his unblinking gray eyes. Duelist's eyes, Theodore Roosevelt had thought. Eyes cold with confidence that the laws of logic, not emotion, governed revolution. Or so Bunau-Varilla needed to be true, for he was counting on the scientific method to see through his revolution in Panama.[2]

One might not have expected a Frenchman to be leading a Panamanian revolution, but Bunau-Varilla was no ordinary Frenchman. Born in Napoleon III's Paris on July 26, 1859, he had received the most advanced mathematical education in the world at L'École Polytechnique, France's preeminent launching pad for state engineers. He had also received his life's purpose. His final year, Ferdinand de Lesseps, the famed builder of the Suez Canal, had spurred him and his spellbound peers on to the next grand adventure—building a canal through Panama.[3]

Four years later Bunau-Varilla had sailed for Colón, the latest recruit to de Lesseps's canal company, the Compagnie Universelle du Canal Interocéanique. By age twenty-six, Bunau-Varilla was the company's chief engineer—a meteoric ascent attributable both to his talent and to the malaria and yellow fever that ran riot through upper management's ranks.[4]

By 1889, however, the Compagnie had dug itself into a financial hole. It declared bankruptcy and the aged de Lesseps fell into disgrace. Nearly everyone wrote the Panama canal off as a boondoggle that would never be finished.[5]

Bunau-Varilla, however, did not give up. Partly, he had no choice—following the Compagnie's collapse, French courts had forced the engineering firm he ran to capitalize the Compagnie's successor with more than two million francs. Bunau-Varilla would never see that money again unless someone bought the new company's assets and finished the work de Lesseps had begun.[6]

But it was about more than just money. Somewhere deep in Panama's pestilential swamps, the idea of the canal had seeped into Bunau-Varilla's soul. He had emerged from the jungle a zealot. Constructing the canal was not just a question of Good triumphing over Evil; it was also his personal, divinely ordained mission. So absolute was his faith that the Frenchman would do almost anything to get the canal built—even rip a sovereign state apart.[7]

Such a step seemed regrettably necessary by 1903. Panama was still a province of Colombia. Colombia, however, had refused to allow the Americans to build a canal in Panama, even though they were the only ones who could do the job. If nothing were done, the Americans would inevitably build elsewhere. But if Panama could be induced to secede, then perhaps a new, independent Republic of Panama would strike a deal with Washington and finally realize Bunau-Varilla's vision.

From his perch in the United States, Bunau-Varilla had been planning a separatist uprising on the isthmus until, at the last moment, his Panamanian co-conspirators had seemingly lost both their nerve and their faith in him. With only one shot at getting his revolution back on track, Bunau-Varilla thought through his plan for the last time. Certain that he had gotten it all exactly right, he marched to the Central Telegraph Office in Baltimore, Maryland. At ten minutes past noon on October 30, 1903, he handed a coded message over for immediate dispatch:

Philippe-Jean Bunau-Varilla: "He didn't just come into a room, he made an *entrance*."

"Pizaldo, *Panama*. All Right Will Reach Ton And Half Obscure. Jones."[8]

Bunau-Varilla took a moment to reflect. He had estimated every variable, drawn every rational inference, relied on every possible logical conjecture. "I have made diplomacy as it were by trigonometry," he thought, all devised to "fire the slow match." Whether an explosion would follow depended on how well he had taken the measure of his co-conspirators—as well as the new president of the United States. But Bunau-Varilla never doubted himself. Panama *would* blow up in four days' time.[9]

The Empire of the American Seas

For centuries, Central America's narrowness—Pablo Neruda called it "America's sweet waist"—had made it a crossroads between West and East, Atlantic and Pacific, great powers and local weaklings. Panama, as the narrowest part of the isthmus, had always attracted special interest. It was there that the treasure carts of the Spanish Empire rumbled along the *Camino Real*, laden with Peruvian silver and other ill-gotten gains, on their way to galleons creaking in the Caribbean. It was there that the great powers scuffled in the shadows for influence and power during the nineteenth century. And it was there that, in 1903, the United States launched one of the most controversial and brazen interventions in its history.[10]

The Panama intervention stands out as a pivotal moment in the rise of the United States. After Colombia refused to ratify a canal treaty, the United States forcibly pried Panama from Bogotá's grasp and then pocketed the canal line, the hemisphere's single most geopolitically important position. Strategically, it was an accomplishment of untrammeled proportions. But it was also unusually gratuitous. Other American interventions of the period were, if not last resorts, at least often seen as the only reasonable option left by the men who ordered them. By contrast, the United States galloped into Panama despite having less forceful ways of achieving its objectives. Part of its haste reflected the moment's passions. But the intervention in Panama was also a story of domestic constraints, miscommunications, great-power rivalry, and the pressure of pent-up desires stretching back decades, all the way back to the moment Latin America first liberated itself from Spain.

━

FOLLOWING INDEPENDENCE IN the early 1820s, Panama had joined the superstate of Gran Colombia to the south, but the union quickly splintered into Ecuador, Venezuela, and New Granada. Civil war meanwhile rocked the rest of Central America. In the chaos, Panama stayed with New Granada, but the political connection was thinned by geographical isolation: the Panamanian isthmus barely touched the roof of South America, and impassable wilderness blunted what little contact there was.[11]

Spying an opportunity in the chaos, the British Empire snaked commercial and political tentacles into the region throughout the 1830s and 1840s. By 1846, the threat had become serious enough that New Granada's leaders turned to the United States for help. On December 12, 1846, the two countries signed the Bidlack-Mallarino Treaty, whose Article 35 promised the United States free "transit across the *Isthmus of Panamá*, upon any modes of communication that now exist, or that may be, hereafter, constructed." In exchange, the United States would guarantee "the perfect neutrality of the before mentioned Isthmus," as well as "the rights of sovereignty and property which New Granada has and possesses over the said territory."[12]

The Bidlack-Mallarino Treaty came at an auspicious moment. Americans were just then clobbering their southern neighbor in the Mexican-American War, and it was becoming clear that the conflict's spoils would include a massive swath of real estate fronting the Pacific.

But Americans on the Eastern Seaboard could not reach these new holdings quickly, cheaply, or reliably. The treaty was providential, offering the country a route from one coast to another just as that second coast was being acquired.[13]

Great Britain was rattled by the escalating competition with the United States, and in 1850 it agreed to a diplomatic cease-fire in the Clayton-Bulwer Treaty. The treaty was another major coup for Washington, at least for a time—it neutralized Central America and prevented either power from gaining "exclusive control" over any future canal.[14]

Over the next few decades, however, the Clayton-Bulwer Treaty became increasingly unpopular in the United States. Americans completed the world's first transcontinental railroad in Panama in 1855, but they soon wanted to trade in their isthmian railroad for a full-blown canal. Not only would a canal dramatically slash the cost of transporting goods from one coast to the other, but it would also open up new fields for American investment and trade, both in the hemisphere and beyond. Even more significantly, a canal would solve the central dilemma of American naval strategy. Rather than fretting constantly about how to divide its warships between the Atlantic and the Pacific, the United States could concentrate its vessels together and use the canal to rotate them from ocean to ocean as needed.[15]

Meanwhile, the United States was fast becoming entangled in Panamanian affairs. The State Department interpreted Article 35 of the Bidlack-Mallarino Treaty to permit the United States to keep traffic across the isthmus open by any means necessary, including force. But few had anticipated how often that would be required. Panamanians, it turned out, had never reconciled themselves to being part of either New Granada or its successor state, Colombia. Between 1840 and 1903, there would be at least fifty Panamanian attempts at revolution, and Bogotá was often unable to rush reinforcements there in a timely manner. The responsibility for maintaining order would then fall to the nearest American naval commander, who would invariably land troops, secure the railroad, and forbid any armed force from endangering isthmian transit. Colombia generally consented to this practice, shrewdly realizing that nearly every American intervention would redound to its benefit by freezing rebel troops in place until an army could arrive from the mainland to quash them.[16]

Given this escalating involvement and the interests at stake, Americans naturally assumed that any future canal would be built under their auspices. So when French engineer de Lesseps organized his Compagnie

Universelle in the late 1870s, the United States went ballistic. "The policy of this country," barked President Rutherford B. Hayes, "is a canal under American control."[17]

The nation, however, was stuck. It could not abide a European canal, and it cheered the eventual collapse of the Compagnie Universelle while spiking the French government's efforts to rescue the project. At the same time, the American government would not yet pick up the spade itself. Too many barriers still stood in the way—a national parsimony, the Clayton-Bulwer Treaty, and even disagreement over where the continent should be split.[18]

——

EACH OF THOSE barriers began falling at the turn of the century. First, the nation received an object lesson in the canal's necessity during the Spanish-American War. On the conflict's eve, the USS *Oregon*, one of the navy's few first-class battleships, found itself parked on the wrong coast. On March 19, 1898, it left its berth at San Francisco and headed to Key West as fast as possible. Unfortunately, "as fast as possible" meant steaming all the way down to Cape Horn at the southern tip of South America and then all the way back up to Caribbean latitudes. It was a perilous voyage of nearly 13,792 miles, and it would take the *Oregon* sixty-six days.[19]

Each day, the nation watched, transfixed, tracking the battleship's progress and hoping that it would make it in time for the decisive clash with the Spanish. As luck would have it, the *Oregon* arrived shortly before the Battle of Santiago, in which it played a critical role. But it was the battleship's sixty-six-day voyage that proved more significant in the long run. For years Captain Alfred Thayer Mahan and his acolytes had struggled to convince an often apathetic public that an isthmian canal was strategically indispensable. But their arguments had been too theoretical to stick until the *Oregon* started sailing across the front pages of newspapers. All at once there were, as one senator observed, "ten thousand arguments" in favor of a canal. Americans realized they could not afford two-month delays in future crises with European powers, especially not with their new insular possessions at stake.[20]

Capitalizing on the burst of public opinion, Secretary of State John Hay approached London about annulling the Clayton-Bulwer Treaty. The Foreign Office proved surprisingly receptive. Great Britain was isolated in Europe and eager to compensate by stoking the growing warmth in Anglo-American relations. Whitehall was also starting to conclude that the British Empire was badly overstretched. Gradually ceding influence in the Western Hemisphere—where the empire had relatively few interests—would allow it to pivot toward rising threats elsewhere, especially Germany. Finally, both the British Foreign Office and the Admiralty realized that the United States was determined to unite the oceans. Great Britain could either yield gracefully or be trampled underfoot. On November 18, 1901, Great Britain yielded gracefully, agreeing to abrogate the Clayton-Bulwer Treaty and opening the door to an American canal.[21]

Shortly thereafter, Congress settled on where it wanted that canal. For decades most Americans had assumed that the waterway would flow through Nicaragua. Every American survey had endorsed that route, American investors had already sunk millions into it, and Managua promised to be a friendly partner. Panama, the next-best option, was seen as "unholy ground" after the French canal company's collapse. When the leading proponent of the Nicaragua route, Senator John Tyler Morgan of Alabama, was asked about Panama's chances in late 1901, he drawled, "I haven't even heard a brush crack in the woods about it."[22]

But Morgan's ears had missed the stealthy approach of Bunau-Varilla and an unlikely coalition of Panama supporters. Bunau-Varilla knew full well that his fate and fortune were bound up with the destiny of the Compagnie Nouvelle du Canal de Panama, the Compagnie Universelle's corporate successor. The Compagnie Nouvelle's only value came from the possibility that the United States might acquire its assets; if the republic chose Nicaragua instead, then the company (and Bunau-Varilla's investment) would be worthless.

Bunau-Varilla lobbied hard for Panama, but his efforts would have gone nowhere save for the anarchist's bullet that took the life of President McKinley in September 1901. "Now look," one senator exclaimed, "that damned cowboy is President of the United States!"[23]

So he was. Theodore Roosevelt had accepted the vice presidential nomination in 1900 with great trepidation, grumbling that it was "not a stepping stone to anything except oblivion." But his friend Lodge's counsel had prevailed, and Roosevelt was no longer grumbling. "It is a dreadful thing to come into the Presidency this way," he told Lodge, "but it would be a far worse thing to be morbid about it."[24]

One of Roosevelt's priorities in his first few months as president was to consult the members of a commission appointed by McKinley to consider the best canal route. The conversations affirmed Roosevelt's sense that the Panama route was technically superior, and he strong-armed the commission into endorsing it over the Nicaraguan alternative.[25]

Over the spring of 1902, the "Battle of the Routes" was joined in the halls of Congress. It was a true David-and-Goliath affair for Panama's partisans. In January, the House of Representatives had approved the Nicaragua route 308 to 2. Bunau-Varilla nonetheless engaged in a lobbying campaign in the Senate of such skill and creativity that on June 19, the battle was effectively decided. By a vote of 42 to 34, the Senate narrowly endorsed Panama over Nicaragua. But there was a catch. If Roosevelt could not negotiate a canal treaty with Colombia "within a reasonable time and upon reasonable terms," he would be obliged to proceed with Nicaragua instead.[26]

Nailing Currant Jelly to a Wall

Roosevelt did not anticipate much difficulty negotiating a canal treaty with Colombia. Opportunities like this came by once a century, and Colombians would be fools to play coy. But Washington badly misjudged Colombia's negotiating position, and before long the talks had sunk into an agonizing quagmire.

Roosevelt and Hay entered into negotiations determined to win the best deal for the United States they could. The margin of victory for the Panama route in the Senate had been a slim eight votes, enough for a majority but far short of the two-thirds necessary for the Senate's ultimate approval of a canal treaty. If the administration did not secure an ironclad agreement with Colombia, Morgan and the other Nicaragua advocates could shoot it down.[27]

Colombia, in contrast, was utterly unprepared to begin talks. Bogotá was busy putting down one of the country's perennial revolutions, and President José Manuel Marroquín could spare little time for discussions in far-off Washington. Marroquín did want a canal—both for its financial benefits and to keep the restless Panamanians happy—but more than anything he wanted to put off a deal until he had consolidated control domestically.[28]

For Hay and the Colombian Legation alike, Marroquín's attitude was exasperating. Colombia's negotiators were given neither clear instructions nor the power to act independently. They were forced into a defensive posture, rejecting Hay's terms but rarely proposing their own.

Occasionally they bucked their orders and tried to meet Hay halfway, only to have their concessions countermanded by Marroquín weeks or even months later. Roosevelt later fumed: "You could no more make an agreement with them than you could nail currant jelly to a wall." Colombia's three successive negotiators had it even worse: the first departed drained and died a year later; the second reportedly had a nervous breakdown and left New York in a straitjacket; and the third, Tomás Herrán, dubbed the entire course of negotiations a horrible nightmare before also dying within a couple of years.[29]

One of the primary sticking points was the rights of the Compagnie Nouvelle. Congress had appropriated $40 million for the French company's assets, but the company needed Colombia's approval to sell, and Bogotá was demanding a cut of the purchase price. That should have been a matter solely between Colombia and the Compagnie—either way, the United States would pay $40 million. Roosevelt and Hay nevertheless insisted that the final treaty authorize the Compagnie to sell its assets without paying a cent to Colombia. This demand was not only inappropriate but also wildly out of character—neither the trust-busting president nor his secretary of state sympathized with big corporations, much less big *French* corporations.[30]

William Nelson Cromwell, a Wall Street attorney and the Compagnie's general counsel, undoubtedly helped coax the administration to his side, having wormed himself so thoroughly into Hay's confidences that he was drafting documents on the Department's behalf. Behind the silver-tongued Cromwell, however, hovered the ghost of Monroe. Assistant Secretary of State Francis B. Loomis later explained how Roosevelt had feared that France might respond to "the looting of the French company" by dispatching a squadron from Martinique and landing marines all along the canal line. Paris would have stayed "for a long period," and any resulting conflict might have drawn in other European powers. By protecting the Compagnie's assets, Roosevelt hoped to snuff out that possibility.[31]

Gallic retribution was only one of many possible foreign headaches. During negotiations, Colombia surreptitiously solicited competing canal offers from Europe. None came in, but the attempt spawned ominous rumors that wafted back across the Atlantic and into the headlines of American newspapers. Especially concerning was the news that Germany was going to swoop in and buy out the Compagnie Nouvelle's rights. One year earlier, the Naval War College had gamed out a similar scenario that led to war with the Kaiser. Berlin denied any interest or involvement, but Roosevelt was not pleased that Colombia had risked turning a paper crisis into a real one.[32]

On January 21, 1903, after almost two years of rancorous negotiations, Hay told Herrán that Colombia's "reasonable time" was finally up. The following afternoon the Hay-Herrán Treaty was signed. By its terms, the United States received a hundred-year franchise, renewable at its option, and control of a canal zone approximately six miles in width. Inside the canal zone, American authority would coexist uneasily with Colombian sovereignty. In turn, Colombia would pocket $10 million up front and an annual rent of $250,000 starting nine years after ratification. Finally, in a provision targeted at Europe, the treaty forbade Colombia from alienating "to any foreign government any of its islands or harbors" near the canal zone for military purposes; it also committed the United States to giving Colombia "the material support that may be required in order to prevent the occupation of said islands or ports."[33]

———

COMING TO AN agreement was only half the battle. Both the United States and Colombia now had to ratify it, and Roosevelt threw himself into the effort with his usual energy. As expected, the forces backing the Nicaragua route put up a stiff fight, and Senator Morgan alone marshalled no fewer than sixty amendments to kill the treaty. Undeterred, Roosevelt cheerfully informed Hay that he was "sweating blood" to win the Senate's consent. On March 17, 1903, he got it: the treaty was approved without a single amendment.[34]

Colombia was expected to quickly follow suit. But just as Morgan was being routed in Washington, the American minister in Bogotá, Arthur M. Beaupré, began reporting problems. On March 30, Beaupré alerted the State Department that Colombian public opinion was turning "strongly" against the treaty. On April 15, he wrote of "a sudden outburst of controversy"; sentiment on the agreement had gone "from approbation to suspicion and from suspicion to decided opposition." On May 4, he observed that the opposition was "intensifying."[35]

Hay could not understand the souring mood. German intrigues came naturally to mind, but as far as Beaupré could tell, "no direct hostile influence is being used here." Instead, Colombians seemed genuinely grieved by what they saw as the treaty's inadequate compensation and extensive imposition on their sovereignty. Beaupré nevertheless assured the Department that public opinion notwithstanding, "any legislation seriously desired by the [Colombian] Government will pass."[36]

Overestimating Marroquín's authority, Hay and Roosevelt decided to force the Colombian president's hand. On June 9, Hay warned him that rejecting the treaty would "seriously" compromise diplomatic relations and potentially lead to actions by "Congress next winter which every friend of Colombia would regret." Simultaneously, Roosevelt leaked word to remind Marroquín that the treaty's rejection might trigger Panama's secession. Roosevelt was not seriously considering this possibility yet, but the threat brought into sharp relief a danger that had long prowled along the periphery of the negotiations.[37]

Hay and Roosevelt's tactics backfired. Colombia's public, already up in arms about the country's jeopardized sovereignty, grew even more incensed at the United States's bullying. Caught between Roosevelt and his own population, Marroquín chose the latter.

On August 12, 1903, the Colombian Senate rejected the Hay-Herrán Treaty unanimously. Even Marroquín's son voted no.[38]

Little Wildcat Republic

Roosevelt was apoplectic. He dedicated much of his summer and fall correspondence to vindictively sorting Colombia's politicians into various branches of the Linnaean taxonomic tree. Marroquín, he informed Rudyard Kipling, was a deceitful "Pithecanthropoid." Colombia itself was a "little wildcat republic." Bogotá's politicians were "contemptible little creatures," though he went back and forth on whether to classify them as "cat-rabbits" or "jack rabbits." Either way, they were completely intolerable.[39]

Between epithets, Roosevelt found time to consider next steps. The easiest option was to negotiate a canal with Nicaragua instead, and Hay reported that it would be "quick work" to make a deal. But Roosevelt resisted. Some of the country's best engineers had stated flatly that "we had better have no canal at this time" than one in Nicaragua, and the president was loath to ignore their advice. Roosevelt also had geopolitical risks on his mind. If the United States renounced the half-dug Panama route, it could be scooped up and finished by a European rival. Letting the Nicaragua route lie fallow, by contrast, seemed less dangerous: it was far further from completion, and Managua had not yet tried to solicit other buyers.[40]

Roosevelt was instead drawn to a second option proposed by John Bassett Moore. Moore, a highly regarded international law professor, argued that whether Bogotá ratified the canal treaty was irrelevant because

Colombia had *already* given the United States permission to dig a canal in Article 35 of the Bidlack-Mallarino Treaty. By giving the United States the power to maintain free transit across the isthmus, Moore claimed, Colombia had also impliedly given it the right to "construct the great means of transit which the treaty was chiefly designed to assure." The difficulty with Moore's proposal, however—other than its fanciful reasoning—was that Colombia would vigorously oppose any attempt to act on his interpretation. Not that Roosevelt minded; at this point he was spoiling to personally lead the Rough Riders against "the foolish and homicidal corruptionists in Bogota." But the president realized that "as yet, the people of the United States are not willing to take the ground of building the canal by force," and Congress would probably share their timidity.[41]

Roosevelt also considered a third option—secession. If Panama seceded, the Panamanians would surely make signing a lucrative canal treaty their first priority. But Roosevelt had to tread carefully. Panama's secession would resolve his conundrum, but the president could not openly encourage revolution. "Whatever other governments can do," Roosevelt told a friend, the United States could not employ "such underhand means." He admitted privately that if Panama seceded he would be "delighted," but "for me to say so publicly would amount to an instigation of a revolt, and therefore I cannot say it."[42]

If a revolt were to begin of its own accord, however, well, *then* the United States might be able to do something about it. For years, the United States had landed forces on the isthmus under Article 35 to help Bogotá maintain authority over its rebellious province. Now, however, Roosevelt and his secretary of state began to think about using Article 35 in a different way. If—when—another revolution occurred, Hay suggested, "our intervention should not be at hap-hazard, nor, this time, should it be to the profit, as heretofore, of Bogota." Hay ventured ominously that "nothing can be lost, and something may be gained, by awaiting developments for awhile."[43]

One final option was obvious—compromise. Colombia wanted better terms, and it intimated that even $5 million more would be enough (along with a $10 million cut of the French company's fee) to secure its acquiescence. But Roosevelt refused "to have any further dealings whatever with those Bogota people," having already gone "further in their interests than we by rights ought to have gone." Even had Roosevelt been inclined to compromise, however, his back was up against a congressional wall—further concessions to Colombian cupidity would have made the Nicaraguan alternative more attractive, making it even harder for any treaty with "those Bogota people" to survive the Senate.[44]

By early October, the administration had settled on a basic strategy. Once Congress reassembled in December, Roosevelt would ask for permission to build a canal without Colombia's consent. If Congress balked, he would then build in Nicaragua. In the meantime, the administration would wait and see what turned up on the isthmus. "The teeth of the children at Panama are getting a fine edge on to 'em," a State Department official noted.[45]

A Man Who Would Act

Dr. Manuel Amador Guerrero did not strike most of his fellow travelers as a sharp-toothed revolutionary. Since chugging out of Panama's port town of Colón, the *Segurança*'s passengers had observed a thin, frail man who had just celebrated his seventieth birthday. Small, circular, steel-rimmed glasses framed his warm eyes, and an enormous, bushy white walrus mustache made amends for a thinning hairline. Puttering around on the steamer's deck, Amador appeared more kindly grandfather than cunning insurrectionist leader.[46]

In truth, the septuagenarian doctor had gladly joined the ranks of the Panamanian separatists. Amador had long been the Panama Railroad Company's chief physician and understood better than most the value of a canal to Panama. When another railroad employee had reported in early August that Cromwell was ready to "go the limit" for the conspirators, Amador had volunteered to go north to negotiate a final deal with the lawyer and—ideally—win the State Department's blessing.[47]

Shortly after Amador landed in New York on September 1, 1903, however, the plan went awry. Cromwell showered Amador with promises of support at their first meeting, but when Amador came back for a second conference, Cromwell inexplicably threw him out of the office. One of Amador's fellow passengers, it later emerged, had ratted the doctor out to the Colombian chargé in Washington, who had warned Cromwell that the Compagnie Nouvelle would lose its concession if he did not cut ties with Amador instantly.[48]

Amador knew none of this, however. After cabling a single word back to his friends in Panama—"disappointed"—the baffled doctor spent the next three weeks wandering the streets of New York aimlessly, tailed by detectives in the Colombian chargé's pay, hoping for something, anything, to turn up.[49]

ON SEPTEMBER 22, Bunau-Varilla stepped off a transatlantic steamer. He had escorted his wife to New York at her request, or so he said. But the French engineer admitted to a friend that he had actually come to guarantee "the Washington govt. makes no mistake in dealing with Columbia [*sic*]."⁵⁰

Bunau-Varilla had a knack for serendipitous timing. Amador was about to return to Panama empty-handed. Instead, at 10:30 a.m. on September 24, Bunau-Varilla heard a soft knock at the door of Room 1162 of the Waldorf-Astoria.⁵¹

Amador shuffled in and laid out the separatist dilemma. The revolutionaries could seize Colón and Panama City, Panama's two major political centers, without much effort; the Colombian garrison was greatly outnumbered and easily corrupted. But Colombia controlled the sea, and unless the Panamanians found a way to keep its warships at bay, Bogotá could retake the province at its leisure.⁵²

For the moment, Bunau-Varilla had no solution to Amador's dilemma. But he knew just the man to see.⁵³

ON OCTOBER 10, 1903, Bunau-Varilla was ushered into President Roosevelt's office. Everyone present would later insist that the subsequent discussion of Panama was limited. Roosevelt asked Bunau-Varilla ("a most interesting fellow") what he predicted would happen. Bunau-Varilla paused melodramatically, then declared: "Mr. President, a revolution." He elaborated: "Colombia has decreed the ruin of the people of the Isthmus. They will not let things go any further without protesting according to their fashion. Their fashion is—revolution."⁵⁴

And that was it. When Bunau-Varilla asked what the United States would do if a revolution erupted, Roosevelt demurred. Assistant Secretary of State Loomis claimed afterward that "nothing was said that could be in any way construed as advising, instigating, suggesting, or encouraging a revolutionary movement."⁵⁵

For Bunau-Varilla, however, it was more than enough. He concluded from what Roosevelt had said—and left unsaid—that the president would support Panama's independence if the opportunity presented itself. Roosevelt, in turn, suspected that Bunau-Varilla had dropped by to learn whether the president "was a *man who would act.*" Few who met Roosevelt ever walked away doubting it.⁵⁶

OVER THE NEXT couple of weeks, Bunau-Varilla shuttled between New York and Washington while devising a plan. From his time in Panama, he knew that the Americans always came running at the first sign of revolutionary trouble on the isthmus. Given Roosevelt's evident loathing for the bandits of Bogotá, Bunau-Varilla doubted that any American intervention this time around would favor Colombian interests. Instead, the U.S. Navy would probably position itself between the revolutionaries and the Colombian warships, thereby guaranteeing the revolution's success.[57]

So solving the separatist dilemma boiled down to game theory. If the Panamanians revolted, the United States would intervene. If the Panamanians knew the United States would intervene, they would revolt. But the Panamanians did not know whether the United States would intervene, and the United States could not tell them. What was missing was a middleman, someone who could convince both sides that he spoke for the other, even when he emphatically did not.[58]

Bunau-Varilla was born for the role. Literally bristling with confidence, the mustachioed Frenchman baselessly assured Amador "that you will be protected by the American forces forty-eight hours after you have proclaimed the new Republic." Bunau-Varilla also promised to secure $100,000 for the revolutionaries to bribe the Colombian garrison, but in exchange he wanted to become the isthmian republic's first diplomatic representative. Gradually and grudgingly, the doctor was won over to Bunau-Varilla's plan, and he promised to convince his co-conspirators. The revolution would start no later than November 3.[59]

Shortly before Amador's departure back to Panama, Bunau-Varilla unveiled a surprise. In his spare time, the engineer had packed the doctor a revolutionary kit, complete with a codebook, plan of military operations, and draft declaration of independence. Bunau-Varilla's wife had even used material from Macy's to sew a flag for the new republic.[60]

If Amador was surprised by the Frenchman's presumptuousness, he kept it to himself.

Her Destination Is Believed to Be Colombia

On October 29, Bunau-Varilla received an encrypted telegram from Panama: "TOWER, *NEW YORK*—FATE NEWS BAD POWERFUL TIGER. URGE VAPOR COLON.—SMITH."[61]

Bunau-Varilla, using the codebook he had given Amador, translated the message as best he could. It was for him ("Fate") from Amador

("Smith"). "News" indicated Colombian troops were coming, and "bad powerful tiger" revealed how many, when, and where: more than two hundred, in five days, to Colón. But the end of the message—"Urge vapor Colon"—did not correspond to anything in the codebook. Bunau-Varilla relied on his Spanish to translate it roughly as "Press steamer Colón."[62]

Suddenly, Bunau-Varilla understood. It was a test. Amador wanted Bunau-Varilla to demonstrate Roosevelt's support for the Panamanian secessionists by sending an American warship ("steamer") to Colón. Bunau-Varilla panicked. The U.S. Navy was beyond his control, but if a ship were not sent, the revolution was finished.[63]

———

BUNAU-VARILLA WAS RIGHT. Back in Panama, Amador had unveiled Bunau-Varilla's plan. His co-conspirators were crestfallen. They had expected cash and a promise of official American support, not a homemade flag and the word of a high-strung Frenchman. It was not even a *good* homemade flag; Mrs. Bunau-Varilla had simply yellowed Old Glory's stripes and swapped out the white stars for some vaguely isthmian imagery.[64]

Amador saw an opportunity to kill two birds with one cable. If Bunau-Varilla sent an American warship, it would simultaneously reassure his friends of Washington's support and protect them from the incoming Colombian troops.

In the meantime, his son would begin work on a new flag.[65]

———

BY THE TIME he arrived in Washington, Bunau-Varilla had a plan. Pursuant to Article 35 of the Bidlack-Mallarino Treaty, the United States sent forces to Panama whenever turmoil there threatened to disrupt free transit across the isthmus. If Amador was right, and Colombian troops were indeed bound for Colón, then fresh turmoil seemed imminent. Bunau-Varilla would spend the day convincing anyone he met of that fact in the hopes that it would get the administration to send a warship as a precautionary measure.[66]

Bunau-Varilla learned the next morning that his warnings had hit home. "I have thought over what you said," Assistant Secretary Loomis told him. "This situation is really fraught with peril." That was all Bunau-Varilla needed to hear. He decided that Loomis's remark could mean only one thing: the United States had sent a cruiser to Colón.[67]

On the eleven o'clock train back to New York, Bunau-Varilla did some quick math. He knew from public reporting that the closest gunboat to Colón was the USS *Nashville*, stationed about five hundred miles away in Jamaica and capable of ten knots. Factoring in an extra twelve hours for preparations, that meant it would reach Panama in roughly two and a half days, on the morning of November 2—if, that is, Bunau-Varilla had picked the right warship, and if he had fathomed Loomis's intentions correctly.[68]

Calculations complete, Bunau-Varilla got off at the next stop and marched to Baltimore's Central Telegraph Office. At ten minutes past noon on Friday, October 30, 1903, he handed a coded message over for immediate dispatch: "PIZALDO, *PANAMA*. ALL RIGHT WILL REACH TON AND HALF OBSCURE. JONES." Translated, it responded to Amador's request for a cruiser as follows: "All right. Will reach two days and a half."[69]

TWO DAYS LATER, Bunau-Varilla's eye caught a notice buried on the fourth page of the *New York Times*. It read: "KINGSTON, Jamaica, Oct. 31.—The United States gunboat Nashville sailed from here this morning under sealed orders." His heart skipped a beat. "Her destination is believed to be Colombia."[70]

Long Live the Republic of Panama!

Panama's revolution nearly ended before it began. On November 2, the USS *Nashville* glided into Colón shortly before sunset, only half a day behind Bunau-Varilla's schedule. The Panamanian revolutionaries were ecstatic; here, finally, was the proof they needed of American support for the next day's planned revolution. But the plan began going awry when a second ship joined the *Nashville* at midnight. It was the *Cartagena*, carrying General Juan Tovar and a detachment of four hundred crack Colombian riflemen, the *tiradores*. Early revolutionary celebrations crumbled into disillusionment at daybreak the following morning when, contrary to the revolutionaries' expectations (and contrary to orders belatedly sent from the U.S. Navy Department), the *Nashville* did nothing to stop Tovar from disembarking his sharpshooters at Colón's old railroad wharf.[71]

Terror flashed through the hearts of the revolutionaries. Few had known that so many Colombian troops were coming, but far worse was that the *tiradores* had landed unmolested. Even Amador, who had been energetically pacing the streets of Panama City at six that morning, had flopped back into his hammock by eight, completely deflated. At that gloomy moment, the revolution was saved twice over by Amador's intrepid wife. She first roused the doctor from his languor and then hatched a plan to divide and conquer General Tovar's battalion.[72]

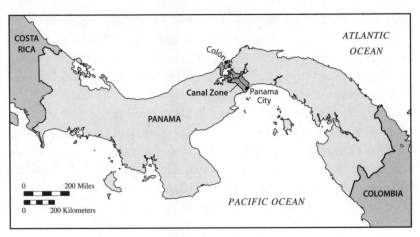

Panama

James Shaler, a co-conspirator and the general superintendent of the railroad, lied and told Tovar that there were not enough train cars currently available in Colón to transport all of Tovar's troops to Panama City. Shaler pretended, however, that he had managed to rustle up a special coach for the general and his fellow officers to use, on the understanding that the rest of their battalion would follow a few hours later.[73]

Once lured aboard the coach, Tovar and his officers began having second thoughts about being separated from their men. Sensing a trap, Tovar's second-in-command suddenly became agitated and demanded to get off. Before he could, Shaler blew his whistle and the train lurched toward Panama City, startled human cargo in tow.[74]

Isolated from their battalion, Tovar and his fellow officers were easy pickings. That afternoon, as they were sunning themselves near the Panama City seawall, wondering where the rest of their men were, a company of supposedly loyal Colombian soldiers approached them. One file passed in front, the second behind, and then both lines turned, lowered their bayonets, and formed a ring of steel around the surprised officers. Tovar tried to push his way out, but a dozen blades blocked his path. He and the other prisoners were disarmed and arrested. Shortly afterward, the revolutionaries formally proclaimed Panama's independence.[75]

The next morning, Amador doled out eight boxes of Colombian silver to the defecting soldiers. "Boys, at last we have carried through our splendid work," he praised. He led them in three cheers: "Long live the Republic of Panama! Long live President Roosevelt! Long live the American Government!"[76]

PANAMA CITY IN hand, all that remained was to liberate the province's other major city, Colón. But the revolution's second act was complicated by the continued presence of the *tiradores* whom Shaler had stranded there the previous day. For the revolution to succeed, the garrison had to be eliminated.

Colón's insurrectionist leader, Porfirio Meléndez, hoped to do so peacefully. Around noon, he invited Colonel Eliseo Torres, the inexperienced officer left in charge of the *tiradores*, to a local watering hole. Over a drink, Meléndez revealed to the still-clueless Colombian colonel that, first, Tovar had been imprisoned; second, Panama was seceding; and third, the United States backed the uprising. If Torres did not pack up and go home, Meléndez bluffed, several incoming American warships would eject him and his men by force. Seemingly on cue, orders came from the *Nashville* forbidding Torres from using the railroad to retake Panama City.[77]

Torres did not take the news well. Flying into a rage, he swore that unless the imprisoned Colombian generals were released by two o'clock that day, he was going to kill every American in Colón, burn the town down to the ground, and forcibly commandeer a train to Panama City to rescue his superior officers and smother the revolution in its own blood.[78]

That was not the response that either Meléndez or the Americans had been looking for. The *Nashville* promptly beached forty-two blue-jackets, and in minutes they had barricaded themselves and the town's American men inside a stone warehouse. (Women and children were bundled onto civilian steamers in the harbor.) Torres instantly surrounded the warehouse with his four hundred sharpshooters. The *Nashville*, hoping to even the odds, cleared its decks for action and closed in on the waterfront. As it did, the crew of the *Cartagena*, the Colombians' troopship, lost their nerve and bolted out of the harbor, leaving Torres stranded for the second time in as many days.[79]

Cut off now from both his superior officers and his only means of escape, Torres found himself in an unenviable position. Minutes seemed to span hours as the two sides fiddled with their triggers and stared nervously at each other through gunsights. Finally, at around 3:13 p.m., Torres approached the warehouse gingerly. Over the barrels of the rifles pointed at him, he explained that it was all a big misunderstanding; he was actually quite "well disposed" toward Americans and wished only to talk to his commanding officer.[80]

Negotiations would continue for another day, but the hotheaded colonel had lost control of the standoff. Early in the evening of November

5, Torres gave up entirely and ordered his battalion onto a British mail packet headed south to Cartagena. For his trouble, he received two clinking sacks of American twenty-dollar gold pieces.[81]

FROM THE PANAMANIAN perspective, it had been a near-run thing. As long as revolutionaries held one end of the railroad and Colombian forces the other, Roosevelt had to at least feign neutrality between the two sides. When Torres sailed away with his sacks of gold, however, the entire province fell into secessionist hands.

On the morning of November 6, the State Department learned of Torres's departure. Fifty-six minutes later, it instructed the Panama City consul-general to recognize the de facto independence of the new Republic of Panama. Roosevelt then moved to safeguard that independence by ordering ten warships to Panama, while the remainder of the U.S. Navy prepared to repel any foreign power inclined to exploit this delicate moment.[82]

Colombia, as expected, dispatched troopships to restore control over its wayward province. But Roosevelt refused to let them land, explaining that if he did, a fight would inevitably break out on the isthmus and endanger free transit contrary to the United States's obligations under the Bidlack-Mallarino Treaty. Colombia stormed at this twisted interpretation of Article 35—which had, after all, been designed to guarantee Bogotá's "rights of sovereignty" over the isthmus—but its forces could not surmount the 42,560-ton wall of armor and gunmetal that now protected the secessionists. Whether Colombia liked it or not, Panama was gone for good.[83]

I Am Ready to Sign the Treaty

One final drama remained. Panama had freed itself from Colombia but not the world's expectations, and no expectation weighed as heavily on the renegade republic as the need for a canal treaty. Even more than the Americans, Amador and his compatriots wanted a canal. But the revolution's course had constrained their bargaining position and left them burdened by obligations about who would bargain on their behalf. Bluffs, bayonets, and bribery had won Panama its independence, but new fetters were about to be imposed at the negotiating table.

Bunau-Varilla had conditioned his support for the revolution on being appointed the republic's first diplomatic representative. Panama's new junta dragged its feet on crowning the Frenchman with that kind of authority, not least because he hadn't set foot on the isthmus since 1889. But Bunau-Varilla kept the wires hot and withheld funds until, thoroughly exasperated, the junta agreed to make him envoy extraordinary and minister plenipotentiary. Simultaneously, however, it dispatched Amador and one of its own members, Federico Boyd, to link up with the Frenchman in Washington and wrest control of the canal treaty negotiations before Bunau-Varilla could do too much damage.[84]

But Bunau-Varilla was never one to be a placeholder. Once he learned that Amador and Boyd were on their way to Washington, he begged Hay to accelerate the pace of negotiations and deny Panama City's politicians the chance to intrigue in ways that could endanger a canal treaty.[85]

Hay sensed Bunau-Varilla's desperation. On Sunday, November 15, the secretary dropped off for the Frenchman's consideration an updated version of the Hay-Herrán Treaty that substantially expanded American perks. But Bunau-Varilla had something even grander in mind. Sleeping only a few hours, he spent the entire night and next day tossing off treaty revisions. By Tuesday morning, a new draft was ready, and he sent it to Hay with his impatient regards. "I am ready to sign the Treaty," he pleaded.[86]

As the secretary deliberated on the new draft, Bunau-Varilla felt his stomach sinking. The delegation from Panama had just landed in New York. There was not a moment to lose.[87]

———

AMADOR HAD INDEED just returned triumphantly to the United States. So much had happened in the month since he had left—Panama's independence, Colombia's humiliation, and, most recently, the news that he would be the first president of the new republic. But Amador and Boyd became uneasy when they realized that their country's envoy extraordinary was, rather extraordinarily, not on hand to greet them. Even more disturbing was a telegram from Bunau-Varilla chiding them to "remain in New York, to observe the greatest secrecy with regard to their mission, [and] not to say a thing to the newspapers."[88]

Suspicions aroused, the delegates hastened the following evening to the capital. But it was too late. Bunau-Varilla met them at the train station, grinning from one mustache tip to the other.

"I have just signed the Canal Treaty," he beamed as they stepped onto the platform. "Panama is henceforth under the protection of the United States."[89]

Amador nearly fainted. Boyd reportedly struck the smug Frenchman in the face.[90]

ONLY HOURS EARLIER, Bunau-Varilla had indeed signed what everyone recognized would be the most important treaty in Panama's history.
Technically, the Frenchman had acted within the scope of his authority.
But no one in Panama City had foreseen that their determined representative would force the issue so quickly, before a single Panamanian even
arrived on the scene.

Panama would rue the oversight for decades. Contrary to what Bunau-
Varilla would later say, the new treaty was not practically "identical" to
the old Hay–Herrán Treaty with Colombia. True, there were superfi-
cial similarities, even improvements: the new treaty did not change the
amount of compensation, and it obligated the United States to maintain
Panama's independence. In exchange, however, the new treaty extended
the canal concession from one hundred years to perpetuity and widened the canal zone from roughly six miles to ten. Most importantly, the
treaty gave the United States practically sovereign authority over the canal zone, as well as a Platt Amendment–like power to intervene "for the
safety or protection of the Canal ... at all times and in its discretion."[91]

From the perspective of the United States, the Hay–Bunau-Varilla
Treaty was so favorable it was almost embarrassing. Hay confessed
sheepishly that although the agreement was "vastly advantageous to the
United States," it had "many points ... to which a Panaman patriot could
object."[92]

But Bunau-Varilla was no "Panaman patriot," and he had not objected. Only one thing mattered to Bunau-Varilla—building the canal.
During negotiations, that had meant loading the treaty with as many
pro-American provisions as possible. Panama would ratify regardless; the
little republic had no choice, with Colombian forces hovering ominously
over the horizon. But the U.S. Senate was a different matter, especially
given the controversy that Roosevelt's intervention was bound to stir up.
Both Hay and Bunau-Varilla therefore wanted to bulletproof the new
treaty before it ran the senatorial gauntlet—to make it, in the latter's
words, "so well adapted to American exigencies, that it could challenge
any criticism in the Senate."[93]

The results spoke for themselves. Even an erstwhile congressional
opponent was forced to concede that the treaty gave the United States
"more than anybody in this Chamber ever dreamed of having.... We
have never had a concession so extraordinary in its character as this."[94]

WHILE THE AMERICANS marveled at their good luck, Bunau-Varilla ensured that Panama would not reverse its misfortune. He assailed the junta with dire cables urging Panama to ratify his canal treaty *immediately*, before Colombia underbid it. Bunau-Varilla was exaggerating the urgency, but to the isolated junta, the emergency appeared real enough.[95]

On the afternoon of December 1, an iron strongbox arrived in Panama City. Inside, a typewritten copy of the Hay–Bunau-Varilla Treaty had been symbolically nestled inside the new Panamanian flag. Equally symbolically, both the treaty and the Panamanian standard were then swallowed up in the folds of an American flag.[96]

As far as metaphors go, it was hard to imagine one more telling. Panama's junta officially approved the treaty the next morning. Town councils across the isthmus heralded the decision with understandable enthusiasm; it ensured the separatist republic's survival. But in securing Panama's sovereignty against the immediate threat to its south, the treaty opened up the country's independence to a longer-term threat from the north. One day shy of one month old, the fledgling republic had already subordinated its fate to the strategic needs of a rising colossus.[97]

I Took the Isthmus

On March 23, 1911, Roosevelt faced a packed audience in the Greek Theater at the University of California, Berkeley, and defended the start of what he described as one of "the greatest feat[s] ... that has ever been attempted by civilized mankind." If he had followed traditional methods, the former president exclaimed, he would have submitted a long state paper to Congress urging the construction of an isthmian canal. The debates would still be ongoing, "and the beginning of work on the canal would be fifty years in the future." Instead, Roosevelt reportedly bellowed to laughter and applause, "I took the isthmus, started the Canal and then left Congress not to debate the Canal, but to debate me." Some still debated the propriety of his actions, "but while the debate goes on the Canal does too."[98]

Few of Roosevelt's actions have been as heavily debated as the taking of Panama. For Roosevelt, it was "by far the most important action I took in foreign affairs during the time I was President." Every step "was not merely proper," he argued, "but was carried out in accordance with the highest, finest, and nicest standards of public and governmental ethics." Roosevelt's critics thought otherwise. The president, according to one senator, obtained "a pretended claim ... by the methods of a sneak thief and then defend[ed] it by the attitude of a bully." "Even the buccaneers who sailed the Spanish Main would have found it too much for them," agreed *The Nation*. Former Secretary of State Richard Olney, who had once boasted that Washington's "fiat is law" in the Americas, moaned that "we now stand before the world as a bullying, land-grabbing, treaty-breaking, unscrupulous power, all the more offensive for the unctuous and pharisaical professions of the public functionaries who represent us."[99]

Such criticism bounced harmlessly off Roosevelt in the immediate aftermath of the revolution. Late in February 1904, the administration wrung approval out of the Senate for the Hay–Bunau-Varilla Treaty. Republican lines held firm in an election year, and many southern Democrats defected to Roosevelt's side because a canal would benefit their states in particular. Critics also faced the same problem they had encountered in the Philippines: what, exactly, was the alternative? Roosevelt had presented them with a fait accompli, and unless they wanted to toss both a favorable treaty and thousands of Panamanians to the wolves, there was little they could do.[100]

Over the longer term, however, the president's intervention became infamous. His 1911 speech at Berkeley unleashed new torrents of criticism, sparking a congressional investigation that revealed for the first time the extent of Bunau-Varilla and his compatriots' machinations. Bogotá, too, interpreted Roosevelt's remarks as a plea of guilty to the charge of international assault and battery. It demanded reparations and eventually received $25 million in what one wag called "canalimony." At $6.25 million a word, "I took the isthmus" became the costliest boast the president reportedly ever made.[101]

Even Roosevelt's most ardent defenders have struggled to excuse his actions on the isthmus, especially his decision to turn a treaty guaranteeing Colombian sovereignty into a shield for secession. Setting aside the president's self-serving rhetoric about fairness, morality, and civilization, it is clear that he took the Panamanian isthmus because that's where he wanted the canal built. Roosevelt himself admitted as much, defiantly arguing to his cabinet that he could not possibly have conspired to incite revolution in Panama because, Congress permitting, he had planned to seize the province outright. "Excellent!" Elihu Root congratulated him on behalf of the stunned cabinet. "The defense is complete. To clear yourself of a charge of seduction you confess to rape!"[102]

Root's quip understated the problem. Roosevelt's intervention was worse than a crime—it was a blunder. He could have continued to negotiate with Colombia, perhaps securing a canal treaty for a mere $5 million more (pennies on the dollar compared to the ill will and $25 million reparations bill that the United States eventually picked up). Or he could have gone forward with the Nicaragua route, which was a viable alternative even if technically inferior. Either option would have delayed the canal's opening by a few years at most, a trifling setback.[103]

Of all the American interventions in the region, Panama in 1903 thus stands apart. Elsewhere, the United States generally avoided intervening in its neighbors' affairs except in response to serious threats and the problem of order. Sometimes, as in Hawai'i, those threats were clear, direct, and imminent; other times, as with the Platt Amendment, policymakers instead calculated that they would run intolerable risks in the future by failing to intervene in the present. Such risks did shape the administration's thinking on Panama, but they did not ultimately drive Roosevelt to support secession; after all, the United States had other, equally safe ways to keep Europe's powers at bay. Strategic imperatives made a canal under American control a necessity, but they did not demand this canal at this time in this way.[104]

Colombia's weakness had offered temptation, and Roosevelt had succumbed. Secretary Seward had once been ready to launch a world war if the great powers recognized the secessionist South. Four decades later, Roosevelt advanced his objectives by allying with foreign secessionists and using military force to protect them. Roosevelt missed that irony, as well as one other: that, like its despised European rivals, the United States had taken advantage of local dissensions in order to expand its influence in the region.

—

ROOSEVELT WAS RIGHT about one thing, though—while the debate went on, the Canal did too. Shortly after the Hay–Bunau-Varilla Treaty was ratified, the U.S. Treasury completed the world's costliest real-estate transaction to date when it bought the Compagnie Nouvelle's assets for $40 million. Bunau-Varilla and his firm received their cut, recouping millions of francs plus 3 percent annually. Soon American engineers were brushing the rust and vines off abandoned French dredges and locomotives, and before long the isthmus was alive again with the sound of clanking machinery, dynamite blasts, and hollering foremen.[105]

On August 15, 1914, nearly eleven years after Panama's revolution, the Panama Canal would finally open. British Ambassador James Bryce called it "the greatest liberty Man has ever taken with Nature." Excluding wars, it was also the single most expensive endeavor in human history to

The Panama Canal: "If [a canal] be made, and fulfil the hopes of its builders, the Caribbean will be changed from a terminus, and place of local traffic, ... into one of the great highways of the world."

that point. American expenditures alone came out to a staggering $352 million—almost five times the amount the republic had paid for all of its previous territorial acquisitions, *combined.*[106]

For a rising United States, though, that cost was trivial. Not only did the canal pay for itself many times over through tolls and trade, but it also cracked the central dilemma of American naval strategy. By connecting the Atlantic and Pacific oceans, the canal effectively doubled the size of Roosevelt's beloved navy. Pilloried or not, the president could rest content. The United States controlled the economic and strategic crossroads of the hemisphere. All that remained now was to ensure that Europe's great powers never launched another major intervention in the region ever again.

CHAPTER 7

AN INTERNATIONAL POLICE POWER

The Second Venezuela Crisis and the Dominican Republic, 1902–1905

From behind closed doors and cracked windows, scared eyes peeked out at the soldiers trooping past. *Alemanes*, recognized the more cosmopolitan residents of Caracas's port city, La Guaira. The Germans paraded past so efficiently, so robotically, that it was easy to lose count of how many there were: *diez, veinte, treinta*, on and on, at least one hundred German soldiers marching on Venezuelan soil. Landing after dark on the night of December 9, 1902, the columns had penetrated La Guaira's suburbs. They were now returning to the waterfront, escorting their prize—the German consul and his family—to a waiting cruiser.[1]

Some of La Guaira's residents knew that Europe's great powers had amassed a long list of claims against Venezuela stemming from its civil wars and fiscal mismanagement. But it had still come as a shock when, earlier that afternoon, the port city had fallen under the shadow of the German and British cruisers that had come to collect. Shortly after 4:15 p.m., the warships had launched a dozen cutters filled with 240 sailors and marines toward La Guaira's docks, where most of what passed for Venezuela's ramshackle "navy" was moored. Flourishing revolvers and a Maxim gun, the Europeans had chased off the native crews, cut the anchor chains of three steamers—the *Ossun*, the *Totumo*, and the *General Crespo*—and then, like pirates of old, towed the Venezuelan vessels away.

British sailors stumbled on a fourth steamer still in the middle of repairs. Swarming over it like locusts, they smashed instruments, machinery, and torpedo tubes until the ship was left permanently crippled.[2]

La Guaira was now deathly still, apart from the sound of boots stepping briskly back toward the landing boats.

By contrast, all was chaos ten miles away in Caracas. The capital's boulevards were thronged with rowdy demonstrators, a sea of angry, roaring faces occasionally broken by a waving banner or the blistering flash of a European flag going up in flames. From the palace, General José Cipriano Castro railed against "the insolent feet of foreigners" desecrating Venezuela's "sacred soil." He called for resistance to the death. Men of every class and creed obligingly pulled Mauser rifles out of storage as stones crashed through the German Legation's windows.[3]

At 10 p.m., the order went out to arrest every German and Briton in the city. Within an hour, Caracas's police station was packed with over two hundred frightened foreigners. Outside, a mob chanted, "Death to Germans! Death to foreigners! English sons of bitches!" One British warehouse owner kept a stiff upper lip. "Well, they always shout these things, old boy," he reassured another captive. "It makes them feel better. We're going to give them a hiding, you know."[4]

On cue, the aptly named HMS *Retribution* was just then helping tow the three captured Venezuelan steamers out of La Guaira. One of the steamers, the *Ossun*, would be retrofitted for blockade duty. The other two were less lucky. Sentries atop La Guaira's fort spotted lights flickering across the decks of the *Totumo* and the *General Crespo*, but the guards were too far away to make out the German sailors cramming charges into the ships' atria and ventricles. Suddenly, all the lights fled the condemned vessels, save for the dim glow cast by a handful of sputtering fuses. Seconds later, the dynamite exploded, blasting the ships' innards out into the inky deep. Black water rushed in to cauterize the gaping wounds. Within minutes both ships had slipped beneath the ocean's midnight surface, leaving just a few eddies and some foam to ephemerally mark their final resting place.[5]

Somewhere to the north, the American giant stirred fitfully. President Roosevelt had spent a year watching this intervention develop. It was a trap, he knew that, but he couldn't be sure yet who was trapping whom. The Kaiser had pledged to respect the Monroe Doctrine, but he could be lying. Either way, Roosevelt had seen enough war games to know how easily innocent expeditions could escalate into something more menacing than even the French occupation of Mexico. He would go to war to prevent that.

One thing Roosevelt could be sure of—whatever happened next, there was no going back. He would do whatever it took to make this the last major European intervention in the hemisphere, even if that meant staking an unprecedented claim to control of the New World. It was time for a new corollary to the Monroe Doctrine.

The Grizzly Terror

On that night, Roosevelt must have thought back to how much the last few years had changed Washington's relationship with each of the intervening powers.

Great Britain had loomed since the Revolutionary War as the bête noire of American foreign policy. But after more than a century of enmity, a remarkable series of events had coincided with cultural and ideological affinities to push the two nations into a rapprochement. Great Britain had capitulated during the last Venezuelan crisis, sympathized with Washington throughout the Spanish-American War, and practically ceded supremacy over American waters when it abrogated the Clayton-Bulwer Treaty. Several factors drove these decisions, but the basic one was geopolitical. British leaders, especially in the Admiralty, had concluded that the United States had grown too powerful to resist. If it ever came to war, Great Britain could neither defend Canada nor defeat the United States; given that reality, the Admiralty was starting to rebalance its forces away from the hemisphere toward new threats in Europe and Asia, in effect abandoning Latin America to the United States. Americans noticed and applauded these moves; Roosevelt cheerfully observed in 1901 that "there is no danger to us from England now in any way."[6]

Closely linked to Great Britain's withdrawal, however, was the rise of what Henry Adams called "the grizzly terror." Great Britain, he wrote, had been "frightened ... into America's arms" by the "sudden appearance" of Germany, Europe's newest and most ambitious great power. But London was far from alone in its anxieties.[7]

Germany and the United States had gotten along well enough during the Teutonic giant's first decade on the international scene. Starting in the 1880s, however, relations had turned rocky as the pair clashed over tariffs and other trade matters. Still, Americans saw their

Kaiser Wilhelm II of Germany: "The Kaiser, like Carlyle,
is 'gey ill' to live with, on occasions."

German competitors more often as an economic challenge than a security one.[8]

All that changed in 1897 when Kaiser Wilhelm II announced *Weltpolitik*, his world policy. Casting aside the small-mindedness of previous
decades, *Weltpolitik* demanded German greatness on a global scale. The
Kaiser already commanded the world's greatest army; now he wanted to
wield the trident of the sea as well. In April 1898, the Reichstag passed
the First Fleet Bill, expanding the imperial fleet by seven battleships and
nine cruisers. Two years later, the Second Fleet Bill ordered an additional
nineteen battleships and twenty-three cruisers constructed. Germany,
too, would have its place in the sun.[9]

Weltpolitik did not bode well for the Americas. Like Shakespeare's
Cassius, Germany had a lean and hungry look. It had entered the colonial game late and was determined to make up for lost time. By 1901,
the great powers had already established 140 colonies, protectorates, and
dependencies over two-thirds of the world's surface and one-third of
the world's people. Only two areas remained for the taking: China and
Latin America. Germany was already making inroads into the former—
it seized a "temporary" ninety-nine-year lease on the Chinese port of

Kiauchau in 1898—and if *Weltpolitik* was to mean anything, a play for the latter did not seem long in coming.[10]

Guided by arrogance and enthralled by power, Kaiser Wilhelm II increasingly resented the Monroe Doctrine. "We must be paramount in South America," he proclaimed across the margins of one memorandum. On another, he scrawled: "South America is no concern of the Yankees!" When an underling dared mention Monroe's Doctrine, the Kaiser scoffed: "We will do whatever is necessary for our navy, even if it displeases the Yankees. Never fear!" In 1899, Wilhelm personally directed his military to draw up war plans against the United States. Over the next few years, he monitored "Operations Plan III" closely, even outlining the concessions that the German Empire would demand in Latin America after its inevitable victory. Privately, the Kaiser assured his uncle King Edward VII that "German naval construction is directed not against England but America."[11]

Others in Berlin shared the Kaiser's acquisitive interest in the Western Hemisphere. German pundits and parliamentarians dismissed the Monroe Doctrine as "a non-binding monologue" or worse. Otto von Bismarck came out of retirement to call it "a species of arrogance peculiarly American and inexcusable." German naval commanders urged the fleet to seize a base somewhere in the Americas, and Germany's foreign minister salivated over the "very promising strips of land" to be found there. One captain of the German Grand General Staff complained that "in the last century we were too late to partake of the general partition." Happily, however, "a second partition is forthcoming. We need only consider the fall of the Ottoman Empire, the isolation of China … , [and] the unstable condition of many South American States, to see what rich opportunities await us."[12]

It became an article of faith among Germany's political and military classes that war with the United States over the New World was inevitable, even if the moment had not yet arrived. For now, the imperial navy would content itself with pinpricks: gunboat diplomacy in Haiti in 1897 and 1902; surveys of Caribbean harbors from 1900 on; inquiries about purchasing a strategic harbor in Mexico in 1902; and the decision in 1902 to form a permanent "American Naval Squadron." German marks, immigrants, and military trainers meanwhile continued flooding the hemisphere.[13]

Berlin's objective appeared obvious to most American military officers. "Everything points to the acquisition of territory on the South

American continent," the *Army and Navy Journal* judged. The General Board, the Navy Department's top advisory body, agreed. "Germany wants to expand her colonial possessions," the Board assessed. "She is planning to test the Monroe Doctrine by annexation or establishment of a protectorate over a portion of South America, even going to the extent of war with the United States when her fleet is ready."[14]

Senior civilians echoed these concerns. Secretary of War Root warned in April 1900 that "the American people will within a few years have to either abandon the Monroe Doctrine or fight for it, and we are not going to abandon it." Secretary of State Hay, too, was alarmed. He reported that "the jealousy and animosity felt toward us in Germany is something which can scarcely be exaggerated ... the *Vaterland* is all on fire with greed and terror of us."[15]

For his part, Roosevelt was no alarmist. "I have a hearty and genuine liking for the Germans both individually and as a nation," he assured Lodge. Even so, the president agreed that Berlin was "the only power which may be a menace to us in anything like the immediate future." Roosevelt saw some opportunities for cooperation—he hoped, for instance, that German trade could help stabilize the Americas—but he remained wary of where Germany's appetites might lead it. He, too, emphasized "the extreme desirability of keeping Germany out of this hemisphere."[16]

American policymakers were not stupid. Germans might dream of supremacy over Latin America, but for now it was just that—a dream. Berlin could not readily adventure across the Atlantic while it was fending off French probes, British prods, and Russian pokes at home. But American policymakers also realized that even though the European balance of power would keep Germany in check most of the time, it was not foolproof. They remembered the French intervention in Mexico well, and they saw the parallels between the reckless ambition of Napoleon III's Grand Design and that of Kaiser Wilhelm's *Weltpolitik*. Germany, moreover, did not need to send its entire navy to the hemisphere to be dangerous. The *Kaiserliche Marine* had qualitative and quantitative advantages—superior training and 50 percent greater tonnage—that had enabled it to repeatedly trounce the U.S. Navy in war games, even in the latter's home waters and even with the former operating at less than full capacity. Finally, American policymakers concluded that German expansion was driven by a search for economic and demographic *lebensraum*, an outlet for Germany's bursting factories and exploding population. Even if the Reich wanted to, perhaps it could not resist the great historical currents sweeping its warships toward the New World.[17]

German officials weren't blind to the fears they were provoking. Sometimes they even cared. But efforts to alleviate American concerns were rare and often spectacularly ill-conceived. When the Kaiser clumsily tried to present the United States with a goodwill statue of Prussian autocrat Frederick the Great, the *Army and Navy Journal* advised sending back the likeness of James Monroe.[18]

In Case of Sudden War

German ambitions finally collided with American fears in late 1902. The United States had never previously dreamed of barring European powers from forcibly intervening in the hemisphere. But Washington began rethinking that age-old stance when Germany announced its intent to attack Venezuela.

Americans had always been jumpy at the prospect of European military expeditions in the Western Hemisphere. But little could be done: international law permitted countries to forcibly recover from those who had wronged them. For decades, then, the United States had clenched its teeth and reluctantly allowed Europe to send gunships to collect on the claims racked up by the "turbulent little republics" of Latin America. Roosevelt summed up the state of affairs in 1901 with typical color: "If any South American State misbehaves towards any European country, let the European country spank it."[19]

Few countries deserved a "spanking" in Roosevelt's view as much as Venezuela. Cursed with a long history of political instability, Venezuela had been particularly troubled and troublesome since General Castro had seized power in late 1899 and established a regime built around corruption, incompetence, and cheeky populism. Roosevelt thought the general was "unspeakably villainous," a sentiment most foreigners shared. One British newspaper complained that Castro had "the insolence of infinite littleness."[20]

Germany had suffered greater indignities at Castro's hands than most. Its merchants and bankers had invested over 150 million marks in Venezuela and received mostly contempt in return. Castro defaulted on multiple German loans, refused to protect a German-owned railroad from rebels and bandits, and generally spat on German requests for compensation. By late 1901, Berlin was fed up and began thinking seriously about exporting less gold and more lead into the country.[21]

On December 3, 1901, Germany saw the opening it had been waiting for. Earlier that day, Roosevelt had reiterated to Congress that the United States would "not guarantee any [Latin American] state against punishment if it misconducts itself," as long as there was no "acquisition of territory." Eleven days later, German Ambassador Theodor von Holleben informed the United States that the Wilhelmstrasse considered further negotiations with Castro "hopeless," and that it planned to demand a final settlement from Caracas before applying "measures of coercion." Naturally, Berlin promised, it had no plans to acquire or permanently occupy any Venezuelan territory.[22]

Despite the disclaimer, there were worrying signs that something more ominous than debt collection might be afoot. Over the previous year, the German flagship *Vineta* had been scouting the island of Margarita off the Venezuelan coast, one of the few spots that the German navy could reach in the Caribbean without coming near established American bases. Von Holleben also admitted that Berlin was considering "the temporary occupation" of Venezuelan ports as part of its intervention. What the Wilhelmstrasse considered "temporary," however, was anyone's guess. It soon became clear that several German officials in the region hoped the intervention would reap "something of a permanent administrative nature."[23]

Roosevelt, however, had just blessed punitive expeditions generally, and he had not objected to forcible measures taken by other powers in the neighborhood. So despite his misgivings, the president had little choice but to blandly thank Berlin for its pledge of abstinence and green-light Germany's planned intervention.[24]

———

ROOSEVELT IMMEDIATELY BEGAN preparing for the worst. One day after approving the German intervention, he ordered Culebra, an island off Puerto Rico, turned into a naval base; the General Board had previously asked for this step "in case of sudden war." Roosevelt then demanded that Congress appropriate $120,000 so the U.S. Navy could, for the first time in its history, converge in the Caribbean for combined exercises. The president scheduled this Mahanian show of force for the following autumn, when the German intervention was most likely to occur. In June 1902, he took the unusual step of asking Admiral of the Navy George Dewey—a notoriously rabid Germanophobe after his experiences in Manila Bay—to personally command the upcoming fleet maneuvers. The General Board, meanwhile, drew up war plans for the defense of Venezuela's coast.[25]

Germany had found an ally in the interim. Great Britain had amassed its own mountain of complaints against Castro, and over the summer Whitehall agreed to a joint intervention in principle. First, the allies would seize Castro's navy; then, if he still refused to cooperate, they would blockade his coast.[26]

British involvement did not allay Roosevelt's concerns. "Germany," he later wrote, still planned "to seize some Venezuela harbor and turn it into a strongly fortified place of arms." He believed that the British, "with their usual stupidity, [had] permitted themselves to be roped in as an appendage," much like France had used Spain and Great Britain as diplomatic camouflage during its expedition to Mexico in 1861.[27]

Even if not, Roosevelt was aware of a second, more subtle danger. Rear Admiral Henry Clay Taylor, the nation's second-ranking naval officer, explained to Roosevelt in late autumn how even an innocent intervention would likely spiral out of control. Castro, being "a perfectly irresponsible dictator," would resist any punishment, precipitating a war. But victory would not come cheaply, and Venezuela, when it eventually lost, could indemnify Berlin only by offering territory or mortgaging customs revenues, thereby "plac[ing] herself in complete political dependence on Germany." Either way, the Kaiser would control part of the Americas. War with the United States, Taylor warned, was the "most probable" result.[28]

━━

BY LATE NOVEMBER 1902, all the chess pieces were on the board. Every battleship in the U.S. Navy, every torpedo boat, every cruiser, was now stationed in the Caribbean, an armada of fifty-three vessels in all. Never before had the country assembled so many men of war in one place; indeed, such a massive fleet would have been inconceivable to the men of Blaine's era.[29]

On December 1, Dewey received final secret instructions from Roosevelt before sailing to take command of the combined fleet. One week later, on the same day the admiral hoisted his four-star ensign, Germany and Great Britain severed diplomatic relations with Castro's government and prepared to attack La Guaira the next day.[30]

Tell the Kaiser

Coincidentally—and in Roosevelt's world, such coincidences abounded—the German ambassador was visiting the White House that very morning with a national delegation. Seizing the opportunity, Roosevelt pulled von Holleben aside to the southwest corner of the room, where a massive globe, half the president's height and twice his girth, stood on a wooden tripod near the fireplace. The president spoke softly but urgently as he triggered a showdown one year in the making.[31]

"Tell the Kaiser," Roosevelt hissed through a smile, that although the world saw Dewey's fleet "merely as a maneuver," the admiral would "interfere, by force if necessary, if the Germans took any action which looked like the acquisition of territory."[32]

Von Holleben, caught off guard, insisted that Germany did not intend to take any "permanent" possession of Venezuelan territory.[33]

Roosevelt was not placated. The Chinese port of Kiauchau, the president observed witheringly, was also "not a 'permanent' possession of Germany's"—"merely held by a ninety nine years lease." And Roosevelt "did not intend to have another Kiauchau, held by similar tenure, on the approach to the Isthmian Canal." Roosevelt accordingly delivered his ultimatum: Berlin had ten days to agree to arbitrate its dispute with Venezuela, or else the entire massed American battle fleet would be ordered south along with its Germanophobic commander.[34]

Von Holleben was horrified. Did the president understand what he had just threatened, "consequences so serious" that the ambassador "dreaded to give them a name"? In response, Roosevelt jabbed at the blue patch on the globe next to them where the joint expedition was preparing to raid La Guaira. Even a glance, the Rough Rider said steadily, would reveal that "there was no spot in the world" where Germany would fight the United States "at a greater disadvantage."[35]

Minutes later, a smiling Roosevelt ushered the dumbstruck ambassador and his none-the-wiser compatriots out of the office.[36]

———

GERMAN AND BRITISH soldiers seized and sunk most of the Venezuelan navy at La Guaira the next day. Four days later, the allies bombarded the castle and fortress at Puerto Cabello. Castro refused to give in, demanding that the allies instead arbitrate their disagreements. Dewey meanwhile kept the American fleet on high alert and ready to move at a moment's notice. Anticipating imminent combat operations, he ordered a marine hospital ward in Puerto Rico expanded tenfold in size.[37]

Given Castro's intransigence, Germany and Great Britain had two options if they wanted to continue the intervention. Either they could blockade Venezuela indefinitely until Castro capitulated, or they could turn up the heat by landing more forces, seizing customhouses, and even driving inland toward Caracas.[38]

Neither option appealed to London. British public opinion was turning sharply against the alliance with Germany, the country's hated rival. Committing to an indefinite blockade of Venezuela was politically suicidal. So was escalating, which risked rupturing the Anglo-American entente and bringing Dewey down on everyone's heads. Great Britain thus began leaning toward accepting Castro's offer to arbitrate.[39]

Similar calculations were unfolding in Berlin, and that was before the Kaiser even learned about Roosevelt's ultimatum.[40]

CRISES HAVE A center of gravity that can warp the judgment of even the strongest psyches. And German Ambassador von Holleben was no *übermensch*, just a stiff, unimaginative officer who lived in mortal terror of crossing the Kaiser. Shocked by Roosevelt's ultimatum, terrified of bearing bad news, and distressed by plummeting American public opinion, von Holleben had decided not to forward the president's threat on to Berlin. He sat on it, convinced that because he so badly needed it not to be true, it therefore *must* not be true.[41]

This was no way to run a foreign service. Early Sunday afternoon, December 14, with only four days to go on Roosevelt's ten-day ultimatum, von Holleben stopped by the White House. He chatted lightly with the president about the weather—the season's first snowfall had just dusted the capital—and then rose to go.[42]

Roosevelt stopped him. He asked if Berlin had responded to the ultimatum. Von Holleben told him, truthfully enough, "no."[43]

Roosevelt did not miss a beat. He said he was very definitely threatening war, but since it was apparently "useless to wait as long as I had intended," he was going to move up the deadline by twenty-four hours. Dewey would now sail south on the seventeenth, in three days' time.[44]

Shaken out of his stupor, von Holleben raced to New York to confer with German Consul General Karl Bünz, a friend of the president's. Bünz was unequivocal. Roosevelt did not bluff, and the Reich should "count on his doing as threatened." Von Holleben felt his world collapse as reality clawed its way in.[45]

On December 16, one day before Roosevelt's deadline, the ambassador finally passed the threat of war on to Berlin. By this point, the Kaiser was already worried about slumping British and American public opinion. He did not want to be left in the lurch by his British ally, especially not with Roosevelt's threat on the table.[46]

Only hours before Roosevelt's deadline was set to expire, Wilhelm folded. Berlin informed the United States that it would accept Castro's arbitration proposal.[47]

———

PEN BURSTING WITH pride, Roosevelt wrote a week later to the only other person who could understand what it meant to win a showdown with Europe over Venezuela. "I congratulate you heartily on the rounding out of your policy," Roosevelt whooped to ex-President Cleveland.[48]

All that remained was for Castro and the allies to hammer out a settlement. Roosevelt declined the allies' invitation to arbitrate the dispute himself because the United States had its own claims against Venezuela. So Germany and Great Britain—belatedly joined by Italy—blockaded the Venezuelan coast while they negotiated with Castro to see what everyone could agree to and what needed to be sent instead to the Permanent Court of Arbitration at the Hague.[49]

The British Foreign Office remained conciliatory throughout the negotiations. Being allies with Germany rankled the American and British publics, and Prime Minister Arthur Balfour tried to soothe both by prostrating himself before the idol of Monroe. "The Monroe doctrine has no enemies in this country that I know of," he declared to a cheering crowd in Liverpool. "We welcome any increase of the influence of the United States of America upon the great Western Hemisphere."[50]

Berlin was less publicly obsequious, but it, too, was looking for a face-saving way out. On January 5, the Wilhelmstrasse canceled von Holleben's credentials and forced the disgraced ambassador into early retirement. He was replaced by Roosevelt's good friend Hermann Speck von Sternburg, who declared that Germans would no sooner violate the Monroe Doctrine than "colonize the moon." Few believed him—and Germany did not help its case when, in mid-January, its gunboats reduced another Venezuelan fort to pebbles—but negotiations ground steadily on.[51]

By early February 1903, Caracas had agreed to recognize the allies' claims. The only sticking point was the issue of "preferential treatment"—whether Castro had to pay back the claims of the allies *before* it settled the claims of other non-blockading countries. Caracas argued against preferential treatment, reasoning that it would reward the use of violence. But the allied powers were adamant. After Roosevelt declined to break the deadlock, the parties agreed to submit the question to the Hague Court.[52]

Roosevelt had welcomed the Hague's involvement all along, subject always to one caveat—that there be "no possibility of the Court rendering a decision which might be in conflict with the Monroe Doctrine." It is unclear why the president nevertheless recommended submitting the preferential treatment question to the Court. Either he trusted the Court not to reward intervention, or he overlooked the consequences if it did so. Whatever the reason, it would prove a serious mistake.[53]

On February 13, 1903, the parties signed a final protocol, and the blockade of Venezuela ended. By a gentlemen's agreement, the State Department and the Wilhelmstrasse bleached their records of any evidence of the American ultimatum, leaving only a documentary silhouette as evidence of the crisis that had nearly sparked great-power war.[54]

Speak Softly and Carry a Big Stick

Roosevelt and the United States had safely navigated another European intervention, with the Monroe Doctrine no worse for the wear. But as is so often the case, the resolution of one crisis only deepened fear of the next. Germany, Roosevelt was sure, had been probing the hemisphere's defenses. He could not know whether Berlin's retreat was "a case of *post hoc* or *propter hoc*," but he increasingly felt that only his firm warning had kept the Kaiser at arm's length.[55]

Some of his mistrust may have been misplaced. Though incomplete, German archives suggest that while many German officials did pine for a Venezuelan foothold, the Kaiser thought it was not yet the right time. Despite his occasional outbursts about dominating South America, Wilhelm consistently accommodated American concerns before and during the crisis.[56]

Of course, Roosevelt could not access the German archives, and it would have been foolish for him to ignore what evidence of German intent he did have. Even if the Kaiser had not planned on expansion, moreover, a combination of bad luck and the Kaiser's more belligerent subordinates could easily have forced Germany's hand. Perhaps it had been a close call, perhaps not. For all his preparations, however, Roosevelt had still been reacting to events rather than shaping them, and he could not guarantee that the United States's lucky streak would continue.

Post-Venezuela crisis, the president's thoughts thus began to turn toward figuring out how the United States should handle the threat of future European interventions. Half of the solution was straight-forward: ensure the U.S. Navy remained the ultimate backstop. But Roosevelt struggled with the second half of the puzzle—how to prevent European powers from intervening in the first place. He, like his predecessors, understood the danger posed by weak neighbors. But he saw no clear way to eliminate that danger short of claiming an exclusive right to intervene in the region—a course that he hesitated to adopt, at least for now.[57]

———

SHORTLY AFTER THE end of the Venezuelan intervention, Roosevelt hailed what he saw as the ultimate line of defense against future European sallies into the hemisphere. "There is a homely old adage which runs: 'Speak softly and carry a big stick; you will go far,'" the president told a packed auditorium in Chicago. "If the American Nation will speak softly, and yet build ... a thoroughly efficient navy, the Monroe Doctrine will go far."[58]

The proverb was an immediate hit. Within a day, the presidential train was chugging through gauntlets of shaking bats and homemade clubs. Roosevelt and his military advisors had long believed that the Monroe Doctrine needed a spine of steel. After the Venezuelan crisis, much of the public agreed. "The country has just been given a vivid reminder that the Monroe Doctrine is not self-enforcing," opined the *Boston Journal*. "A heavier battle-line is sure to follow."[59]

Critics tried to draw the opposite lesson. They claimed that the naval stick was already big enough—that American shipyards had been showering sparks nonstop since the days of Blaine, and that the sheer size of Dewey's armada attested to the result. Surely such a massive fleet could fend off any interlopers.

For American navalists, however, the size of Dewey's fleet was meaningless in and of itself. What mattered was relative, not absolute, power. As long as new German keels kept splashing into the Baltic's icy waters, the U.S. Navy had to keep pace, whether it wanted to or not. Furthermore, the British Admiralty was starting to draw down its forces in Latin America in line with its broader withdrawal from the hemisphere. The U.S. Navy needed to compensate for this withdrawal if it hoped to maintain a favorable balance of forces.[60]

So the naval buildup continued. Eighteen first-class battleships were already authorized, under construction, or in operation when

Roosevelt became president. He wanted more. In his first four years, Roosevelt would coax funding for another ten first-class battleships, four armored cruisers, and seventeen other vessels. He paused in 1905, but only temporarily. In October 1906, a new leviathan called the HMS *Dreadnought* swam out of the British Admiralty's navy yards and instantly rendered every other capital ship obsolete. Roosevelt insisted the U.S. Navy stay abreast of these new giants, and by the time he left office, six *Dreadnought*-class vessels would be in commission or under construction.[61]

Roosevelt was too proud of the fruits of his labors not to share them, and toward the end of his administration he dispatched much of his new navy on a worldwide cruise. "Perfectly bully," he sang as he watched the Great White Fleet sail out. "Did you ever see such a fleet?"[62]

A HEAVIER BATTLE-LINE had few downsides as far as Roosevelt could tell, but the same could not be said of the president's options for discouraging European interventions in the first place.

Like many before him, Roosevelt understood how the weakness of Latin American states could encourage and facilitate foreign intervention. He was especially concerned by one aspect of the problem that Germany and Great Britain's intervention in Venezuela had highlighted: how interventions could lead European creditors to seize territory, as either direct payment or a "temporary" way of collecting money. During this era, Latin American states raised practically all their revenues by taxing foreign trade at customhouses. So if a foreign power wanted to collect payment by force, it could seize its debtor's customhouses and

The Great White Fleet Enters the Straits of Magellan:
"This is indeed a great fleet and a great day."

help itself to whatever cut of customs revenues it wanted. That practice was as distressingly common elsewhere in the world as it was dangerous. Once a European power controlled a state's customhouses, it effectively controlled that state's revenue stream and, by extension, the state itself. Great Britain had partly taken over Egypt in just that way.[63]

Seeing the problem, however, was not the same as solving it. Roosevelt and his administration needed a new solution, something that— consistent with his philosophy that "nine-tenths of wisdom is to be wise in time"—would allow Washington to act "sufficiently far in advance of any likely crisis to make it improbable that we would run into serious trouble."[64]

Luis María Drago, Argentina's distinguished foreign minister, was among the first to offer Roosevelt a solution. The Venezuelan intervention unnerved Drago, who, like Roosevelt, thought that "the collection of loans by military means implies territorial occupation." During the crisis, Drago therefore proposed a new rule of international law: that "the public debt of States should not serve as a reason for an armed attack."[65]

The Drago Doctrine, as it came to be known, reflected long-standing American practice and would soon be championed by Washington. But it was an imperfect solution at best. Even if the United States supported it, other great powers might not. Furthermore, the rule forbade only *some* interventions—those stemming from defaulted loans and other state-issued debt. But European powers generally cared far less about the financial travails of adventurous investors than they did about injuries to their nationals and property, and it was those claims that sparked most European interventions.[66]

Of course, the Drago Doctrine could theoretically be stretched to prohibit any intervention based on any type of claim. Another Argentine jurist, Carlos Calvo, had gone just that far in the 1860s, denying that a state was financially responsible if its intestinal troubles harmed foreign nationals or their property. If accepted, the Calvo Doctrine would have banned most gunboat diplomacy in the Americas. But it was too radical to be realistic. Europe would never agree to absolve states of all responsibility for foreign nationals in their midst, and Roosevelt himself considered the rule immoral and ill-conceived. Indeed, by removing the financial incentive to protect foreigners, the Calvo Doctrine could paradoxically put foreigners in greater danger and ultimately make intervention *more* likely.[67]

Germany's new ambassador, Hermann Speck von Sternburg ("Nice little Baron Speck"), offered Roosevelt a second solution to the problem of order. Speck von Sternburg proposed creating a syndicate through which the United States and other great powers would collectively take over the finances of the region's reprobate nations, presumably by controlling their customhouses. He argued that in so doing, the powers "would do away with the chance for a repetition of punitive expeditions by European powers to collect debts."[68]

Speck von Sternburg's solution held no appeal for Roosevelt. Giving Europe control of Venezuela's finances "would pave the way for reducing Venezuela to a condition like that of Egypt," Roosevelt told his German friend, something that "our people would view with the utmost displeasure." If the Monroe Doctrine meant anything, it had to exclude European powers from even partial "control of any American republic."[69]

Great Britain pointed Roosevelt toward a third solution. British statesmen had long emphasized the gulf separating American regional interests from American regional responsibility. Lord Salisbury had argued during the first Venezuelan crisis in 1895 that Washington should tone down its interests to match the level of regional responsibility it was willing to accept. Eight years later, Salisbury's successor (and nephew) argued the opposite during the second Venezuelan crisis—that Washington needed to level *up* its responsibility to match its interests. "It would be a great gain to civilization," Balfour declared, if Washington would preempt "these constantly recurring difficulties between European Powers and certain States in South America."[70]

Great Britain was effectively telling the United States that if it disliked foreign powers intervening in its neighborhood so much, then it had better make sure that its neighborhood did not give those powers any reason to intervene. If—*when*—its neighbors failed to live up to that standard, the United States would have to intervene on Europe's behalf as a way of preempting European intervention. In practice, Great Britain was saying, Washington should become Europe's debt collector, its claims executor, the guarantor of regional order, and the policeman of the Western Hemisphere.

For this arrangement to work, the United States would need to commit to an economic "open door" in Latin America. If the United States attempted to exploit its dominant position for commercial ends, then the British solution would no longer serve Europe's purposes and might spark a clash. Washington could claim an exclusive sphere of political influence, in other words, only by giving up any pretensions to an exclusive sphere of commercial influence.[71]

Roosevelt was drawn to the logic of the British position. As a former policeman, he already thought that the world's "increasing interdependence and complexity" required "all civilized and orderly powers to insist on [its] proper policing"; the president also had strong views about the proper relationship between "civilized" powers and other (usually non-white) nations who supposedly had yet to attain the same level of material growth, moral fiber, and political development. Roosevelt also liked the British proposal because it would help address the concern among many Americans that the Monroe Doctrine encouraged bad behavior in the region by shielding local states from the consequences of their wrongdoing. Finally, Roosevelt understood how the British position aligned with the long-standing objective and trend of Washington's regional policy, including the recent Platt Amendment. The Platt Amendment had given the United States the right to keep order in Cuba so as to preempt foreign intervention there; the British essentially wanted the same thing, only region-wide.[72]

But there were also reasons for caution. Roosevelt hated the idea of rescuing investors, whether foreign or American, from their mistakes. "If they lose their money, they should take the consequences," he believed. He also did not want the United States to overextend itself; the republic had enough problems at home without trying to make a dozen neighbors live up to their international obligations.[73]

Some of Roosevelt's advisors were similarly hesitant. Captain Mahan, for instance, argued that "the United States is inevitably the preponderant American Power; but she does not aspire to be paramount. She does not find the true complement of the Monroe Doctrine in an undefined control over American States, exercised by her and denied to Europe."[74]

Over the next year, these misgivings won out. Roosevelt wanted to prevent future European incursions, but the British approach was riddled with trouble. For now, it seemed easier to push the question off until some new crisis forced a decision.

A Premium on Violence

Going into 1904, Roosevelt still remained reluctant to embrace the British proposal. In February, however, two seemingly unconnected events—

one in the Dominican Republic, the other in the Hague—convinced him that its logic was inescapable. To protect the hemisphere, the United States would first have to police it.

Since declaring independence in 1844, the Dominican Republic had split the island of Hispaniola with Haiti. Haiti was not a good sharer, and the Republic spent most of its first three decades beating back attacks from its neighbor while begging foreign powers for a protectorate or outright annexation. Only Spain and the United States ever answered the call, but Dominicans expelled the Spanish in 1865, and President Grant failed to consummate his attempt to annex the island in the 1870s. All the while, Dominicans bounced one *caudillo* after another out of the presidential palace in a whirling carousel of bloody revolutions and civil wars. Between 1874 and 1879 alone, thirteen governments went into (and then out of) office.[75]

The Dominican Republic's troubles mounted after Ulises Heureaux seized control in the 1880s. Persuaded that Machiavelli's *The Prince* exemplified good governance, Heureaux brought a brutal peace to the island but let its financial situation go from bad to worse. The Dominican Republic was no stranger to predatory loans, but Heureaux signed on to them at record levels, confident that he would enjoy the resulting payoffs and creature comforts while his country would be left holding the bag once he was gone. He was right. By the time a rival named Ramón Cáceres assassinated Heureaux in 1899, the Dominican Republic was drowning in a sea of red ink.[76]

Heureaux's killing triggered new spasms of bloodshed that combined with the island's financial flailing to attract unwelcome attention. Since 1893, the State Department had kept a lid on foreign influence by supporting the San Domingo Improvement Company, a private American firm that ran the island's customhouses, floated its loans, indulged Heureaux's appetite for cash, and generally reined in European bondholders. But Dominicans did not believe the Improvement Company was living up to its name, and they ousted "the nefarious company" (*la nefasta compañía*) after Heureaux's death. The country's finances became as disorderly as its politics, and European bondholders—along with their governments—grew correspondingly agitated. Foreign warships began making regular stops at the island.[77]

None of this reassured Washington. Since the navy suspected that any European attacker would use the Dominican Republic—which guarded the entrance to the Caribbean—as a staging ground, the navy's General Board drew up detailed plans to preemptively seize the island in the event of hostilities. The Board also warned that the Dominican Republic's "feeble and chaotic conditions" could make "it easy for any country to obtain concessions" of a strategic nature. Sure enough, the American minister reported in September 1903 that the Dominican foreign minister was trying to trade two coaling stations for an alliance with Germany. Before the talks could progress any further, however, the Dominican government was overthrown.[78]

The Republic's new government looked north for help. In January 1904, a delegation arrived in Washington with a surprising request. Thirty-two million dollars of debt had turned the country's balance sheets scarlet, and the new president, Carlos F. Morales Languasco, thought that only an American protectorate—complete with loans, naval stations, and special trade relations—could stabilize the island. Morales thus implored Roosevelt for a Dominican Platt Amendment, even alluding to eventual annexation.[79]

Roosevelt rejected the proposal out of hand. "Santo Domingo is drifting into chaos," he admitted to his son, using a common nickname for the island. The president feared it was "inevitable" that, as the British had suggested, the United States should "sooner or later ... assume an attitude of protection and regulation in regard to all these little states." But he prayed that moment would "be deferred as long as possible." On February 23, he confided to a friend with disgust: "If I possibly can I want to do nothing to them. If it is absolutely necessary to do something, then I want to do as little as possible." The Dominicans had been "bedeviling" him to establish a protectorate and "take charge of their finances," but he had insisted "that we could not possibly go into the subject." Even less appealing was anything permanent: "I have about the same desire to annex [the island] as a gorged boa constrictor might have to swallow a porcupine wrong-end-to."[80]

———

EVEN AS THAT uncomfortable prospect crossed his mind, however, Roosevelt was receiving news that would make involvement unavoidable. One year earlier, Venezuela and its European adversaries had asked the Hague Court to decide whether Caracas should repay the blockading powers ahead of other creditors. In February 1904, the Court decided in the affirmative. By blockading Venezuela, it said, the allies had won the right to see their claims repaid first.[81]

The decision sent alarm bells ringing throughout Roosevelt's administration. If intervention meant preferential treatment, then many more interventions were likely in the near future. One State Department official protested that the Hague's decision placed "a premium on violence."[82]

The Dominican Republic could ill afford that premium. In mid-April, the American minister learned that Italy was about to seize the nation's customhouses. "The action of the Italian Government," he reported, "is based upon the recent decision at the Hague." Italy was not itself a menace, but once the interventionist ball got rolling, it would be hard to prevent other, more dangerous powers from piling on.[83]

Given the Hague's decision, Roosevelt finally accepted that "it is our duty, when it becomes absolutely inevitable, to police these countries in the interest of order and civilization." But in his view, that moment had not yet arrived. Even though the Dominican Republic was "on the point of dissolution," Roosevelt saw no way for the United States to involve itself "without establishing precedents which would be equally inconvenient and undesirable for both countries." He did not change his mind even after President Morales offered Washington preemptive control of Dominican customhouses. It was long-standing State Department policy not to "interfere with the management by foreign governments of their own fiscal systems," and since Italy had denied any intent to intervene, Roosevelt thought he could still hold back.[84]

Roosevelt's qualms were reinforced by domestic concerns. "Theodore thinks of nothing, talks of nothing, and lives for nothing but his political interests," observed Henry Adams. "If you remark to him that God is Great, he asks naïvely at once how that will affect his election." Eager to be elected in November, Roosevelt knew that the path to victory did not pass through the Dominican Republic. Panama's revolution was only a few months behind him, and the Rough Rider did not want to aggravate his trigger-happy reputation. So although "the best people of the island" demanded American interference, he told one correspondent, he felt "obliged to put off the action until the necessity becomes so clear that even the blindest can see it."[85]

Sometimes, though, national vision requires a bit of guidance. Roosevelt asked Elihu Root, who had left his post as secretary of war in January, to read a letter on his behalf at an upcoming banquet celebrating the two-year anniversary of Cuba's independence. Root agreed, and on May 20, 1904, he announced that the United States could no longer ignore its duty to keep order in the hemisphere. "Our interests, and those of our southern neighbors, are in reality identical," he read. "All that we ask is that they shall govern themselves well, and be prosperous and orderly. Where this is the case they will find only helpfulness from us."[86]

The trial balloon had barely cleared the roof of the banquet hall before it was popped by a fusillade of critical press coverage. "A flagrant exhibition of jingoism," scolded the *New York Herald*. Roosevelt couldn't understand it. "What I wrote is the simplest common sense," he told Root. "If we are willing to let Germany or England act as the policeman of the Caribbean, then we can afford not to interfere when gross wrongdoing occurs. But if we intend to say 'Hands off' to the powers of Europe, then sooner or later we must keep order ourselves. What a queer set of evil-minded creatures, mixed with honest people of preposterous shortness of vision, our opponents are!"[87]

The Roosevelt Corollary

Roosevelt vanquished his evil-minded and preposterous opponents that November in a record-breaking electoral landslide, with 50 percent more votes than his opponent. Shortly before the returns started coming in, he privately admitted to his sister that he "had never wanted anything in his life quite as much as the outward and visible sign of his country's approval." Now he had it, and along with it came the power to modernize the Monroe Doctrine.[88]

On December 6, 1904, in his fourth State of the Union message, the president announced to the world what would become known as the Roosevelt Corollary to the Monroe Doctrine. Borrowing liberally from his May letter, Roosevelt declared that the United States desired only to see its neighbors "stable, orderly, and prosperous." No neighbor needed to fear interference from the United States, he promised, as long as it "shows that it knows how to act with reasonable efficiency and decency in social and political matters, if it keeps order and pays its obligations"—if, that is, it showed the "progress in stable and just civilization" that "so many of the republics in both Americas are constantly and brilliantly showing." But the United States could no longer tolerate those failing or failed states who "invited foreign aggression" through either "chronic wrongdoing" or "an impotence which results in a general loosening of the ties of civilized society." Such cases could "ultimately require intervention by some civilized nation," and in the Western Hemisphere, only one nation could safely do the job. Adherence to the Monroe Doctrine, Roosevelt concluded, "may force the United States, however reluctantly, ... to the exercise of an international police power."[89]

It was an awesome assertion of American power. Until this point, the United States had tried to uphold the Monroe Doctrine mostly without force. Where force was used, it was aimed primarily at the perceived threat—the European great powers. Now, however, the United States was turning its guns against its own neighbors, the very states that the republic had sworn to protect.

Generations of historians have criticized the Roosevelt Corollary as an unnatural extension of the Monroe Doctrine, even a perversion. In truth, it was nearly the opposite—the Corollary was the Doctrine's inevitable outgrowth, the next trial in a decades-long experiment that had seen the country cycle through less intrusive means of regional defense one by one. Since the Civil War, American grand strategy had sought to prevent great-power rivals from using the region's failed or failing states to expand into the hemisphere. Secretary Seward and his immediate successors had tried to strengthen those states through trade links and friendly relations. Secretary Blaine had deepened and systematized that effort through bilateral reciprocity treaties, and he had also tried to settle regional conflicts through arbitration and Pan-American cooperation. By the 1890s, these approaches appeared woefully insufficient; Latin America was no more stable than before, and the great powers seemed about to kick in the door. After the Spanish-American War, the United States had moved on to the next logical step—stabilizing its neighbors from the inside out. Through the Platt Amendment, the United States had preemptively curtailed Cuba's authority over its external relations while giving itself the right to intervene if anarchy erupted. It seemed only natural for Roosevelt to now extend that policy to the whole region.[90]

In fact, Roosevelt was doing little more than making explicit what had always been implicit. President Monroe had set the ends of the Doctrine but said nothing about its means, and American statesmen had long understood those means to include, as a last resort, intervention. General Sheridan had wanted to invade Mexico not only to boot out Emperor Maximilian, but also to give the country a stable, "permanent government." Seward had threatened to annex Haiti if Europe came too close. Senators had opposed Grant's attempt to annex the Dominican Republic but conceded that an actual foreign threat might make them reconsider. Several anti-imperialist senators had then lived up to the spirit of that concession when Japan menaced Hawai'i. Olney, in an unused draft of Cleveland's 1896 State of the Union message, had written that the Monroe Doctrine "not merely asserts rights but entails correlative obligations—not merely declares the right of the United States to regulate the affairs of Cuba to the exclusion of European powers, but requires it to do so whenever such outside regulation becomes imperative." It was the Roosevelt Corollary in all but name.[91]

Much as intervention had been lurking in the background all along, however, Roosevelt had also lost little of his predecessors' reluctance to actually deploy violence. He studded his corollary with limiting language—local states' wrongdoing had to be "chronic," the cases "flagrant," before the United States would intervene "reluctantly" and as a "last resort." Each of these terms was malleable, but Roosevelt meant them to be read narrowly, and Root amplified the limitations a few weeks later. In a speech, he pruned the worst rhetorical excesses of Olney's twenty-inch gun, including its infamous declaration that the United States was sovereign upon this continent. "We arrogate to ourselves, not sovereignty over the American continent, but only the right to protect," Root pledged. "Above all things let us be just."[92]

Such public handwringing might have seemed contrived were it not also reflected in months of Roosevelt's most personal conversations and correspondence. He had admitted to Speck von Sternburg that a protectorate over the Americas often seemed like "the only way out," but he was nonetheless "absolutely against it," adding melodramatically that he would sooner "sponsor a retrocession of New Mexico and Arizona." Brooding over involvement in the Dominican Republic, Roosevelt insisted to another friend: "I won't do it as long as it can be helped." Indeed, the president would "be greatly relieved" if the United States could—without intervening—"get Santo Domingo to behave, internally and externally, with any kind of decency and efficiency."[93]

By the time Roosevelt announced his Corollary, however, it was already too late.

Order Out of Chaos

Europe's patience with the Dominican Republic had finally run out in December 1904. Summoning the ghost of Emperor Maximilian, France warned that if the United States did not resolve the island's debt crisis, the French navy would. Other European powers echoed those sentiments, and Secretary of State John Hay detected "a concert among them." A repeat of the Venezuelan crisis was imminent, with Germany once again foremost on the administration's mind.[94]

Out of options and "after infinite thought and worry and labor," Roosevelt ordered the State Department to approach the Dominican Republic with an offer to take over the island's customhouses. This would be interference by invitation, as Morales had been begging for this step (and more) for over a year. Still, not every Dominican was as excited as Morales about American involvement, and on the advice of his minister Roosevelt sent warships to the island to exert a good "moral effect upon [the] malcontents."[95]

On February 15, 1905, Roosevelt sent a finalized treaty to the Senate. Under the agreement, American officials would collect the Dominican Republic's customs revenue and divvy it up between the island's government and its creditors, with no less than 45 percent going to the former. Since the Dominican government had no real source of revenue other than customs duties, this customs receivership would effectively give the United States control over the Republic's fiscal system for as long as it took to amortize the country's debt.[96]

Roosevelt warned the Senate that there was no alternative. Pronouncing the situation in the Dominican Republic "hopeless," he revealed that several European powers were about to intervene "to bring order out of the chaos." If they did, they would necessarily seize the customhouses, and that "would mean a definite and very possibly permanent occupation of Dominican territory." So the United States faced a choice: either "submit to the likelihood of infringement of the Monroe doctrine," or agree to stabilize the island's finances itself.[97]

Despite Roosevelt's pleas, the Senate refused to act on the treaty. Democrats wanted to torpedo the president's second term, and the Senate more broadly wanted to throttle the vigorousness of Roosevelt's policies and the republic's entanglements abroad.[98]

Roosevelt, as usual, was spectacularly indifferent to what the Senate wanted. Bypassing Congress, he arranged a temporary customs receivership directly with Morales. He then kicked the American-owned San Domingo Improvement Company to the curb; it would not do to promote American interests over foreign ones, especially when those interests had aided and abetted the Dominican Republic's financial extravagance. Roosevelt also ordered the navy secretary to stop any revolutions until the Senate finished deliberating. "That this is ethically right I am dead sure," he explained, "even though there may be some technical or red tape difficulty."[99]

Roosevelt continued disregarding red tape (and congressional cries of tyranny) for the next two years. Finally, in February 1907, the Senate gave up and consented to a modified version of the original treaty, and the Dominican Republic formally joined Cuba and Panama inside the perimeter of the United States's ever-expanding sphere of regional influence.[100]

A Precedent for American Action

Historians sometimes mark the Roosevelt Corollary as a turning point in American foreign policy, the moment when everything began to go wrong for the republic and the region. But while the Corollary was surely a step toward eventual hemispheric hegemony, the United States had set foot on that path long before Roosevelt arrived and would continue treading it long after he left.

One of the Corollary's many peculiarities is that it was invoked only once by the president who lent it his name. After the Dominican Republic, Roosevelt never relied on his Corollary again. In fact, he continued to handle potential European interventions on a case-by-case basis, often letting them go forward. In late 1905, for example, Roosevelt acquiesced to a French punitive expedition against General Castro after first extracting a written promise of no permanent occupation. Similar permission slips were handed out to Great Britain (Uruguay) and the Netherlands (Venezuela again). None of these planned interventions came to pass, but the fact that Roosevelt refused to invoke the Corollary to block them underscores his administration's commitment to reserving American intervention as a last resort.[101]

Such reticence reflected a broader reluctance to interfere too much in the region. Roosevelt carped to Lodge about one critic who had argued that Washington should reverse course and interfere in its neighbors' affairs only to "the minimum" necessary, and that any interference should be "so veiled as to avoid hurting the feelings of those in whose behalf we are interfering." Roosevelt rolled his eyes at that gratuitous advice. "This," he underscored irritably, "exactly describes what has been done in Santo Domingo."[102]

Still, Roosevelt came to believe that however veiled and minimal, his interference in the Dominican Republic had produced "incalculable" benefits for the island. Even though Roosevelt had agreed to the customs receivership first and foremost to stop Europe's powers from intervening, he had hoped it would also help the island in the long run by eliminating corruption and mismanagement of customs revenues. Even more importantly, the receivership promised to tamp down future disorder.

Civil wars in the Dominican Republic had always been fought over the customhouses, Roosevelt believed; they were the pot of money that financed insurrections and inspired insurrectionists. But no revolutionary in his right mind would try to seize a customhouse from American officials. Roosevelt thus anticipated that the receivership would mean more money coming in and less being wasted on revolution, allowing the Dominican government to spend more on public goods, jump-start growth, and increase customs revenues. Over time, that virtuous cycle would ideally develop the Dominican Republic into a politically stable and economically prosperous state.[103]

At first, the receivership bore out those heady expectations. Washington helped adjust the Dominican debt down from a high of $32 million to $15.5 million, and repayments began occurring regularly. Customs revenues soared from $1.85 million before the receivership to $3.65 million in 1907–08. Even with its 45 percent cut, the central government now had more cash on hand than ever before, and it began financing public improvements for the first time in years. The Dominican Republic stabilized politically as well; there were fewer revolutions and civil wars, each more anemic than the last. It became conventional wisdom in Washington that the customs receivership had been an unalloyed success.[104]

Some began to see the Dominican receivership as a template for further regional change. By 1909, Roosevelt was telling Andrew Carnegie that the receivership was "literally invaluable in pointing out the way for introducing peace and order in the Caribbean and around its borders." "The action there taken," he later reiterated, "should serve as a precedent for American action in all similar cases."[105]

===

IF ROOSEVELT HAD looked a little closer, however, he might have realized that while his policies had solved some problems, they were also creating new ones. For instance, the Roosevelt Corollary risked making the United States into Europe's cat's-paw. All else being equal, European powers wanted to avoid interventions, which were costly in treasure and goodwill. If Washington was going to bear the brunt of those costs on their behalf, however, then these powers had every incentive to provoke American interventions more often, even where they ordinarily might have turned the other cheek.

Worse, the Roosevelt Corollary also incentivized the very threats to the Monroe Doctrine that it aimed to prevent. Since the Corollary conditioned American intervention on the risk of European intervention, it encouraged anyone who *wanted* American intervention to exaggerate, invent, or even provoke foreign threats. Great Britain had already exploited that dynamic, playing down its interest in Hawai'i in 1893 to ward off American annexation, but playing up the threat to the Philippines in 1898 to persuade Americans to take the archipelago. By making the threat-intervention link more explicit, the Roosevelt Corollary left the United States open to manipulation, unable to determine which of the many threats it perceived were actually real.[106]

Roosevelt also intended his Corollary to apply only to the most extreme cases. That was, in truth, not much of a constraint. Instability was endemic to the hemisphere, and Roosevelt often griped about the region's many "small bandit nests of a wicked and inefficient type." By late 1908, the president was muttering about the need to "put a stop to crying disorders at our very doors" in Haiti, Venezuela, and "at least one Central American State." But he desisted, knowing that "tho the need was great," there was no immediate threat—for now.[107]

The Dominican customs receivership also spawned its own problems, starting with mission creep. American officials were supposed to only be collecting and distributing the island's customs revenues. But they gradually took on additional responsibilities, like stamping out smuggling by training a frontier guard and lending four revenue cutters for maritime interdiction. The Dominican government soon repurposed both: the guard became a paramilitary police force, and the cutters turned into a proto-navy used to transport troops, intimidate domestic enemies, and even lance the occasional revolutionary boil. Ever so slowly, the United States was getting drawn into the Dominican Republic's day-to-day politics.[108]

Furthermore, the path from chronic wrongdoing to model state was proving a little more crooked than Americans had imagined. Roosevelt expected that the Dominican receivership would end revolutions by taking the biggest pot of money off the table. But revolutions were always about more than money, and in any event the prize still existed; winning it just required Dominicans to point their rifles away from the ports and toward the presidential palace.[109]

Roosevelt got his first taste of what these incentives could look like in December 1905. Seeking to expand his authority, Dominican President Morales engineered a fake coup against himself that accidentally turned into a real one. Following a brief period of conflict, Cáceres—Heureaux's assassin—became president. He declared that he would cooperate with the Americans and their beloved receivership, and Washington decided not to oppose his grab for power. Things soon went on as before, with few yet concerned about how this executive shuffle reflected the introduction of American power. It would take another year before the law of unintended consequences really hit home, this time back in Cuba.[110]

CHAPTER 8

THE CREATION OF A REVOLUTIONARY HABIT

The Return to Cuba and Panama, 1906–1909

Theodore Roosevelt could barely contain his rage. Stomping around his Oyster Bay vacation home in mid-September 1906, the fuming president was complaining to anyone who would listen that he had done what he could, that the United States had lived up to its end of the bargain, and that whatever was happening in Cuba was, most emphatically, *not* his fault.

Over four years had passed since that promising day when the United States had left the island. In his diary, Military Governor Leonard Wood had remembered that day as "a fine clear day, the best sort of a Cuban May day." For a week prior, jubilant crowds had paraded along Havana's gaily decorated streets to the beat of exploding firecrackers. At noon, though, everything had gone still as Wood read out the document of transfer. American soldiers had slowly lowered their country's colors and hoisted the Cuban flag; in the harbor, the guns of American warships had begun booming in celebration. Cuba was free at last.[1]

Cubans, to be sure, had won independence only with an asterisk. The Platt Amendment meant that another American takeover remained theoretically possible, and some cynics, like Senator Joseph B. Foraker of Ohio, had even warned at that time that the Amendment would incentivize political "outs" to create exactly the sort of disorder that would bring the Americans running back to the island.[2]

On that bright, brilliant Cuban day, however, such concerns had seemed as wispy and far off as the clouds hanging on the horizon. Certainly no one in the newly installed Roosevelt administration had given them much thought.

Four years later, though, Cuba was very much on Roosevelt's mind. "Just at the moment I am so angry with that infernal little Cuban republic that I would like to wipe its people off the face of the earth," he stormed. "All that we wanted from them was that they would behave themselves and be prosperous and happy so that we would not have to interfere. And now, lo and behold, they have started an utterly unjustifiable and pointless revolution."[3]

So they had, at least from Roosevelt's perspective. Quarreling between Cuba's two political parties, the Moderates and the Liberals, had led the latter into revolt in August 1906. Now the Liberal revolution was metastasizing quicker than Havana could contain it. Worse still, it was becoming clear that, for all their differences, the warring parties wanted the same thing: a second American occupation of the island.

Cuba was not even the only "infernal little republic" causing trouble. Senator Foraker's prediction—that American interventions might generate their own sequels—was also coming true in the republic's second protectorate, Panama. It was infuriating. Cuba and Panama were supposed to be the poster children of American regional stabilization. Instead, lo and behold, they were unraveling in ways that would draw the United States further into their affairs—at the very moment, no less, when the administration was struggling to communicate its benign intentions to a wary region.

Roosevelt just could not understand what had gone wrong.

No Victories but Those of Peace

If someone had asked Elihu Root a year earlier whether he would soon find himself on a precedent-smashing goodwill tour through South America, the high-flying attorney would have arched an eyebrow. He had resigned as secretary of war in early 1904, intending to return to private practice for good. Seventeen months later, however, Secretary of State John Hay passed away, and on the presidential train back from the funeral, Root heard the request he had hoped would never come.[4]

"Elihu," Roosevelt said, fixing him with a stare, "you have got to come back into my Cabinet." Root began running in his mind through all the reasons why he would say no. He had just traded an $8,000 public salary for a $200,000 private one. His wife hated Washington. They had just started building a new house on Park Avenue. Even the thought of returning to government service exhausted him.[5]

Instead, he looked up at Roosevelt and said yes.[6]

——

FOR HIS SINS, the new secretary of state had assumed responsibility for rehabilitating the country's standing in Latin America. Not that the United States was hated, exactly. While the Roosevelt Corollary had disturbed some countries, most believed that it would never apply to them, and Roosevelt had gone out of his way to stress that fact. As for Panama, many Latin Americans suspected that Colombia had gotten what it deserved; foolish nations and their sovereignty are soon parted, after all. And hadn't Washington stood up for Venezuela, twice? Most importantly, hadn't it left Cuba?[7]

Still, there was considerable room for improvement. Since the 1890s, the American relationship with the region had been deteriorating. If nothing changed, the United States risked being seen not as an occasionally overbearing neighbor but as an outright enemy.

Contrary to his reputation, Roosevelt cared deeply about reversing the decline. In private, the president was sometimes condescending about Latin Americans, especially when piqued (in fairness, he was condescending about practically everyone when piqued), and he could revert to racist stereotypes. Publicly, however, Roosevelt usually kept his tongue in check and his tact engaged. "Nothing is of greater importance from a political point of view," the president emphasized to his diplomats, "than that the United States should be understood to be the friend of all the Latin-American republics and the enemy of none."[8]

Root felt even more strongly. "The South Americans now hate us," he reflected sadly, "largely because they think we despise them and try to bully them. I really like them and intend to show it. I think their friendship is really important to the United States, and that the best way to secure it is by treating them like gentlemen."[9]

Root was no fool. Like Roosevelt, he recognized that the country's strategic objectives—especially its determination to control the Panama Canal—would inevitably require it "to police the surrounding premises." But there was policing and then there was *policing*. Root wanted Washington to ease off the nightstick and instead keep order in Latin America through "a little genuine interest combined with respectful consideration," which he was sure would "give us in that part of the world the only kind of hegemony we need to seek or ought to want." Otherwise, Root feared the consequences. "The key-stone of our Latin-American policy is anti-imperialism," he concluded. "If we step one foot off that basis we are gone."[10]

———

As SECRETARY OF state, Root therefore prioritized winning back the affection of Latin America. He began by seeking out the friendship of its diplomats, taking small but welcome steps to integrate them into Washington high society. Root then devised a more ambitious initiative: traveling to Rio de Janeiro over the summer of 1906 to headline the Third International Conference of the American States.[11]

Since Secretary Blaine had hosted the equivocal First Conference in 1889, the Pan-American movement had fallen into a slump. For over a decade the American republics had not met, and when Mexico finally hosted the Second Conference in 1901, it accomplished little.[12]

Root was determined to make the Third Conference a success, though not by reviving Blaine's far-reaching policy proposals. Instead, Root intended to publicly bind the United States to a new regional policy. His physical presence alone would demonstrate his nation's commitment to better relations, not least because it would be unprecedented—the first time in history that a sitting secretary of state had ever visited South America.[13]

On July 31, 1906, as night settled over Rio, Root delivered the Conference's keynote address. He spoke to the deepest fears of the assembled delegates and promised soothingly and sincerely that those fears would never come to pass. "We wish for no victories but those of peace," he pledged, "for no territory except our own; for no sovereignty except the sovereignty over ourselves. We deem the independence and equal rights of the smallest and weakest member of the family of nations entitled to as much respect as those of the greatest empire, and we deem the observance of that respect the chief guaranty of the weak against the oppression of the strong."[14]

We wish for no victories but those of peace. Few who heard Root's words that night would forget them, and his promises were soon being reprinted and repeated across the hemisphere. Even skeptics of American power and purpose were momentarily enchanted. The *Jornal do Brazil*, which had attacked the secretary vigorously before his arrival, admitted that his speech had "never failed to hit the mark." A new era of regional cooperation seemed at hand.[15]

Root was pleased. He told Roosevelt that he saw his speech as encapsulating "the true theory of relations between the American Republics."

His promises, he knew, would fix "a standard which the United States is bound to live up to." Good, he thought. "I meant to have it so, for I think we ought to live up to that standard."[16]

━━

Root's speech in Rio was only the start of a grand continental tour. Two weeks later, the secretary stood next to Argentinian Foreign Minister Luis María Drago in the Buenos Aires Opera House and formally pledged his country to the Drago Doctrine, promising the United States would never "use her Army and Navy for the collection of ordinary contract debts." Then he was off, on to Chile, Peru, Panama, and even Colombia.[17]

At each stop Root suffered through new levels of pride, pomp, and circumstance. He despised the razzle-dazzle of diplomatic pageantry, and he especially dreaded "the fate of an honored guest in Spanish America"—"drinking warm, sweet champagne in the middle of the day." But the secretary kept his distress to himself, smiling through tedious speeches, lavish meals, glitzy boat trips, and interminable carriage rides over flower-strewn streets.[18]

Everywhere he went, the secretary made friends and influenced people. His message was always the same: the United States was the friend of all Latin America; it had no desire to interfere unnecessarily in its neighbors' affairs. By the time Root returned home, he had sent out twelve thousand Tiffany-engraved invitations, a continent-wide courtship fortified by the ample supply of wines and Havana cigars stocked aboard his ship.[19]

For a sixty-one-year-old, wining and dining at this pace was exhausting. "I am being driven like a battery of light artillery," he groused. Still, despite the pace, despite the pomp, despite even the warm, sweet champagne, Root was happy. He believed his tour was changing the prevailing narrative about the Northern Colossus, and while some of the region's newfound warmth would be as "evanescent" as the bubbles in his champagne, he told Roosevelt that he had "no doubt there will be a residuum of friendly feeling." Others agreed; one American diplomat gushed that the secretary's visit "has resulted in greater good to our relations with Central and South America than any one thing that has heretofore taken place."[20]

As the secretary rounded Cape Horn, however, his trip was interrupted by disturbing news. In mid-August, a revolution had exploded in Cuba.[21]

The U.S. Has a Direct Responsibility

Cuba's revolution caught Root and the rest of the administration completely by surprise because everything on the island had seemed to be going so well. Cuba's economy had taken off from the postwar ashes like a phoenix, expanding by approximately a quarter in just four years. That ascent reflected international confidence in the island's stability; money could at last be had at 6 percent. It also reflected savings from demobilizing the Cuban army, which Americans considered unnecessary after the Platt Amendment. Things were going so well, in fact, that by the fall of 1906 the central government had stocked the treasury with a $13.6 million surplus.[22]

Cuba's apparent success was buoyed by two American decisions. The first was to ratify a reciprocity treaty with the island. Since the days of Blaine, reciprocity had lost much of its caché in Republican circles, but Roosevelt insisted on making Cuba the exception. Partly, it was a matter of honor; Cuba had "agreed" to the Platt Amendment, and every good *quid* deserved a *quo*. "We expect Cuba to treat us on an exceptional footing politically, and we should put her in the same exceptional position economically," the president argued. But it was also a matter of strategic self-interest, as a wealthy Cuba would presumably be a stable Cuba. Roosevelt accordingly jammed through Congress a reciprocity treaty that was tilted heavily in Cuba's favor, including a 20 percent cut in the tariff on Cuban sugar. Cubans were pleased—they favored reciprocity almost uniformly—and the treaty helped fuel the island's economic takeoff.[23]

Of equal importance was the American decision not to abuse its power under the Platt Amendment. Root had promised that the Amendment would "never give rise to intervention in the internal government of Cuba." Since 1902, the United States had largely kept its word. It had let the island chart its own course in most matters, and the one prominent exception—American opposition to a Cuban reciprocity treaty with Great Britain—had been rooted in the text of Cuba's reciprocity treaty with the United States, not the Platt Amendment. Even in matters directly covered by the Amendment, Washington had proved unusually accommodating. For example, the U.S. Navy had wanted Cuba to cede four naval bases under the Amendment, but the administration had compromised and negotiated to rent just two, eventually agreeing to only the lease of Guantánamo Bay. Platt Amendment or not, it was a source of pride for Roosevelt that "we have preserved just so much interest in the islands as to enable us to be of assistance to their people in standing alone."[24]

Beneath the surface, however, all was not well. Cuba's economic growth was impressive but not inclusive. After the rebellion against Spain torched the island's economy and drove its property owners deep into debt, Cubans had needed foreign capital to rebuild. One possible source of that capital, loans, was passed over by occupation forces to avoid saddling Cuba's new government with massive debt right out of the gate—the problem that had tormented and destabilized so many of Cuba's neighbors. But that left only the alternative of private investment. American policies, including reciprocity, ensured that private investors flowed in and helped revive the island's economy. As in Hawai'i, though, the influx of outside capital meant that the returns from Cuba's subsequent economic boom went mostly into the pockets of investors abroad rather than Cubans. Cuba prospered; Cubans mostly did not. One estimate suggests that by 1906, foreign companies owned 60 percent of rural land, with another 15 percent in the hands of resident Spaniards and only 25 percent owned by the Cubans themselves. Foreign investors disproportionately controlled other sectors of the economy too.[25]

Even as Cuba's economic growth became more unequal, it also became less resilient, as more and more of the island's economy became tied to the fate of sugar. Cubans and Americans alike saw the sweet stuff as the ticket to prosperity, and to a certain extent they were right. As in Hawai'i, however, the development of a sugar monoculture made Cuba vulnerable to swings in foreign markets. It also had unintended political and social side effects. Sugarcane is grown in a six-month wet season (typically May to November) and harvested in a six-month dry season (November to May). Cubans stayed frenetically busy during the harvest, but during *el tiempo muerto*, the growing season's dead time, thousands were thrown out of work and onto the streets. Every summer like clockwork, *el tiempo muerto* thus turned the island into a revolutionary powder keg.[26]

BY 1906, CUBA's politics were rapidly approaching the point of combustion. Since independence, the island had been governed by President Tomás Estrada Palma. Palma had spent much of his adult life in the United States, including his wartime service as head of the revolutionary Junta. His exile made him an oddly perfect choice for *Cuba libre*'s first leader—above the island's partisan politics and friendly to the United States, he appealed to Cubans and Americans alike.[27]

Palma initially tried to govern as a nonpartisan. But he became convinced that to accomplish anything, he needed to ally with one of the two political parties, even though both centered more on personalities than policies. In early 1905, Palma threw his lot in with the Moderates. His decision embittered the Liberals, and the always-personal politics of the island grew even more rancorous.[28]

Palma's pride got the better of him as the elections of 1905 approached. Conflating his personal fortunes with Cuba's, Palma persuaded himself—as leaders everywhere so often do—that only his reelection could thwart national catastrophe. Staying in power appeared to him not just desirable, but necessary, even patriotic. Given that end, the means followed naturally: partisan purges, ballot stuffing, intimidation, and political violence. The Moderates swept the elections of late 1905, Palma was reelected, and the Liberals were shut out.[29]

The Liberals began plotting revolt immediately, but the harvest season was upon Cuba. Scattered violence aside, they would have to wait until the summer of 1906 to strike. As surely as *el tiempo muerto*, however, revolution was coming. And the Liberals liked their chances. Palma had no army, only a thinly spread rural guard, while the Liberal leaders were veteran guerrillas skilled in the art of overthrowing oppressive regimes. They had done it once, and they were ready to do it again.[30]

FEW BACK IN Washington took the threat seriously, confident that the Platt Amendment would deter any prospective revolutionary. Far from being dissuaded by the thought of American intervention, however, the Liberals were increasingly counting on it. "The U.S. has a direct responsibility concerning what is going on in Cuba," urged General José Miguel Gómez, the Liberals' defeated presidential candidate. He added ominously: "If the U.S. would intervene and insist that the presidential elections should be held honestly, it would prove that 80% of the Cuban people were Liberal."[31]

But American officials were too busy holding Cuba up as a success story to notice the ill omens. Roosevelt dreamed that "every country washed by the Caribbean Sea would show the progress in stable and just civilization which with the aid of the Platt Amendment Cuba has shown." Root expressed the same complacency shortly before departing on his South American tour. "The Cubans have done admirably in their experiment in self-government," he wrote, "far better than anyone dared to hope."[32]

So it came as a total shock when, on August 16, 1906, the Liberal revolt broke out in Cuba's westernmost province, Pinar del Río, and spread within a week to the provinces of Havana and Santa Clara.[33]

House of Cards

Washington was slow to react even after the Liberal revolution began, in part because officials expected the fuss to peter out quickly. Even Roosevelt, normally hyperactive, did little more than permit Palma's government to buy five million cartridges.[34]

On Saturday, September 8, 1906, a cable finally awoke the administration to the seriousness of the situation. "Government forces are unable to quell rebellion," blared the American consul general in Havana. "President Palma will convene [Cuban] Congress next Friday, and Congress will ask for our forcible intervention."[35]

Administration officials were horrified. "What I have dreaded has come to pass," the president moaned. He saw few good options. "On the one hand," he sputtered, "we cannot permanently see Cuba a prey to misrule and anarchy." The immediate loss of life and property would be bad enough, but even worse would be "the creation of a revolutionary habit" that would destabilize the island for decades to come.[36]

On the other hand, however, Roosevelt "loathe[d] the thought of assuming any control over the island." "We emphatically do not want it," he insisted privately, and "nothing but direst need could persuade us to take it." Cuba had been the shining example of American stabilization policies. If the United States intervened, it would be an embarrassing acknowledgment that the Platt Amendment had failed, with the chilling implication that stronger medicine might be needed. Intervention would also be unpopular at home and abroad, especially if fighting broke out. Roosevelt's generals warned that American forces could beat the world's most experienced guerrillas only by reviving Spanish General Valeriano Weyler's reviled *reconcentrado* tactics. It would be the Philippine-American war all over again.[37]

Roosevelt sought to wriggle out of this dilemma. From his vacation home at Oyster Bay, he sent "a most emphatic protest" against the proposed American intervention. "Out of the question," he chided the American consul. If Havana could not quell the revolt, then Palma would have to compromise.[38]

"I guess I can work it out all right somehow," he told a friend with more force than confidence. "But I do not yet quite see how."[39]

OVER THE NEXT few days, Cuba crept closer to intervention as the Liberal revolution continued to spread. Roosevelt meanwhile struggled to make sense of everything. "These people have had for four years a decent, respectable government of their own," he harrumphed around his vacation home. "They are not suffering from any real grievance whatsoever. Yet they have deliberately plunged the country into civil war." Soon things might get "into such a snarl that we have no alternative save to intervene—which will at once convince the suspicious idiots in South America that we do wish to interfere after all, and perhaps have some land-hunger!"[40]

On Friday, September 14, the snarl worsened. Palma informed Washington that he and his cabinet planned to resign, leaving a black hole where the government of Cuba once sat. Constitutionally, the Cuban Congress would be unable to fill the void, meaning that if nothing were done, Cuba was days away from literal anarchy.[41]

Roosevelt urgently countered on two fronts. First he went public, urging "all Cuban patriots" to set aside their differences and remember "that the only way that they can preserve the independence of their republic is to prevent the necessity of outside interference, by rescuing it from the anarchy of civil war." Citing the Platt Amendment, the president begged Cubans to pull back while they still could.[42]

Simultaneously Roosevelt dispatched a high-level commission to broker a compromise. With Root still on tour, the president deputized Secretary of War William Howard Taft and Assistant Secretary of State Robert Bacon for the sensitive diplomatic mission. Back in Cuba, both sides agreed to a cease-fire while they awaited the mission's arrival.[43]

Taft estimated their odds of success as "about even," but that was a shot in the dark. By his own account, he was "so lacking in knowledge" compared to Root "that it is quite embarrassing for me to go." All he knew was that Cuba "has proven to be nothing but a house of cards."[44]

ON ARRIVING IN Havana on Wednesday morning, September 19, Taft and Bacon learned that the situation was in even greater shambles than they had feared. On top of the slippery steps of the Caballería pier, the Americans found Havana at its placid best: theaters bursting with laughter, live music wafting from the park, urbanites digging decorously into ices and sorbets inside buzzing open-air cafés. Outside the capital, however, a rebel army was massing, and it already outnumbered government forces two to one.[45]

One of the first things Taft and Bacon realized was that Palma's government was finished. Taft reported to Roosevelt that the regime was strongly opposed by a "large majority" in the city and country alike. Furthermore, Palma's government lacked the means to defend itself. At the start of the rebellion, it had had six hundred artillery troops and three thousand rural guards. Since then, it had scraped together a handful of additional troops, but the new recruits were raw and indifferent. Indeed, Palma's government had left itself so defenseless that Taft suspected it had been counting on Washington to crush its domestic enemies under the Platt Amendment all along.[46]

On the other side of the lines, Taft learned, the Liberal rebels grew more powerful each day. Even now they held a gun to the heart of Cuba's economy. One word, one match, Taft realized, and inside of a month $70 million of sugar *centrales* "would go up in smoke." The Liberals were also relatively popular with the people. But Taft objected to the idea of turning Cuba over to them. Not only would doing so encourage future revolutions, but he also "shiver[ed] at the consequences" of rewarding this particular rebellion, "an undisciplined horde of men under partisan leaders."[47]

On Monday, September 24, Taft and Bacon proposed a compromise. Palma would remain president, but the legislature would resign, and new elections—*fair* elections—would be held within months. The Liberals, knowing that they would dominate any free elections, warily agreed. But Palma and the Moderates rejected the proposal as an affront to their government, instead reiterating their plans to resign in a few days' time. Taft was furious. "Palma and the Moderates will now take away their dolls and not play," he cabled Roosevelt mockingly. Taft was even more caustic in letters to his wife, and he confirmed his earlier impression that Palma was "difficult," "quite obstinate," and "a good deal of an old ass." "He doesn't take in the situation at all," the secretary whined.[48]

But it was the Americans who failed to take in their situation. The administration could not back the Liberals without condoning future disorder. Nor could it support Palma and the Moderates without plunging the United States into a bloody counterinsurgency. If Palma could have mustered either popular or military support, Taft mused, Washington could have helped him; as it was, however, intervening on Palma's behalf would mean "fighting the whole Cuban people."[49]

Compromise between the parties was also impossible. Both sides realized that a Liberal regime was inevitable. The Moderates resolved to defer that evil day by triggering an immediate American takeover of

Cuba. The Liberals were also happy to wait; they knew they would take control as soon as the Americans left, and rather than wage war against Palma and likely the United States, they preferred to take the scenic route to power. One rebel leader nonchalantly explained why his side could not lose. "We will overthrow the Palma Administration or make everything in the island American. We would much rather trust Roosevelt than Palma."[50]

So to Taft and Roosevelt's chagrin, the one and only thing that both Moderates and Liberals could agree upon was that the United States should reoccupy the island. "If the Queen should lead Alice straight from Wonderland into the heart of this amazing Cuban war, they would both feel perfectly at home," a journalist marveled.[51]

Desperate to avoid this trip through the looking glass, Roosevelt acted curiouser and curiouser. He burned up the cable wires with increasingly fantastical ideas about how to stabilize the "kaleidoscopic" crisis. He pleaded with Palma not to resign and griped about the Cuban president's "sulky" behavior. He flung battleship after battleship toward Havana as a precautionary measure. He brooded to Lodge and others about how "greatly disheartened" he was, how he could not understand "the criminal folly of this insurrection," how he was at his "wits' end." Baffled, the president instructed Taft, over and over and over again, to grab at any solution and "take no step we are not absolutely forced to." Finally, with one eye on domestic politics, Roosevelt pestered Taft to, at minimum, avoid using the word *intervention* if—when—it finally came.[52]

On Friday, September 28, the moment arrived. "It looks to-day as if intervention would come to-night or to-morrow morning," Taft reported gently. "I know how much you deplore this, but there is really no way out of it. The truth is that the two sides want it now." Roosevelt had lost, and he knew it. He curtly gave the order: "All right land forces ... but if possible emphasize fact that you are landing only at Palma's request and because there is no Government left."[53]

That evening, Palma scuttled the Cuban government. With no central authority left and rebels at the gates of Havana, Taft ordered thirty marines ashore in the early hours of the morning to secure the treasury.[54]

Over the next month, nearly six thousand American forces would garrison the island under Article III of the Platt Amendment. Their first task was disarming and dispersing the rebel forces. Still haunted by the prospect of a Liberal insurgency, Roosevelt reiterated that he was "most anxious that there should be no bloodshed between Americans and

Cubans." He need not have worried: just then, the Liberals were busy soliciting contributions for a new statue of Roosevelt that they planned to erect in Havana.[55]

Doll House

Cuba was not the only place where political "outs" were starting to probe what it would take to bring the United States in. Only by adopting a different approach in Panama was the United States able to avert a military occupation. The trouble was, that new approach still required the administration to get far more involved in Panama's internal affairs than it wanted. It seemed like no matter what Americans did, they could not escape the whirlpool of their neighbors' politics.

Shortly after independence, Panama began following the path marked out by Cuba. In January 1904, soon-to-be President Manuel Amador Guerrero and other members of the Conservative Party proposed inserting a clause into Panama's draft constitution that would give the United States a Platt Amendment–like right to intervene to maintain public order.[56]

State Department officials blanched at the suggestion. Second Assistant Secretary of State Alvey A. Adee dismissed it as "unwise and shortsighted." He thought the United States already had "ample" powers to protect the canal under the Hay–Bunau-Varilla Treaty, and he did not want an additional obligation to "put down any insurrection." The secretary of state agreed, and he ordered the U.S. minister to Panama, William I. Buchanan, to scupper the Panamanian proposal.[57]

Something, however, was lost in communication, for Buchanan cheerfully cabled back a week later with the "glad" tidings that he had secured an article recognizing the right of the United States to intervene. He had told the Panamanians that "it was a matter of entire indifference to us" whether Panama granted such a right. But, violating his instructions, Buchanan had then personally encouraged the Panamanians to grant the right anyway because he thought it would deter future disorder. Panama's constitutional convention apparently agreed; it included a provision in the new Constitution, Article 136, that gave the United States the right to "intervene in any part of the Republic of Panama to restablish [sic] public peace and constitutional order."[58]

Senior State Department officials were annoyed at this unnecessary and provocative concession, but they never asked *why* Panama's leaders had demanded it. To more cynical minds, though, a pattern was emerging.

Like Palma, President Amador and his friends had learned an important lesson from their struggle for independence—American power could be co-opted to crush their enemies. In 1903, it had been the Colombians; in the future, it might be domestic opposition. If the price of keeping the "right" people in power was giving up a little sovereignty, then so be it.[59]

Amador's consolidation of power unnerved Liberal opposition leaders. In November 1905, they appealed to the United States for help, much as the Cuban Liberals were then doing. If the United States did not act, they claimed, the Conservatives would steal the next election.[60]

Root wanted nothing to do with these intramural fights, and he responded icily that while Washington hoped "that there shall be a fair, free and honest election in Panama," it was not going "to help either the party in power or the party of opposition." Undeterred, the Liberals journeyed to the United States to plead their case in person. Root remained firm: even though fraud in the upcoming elections was likely, the Panamanians would have to solve their own problems. Otherwise, it would mean appointing Americans as "agents in the territory of the little Republic of Panama," simply "to intervene in whatever debates about the electoral or civil rights the Panamanian citizens have."[61]

"On that day," Root remarked presciently, "you will have lost your sovereignty."[62]

―――

As EXPECTED, THE Liberals lost the July 1906 elections. Amador's Conservatives took twenty-five of the twenty-eight national assembly seats, even though well over a majority of the country backed their opponents. Cheated of their victory at the ballot box, the Liberals began contemplating revolution.[63]

For American officials, it was déjà vu all over again. They desperately wanted to maintain their hands-off stance. But the administration was haunted by its recent failure in Cuba. Taft privately called it "the greatest crisis I ever passed through," and he had "suffered much from the thought of [Root's] disappointment keen and deep." Assistant Secretary of State Bacon was also "ashamed to look Mr. Root in the face," knowing that the Cuban intervention was "contrary to his policy and what he has been preaching in South America." Root, in turn, did "not see how anything else could have been done," but he too "felt very badly." Each of these traumatized officials now saw events on the island repeating themselves on the isthmus. If they let the Conservatives steal another election in Panama, they feared it would mean a Liberal uprising followed by another unwanted occupation.[64]

Events were certainly headed in that direction. Amador had decided not to run for reelection in 1908, but as the vote approached, he began retooling the electoral machinery to install his chosen successor, Ricardo Arias, into power. The Liberals supported the candidacy of José Domingo de Obaldía, but if they could not secure Obaldía's election, they would settle for revolution. Echoing similar comments in Cuba, a chilling slogan began to make the preelection rounds: "It will either be the Liberals or the United States."[65]

Roosevelt decided it had better be the Liberals. Two years earlier, the United States had refused to get involved on behalf of either party. Now it entered the contest in favor of Obaldía. Washington did not have any particular love for him as a candidate, but it calculated that Panama would be more stable if its government were popularly supported. Given the Liberals' threat of revolution, it also seemed like favoring Obaldía was the safest way to avoid a military intervention.[66]

Taft visited the isthmus in May 1908 to personally deliver the threat. If Panama failed to hold a fair election, he warned Amador, the United States would consider it "a disturbance of public order which under Panama's constitution requires intervention." Taft accordingly "venture[d] to suggest" that Amador allow the Americans to supervise the upcoming vote. "It goes without saying that the United States will be most reluctant to intervene," the secretary of war remarked, but "should the [occasion] arise, I do not see how it can be avoided."[67]

Once upon a time, the United States had spurned the right of intervention that Amador sought. Ironically, it was now using that same right to coerce *him*.

———

Taft's threat worked. Amador formally requested that American agents supervise the election. Arias, recognizing he would not win a fair ballot, withdrew from the race, sniffing about "the imminent peril of ... military occupation." Obaldía and the Liberals claimed total victory.[68]

Some in Washington breathed a sigh of relief. "I am very sure that had we not taken the steps which we did take, Amador and Arias would have forced the election of Arias," wrote Taft. He continued brightly: "Obaldia was the choice of two-thirds of those entitled to vote in Panama, and I think the cause of good government has been helped by securing the return of the man thus the choice of the people."[69]

Others were less sanguine. "If we mean to intervene in this Republic," Representative Edwin Denby of Michigan warned Root, "we are following the right course." Taft had practically told the Panamanians "that their government is a plaything, their republic a doll house in which they may amuse themselves so long as they do not disturb or annoy us." Denby worried that this "overbearing attitude" would tarnish Root's policy of reconciliation with Latin America. "The policy of leading strings having now been established," the congressman concluded darkly, "must always be followed."[70]

Certainly there were worrying signs that Washington was replacing Panama City as the governing authority on the isthmus. Shortly after Arias withdrew, Obaldía cabled Taft to thank him for "the American intervention," which had been "a salutary step that does not inspire fear to patriots." But Obaldía's word choice flabbergasted the State Department, just as similar phrasing had spooked Roosevelt with regard to Cuba. "*Intervention!!!*" scribbled an alarmed Bacon on the telegram in bold red pencil. Second Assistant Secretary of State Adee was equally stunned, if somewhat more articulate. "Obaldia is even more of a fool than a knave," he observed. "His insane claim that he owes his approaching election to American intervention means patriotic revolution, endless trouble and ultimate real intervention as in Cuba."[71]

Obaldía had it right, though. The United States *had* intervened. And in its own way, that intervention was just as "real" as the reoccupation of Cuba. Taft and others had decided that to avoid military intervention, they needed to proactively manage Washington's protectorates. The lesson of "leading strings" would not soon be forgotten.[72]

The U.S. Will Have to Go Back

Officials in Washington could be forgiven for seeing events in Cuba as the more "real" intervention; after all, they still had to manage the island's occupation. Root framed the basic task with his usual clarity: "We do not want Cuba ourselves, we cannot permit any other power to get possession of her, and to prevent the necessity of one and the possibility of the other of those results, we want her to govern herself decently and in order." But Root's framing left open just how far Washington would go to ensure that Cuba governed itself decently, and the administration remained torn between that objective and extricating itself as quickly as possible from an intervention it had never wanted. In the end, the administration rushed to withdraw from the island despite having resolved few of Cuba's underlying political problems.[73]

Occupation forces tried to reform Cuba's politics and society up to a point. Setting the domestic American model as a paradigm, the

occupation government eagerly began "fixing" the island by strengthening its electoral laws, augmenting the judiciary's independence, and
enhancing public employees' protections against political retribution.
Such nonconsensual reforms seemed fundamentally at odds with American paeans to Cuban liberty, but Roosevelt squared the circle as best he
could. "We must try to make them understand that our purpose is not to
interfere with the design of limiting their independence, but to interfere
so as to enable them to retain their independence," he wrote to Root.
"We must try to make them understand, what is the exact truth, that we
would object to having to take charge of the Island quite as much as they
would object to our doing so, and that our sole and genuine purpose is
to help them so to manage their affairs that there won't be the slightest
need of further interference on our part."[74]

Roosevelt, however, would help the Cubans manage their affairs only
so much. He was "seeking the very minimum of interference necessary
to make them good," he assured one audience, and he displayed little
appetite for long-term nation building. Roosevelt told Taft, for instance,
that "our business is to establish peace and order on a satisfactory basis,
start the new government, and then leave the Island." It was critical, the
president thought, for American forces to withdraw before he left office
in early 1909.[75]

Some, both in Cuba and the United States, wanted Washington to
stay on in a more permanent supervisory role. Others pushed for outright annexation. But the administration flatly rejected both proposals.
"It is not a thing we can do," Roosevelt wrote a correspondent. "The
Cubans are entitled to at least one more trial for their independent republic." Root, hearing "a good deal of talk in the newspapers about the
annexation of Cuba," responded even more definitively: "Never!"[76]

Over time, however, officials on the ground became increasingly
doubtful that the administration's two objectives—Cuban stability and
American withdrawal—were compatible. Cuba's political pathologies
ran deep; the island needed thoroughgoing economic and social reforms,
including an end to its sugar monoculture and winner-take-all political
culture. Occupation officials were also disheartened to learn that several
pro-annexationist groups on the island—especially wealthy foreigners—
had concluded from recent events that revolt and rebellion were the best
way to draw the United States into Cuban affairs. Cuba's provisional
government thus had to suppress several foreign-funded attempts to
promote disorder.[77]

Solving these problems permanently, however, required far more time, effort, and resources than Washington was willing to invest. Occupation officials grew steadily more frustrated at the administration's desire to leave the island helter-skelter, but there was little they could do as evacuation day approached. "The U.S. will have to go back," one lieutenant colonel recorded presciently in his diary. "It is only a question of time."[78]

God Given January Day

Governor Charles E. Magoon remembered January 28, 1909, as a fine clear day, "a God given January day," in one journalist's words. After twenty-seven months, Magoon's tenure as Cuba's provisional governor was finally coming to an end, and jubilant crowds were again parading along Havana's gaily decorated streets to the beat of exploding firecrackers.[79]

But this time, the festivities had an edge to them. Magoon could not understand it. Cubans had *wanted* the occupation, and his administration had been utterly conciliatory. So why, in the recent elections, had Cuba's political parties all run on virulently anti-American platforms? General José Miguel Gómez, the Liberal architect of American intervention in 1906, excused the politicos' rabid rhetoric by observing genially that there "must be some pepper in the food." Gómez apparently understood his people's palate well, for he had been elected president in the subsequent elections.[80]

At noon, everything went still as Magoon transferred control of Cuba's government to Gómez. The Cuban flag was hoisted; in the harbor, the guns of American warships began booming in celebration. But the moment had none of the optimism, none of the shared excitement for the future, that had brightened Cuba's first independence day. This time, no one could quite bring themselves to believe that Cuba really was free at last.[81]

――

SOMETHING WAS GOING terribly wrong. Cubans had deliberately lit a match under their own country. Only a last-minute gust from the north had prevented the Panamanians from doing the same. Why were the United States's protectorates and Platt Amendments, its vaunted international police power, not stabilizing the hemisphere?

Senator Platt had argued in 1901 that his Amendment would "constitute the balance wheel in the governmental machinery"; Root had likewise believed it would thwart "such revolutions as have afflicted Central and South America." Cubans would not rebel, the theory went, knowing that they would "be confronted by the overwhelming power of the United States."[82]

Overwhelming power, however, corrupts not only those who have it, but also all who crave it. Taft was right that by 1906 Cuba had become a house of cards. That was unavoidable as long as the Cuban government could be knocked down and reshuffled at American command. By committing American power to the task of keeping Cuba stable, the Platt Amendment created perverse incentives—for the government, not to prepare for instability; for the opposition, to create it. Each sought to wield the Amendment's promise of overwhelming American power to accomplish factional ends, even at the expense of the nation as a whole. The Platt Amendment, far from stabilizing Cuba, had upended it.[83]

Cuba would also not be an isolated case. Panama demonstrated as much, and Roosevelt had effectively also brought the rest of the region under the aegis of the Platt Amendment when he announced the Roosevelt Corollary. As long as the pull of factionalism outstripped the glue of nationalism, each of these countries was now primed to snap. The "revolutionary habit" that Roosevelt so dreaded was being created by none other than the president himself.

—

MOST OF THIS was lost on the outgoing administration. Insisting that the United States had "not caused the evil," Roosevelt retreated to appalling stereotypes to explain away the Cuban intervention. He fumed to his son, for example, that one "never could tell when those ridiculous dagos would flare up over some totally unexpected trouble and start to cutting one another's throats." Taft, Lodge, and others felt similarly. The fault was not in American strategy, they decided—it lay with the Cubans, the Panamanians, and whoever else took up a rifle next.[84]

Even Roosevelt's sharp-witted secretary of state missed the problem. Overlooking Cuba and Panama, Root instead flaunted the showcase of the Dominican Republic, still slumbering peacefully under an American customs receivership. Defending a plan to expand the right of intervention into Central America, Root explained that "the existence of the power would render its exercise unnecessary, just as the existence of such power has rendered unnecessary its exercise in San Domingo." That sounded awfully similar to what he had once said about the Platt Amendment.[85]

Root had misdiagnosed much of the problem, but he nevertheless kept the United States from straying too much further down the interventionist path. One of the lessons of the Cuba and Panama fiascos was that Washington needed to be even more proactive; it needed to nip instability in the bud *before* it escalated to the point where the marines had to be called in. Root appreciated the delicacy of this task. Like the president, he did not want to stabilize the region by force; indeed, he shied away from even the sort of crude interference that Taft had employed in Panama.[86]

So in the waning years of the Roosevelt administration, Root started instead turning to a quintessentially legal solution: building up a consensual set of norms, processes, and institutions that would incentivize good behavior by Europe and Latin America alike. He persuaded Europe's powers to agree to a slightly watered-down version of the Drago Doctrine that barred interventions to collect contractual debts in most cases. He also convinced Central American nations to start developing an institutionalized peace system that, among other things, prohibited them from intervening in nearby civil wars and recognizing revolutionary governments.[87]

Like so many of Root's other initiatives, however, these plans came too little and too late. The Roosevelt administration was drawing to a close, and not everyone else had arrived at the same conclusions as Root about the importance of diplomacy, goodwill, and multilateral institutions.

CHAPTER 9

DOLLAR DIPLOMACY

The Taft Administration, 1909–1913

E lihu Root had presided over the State Department for three and a half years. During that time, he had kept relations with Latin America on an even keel despite Washington's unprecedented level of meddling. Even the president—not often modest—admitted that every regional success had been Root's alone. "To deny Root credit for what the Department of State has done because it has been done under me," Roosevelt wrote, "is a good deal like denying credit to Sherman and Sheridan because they were under Grant."[1]

Some hoped that Root's time at the helm was just beginning. Roosevelt was kingmaker in 1908, popular enough to anoint practically anyone as the next Republican presidential nominee and his likely successor. Topping the president's short list were the men he called his fellow musketeers, Root (Athos) and Taft (Porthos). But despite being better qualified, Athos was both less electable and less ambitious, so Porthos won by default.[2]

Taft was elected as expected, and Roosevelt spent the rest of his life ruing the consequences. His regret stemmed partly from Taft's domestic record, which spurred the ex-president to run the third-party "Bull Moose" ticket in 1912 and seal the electoral doom of both. But Roosevelt and Root were equally disappointed in Taft's legacy abroad, especially in Latin America. Like them, Taft used carrots and sticks to manage the region. But the carrots shrank to baby size, while Roosevelt's big-stick diplomacy grew and grew until it took on the proportions of a redwood.

From Nicaragua to Honduras, Cuba to the Dominican Republic, the new administration tried to brute force its way through the problem of hemispheric order. One of the first casualties was the regional goodwill that Root had so carefully nursed for years.

Root and Roosevelt lamented the rough edges of Taft's "dollar diplomacy," and rightly so. In truth, however, he was largely following their lead. Stability remained the overriding priority, which meant that Taft's senior staff were repeatedly presented with a familiar choice: retreat from the core objective of stability and risk catastrophe, or interfere in the region slightly more than ever before, with the promise that *this* trespass would be the last. Each time, they made the same choice, learning only too late that the road to hell was paved with "good" interventions.

A Nightmare Such as Sinbad Never Dreamed

President Taft would entrust his administration's foreign policy to a two-man team at the State Department, Secretary Philander C. Knox and First Assistant Secretary Francis M. Huntington Wilson. Together, Knox and Huntington Wilson would become the architects of dollar diplomacy.[3]

Knox was not Taft's first choice for secretary of state. Taft had wanted Lodge, but the Massachusetts senator preferred his existing perch on the Senate Foreign Relations Committee. When Taft turned to Knox, the reaction among Washington insiders was decidedly mixed. Some, like Root, Lodge, and Roosevelt, cautiously endorsed the secretary-elect. Others did not. "Four years of Bill Taft will kill me," moaned Henry Adams. "But four years of Bill Taft with Philander Knox on top of him, make a nightmare such as Sinbad never dreamed."[4]

Knox had the right credentials. Born fifty miles south of Pittsburgh on May 6, 1853, he had started out in the legal field before helping guide the republic onto the world stage as attorney general for McKinley and then Roosevelt. (Asked to justify the taking of Panama, Knox had wryly advised the president that such an achievement should be kept "free from any taint of legality.") Since 1904, Knox had been representing Pennsylvania in the Senate.[5]

Observers like Henry Adams were concerned less by Knox's résumé, however, than by his temperament. Everyone agreed Knox was an effective lawyer, but his zealous and supercilious style of advocacy augured ill for the eggshell world of diplomacy. Knox sometimes came across as an impassive gargoyle: cold as granite, slow-moving, with hooded, dark

Secretary of State Philander Knox: "He is an interesting figure,
this Mr. Knox, with his extraordinarily calm and controlled,
almost mask-like countenance."

eyes set in a fixed, humorless mask. Others described him as a "political cardinal," a modern-day Borgia whose large, bald dome of a head
was perpetually held aloft by a stiff, stand-up collar. If necessary, Knox
could laugh at himself—the five-foot-five attorney had endured years of
Roosevelt calling him a "sawed-off cherub"—but he lacked the natural
sociability of a seasoned diplomat. He was, in Root's words, "a peppery
sort of fellow."[6]

Knox's temperamental shortcomings were aggravated by his choice of
second-in-command. Huntington Wilson was born to luxury in Chicago
on December 15, 1875, but he never felt totally secure in his elite status.
He used his father's influence after graduating from Yale to grab a spot at
the American Legation in Tokyo, where he spent nine years until he was
recalled to Washington to serve as Root's third assistant secretary of state.[7]

Root and Huntington Wilson clashed immediately. Root appreciated his subordinate's smarts and diligence, but also found him to be
tactless, arrogant, prissy, paranoid, mean-spirited, and inordinately sensitive to criticism. Toward the end of the administration, Root had the
callow thirty-three-year-old appointed minister to Argentina to get him
out of Washington.[8]

First Assistant Secretary of State Francis M. Huntington Wilson:
"I was a 'snappy' dresser in those days, indulging in fancy waistcoats,
puff-ties and scarf-pins, striped trousers, spats, yellow gloves,
walking-sticks, and brown derbies worn at quite an angle."

Huntington Wilson began packing his bags as Taft's inauguration approached. But Knox caught wind of a blueprint that the young man had drawn up to reorganize the State Department, and the secretary-elect decided to turn the plan's architect into its foreman as well. Huntington Wilson would become first assistant secretary, with control over nearly all Department operations.[9]

———

KNOX AND HUNTINGTON Wilson soon settled into what each saw as the perfect partnership. Knox spent little time at the Department. Coming in at around ten or ten thirty, he would typically head straight for the links after lunch. Once golfing began, he was unreachable; he insisted that nothing "so unimportant as China" interfere with his game. If work had to be done, it would be done at home, on the massive French desk in his library where the secretary could find peace between a bust of Napoleon and a picture of himself.[10]

Such truancy suited Huntington Wilson just fine. "Chiefs are even harder than parents to bring up properly," he had once told his mother.

"One must be firm, you know." Armed with this Rooseveltian attitude, the first assistant secretary handled most day-to-day issues himself. Questions important enough to warrant Knox's input were raised at the duo's thrice-weekly lunches at the Shoreham or Metropolitan Club. Knox would chew over his deputy's recommendations between bites of either terrapin with champagne or canvasback duck, done very rare, washed down with a Romany burgundy.[11]

Unusual as it was, the arrangement worked for both men, and they quickly developed a coherent and comprehensive foreign policy strategy. For the most part, they ignored events in Europe as peripheral to the republic's interests. East Asia held their attention more, given Huntington Wilson's (and Taft's) history there. Like so many statesmen before them, however, Knox and Huntington Wilson gave pride of place to their own hemisphere, which they believed had reached a crossroads.[12]

"Certainly Latin-American affairs were to occupy a goodly proportion of the Department's attention," Huntington Wilson later observed with considerable understatement.[13]

We Had Reason to Be Wary

Latin America occupied a goodly proportion of the State Department's attention in part because of two important changes sweeping the region. First, some threats from Europe were waning while new ones were emerging as the continent drew closer to World War I. Second, the Department was also keeping an eye on a new class of regional players: American corporations.

Taft did not enter office a burning zealot for the Monroe Doctrine. He once wondered whether the creed was worth even "the bones of one Pomeranian grenadier," as Otto von Bismarck had famously asked of the Balkans. By 1909, it was a fair question. Europe had become a continental O.K. Corral, with the great powers stepping into the boots of the Wild West's most fearsome gunslingers: eyes locked, hands twitching near holsters, minds calculating how quickly everyone else could draw. Given the tensions in Europe, Taft dismissed the idea of a German surprise attack on the Western Hemisphere as "absurd." (He was right; Berlin had quietly mothballed the Kaiser's invasion plan three years earlier.) In his first State of the Union address, Taft even suggested that "the apprehension which gave rise to the Monroe Doctrine may be said to have nearly disappeared."[14]

But that was too simplistic, as the president and his foreign policy team soon realized. Europe's rivalries benefited the United States, yes, but they also posed new dangers—including Europe's ever-bigger armies, better navies, and more aggressive foreign policies. Germany already commanded the most powerful fleet after the Royal Navy. By 1911, the *Kaiserliche Marine* would have ten dreadnoughts to the U.S. Navy's four, to say nothing of its incomparable set of battle cruisers. If war broke out on the continent, these military machines could quickly spill into the hemisphere as Europe's powers clawed for any advantage.[15]

Even now, the great powers were laying the groundwork in the region for a future conflict among themselves. Germany was predictably the worst offender. Its officers secretly subdivided the Western Hemisphere into different districts, organizing select German merchants in each into covert naval supply, intelligence, and sabotage networks. Berlin also continued muscling for a greater slice of the region's trade. State Department officials closely watched these developments, which Huntington Wilson termed "the spreading disease of German ambition."[16]

Current tensions aside, Washington also had to plan for the future. The U.S. Navy's General Board expected that when "Germany is strong enough, Germany will insist upon the occupation of Western Hemisphere territory." It was true that Europe had the Kaiser tied down for the moment, but as one admiral noted, "no one can predict what alliances and ententes [*sic*] may exist a year hence." It would be foolhardy for Washington to bet on German distraction indefinitely when naval programs took decades to finish but alliances could shift in days.[17]

Concerns were also mounting about another rising power, Japan. Tokyo was rapidly drawing closer to Latin America and especially Mexico, so much so that rumors of a secret alliance between the two regularly surfaced in American (and Japanese) newspapers. After hearing about a Japanese company's attempt to scoop up a desolate tract of land near Mexico's prime naval harbor of Magdalena Bay, Senator Lodge introduced a resolution expressing "grave concern[s]" if strategically valuable territory in the Americas were possessed by "any corporation or association which has such a relation to another Government, not American, as to give that Government practical power of control." Lodge's resolution passed the Senate fifty-one to four and marked a growing recognition that rival governments might infiltrate the hemisphere through corporate stalking horses.[18]

Knox and Huntington Wilson discounted Lodge's specific anxieties about Magdalena Bay, but they shared his broader suspicions about foreign corporations, especially as they concerned territory around the Panama Canal. Since 1904, steam shovels had been snorting and rooting through the isthmian rock and mud, and the project was now entering its final phases. For decades the State and Navy departments had warned that the canal's completion would whet foreign appetites. Few were therefore surprised when German and French syndicates reportedly tried to snap up land at either end of the canal, including in Haiti, the Galapagos Islands, and even Panama itself. The navy secretary warned Knox that the great powers were "thoroughly awake" to the advantages of "hemming in the approaches to the canal."[19]

State Department officials did not need to be told twice. Huntington Wilson had already concluded that the Germans "were snooping around there and required watching." Evaluating the threat years later, he concluded somberly: "We had reason to be wary."[20]

———

SEPARATE FROM EURASIA'S powers, Knox and Huntington Wilson were also wary of a new set of interlopers on the regional scene: American businesses. Foreign trade and investment had long been bit players in the story of American economic growth. But alongside the rise of the United States came the rise of American companies, who increasingly went abroad to do business. In 1897, Americans had invested only $304 million in Latin America. By 1908, that figure had jumped to almost $1.1 billion, and six years later it blew past $1.6 billion—a fivefold increase in less than two decades.[21]

Some of the most important new commercial players were the banana companies. Bananas had long been shipped to the United States by small firms acting as middlemen for local growers. In 1899, however, natural disasters wiped out most of the crop and all but the hardiest of these companies. For the survivors, the lesson was clear—staying small was suicidal; they needed to grow and grow and grow, big enough to weather any downturns that could affect their sensitive product, ideally by cultivating their own bananas on a massive, cross-country scale.[22]

One company internalized this lesson particularly well: the United Fruit Company, later known to Latin Americans as *El Pulpo*, the Octopus. Incorporated in 1899, United Fruit wrapped its tentacles around twenty-seven other banana companies in its first six months. Once it had squeezed into every nook and cranny of the American market, United Fruit turned its implacable gaze south and persuaded Latin American states to feed it gargantuan cuts of land that the company then developed into state-of-the-art plantations, complete with railroad systems, docks, company towns, schools, housing, and foreign workers. By 1910, *El Pulpo* also commanded a vast 115-vessel fleet.[23]

Companies like United Fruit added a new twist to American regional strategy. On the one hand, officials in Washington believed that the region's instability stemmed partly from its dismal economic record. If American companies could help these turbulent countries develop, then they would do good in addition to doing well. On the other hand, these behemoths were powerful actors with private agendas. If they weren't carefully managed, they could interfere with the government's plans.

———

EVEN AMID THESE changes, one aspect of Latin American affairs stayed regrettably constant. The region's "unstable conditions," Taft sighed, remained the State Department's "perennial occupation." Following Root's lead, the Department worried little about most of South America, which was stable enough to defend itself against European interference and remote enough to affect American security only indirectly. But the same could not be said of the countries just south of the border. "It is obvious that the Monroe Doctrine is more vital in the neighborhood of the Panama Canal and the zone of the Caribbean than anywhere else," Taft noted. Unfortunately, that area's importance was matched only by its turbulence.[24]

"Thus the malady of revolutions and financial collapse is most acute precisely in the region where it is most dangerous to us," Knox concluded. "It is here that we seek to apply a remedy."[25]

Substituting Dollars for Bullets

Like their predecessors, Knox and Huntington Wilson were determined to stabilize Latin America in order to avoid European influence and intervention. But they would no longer wait until the last moment to reimpose order. Instead, the State Department would act promptly and proactively to *prevent* disorder for arising in the first place.[26]

Financial rehabilitation was the key to this preemptive approach. "True stability is best established not by military but by economic and social forces," Knox announced in 1910. "The problem of good government is inextricably interwoven with that of economic prosperity and sound finance; financial stability contributes perhaps more than any other factor to political stability." Huntington Wilson echoed this logic a year later, quipping that the State Department's new policy sought "the substitution of dollars for bullets." By stabilizing the finances of its neighbors, he later explained, the United States would "give those turbulent nations a taste of prosperity in the hope of giving them a taste for peace."[27]

Newspapers quickly branded the policy "dollar diplomacy," and the administration defiantly embraced the epithet as its own. "If the American dollar can ... replace insecurity and devastation by stability and peaceful self-development, all I can say is that it would be hard to find better employment," Knox countered. Taft was equally unapologetic. He thought it "essential" that the Caribbean basin "be removed from the jeopardy involved by heavy foreign debt and chaotic national finances and from the ever-present danger of international complications due to disorder at home." By financially rehabilitating these countries, his administration planned to "remove at one stroke the menace of foreign creditors and the menace of revolutionary disorder."[28]

"Substituting dollars for bullets" was more than a tagline. Taft and the State Department had been traumatized by the second Cuban occupation, and they would do almost anything to avoid a repeat. Dollar diplomacy offered an alternative path to stability, perhaps the only one. Any other course, Huntington Wilson argued, "would involve the mad opinion that an ounce of prevention is not worth a pound of cure."[29]

Equally mad would be continuing to apply the Roosevelt Corollary ad hoc. "These days," Huntington Wilson warned, "the interests of one nation are [so] intertwined with those of all others that the financial recklessness or heresy of one becomes the peril of all. As well leave the slum to manage its own sanitation and thus infest the whole city, as to allow an unenlightened government, unopposed, to create or maintain a financial plague spot to the injury of the general interests." Either dollar diplomacy would be implemented across the board or it would fail. No state could or would be spared.[30]

————

OF COURSE, DOLLAR diplomacy served crasser ends as well. "We are not above being practical and commercial," acknowledged Huntington Wilson. Taft agreed heartily. "Our State Department could not vindicate its existence," the president proclaimed, if it "in any way withheld a fostering, protecting, and stimulating hand in the development and extension of [foreign] trade."[31]

Officials in Washington saw no contradiction between profits and peace. American businessmen would benefit, but so would the nations they interacted with. And if American companies chose to prey on the region rather than partner with it, the State Department could step in and make sure that Latin America got a fair shake.[32]

Knox's State Department particularly wanted to professionalize its relationship with Wall Street's banks. Partly, that was out of necessity. For dollar diplomacy to work, the Department needed dollars, and the only game in town was the private banking community. "When you want to borrow ten millions," Knox explained, "you don't ask the grocer for it or the boot black; you go to the man who has it." But the Department also spied an opportunity. American financial interests had previously run wild in the hemisphere, sometimes using their freedom in counterproductive ways. Growing closer to American banks might allow the State Department to tame them, so that the national interest reliably came out on top. It would also give Latin America access to lower interest rates than would otherwise be available. Early on, Knox acted on this rationale by informing American lenders that the Department would "categorically" refuse to support any loan that was not "equitable and beneficial" for Latin American debtors. He meant it, and the Department consistently worked with independent financial and legal experts either to improve the fairness of proposed loans or to discourage their issuance.[33]

Few things drove the State Department crazier than the accusation that it was trying to exploit Latin America or, worse, that it had become the handmaiden of Big Business. Huntington Wilson believed such charges were silly and "missed the whole point"—"they refused to distinguish between old-fashioned selfish exploitation and the new and sincere and practical effort to help." The State Department was confident it could distinguish between the two, and it was determined to end "the machinations of the United Fruit Company" as well as "the schemes of different Americans in collusion with corrupt Central American politicians."[34]

If anything, businessmen were sometimes so reluctant to work with the government that it had to appeal to their patriotism to get anything done. Knox was sufficiently exasperated by one skittish bank's concerns about loan security that he finally demanded, "Do you expect to have a battleship attached to every bond?"[35]

―――

DESPITE KNOX'S SARCASM, his policies further departed from past practice by attaching new importance to battleships and hard power. Root had waited *years* for Latin Americans to ask the United States to do what he wanted. Knox and Huntington Wilson would not waste that kind of time when they could often achieve the same results through an ultimatum and the well-timed arrival of a warship.[36]

Jettisoning much of Root's work, the new administration ignored his regional institutions and sneered at his efforts to cultivate goodwill among the hemisphere's "dirty so called republics." Knox dismissed "the delicate entente with the Latins" out of hand, observing snidely that it had been "maintained largely in the past upon champaigne [sic] and other alcoholic preservatives." Huntington Wilson agreed that if the United States wanted to secure the region and avoid military interventions, it needed something more definite than "sweetness and light between good neighbors." Root's policies had suffered from an "appalling lack of realism," he thought; "there were words and words and words," "an endless procession of words," but in the end they all "really meant very little."[37]

"Every reasonable man is for peace, just as every man would prefer to go to Heaven," Huntington Wilson declared. "But to secure the one or the other requires something more than aspiration. The millennium will not come for the wishing."[38]

We Are Not Intermeddlers

Over terrapin and canvasback duck, Knox and Huntington Wilson unfurled maps of the hemisphere and set to work bringing about the millennium. Imbued with the Progressive spirit of the day, they saw dollar diplomacy's objective as simplicity itself—to "solve the problem of misgovernment."[39]

First up were outstanding European loans. States around the Caribbean often owed astronomical sums to European creditors, the kind of debts that had invited outside interference from Mexico in 1861 to the Dominican Republic in 1904. So Knox and Huntington Wilson committed to mopping up foreign loans by consolidating and refinancing them through American banks. From their perspective, everyone benefited: European creditors got paid back, American banks expanded their business, Latin America escaped military intervention, and Washington slowly squeezed the Old World out of the New.[40]

Such financial diplomacy was almost unprecedented. Secretary Seward had struggled and failed to refinance Mexico's debt in 1861–1862, and few secretaries had tried to repeat the experiment since. At most, Root had believed American banks should supplant their European competitors on the isthmus to avoid having "ultimate control ... vested in any foreign power." But it was only a suggestion, and Root did not put the Department's full strength behind it during his tenure. By contrast, Knox and Huntington Wilson had no qualms about simultaneously and aggressively trying to expel British loans from Guatemala and Costa Rica, muscle into a European financial consortium in Haiti, and reset the finances of Honduras and Nicaragua. (They also rolled out similar tactics in East Asia.)[41]

Substituting American loans for European ones was just the beginning. On their own, new loans could only staunch bleeding balance sheets; they could not generate new revenues or otherwise rehabilitate the long-term financial prospects of the United States's heavily indebted neighbors. But the State Department had an answer for that problem as well.

Out of the financial chaos engulfing Central America and the Caribbean in 1909, Knox and Huntington Wilson saw one oasis of stability: the Dominican Republic. Roosevelt had taken control of the island's customhouses and thus its fiscal system, and in the four years since, Knox and Huntington Wilson decided, the experiment had been a "signal success." Once, Dominican history had been "a kaleidoscope of revolution interrupted only by despotism"; now, "the annual harvest of revolutions is no longer gathered," customs dues were soaring, and the land was enjoying "domestic tranquillity and prosperity … to a degree never before known." Perhaps most importantly, the customs receivership meant the United States no longer needed "constantly to interfere in the Dominican Republic."[42]

Similar initiatives seemed necessary to remediate other trouble spots in the region, like Honduras. If the United States managed these countries' customhouses for them, it would theoretically eliminate two of the most significant strains on their budgets: corruption and civil wars. Like the Dominican Republic, these countries would then see their revenues mushroom and their debts shrink, delivering the financial stability that the State Department had decided they so badly needed.[43]

Some states, however, needed even more hands-on management than that. The problem, Knox and Huntington Wilson decided, was that the Roosevelt administration had employed too light a touch. Stern warnings and advice were not always going to be enough; instead, stability sometimes had to be engineered from the ground up, through what Knox euphemistically dubbed "benevolent supervision."[44]

Cuba was the primary testing ground for "benevolent supervision." Roosevelt had left the island mostly alone, and the result had been the second American occupation. Taft would not repeat that mistake; he had learned from Panama. He therefore implemented the so-called "preventive policy," a policy of leading strings that the president defined as "doing all within [our] power to induce Cuba to avoid every reason that would make intervention possible at any time."[45]

That meant micromanagement, and a lot of it. Publicly, Knox declared "we are not intermeddlers"; privately, he instructed his minister in Havana "to deter the Cuban Government from enacting legislation which appears to you of an undesirable character, even though it seem improvident or ill advised purely from the Cuban standpoint." Root had promised Cubans that the Platt Amendment would never be used to interfere in their internal concerns. Now Washington reversed course. Benevolently or otherwise, it would supervise Cuban affairs, from high-level foreign policy issues all the way down to the port dues used to finance harbor improvements. *Viva la Cuba Libre*, indeed.[46]

Finally, Knox and Huntington Wilson reserved the most drastic tool in dollar diplomacy's toolkit for last—regime change. If the problem of misgovernment went all the way to the top, there was nothing left to do but to lop the top off and start over. Knox and Huntington Wilson were not particularly keen on this remedy; after all, the whole point of dollar diplomacy was to avoid the kind of hard-hitting interventions necessary to knock incorrigible governments out of their seats. But the Department could not make an omelet without breaking some eggs, and several bad eggs in the region were just crying out to be broken. Far better to endure the quick pain of regime change now than to suffer through more serious and sustained interventions later.

With this in mind, Knox and Huntington Wilson found early on that they could trace most of the region's troubles back to one state, one regime, and one man: President José Santos Zelaya López of Nicaragua. His government, they decided, would become dollar diplomacy's proving ground.[47]

A Blot upon the History of Nicaragua

Zelaya and the United States didn't always hate each other. In fact, Zelaya had once counted himself among Washington's favored regional partners. Smart, competent, and a stabilizing force inside Nicaragua, he had wooed Americans throughout the 1890s while waiting patiently for them to dig a canal through his country. But when Congress chose to dig through Panama instead, Zelaya felt wounded and betrayed. Redefining himself as a provocative, anti-American nationalist, the jilted dictator began to undermine the United States at every opportunity. By 1909, the two countries were barely on speaking terms.[48]

When American officials did speak, they had few nice things to say. Taft publicly branded Zelaya an "international criminal"; Knox pronounced him one of the region's greatest "tyrants." Officials minced even fewer words in private. Huntington Wilson complained that Zelaya remained president only because "no one was publicly spirited enough to risk ... killing him." Zelaya, he added, was "an unspeakable carrion who mulcted his people of a huge fortune ... [over] sixteen years of outrageous despotism."[49]

"Outrageous despotism" was not, in truth, the greatest or even most relevant of Zelaya's sins. Other Latin American strongmen exuded the same authoritarian odors, yet American noses tolerated them all the same. Zelaya, however, had made two additional and fatal mistakes.

First, he had not kept his hands to himself. Zelaya sought to violently overthrow neighboring regimes until he controlled all of Central America. Nicaragua's primary export under his rule became revolution, and the isthmus teemed with Zelayan rebels, saboteurs, and assassins that provoked a new war every year. Zelaya, Knox complained, was chronic wrongdoing incarnate, "the cause of all the unrest which now blocks the material and political progress of Central America."[50]

Zelaya made the further mistake of repeatedly crossing James Monroe. Germany featured especially prominently in Zelaya's vision of a new Nicaragua; the dictator reorganized his army with German advisors and placed a cadet school under their control. But Zelaya also welcomed loans and investors from other European countries. The final straw came in 1909, when Zelaya moved toward building a competing isthmian canal with foreign capital. He sent his private secretary to Europe and Japan to drum up offers; meanwhile, the semiofficial *Diario de Nicaragua* recommended an alliance with Tokyo in exchange for a Japanese right to construct the canal.[51]

Zelaya had finally gone too far. He could thumb his nose at Washington all he liked, but the ever-watchful State Department could not let him subvert both his neighbors and the Monroe Doctrine. It decided that for the good of the United States, Central America, and the hemisphere, Zelaya had to go.[52]

—

ZELAYA'S DOWNFALL BEGAN in October 1909. That month, General Juan José Estrada, a governor on Nicaragua's east coast, banded together

Honduras and Nicaragua

with local Conservatives to revolt against the capital's rule. Estrada's rebellion was serious: he operated out of Bluefields, a seaport screened from faraway Managua by impenetrable bogs and jungle. Estrada's rebellion was also well funded: it could dip freely into the pockets of the port's many foreign concessions, who gave generously in the effort to end Zelaya's wanton autocracy.[53]

Huntington Wilson wanted Washington to aid Estrada's rebellion, but more experienced hands convinced him and Knox to remain grudgingly neutral. The Department's restraint mattered little, however, because the fed-up American consul at Bluefields ignored orders and began aiding the rebels on his own initiative. So did a number of the port's seedy American expatriates, who enlisted in the revolutionary cause looking for a good scrap.[54]

In early November, Zelaya's army caught two of these American adventurers laying mines in the San Juan River. One of Zelaya's ministers counseled leniency to avoid antagonizing the United States. "No, my friend," Zelaya gloated, "we're going to yank Mr. Taft's chain." The dictator personally ordered the Americans executed, and on November 17, a firing squad shot the two bound and blindfolded prisoners in the pelting rain.[55]

The murders electrified the State Department. Here, at last, was a chance to yank Zelaya back. Huntington Wilson toyed with the idea of immediately occupying Managua, but the Department decided to sever diplomatic relations and demand reparations instead. Huntington Wilson acquiesced to this more moderate course, but only if the demands were made so strong that Zelaya could not possibly meet them. "We should not," he warned, "put ourselves in the position not to be able ... to proceed further in the elimination of Zelaya."[56]

He need not have worried. On December 1, 1909, Knox severed relations with Zelaya's government in a jaw-dropping diplomatic note. It cordially informed the general that his regime was "a blot upon the history of Nicaragua," and that the United States would no longer have anything to do with him. Simultaneously, the Navy Department dispatched a thousand marines toward Nicaragua. It was a bluff, but Zelaya could not take the chance. Two weeks later, with rebels marching on the capital and an American expeditionary squadron hurtling toward his coast, the Nicaraguan president angrily resigned and fled to Mexico.[57]

For the first time ever, officials in Washington had openly toppled a foreign government.[58]

———

ZELAYA WAS ELIMINATED, but Zelayaism remained. Shortly before fleeing, Zelaya had handpicked another member of his Liberal party, José Madriz, as his successor. Reasoning that "to substitute any of Zelaya's creatures would be just as bad as to do nothing," the State Department refused to recognize President Madriz and instead waited for General Estrada and his rebels to finish the job.[59]

Optimistic about the rebellion's prospects, Huntington Wilson began ghostwriting dispatches for Estrada to send back to Washington on Nicaragua's behalf after the general took Managua. Estrada, Huntington Wilson decided, would pledge to put Nicaragua's "finances upon a better basis" by "making with American bankers a satisfactory financial arrangement." Meanwhile, Taft and Knox pondered how to secure a Platt Amendment for all Central American states, so that the United States could "knock their heads together until they should maintain peace."[60]

Estrada, however, failed to live up to expectations. His drive on Managua faltered, stopped, and then reversed. By late May 1910, he was down to 350 rebels, all crammed into Bluefields and surrounded by 1,500 government troops. Unless something drastic occurred, Madriz was days away from crushing the rebellion.[61]

———

SOMETHING DRASTIC CAME in the wiry form of Major Smedley Darlington Butler. Butler was a no-nonsense soldier, meaning that if he encountered any nonsense he was liable to shoot at it. Born in West

Chester, Pennsylvania, the lifelong Quaker had joined the U.S. Marine Corps in 1898 at age sixteen. Since then, he had been at the tip of the American spear: ducking Spanish sniper fire on Guantánamo's hills; charging Beijing's walls during the Boxer Rebellion; midwifing Panama's secession; and regularly splashing ashore to soothe what he called the Caribbean's "fidgety spots."[62]

Butler was already a marine legend. He had gotten the service's Eagle, Globe, and Anchor emblem tattooed across his chest during the Philippine-American War. He growled that from that moment forward he was "a Marine from throat to waist," and that "nothing on earth but skinning will remove it." Some doubted his sanity. Fierce and fearless, he had been shot multiple times, including one bullet that, rather symbolically, had gouged out part of Latin America from his tattoo. Like his father, Butler spoke what he called "the plain language of the Quakers," which he garnished "with choice epithets when the occasion demanded high explosives." But the leatherneck also had a softer side. He signed letters to his family "your worshipping adoring Daddie Piddie" and shot off "100 Kisses" to his children between cartridges.[63]

Cynical and sarcastic, the major thought little of the world he policed. He reported to his parents that during Zelaya's "Presidency of 16

Major Smedley Darlington Butler: "The whole attitude of our State Department is beyond me, but of course I am simply a hired policemen and am not supposed to understand affairs of state."

years, term under Constitution being 2, [Zelaya] managed to save, out of a salary of $2500.00 a year, $22,000,000.00, this of course only being accomplished by the strictest of economy." Butler was equally disenchanted with Zelaya's opponents. Butler assumed most American military involvement was the result of local "degenerate Americans" trying to "make their investments good." He concluded that "the whole business is rotten to the core."[64]

———

EARLY ON THE morning of May 31, 1910, before the steam had even started rising from the shore, Butler and his marines arrived in two launches at Bluefields and sized up the situation. Butler recognized that things were desperate: Washington wanted Estrada's rebel forces to win, but Madriz's government forces had them cornered.[65]

Butler decided to guarantee the rebels' success. He informed Madriz's commanders that "they could capture Bluefields if they wanted to—the Marines would not interfere—but there must be no shooting." If they attacked with guns, Butler explained, they might accidentally hit an American in the town, and he could not allow that.[66]

"How are we to take the town if we can't shoot?" demanded Madriz's flummoxed generals. "Won't you also disarm the revolutionists defending the town?"[67]

Butler was ready for that. "There is no danger of the defenders killing American citizens," he answered suavely, "because they will be shooting outwards, but your soldiers would be firing toward us."[68]

Realizing Butler was serious, the government forces lifted the siege in disgust. But Butler was just getting started. "We sent an American beachcomber on ahead to [the next town] to be sure there would be another American life to protect, and then re-enacted the farce," he later reported. Government forces eventually "melted away," knowing they could not fight "revolutionists backed by the Marines."[69]

———

SEEING THE WRITING on the wall, Madriz gave up in late summer and followed Zelaya into exile. On August 28, 1910, Estrada entered the capital triumphantly.[70]

Estrada found a cable from the State Department waiting for him. Inside was the text of a ghostwritten diplomatic note that he was supposed to send back to Washington, in which he committed his country to, among other things, loans from American banks secured by an American customs receivership. It just awaited his signature.[71]

Estrada hesitated, recognizing that he was being invited to compromise his nation's sovereignty. But after a prolonged period of internal struggle and doubt, Nicaragua's new leader gave up and signed the note.[72]

We Are After Bigger Game Than Bananas

Dollar diplomacy had bagged its first success, but Knox and Huntington Wilson saw the job as only half done. Central America would not stay peaceful for long if the isthmus's other trouble spot—Honduras—remained, as Knox put it, "torn with internal dissension and overrun with revolutions."[73]

Honduras was the original "banana republic," a term coined by short story writer O. Henry after six months on the lam in the port of Trujillo. The phrase invoked not only Honduras's economic dependence on foreign fruit conglomerates, but also its weak and corrupt central government. Honduran presidents sometimes changed more often than the season; in 1876 alone, the country had cycled through eight of them. The nation had settled down somewhat by 1909, enduring a mere seven revolutions in the previous fifteen years.[74]

Combatting internal disorder was not cheap, and the country's credit was an international punch line. Honduras owed over $120 million, a surreal sum for a government that collected only $1.6 million in revenue annually. "Honduras," Huntington Wilson pronounced with his usual curtness, "has politically, financially and economically about as bad a record for stability as could be found on the face of the earth."[75]

On its own, that was bad enough, but Honduras's weakness had also turned it into what Knox called "a standing menace." Honduras had the misfortune of being located in the middle of the isthmus. That meant that on the rare occasions Honduras's neighbors were not invading it directly, they were using the nation as a springboard to invade others. If left alone, Knox feared, Honduras would remain the "cockpit of Central America," a "hotbed of most of the internal disturbances of its neighbors." But if dollar diplomacy could work its magic, Honduras would become stable and neutral, "and the peace of the rest of Central America [would] be immensely strengthened."[76]

Saving Honduras seemed especially urgent because British bondholders, exasperated with what passed for Honduras's finances, had persuaded the country to refinance its debt in London at an exorbitant interest rate. If the deal went through, the State Department feared that the British Empire would seize control of Honduras's public finances to the lasting detriment of both Honduras and the Monroe Doctrine.[77]

No one was willing to risk that, so Knox and Huntington Wilson proposed a way "to straighten out Honduras" that everyone could supposedly get behind. Washington would buy out the British bondholders by having the bankers at J. P. Morgan refinance Honduras's loans. That contract, in turn, would require Honduras to sign up for an American customs receivership like the one in the Dominican Republic.[78]

By late summer 1910, the plan was in place, and State Department officials assumed that Honduras would be safely on its way to stability by Christmas. Few would have guessed that the best-laid plans of mice and statesmen were about to go awry thanks to someone nicknamed Sam the Banana Man.[79]

———

SAMUEL ZEMURRAY WAS the son of impoverished Jewish peasants from Bessarabia. He had emigrated to Alabama in 1892 at age fifteen, seen his first banana a year later, and begun peddling unwanted "ripes" from boxcars across the South shortly after that. Grit, sweat, and a Machiavellian sense of morality propelled him up the banana chain, and by 1910 he ran Cuyamel Fruit Company, one of the few competitors to United Fruit's ever-expanding empire of green and gold. United Fruit would eventually buy out Cuyamel years later, but even then Zemurray proved indigestible. He became a legend, the "fish that ate the whale," when he took over United Fruit from inside the belly of the beast in one of the most audacious shareholders' revolts in history.[80]

Over the summer of 1910, however, Zemurray was being driven to a different sort of revolt. He had recently sunk every penny he owned—and thousands of dollars he did not—into the wild banana lands of Honduras. If the United States took over Honduras's customhouses, however, that would spoil everything, ending the sweetheart deals that Zemurray and Cuyamel needed to stay one step ahead of United Fruit's tentacles.[81]

Zemurray's life's work depended on stopping Knox's customs receivership. So he sicced a pack of lobbyists on Washington to sabotage the treaty negotiations between Honduras and the United States.[82]

Knox quickly uncovered the source of the opposition, and he summoned Zemurray to Washington. The two sized each other up across a large wooden desk, the political cardinal glowering at the fruit jobber. Knox's warning was polite but firm, the message unmistakable: stop meddling in affairs of state.[83]

Zemurray agreed, supposedly. But Knox was not convinced. He ordered secret service agents down to New Orleans to keep tabs on the banana man and his associates.[84]

——

OF COURSE, ZEMURRAY had no intention of rolling over. He couldn't change Knox's mind, but he could try to change the Honduran regime. Zemurray thus agreed to help his friend and the ex-president of Honduras, General Manuel Bonilla, overthrow the Honduran government. In exchange, Bonilla would protect Zemurray's interests once in power.[85]

Zemurray and Bonilla conspired with a legendary mercenary named Lee Christmas. Originally from Louisiana, Christmas had spent his early years drifting from one job (and brothel) to another. By 1891, he was running locomotives out of New Orleans. But after falling asleep at the switch—literally—he was fired. Christmas disconsolately wandered down to Honduras, where he ferried ice and bananas along a small gauge line before being captured by rebels during one of the country's periodic revolutions. A drunk rebel general informed Christmas that he would be shot. "This of course was a Bitter pill," Christmas later recalled stoically in his five-page handwritten autobiography. So he told "the Gen all Right if I have to be made a target of give me a Gun so I may kill some S—B—." Surprised, the rebel chief handed Christmas a rifle and pointed him in the direction of the government forces.[86]

Christmas was a poor railroad engineer, but he proved an excellent soldier. His adopted side lost that particular conflict, but he was hooked. Gun smoke became his muse and "revolutin'" his profession, guiding him from one Central American battlefield to another. Over the next decade and a half, he became the isthmus's go-to gun for hire, a soldier of fortune who proved his toughness by chewing on glass. He survived four marriages, three divorces, and too many assassination attempts to name. He now signed up eagerly for the ultimate escapade: restoring his friend and patron, Bonilla, to the presidency of Honduras.[87]

On December 21, 1910, Christmas, Bonilla, and several mercenaries were holed up in Madam May Evan's, a grand bordello in a decaying Victorian mansion in New Orleans's famed red-light district. Outside, Knox's secret service agents shivered as they enviously watched champagne being popped, men guffawing, and kimono-clad prostitutes swaying drunkenly to the jangle of a quarter-hungry pianola. By 3 a.m., the frozen agents had had enough. They phoned the Department that "it's nothing but a drunken party" and went to bed.[88]

As soon as they turned the corner, the mood inside Madam May's sobered up. "Well, *compadre*," Christmas winked at Bonilla, "I've heard about 'em rising from rags to riches, but this here's the first time I've ever heard tell of somebody going from the whore-house to the White House." Cars whisked Christmas and his compatriots from the bordello to the black waters of the bayou, where a yacht was waiting. They were met in the Sound by Zemurray, who presented the revolutionaries with cases of rifles, a machine gun, and enough ammunition to start a war. He also furnished the makeshift army with the *Hornet*, a 160-foot gunboat left over from the Spanish-American War.[89]

On Christmas Eve, Zemurray gave the revolutionaries one last gift. Seeing Bonilla shivering in the slashing Gulf winds, the banana king handed over his coat. "I've shot the roll on you," he said. "I might as well shoot the coat too." Then he was gone, and the *Hornet* was on its way to overthrow the Government of Honduras.[90]

—

CHRISTMAS AND BONILLA stayed one step ahead of an increasingly aggravated State Department. Dodging American naval patrols on its journey south, the *Hornet* made landfall on Roatán, one of Honduras's Bay Islands, where the revolutionaries easily overpowered a skeletal government garrison. That night, Christmas got drunk and led an impromptu invasion of the nearby island of Utila. He rang in the new year by forcing Utila's military governor to run around in his underwear at gunpoint shouting "*¡Viva Bonilla!*" repeatedly. The revolution had officially begun.[91]

From Roatán, Christmas and Bonilla descended on the north coast. Honduras's port cities began to fall one by one, to the mounting horror of both the State Department and Honduran President Miguel Dávila.[92]

Dávila needed American help and knew it. On the day that the revolutionaries took the port of Trujillo, Dávila's agent in Washington signed the long-delayed customs receivership treaty with the United States. Soon afterward, the U.S. Navy finally swatted the wayward *Hornet*. By this point, however, Bonilla no longer needed the gunboat, and his army continued racking up victories.[93]

Scared stiff, and with visions of firing squads dancing in his head, Dávila decided that only a full-scale American intervention could save his tottering regime. He personally begged his handpicked congress to approve the customs treaty, calling it a heaven-sent opportunity "to secure the help of the United States." The response was icy: "There was no applause, not a sound, nothing," one deputy remembered. Two hours later, the congress voted the treaty down thirty-two to four.[94]

═══

KNOX HAD BEEN trying to stop Bonilla's revolution because he assumed it would interfere with the State Department's plans for Honduras. But the situation had changed. Dávila, always less than reliable, had turned out to be nearly worthless. Bonilla, in contrast, was surging, and he had just secretly sent word that if his revolution succeeded, he would promptly agree to "the American loan proposal" and see the country's "European debts paid off." Knox faced a choice: forcibly prop up a fading, impotent president, or help events flow to their natural and apparently tolerable conclusion.[95]

Knox disliked rewarding Zemurray's unsavory tactics. But dollar diplomacy could hardly turn on the karmic fortunes of one fruit jobber. Indeed, State Department officials had once reminded a naval officer that in Honduras, "the banana question is merely one of rivalry of American interests," a "wearisome," "see-saw" squabble. Washington, though, was "not in Honduranean waters on banana-police duty, but to exert a moral influence towards political tranquillity...We are after bigger game than bananas."[96]

Knox made his choice. The State Department pressured Dávila to resign and appointed one of Bonilla's cronies interim president until the general could assume the office himself.[97]

Everyone seemed happy. Bonilla, deep in the banana king's debt, planned not only to shower Zemurray with tax-free concessions but also to have him replace J. P. Morgan as Honduras's new banker. Knox did not much care *which* American entity refinanced Honduras's loans, as long as the country got a relatively fair deal. So the State Department knifed the House of Morgan without a second thought to make room for Zemurray, and the Faustian bargain was complete: Bonilla would get his presidency, Zemurray would get his concessions, and Washington would get its customs receivership. The only losers would be Dávila, J. P. Morgan, and the people of Honduras.[98]

Second Assistant Secretary Alvey A. Adee closed out one of the relevant State Department files with a suitable ditty. "Treason is ne'er successful," he scribbled, "what's the reason? / When it succeeds, it is no longer treason."[99]

There Is a God in Israel

State Department officials reveled in the dizzying thrill of power successfully exercised. In March 1912, Knox published an article titled "The Achievements of Dollar Diplomacy" in which he boasted of the Department's successes in Nicaragua, Honduras, and the Dominican Republic; he was undoubtedly also thinking of Cuba and Panama's continued stability. Meanwhile, the Department was flushing pounds, marks, and francs out of Guatemala and Haiti and replacing them with good old-fashioned, red-blooded American dollars. Best of all, the United States had accomplished all of this with minimum violence.[100]

Knox's high was short-lived, however. By year's end, practically every one of the administration's regional "successes" had been reversed and its policies shot to pieces in the course of three new military interventions in Cuba, Nicaragua, and the Dominican Republic.

The secretary didn't know it yet, but dollar diplomacy was about to enter free fall.

—

DOLLAR DIPLOMACY'S TROUBLES started at home. By mid-1911, the State Department had wrangled customs receivership treaties out of Nicaragua and Honduras. But despite describing the agreements as "test case[s] of utmost importance," the administration could not get the Senate to approve them. Democrats opposed the treaties on a party-line basis, while some Republicans feared taking on any new commitments. On May 8, 1912, the Foreign Relations Committee finally put the treaties out of their suspended misery by refusing to report them favorably out of committee. Forced to improvise, Knox had emulated Roosevelt in the meantime and fastened an "interim" customs receivership on Nicaragua without Congress's approval. Honduras meanwhile escaped the clutches of Washington's financial control entirely.[101]

Congress, however, fast became the least of the Executive Branch's troubles. Knox and Huntington Wilson were baffled—despite their best efforts, the hemisphere was trending toward chaos, even in places they thought had long since attained stability.

Mexico, for instance, had been politically and financially stable ever since Porfirio Díaz took over in 1876 and cemented "order and progress" as the cornerstone of his rule. But his pro-growth policies, as with similar policies in Hawai'i and Cuba, had produced double-edged results. Mexico prospered overall, but the Porfiriato concentrated the country's wealth—especially its land—in the hands of foreign investors and

Mexican elites while concentrating the country's political power in an exclusive, increasingly sclerotic cabal. In 1907, a recession in the United States pushed its southern neighbor into economic crisis, and the stage was set for the Mexican Revolution.[102]

Francisco I. Madero was the unlikely instigator. He was a bookworm who hailed from a privileged Coahuilan family; his own grandfather compared Madero's obstruction to "a microbe's challenge to an elephant." Madero, however, had tapped into a thunderous wellspring of grievances, and he combined middle-class political and social liberalism with a rush of rural populism to throw the country into revolutionary turmoil. By March 1911, Madero's revolution had caught fire, and Taft mobilized twenty thousand troops to the border in part to warn off foreign powers (especially Germany) from exploiting the chaos. Two months later, President Porfirio Díaz was on his way to exile.[103]

Over the next two years, Madero struggled to tame the revolutionary and counterrevolutionary forces he had unleashed. Throughout, the Taft administration remained torn between its desire to avoid intervening and its frustration with Madero's inability to stabilize the country. Madero apparently needed a reminder that "there is a God in Israel and He is on duty," Taft grumbled in late 1912, and he considered putting "a little dynamite in for the purpose of stirring up that dreamer." For all Taft's carping, however, the president withheld divine retribution. "I am not going to intervene in Mexico until no other course is possible," he maintained, and the problem was largely shuffled off to his successor.[104]

———

TAFT DUCKED MILITARY intervention in Mexico, but he would not be so lucky in Cuba. Black Cubans had for years suffered second-class status, a burden that increased as accelerating American investment disrupted Cuba's economy and society. In May 1912, that resentment ignited into a popular uprising, and the movement's leaders threatened to provoke an American intervention if Havana did not meet their demands.[105]

Any parallel to 1906 was quickly dispelled, however; this time, there would be no hesitation, no equivocation. Taft immediately deployed the marines based at Guantánamo Bay to protect American property in the area. Freed from guard duty, the Cuban government unleashed its army on the ill-coordinated uprising. The State Department soon received sickening reports of Cuban soldiers "cutting off heads, pretty much without discrimination, of all negroes found outside of the town limits." By summer's end, Havana had viciously stamped out the revolt, and American marines returned to their barracks to wait for the next intervention.[106]

———

CUBA WAS ONLY a trial run for tribulations in Nicaragua. Shortly after deposing Zelaya and Madriz, the State Department had tried to put the Nicaraguan government back together again. But the troubled republic's politics were not as straightforward as they had seemed from the Potomac's placid shores; for all his faults, Zelaya had been relatively popular, and his Liberal party outnumbered the Conservative opposition by as much as five to one. Concluding that any free and fair election would threaten the return of Zelayaism, the State Department helped slide what amounted to a minority Conservative regime into power.[107]

Over the next two years, that arrangement came under increasing strain. General Estrada, the new president, quickly succumbed to a palace coup. He was replaced by his vice president, Adolfo Díaz, but Díaz's position was even more precarious. He was a political unknown with little support among either political party, and he was menaced by the growing power of his pro-German minister of war, General Luís Mena. Díaz hoped that support from Washington could offset his domestic weakness, but that was a risky bet. One American diplomat reported sheepishly that the United States was despised by "an overwhelming majority of Nicaraguans," who apparently did not look kindly on Washington's meddling or desire to control their country's customs. American bankers were also unhelpfully mortgaging many of Nicaragua's most prominent assets—including its national bank and railroad—as domestic corruption and mismanagement sent the country's previously stable finances off a cliff. By early 1912, Díaz was so unpopular that the American minister warned his regime was "not in a position to withstand, unaided, even a feeble uprising."[108]

When it came, the uprising was far from feeble. On July 29, 1912, Minister of War Mena launched a rebellion of dispossessed Liberals and others opposed to Washington's reach that was so bipartisan, nationwide, and formidable that it bordered on being a social revolution.[109]

For the State Department, Mena's rebellion was about much more than which *caudillo* warmed Nicaragua's presidential chair. Huntington Wilson wrote Taft that "to sit by and see [Mena] triumph would, we fear, be a blow to our prestige in all the neighboring republics," to say nothing of the "disorder" it would sow "throughout all of Central America." "If the United States did its duty promptly, thoroughly and impressively," however, then Huntington Wilson was certain—*certain*—that "it would strengthen our hand and lighten our task, not only in Nicaragua itself in the future, but throughout Central America and the Carribean [*sic*]."[110]

No one in Washington wanted to intervene again, but what choice was there? Like a desperate gambler who loses hand after hand, the United States was constantly being presented with the choice of going double or nothing. Seeing no alternative, Taft directed a full expeditionary force to Nicaragua.[111]

"Revolution was on again, and we marines were off again," Butler quipped. Shortly after the major entered Managua with an advance battalion, Mena's forces cut off the capital's communications. Butler requisitioned a train and spent several sleepless weeks opening up the routes out of the capital. Rebels dogged the marines' every step, but Butler bluffed or battled his way through each hostile encounter. The greatest danger came from an attack of malaria that sent his temperature soaring to 104°F. Too feverish even to stand, Butler insisted on plowing forward. Bowled over by his stamina—and spooked by his crazed, bloodshot gaze—Butler's men began calling him "Old Gimlet Eye."[112]

As Old Gimlet Eye and his marines raced around Nicaragua, something rather unexpected happened—they got shot at. American forces were accustomed to landing in the Western Hemisphere without facing much armed opposition. But times were changing; Latin Americans were tolerating their northern neighbor's meddling less and less, and they had caught on to the *yanquis*' desire to avoid entangling military interventions. So despite the suicidal military odds, Mena's rebels fought back, and for the first time ever, American forces went into open battle to suppress a regional revolution. Casualties were relatively low on both sides, but the skirmishing signaled a raised ante; henceforth, the United States would rarely again enjoy the privilege of bloodless interventions.[113]

Butler and his men eventually cornered Mena inside the Church of San Francisco, an ancient stone vault in the center of Granada. Shortly before midnight on September 24, 1912, Old Gimlet Eye went in alone to confront the rebel general. "It certainly was weird, the great emptiness of the Cathedral, lighted only by two ordinary American lanterns, suspended from long ropes to the dome," Butler remembered. He was startled by Mena's condition. Once, the general had been "an ox driver, a rough giant of a man"; now, he was moaning and writhing in pain on an old canvas cot, laid low by rebellion and rheumatism. Butler and Mena spoke through an interpreter, their words bouncing softly through the cavernous gloom. The jig is up, the major told the general, and it was true. Mena surrendered unconditionally in the early hours of the morning.[114]

With that, the rebellion flickered out. Mena was quietly bundled off to Panama, and the marines mopped up the remainder of his forces within two weeks. By late November, most of the 2,350 American soldiers sent ashore had been withdrawn.[115]

Only a company of marines remained at Managua. Ostensibly, these hundred soldiers were there to guard the American legation. In truth, they were kept in the capital as a warning, a reminder that Washington would brook no disagreement with the minority regime it had installed. The marines would remain there for the better part of the next twenty years.[116]

——

THE STATE DEPARTMENT'S very long summer was capped by the greatest embarrassment of all. The Dominican Republic had served for years as the poster boy of American-imposed stability in the Caribbean. Difficulties had arisen, but Washington had been able to paper over any cracks branching across its treasured showcase so long as Dominican President Ramón Cáceres continued keeping a tight, competent, and cooperative grip on power.[117]

On November 19, 1911, however, assassins gunned Cáceres down in a stable next to the American Legation, and Washington quickly learned how much the country's relative peace and prosperity had been due to the slain president's rule rather than the American receivership. In the capital, a young colonel named Alfredo Victoria seized power and installed his uncle, Eladio Victoria, as president. Few outside San Domingo City accepted the Victorias' takeover, and by early 1912 gun smoke blanketed large pockets of the Dominican countryside.[118]

For several months the State Department resisted intervening. But Victoria's government could not squelch the rebellions; indeed, it was barely even trying, instead using the war to mask its embezzlement of treasury funds. By summer, corruption and war expenditures had erased almost seven years' worth of progress on repaying the country's debts. Politically and financially, the Dominican Republic was back to square one, as if the American customs receivership had never happened. By mid-September 1912, the American minister pronounced the situation "hopeless" and cabled in despair: "Only complete control by our Government would permanently insure order and justice."[119]

Complete control was impossible, but so was doing nothing. Panicked, Huntington Wilson informed the president that the Dominican

Republic's collapse would strike "a very severe blow to American diplomacy." As he saw it, Washington had to decide whether to "sit by and see its whole Dominican policy fail and carry with its failure the wreck of the broad policy pursued in Central America," or, instead, to intervene. The Dominican Republic had become too important to fail.[120]

Taft dispatched two commissioners and 750 marines to "negotiate" with the Victoria regime. Victoria refused to meet American demands, so Washington used its control over the island's customs to cut off revenues to Victoria's regime. By the end of the year, the Victorias had joined Zelaya, Madriz, and Dávila on the growing list of leaders toppled by the United States.[121]

From one perspective, the intervention in the Dominican Republic was less serious than the Cuban and Nicaraguan interventions earlier that summer, which had seen more troops and more violence. But the Dominican intervention was nevertheless especially devastating for dollar diplomacy because it revealed that customs receiverships were not the silver bullet the administration had believed them to be. Controlling its neighbors' customs was not enough; if the United States wanted regional financial stability, it would apparently also have to ensure that its neighbors' governments were honest and responsible.[122]

It seemed as if the more involved the United States got, the worse things became, and the worse things became, the more involved the United States got. Latin America was spiraling out of control and taking American foreign policy down with it.

CHAPTER 10

GOD SAVE US FROM THE WORST

The Wilson Administration, 1913–1918

O n March 4, 1913, at 1:34 p.m., Latin America sighed in relief as Thomas Woodrow Wilson placed his right hand on the Bible, locked eyes with the chief justice, and swore the oath that would elevate him to the presidency.[1]

Twenty years had passed since the last Democratic inauguration. During that time, the Colossus of the North had hurled the Spanish out of the hemisphere, seized Madrid's crumbling empire, and swung the big stick in an ever-widening gyre. The last four years had been particularly unkind: under Taft's dollar diplomacy, American bayonets had left deep scars as they pirouetted across the face of the region.

All that, however, was supposedly coming to an end. Wilson had signaled in word and deed that a new moralism was at hand, one that permitted no exploitation of weaker neighbors. He believed that the republic's interventionism until now had reflected the misguided—even corrupt—motives of his predecessors, and he was confident that his own benign intent would be enough to shepherd the republic back onto a more righteous path.

On that day, it was easy to believe him. Wilson looked every bit the redeemer, standing tall and determined with his penetrating blue-gray eyes, square jaw, and high cheekbones. Indeed, the moment was almost too perfect. Just as Wilson took the oath, the sun broke through the clouds. He kissed his inaugural Bible at the 119th Psalm.

And take not the word of truth utterly out of my mouth;
for I have hoped in Thy judgments.
So shall I keep Thy law continually forever and ever.[2]

This Hardened Saint

Wilson had undergone two great baptisms in his life. The first occurred shortly after December 28, 1856, when he was born the son of a southern Presbyterian minister. Calvinism suffused young Woodrow's childhood, and he grew to believe that God presided over a just universe, His laws governing men and nations alike. Morality was no trifle, but the highest ideal, the yardstick against which all human actions were measured.[3]

Wilson's second baptism was secular and gradual, but no less revelatory. After graduating from Princeton College, he found his calling as a scholar of law, history, and government. His studies converted Wilson to the cause of democracy, whose virtues he came to believe in as devoutly as his Christian faith.[4]

Earning a doctorate in history, Wilson returned to Princeton as a professor in 1890. From his new pulpit, Wilson preached the creed of

President Woodrow Wilson: "Once he made up his mind that
a particular course of action represented the will of God, nothing
could shake him loose from it. 'God save us from compromise,'
he used to say."

self-government to his students and the public. His ideas resonated, and Wilson became Princeton's president in 1902 and New Jersey's governor in 1911. When Roosevelt and Taft split the Republican vote in the 1912 election, Wilson stepped through the breach into the White House.[5]

Wilson's idealism was both his greatest strength and his greatest weakness. His principles told him what to do, and they gave him the strength to do it. They also inspired his many supporters. But to others, his Puritanism was alienating. Wilson often seemed cold and egotistical, supremely confident in his moral superiority. He would approach policy problems carefully, seeking wide counsel and evaluating any proposal against the high standard to which he held himself and the world. Once his mind was made up, however, little could change it; Wilson had found the essential truth as surely as if it were manna fallen from heaven. Any dissent, any concession, was suspect, bordering on blasphemy.[6]

Such stubbornness made any give-and-take relationship—like diplomacy—challenging. "He does not seem to have the slightest conception that he can ever be wrong," observed the French ambassador disgustedly. The British ambassador agreed: "There is nothing to do with this hardened saint." Shades of gray did not exist in Wilson's international politics any more than in his personal affairs. "The world is *run* by its ideals," he snapped toward the end of his life. "Only the fool thinks otherwise."[7]

———

LATIN AMERICANS AT first welcomed Wilson and his ideals, which they hoped would check the implacable force that had been dragging relations with the United States downward. If a simultaneous change in party, personnel, and principles could not arrest the capsizing relationship, then perhaps nothing could.[8]

For over a decade, the Democrats had been the self-proclaimed party of anti-imperialism. They had stalled Roosevelt's customs receivership over the Dominican Republic and scuppered Taft's treaties for receiverships over Nicaragua and Honduras. Some of that was reflexive partisanship, but the party's views also reflected the convictions of Wilson's new secretary of state, William Jennings Bryan. Following his notorious "Cross of Gold" speech in 1896, Bryan had become the party's leader and three-time presidential nominee, including in 1900 when Democrats declared imperialism the campaign's "paramount issue" in response to the annexation of the Philippines. Bryan lost that election but none of his fervor for supporting democracy in its "mortal combat" against "the swaggering, bullying, brutal doctrine of imperialism." "The

Secretary of State <u>William Jennings Bryan</u>: "His heart often leaped to
conclusions in fields of thought which his mind
had scarcely explored."

fruits of imperialism, be they bitter or sweet, must be left to the subjects
of monarchy," he counseled his fellow citizens. "It is the voice of the serpent, not the voice of God, that bids us eat."[9]

Other members of the new administration had also abstained. Secretary of the Navy Josephus Daniels was a pacifist, and Colonel Edward
House, the president's closest advisor, disparaged Roosevelt and Taft's
Latin American policies as "futile." "In wielding the 'big stick' and dominating the two Continents," House observed, "we had lost the friendship
and commerce of South and Central America."[10]

Wilson was determined not to make the same mistake. Shortly after
entering office, he issued a public statement declaring that "one of the
chief objects" of his administration would be "to cultivate the friendship
and deserve the confidence of our sister republics." The president did not
look kindly on Latin American revolutions—"he was not going to let
them have one if he could prevent it," he told his cabinet sternly—but he
did not plan to perpetuate dollar diplomacy's failures. "The United States
has nothing to seek in Central and South America except the lasting
interests of the peoples of the two continents," he pledged, and Bryan
confirmed that dollar diplomacy was now "dead."[11]

Wilson doubled down on those promises later that year. "The future,
ladies and gentlemen, is going to be very different for this hemisphere
from the past."[12]

Sunday School Superintendents

Shortly after his new administration began, Wilson called in his personal physician to announce with a wink that he was experiencing "turmoil in Central America." Wilson's stomachache soon passed, but the same could not be said for the upheavals afflicting the hemisphere.[13]

For all the distance Wilson would try to put between himself and his predecessors, he shared their healthy appreciation for the problem of order. From the start Wilson grasped the threat posed by Germany and the other great powers. He also recognized the vulnerability created by the region's instability, especially in and around the Caribbean. Wilson believed that "with the opening of the Panama Canal it is becoming increasingly important that the Governments of the Central American Republics should improve, as they will become more and more a field for European and American enterprize." If those troublesome nations did not soon come by "fairly decent rulers," he feared their mischief would "lead to friction" and trigger "such incidents as [the] Venezuela affair under [Cipriano] Castro."[14]

Curing the region's gastrointestinal distress would require a new approach, however. Previous administrations had floundered, Wilson believed, because they had treated only instability's *symptoms*. The United States had been managing customs, putting down rebellions, and deposing rancorous leaders, all without ever diagnosing *why* its neighbors remained turbulent, *why* they threw up revolutions so regularly. If Washington truly wanted to soothe conditions south of the border, it needed to remove the irritants at their source. And for Wilson, that meant a new regimen centered in equal part on the virtues of self-government and the vices of concentrated economic power.

—

FOR GENERATIONS, THE United States had steadfastly ignored the unsavory character of neighboring governments. Ballot boxes could be stuffed, dissidents disappeared, and elections stolen; none of it mattered until it threatened to trigger revolution. On rare occasions, Roosevelt and Root had grudgingly supervised an election, but only to end an American occupation (Cuba) or avoid the need for one (Panama).[15]

For its part, the Taft administration had criticized Roosevelt and Root for being too squeamish about digging into the entrails of foreign governments' domestic policies. For all its heavy-handed micromanagement, though, Taft's team had shown little interest in democratizing those governments wholesale. "We cannot be too careful to avoid forcing our own ideas of government on peoples who, though favoring popular government, have such different ideas as to what constitutes it," Taft observed publicly. Privately, he was less delicate: "They are not Sunday School superintendents down there, and we can not make the qualifications of Sunday School superintendents square with the necessities of [a] situation where anarchy prevails."[16]

Wilson disagreed. He believed that anarchy prevailed precisely *because* the region squirmed under the thumb of repressive dictators, who seized "the power of government to advance their own personal interests or ambition." Such usurpations, Bryan agreed, "menace the peace and development of America as nothing else could." As long as Latin Americans struggled to achieve self-government, instability would remain endemic.[17]

Stability therefore meant centering hemispheric strategy around democratic principles. "We shall look to make these principles the basis of mutual intercourse, respect, and helpfulness between our sister republics and ourselves," Wilson announced. In practice, that meant his administration would no longer support or even recognize regimes that had come to power extraconstitutionally. That policy broke with centuries of diplomatic norms, which had understood diplomatic recognition as a routine acknowledgment of a foreign government's de facto existence, rather than as a moral judgment on its legitimacy.[18]

Contrary to later characterizations, Wilson was no crusader. He wanted to encourage the growth of democracy in Latin America, but he had no illusions about doing so at the tip of a bayonet. Earlier in his career, Wilson had opined that in politics there was "one rule ... which may not be departed from under any circumstances, and that is the rule of historical continuity"—that "each people, each nation, must live upon the lines of its own experience." Accordingly, only "slow habit" could build up democratic institutions, whether in Latin America or elsewhere. Self-government could not be adopted, much less imposed; it had to be cultivated.[19]

Even so, Wilson thought the United States could help nudge the process along. For one, the president saw many malign influences choking off democracy's growth in Latin America. Washington could help uproot those weeds to give self-government the space it needed to flourish.[20]

Wilson also envisioned the United States descending from the city upon the hill to educate its neighbors and share its experiences in self-government with them. He wanted to extend a "strong guiding hand" to steer the region's most troubled countries "back into the paths of quiet and prosperity." Of course, Washington would let these nations "work out their own destiny"—anything less would flatly contradict his principles—but the region was remarkably fortunate in that Wilson had already figured out exactly where its destiny lay.[21]

Wilson never doubted his ability to toe the line between friendly guidance and dictatorial instruction because he never doubted his good intentions. So when the president was asked by a British diplomat to sum up his regional policies, he did not hesitate: "I propose to teach the South American Republics to elect good men."[22]

───

ELECTING GOOD MEN would be impossible as long as bad men stayed in charge, and bad men would stay in charge as long as they retained the support of foreign economic interests. That was Wilson's second revelation—that the chief obstacle to democracy, "the root cause ... of instability," was Big Business. Its interests were the "dominating forces to-day in most of the Latin-American republics" and "more dangerous to the peace, prosperity, and welfare of those countries than any other one thing." By corrupting local politics, foreign business interests squelched self-government and bankrolled instability, all to the ultimate detriment of American security. "There will never be any peace in Latin America," Wilson believed, "so long as the Presidents of those States are put into office and maintained in office by one set of concessionaries, while another set of concessionaries, being out of favor, is striving by every expedient to pull down the Government and erect another more friendly in its place."[23]

Wilson concluded that American companies had contributed greatly to the turmoil. He accused them of bringing about "the recent troubles in Honduras, Nicaragua, and Santo Domingo." He also blamed them for "the recurrent demand" that Washington "take over or exercise a veiled protectorate over one or another of the republics south of us." But those days were gone; the Wilson administration would banish Wall Street from the councils of power and even begin prosecuting the United Fruit Company for antitrust violations. "Dollar diplomacy," the president decided, "has been supplanted by diplomatic welfare work."[24]

If Wilson found dollar diplomacy odious, he downright despised the economic imperialism being pumped out of Europe's chancelleries. Bad as American corporations were, he thought, they were at least partially checked by the inherent goodness of the American people. The same could not be said for European enterprises and their state handlers, who exploited the region ruthlessly. Latin Americans, Wilson believed, "have had harder bargains driven with them in the matter of loans than any other peoples in the world."[25]

Secretary of State Bryan shared his chief's views. He observed to Wilson that the Monroe Doctrine had originally been designed "to protect the republics of America from the political power of European nations." Over the past century, however, new dangers had arisen, and "the right of American republics to work out their own destiny ... is just as much menaced today by foreign financial interests as it was a century ago by the political aspirations of foreign governments."[26]

━━

CONVINCED THAT HE had "discovered the germ that causes [the] revolutionary disease," Wilson set out to eradicate it. He would curb the power of American companies, expel European ones, and cold-shoulder local strongmen. Once those strongmen had been stripped of their external support, they would be toppled by their own people, ushering in a wave of free and stable self-government across the region. It was destiny, and Wilson rejoiced at the role he and the United States would play in what he described as the coming "emancipation."[27]

The Good Samaritan

One of the first proving grounds for this emancipation would be Nicaragua. Taft had left the Central American republic in a state of suspended chaos: debts dragging its economy down, American bayonets propping its government up. Nicaragua thus offered the new administration a perfect opportunity to repudiate dollar diplomacy. But it would turn out that breaking with the past requires more than good intentions.

Secretary Bryan had one overarching rule as he dealt with Nicaragua during the administration's early months: the less involvement from bankers, the better. Bryan thought that these financial pirates had shamelessly "plundered" Nicaragua and other republics, their tactic being to "first demand a high rate of interest and a big discount to cover risk taken and then appeal to their governments to eliminate the risk." He spat: "We see in these transactions a perfect picture of dollar diplomacy."[28]

If not Wall Street, however, Nicaragua needed money from *somewhere*. Since Zelaya's time, it had collapsed into a black hole of corruption and mismanagement, and Bryan's State Department did not want Nicaraguans patching that hole with European funds.[29]

Bryan first tried funding Nicaragua directly from the U.S. Treasury. On its way out, Taft's State Department had negotiated a treaty to pay

Nicaragua $3 million for exclusive rights to any canal route through the country. The logic was clear: the purchase price would shore up Nicaragua's tottering finances, while the canal rights would prevent Nicaragua from mortgaging its territory to a foreign power—a neat solution that would, as one minister put it, "forever dispose of the bogy of a German or Japanese canal anywhere on the American continent."[30]

Bryan, however, would make the draft treaty even more comprehensive. At the urging of Nicaragua's negotiators, he agreed to incorporate into the treaty a few provisions borrowed from the Platt Amendment, including the infamous right to intervene. Bryan never asked *why* the Nicaraguan regime was so eager to sell off its country's sovereignty; the secretary was too kindhearted and naive to recognize the long history of local Sunday-school superintendents exploiting American power for their own ends. Bryan instead thought that turning Nicaragua into an American protectorate would help it escape the grip of Big Business by eliminating the political risk that justified high interest rates.[31]

Wilson, the committed critic of interventionism, read over Bryan's draft treaty "very carefully" before giving his "entire approval." "I sincerely hope that the Senate may approve it," he remarked, "as well as our friends, the Nicaraguan government."[32]

IF BRYAN AND Wilson missed the irony, others did not. "Dollar Diplomacy Outdone," hooted the *New York Times*, adding snidely that by comparison Taft's policies "more nearly resemble[d] ten-cent diplomacy." Senate Democrats generally blanched at the prospect of establishing another protectorate, as did many Republicans, and Bryan's treaty was left dead in the water.[33]

Nicaragua still needed money, however, and Bryan still loathed banks. So as the summer of 1913 progressed, the secretary developed a second alternative.

Bryan had observed that banks often charged a much higher rate of interest for unstable Latin American countries than for the United States. He wanted to exploit that difference by having Nicaragua issue bonds at a 4.5 percent rate of interest; the United States would then scoop those bonds up while issuing its own parallel set of bonds at 3 percent. Over time, Washington would use the difference paid by Nicaragua (1.5 percent) to repay the bonds' principal. In effect, the United States would be loaning its lower credit rating to Nicaragua.[34]

Bryan crowed that his plan "would furnish a modern example of the Good Samaritan," "helping those who have fallen among thieves."

Economically, he argued, the proposal would "confer a material and substantial benefit" on Nicaragua. But Bryan also saw political upsides. "The
plan would give our country such an increased influence," he assured
Wilson, "that we could prevent revolutions, promote education, and advance stable and just government." It would, in short, "make absolutely
sure our domination of the situation."[35]

Once Nicaragua accepted the plan, Bryan believed the other countries in the region would soon clamor for "the same neighborly assistance." How could they not? Like Wilson, Bryan knew to a moral
certainty that greedy foreign financiers had caused the region's troubles.
If Washington pushed those interests aside, its own expanded influence
would naturally be "welcomed because obviously beneficial."[36]

Bryan did not apparently understand what he was proposing. The
secretary insisted that his plan was "perfectly safe," with no risk of loss.
But the United States enjoyed lower rates of interest because it was
objectively a much safer credit risk. For the republic to lend its credit
risk free, it would have had either to dramatically reform its unstable
neighbors ex ante, or to intervene ex post, following up any default with
gunships to forcibly extract the money owed. Bryan's proposal, in other
words, would have eliminated private banking interests only by drawing
the United States further into its neighbors' affairs.[37]

For Wilson, it was all too much. He refused to support Bryan's plan,
eventually telling the crestfallen Nebraskan that turning the United
States government into the region's banker "would strike the whole
country, I am afraid, as a novel and radical proposal. I think that for the
present there are enough difficult questions on the carpet."[38]

———

BY PROCESS OF elimination, Bryan thus arrived at the same answer to
Nicaragua's financial woes as his predecessors. He could neither permit
European loans nor use the American government's money or credit.
That left only one option.[39]

On October 8, 1913, Nicaragua took out another loan from the
bankers Bryan so despised. Bryan had bargained hard for fair terms for
Nicaragua, and its government expressed gratitude for his strenuous efforts on its behalf. From the outside, however, it was hard to see the
promised deliverance from dollar diplomacy. Taft's State Department
had also haggled with banks for better deals, and in any event, a percent-
age point or two of interest either way was not what separated Nicaragua
from financial ruin. Even more ominously, the episode suggested that

the administration was so determined to expel financial interests that it had lost sight of an obvious truth: once those interests were gone, the Good Samaritan who took their place would inevitably be none other than the United States itself.[40]

All Hands off Excepting Our Own

Of the administration's inherited crises, Nicaragua was a relatively minor affair. Far more consequential was Mexico, where the Mexican Revolution had taken a reactionary turn only weeks before Wilson's inauguration. Mexico would demand the president's attention continuously and, more than anywhere else, put his anti-interventionist ideals to the test— only to find them deeply wanting.

Francisco Madero had overthrown longtime Mexican President Porfirio Díaz in 1911. Since then, Madero had teetered atop a shaky coalition government made up of two implacably hostile groups: reactionaries who yearned to return to the Porfiriato, and old comrades-in-arms who wanted the Revolution to blaze into new areas. Madero had successfully suppressed revolts launched by disaffected elements on either side, but his path forward was narrowing. Every day, Madero relied more and more on the military to hold the balance, but there was always the risk that one day, the generals would begin wondering why they needed Madero at all.[41]

On February 9, 1913, that day arrived when Félix Díaz, Porfirio Díaz's nephew, attempted a coup. At first, it seemed destined for failure. Loyalist forces killed Díaz's co-conspirator and quickly cornered the remaining rebels in Mexico City's fortified arsenal. Madero then ordered one of his generals, Victoriano Huerta, to finish the job.[42]

It was a fatal mistake. Over the next week and a half, known as the *Decena Trágica*, Huerta and Díaz pretended to attack each other while secretly working toward an understanding. Even though their hostility was staged, their artillery duels were not. Scores died as shells exploded across the city center, conveniently striking everywhere except where their forces were concentrated. Finally, on February 18, Huerta's men rushed into the National Palace and after a short gun battle seized Madero and his cabinet.[43]

Huerta and Díaz were supported throughout the *Decena Trágica* by American Ambassador Henry Lane Wilson. Ambassador Wilson had previously raised alarm bells for his tendency, as Knox put it, "to drive the [State] Department to action along the lines which he, for reasons of his own, seems set upon." True to form, Ambassador Wilson had ignored Knox's instructions to stay neutral, instead pressuring Madero to resign, and facilitating Huerta and Díaz's treacherous negotiations. Once Madero was detained, the ambassador capped off his partisan meddling by brokering a power-sharing agreement in the smoking room of the American Embassy, clearing the way for Huerta to become provisional president.[44]

Knox had sanctioned none of this, but he acquiesced in the fait accompli while ordering Ambassador Wilson to protect Madero's life. But once again, the diplomat had other priorities, and he told Huerta to do whatever was "best for the peace of the country."[45]

Shortly before midnight on February 22, Madero was gunned down behind the capital penitentiary while supposedly trying to escape. Ten days later, Woodrow Wilson became president of the United States.[46]

—

MADERO'S ASSASSINATION UNSETTLED Wilson's cabinet. Here was a prime example of a destabilizing, antidemocratic retrogression in an important neighbor. Even worse, the cabinet thought it spied the slippery hand of big oil companies behind Huerta. Most of Wilson's advisors opposed military intervention—"unthinkable," sniffed Navy Secretary Daniels—but something had to be done.[47]

Wilson moved swiftly. After sending an emissary south to "find out just what is going on down there," he unceremoniously sacked Ambassador Wilson for his numerous indiscretions. Simultaneously, the president developed a visceral antipathy toward General Huerta and his loathsome "government of butchers." Europe's powers had all recognized the blood-spattered regime, but Wilson decided that basic morality prevented Washington from following suit. It was also a question of stability. Huerta's coup had sparked fresh revolts, including the rise of a formidable Constitutionalist army in the north led by "First Chief" Venustiano Carranza. The only way to avoid further civil war, Wilson determined, was for Huerta to peacefully transition power to a new, freely elected government.[48]

Wilson set his plan in motion in early August 1913. He dispatched the former governor of Minnesota, John Lind, with instructions to "counsel Mexico for her own good." Lind—a virulently racist, anti-Catholic bigot—was not the best choice of emissary. "When I met Mr. Lind," one expat recalled, "I thought he was after the facts. Later on I sort of got the impression that the facts were after him and that he was not anxious to meet them." But Lind was loyal to the president, so off he went with a peace plan recommending an immediate armistice and early elections in which Huerta would not take part. "If Mexico can suggest any better way in which to show our friendship," Wilson concluded the message imperiously, "we are more than willing to consider the suggestion."[49]

In fact, Huerta did have a suggestion: Wilson could try recognizing the general's regime before telling him how to run his country.[50]

Surprisingly, it had never occurred to Wilson that Huerta might not agree to step down, and he took the general's rebuff personally. "Our friend Huerta is a diverting brute!" Wilson stormed. "One moment you long for his blood, out of mere justice for what he has done, and the next you find yourself entertaining a sneaking admiration for his nerve." Sneaking admiration or not, Huerta had to go. "We shall now simply take hands off, isolate Huerta, ... and give [Mexicans] a certain time in which to settle their own affairs," Wilson decided. He would not, however, consider removing Huerta forcibly—not yet. "Intervention must be avoided," the president insisted. "God forbid!"[51]

On August 27, 1913, Wilson delivered a message to Congress on "the deplorable posture of affairs in Mexico." Huerta had rejected his peace plan, but Wilson was willing to wait. In the meantime, the president would embargo arms sales to the regime and rebels alike. Such evenhanded neutrality was necessary, Wilson explained, because Americans could not justly become "the partisans of either party" or "the virtual umpire between them."[52]

In righteous tones, the president pledged, "We shall yet prove to the Mexican people that we know how to serve them without first thinking how we shall serve ourselves."[53]

WILSON'S POLICY OF "watchful waiting"—or, as his detractors preferred, "deadly drifting"—did not last two months. He had counted on the one-two punch of an embargo and nonrecognition to persuade Huerta to sit out the national elections scheduled for late October 1913. To Wilson's great surprise, however, the general again refused to cooperate in his own destruction. On October 10, Huerta marched a battalion of soldiers into the Mexican Congress, arrested 110 deputies, and dissolved the last formal check on his authority.[54]

Wilson was stunned. But the bigger shock came a day later, when the new British minister to Mexico, Sir Lionel Carden, formally presented his diplomatic credentials to Huerta. Carden was a notorious Yankee-phobe who scorned the Monroe Doctrine (Huntington Wilson had once described him as "always pro anything anti-American"). Carden's timely appearance struck the president like a calculated show of British support for Huerta's latest power grab.[55]

Wilson had long suspected that British oil interests backed Huerta, but the coup-Carden coincidence revealed just how far the rot had spread. "The Huerta regime was practically at the end of its rope," the president fumed, "when Sir Lionel Carden gave it renewed life."[56]

Wilson had intended to take "hands off" Mexico—to avoid becoming "the virtual umpire" of its future. But the president was realizing it was not that simple. Transitions from military dictatorships to self-government were messy, back-and-forth affairs even at the best of times, and they presented limitless opportunities for foreign meddling. In an ideal world, Mexico would be hermetically sealed off while it sorted out its problems, in which case Wilson would "trust the [Mexican] people to protect themselves." But Mexico was not sealed off, and it was increasingly obvious to the president that foreign influences were seeping in. "Watchful waiting" had been appropriate when everyone else was waiting as well. But if foreign powers were dealing themselves in, the United States had to get more involved, too.[57]

By late October, Wilson had decided that Washington "would be derelict in its duty" if it did not "assist in maintaining Mexico's independence." British oil interests and banks had formed an unholy alliance with Whitehall to sustain Huerta, and other European states were undoubtedly trespassing too. The solution was obvious: the United States would cast Huerta down by whatever means necessary.[58]

Smiting Huerta would not be intervention, not exactly—more like *anti*-intervention, Wilson thought, to counter the malign foreign interests holding Mexico back. Lind agreed, later explaining nonchalantly that because Washington wanted only "to afford the Mexican people an opportunity to resume orderly government," even an American invasion that culminated in taking Mexico City would not be "intervention in the offensive sense."[59]

Wilson planned to challenge the European powers directly by sending them an ultimatum: either cooperate with the United States, or "antagonize and thwart us and make our task one of domination and force." The State Department talked him out of the intemperate threat, but Wilson still made a well-publicized speech in Mobile, Alabama, on October 27, 1913, in which he warned ominously of "foreign interests" dominating Latin America, "a condition of affairs always dangerous and apt to become intolerable." Wilson then sent diplomatic notes to

Europe in which he proclaimed it "his immediate duty to require Huerta's retirement."[60]

Privately, Wilson began readying himself to declare war against Mexico. During the day, he plotted out naval blockades and drafted war messages to Congress; at night, he had trouble sleeping, with all manner of "fateful possibilities" chasing each other round and round inside his head. Complaining of the strain, he confessed to a confidante that "no man can tell what will happen while we deal with a desperate brute like the traitor, Huerta. God save us from the worst!" Colonel House, Wilson's national security advisor, recorded that the president knew "his course may possibly bring about a coalition of the European Powers against this Government." No matter: "He seems ready to throw our gauntlet into the arena and declare all hands must be kept off excepting our own."[61]

Pacifists at Heart

Though genuine, Wilson's fears about Mexico were misguided. Huerta's survival owed more to factional politics and his grip on the military than to European influence. Europe's diplomats did support Huerta, and Carden in particular was a close confidant. Carden's wishes notwithstanding, however, the great powers had little interest in fighting a proxy battle against the United States in Mexico. All they asked was that order be restored, one way or another.[62]

Europe responded deferentially to Wilson's diplomatic notes, and the president inched back from the brink. But the self-spun war scare had convinced him that every day Huerta remained in office posed unacceptable risks. Wilson didn't want to intervene militarily, but he couldn't afford to keep waiting.[63]

One middle ground was to aid Carranza and his Constitutionalist rebels, much like General Sheridan had once aided Benito Juárez's rebels against the French. In mid-November 1913, Lind urged that step over military intervention, which the ex-governor worried would not suitably chasten the Mexico City elites he loathed. "To make a dog feel that he really is a cur he must be whipped by another dog and preferably by a cur," Lind explained. "Consequently let this house cleaning be done by home talent."[64]

By early 1914, Wilson was ready to lend "home talent" a hand. Huerta had suspended interest payments on Mexico's debt, prompting the *New York Times* to recall how a similar debt suspension in 1861 had led the French to invade. Nothing so dramatic was in the offing now, but "there is danger of serious complications." Wilson agreed, telling a friend that he was feeling "all but unbearable strain" managing the threat of European intervention alongside numerous other perils. "I am growing cross-eyed with watching people in so many separated quarters at the same time," he complained.[65]

On February 3, 1914, Wilson lifted the arms embargo; the Constitutionalist rebels could henceforth buy as much arms and ammunition from the United States as they could cart across the border. "Mexico," Wilson lectured the British, "had best be left to find her own salvation in a fight to the finish."[66]

Fighting continued, but salvation seemed as remote as ever. Every day brought new dangers and potential threats from Europe. Shortly after the arms embargo was lifted, the most powerful *caudillo* in Carranza's army, Pancho Villa, murdered a British citizen. Europe was scandalized; from Mexico City, British Minister Carden gleefully called for strong measures. London restrained itself, but there was no guarantee that other powers would be as self-disciplined. Germany's foreign minister informed Washington that "if one German citizen should be killed in Mexico ... [Berlin] would be forced to take some drastic action." A senator inquired, "Mr. President, is not our Monroe Doctrine ... in jeopardy now?"[67]

American patience had nearly run out. Behind closed doors, men in braided uniforms began drawing up plans. One of the most spectacular came from the republic's foremost veteran of small wars, Major Smedley Darlington Butler. Butler went undercover into Mexico to plot out the seemingly impossible—a lightning strike on the capital by a thousand American soldiers, who would cover 260 miles in twenty-two hours to decapitate Huerta's regime before it knew what hit it.[68]

If Carranza, Villa, and the other Constitutionalists could not finish the fight, Wilson would finish it for them. All he needed was a pretext.

TAMPICO WAS AN unlikely setting for the casus belli. American warships had been sleepily anchored there for months, and relations with Huerta's forces were friendly. Each day, the bluejackets went ashore to play baseball.[69]

On April 9, 1914, eight American sailors set out in a whaleboat to pick up gasoline. Huerta's soldiers arrested them mid-errand for trespassing. Less than an hour later, the sailors were released with the military governor's apologies, and the incident seemed closed. But the commanding American admiral wanted more than an oral apology; he believed the sailors had been unlawfully removed from a vessel, however small, flying the American colors—the equivalent of American soil.[70]

Spying the pretext he'd been waiting for, Wilson rebuffed Huerta's attempts to de-escalate what was now a crisis. On April 20, the president asked Congress for the authority to forcibly punish Huerta.[71]

As far as the public knew, the plan was to seize Tampico, where American honor had been impugned. Shortly before his address to Congress, however, Wilson had learned that a German freighter, the *Ypiranga*, was headed to Veracruz with almost eighteen thousand cases of guns and ammunition for Huerta in its holds. Plans were hurriedly revised. That night, Wilson was awakened at 2:30 a.m. for a four-way call with Bryan, Daniels, and Wilson's private secretary, Joseph P. Tumulty. Bryan told the president that the *Ypiranga* had just left Havana and would dock at Veracruz in a few hours. If the arms shipment was to be stopped, the United States had to act, *now*. Wilson gave the order: "*Take Vera Cruz at Once.*" He then hung up and went back to sleep.[72]

Silently, Tumulty wondered at the incongruity of the three pajama-clad men, all "pacifists at heart," deciding upon armed intervention. But Wilson slept soundly because he knew—to a moral certainty—that no harm would befall the men and boys he had just ordered ashore. Surely Mexicans would understand that the Americans came not as war makers, but as liberators, ready to deliver Mexico from Huerta and Europe alike.[73]

———

ON APRIL 21, 1914, at 11:20 a.m., the first American soldiers landed in Veracruz under gray skies. Originally, they had intended to seize only the harbor facilities, but a limited incursion proved impossible once snipers began firing at the Americans. Butler and a mix of battle-hardened marines and raw bluejackets occupied the whole city after a day of bloody street fighting. Nineteen Americans were killed and forty-seven wounded; on the Mexican side, the corresponding figures were in the hundreds.[74]

Mexicans, divided for years by civil war, united in hot anger against the *yanqui* occupation. Support for Huerta's regime spiked, and rebel officers briefly contemplated supporting him against the invaders. "Three years of fratricidal war was forgotten in a day," reported the *London Daily Telegraph*; even Carranza heatedly demanded that Wilson withdraw. Across Mexico, mobs looted American consulates, bellowed "Death to the Gringoes!" and smashed doors and stoned windows. In Mexico City, demonstrators pried a statue of George Washington from its pedestal. Anti-American riots also broke out in Chile, Costa Rica, Ecuador, Guatemala, and Uruguay.[75]

On April 23, Wilson appeared in public. One reporter thought he looked "preternaturally pale, almost parchmenty," and "positively shaken." "I cannot get it off my heart," Wilson confessed to his secretary. "It was right. Nothing else was possible, but I cannot forget that it was I who had to order those young men to their deaths." His nerve lost, Wilson forgot why he had intervened. He ignored new and far graver slights to American honor, including when a mob ransacked the American consulate in Monterrey, burnt its flags, and imprisoned its consul. Nor did the president stir when the *Ypiranga*, blocked in Veracruz, offloaded its deadly cargo in Puerto México instead. Instead, Wilson seized an invitation to mediate extended by Argentina, Brazil, and Chile, welcoming it as "an exit" from the "blind alley" into which he had unwittingly plunged.[76]

Wilson could not withdraw from Veracruz, but he had lost interest in going any further. It took the Mexicans themselves to accomplish his objectives. On July 15, 1914, as Constitutionalist armies neared the capital, Huerta resigned and fled the country.[77]

———

LATER THAT SUMMER, the secretary of war pushed the president to reinforce Veracruz against a possible Constitutionalist attack. Wilson waved him off. "We shall have no right at any time to intervene in Mexico," he explained with a serene lack of self-awareness. "There are in my judgment no conceivable circumstances which would make it right for us to direct by force or by threat of force the internal processes of what is a profound revolution."[78]

The World Is on Fire

Over four thousand miles away, on the sun-dappled morning of June 28, 1914, a young Bosnian Serb named Gavrilo Princip stepped out from under a Sarajevo shop awning and fired twice at the automobile in front of him. His first bullet tore Duchess Sophie Chotek's abdominal artery; the second bullet caught her royal consort in his jugular vein. Blood began spilling from the archduke's mouth, and his helmet, plumed with iridescent green ostrich feathers, flashed as it slipped from his head.

Asked about his pain, Franz Ferdinand whispered his last words. "It's nothing."[79]

It was everything. Princip's shots reverberated throughout Europe, triggering a monthlong crisis in which even the greatest of the powers lost agency, each little more than an axis in a doomsday device whose gears had started to turn. Blame was assigned, culpability denied; demands made, demands ignored. Treaties were consulted, then troop mobilization schedules. Finally, without anyone seemingly intending it, orders were issued setting off with mechanical precision one of the greatest tragedies in human history.[80]

Senior American policymakers reacted to the start of the Great War with shock and incredulity, followed closely by a secret undercurrent of relief. For years they had worried Europeans might descend on the hemisphere; suddenly, those Europeans were busy burying each other in the mud of Flanders Fields. Wilson, when reminded that autumn of Germany's ambitions in Latin America, mused that the war in Europe "was perhaps a Godsend to us, for if it had not come we might have been embroiled in war ourselves."[81]

Wilson's relief, however, would be short-lived.

———

WORLD WAR I initially posed three major challenges for the United States. The first was obvious: how to stay neutral. It was a struggle that would take place not only on the high seas but also inside the country's borders, as German saboteurs smuggled time bombs onto Allied ships, set munitions factories and depots alight, and cultured anthrax and glanders bacilli for Europe-bound livestock.[82]

Second, the administration also had to worry about the rest of the hemisphere. "The world is on fire," Wilson fretted, "and there is tinder everywhere." Latin America remained as combustible as ever, and any sparks from Europe's clash had to be stamped out before they ignited the whole region. The danger was especially acute because the Panama Canal was finally open and thus potentially a target. Senior American officials also worried that the Kaiser planned to sprinkle covert submarine bases across the Caribbean to supercharge his war against British commerce.[83]

Finally, the administration faced the greatest challenge of all: how to avoid not this war but the next one. The United States had long benefited from a continental cold war that kept British, German, and French forces frozen in place on the other side of the Atlantic. That rough equilibrium was now being, to use the bloodless term, "recalibrated." Each burst of shrapnel, each zing of a railway gun, each silhouette spasming in hazy, pale green gas was one more violent jolt to a balance of power already spinning wildly out of control. It was impossible to know where the European scale would finally settle, but its resting place would surely not be where it began.[84]

Americans had felt their strategic position was precarious enough when Europe's powers nearly counterbalanced each other. Once they no longer did, things would become markedly more dangerous. A lopsided postwar balance of power could spark a new European race for territories and influence abroad, much as Germany's rise had set off the second Age of Imperialism decades earlier. Furthermore, win or lose, Europe's great powers would find themselves destitute at war's end, struggling with poverty, inflation, and unemployment at home, but armed with millions of veterans accustomed to venturing abroad. The temptation to solve domestic problems with foreign expansion could prove irresistible, and as always, Latin America would beckon as one of the last unclaimed treasure houses of the world.[85]

Germany, as ever, was the main concern. "A victorious Germany," warned the Atlantic Fleet's chief of staff, "means a great army and a great navy flushed with success and animated by the spirit of Bernhardi." The Kaiser would likely not rest "until he has practically attained the dominion of the world." Wilson's ambassador in London agreed. "If Germany should win," he observed in September 1914, "our Monroe Doctrine would at once be shot in two."[86]

If the Kaiser were defeated, however, the situation appeared no less dire. For one thing, Germany might try to recoup its fortunes in the New World; few things are more dangerous than a great power grown desperate. There was also the risk that the British—whose warmth toward their American cousins had been kindled by the rise of the "grizzly terror"—might suddenly turn cold in victory and attempt to return to the hemisphere. "Should the Allies be successful," reported the Atlantic Fleet chief of staff, "it is difficult to see what would restrain England in her ambition[s]."[87]

The United States needed to intervention-proof the region while it still could. "When the European war is over there will be in all probability an intensification of colonial ambitions," observed the *Chicago Daily Tribune*. "If we are wise we shall get a better control over events in Central America and the Caribbean than we have now, and get it while we are comparatively free from interference." Europe was demonstrating in spectacular fashion the follies of great-power competition. If the United States wanted to avert a similar cataclysm closer to home, it had better batten down the hemispheric hatches.[88]

OVERSEEING THE REGION's weatherproofing would be new Secretary of State Robert Lansing. Lansing had entered the State Department as counselor in April 1914, a few months before the guns of August sounded. Once the war began, he became indispensable, and he replaced Bryan as secretary in June 1915.[89]

Some saw the new secretary as bland and dull. He had gray hair, gray eyes, and a well-trimmed gray mustache; he wore gray trousers and gray tweeds. His personality was equally colorless. Lansing was proper without being prim, civil without being chummy. Over a lifetime he had mastered the technicalities of international law; in his free time, he collected coins and tended his garden. One cabinet colleague dismissed him as "meticulous, metallic, and mousy."[90]

Lansing's drabness, however, helped him stand out. He shared his chief's morals but not his fundamentalist fervor, having instead spent his career stripping matters down to their unvarnished essentials. Good and evil, black and white—these were dangerous ways to think about the world at a time when the United States was being pressed to take

Secretary of State Robert Lansing: "Lansing was trained to the law, an authority on international law, a devotee of tradition, technique and precedents."

sides in a great war. True to his appearance and personality, Lansing was happy to inhabit a gray world.[91]

—

LIKE WILSON AND Bryan, Lansing feared a European power using financial influence to dominate a local government "almost as completely as if it had acquired sovereign rights." German ambitions especially disturbed him. So with wartime exigencies in mind, he and Wilson set two conflicting priorities for the administration's regional policy.[92]

First, the United States would improve relations with its neighbors. "Nobody seriously supposes," Wilson explained to one audience, "that the United States needs to fear an invasion of its own territory. What America has to fear, if she has anything to fear, are indirect, roundabout, flank movements upon her regnant position in the Western Hemisphere." If the United States menaced the region, it would open the gates to exactly that sort of flank movement by pushing its neighbors into Europe's arms. But if Washington won back its neighbors' confidence, it would earn "the only sort of safety that America covets." Echoing this logic, Lansing prioritized "alienating the American republics from European influence."[93]

Lansing and Wilson built their public relations strategy around rehabilitating the Monroe Doctrine. Wilson wanted to turn the unilateral mantra into a shared system of collective security, and in late 1914 he typed out plans for a grand peace alliance that would bind the region together through a "mutual guarantee of political independence under republican forms of government." Over the next few years, Washington would push this Pan-American Pact under the banner of regional solidarity.[94]

Lansing realized, however, that this renewed enthusiasm for Pan-Americanism fit uneasily with the administration's second wartime priority: regional stability. Lansing explained in two long memoranda that he was "concerned" by—even "prejudice[d] against"—Washington's recent turn toward interventionism. But careful consideration had persuaded him "that the logic of the situation is irresistible." If the United States wanted to uphold the Monroe Doctrine, "the surest if not the only means" was establishing "stable and honest government[s]" across the region. Doing so required taking "control of the public revenues," flushing out "foreign financiers," and helping local governments build up "reliable and efficient military force[s]."[95]

If a conflict ever arose between the administration's two priorities of neighborliness and stability, Lansing had few illusions about which should win out. He believed that the sovereignty of his country's neighbors was only "an incident, not an end," a happy by-product of the Monroe Doctrine that might theoretically have to give way to the Doctrine's actual objectives. "The primacy of one nation," Lansing acknowledged, "is out of harmony with the principle of the equality of nations which underlies Pan-Americanism, however just or altruistic the primate may be."[96]

Lansing did not doubt that the United States was a just and altruistic primate whose policies had helped the rest of the region. But he refused to justify his policy on those grounds. "The argument based on humanitarian purpose does not appeal to me," he confessed to Wilson. "Too many international crimes have been committed in the name of Humanity."[97]

Wilson reviewed Lansing's analysis carefully. Lansing had glossed over the precedents, but he was effectively recommending the Roosevelt Corollary and dollar diplomacy in all but name. If that bothered Wilson, he gave no sign. "The argument of this paper seems to me unanswerable," the president responded.[98]

———

SOMETIMES, WASHINGTON WOULD be able to paper over the conflict between its two goals of neighborliness and stability. In Nicaragua, for example, the State Department rescued Bryan's canal treaty from legislative purgatory by eliminating its Platt Amendment–like provisions. Senators still had misgivings about the propriety of signing a treaty with a government that was, as now-Senator Elihu Root put it, "maintained in office by the presence of United States marines." But in February 1916, rumors of a competing bid by Germany caused the Senate to swallow its doubts, and the United States soon cornered the market on Central American canal routes.[99]

Other times, the conflict between the administration's priorities would be a little more obvious, as in the Danish West Indies. The United States had signed treaties to purchase the strategically positioned islands twice before, but to no avail: once, under Seward, the Senate had refused to consent; then, under Roosevelt, it was the Danish Parliament's turn to object. Even though the United States no longer needed the islands for naval bases, Lansing and Wilson wanted to keep them from Germany. Lansing bluntly informed the Danish minister that Washington would seize the islands if control of them threatened to pass to "one of the great powers of Europe." Shocked and embarrassed, Denmark agreed to sell. Wilson was pleased. "I am glad the Danish Minister gave you an opportunity to be so frank with him," he told Lansing brightly. "I hope he realizes how entirely friendly to Denmark the frankness was." On March 31, 1917, the United States annexed the newly rechristened U.S. Virgin Islands. It would be the republic's last major territorial acquisition in the Western Hemisphere, and, British-held Jamaica aside, it buttoned up American control of the Greater Antilles and the major sea-lanes approaching the Panama Canal.[100]

Least of the Evils in Sight

Lansing and Wilson would take their wartime policy to its extreme in Haiti and the Dominican Republic. Lansing saw German agents "plotting and intriguing" everywhere, and he had no doubt that the Kaiser planned to exploit those two nations' disorder in particular, in the hope of expanding Germany's influence, securing submarine bases, and perhaps even paving the way for intervention. But the United States would sooner extinguish those nations' independence entirely than permit them to fall under Germany's sway.[101]

Haiti had never been a byword for peaceful democratic transitions, but since 1889 most of its presidents had at least come respectably close to serving out their full seven-year terms. Starting in 1911, however, the Haitian presidency became an actuary's worst nightmare. Over the next five years, Port-au-Prince would burn through seven different presidents in a blur of revolutions and assassinations.[102]

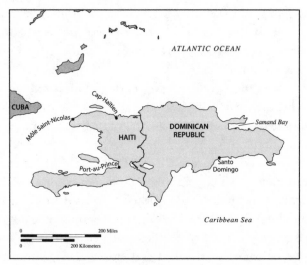

Haiti and Dominican Republic

Simultaneously, Haiti was losing its grip on its once-stable finances. By 1915, Haiti's foreign debt had bulged to $21.5 million, with 80 percent of government revenues going to service it every year. Such extreme financial dependency was worrying even if Port-au-Prince never missed a payment: with official funds tied up, Haitian leaders hungered for new sources of foreign funding, no matter how usurious or politically compromising.[103]

Officials in Washington found Haiti's growing political and financial disorder intolerable given long-standing European influences in the country. France was Haiti's chief market abroad, as well as a cultural role model for its elite. Meanwhile, German businessmen owned many of the nation's public utilities, carried most of its trade, and were notorious for financing Haiti's many revolutions.[104]

At first, the Wilson administration worried primarily about the foreign threat to Môle Saint-Nicolas, a strategic harbor perched opposite the Windward Passage from Guantánamo Bay. In June 1913, Bryan urged Wilson to take the Môle "out of the market so that no other nation will attempt to secure a foothold there." Wilson agreed, and the administration made the incumbent Haitian regime promise to never alienate the harbor to a foreign power.[105]

Such a promise, however, was only as good as the government that gave it. A revolution wiped both away in early 1914, and the State Department was left scurrying to secure another pledge of non-alienation from the new president. The Department went through the rigmarole again after another successful revolution in late autumn; then again in February 1915. Roosevelt had once compared negotiating with Colombia to nailing currant jelly to a wall; for Wilson, negotiating with Haiti entailed the additional frustration of the wall itself falling down every few months.[106]

Concerns about the Môle reinforced growing concerns about Haiti's independence more broadly. Just before World War I began, France and Germany had each proposed patching up Haiti's finances through joint customs receiverships with Washington. Wilson rejected the proposals out of hand, upbraiding Berlin's ambassador for contemplating such "a very serious departure" from the Monroe Doctrine. Like the Dominican Republic in 1905, though, Haiti had suddenly surfaced as a target of foreign interest.[107]

Wilson decided Haiti needed his help. Suitably alarmed at being made into the president's next project, Haitians countered the administration's proposed customs receivership by offering economic concessions instead. Bryan was indignant at the attempt to buy Washington off, and he informed Port-au-Prince that "while we desire to encourage in every proper way American investments in Haiti, we believe that this can be better done by contributing to stability and order." That, of course, was exactly what Haitians had been afraid of.[108]

Once it became clear that Haitians would not accept a customs receivership voluntarily, Bryan and Wilson began considering forcible measures. In early January 1915, Bryan judged the prospects for stability slim unless Washington supervised an election. Before Bryan could get his plan going, however, Haiti's revolving door of governments whirled once more, bringing a new regime—led by upstart Vilbrun Guillaume Sam—into power.[109]

By now, Haiti's instability was taxing not only Washington's patience, but also Wall Street's. Roger L. Farnham of National City Bank (modern-day Citibank) began withholding funds due Port-au-Prince in the hopes of forcing the American intervention that he believed was the only answer to Haiti's problems. Farnham also warned the administration of an imminent European threat, including a fantastical supposed plot by France and Germany—then at war with each other—to seize joint control of the Môle.[110]

Wilson and Bryan had grown so concerned that they bought Farnham's broader story without a second thought. "This whole matter has a most sinister appearance," Wilson told Bryan. "The more we go into it the more unpleasant and unpropitious it looks." Sounding like the dollar diplomats he despised, the president concluded that "American interests should stay in and that we should sustain and assist them in every legitimate way." Time was running short, and the European threat had put him on edge. "The sooner we get our plans going in Haiti for a stable arrangement that will preclude anxieties such as we have recently felt the better," he remarked.[111]

The State Department dispatched a special envoy to offer President Sam a protectorate. By its terms, Sam would take the American Legation's advice in exchange for Washington employing any force necessary to prevent insurrections.[112]

Sam declined the offer. For better or worse, he would play by his own rules.[113]

—

ON JULY 28, 1915, Sam's dismemberment outside the French Legation forced the issue. U.S. Navy Rear Admiral William B. Caperton landed his forces at twilight in Port-au-Prince and cabled for reinforcements the next morning.[114]

For months, the administration had been preparing to forcibly stabilize Haiti. But now, with its capital already occupied, Wilson and his new secretary of the state were suddenly stricken with doubt. Lansing called the situation "distressing and very perplexing. I am not at all sure what we ought to do." Wilson responded that "my own judgment is as much perplexed as yours." He did not want to follow Roosevelt's example in Panama or the Dominican Republic, but he also felt compelled "to bring some order out of the chaos."[115]

For all the administration's hand-wringing, however, the strategic logic remained as inescapable as ever. Lansing explained to the Haitian minister in a long conversation how the United States had had no choice; if it had not landed marines, "in all probability some other nation would have felt called upon to do so." On August 4, Wilson wearily accepted the inevitable: "I suppose there is nothing for it but to take the bull by the horns and restore order."[116]

Admiral Caperton was instructed to let the Haitian Congress elect a new president but told that Washington "prefer[red]" the candidacy of the pliable Senate president, Philippe Sudré Dartiguenave. One cabinet member needled Navy Secretary Daniels ("Josephus the First, King of Haiti!") by salaaming and inquiring innocently: "Will the candidate you and Lansing picked out manage to squeeze in?"[117]

On August 12, the administration found out. Caperton had dotted the two-block radius around the Haitian Congress with sandbags, field guns, and a regiment of American bluejackets. Everyone admitted into the chamber that day was frisked, though the admiral permitted congressmen to keep their pistols on "the understanding that they would be free to shoot themselves while in session, but not others." Marines stood at parade rest in the aisles while the congressmen voted. Major Butler, displaying deft use of the passive voice, summarized the result: "I won't say we put [Dartiguenave] in. The State Department might object. Anyway, he was put in."[118]

Dartiguenave installed, Lansing next drew up a treaty granting Washington what he described as "extensive control" over Haiti, with the objective of preventing "foreign intervention in the future based on political and financial disorders." Borrowing heavily from the Platt Amendment, the treaty gave Washington the unfettered right to intervene in Haitian affairs and all-but-complete control of its fiscal system; it also mandated an American-officered constabulary.[119]

Lansing did not like the way things were turning out. "I confess that this method of negotiation, with our marines policing the Haytien capital, is high handed," he fretted to Wilson. "It does not meet my sense of a nation's sovereign rights and is more or less an exercise of force." But, he shrugged, "from a practical standpoint ... it is the only thing to do if we intend to cure the anarchy and disorder which prevails in that Republic."[120]

Wilson, too, suffered pangs of doubt. "I do not like the argument that the end justifies the means," he remarked uneasily. Still, "we must insist." Haiti would experience "the most sordid chaos" if the United States did not "amicably take charge," even through means that were "nothing less than high-handed."[121]

"High-handed" was putting it mildly. Dartiguenave balked at the treaty, but he was in no position to argue after American forces declared martial law in Port-au-Prince and started occupying other cities. Legend has it that Dartiguenave finally relented after Butler—who else?—climbed up through a palace window and accosted the beleaguered Haitian president in the bathroom where he had been hiding. With Butler glowering over him, Dartiguenave was forced to sign the treaty there and then, and Haiti was added to Washington's growing portfolio of nations under management.[122]

SOON IT WAS the Dominican Republic's turn. General José Bordas Valdez had become provisional president in mid-April 1913, but his political maneuvering and attempts to hold onto power spawned new rebellions. The Wilson administration initially supported Bordas, encouraging rebels to register their opposition through ballots rather than bullets. From the sidelines, the American minister unhelpfully chimed in that Dominicans could find "a real substitute for the excitement of revolutions" in baseball, demonstrating a profound misunderstanding of revolutions, baseball, or both.[123]

By summer 1914, Bordas had lost control of the country. Wilson decided to reset Dominican politics through the so-called "Wilson Plan," which demanded an immediate cease-fire, Bordas's resignation, and American-supervised elections. Washington would then back the newly elected president against future rebellions. The State Department forced Bordas out and implemented the Plan, and in early December 1914, General Juan Isidro Jimenes became president.[124]

Jimenes found himself in an impossible position. Wilson insisted that the new president dissolve the Dominican army, create an American-led constabulary, and let Americans control all public expenditures, public works, and internal revenues. For Washington, anything less would condemn the island to continued instability. "We have Constitutional Government and Constitutional reforms jacked up here and resting upon props," the American minister had advised earlier that year. "We should build our foundation at once." Only once that foundation was built, reasoned one receivership official, could "our Dominican friends ... be safely left to play the game of self-government to their heart's delight." Dominicans, however, did not look kindly on this condescending attitude, and they opposed the reforms vehemently.[125]

Jimenes tried to meet the State Department halfway, but he only destroyed his legitimacy at home while failing to budge Washington. The Department continued to demand that Jimenes accept its proposed reforms while throttling his government's access to funds from the customs receivership, which constituted roughly 90 percent of the government's revenues.[126]

The Dominican political situation finally gave way in April 1916. The minister of war, a powerful *caudillo* named Desiderio Arias Álvarez, seized the capital while Jimenes was away. The State Department had long seen Arias as the worst of the bomb throwers in Dominican politics, not least because of his pro-German sympathies. In keeping with the Wilson Plan's pledge, Washington landed 150 marines to support Jimenes.[127]

Arias was unfazed. Smiling, he taunted the marine captain who came to demand his surrender: "Has the United States sent people down here to teach us how to behave?"[128]

In fact, that was exactly what Wilson proposed to do. But his plan hit a snag when President Jimenes decided enough was enough and resigned instead.[129]

Washington, however, would not be stopped by anything so pedestrian as the resignation of the president it had landed forces to support. The Dominican Republic needed to be stabilized, Dominicans were not up to the job, and so the United States would do what needed to be done. Caperton was summoned from Haiti to defend the no-longer-existent Dominican government, and the admiral chased Arias out of the capital. By mid-July, American forces had completely routed Arias's forces and occupied most of the nation's key cities.[130]

Casting a wary eye at Haiti's fate next door, the Dominican Congress elected another provisional president. But attempts to find a middle ground remained fruitless. Washington refused to dilute its absolutist demands and attempted to starve the Dominican government into reform, this time by cutting off both its internal and external revenues.[131]

The Dominican Republic plunged into economic crisis, but Dominicans still refused to bend. Even in Haiti, Washington had found willing collaborators like Dartiguenave. But Dominican leaders preferred flirting with complete catastrophe over cooperating with the *yanquis*. "I have never seen such hatred displayed by one people for another as I notice and feel here," Caperton reported. "We positively have not a friend in the land."[132]

What choice did Wilson have? The Dominican Republic was melting down at a time when its stability seemed more crucial than ever. The final straw came with the scheduling of national elections that threatened to bring the pro-German Arias to power. With "the deepest reluctance," Wilson authorized a full-scale military occupation as "the least of the evils in sight."[133]

On November 29, 1916, a U.S. Navy captain declared martial law. "This military occupation," he swore, "is undertaken with no immediate or ulterior object of destroying the sovereignty of the Republic of Santo Domingo." It was an ironic epitaph for the end of another nation's independent existence.[134]

We Must Not Intervene

Even as it helped drive Haiti and the Dominican Republic's occupations, World War I also shaped American policy toward the Mexican Revolution. In July 1915, Wilson complained that "the Mexican situation grows ominously worse and more threatening day by day," and that it sometimes concerned him more "than even our correspondence with Germany." Lansing agreed, and in his first four months as secretary he dedicated as much time to Mexico—25 percent—as he did to Germany. In truth, the two problems were intimately connected. "The German Government desires to keep Mexico in a state of ferment and anarchy," Lansing explained, "so that the United States will have ... [to] intervene, and have its attention concentrated on Mexico" rather than Europe. Lansing and Wilson therefore agreed on one thing—"that no matter what happens, we must not intervene in Mexican affairs."[135]

Mexico's continuing disorder made it difficult to keep that pledge. General Huerta's exile in July 1914 had not ended the Mexican Revolution. Instead, the prevailing Constitutionalists had fallen out among themselves in a war of the winners. Small, vicious factional fights blazed across the country, but the defining clash occurred in central Mexico between the armies of First Chief Carranza and his former lieutenant, Pancho Villa.[136]

At first, Villa appeared unstoppable. But Carranza's retreat east coincided with Wilson's evacuation of Veracruz in November. Carranza reclaimed the abandoned seaport along with a massive arms cache left behind, and then used both to strike back at Villa.[137]

Seeking to exploit this ongoing fighting to trap the United States in another intervention, German agents approached General Huerta in exile and agreed to help the ex-dictator return to power. Once the counterrevolution succeeded, Huerta promised to repay Germany by going to war with the United States. Huerta likely never intended to keep up his end of the bargain—he had broken less suicidal pacts before—but German officials hoped that Huerta's mere return to Mexico would goad Wilson into military action once again.[138]

American intelligence agents, however, were one step ahead. For months, they monitored the unfolding conspiracy: the hushed meetings, the transfers of small fortunes, the purchase of guns and ammunition. In late June 1915, when Huerta suddenly bolted for the border, federal agents were waiting for him. He was arrested and detained.[139]

Germany, however, had already moved on. Arms originally intended for Huerta were now secreted in coffins and oil tankers for Villa instead. Other generals, revolutionary and reactionary, also benefited from the Kaiser's largesse. Laying chips on red, white, and everything in between felt like a wager the Wilhelmstrasse could not lose.[140]

Germany's gambits prompted Wilson to go all in. For months the administration had vacillated between backing the relatively pro-American Villa and finding a compromise leader. Few officials ever warmed to the obvious third option, Carranza, who remained stubbornly resistant to American charms even as he crushed Villa's army. But in October 1915, the administration suddenly extended Carranza de facto recognition. Following his victories over Villa, he had become the best hope for a stable—if hypernationalistic—Mexico. "Germany does not wish to have any one faction dominant in Mexico; therefore, we must recognize one faction as dominant," Lansing explained in a private memorandum. "Germany desires to keep up the turmoil in Mexico until the United States is forced to intervene; therefore, we must not intervene."[141]

Following that advice would prove unexpectedly difficult, however. For two decades the United States had been sowing the seeds of interventionism in the region, and those seeds were about to start bearing their bitter fruit.

———

WILSON EMPHATICALLY DID not want to intervene in Mexico again. "If the Mexicans want to raise hell, let them raise hell," he muttered in December 1915. "We have got nothing to do with it. It is their government, it is their hell."[142]

On March 9, 1916, however, Mexico's hell spilled over onto American soil. That night, Villa and nearly five hundred horsemen thundered across the border and sacked the tiny town of Columbus, New Mexico. It was such a brazen attack that Wilson felt he had little choice but to immediately dispatch a "Punitive Expedition" to pursue Villa's band into Mexico and bring the bandit-general to justice. At its height, the Punitive Expedition involved ten thousand American soldiers operating hundreds of miles inside Mexico. Each step they took risked open war with Carranza's increasingly hostile forces.[143]

German intelligence watched the Punitive Expedition's progress with ill-concealed glee. Berlin had not organized the attack on Columbus, but it had armed Villa and egged him on. The Wilhelmstrasse prayed the Punitive Expedition would spark a war between the neighbors, and for a while, Germany seemed likely to get its wish. Tensions between the Expedition and Carranza's forces exploded in a skirmish on June 21 near the town of Carrizal. Thirteen Americans were killed and twenty-three captured in a humiliating defeat. For several days, a full-scale American invasion seemed unavoidable. Wilson despaired while drafting another war message. "The break seems to have come in Mexico," he told an advisor. "I am infinitely sad about it."[144]

Germany was to be disappointed, however. Carranza released the American prisoners and worked with Wilson to sidetrack the crisis onto diplomatic rails where it could be safely neutralized. After winning reelection in November, and with Germany foremost in mind, Wilson ordered the Expedition withdrawn.[145]

From one perspective, Wilson could not be seriously faulted for his second major intervention in Mexico. Carranza was either unable or unwilling to control the borderlands, and Wilson could not let Villa's depredations on American soil go unanswered.[146]

From another perspective, however, the Punitive Expedition was the natural consequence of years of American interventionism. Villa did not attack Columbus out of lifelong hatred for the United States. In fact, his relatively pro-American views had once made him an

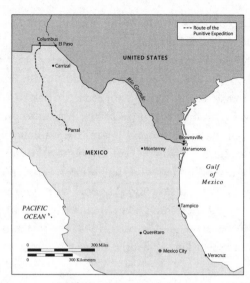

The Punitive Expedition

administration favorite. Villa, however, reversed course in early 1916 for two reasons: first, he was angry at Wilson's decision to recognize Carranza; and second, he correctly calculated that his raid would provoke an American invasion, which would drive a wedge between Washington and Carranza while simultaneously restoring Villa's fading reputation. Each rationale stemmed from earlier American meddling, which had set Villa's expectations for American support unrealistically high while priming Mexicans for his reinvention as an anti-American folk hero.[147]

EVEN THOUGH THE Punitive Expedition had not sparked the war Germany wanted, it had still pushed Mexico into Berlin's open arms. Carranza had long mistrusted Germany because it had supported his domestic foes. But the old "enemy of my enemy" adage had irresistible force, and in the wake of the Punitive Expedition, Carranza needed a powerful foreign friend to counterbalance the threat of a full-scale American invasion. Over 1916, he secretly began cooperating with Berlin, and by year's end, Carranza was dangling the possibility of building a German submarine base in Mexico.[148]

Berlin did not take the bait—not yet. German officials worried that violating the Monroe Doctrine so brazenly would aggravate Washington unnecessarily. Such concerns, however, became moot in January 1917 when the German High Command decided to resume unrestricted submarine warfare. It was a red line for Wilson, and German military planners understood that by crossing it they had very likely ensured American entry into World War I. The gamble was that their U-boats would defeat the Allies before the United States could save them.[149]

Following the decision, Berlin's appetite for risk in Mexico soared. In mid-January, German Foreign Secretary Arthur Zimmermann sent a telegram to Carranza that proposed a military alliance between Germany and Mexico (and possibly Japan). Even more audaciously, the telegram stated that it was "understood that Mexico is to reconquer the lost territory in New Mexico, Texas, and Arizona" with the Kaiser's financial support. Germany did not think that Mexico could actually defeat the United States; instead, the goal once again was to instigate war between the two neighbors in order to absorb American forces and distract the United States.[150]

The Zimmermann Telegram seemed miraculous to the British intelligence agents who intercepted and deciphered it. By that point, Germany's unrestricted submarine warfare had led Washington to—but not quite over—the brink of war. Frustrated, the British ambassador in Washington reported that the United States's reluctance to enter the war approximated "a soda water bottle with the wires cut but the cork unexploded." Zimmermann's telegram was just what London needed to pry the cork loose and bring Americans rushing into the war.[151]

On February 24, 1917, British intelligence shared the telegram with the administration, who furiously passed it on to the press. The public was initially incredulous; surely Germany was not seriously proposing to carve up the American southwest? But after Berlin confirmed the message's authenticity, the reaction turned to rage. Historians debate just how much the telegram contributed to the final decision for war, but at minimum it accelerated the process by weeks at a moment when every day counted. On April 6, the United States declared war on Germany.[152]

Often forgotten is what the Zimmermann Telegram revealed about the republic's regional policies. Since Seward, the United States had centered its grand strategy on the assumption that strong, stable neighbors were the best bulwark against Europe's great powers because they would naturally resist any expansion of foreign influence. But American efforts to stabilize and strengthen its periphery had led the region to hate and fear the Northern Colossus, so much so that some of its neighbors considered siding with its enemies against it—the exact "indirect, round-about, flank movement" that Wilson had feared. Germany had pulled the trigger on an anti-American alliance, but it was Washington who had loaded the gun and cocked it.

Unhindered, Unthreatened, and Unafraid

On January 22, 1917, when it still seemed possible for the United States to remain neutral, Wilson gave his famous "peace without victory" speech. He promised a postwar world freed from distinctions "between big nations and small." "I am proposing," he explained, "that the nations should with one accord adopt the doctrine of President Monroe as the doctrine of the world: that no nation should seek to extend its polity over any other nation or people, but that every people should be left free to determine its own polity, its own way of development, unhindered, unthreatened, unafraid, the little along with the great and powerful."[153]

Eloquent—and genuinely felt—though Wilson's words were, they did not reflect the lived experiences of those "little nations" who were enduring the doctrine of President Monroe firsthand. On the eve of its entry into World War I, the United States was intervening across the hemisphere as never before. In Cuba, another stolen election had led to another uprising partly intended to trigger another American intervention. After telling his cabinet "we cannot afford to let Cuba be involved by G[erman] plots," Wilson sent hundreds of marines to support the Cuban regime; he then ordered portions of eastern Cuba occupied. Washington encountered turbulence in Haiti as well when a rebellion broke out against the new American occupation. Major Butler earned his second Medal of Honor bloodily suppressing the uprising, and then earned further notoriety when he forcibly dissolved the national legislature after it refused to revise the Haitian constitution as Washington wanted. Meanwhile, Washington tried vainly to stamp out a third insurgency next door in the occupied Dominican Republic.[154]

On the isthmus, the situation was not much better. In Panama, Washington moved troops into Colón and Panama City after an electoral crisis in 1918; it then supervised the subsequent election, took over Panama's police force, installed an American "fiscal agent" to run Panama's finances, and forcibly occupied parts of Chiriquí Province. In Nicaragua, the United States remained torn between its conflicting desires to elect good men and to keep the minority Conservative regime in power. In February 1916, the American chargé d'affaires referred unabashedly to the ruling "oligarchical ring" who had "been strangling Nicaragua for these four years past and who, without outside help, can only be overthrown by revolution." But when the opposition party nominated a known Zelayista for the upcoming presidential election, Washington saw no choice but to unite the "oligarchical ring" behind its chosen candidate and help rig the subsequent election.[155]

American leaders felt trapped in a cycle of intervention, and the more they flailed, the more ensnared they became. Wilson wanted Americans to serve the world as they had served their neighbors, but as the wife of an American diplomat in Mexico observed dryly, "we can but express the pious hope that with the help of God no foreign nation will ever have a chance to serve us to the same extent."[156]

CHAPTER 11

ALL THE NUISANCE OF EMPIRE

Two decades earlier, in 1898, the United States had adopted a new security strategy: stabilizing its neighbors through internal reforms. Officials in Washington had wanted to achieve that stability with as little interference as possible, and they had especially hoped to avoid using armed force.

Over time, however, that new strategy had led the country up a ladder of interventionism. Beginning with the Platt Amendment, Washington had imposed debt limits, forbidden its neighbors from negotiating away their independence, and promised to protect them against foreign intervention and catastrophic failures of governance. Politically, however, these new policies encouraged states to engage in risky behavior abroad and maladministration at home. In an effort to realign skewed incentives, the Roosevelt administration had threatened to forcibly correct "chronic wrongdoing," but that corollary generated its own perverse incentives. Economically, meanwhile, debt limits were not resolving the underlying problems in the region's balance sheets. Once again, the Roosevelt administration had adopted a new and more invasive approach: collecting its neighbors' customs revenues for them. But as officials soon realized, customs receiverships could not control what happened to a nation's funds after they entered the national treasury.

Seeking to resolve these issues, the Taft administration had begun micromanaging its neighbors' internal affairs. But the administration's "benevolent supervision" had created new problems, including moral hazards and nationalistic backlashes that led to governments that were so incompetent, so unpopular, or so anti-American that Washington concluded they needed to be put down. Once those regimes had been

273

toppled, the United States had to build new, stable governments from scratch—a project that became increasingly impossible as local resentment grew. Eventually, in the most extreme cases, it seemed as if the United States could stabilize its neighbors only by governing them outright.[1]

This account oversimplifies the messy complexities of this two-decade period of American policy. Oftentimes, the United States would jump up to the middle of the interventionist ladder or have its feet on multiple rungs simultaneously. But it nevertheless captures in broad strokes the American experience in Latin America from 1898 to the end of Wilson's tenure. Each administration believed it had found the silver bullet for stabilization. But when each metaphorical bullet failed to hit home, Washington turned to higher calibers and faster rates of fire. By the end, the United States had crossed the line from metaphor to reality as it unsuccessfully attempted to impose stability through barrages fired by bluejackets and leathernecks.

What had gone wrong?

The Only Possible Way for a Foreign People to Be Happy

First, there was poor execution. Americans didn't know what they were getting into, and they made a terrible mess of things once they got there.

Officials and administrations were ignorant. Each of the United States's neighbors had intricate political ecosystems. Bureaucrats in Washington wanted to "fix" those systems but rarely understood what made them tick, much less how to resolve their dysfunctions.[2]

Compounding that ignorance were several blinders—especially racial, cultural, and religious prejudices—that obscured the causes of instability. For example, when Cuba's political system collapsed in 1906, Americans could have interpreted the crisis as a warning about the perverse incentives the Platt Amendment had created. Instead, Taft spoke for many when he concluded disgustedly that "the whole thing demonstrates the utter unfitness of these people for self-gov't." Such judgments often became self-fulfilling: disorder reaffirmed underlying prejudices, which led to wrongheaded "solutions" that generated more disorder.[3]

Officials in Washington also paired their blinders with rose-colored glasses. High on the can-do spirits of Progressivism and American exceptionalism, they overestimated their capabilities while grossly underestimating the problems confronting them. Both at home and abroad, Progressives sought simple solutions to complex problems, not realizing how often their quick fixes only made things worse.[4]

Closely related was the issue of domestic imaging. Contrary to some later accounts, the United States did not intervene in order to "Americanize" its neighbors. But once officials in Washington found themselves in control of their neighbors' affairs, they naturally fell back on their domestic experiences in deciding what to do next. One critic observed sarcastically how well-intentioned bureaucrats in the State, Navy, and War departments believed their country represented "the final word in human perfection." Given that assumption, it was obvious to these bureaucrats that "the only possible way for a foreign people to be happy is to be standardized into the mold already created in the United States." Sure enough, during this period every American occupation shared certain common elements, including a focus on education, sanitation, law enforcement, public works, judicial reforms, and electoral improvements. Not coincidentally, these were also the priorities of Progressive reformers at home. But Americans could not always export their domestic experiences successfully, and much of Washington's social engineering foundered on the shoals of different cultures, societies, and institutions. In trying to replicate its image abroad, the United States was often trying to pound a square peg into a round hole.[5]

Other cognitive biases clouded the picture further. Officials were operating on short time frames with small sample sizes, and it was easy for them to focus on initial successes while missing countervailing failures and longer-term consequences. Roosevelt, for example, famously contemplated involvement in the Dominican Republic with the enthusiasm of "a gorged boa constrictor" looking "to swallow a porcupine wrong-end-to." But he overcame his doubts and decided after a few years of growing revenues and political stability that the island's customs receivership should become a model for other troubled neighbors. In hindsight, however, the evidence suggests a case of post hoc, ergo propter hoc: the Dominican Republic owed its stability to President Ramón Cáceres's adroit leadership, not the receivership. Once Cáceres was assassinated, the Republic fell to pieces—but by that point, it was too late; the United States had already begun exporting the flawed Dominican model to the rest of the region.[6]

Officials in Washington were also making policy based on slanted and incomplete information. Most of what they knew about Latin America came from the region's political and economic elites. But those elites had different interests than their countrymen and were misleading sources at best. For example, Washington often expected its interventions to be welcomed, and in a narrow sense they were—but only by the local leaders those interventions propped up, and not by the rest of their nations. Likewise, American officials often bought into local leaders' inflated threat assessments and thus considered interventions more urgent and necessary than they really were.[7]

Similar misinformation problems arose with business interests. For example, National City Bank's representative repeatedly informed officials in Washington that European powers were conspiring to seize a strategic harbor in Haiti. That was untrue, but the Bank wanted to push the Wilson administration into occupying the country because it believed American control would lead to greater profits.[8]

Finally, Washington also made its mission immeasurably harder through its cautious, piecemeal approach. Early interventions were too minimal to be effective, but they nevertheless stirred up nationalism and pushback, upping the ante for future interventions. So while at the outset the United States could convince its neighbors to enact reforms with relative ease, later on those same reforms had to be negotiated and finally compelled. By the 1910s, Washington could no longer count on even the grudging acquiescence—much less the support—of the nations it was trying to stabilize. Since its stabilization tools often required at least a modicum of cooperation, that meant the United States had to intervene more and more invasively just to implement the same reforms as before—reforms that were considered inadequate by that point anyway. Washington thus ended up shooting at a rising target from a falling platform. Closing the gap often required coercion and direct occupation.[9]

Combined together, all these shortcomings blinded Americans to an obvious truth: stabilizing failed or failing states was a monumental task without any easy fixes. In 1900, officials had naively believed that the United States could stabilize the region quickly and efficiently by applying American power decisively in a few narrow areas. Two decades later, it was becoming obvious that if forcible stabilization were even possible, it required total overhauls of the afflicted societies. Roosevelt had imagined his country as the policeman of the Western Hemisphere, but his successors would belatedly realize that the United States needed to act as lawgiver, judge, financier, social worker, and health inspector too.

The Odor of Imperialism

Even if American officials had gone in with clear eyes, however, they still would have failed to stabilize the region because their interventionist strategy was likely doomed from the start.

First, efforts to forcibly stabilize the region paradoxically encouraged instability by giving local opposition leaders an easy way to undermine ruling regimes. Americans got a taste of this dynamic in Cuba in 1906, when the Liberals rebelled with an eye toward provoking an American intervention that would sweep away the ruling Moderate regime. Similar dynamics played out in Cuba in 1912 and 1917, as well as in Panama in 1908 and Mexico in 1916. Occasionally, the instigators were not local politicians but outsiders. For example, National City Bank helped destabilize Haiti in 1915 to encourage an American intervention; likewise, foreigners caused trouble during Cuba's second occupation in an unsuccessful bid for annexation.[10]

Officials in Washington also never understood that external intervention, almost by its very nature, undermines a country's long-term stability. When a country is unstable, that usually reflects weak political institutionalization—a failure to create those norms, rules, and practices that can reliably produce political order, economic growth, and social justice in the long run. For political institutions to be durable, however, they must enjoy support among the governed, which in turn requires a sense of local ownership and buy-in. It is thus inherently difficult for outsiders to impose the kinds of institutions needed for long-term stability.[11]

Still worse, interventions usually corrode and destroy what few stabilizing institutions a country has. Every time the United States squeezed itself into the internal affairs of a neighbor, it displaced some local authority. In the short term, that was fine; the United States could fill the resulting vacuum with its own power. But since Americans were not looking to stay for the long haul, they ended up smashing their neighbors' existing institutions while crowding out opportunities to build new ones.[12]

Furthermore, even when the United States was not directly displacing local institutions, it was warping existing ones through its mere proximity. Ordinarily, a country's leaders must work with other leaders and factions to bridge gaps, find compromise, and build sustainable coalitions—the day-to-day work that provides the grist for long-term political development. Even dictators cannot rule alone, and politicians everywhere must respond to the needs of at least some domestic constituencies. Once the United States involved itself in the internal affairs of Latin American states, however, it offered local elites an alternative base of power. Rather than building support domestically, local elites could seek the support of Washington; rather than responding to their citizens' demands, they could cater to the State Department's whims. So from Haiti to Honduras, local leaders frequently volunteered to compromise their nations' sovereignties, in ways big and small, in exchange for American support. Such Faustian bargains could extend these regimes' leases on life in the short term, but in the long run, they eroded the capacity for self-governance even further.[13]

These problems worsened over time as Washington shifted from setting limits within which its neighbors could govern to governing directly in their stead. That was no way to spur organic political development, which requires responsibility, participation, and the opportunity to make and learn from mistakes. Left with smaller and smaller slices of sovereignty to manage, local elites were effectively told they were incapable of governing well. It was not a message calculated to inspire real statesmanship.[14]

Finally, Americans also faced an inherent mismatch between their maximalist objectives and their preferred minimalist toolkit. For stability

U.S. Marines on Patrol in Haiti: "In case of intervention, as in Haiti or Nicaragua, political power is divorced from all organic connection with the politics, the government, and the culture against which it is exercised."

to stick, Washington needed to remake its neighbors' governments from top to bottom. But it could not rely on local elites to help implement reforms that, almost by definition, impinged on elite interests. Nor could Washington force elites to cooperate through external pressure, because it was too easy for elites to evade or subvert desired reforms. So although the United States wanted to avoid governing these societies directly, direct governance—including armed occupation—was often the only path to the social overhauls that Washington really wanted.[15]

One example of this dynamic was the republic's attitude toward revolutions. In effect, the United States wanted to ban revolutions in Latin America. But in many places, revolutions were the traditional—and often the only—way of ousting incumbent regimes. So to succeed, Americans needed to find some plausible substitute.

One approach, favored by Roosevelt and Taft, was to support local strongmen who could stabilize their countries in the mold of Mexico's Porfirio Díaz. But Díaz's fate and the decade-long chaos of the subsequent Mexican Revolution demonstrated the shortcomings of this approach; as President John F. Kennedy would later observe, "those who make peaceful revolution impossible will make violent revolution inevitable." If anything, American support for strongmen only encouraged long-run instability, as it made autocrats less popular and less accountable. That led to a vicious cycle. The more Washington supported a strongman's regime, the more unpopular the regime became; the more unpopular the regime became, the more Washington needed to support it. Often, these ever-deepening commitments would culminate in the United States sending its citizens to fight and die on behalf of foreign autocrats it despised. This problem emerged in Cuba and elsewhere during the 1910s, but it would peak in Nicaragua during the late 1920s and, later, in Vietnam.[16]

On the other hand, a different if equally grave set of problems hindered American efforts to substitute democracy for revolution. First there was the difficulty of determining *which* leaders were popularly supported—no easy task in unstable nations awash with guns and political violence. Wilson attempted to solve this difficulty through the Wilson Plan in the Dominican Republic (and similar plans for Haiti and Mexico), but that approach required foisting elections on nations that were culturally, socially, and institutionally ill-prepared for them.[17]

Once a "popular" government entered office, the problems only multiplied. Governments were often popular precisely because they stood up to Washington. That risked turning the United States against them, and few regimes could survive without American recognition, loans, and trade. If Washington did embrace a "popular" regime, however, that was often the kiss of death for that government's domestic legitimacy. So by the end of the Wilson administration, the United States had boxed itself into the ultimate catch-22: any leader who cooperated with the United States lost the domestic legitimacy needed to govern, but without the United States's support, no leader could hold onto power. In the most extreme cases, the logical result was direct American rule.[18]

One contemporary critic, Walter Lippmann, summarized the end result. American policy, he wrote, "is designed to prevent interventions and it simply makes intervention more elaborate and costly. It gives us the odor of imperialism, and yet our intention, I believe, is not to create an empire." Not only had the policy boomeranged, Lippmann noted, but it had also brought down on the United States "all the nuisance of empire without the constructive advantages of a well-managed imperialism."[19]

A Far-Reaching Effect

Even once the flaws in its stabilization strategy had started to emerge, it was hard for the United States to reverse course. Credibility was one reason why. Having signed treaties, proclaimed policies, and sunk many resources into its regional strategy, Washington could not backtrack in one location without risking serious consequences elsewhere. If the United States failed to suppress one revolution, what would stop other disaffected factions from trying their luck and also rising up? If the United States did not respond to instability in one country, why should Europe's powers expect it to respond to instability elsewhere?[20]

On that score, the Taft administration marked an important turning point. Roosevelt had applied his Corollary rarely and ad hoc, so if he chose not to intervene in any given case, that mattered little either for him personally or for the overall credibility of the Monroe Doctrine. But the Taft administration departed from that loose approach and froze the Roosevelt Corollary into place as a formal and comprehensive policy. Every intervention became linked, and failure anywhere began to mean failure everywhere. Huntington Wilson acknowledged as much when he urged Taft to depose the Dominican president because failing to do so would "wreck ... the broad policy pursued in Central America." Similar considerations pushed the Wilson administration to insist on control of the Dominican Republic's finances and police; the chief of the Latin American Division observed that "at stake" was "the entire principle that control of customs in turbulent countries precludes the possibility of revolution." "Should it fail," he added, "it will have, I fear, a far reaching effect upon the countries of Central America and ... Haiti."[21]

Officials were also slow to reevaluate their failing policies because the costs were not always immediately obvious. For most of the 1900s and 1910s, it was relatively easy for American policymakers to throw good money after bad under the delusion that success was right around the corner. Only once the United States had clambered up the ladder of escalation several times did the meager benefits and high costs start to become clear. As Winston Churchill might have said, American officials could be counted on to do the right thing in the region, but only after they had tried everything else.[22]

Changing course was also made more difficult by partisanship. By 1913, the failures of American regional strategy were glaring. But influenced by partisan suspicions, Wilson and many of his fellow Democrats attributed the failures to the previous administration's intentions rather than its policies. The stage was thus set for a repeat of dollar diplomacy's prescriptions—and its problems. Only after both political parties had made the same mistakes was a new, bipartisan consensus possible.

Finally, and most importantly, the United States did not reverse its interventionist course because it did not see any better options. Above all, the United States had been intervening to fill the region's power vacuums before its rivals could. If the United States stopped, and suddenly pulled out, it would have re-created those vacuums, and that was not a risk Washington was willing to take at a time of escalating imperial rivalries and, eventually, world war. In the end, it seemed better to destabilize and then occupy vast swaths of the hemisphere—no matter how costly, immoral, and aggressive that option was—than to let it fall under the sway of foreign powers.

By the end of Wilson's tenure, however, this calculus was beginning to change.

PART III
HEGEMON

CHAPTER 12

AT THE POINT OF BAYONETS

Retrenchment, 1918–1933

O n July 4, 1821, then Secretary of State John Quincy Adams boasted that his beloved republic had—"without a single exception"— respected other nations' sovereignty. The United States would sacrifice much for the cause of freedom, he swore, but never "under other banners than her own," not even those of "foreign independence." Otherwise, Adams warned, the republic would become trapped in endless wars, intrigues, and interventions; over time, "her policy would insensibly change from *liberty* to *force*," until at last there lay on her head "an Imperial Diadem, flashing in false and tarnished lustre the murky radiance of dominion and power."[1]

So, Adams concluded memorably, "wherever the standard of freedom and independence has been or shall be unfurled, there will her heart, her benedictions, and her prayers be. But she goes not abroad in search of monsters to destroy."[2]

One century later, Americans were battling monsters, real and imagined, in nearly a dozen states across the New World. Their soldiers and diplomats were occupying two entire nations, garrisoning parts of three more, running half a dozen protectorates and customs receiverships, prosecuting several bloody counterinsurgencies, and deposing regimes with a frequency that bordered on the gratuitous. Over two decades, the United States had used force in the region more than three dozen different times.[3]

For its trouble, the republic had at last attained regional hegemony, its power unrivaled in half the world. Finally, there were no more enemies left, no one for the United States to fight and fear but itself. As Adams had anticipated, however, the nation's new crown did not sit well—not with the neighbors it ruled, not with its own people, and not even with its own security needs.

Over the course of the 1920s and early 1930s, the United States thus did something unprecedented. At the peak of its regional power—when it could easily have turned hegemony into the murky radiance of outright dominion—the republic instead started surrendering control over its neighbors' affairs. It was a halting and gradual process, and it involved one of the country's largest interventions to date. But the policies of the previous two decades had proved grossly ineffective, and they were no longer necessary or sustainable. If the republic's newfound hegemony was to avoid collapsing under its own weight, something new was needed.

Conquest of the World

Several factors drove the end of the United States's interventionist streak, but two were especially important: the republic's changing security situation and the backlash its interventionist policies had provoked.

Since 1898, the United States had been intervening to prevent its rivals from expanding into the hemisphere. On November 11, 1918, however, the guns of August had fallen silent, marking not only the end of the First World War but also the culmination of American grand strategy. For many years, Americans had been dominant in the Western Hemisphere, but it was only now that they so overshadowed their great-power rivals that they saw no chance they could be meaningfully challenged in the hemisphere in the near future. The United States was, at last, supremely powerful in its own neighborhood—a regional hegemon.

Few Americans had expected that result at the start of the war. To the contrary, the Wilson administration had feared the conflict would either spill into the hemisphere or propel the great powers into Latin America afterward.

Such fears, however, had not foreseen the magnitude of the war's destruction. Germany—for two decades the bête noire of American strategists—had been decisively defeated, its Kaiser overthrown, its military machine dismantled, and the much-vaunted *Kaiserliche Marine* of the First and Second Fleet Bills scuttled at the bottom of Scapa Flow.

Shorn of territory and saddled with staggering reparations, Berlin would not be rebuilding its expeditionary forces anytime soon.

Germany's opponents were not much better off. France had borne the brunt of the fighting on the Western Front, and its countryside was pockmarked by shells and corpses. Russia had lost its czar to revolution, and Vladimir Lenin's crusade to turn the country red was bleeding it white. Even the British Empire was looking shaky, though its war deaths—908,000—paled next to France's 1,357,000, Russia's 1,700,000, or Germany's 1,773,000.[4]

By contrast, the United States stood tall. Americans counted only 126,000 dead out of a population of over one hundred million. They were also brimming with self-confidence, and they held the world spellbound with the Wilsonian creed of democracy, liberalism, and self-determination. Even as Wilson drove Europe's leaders up the wall personally—the French prime minister moaned that "talking to Wilson is something like talking to Jesus Christ!"—the continent's masses idolized the American president. Once an isolated city on a hill, the United States had become a global beacon of hope, and Wilson imagined the Founding Fathers "looking on with a sort of enraptured amazement that the American spirit should have made conquest of the world."[5]

"Conquest of the world" was characteristically grandiose, but Wilson was not far off. A net debtor at the war's start, the United States finished it the world's greatest creditor, owed $12.6 billion. Meanwhile, American businesses had feasted on wartime opportunities; from 1914 to 1918, the United States grew its manufacturing by 25 percent and its gross national product by 21 percent, even as modest firms like DuPont and Bethlehem Steel sprouted into multinational giants. By 1919, the United States boasted an economic output that rivaled that of the entire European continent.[6]

American ascendancy was even more stunning closer to home. Once the war began, the British blockade had snipped Germany's economic links with Latin America, while German U-boats, wartime exigencies, and the demands of the front had slowed the Allies' regional trade, credit, shipping, and investment to a trickle. Europe could scarcely have chosen a worse time to go missing in action, as the opening of the Panama Canal was just then resetting the region's trade patterns.[7]

Americans had made short work of this opportunity. In 1913, the United States had accounted for roughly 25 percent of Latin America's imports and 31 percent of its exports; by 1917, it was 54 percent and 51.7 percent, respectively. Americans meanwhile caught up to Europe in areas like investment, shipping, and banking, while beginning to break (with Washington's help) British regional monopolies on cable and radio services. Even the region's media fell within Americans' grasp; by 1922, Hollywood made over 95 percent of all movies in the Latin American market.[8]

Such local and global leverage was too tempting to leave unused, and Wilson for one had never been very good at keeping his values to himself. He dominated the peace negotiations at Versailles and designed a new international organization, the League of Nations, to preserve the postwar order. The League was centered around the concept of collective security Wilson had first floated in his aborted Pan-American Pact, and it exemplified his idealism and American power in equal measure. Nothing illustrated the latter like the League's Covenant, which in Article XXI expressly disclaimed any impact on "regional understandings like the Monroe Doctrine." For the first time, the world had formally legitimized the Doctrine's existence—indeed, "swallowed [it] hook, line, and sinker," in Wilson's words. Congress ultimately prevented the United States from joining the League, but that decision only further underscored the republic's outsized freedom of action.[9]

So complete was postwar American power that the United States could afford to treat Europe like one of its Caribbean dependencies. After the war, Europe's powers resembled the troubled states of Latin America in many ways: war-torn, politically polarized, and staggering under debt loads that kept them in financial thrall to the United States. Officials in Washington took swift advantage of this situation. In 1924, Washington booted France out of German territory it had seized by leveraging Paris's need for a new loan. Germany, meanwhile, got its own taste of dollar diplomacy when it accepted American-arranged credit in exchange for internal reforms and a promise to pay its debts. Chronic wrongdoing was chronic wrongdoing, in Haiti or on the Rhine.[10]

———

OVER THE NEXT decade, the United States would continue outpacing its onetime rivals. "Great Britain is faced in the United States of America with a phenomenon for which there is no parallel in our modern history," the British Foreign Office croaked in 1928—"a state twenty-five times as large, five times as wealthy, three times as populous, twice as ambitious, [and] almost invulnerable." "If ever there is to be a trial of strength between the Empire and the United States," the Foreign Office added unnecessarily, "this is not the moment."[11]

Strength like this opened space for second thoughts. With the neighborhood secure, the international policeman could safely hang up his nightstick. It was suddenly no longer clear why the United States needed to keep intervening in its region at all.[12]

Confession of Deeds Such as This

On its own, this newfound security may not have reversed the United States's interventionist streak. But it coincided with enough resentment and resistance to the country's policies to compel a change in course.

Opposition developed slowly. Since the turn of the century, the anti-imperialist movement inside the United States had largely lain dormant. Outside the United States, the story was much the same, with most South American capitals ranking the adventures of the *norteamericanos* a secondary—even tertiary—concern as late as the end of the Roosevelt administration.[13]

Over the 1910s, however, the situation began to change. Taft's dollar diplomacy was traumatizing, Wilson's democracy promotion even more so. One decade on, mothers would still be frightening misbehaving children in Nicaragua by hissing, "Hush! Major Butler will get you."[14]

Serious opposition finally crystallized around the occupations of Haiti and the Dominican Republic. Not only were they brazen examples of American power run amuck, but they also generated new friction constantly. Occupation forces were arrogant, demeaning, and racist; they also seethed at being left to babysit Caribbean dependencies while their peers fought across the pond in the First World War. Occupations are never spotless, but the prejudices, low caliber, and pent-up frustration of these troops all contributed to widespread and horrific abuses of the local population, including rape, arson, torture, and murder.[15]

Occupation forces stuffed these skeletons into closets as best they could, but with the end of the Great War came new efforts to drag the occupations' misdeeds out before the world. Haitian and Dominican protests caught the attention of *The Nation*, which unleashed muckraking exposés and damning comparisons of American ideals as preached to the Old World and practiced in the New. By 1920, most American periodicals had turned against the occupations, just in time for election season.[16]

On August 18, 1920, the Democratic vice presidential candidate committed the cardinal sin of politics: he said too much. "You know I have had something to do with the running of a couple of little republics," Assistant Secretary of the Navy Franklin D. Roosevelt bragged at a rally. "I wrote Haiti's constitution myself, and, if I do say it, I think it a pretty good constitution."[17]

Ten days later, Senator Warren G. Harding pounced. If elected, the Republican presidential candidate thundered back, "I will not empower an Assistant Secretary of the Navy to draft a constitution for helpless neighbors in the West Indies and jam it down their throats at the point of bayonets." Harding attacked again three weeks later. "Talk about self-determination! Talk about American ideals! Talk about equal rights for small nations! Before confession of deeds such as this, what becomes of the smooth rhetoric of vaunted righteousness to which we have so long been accustomed?"[18]

Soon-to-be President Harding may have been only "the best of the second raters," as one senator put it, but he was a first-class political weather vane. Following his landslide victory, the Senate began investigating the two occupations, in turn encouraging the occupied to ally with organizations like the NAACP and protest still louder.[19]

Critics were everywhere merciless. Emissaries from occupied countries fanned the region's anti-Americanism until it burned white-hot, and Latin Americans founded new papers from Argentina to Honduras just to attack the endless chain of indignities meted out by the Colossus of the North. Mexico meanwhile began organizing a united regional front against the United States. "We are piling up hatreds, suspicions, records for exploitation and destruction of sovereignty in Latin America, such as have never failed in all history to react in war, suffering, and defeat of high moral and spiritual ideals," one American observer warned.[20]

On the ground, it was even worse. Dominicans and Haitians resisted the occupations in every way, from launching uprisings to making American soldiers patrol in the middle of streets to avoid getting hit by garbage bags thrown at their heads. One fed-up marine was approached by a Dominican woman selling tickets to a benefit performance. "How much," he asked, "and what's it for?" For getting the Americans out of the Dominican Republic, she replied. "Gimme two," said the marine, "and I don't care how much they cost."[21]

Officials in Washington worried that this rising tide of resistance was not just annoying, but dangerous. Washington had wanted strong, stable neighbors on the assumption they would help defend against the mutual threat of European imperialism. Once the United States replaced European imperialism as the greatest threat to Latin America, however, that reasoning went out the window.[22]

Someday, a rival would again arise across the oceanic moat, and when that day came, the United States could not afford to have its neighbors enthusiastically lowering the drawbridge. "The complaisant North American may smile at … the possibility of our losing our position of dominance," one critic cautioned, but "Latin Americans are betaking themselves as fast as they can to Europe for protection against us." "Sooner or later," agreed a former minister to the Dominican Republic, "an alliance will be formed to enable [Latin America] to break away from the Monroe Doctrine or fight it. I can see no other peril to our country so great or so imminent." Change was clearly needed.[23]

Let Them Work Out Their Own Salvation

Together, the republic's newfound security and the resistance it faced forced a course correction. Roosevelt's porcupine had won, and the engorged American boa constrictor would regurgitate each turbulent little republic it had swallowed.

Retrenchment was slow, messy, and exceedingly uncomfortable for everyone involved. Even though American policymakers wanted to interfere less in their neighbors' affairs, they were unsure how far or fast to pull back. They were also still coming to terms with what had gone wrong, and even under retreat they often repeated past mistakes or blundered into new ones. But constantly pressured by both its public and its neighbors, Washington wound back the clock: first liquidating Wilson's occupations, then phasing out Taft's dollar diplomacy, and finally questioning even the fundamentals of Roosevelt's policies.

———

CHASTENED BY HIS failed interventions, Wilson had started musing in late 1918 on the need to let foreign peoples "work out their own salvation, even though they wallow in anarchy for a while." Electing good men was no longer his priority, and he refused to intervene to stop a coup in Costa Rica, election rigging in Cuba, or new outrages from revolutionary Mexico. In late 1920, Wilson also announced his intent to end the occupation of the Dominican Republic. The State Department explained that the status quo was untenable, citing "the increasing agitation among the Dominicans" and "the anxiety expressed by the governments of other American republics."[24]

Characteristically, however, Wilson doubted whether his opponents had also seen the light. "If Harding is elected," he scowled, "the prospects that we shall have war with Mexico [are] very great."[25]

But Harding's administration was even less interested in new adventures abroad. Harding appointed eminent Republican statesman Charles

Evans Hughes as his secretary of state. Roosevelt had once called Hughes "a whiskered Wilson," but the former Supreme Court justice displayed little of Wilson's interest in hemispheric emancipation. On the Monroe Doctrine's centennial year, Hughes reaffirmed Washington's interest in regional stability but "utterly disclaim[ed]" any intent "to superintend the affairs of our sister Republics, to assert an overlordship, ... [or] to make our power the test of right in this hemisphere."[26]

Such promises were by now a rite of passage for secretaries of state, but Hughes was determined to live up to his words. He tried to repair the United States's damaged reputation in numerous ways, including by paying Colombia $25 million in reparations for Panama's secession. But he would ultimately make ending Washington's many occupations the calling card of his regional policy.[27]

Sumner Welles was the junior diplomat who masterminded the withdrawals. Born in 1892, Welles was an American aristocrat by both breeding and belongings. As a child, he showed up to playdates wearing white gloves; as a State Department official, he pierced his black cravats with jeweled stickpins, marched with a gold-headed Malacca cane, and was tailed by a British valet surnamed (alas) Reeks. Educated at Groton and Harvard, Welles acquired a haughtiness that tried the patience of

Chief of the Latin American Division Sumner Welles: "Welles is a man of almost preternatural solemnity and great dignity. If he ever smiles, it has not been in my presence."

everyone he met. "He conducts himself with portentous gravity," observed one cabinet secretary, "as if he were charged with all the responsibilities of Atlas." Even a British earl's son lamented how Welles must have inadvertently "swallowed a ramrod in his youth."[28]

Few knew what to make of this wealthy loner. State Department functionaries feigned shivers when leaving his office, and newspapers likened his criticism to "being stabbed to the heart with an icicle." But Welles complemented his glacial manners with a blazing intellect. "He is brilliant, tireless," marveled one boss. "When there is work to be done—the clock does not exist." *Time* called him a "casting director's dream of a diplomat," a six-foot-three giant who was precise, immaculately dressed, and prodigiously disciplined, and in the end seemed almost "too impressive to be real."[29]

Such superhuman qualities did indeed have their dark mirror image. Like Dorian Gray, Welles achieved outward perfection only by siphoning strength from his private life. He had regular heart attacks starting at age thirty-three and eventually drank himself into an early grave. Welles also engaged in an endless series of extramarital flings. Sexual affairs were nothing new in American politics, of course, but Welles crossed several puritanical lines in his appetites. Most fatefully, he did not limit his romances by either sex or race, and the resulting scandals would eventually rip his career apart.[30]

For now, however, Icarus flew high. In 1920, at the precocious age of twenty-seven, Welles became the acting chief of the State Department's Latin American Division, where he oversaw the end of most of the country's regional occupations.[31]

Some of the withdrawals were straightforward. American forces had occupied parts of Cuba in 1917 and Panama in 1918, but since those occupations were informal and limited, it was easy enough to pull American soldiers back to their bases in 1922 and 1921, respectively.[32]

Getting out of the Dominican Republic was harder. The island teetered on the tips of American bayonets; if Washington withdrew precipitately, it would mean chaos. So the question for Welles and his compatriots was how to devolve power in a stable and sustainable way while getting local buy-in and also preserving American interests.[33]

Welles handled this delicate task with aplomb. He patiently negotiated his country's withdrawal over four years, including two in the field. On July 1, 1924, the occupation formally ended, and the last American marine left the Dominican Republic soon after.[34]

Even as Washington ended some occupations, however, it was not yet ready to leave its interventionist days entirely behind. Before withdrawing from the Dominican Republic, for example, Washington insisted on continuing the American customs receivership.[35]

Washington also refused to withdraw from Haiti. It had some ostensibly valid reasons for treating the nation differently—for instance, Haitians had never had the same tradition of organized political parties—but it mostly came down to skin color. Contrasting the occupations of Haiti and the Dominican Republic, one State Department analyst explained that the two "demand[ed] different treatment" because Dominicans "have a preponderance of white blood and culture," whereas Haitians "are negro for the most part" and "are almost in a state of savagery." Washington would periodically make noises about leaving Haiti, but these "someday" dreams would take another decade to turn into reality.[36]

Washington kept its fingers in other regional pies as well. In 1923, Welles persuaded the states of Central America to refuse to recognize revolutionary regimes, an attempt to resurrect the Central American peace system that Secretary of State Elihu Root had created in 1907 but which had decayed since. One year later, however, the dangers of this nonrecognition policy became clear when United Fruit funded a revolution against Honduras's government. (Samuel Zemurray's Cuyamel Fruit Company backed the incumbents.) Instability beckoned, and despite Hughes's desire to stay out, the United States was once again powerless to resist the call. Welles and the marines went in, and over several sleepless days, the Groton-Harvard alumnus trekked inland using whatever means he could find, including a banana train, a rickety Ford, a rented launch, and for the final stretch, a mule. Welles mediated the conflict and the marines left, but the episode foreshadowed future troubles.[37]

ELSEWHERE, THE HARDING administration tried to fall back on the familiar routine of dollar diplomacy, arranging private loans to Latin America in exchange for stabilizing internal reforms. The intent, somewhat counterintuitively, was to shrink American influence; stung by Wilsonian militarism, Washington was once again trying to substitute dollars for bullets.[38]

Starting around 1923, however, the State Department began backing away from even dollar diplomacy. Some administration officials had grown disenchanted working with self-interested financiers; in several cases, banks had maneuvered the Department into supporting loans of dubious merit. Official support also seemed less and less necessary. For ages, American companies had been fighting to make headway against established European commercial interests in the region, but in the wake of the First World War, it was American businesses who had the upper hand. With American companies increasingly able to fend for themselves, officials in Washington saw less need to get involved on their behalf.[39]

Ending dollar diplomacy was also made easier by the rise of a privatized alternative: the "money doctors." Epitomized by Princeton economist Edwin Kemmerer, the money doctors were American financial consultants who visited foreign countries, diagnosed their economic ills, and prescribed a rigorous cocktail of reforms as a cure. Latin American states invited these house calls in hope of using the resulting bill of clean health to enter the frothy American investment market. In effect, the money doctors gave the State Department a way to outsource dollar diplomacy while making it more consensual, and the Department unsurprisingly jumped at the opportunity.[40]

Once again, however, it was external criticism that drove most of the government's retreat. State Department officials had hoped ending the country's occupations would appease the raging anti-imperialist movement. But critics showed no signs of letting up, and their fire shifted instead to the cozy relationship between Wall Street and Washington.[41]

By 1925, dollar diplomacy had faded to a shadow of its former self. Even as Washington continued promoting private loans and consultants, it pared back its links to the banking community and got out of the sordid business of micromanaging its neighbors' internal affairs. Welles publicly declared that "the day of 'dollar diplomacy' … is past," and internal memoranda confirmed the State Department's sincerity. "The United States will get better results," stressed one official, if it "let the natives work out their solution."[42]

Sound advice, but officials in Washington would appreciate its full wisdom only after a disastrous new intervention in Nicaragua.

Butchered in the Jungle

Consistent with its broader retreat, the United States also sought to evacuate Nicaragua in the mid-1920s. But its withdrawal was clumsy and rushed, and Americans were sucked right back in. Catastrophic in most respects, the resulting intervention did have one virtue: it reinforced Washington's commitment to ending its interventionist policies.

Since 1912, the United States had prevented revolutions in Nicaragua by garrisoning marines in its capital. By the early 1920s, Washington was ready to bring those marines home, but a premature withdrawal risked sparking a revolution against the embattled Conservative government. So the State Department devised a two-part withdrawal strategy: first, free and fair elections that would presumptively bring a popular Liberal government to power; second, the creation of a nonpartisan constabulary that would defend that new government once the marines left.[43]

Little of this plan survived contact with Nicaraguan politics. Conservatives knew they maintained power by the grace of American arms alone, so they sabotaged the withdrawal plan at every turn. By 1924, the State Department had lost the will to fight back; officials preferred to see their plan fail rather than to forcibly compel its success through additional interventions in Nicaraguan politics.[44]

On October 5, 1924, Nicaraguans voted, and as always, force and fraud swept the regime's preferred ticket to victory. On the way to election day, however, something unexpected had happened. Conservatives had nominated former President Emiliano Chamorro as their candidate, but the sitting president—a Chamorro archrival—had instead backed a fusion ticket of Conservative Carlos Solórzano and Liberal Juan Bautista Sacasa. Conservatives generally supported Chamorro while most Liberals favored Solórzano and Sacasa, so when the latter won, it was a Liberal victory in all but name.[45]

This was nowhere near the free and fair election the State Department had wanted, but it was close enough. For over a decade Washington had allowed Conservatives to win rigged elections, and in a perverse sort of way, it seemed only fair to give Liberals the same opportunity. Washington recognized Solórzano's government, slapped together a semi-functional constabulary, and pulled its marines out of Nicaragua on August 3, 1925.[46]

Slipshod or not, the withdrawal was complete. But the State Department's celebrations were short-lived. On August 28—barely three weeks later—Managua's International Club was hosting a grand gala for Nicaragua's most distinguished citizens, including most of the new cabinet, when a band of drunken men burst in. Shooting their guns into the air, the uninvited guests announced amid screams and fainting that they had come to free the government from Liberal domination.[47]

EVENTS MOVED QUICKLY in the following months. Chamorro, the jilted Conservative candidate, usurped the presidency from Solórzano, while Liberal Vice President Sacasa went to Washington to plead for American help. But the State Department refused to get involved. "As long as the people of Central America feel that the 'last word' comes from the Department," one official said firmly, "the attainment of political stability will be postponed." Rebuffed, Sacasa returned to Nicaragua to lead a Liberal revolution against Chamorro.[48]

As Nicaragua descended into civil war, the State Department struggled to maintain its hands-off attitude. Efforts to broker a settlement led Chamorro to resign in favor of Adolfo Díaz, the Conservative ex-president who Americans had propped up during the Taft administration. Sacasa kept fighting, however, much to Washington's growing annoyance.[49]

Sacasa further alienated Washington by letting slip that Mexico was supplying his forces. Mexico had settled down since the 1910s, but one of the final acts of the Mexican Revolution had been a sharp turn toward radical economic nationalism. Sacasa's alliance with Mexico thus raised concerns that Mexico was trying to pump bolshevism into Central America. Combined with lingering trauma from the country's last Red Scare, some in the State Department even saw Sacasa's war as the tip of a revolutionary spear being thrust into the hemisphere by the Soviet Union itself.[50]

Mexico and the United States would soon patch up their differences, but their reconciliation came too late for Nicaragua. Over the fall and winter of 1926, Sacasa's rebels continued gaining ground. American expats demanded boots and boats, and President Díaz shrewdly reinforced these pleas with his own calls for help. Washington understood it was being manipulated, and it refused to fight Sacasa's rebels directly. But it saw no alternative to sending forces to establish neutral zones in cities threatened by the Liberal advance, even though doing so helped the Conservatives.[51]

On January 10, 1927, President Calvin Coolidge tried to justify his country's escalating involvement. Citing the "position of peculiar responsibility" the United States held because of its canal interests, Coolidge argued Washington could not permit "any serious threat to stability and constitutional government in Nicaragua," especially not from "outside influences" or "foreign power[s]." He also could not ignore American and European calls for protection.[52]

Coolidge was hoping that Díaz could win the war on his own, but Sacasa's rebels advanced relentlessly. By late February, Washington had dispatched 5,414 marines to Nicaragua and stationed eleven cruisers and destroyers in its ports. By mid-spring, American forces were "neutralizing"—that is, occupying—most of the country's major cities. Sooner or later, a clash between leathernecks and Liberals seemed inevitable, so a desperate Coolidge instructed Henry L. Stimson, Taft's former secretary of war, to "go down there" and "straighten the matter out."[53]

Stimson hammered out a deal that would become known as the Peace of Tipitapa. Under its terms, Díaz would remain president but would pardon the Liberal rebels and bring them into his cabinet. Even more importantly, the United States would supervise elections the following year while resuming its efforts to organize a nonpartisan constabulary.[54]

On May 12, 1927, under threat of forcible disarmament, the Liberal commander-in-chief sent Stimson a telegram accepting the peace terms. Signed by nearly all of the commander's generals, the message signaled the end of the war, or so everyone thought. One thirty-one-year-old general, however, had refused to endorse the deal. His name was Augusto César Sandino.[55]

———

SANDINO WOULD BOG American forces down in a bloody insurgency for the next six years. Operating out of the remote northern mountains,

General Augusto César Sandino [center]: "Either you will fill yourself with glory killing a patriot, or I will make you eat the dust."

the charismatic and ruthless guerrilla leader never seriously threatened the American-supported regime. But Sandino's solitary war against Goliath nevertheless unleashed a landslide of opposition abroad that pushed American forces out of Nicaragua and finally buried the big-stick policies of the previous three decades.[56]

Sandino's insurgency quickly captured the hearts of Latin Americans, who ferociously condemned the American intervention. Ex-Secretary Hughes was forced to play defense at the Sixth Pan-American Conference in 1928. "What are we to do," he pleaded, "when government breaks down and American citizens are in danger of their lives? Are we to stand by and see them butchered in the jungle"? Hughes temporarily silenced his country's critics, but few ultimately bought his emotional defense of the republic's latest "interposition of a temporary character."[57]

Sandino and his cause were also idolized by many Americans. Congressional Peace Progressives, socialists, churches, pacifists, and African American groups united around the latest anti-imperialist cause célèbre, fundraising for the Sandinistas and picketing the White House with signs declaring that "Wall Street And Not Sandino Is The Real Bandit." Further down Constitution Avenue, many lawmakers were equally censorious. "What are we going to accomplish by killing those men and those women and those children and burning those little hovels and those little homes?" one senator demanded. "What are we going to accomplish?"[58]

Officials in Washington had few good answers. In March 1928, the secretary of state wrote the Managua Legation about the marines' failure to pacify the country. "People cannot understand why the job cannot be done," he huffed. "Frankly I do not understand myself."[59]

Efforts to get out of Nicaragua, however, were haunted by memories of the failed first withdrawal. In 1924, the State Department had botched its plan for free elections and a nonpartisan constabulary, and the result had been coups, civil war, and a new occupation. In the Peace of Tipitapa, Stimson had essentially recommitted the Department to the same two-part plan, and this time, policymakers were determined to get it right.[60]

Even so, the State Department refused to meddle more than necessary. Some officials on the ground wanted extensive reforms resembling the "benevolent supervision" of previous years. Washington would have none of it. American officials supervised elections in 1928, 1930, and 1932, but the head of the last electoral mission advised that Washington should "seek, by every means possible, to avoid again becoming involved in a commitment of [this] nature." The State Department did not need to be told twice; it had already decided in another context that "the last thing we want" is "participation in or even supervision of ... elections."[61]

Efforts to withdraw spurred other policy changes too. Coolidge had sent the marines in partly to protect Americans and their property. But when the Sandinistas began murdering their way through Yankee settlements in early 1931, the State Department refused to act. American expats were furious. "I fail to see why our Government cannot give American citizens full protection," observed one testily. "What have you got gun boats *for*?" Exhausted by this "pampered lot of people," Stimson—now secretary of state—announced that Washington would no longer protect all Americans in Nicaragua. Better to stand by and see them butchered in the jungle, apparently, than run the risk of deepening the intervention.[62]

On January 2, 1933, the last American soldiers sailed from Nicaragua. Their return had bucked the overall trend of American retrenchment. But in the long run, the intervention—and the resentment and frustrations it caused—had accelerated the basic drift of American policy. Washington was sick of supervising elections, sick of governing its neighbors, and above all sick of deploying marines and warships. When Stimson was asked in 1932 whether he would consider landing forces elsewhere in the hemisphere, he did not hesitate: "Not on your life."[63]

The Good Neighbor

On November 19, 1928, two weeks after being elected president, Herbert C. Hoover set out on a ten-week tour of ten Latin American nations. It was unprecedented for a president-elect to journey outside the United States for so long, but Hoover hoped to send an unprecedented message. At his first stop, he explained how he wanted his trip to "symbolize the friendly visit of one good neighbor to another."[64]

Hoover practiced what he preached. During his tenure, the Quaker president refused to send marines to restore or maintain order in Latin America, and he even cut back on landings to protect American lives. He also withdrew American forces from Nicaragua, disapproved of new customs receiverships, ended Washington's remaining attempts to promote fiscal reform (including through money doctors), repudiated much of Wilson's nonrecognition policy, and set in motion the end of Haiti's occupation.[65]

Such good-neighborliness came not a moment too soon. On October 24, 1929, a stock market crash announced the start of the Great Depression. As the world buckled, critics vilified Wall Street with new gusto. Senate investigations purportedly revealed major banking abuses, especially in the flotation of foreign securities in Latin America. Conspiracy theorists quickly unspooled enough yarn to connect these allegations, however tenuously, to three decades' worth of foreign policy failures. Major General Smedley Butler—now retired—led the charge, claiming he had "helped make Haiti and Cuba a decent place for the National City Bank boys." In truth, the maverick marine had little more insight into why he had terrorized Latin America than did the privates under his command. But to many angry and unemployed Americans, it did not matter; Butler had the rare credibility that comes from having as many stars on his shoulders as Medals of Honor around his neck.[66]

Even as Washington continued sloughing off its interventionist policies, however, it refused to renounce its theoretical right to intervene. In 1930, the administration published a memorandum that disassociated the Roosevelt Corollary from the Monroe Doctrine but maintained that intervention could still potentially be justified by "the necessities of security or self-preservation." Few officials wanted to keep on forcibly stabilizing Latin America, but they hesitated to promise that they would never again need to do so.[67]

Behind this final reluctance lay concerns about the future. Washington could afford to dismantle its vast sphere of influence because it currently faced no serious threats from abroad. But if—*when*—a new danger arose, what would Washington do? "If the need to interpose to correct bad conditions seemed less urgent in 1930," a State Department official later recalled, "it was because there seemed to be little immediate probability that some unfriendly power would attempt to get a foothold there."[68]

Stimson, Welles, and others worried that the recent surge of withdrawals was thus not so much a new strategy as the repudiation of an old one. Intervention was not sustainable. But neither was isolationism, not while the problem of order could still reemerge. And Latin America seemed more unstable than ever. The Great Depression was cutting its way through the region like the Grim Reaper, and by February 1931, revolutions had claimed one of every three governments as economic distress triggered political upheaval. In response, Washington wrung its hands. "I am getting quite blue over the bad way in which all Latin America is showing up," Stimson wrote mournfully. Governments struggled to stay upright, "yet if we try to take the lead for them, at once there is a cry against American domination and imperialism."[69]

Welles recognized that Washington could not ignore this rising disorder forever. He had concluded that another world war was inevitable, and that the region had to be made ready for a new set of threats. But time was starting to run out, and as Welles looked to Europe and Asia in the last days of the Hoover administration, he could already see something dark and ugly beginning to stir.[70]

CHAPTER 13

THE COLOSSUS

The Good Neighbor Policy, 1933–1945 and Beyond

O n February 17, 1941, the country's mightiest media mogul, Henry R. Luce, penned a call to arms in *Life* magazine. Born days before the start of the Spanish-American War, Luce had spent his entire life in the shadow of a nation growing from great power to colossus. In his eyes, however, Americans had been shirking the responsibilities they increasingly owed the world. The result was "tragic disappointment," he wrote—a century "so big with promise," now wrapped in the flames of World War II.[1]

Americans were not yet at war, but Luce had no doubt they would soon be presiding over its aftermath. He knew Washington could never underwrite "the good behavior of the entire world," but he nevertheless argued that the United States needed to benevolently supervise "the world-environment in which she lives."[2]

To that end, Luce sketched out a four-part program. First, the United States would need to champion "a system of free economic enterprise." Second, it would need to share "its technical and artistic skills." Third, it would need to aid the world as a global Good Samaritan. Finally, and most importantly, it would need to become "the powerhouse of the ideals of Freedom and Justice." Luce concluded triumphantly: "It is in this spirit that all of us are called ... to create the first great American Century."[3]

Luce may not have realized it, but his breathtaking vision of an American Century owed much to the United States's regional experience. Since

President Franklin D. Roosevelt's inauguration a decade earlier, the United States had been test-driving Luce's blueprint in its neighborhood—bolstering the region's economies through free trade, dolloping American expertise onto its societies, and directing aid where needed. Above all, FDR had promised unprecedented fidelity to the ideals of noninterventionism and noninterference.

At first glance, this Good Neighbor Policy appeared a sterling success. Despite an uncertain start in Cuba, the Policy had improved relations with Latin America dramatically, and as storm clouds gathered over Eurasia, the hemisphere had become one of the world's few bright spots. When the storm had finally broken and the Old World had plunged into Armageddon, Latin Americans followed Washington into isolation and then war. Just as Luce had predicted, the United States would emerge at conflict's end as the indispensable nation, ready to scale its regional policies up into a new world order.

But the more things changed, the more they stayed the same. Before the Second World War, the United States enjoyed a rare reprieve from great-power competition that allowed it to ignore—but not escape—the problem of order. Once the problem returned, however, so did the republic's old habits; far from being a turning point, the Good Neighbor Policy completed a circle. As Americans marched confidently into their new Century, they would encounter the same challenges and make much the same mistakes as before, only this time on a global scale.

Sneak Up Behind Him and Cry "Boo"

On March 4, 1933, FDR used his inaugural address to announce "the policy of the good neighbor," a phrase that quickly became the tagline for the administration's new approach to Latin America. In time, the Good Neighbor Policy would be remembered as a golden age of regional relations, when the United States finally came close to treating its weaker brethren with the respect they deserved. But in 1933, the Policy was still in its infancy, and it nearly ended before it even began.[4]

Cuba, appropriately enough, was the scene for the Policy's brush with oblivion. Since the start of the Great Depression, the plummeting price of sugar and tobacco had dragged Cuba's economy into the abyss. Economic misery had contributed to political instability and then repression; by the early 1930s, Cuba's dictator, General Gerardo Machado y Morales, was presiding over a regime so tyrannical that it approached

<u>President Franklin D. Roosevelt</u>: "To encounter Roosevelt, with all his buoyant sparkle, his iridescent personality, and his sublime confidence, was like opening your first bottle of champagne."

caricature, right down to the way his henchmen fed opposition leaders to the sharks swimming in Havana Bay. But Machado's state-sponsored terrorism only prompted an equal and opposite reaction from his political opponents, who began assassinating government officials with abandon. By late 1932, American embassy staff were reporting "feelings of horror and terrified apprehension to a degree which it would be difficult to exaggerate."[5]

Even as Cuba's politics disintegrated, however, the Hoover administration refused to get involved. Still scarred by the intervention in Nicaragua, Secretary of State Henry L. Stimson did not want to interfere in Cuba, no matter how bad Machado's reign of terror became.[6]

FDR had no such compunctions. Shortly after entering office, he dispatched his close family friend and perennial Latin American troubleshooter, Sumner Welles, to sort out the situation.

FDR and Welles were, like everyone else, still figuring out exactly what it meant for the United States to be a good neighbor. Both men opposed the hyper-interventionism of previous administrations, but they still drew a hazy distinction between the evils of such "remedial" interventionism and the benefits of "preventive" interference that would preemptively "eliminate [any] causes for unrest." From their perspective,

Cuba needed a dose of the latter, especially because the State Department was desperate to avoid another occupation of the island right before the next Pan-American Conference, only a few months away. Welles accordingly arrived in Havana with instructions to do whatever it took to "prevent the necessity of intervention."[7]

By midsummer, Welles concluded that Machado was unwilling to compromise with his political opponents and that a political settlement was impossible. If FDR wanted Cuba restored to stability, only one option was left: Machado had to go. Surviving mainly on coffee and chain-smoked cigarettes, Welles worked to secretly unite opposition leaders, peel away what remained of the beleaguered president's support, and assure the Cuban military of American acquiescence if it took action. In early August, following a general strike and island-wide protests, Welles triggered a final showdown by demanding Machado's resignation.[8]

Machado's fall was quick. In a final act of desperation, the general reportedly assigned a hit squad to kill Welles, but Machado realized he had been outmaneuvered when even the military refused to support him. On August 12, 1933, he resigned. After narrowly escaping an ambush by troops at the airport, the ex-dictator flew out of Cuba on a bullet-riddled plane, taking with him five revolvers, seven bags of gold, and half a dozen friends still in their pajamas.[9]

———

WELLES WAS PLEASED. He had retired Machado without open intervention. Better yet, the new government seemed stable: it had united Cuba's traditional political forces behind it while sidelining radicals in the labor and student movements.[10]

On September 4, 1933, however, everything fell apart again. That night, noncommissioned officers in the army mutinied under the leadership of a stenographer named Fulgencio Batista y Zaldívar. Batista and the other sergeants at first wanted only modest military reforms like higher pay. Some marginalized student activists, however, saw the revolt as a vehicle for their wider ambitions. Rushing to the barracks, the students talked the noncommissioned officers into dreaming bigger, and the mutiny morphed into a full-fledged revolution. Together, the sergeants and students overthrew the government and installed a five-man junta.[11]

Stunned, Welles cabled Washington that "the most extreme radicals of the student organization" ran Cuba's new government, and that the army was now "under ultra-radical control." If nothing were done, he feared the "complete collapse of government." Welles thus demanded the unthinkable: military intervention.[12]

Historians have long wondered what led Welles, the Good Neighbor Policy's future architect, to try to raze his creation before it ever got off the ground. Partly, it was the press of events—Welles was strained, sleepless, and caught off guard. Partly, too, it was a question of ego. He had helped organize the previous government and took its fall personally. And partly, it was the fact that Welles had not yet shaken his belief in the benefits of "preventive" interference. So while he opposed all intervention on principle, he decided that a "limited and restricted form of intervention" in Cuba would be "infinitely preferable" to waiting "until complete anarchy prevails" and a full-scale occupation became unavoidable.[13]

FDR and Secretary of State Cordell Hull, however, saw the situation as less dire, and they pulled the emerging Good Neighbor Policy back from the brink. "If we have to go in there again," Hull warned Welles, "we will never be able to come out."[14]

Just because the administration would not land marines, however, did not mean it had made peace with Cuba's new revolutionary regime. Welles in particular was determined to bring the junta down. He convinced his superiors that it had not consolidated control and therefore should not be recognized. But Welles's reasoning was circular: by not recognizing the regime, Washington ensured its failure, because as Welles conceded, "no government here can survive for a protracted period without recognition by the United States." Just to make the revolutionary government's demise triply sure, Welles also organized political opposition against it, shut off aid, and ringed the island with American warships.[15]

At first, this hostility accomplished little. On September 10, student leaders dissolved the five-man junta and elevated one of its members, a physiology professor named Dr. Ramón Grau San Martín, to the presidency. Grau's government quickly survived two crises: a shoot-out in downtown Havana with deposed army officers and a ham-handed revolt by the political opposition.[16]

Each success, however, underscored the real power behind Grau's throne: the army's new leader, Batista. Welles began cultivating Batista, ostensibly opposing a coup but nevertheless pointing out that a "swing" in Batista's support could lead to a new "government which had the confidence of all."[17]

In mid-January 1934, Batista overthrew Grau's government. After demanding and receiving Grau's resignation, Batista arranged for a transitional government that lasted thirty-nine hours before a hand-picked candidate took power. "The method of changing a president in Cuba has been solved," mocked the *Miami Herald*. "You sneak up behind him and cry 'Boo.'"[18]

Grau had a different take. "I fell because Washington willed it," he remarked bitterly.[19]

Ah'm Against Intervention

Cuba was not the most auspicious start for the Good Neighbor Policy. Welles had helped unseat two governments—hardly neighborly behavior. But Washington *had* resisted the impulse to land armed forces, and in so doing it had suggested a bedrock for the emerging Good Neighbor Policy: nonintervention. The question was how much the new administration could and would build on that foundation.[20]

In December 1933, Secretary of State Hull took the first step in Montevideo, Uruguay, where the hemisphere had gathered for yet another Pan-American Conference. On the way down, an advisor informed Hull that American interventionism would again be in the crosshairs. "Ah'm against intervention," Hull responded in his thick Tennessee drawl, "but what am Ah goin' to do when chaos breaks out in one of those countries, and armed bands go woamin' awound, burnin', pillagin' and murdewin' Amewicans?" "Mr. Secretary," the advisor pointed out, "that usually happens *after* we have intervened."[21]

Confronted by "wild and unreasonable" regional pressure in Montevideo, Hull took the unprecedented step of agreeing that "no state has the right to intervene in the internal or external affairs of another." FDR confirmed the policy change a few days later. "The definite policy of the United States from now on," the president declared, "is one opposed to armed intervention." After a three-and-a-half-decade binge, Washington was swearing off intervention for good.[22]

The next step was tying up loose ends. Now back in Washington, Welles picked up where he had left off during the 1920s and finished liquidating the country's sphere of influence. He started with the Platt Amendment, which he knew from his time in Cuba offered dangerous temptations. In early June 1934, the two nations abrogated the Amendment and ended Washington's protectorate over Cuba. Next, in August, the United States ended its occupation of Haiti, although certain fiscal controls would remain into the 1940s. In 1936, Welles then negotiated a treaty ending the American protectorate over Panama. FDR was sufficiently impressed by these and other results to promote Welles to undersecretary of state, second-in-command of the State Department. Finally, in 1941, Welles wound up the republic's customs receivership in the Dominican Republic.[23]

Ending interventions and protectorates was one thing; shunning more subtle forms of meddling was another. Surely, one incredulous diplomat asked in early 1936, the Good Neighbor Policy did not mean taking a "completely negative position" on other states' internal matters? No one wished to repeat "the former sins of commission," but if Washington failed to use "its immense power and moral influence," it risked committing "a sin of omission with consequences fully as grievous."[24]

At first, Welles agreed, in keeping with his long-standing faith in "preventive" interference. But after consulting with his staff (and presumably reflecting on his Cuban experience), he had a change of heart, and the Good Neighbor Policy took another step forward. In March 1936, Welles instructed American diplomats to follow "a new precedent" in the unsettled Caribbean area—they should "conduct themselves exactly as if they were dealing with ... any non-American power; that is to say, that they should religiously abstain from offering advice as regards any domestic question." Noninterference had joined nonintervention at the heart of the Good Neighbor Policy.[25]

Finally, the administration rounded out the growing Policy with an economic component. Global trade had seized up from 1929 to 1934, collapsing 66 percent in value. To get the system moving again, the State Department dusted off former Secretary of State James G. Blaine's great love: reciprocity. Officially, this campaign for lower trade barriers was not limited to Latin America; in practice, though, American policymakers focused their efforts close to home, not least because doing so dovetailed perfectly with the emerging Good Neighbor Policy. "There is no more effective means of enhancing friendship between nations than in promoting commerce between them," Welles reminded FDR. From 1933 to 1945, the United States would sign over two dozen reciprocity treaties, the majority of them with Latin America.[26]

Latin America had greeted the election of Woodrow Wilson's former assistant navy secretary with understandable anxiety. But as FDR and his team developed the Good Neighbor Policy, they quickly won the region over with a deft mix of substance and style. FDR did not simply proclaim the end of Haiti's occupation; rather, he went to the island to personally deliver a farewell speech—in French. It was the first time *any* foreign head of state had ever visited Haiti, and it left the kind of impression that few statesmen since Elihu Root had managed to make. FDR had come a long way since boasting about writing Haiti's constitution.[27]

———

LATIN AMERICANS CHEERED the Good Neighbor Policy, but it had a dark side. For the policy to mean anything, the United States had to be a good neighbor to *all* its neighbors, not just the ones it liked. Washington thus did little to stop the rise of dictators in the region, even when they came to power on the backs of armed forces the United States had helped create.

Constabularies—armed forces that did double duty as both police and militaries—first became a fixture of the United States's regional policy in the early 1910s, when it became clear that protectorates and customs receiverships could not ensure stability on their own. Washington's reasoning was earnest, if tragically oversimplified. Latin America was imploding at the hands of either tyrannical leaders or greedy revolutionaries who flipped regimes over in search of loot within. Either way, the solution was the same: Washington needed to establish democratic governments guarded by nonpartisan constabularies. Both were necessary—without democracy, constabularies would just breed oppression and revolution; without constabularies, democracies would be defenseless against ambitious and unscrupulous men.[28]

So during its many occupations, the United States assembled, armed, trained, and disciplined constabularies that could maintain order once American forces withdrew. Simultaneously, American officials stamped out competing centers of power.[29]

Carried out with the best of intentions, the program never fully grappled with how to stop constabularies from taking over once the United States left. Giving out guns was easy; ensuring they stayed pointed in the right direction was harder. Efforts to instill nonpartisan values ran up against ingrained norms, values, and history, to say nothing of fundamentally different interests.[30]

One Nicaraguan officer named Anastasio Somoza García illustrated the problem. "You Americans are a bunch of damn fools," Somoza scoffed to a marine during the occupation of Nicaragua. For years, Americans had been chasing the rebel general Augusto Sandino, but they would never catch him until they understood "the Latin American way of doing things." Asked to elaborate, Somoza laid out his plan. "It'd be very simple. I would declare an armistice, I would invite Sandino in, and we'd have some drinks, a good dinner, and when he went out one of my men would shoot him."[31]

Somoza's advice went over Washington's head. In 1933, the United States withdrew from Nicaragua, and Sandino ended his insurgency after the newly elected Nicaraguan president, Juan Bautista Sacasa, extended amnesty. But as time passed, Sandino grew concerned about the expanding power of the American-trained constabulary, and even more concerned about its new director, Somoza. Sandino returned to the capital in 1934 to discuss his anxieties with a sympathetic President Sacasa over drinks and dinner. But after Sandino left the president's home, he was seized by Somoza's men and shot—just as Somoza had planned years before.[32]

Sandino's assassination was a portent of things to come, but Washington hesitated to do more than wag its finger. One official traced the State Department's reserve to "its reluctance to interfere in the [region's] internal affairs." Given the choice between being a good neighbor and electing good men, Washington was increasingly opting for the former.[33]

Some Latin American leaders tried to convince Washington to take responsibility for the forces it had created, nurtured, and then unleashed. But no matter how anguished their pleas, they could not move the implacable Good Neighbor, who did little more than watch as its creatures lumbered, jaws open, toward the helpless civilian governments the republic had so carelessly left behind.[34]

Democracies fell like ripe fruit during the Great Depression, and by 1933, dictators ruled at least fifteen out of the twenty states in Latin America. In most cases, the regime changes were homegrown. But it was no coincidence that in nearly every nation the United States had occupied, military men eventually seized power. Nor was it surprising that the resulting dictatorships proved unusually durable and tyrannical. In Cuba, it was General Machado and Sergeant Batista. In the Dominican Republic, the head of the constabulary, Rafael Trujillo, overthrew the government in 1930 and established a three-decade-long dictatorship. In Haiti, the constabulary controlled national politics for decades until it brought François "Papa Doc" Duvalier to power. And in Nicaragua, Somoza followed up his assassination of Sandino by overthrowing Sacasa's government in 1936, establishing a political dynasty that would last until the Sandinistas—taking their name from one of Somoza's first victims—finally toppled it in 1979.[35]

Some Americans cheered the rise of "strong" regional rulers like Somoza and Trujillo. Most, however, were disappointed by democracy's ebb. But the takeaway was not that Washington should do something about it; it was that Washington should never have gotten involved in the first place. One diplomat considered Nicaragua's constabulary "one of the sorriest examples on our part of our inability to understand that we should not meddle in other peoples' affairs." But the United States had finally learned its lesson. It would redeem itself through the Good Neighbor Policy, even as it left others to pay for its earlier sins.[36]

FOR ALL ITS popularity, the Good Neighbor Policy so far was still fundamentally negative in nature. It was a list of prohibitory commandments: thou shalt neither murder thy neighbors nor trespass onto their land, thou shalt neither covet nor steal their resources, and above all, thou shalt not depose thy neighbors' governments to rule in their stead. Rather than enacting a positive program, Washington was mostly ending practices it had never liked undertaking in the first place. "In general, the Good Neighbor Policy does not enunciate any new concepts," one official confirmed. "What is new is a new and more far-reaching application of [neighborly] principles."[37]

For the moment, that was just fine. Secure in its hegemony, the United States could settle comfortably into the hemisphere and enjoy the sort of friendly, peaceful, and profitable regional relations it had always wanted. Stability was nice; so was democracy. But they were no longer necessary, and policies prioritizing them went mostly by the wayside. Meanwhile, the republic jealously guarded what few security interests it had left. Soldiers still patrolled the Canal Zone, warships still hove into Guantánamo Bay, and Congress still insisted on the American right to secure the Panama Canal in an emergency. Each of these exceptions underlined the larger point: the United States could be a good neighbor because it lived in a good neighborhood.[38]

Some, however, had already begun thinking about how the Good Neighbor Policy would have to evolve if extra-hemispheric intruders ever came knocking again. Welles, for instance, had long wanted to soften the blowback from future interventions by getting other neighbors involved—in effect, by multilateralizing the Monroe Doctrine, as Wilson had once tried to do. But most officials, including FDR, were happy to let the Good Neighbor Policy coast along right up until the moment that a new threat jolted them out of their complacency.[39]

Whole Hog on the Monroe Doctrine

Starting in the late 1930s, the rising threat from the fascist great powers—especially Nazi Germany—forced the United States to reckon with the problem of order once more. At first, Washington doubled down on a hemisphere-centric defense strategy and tools of indirect stabilization. But as the threat grew sharper, and the indirect tools proved as inadequate as ever, Washington reconsidered its choice of defensive line even as it began nervously fingering many of the interventionist weapons that the Good Neighbor had supposedly locked away for good.

Earlier that decade, German Chancellor Adolf Hitler had launched his nation on a staggering rearmament program far exceeding anything in the annals of modern militarism. The Führer wanted nothing less than German control of all Europe—followed, in short order, by world domination.[40]

Since world domination included the New World as much as the Old, Americans once again became concerned about their region's security. Germany had already started cutting into Latin American trade by the mid-1930s through unsavory means. FDR feared that if Hitler also conquered Europe, he could put South America's export-oriented economies into a headlock and exact political concessions in violation of the Monroe Doctrine. FDR's fears grew after Great Britain and France appeased Hitler at Munich. "For the first time since the Holy Alliance in 1818," the president told his cabinet, "the United States now face[s] the possibility of an attack on the Atlantic side in both the Northern and Southern Hemispheres."[41]

German ambitions were especially alarming because of the familiar problem of order. How could Americans stop Hitler from moving on the hemisphere when the hemisphere seemed ready to implode at the slightest touch? Washington did not sweat the usual Caribbean suspects, now firmly under the thumb of pro-American dictators. But South America, long a bastion of regional stability, was looking less and less reliable. It had ever-tightening economic links with the Nazis, and it was home to many with German blood. FDR thus expected that, at the touch of "a button from Berlin," revolutions could bring much of South America into the fascist fold. Citing "literally hundreds of concrete instances," Hull agreed the danger was "real and imminent."[42]

Such worries seemed warranted by hemispheric headlines. In 1938, Brazil and Chile beat off attempted coups by local fascist parties. In 1939, Argentina learned of a Nazi annexation plot; the following year, there was evidence of a fresh pot of conspiracies brewing in Argentina, Uruguay, and Brazil. With the benefit of hindsight, it is now clear that some of these intrigues were likely faked by British intelligence, others were the fevered dreams of German expatriates, and the remainder reflected local actors and grievances rather than masterminds in Berlin. But to Americans at the time, these plots only confirmed the region's susceptibility to German subversion, and they unsurprisingly led to a wave of articles and books on "The Coming Struggle for Latin America."[43]

On the other side of the world, meanwhile, Imperial Japan was making its own run at regional hegemony. If successful, the Japanese—who "always like to play with the big boys," FDR smirked—would then look east. Dangling between the jaws of fascist hegemons in Asia and Europe, the Western Hemisphere would rapidly become, as one popular author put it, "the ham in the world sandwich."[44]

=====

SOMETIMES HISTORIANS IMAGINE the tense years before Pearl Harbor as a battle between isolationists and interventionists, pitting Americans who wanted to hunker down behind the country's borders against those who would hurdle over them at the first opportunity. But the debate was never really over Fortress America; it was over the hemisphere. So-called "isolationists" did reject the interventionists' call to defend free Europe, but not so they could hide behind the republic's borders. Instead, many wanted to draw a defensive line around most or all of the hemisphere. "It isn't isolation to prepare to defend ... half a world," noted one crossly.[45]

Like most Americans, FDR agreed and focused on hemispheric defense at first. By 1937, he had privately concluded that the fascist threat meant the United States needed to go "whole hog on the Monroe Doctrine," a point he soon began stressing publicly at every available opportunity. "The epidemic of world lawlessness is spreading," he warned late that year. "Let no one imagine that America will escape, that America may expect mercy, that this Western Hemisphere will not be attacked."[46]

On September 1, 1939, Germany invaded Poland. Two days later, FDR expressly committed his nation to a hemisphere-centric defense strategy. In his first fireside chat in over a year, he reiterated that the country's security "is and will be bound up with the safety of the Western Hemisphere." Like most Americans, the president sympathized with the Allied cause. But it was not yet the republic's fight, and he would do everything in his power "to keep war from our own firesides by keeping war from coming to the Americas."[47]

FDR meant it. On the day war broke out, his administration began organizing another Pan-American Conference to establish a maritime neutrality zone stretching hundreds of miles around the Americas. Meanwhile, Welles began to multilateralize hemispheric security by engineering a Pan-American collective security system. Closer to home, FDR assembled an interagency committee of State, Navy, and War Department officials to coordinate defensive plans. Of the committee's nearly one hundred meetings through 1940, nearly all would prioritize Latin America.[48]

Americans largely followed FDR's lead. Only one month after war started, they were ready to go to war with Germany—just not in or for Europe. Polls reported that even as a bare majority of Americans (54 percent) supported strict neutrality, an overwhelming majority (72 percent) favored forcibly repelling any German incursion within 1,500 miles of the Panama Canal. Every poll over the next two years would show essentially the same thing: if it came down to it, Americans would defend most or all of Latin America by force.[49]

For now, the republic's priority was containment, the plan to build the hemisphere's defenses, and the hope that Axis aggressions would burn themselves out. FDR would sell supplies to the Allies, but in exchange he needed them to buy something much more valuable—time.[50]

A Nazi-Dominated World

Great-power wars usually last years, sometimes decades. Germany cut through France in six weeks. On May 10, 1940, the *Wehrmacht* ended the awkward standstill on the Western Front when it struck thunderously through the Low Countries, quickly steamrolling the French army and shoving the British off the continent at Dunkirk. By June 14, Paris was gone; a week later it was all over.

France had fallen, Great Britain was seemingly next, and after that it would be Latin America's turn. Each step in the chain seemed inevitable, and FDR's head spun at the sudden danger. "If Great Britain goes down," the president calculated, "the Axis powers will control the continents of Europe, Asia, Africa, Australasia, and the high seas—and they will be in a position to bring enormous military and naval resources against this hemisphere. It is no exaggeration to say that all of us, in all the Americas, would be living at the point of a gun."[51]

FDR did not expect Hitler to pull the trigger immediately. FDR conceded in his famous "Four Freedoms" speech that no "enemy would be stupid enough to attack us by landing troops in the United States"—at least not "until it had acquired strategic bases from which to operate." And therein lay the threat—that, like "the Maximilian interlude in Mexico," a foreign power would grab a foothold and then look north.[52]

FDR and other Americans were nearing the end of a revolution in their strategic thinking. Since its earliest days, the republic had sought to expel Europe's powers from the hemisphere and raise the drawbridge behind them. But as the German blitzkrieg was proving, new technologies were dropping new drawbridges, ones that could never be pulled up. France's fall thus forced Americans to reconsider their choice of defensive line—the hemisphere, or the world? FDR could abandon Europe to its fate and concentrate the republic's formidable resources on protecting its own region. Or the president could acknowledge that not even the most formidable defense of a region honeycombed with weak and unstable states could long withstand the might of a European continent united under the Third Reich.[53]

FDR made his choice. Since the best way to protect the republic was to protect the hemisphere, and the best way to protect the hemisphere seemed to be to defeat Nazi Germany in Europe, the president gradually swung the power and might of the United States behind the Allies. One of the president's first moves was to slip fifty aging destroyers into the pocket of the Royal Navy in exchange for rights to military bases on British colonies throughout the Western Hemisphere. Soon FDR shifted the economy onto wartime footing and christened the United States the "Arsenal of Democracy." By mid-1941, the nation had gone from making arms to wielding them as part of an undeclared naval war against Germany.[54]

America Firsters howled at each step away from neutrality. But the president kept his countrymen with him by linking the Allies' desperate fight to hemispheric defense. In speech after speech, he hammered home the same point—that "unless the advance of Hitlerism is forcibly checked now, the Western Hemisphere will be within range of the Nazi weapons of destruction." "It is time for all Americans," he added, "to stop being deluded by the romantic notion that the Americas can go on living happily and peacefully in a Nazi-dominated world."[55]

———

FDR's NEW EUROPEAN focus did not mean he had forgotten about his country's flanks. His first priority was safeguarding the hemisphere's remaining European colonies, which threatened to become Nazi beachheads overnight as Hitler overran the continent.[56]

Washington moved swiftly. Just days after Paris fell, Congress almost unanimously reaffirmed the country's long-standing rule prohibiting transfers of colonies in the region from one European power to another. The State Department then convinced Latin America to permit any state in the region to preemptively seize any European colony in an emergency. Since only the United States could feasibly do that, Latin

America was essentially authorizing Washington to invade, occupy, and administer endangered colonies throughout the hemisphere.[57]

The issue was not academic. Only a blockade and last-minute capitulation saved Vichy French colonies in the Caribbean from an American invasion. Meanwhile, ostensibly neutral American forces were quietly seizing control of nearby European outposts. In April 1941, the United States established a protectorate over Greenland; three months later, American forces landed in Iceland, and four months after that, American soldiers were on their way to Surinam (Dutch Guiana).[58]

FDR also revamped the Good Neighbor Policy to focus on stabilizing the republic's neighbors, including through a new twist on the old favorite of dollar diplomacy. As originally conceived, dollar diplomacy involved Washington extending political loans through Wall Street. In 1913, Secretary of State William Jennings Bryan had proposed cutting out the middleman, but Wilson had dismissed the idea of direct government loans to foreign nations as "novel and radical." Since then, however, the Great Depression had weakened the public's faith in private bankers while familiarizing it with the idea of the federal government taking their place. Now, for the first time ever, the United States began aiding foreign countries directly.[59]

One of the most important vehicles for this project was the Export-Import Bank. Originally created in 1934 to help American exporters, the Bank began loaning money four years later directly to Latin American governments. Once France fell, Congress nearly quadrupled the Bank's lending limits, and the Bank began intentionally trying to shore up Latin America's stability against foreign threats by investing in developmental projects, industrialization, exchange stabilization, surplus distribution, and economic diversification. Outside the Bank, Washington pioneered or returned to other forms of stabilizing aid, including favorable reciprocity deals, military assistance, health and sanitation programs, education projects, and construction of public works. FDR would not admit it, but dollar diplomacy was back in business, bigger and better than ever.[60]

Foreign threats also prompted new levels of tolerance for regional misbehavior toward American business interests. In 1937, Bolivia had seized Standard Oil's properties; a year later, Mexico followed suit and expropriated all foreign oil holdings. Officials in Washington decried what they saw as nationalist smash-and-grab operations. But since the administration needed to keep the hemisphere's governments happy and stable, it eventually decided Latin American economic nationalism was better appeased than opposed. After France fell, Hull and Welles strong-armed the luckless oil companies into settling the expropriation disputes; elsewhere, the State Department forced American creditors to resolve lingering debt disputes on unfavorable terms. Commercial interests were nice, but as always, they came second to hemispheric defense.[61]

SOME OF THESE new policies were welcomed in Latin America, but there were also disturbing signs that the Good Neighbor was one bad day away from transforming back into a big-stick-thumping colossus.

FDR had revealed something of his attitude a couple years earlier. "Suppose," he told reporters off the record, that "certain foreign governments, European governments, were to ... organize a revolution, a fascist revolution in Mexico." He asked pointedly: "Do you think that the United States could stand idly by and have this European menace right on our own borders? Of course not. You could not stand for it."[62]

And, indeed, FDR did not stand for it. In mid-1941, his administration published a "Proclaimed List" and instructed the region to boycott and sanction the nearly two thousand listed Latin American entities or else face sanctions themselves. Meanwhile, the return of dollar diplomacy predictably led to renewed interference in Latin America's internal affairs, including embedded financial advisors, control over development projects, and pressure to enact internal reforms.[63]

Other, more invasive policies were also readied. American military planners drew up numerous plans to preemptively occupy strategic locations in the hemisphere. In May 1940, FDR personally ordered his military chiefs to plan Operation Pot of Gold, a 110,000-man invasion of Brazil's eastern bulge. One month later, the president floated the equally ambitious idea of a hemispheric cartel in which Washington would effectively regulate the trade of every Latin American state by setting internal production numbers and controlling who they sold to.[64]

FDR did not need to implement these plans, especially after Germany foolishly invaded the Soviet Union in June 1941. But the plans' mere existence revealed it wouldn't take much for the Good Neighbor to once again break bad.[65]

If Ever a Policy Paid Dividends

On December 7, 1941, the rising sun had just begun warming the gray battleships moored in Pearl Harbor when the first Japanese planes appeared. Almost forty-five years earlier, the Japanese minister in Washington had urged Tokyo to launch a surprise attack on Hawai'i. Long deferred, his dream now came true. Japanese bombers screamed out of the sun and Mitsubishi Zeroes strafed the base's airfields. Elsewhere in the Pacific, the Japanese Empire made good on its self-proclaimed "Asian Monroe Doctrine" and began conquering British, Dutch, and American possessions.[66]

One of the few bright spots in the months that followed was the unity of the Western Hemisphere. Nine Latin American states declared war on Japan within days of the attack, and by the end of an emergency Pan-American conference in January 1942, every state but two— Chile and Argentina—had at least broken relations with the Axis. "If ever a policy paid dividends," cheered one of FDR's advisors, "the Good Neighbor Policy has."[67]

One of those dividends was the ability to wage world war mostly on foreign soil. The United States was the only great power that became wealthier during the war; while others burned and bled, the republic manufactured its way out of the Great Depression and actually raised its standard of living and per capita productivity. Since the United States faced no enemy at its continental gates, it could also devote its full attention and resources to defeating its rivals abroad. In mid-1942, the U.S. Navy checked the Japanese at Coral Sea and Midway; later that year, the United States struck back in both the Pacific and North Africa. Once the republic roared into action, it was practically unstoppable. Imperial Japan, Fascist Italy, Nazi Germany—all would be ground to dust; the only question was how fast and at what cost.[68]

Officials in Washington understood how much that war effort depended on a stable and friendly hemisphere, and they were ruthless in making sure the region continued to support them. The State Department demanded that neighboring nations round up thousands of suspect individuals, confiscate their properties, and deport them and their families to the United States for detention in small-scale versions of the West Coast's Japanese internment camps. Meanwhile, FDR kept the region's governments in line through the carrot of economic aid and—if any began to stray—the big sticks of sanctions, nonrecognition, and even intervention. Chile, which hesitated to declare war, was forced to break relations with the Axis through a public pressure campaign. Bolivia, after a revolt with supposed Axis links, was denied aid and recognition until the new government purged its ranks of suspected fascists. And Argentina, by maintaining strong links with the Axis, earned the State Department's ire as well as heavy sanctions, a recognition boycott, and gunboat diplomacy, all aimed at regime change.[69]

FDR continued paying lip service to earlier promises of nonintervention, but his words rang increasingly hollow. Welles, who had lost his
job in 1943 after a sex scandal, cast a critical eye on what remained of the
Good Neighbor Policy. "'Intervention,'" he observed waspishly, "seems
again to be becoming almost synonymous with 'nonintervention.'"[70]

═══

SOON THE SECOND World War ended, its final acts a gunshot in a
bunker and two mushroom clouds over Japan. Once again, most of the
world's centers of power lay smoldering and in ruins; once again, the
United States emerged with its economic, political, and military might
supercharged. By 1945, the republic commanded half the world's gross
product, half the world's shipping vessels, and two-thirds of the world's
gold reserves. It wielded a navy and air force larger than everyone else's
combined. Only the Soviet Union had a larger army, but that scarcely
mattered, for Americans monopolized that destroyer of worlds, the
atomic bomb.[71]

"America bestrides the world like a colossus," gasped one prominent
British politician. "Neither Rome at the height of its power nor Great
Britain in the period of economic supremacy enjoyed an influence so
direct, so profound, or so pervasive."[72]

Just as Henry Luce had foreseen, the first great American Century
had dawned.

A Global Monroe Doctrine

Since 1823, easing Europe's great powers out of the hemisphere had
been the north star of American grand strategy. Once the region was
cleansed of foreign influences, the thinking had run, the republic would
at last enjoy permanent security.

On the eve of its success, however, the dogma of James Monroe
appeared woefully obsolete. Any separation between the Old World and
the New disappeared in the fires of the Second World War, and barring
foreign powers from the neighborhood seemed small-minded in the
coming era of ICBMs and thermonuclear weapons. Americans could no
longer "sit in the parlor with a loaded shotgun, waiting," as Secretary of
State Dean Acheson put it in 1950. Instead, to preserve their security,
they had to go out and build a safer world.[73]

As American planners began designing that postwar world, they
found themselves returning again and again to the lessons they had
learned managing their own neighborhood. The Good Neighbor Policy

had sought to reconcile the republic's security needs with its ideals; however imperfect the result, it represented the country's best effort at the sort of world it wished to see. One Commerce Department official observed to Welles in 1942 that "the Good Neighbor Policy in this hemisphere has been the laboratory in which have been distilled the essences from which a post-war plan can be realistically brewed for the entire world." Welles and FDR emphatically agreed, and British diplomats predicted early on that they would use "Pan-Americanism as a model for the post-war world."[74]

Sure enough, after the war the United States scaled up its regional policies and institutions to create the new international order. It is no coincidence that the Atlantic Charter—FDR and Winston Churchill's celebrated blueprint for the postwar world—was drafted in large part by Welles, the State Department's preeminent Latin American expert. Welles also drafted the United Nations Charter, a document that reflects Welles's Latin American experience through and through, from the emphasis on collective security to the prohibition against external armed aggression. Elsewhere, American officials expanded Hull's reciprocity programs into a full-blown free-trade program, structured originally around the General Agreement on Trade and Tariffs but eventually institutionalized in the World Trade Organization and preached as the Washington Consensus. Latin American specialists also used the Export-Import Bank and other regional initiatives as a template for the developmental program of the World Bank, while decades of dollar diplomacy were recast as the International Monetary Fund and its permanent staff of money doctors.[75]

Collectively, the result was an international order informed by—and often directly transplanted from—the regional order first pioneered by Welles, FDR, and their predecessors. The new world order was, in many ways, a New World order.

OFFICIALS IN WASHINGTON at first hoped that their new order could safeguard the peace of the world on its own. On Memorial Day 1942, Welles publicly acknowledged that postwar "social and economic chaos" would force the United States and its allies, however reluctantly, to the exercise of "an international police power." But that Rooseveltian assertion of power would be temporary, Welles thought—a bridge to a self-sustaining "permanent system of general security."[76]

Welles should have known better. Chaos was indeed coming, but on a scale that would make it nearly impossible for the United States to avoid a permanent global role. By the time Welles made his speech, Hitler's legions had already taken down one great power, France, while leaving another, Great Britain, on its knees. Scores of smaller states had been devastated as well, and soon the Axis powers themselves would collapse under the Allies' blows. By 1945, Europe was blackened from Brest to Bucharest, a power vacuum stretching an entire ruined continent. Only two great powers remained standing: a supercharged United States and a bloodied but unbeaten Soviet Union.[77]

For generations, American statesmen had contended with the problem of order in their neighborhood. Now they confronted the same problem worldwide. If they did nothing, the Red Army could overrun all Eurasia, achieving the same regional hegemony that Americans had just spent countless lives and dollars denying Hitler's Germany and Hideki Tōjō's Japan.[78]

Stopping that from happening became the new north star of American grand strategy. On March 12, 1947, President Harry S. Truman announced the Truman Doctrine; henceforth, the republic would support "free peoples who are resisting attempted subjugation by armed minorities or by outside pressures." Four months later, George F. Kennan gave this strategy its name. "The Russians look forward to a duel of infinite duration," he wrote. "In these circumstances it is clear that the main element of any United States policy toward the Soviet Union must be that of a long-term, patient but firm and vigilant containment."[79]

"Containment" became the watchword of the new twilight struggle, but in many ways Americans were just pouring old wine into new bottles. In 1823, President Monroe had cautioned Europe's great powers against "extend[ing] their system to any portion of this hemisphere." From one perspective, Monroe was excluding Europe from the New World. From another, he was containing it in the Old.[80]

Transitioning to the Cold War was thus easy for American policymakers. The old ideological threats of monarchism, colonialism, and fascism were swapped out for the creed of communism; the French, British, Spanish, Japanese, and German empires supplanted by the looming Soviet one. The new dividing line would be not the Atlantic Ocean but the Iron Curtain, and the United States would be playing not for a hemisphere but for the free world. In the mid-1970s, a young senator from Delaware named Joe Biden identified containment for what it really was—"a global Monroe Doctrine."[81]

So it is unsurprising that the "new" strategy of containment bore the unmistakable stamp of the republic's long struggle with the problem of order in its neighborhood. Above all, there was the same obsession with instability and disorder, along with the familiar fear that such power vacuums could tempt the United States's adversaries into expansion. One CIA analysis concluded in late 1947 that the greatest danger to American security came from the Kremlin's "unprecedented opportunity" to "exploit the weakness, instability, and confusion prevalent in neighboring countries to bring to power therein Communist or Communist-controlled governments." Analysts all along the political spectrum would echo the point for decades.[82]

Equally unsurprising, American officials dealt with this "new" problem of order in ways not very different from how they had long dealt with disorder and instability in their own hemisphere. Most obviously, there was the willingness to go to war to prevent the expansion of hostile influence into vulnerable but strategically important areas. Once, it had been General Philip Sheridan on the Rio Grande; now, it was General Douglas MacArthur at the 38th parallel. Indeed, NATO and other Cold War alliances were modeled in large part on the Rio Treaty, a mutual defense alliance signed by the hemisphere in 1947 that in turn traced its lineage back through Welles and FDR all the way to Wilson's aborted Pan-American Pact.[83]

Cold War officials also retained the same unrelenting focus on removing opportunities for hostile expansion by stabilizing and strengthening weak areas of the world. "It should be a cardinal point of our policy," Kennan argued in 1947, "that other elements of independent power are developed on the Eurasian land mass as rapidly as possible." Acheson agreed, reasoning that since the Soviets entertained "hopes for early expansion into areas of weakness," the United States needed to launch "a program for strengthening the free world." Soon American diplomats were saying similar things about the rest of the world, where Secretary of State Dean Rusk noted "there is a great deal that can be done by preventive action."[84]

Officials in Washington hoped to rely mostly on peaceful "preventive action," stabilizing through aid and trade rather than the bayonet blade. So, drawing on political instincts honed over the better part of a century, the United States spent much of the Cold War bankrolling development projects and reconstruction assistance for strategically important areas—most famously, the Marshall Plan for Europe, followed by programs like Point Four and the Alliance for Progress elsewhere. Government agencies like USAID meanwhile spread American technical expertise across the four corners of the globe. Each of these efforts was in turn reinforced by the global economic and financial institutions Washington had established. In "The American Century," media mogul Henry Luce had promised that Americans would share their bountiful wealth, "technical and artistic skills," and "system of free economic enterprise" with the world, and in the name of both anti-communism and humanitarianism, that pledge was coming true.[85]

Officials in Washington remained split, however, over the fourth and final component of Luce's program—the need for the United States to spread "the ideals of civilization" and especially the ideal of democracy. Some hewed to Wilson's earlier insights and preached the gospel of self-government not just as an inherent good, but also as a way of averting communist-tempting societal instability and collapse. Most policymakers, however, approached democracy promotion cautiously. Going from autocracy to democracy requires demolishing existing power structures and creating new ones, a delicate process in which it is all too easy for reform to slip into revolution. One U.S. Army intelligence report summed up the familiar problem: "Where dictatorships have been abolished, the resulting governments have been weak and unstable." Or, as President John F. Kennedy outlined after Dominican dictator Trujillo was assassinated and a new government was needed: "There are three possibilities in descending order of preference: a decent democratic regime, a continuation of the Trujillo regime, or a [Fidel] Castro regime. We ought to aim at the first, but we really can't renounce the second until we are sure that we can avoid the third."[86]

Efforts to avoid the third quickly took priority over establishing "decent democracies" or promoting self-government. Originally, FDR and other senior policymakers had planned to dismantle their allies' colonial empires once the Second World War ended. But in his famous Long Telegram, Kennan warned that Moscow wanted the same thing, on the familiar grounds that "there will be created a vacuum which will favor Communist-Soviet penetration." Similar concerns haunted Americans' postwar drive to cool relations with dictatorships worldwide. In both cases, Washington soon reversed course. Luce had charged Americans with helping lift "mankind from the level of the beasts to what the Psalmist called a little lower than the angels," but in practice the United States was willing to work with any leader, angel or beast, who promised to keep their country stable and non-communist.[87]

Even with American backing, however, local authorities could not always hold the line against disorder and revolution, and the result was a slow but seemingly inexorable expansion of American influence. The world was filling up with poor, war-torn, and factionalized nations, especially as anti-colonial movements gained steam and then independence. In American eyes, these countries' vulnerability made them fertile fields for communist expansion, which in turn required the antidote of American involvement. It didn't take long for the United States to fall back into its interventionist rut, and from Korea to Vietnam, the republic again ended up far more involved in the internal affairs of foreign countries than it had ever wanted to be.[88]

Of course, in all the excitement, Washington never forgot about its old neighborhood. In July 1960, Soviet leader Nikita Khrushchev made the mistake of thinking otherwise when he declared that "the Monroe Doctrine has outlived its time, has outlived itself, has died, so to say, a natural death." But reports of the Doctrine's death were greatly exaggerated, as Khrushchev learned when he tried to sneak nuclear missiles into Castro's Cuba two years later. Even in its original form, the Doctrine still had enough kick in it to take the world to the brink of nuclear war.[89]

Efforts to stop Latin American states from going red—and rolling back those that did—would feature prominently in the republic's Cold War policies. Just like old times, Washington overthrew governments left and right (but mostly left) while intervening in the internal affairs of many more. Cuba's turn toward communism was bad enough, but at least the island could be quarantined before it became a true Soviet outpost. If other states in the region followed Cuba's example, however, then the United States could suddenly find *itself* being contained.[90]

Even at its most neighborly, the Colossus of the North always had its limits. Over vociferous domestic opposition, the Carter administration agreed in 1977 to hand control of the Panama Canal to the Panamanians. But when Congress asked what would happen if the Panamanian government tried to close the canal down "for repairs," National Security Advisor Zbigniew Brzezinski did not mince words. "In that case," he replied tartly, "we will move in and close down the Panamanian government for repairs."[91]

Sometimes it seemed like the republic had learned little from its earlier experiences in the Western Hemisphere. Cold War officials remained prone to paranoia, spying the hand of the Kremlin behind every foreign setback and often responding disproportionately in ways they would later regret. Interventions to prop up unstable governments became as routine as they had been during the 1900s and 1910s, with results no more gratifying than before. And as previously, the United States never ended up being the nation that bore the ultimate costs.

But from another perspective, Americans were just reencountering the iron law of international politics—there are no good choices, only trade-offs. Speaking of his country's role in world affairs, Secretary Acheson once observed irritably that "we cannot direct or control; we cannot make a world, as God did, out of chaos." But, driven by the problem of order, Americans sometimes felt like they had no choice but to keep trying, however fallible and imperfect the results.[92]

CONCLUSION

From his perch in Paris, the Tenth Count of Aranda could see the future. One of the Spanish Empire's ablest diplomats, he had been entertaining powerful statesmen at his ambassadorial residence throughout 1783. His guests had included such American notables as Ben Franklin, John Adams, and John Jay, who had worked closely with the Count to negotiate the treaties officially ending the Revolutionary War. The Americans thought they knew their Spanish friend well, and above all they appreciated his warmth for their new nation.[1]

But that warmth was a lie. Spain had helped midwife the birth of the fledgling republic, but the Count thought it had been a terrible mistake. Shortly after the Revolutionary War ended, the Count unburdened himself in a secret memorandum to King Charles III. "I'm struck with grief and dread," he began. Spain was already declining, and its colonies in the New World would soon demand their independence. Now, the Count argued, the appearance of the United States had made a difficult situation impossible. Even though the republic had been born "a pygmy," it would eventually consolidate its power, turn on its neighbors and onetime benefactors, and become "a giant and then a colossus, devastating in all those regions."[2]

Such dark premonitions would have struck most contemporary Americans as overblown, at least once their neighbors gained independence. The United States was rising, but it was different, *exceptional*, a nation conceived in liberty, opposed to colonial control, and dedicated to sovereignty and self-determination. The Count knew better. "Man is the same in all places and in all climes," he wrote cynically, and the future would surely reflect "what has happened in all ages with nations that begin to rise."[3]

Time proved the Count right. In the decades following, the United States snatched Florida from Spain before marching westward and

subjugating the rest of the continent. By 1865, the United States had resolved its paralyzing sectional conflict, and it was ready to look outward
with united eyes.

Over the next ninety years, the republic grew into the colossus of
the Count's prediction. It dispossessed Spain of its last Caribbean colonies, shoved France and Russia off the continent, and regularly threatened war against Europe's other great powers. It severed a country and
then a continent, helping Panama secede and digging a canal there while
maintaining monopolistic rights over competing routes. In the west, the
United States seized the most important strategic position in the Pacific
Ocean; in the east, it annexed or fastened protectorates over every island
in the Greater Antilles not already possessed by its ally Great Britain. It
came to control every major sea-lane in its immediate neighborhood, and
by 1919 it patrolled them with the world's most powerful navy. It flushed
foreign currencies out of the region's circulatory system, replaced them
with dollars, and helped its capitalists and corporations claim ascendancy in the region's economic affairs. And, of course, it intervened—it
intervened over and over and over again, deposing and setting up presidents, breaking and remaking nations, turning its fiat into law and its
strength into hegemony.

Time proved the Count of Aranda right, but why? What caused a
rising United States to act so aggressively, and what does it mean for us
today?

A Giant and Then a Colossus

From the Founding to the dawn of the Cold War, securing the neighborhood was one of the central objectives of American foreign policy.
Originally framed in defensive terms, that objective led the republic to
adopt increasingly aggressive tactics, thanks in large part to the problem
of order.

States in the international system generally fear their neighbors
growing too strong, but that concern never really crossed the minds of
most Americans. Instead, early on, the United States found itself in a
charmed situation: it was a rising power surrounded by a handful of
foreign colonies and many weak neighbors, but no serious locally based
rival. In fact, the only real threat lay well over the horizon, in distant
Europe. Given that balance of forces, the optimal grand strategy came
naturally to the young nation—to survive and grow, the United States

needed to contain the region's outside powers while gradually clearing the hemisphere of their flags.

Statesmen in Washington realized that, for purposes of this strategy, the weakness of the country's neighbors was both a blessing and a curse. On the one hand, American strategy was premised on the idea that the United States's neighbors were too weak to harm it directly, and that weakness allowed the United States to grow until it had filled up a continent. On the other hand, that very weakness was itself a menace, inviting the kind of foreign influence that Washington was struggling to keep out. The United States accordingly centered much of its post–Civil War foreign policy around ensuring that its neighbors were, if not strong, then at least stable.

Over the course of the late nineteenth and early twentieth centuries, the United States had mixed success in keeping its grand strategy on track. On the plus side, the republic achieved its ultimate objective and pushed Europe's powers out of the hemisphere one by one. Europe's internal rivalries and wars were a big help, distracting and dividing Europe's great powers and making it easy for the United States to continue fattening on their follies. But the United States also helped itself by making sure that Europe's stake in Latin America remained tiny, and that Europe never had an especially good reason to send a large military expedition into the region or to complain about the United States's growing hegemony. Some of that reflected clever economic statecraft; for example, Washington substantially cut down Europe's regional stake by refunding its neighbors' European debts through American banks. Some of it was clever diplomacy; by policing the Monroe Doctrine fanatically, the United States never allowed "Scramble for Africa"–like dynamics to begin in Latin America. By 1945, Washington had torn down almost every great-power outpost in the hemisphere, and the few that remained were relics of a bygone age.

On the other side of the ledger, however, the United States never figured out how to keep the region permanently stable at a cost it was willing to bear. The basic problem was that the republic had no good options. If one of its neighbors imploded, the United States could not safely ignore the resulting power vacuum for fear that one of its great-power rivals might step in. Nor could the United States count on the mere threat of war to keep its rivals out; that approach ran too high a risk of actual great-power bloodletting, even assuming that Washington could always tell what its rivals were up to before it was too late. So that left the United States to either quell local disorder as it developed or prevent it from bubbling up in the first place. In an ideal world, Washington would have accomplished either task by working with local authorities. In practice, however, local authority was rarely a sustainable—or even available—option. Logic and experience thus led American policymakers to a zero-sum conclusion that seemed as tragic as it was inescapable: the safest way—sometimes the only way—to stop its rivals from filling local power vacuums was for the United States to fill them first.

On its own, that conclusion was jarring. Making matters worse was the fact that, just as the United States was rising to power, the region was slipping into new bouts of chaos and instability. The timing was no coincidence, as the United States ended up massively destabilizing the region in its clumsy attempts to stabilize it. The result was a self-reinforcing loop—disorder caused interventions and interventions caused disorder—that sucked the United States deeper and deeper into the region's affairs.

But the timing was no coincidence for a second reason as well: the United States was also destabilizing the region through its rise alone. As the republic grew, it naturally and often inadvertently pulled its neighbors further into its orbit, a deepening gravitational well that stressed those neighbors' economies, societies, politics, and cultures and sometimes caused them to break.

One example was trade. Sometimes with American encouragement, sometimes not, Latin Americans reoriented their economies north to reap the riches offered by the growing American market. But the United States was insatiable, and local monocultures developed throughout the region. When economic conditions were favorable, the region profited handsomely; when things went wrong, however, they went very wrong indeed. For example, when Congress changed the sugar tariff in 1890, it sent Hawai'i spiraling into economic crisis and eventually revolution; when Congress changed the tariff back four years later, it plunged Cuba into its own economic crisis and eventually revolution.

These destabilizing trends fed off each other and a growing sense of threat to fuel the United States's accelerating takeover. Somewhere, sometime, stability would collapse—perhaps because of pressures caused by the United States's rise, perhaps for unrelated reasons. Fearing foreign influence, Washington would intervene to restore stability, but its meddling would only make things worse, leading to a cascading failure of self-perpetuating destabilization and intervention.

Characters differed, pacing fluctuated, and emphases changed, but the same basic plotline runs throughout most American interventions of this era. Concerns about imminent foreign intervention or involvement pushed the United States to annex Hawai'i, occupy Haiti, take over Dominican customs, and purchase the Danish West Indies. Other times, the United States jumped in to preempt foreign threats in the not-so-distant future, including when Washington overthrew Nicaragua's regime in 1909 and again in 1910, retired Honduras's president in 1911, occupied Veracruz, and ratified a canal treaty with Managua. Other interventions involved situations where no foreign interference appeared on the horizon, but policymakers nevertheless acted either to preempt future instability or to uphold the broader credibility of the Roosevelt Corollary and related policies. Examples include the many interventions in Panama, the post-receivership interventions in and eventual occupation of the Dominican Republic, and the post-Zelaya interventions in Nicaragua.

Of course, the problem of order did not cause *every* regional intervention; for example, the United States did not liberate Cuba or help Panama secede primarily to preempt foreign intervention. Instead, the point is simply that the problem acted as a constraint: it consistently channeled American policy in one specific direction, and Washington was rarely (if ever) able to deviate from its strictures, even if other factors also pushed in the same direction. Even in the initial interventions in Cuba and Panama, for instance, the problem of order was very much on the minds of American policymakers, and it directly shaped the aftermath of both interventions.

By 1919, however, the republic's instability-fueled expansion began drawing to a close as its underlying assumptions faded. Officials in Washington started to understand how much their stabilization strategy was destabilizing the region, even as they also realized that the region no longer faced a serious foreign threat, and that the United States thus no longer needed to preemptively fill the region's power vacuums to ensure its own security. Finally, officials were stung by the backlash their meddling had provoked, and they feared that if nothing changed, some foreign power could someday gain a foothold by invitation rather than intervention.

With no reason to continue its stabilization strategy and many reasons to stop, the United States stood down and transitioned to the Good Neighbor Policy. As long as the problem of order stayed dormant, the republic would prioritize consolidating its hegemony by repairing its tattered relationship with the region. But the Good Neighbor Policy was only as good as the idyllic conditions on which it rested, and when foreign threats returned, so did the hard choices that had driven American policy for the better part of a century.

The Only Kind of Hegemony We Need to Seek or Ought to Want

Over time, several misconceptions have sprung up about this era of American foreign policy. One of the most common is that the United States set out to dominate the region. That misconception is understandable; Americans, after all, had been dreaming of regional hegemony since the earliest days of the republic, when Alexander Hamilton urged the country to become "ascendant in the system of American affairs." But the choice of means was critical. By definition, regional hegemony required only that the United States become the sole great power in the region; it did not require the republic to control or bully its neighbors, none of whom stood a realistic chance of becoming great powers in their own right. So in the decades after the Civil War, Americans largely expected to achieve regional hegemony through a process of elimination: by pushing Europe's great powers out of the hemisphere.[4]

Officials in Washington had no premeditated plan to reduce the whole region to vassal status. As impressive as the number of American interventions is, the more revealing figure is the far greater number of times that Washington *declined* its neighbors' invitations to send troops, annex territory, or establish protectorates. For all its interventionism, Washington proved remarkably reluctant to take advantage of opportunities to extend its regional control. Root once underlined the point: that "patience and a few years of the right kind of treatment ... will give us in [the region] the only kind of hegemony we need to seek or ought to want."[5]

Obviously, that is not how things turned out. Far from leading a community of friendly nations, the United States ended up clutching many of its resentful neighbors in its terrible thrall. On one level, that was still success of a sort; the United States had kept its European rivals out of the hemisphere in the process and attained regional hegemony. But, tellingly, few American leaders saw it that way. Instead, the endless cycle of interventions was seen as an abject failure of policy, a grand strategy that had badly miscarried and brought the country to the right destination but via the wrong path.

Americans had wanted hegemony over the New World, yes—but not like this.

—

A SECOND POPULAR misconception is that the United States intervened in the region primarily for cultural, personal, or ideological reasons. Some historians emphasize any number of faddish theories that supposedly led the republic to hack and slash its way through its neighborhood in a misguided attempt to "civilize" it, or as part of a search for the next great frontier, or in conjunction with a global Social Darwinian struggle for survival. Other scholars will stress the quirks and personalities of the individuals who ultimately launched the interventions: Roosevelt's mania for order, Taft's penchant for business, Wilson's missionary moralism. But these explanations—and many others like them—suffer from serious shortcomings.[6]

First, there is the sheer continuity of American policy. From 1860 to 1945, the United States was led by Democrats and Republicans, progressives and conservatives, internationalists and isolationists. Some presidents were soldiers; others were Quakers or the sons of preachers. But all found themselves drawn deeper and deeper into the region's affairs until the United States achieved regional hegemony, at which point all reversed course and withdrew. So Republicans ended up presiding over both interventionism's rise (Roosevelt and Taft) and its fall (Harding, Coolidge, and Hoover), while the extremes of American policy were reached under two Democratic administrations (Wilson and FDR). These trends point toward a deeper, more structural explanation for American behavior than personal quirks or passing ideologies.

Similarly, there is the consistency of American public opinion. Save for during the Spanish-American War, Americans did not hunger for their government to police nations beyond their borders. Quite the opposite, as electoral campaigns regularly demonstrated. Candidates of both parties, rather than promising bigger and better interventions, consistently promised restraint and ran against their opponents' interventionist records. Sometimes, leaders delivered on those promises; other times, they did not. But their campaign rhetoric alone reinforces just how little interest the electorate had in going abroad in search of monsters to destroy.[7]

Cultural, personal, and other ideological explanations also fit poorly with the often extreme reluctance of American officials to use force in the region. Roosevelt, for example, sometimes spoke flippantly about administering "spankings," but when push came to shove, he recoiled at the thought of creating a customs receivership in the Dominican Republic ("I want to do nothing to them") or reoccupying Cuba ("I loathe the thought"). Cuba's reoccupation also upset Taft ("the greatest crisis I ever passed through") and Root ("I felt very badly"). Taft and Wilson likewise dreaded the prospect of intervening in Mexico ("God forbid!"), and Wilson felt forced into the occupations of Haiti and the Dominican Republic (with "the deepest reluctance" and as "the least of the evils in sight"). Officials were generally less reluctant to launch nonviolent interventions, but that was precisely because they hoped such interventions would make the use of force less necessary later on.[8]

Finally, cultural, personal, and other ideological explanations try to make too much out of too little. Nearly all contemporary ideologies were indeterminate: they could justify any number of competing and often mutually exclusive policy proposals. Frederick Jackson Turner, for example, famously argued that with the closing of the American frontier in 1890, Americans would need to look abroad. But that was fortune-cookie wisdom, not a specific policy program. Framed at different levels of generality, Turner's conclusion could have justified anything from trade agreements and tourism to berserker annexationism. At most, one can argue that American policy was consistent with many different ideologies, but that is a far cry from saying that it was *caused* by those ideologies.[9]

None of this is to suggest that ideology never played a role. Officials in Washington, for example, overestimated their ability to stabilize foreign societies thanks to everything from cognitive biases to their deep-seated faith in American exceptionalism. On the margins, these and other ideological factors helped determine which specific stabilization approaches the republic pursued and how those approaches progressed. But they were not the primary factor motivating Washington during this period.

One ideological factor, however, deserves independent consideration: racism. Of all the ideologically tinted explanations, racism contributes most to explaining why Americans meddled in their neighbors' affairs so often and so much, in large part because racism was omnipresent and deeply rooted among American leaders throughout the relevant period. But as recent scholarship suggests, racism had a more complicated and sometimes counterintuitive effect on American interventionism than is often realized.[10]

First, it is important to distinguish between decisions to intervene and the interventions themselves. Once an intervention began, racism often shaped how it unfolded. But there is far less evidence that racism played much of a role in initiating interventions in the first place. Calls to take up the "White Man's Burden" were the stuff of stump speeches and polemics in the park, not cabinet meetings and departmental memoranda. On occasion, some policymakers voiced interest in "uplifting" their neighbors, but such views were rare and usually used to justify interventions already begun.[11]

Racism did encourage interventions in one significant way, however. By and large, American policymakers believed that their non-white neighbors were inherently ill-suited for self-government. That belief aggravated Americans' concerns about the stability of their neighbors and thereby made intervention both more likely and more invasive when it occurred. Cubans, for example, had no history of unstable independent government in 1901 (or any history of independent government at all), but officials in Washington nevertheless imposed the Platt Amendment on the island because—partially for racial reasons—they judged *Cuba libre's* prospects for stability slim.[12]

At the same time, it is easy to overstate how much this ultimately mattered. The truth is that parts of the region *were* chronically unstable (though obviously not because of their inhabitants' skin color), and it was the fact of instability—not race—that primarily led to interventions. And even if racism made Americans more pessimistic about their neighbors' political prospects, many policymakers never believed that race was destiny. Countries like Costa Rica proved that "Latin American stability" was not an oxymoron, and policies like the Platt Amendment would have made little sense if alleged racial inferiority made self-governance completely impossible.[13]

On balance, racism instead likely curbed American adventurism. As discussed in previous chapters, racism led most Americans to want nothing to do with the region, which in turn dampened their enthusiasm for intervening in it. It is no coincidence that the political party most affiliated with the anti-imperialist movement during this time—the Democrats—was also the party most associated with lynchings and institutionalized segregation.[14]

So as widespread, deep-seated, and abhorrent as American racism assuredly was, the evidence suggests that it made interventions less likely to start (but more destabilizing once begun).

ONE OTHER COMMON misconception portrays Washington as little more than a muscleman for Big Business, a debt collector with a big stick. Major General Smedley Darlington Butler famously espoused this view after retiring. "I helped in the raping of half a dozen Central American republics for the benefit of Wall Street," Butler growled. "Looking back on it, I feel I might have given Al Capone a few hints. The best *he* could do was to operate his racket in three city districts. We Marines operated on three *continents*."[15]

For all its polemical appeal, however, Butler's account has never found much favor among most scholars. Like other nations, the United States would land troops to protect its citizens and their property during conflicts, but it is hard to find examples of more invasive interventions at businessmen's behest. Officials regularly treated commercial interests with skepticism or disdain, even while—especially while—working alongside them. Indeed, American interventionism crested during the Progressive Era, when suspicion of concentrated economic power peaked, while reaching troughs during the Gilded Age and the Roaring Twenties (when, as Coolidge quipped, the business of America was business). American interventionism also did not correlate with levels of American investment; the United States often intervened in places—Haiti, Nicaragua, and the Dominican Republic—where Americans had minuscule commercial interests. And even when American companies were directly involved, it was not unusual for the government to neglect, oppose, or even double-cross them. Simply put, Washington was usually after bigger game than bananas, even if it occasionally partnered with private companies to pursue a mutual quarry.[16]

Some scholars have instead gravitated toward the more sophisticated "New Empire" thesis. According to this account, American businessmen were just too good at their jobs, regularly producing more than what the saturated domestic market could bear and thereby triggering economic downturns and social unrest. In essence, too many goods were chasing too few customers in a republic bursting at the seams. If Americans could not find a release valve, then, as one Gilded Age economist put it, "we are certain to be smothered in our own grease." The solution was obvious: the United States should dispose of its production glut abroad. Nineteenth-century policymakers thus purportedly pursued a policy of commercial expansionism that peaked in the 1890s with the inauguration of the "New Empire"—a postcolonial effort focused on controlling foreign markets rather than foreign territory. Over time, this effort evolved into a global "Open Door" policy, an attempt to make the world safe for corporate capitalism by breaking down obstacles to American commercial penetration.[17]

Despite its popularity, the New Empire thesis has serious flaws. To start, there is remarkably little concrete evidence that nineteenth-century officials let the "overproduction" thesis guide their decision-making. Overproduction was one economic theory among many, and it jostled for policymakers' attention alongside conflicting theories about corporate monopolies, speculation, immigration, monetary policy, and tariff schedules. Context matters too: "gluts" and "overproduction" were hot buzzwords in speeches before the National Association of Manufacturers, but the closer one gets to private letters and policy memoranda, the less often and important the underlying theory appears. Indeed, nineteenth-century American companies themselves did not really need or want the government to secure foreign markets on their behalf, preferring to focus instead on the domestic market. So it should come as little surprise that the government pursued overseas commerce with lackluster effort at best, except where doing so aligned with other, more important objectives.[18]

New Empire scholars have also struggled to explain how or why a search for markets would have entangled the United States in some of the poorest, most war-torn countries in the hemisphere. If commerce had been front and center in American foreign policy, Washington would presumably have focused its efforts on moderately wealthy countries with business-friendly environments—the kinds of countries that needed American products and could afford to buy them. Instead, the United States intervened in its most unstable neighbors, where export opportunities were slim, and in the process alienated potential consumers in other, more promising markets.[19]

Commercial ambitions certainly affected American policy on the margins; indeed, since the republic's earliest days, every American administration has promoted foreign trade to some extent. But that's the point—expanding trade has always been important, and it was not a special priority during this time.[20]

———

FINALLY, SOME HISTORIANS have critiqued a security-based account of American policy by arguing that rival great powers posed no real threat to the hemisphere, and that officials' security concerns must therefore have been makeweights. But that critique falls flat too.

If nothing else, American fears were genuine. Officials in Washington did not make up threats in order to mask their "real" reasons for intervening, even if they on rare occasion played up the magnitude of foreign threats for public consumption. Rightly or wrongly, American leaders were obsessed with the great-power threat to the hemisphere, and concerns about it pervaded not only their speeches but also their diaries and most private correspondence. If policymakers were fooling the public, it was only because they had first fooled themselves.[21]

But American policymakers were not fooling themselves. Great powers *were* gunning for the hemisphere during this time, even if not always, and even if not all at once. Kaiser Wilhelm II eagerly anticipated the day when Germany would break Monroe's monopoly on the hemisphere. Adolf Hitler likewise panted for world empire, and Japan, along with many of Europe's powers, had long appreciated Hawai'i's unrivaled strategic value. And, of course, Emperor Napoleon III supplied the precedent when he invaded and occupied Mexico as part of a Grand Design that contemplated a vast expansion of European influence in the region. Each of these aspirations mirrored the grim reality outside the hemisphere, where the great powers were actively carving up the world into their private colonial preserves.

Some historians dismiss these threats to the region as flights of fancy, someday dreams scarcely worth bothering about today. It would have been irrational, the argument goes, for Europe's great powers to have challenged the Monroe Doctrine when they were consistently obliged to tend to the balance of power in Europe, and it was therefore irrational for Americans to take these supposed threats seriously.[22]

Americans did benefit from Europe's balance of power, but they also knew it was far from a surefire guarantee of their own security. Even though European powers were consumed by internal rivalries, they channeled that intracontinental competition into an *extra*continental race for colonies and influence. For that reason, contemporary European crises often centered on events outside Europe's borders, including in Asia, Africa, and the Middle East. Officials in Washington thus did not fear that European great powers would colonize Latin America during a break from their competition; they feared that the great powers would colonize Latin America as *part* of their competition. And if even one great power eked out a foothold in Latin America, that incursion could set off a free-for-all since no other great power could risk being left behind.[23]

Europe's balance of power was also no static constraint. Europe was a kaleidoscope: coalitions shifted frequently and dramatically; great powers rose and fell with startling speed. One year one nation stood atop the continent; the next, it was friendless and isolated. In 1855, Europe's great powers were busy slashing at each other in the Crimean War, and few would have predicted France dispatching a massive expeditionary force to Mexico. Six years later, France did just that.[24]

Europe's leaders also did not need to be looking to expand into the Western Hemisphere to end up doing so anyway. Europe's chancelleries rarely controlled events at the periphery of empire, and crises on the ground could and often did force foreign capitals to take aggressive steps beyond what they had originally planned. (Officials in Washington knew this dynamic well from their diplomats' freelancing in Hawai'i, Panama, Nicaragua, and Mexico.) That meant that any European intervention in the region, no matter how innocently begun, could easily spiral out of control.[25]

Complicating the picture still further was the uncertainty that dogged Washington's every step. Modern historians, armed with archival access, perfect hindsight, and comfy armchairs, can parse the scope and magnitude of the threats the United States faced at their leisure. Not so for the policymakers of the day. During this time, Washington was flooded with reports of European intrigues stretching across half the world, and it was seldom obvious which of those reports mattered. Were European soldiers being landed just to collect debts—or to occupy a strategic harbor? Was a European bank just trying to make a quick buck—or fronting for a foreign ministry's grab for a financial leash? And however benign the motives behind today's intervention, what guarantee did Washington have about where that intervention was going tomorrow?[26]

One of the most compelling pieces of evidence supporting the existence of a great-power threat is the extra-hemispheric control group. From 1870 to 1914, Europeans seized political control over at least 85 percent of previously independent nations in Africa, the Middle East, and Asia, including China. Latin America, however, maintained its independence from Europe during that same period despite offering essentially identical opportunities for European expansion. One can and should question the ways in which the United States tried to safeguard the hemisphere, especially its decades-long streak of interventionism. But it is surely no coincidence that the only part of the world to survive Europe's imperialism practically unscathed was the one region home to a jealous great power that drew the line at *any* foreign expansion.[27]

None of this is to suggest that every perceived threat was real. Sometimes policymakers overestimated threats or spied dangers where none existed. Some of these mistakes were reasonable; others, less so. Given the uncertainties, however, it is understandable why the United States

jumped at every creak of the hemispheric floorboards. Being overly cautious appeared to have little downside, even when it led to interventions.
If the United States missed even one real threat, however, the costs could
be catastrophic—from setting off a hemispheric partition to sparking a
great-power war. Seeing threats everywhere was accordingly not paranoia; it was a rational response to a world full of potential danger. That,
of course, is the tragedy of great-power politics: the international system
incentivizes rational actors to fear for their safety and act in ways that
result in less safety—and much more violence, bloodshed, and war—for
everyone.[28]

Threatened Less by Conquering States Than by Failing Ones

Over a century ago, the United States intervened across the Western
Hemisphere primarily in response to the problem of order. But nothing
about that problem is specific to the United States, its region, or that era.
Great powers, like nature, always abhor a vacuum, and the problem of
order has shaped and ordered international politics for a long time.

Consider the same era, but from Europe's perspective. One can easily understand the contemporaneous wave of European imperialism in
the rest of the world as the problem of order writ global. Europe's great
powers did not want their rivals pocketing what Senator Lodge called
"the waste places of the earth," and they concluded that the best way
to keep their rivals out of those areas was to colonize them first. Hence
what one historian has dubbed "preclusive imperialism": the panicked
Scramble for Africa, as well as the race for footholds in Asia and the
Middle East. Other motivations—economic, racial, and social—entered
the picture too. But European powers often did not want to lay hands
on foreign lands so much as keep those territories from being grabbed
by others. Consider that when President McKinley was debating what
to do with the Philippines in 1898, few powers affirmatively wanted the
islands, but several were ready to take the islands to prevent them from
going to anyone else.[29]

Fatefully, that same dynamic also ate away at the heart of the European balance of power. For decades, Europe had confronted its own
problem of regional order in the form of the "sick man of Europe," the
Ottoman Empire. As the Ottoman Empire slowly declined, its edges
began to fray, posing the infamous Eastern Question: how could Europe

maintain a stable balance of power when one of its component parts was collapsing? Europe never found the answer. Instead, in a mirror image of the forces driving the United States to expansion in the Western Hemisphere, Europe's great powers and their proxies intruded further and further into formerly Ottoman-controlled territory partly for fear that if they did not, someone else would. The result was several rounds of interventions, revolutions, and proxy conflicts that culminated in three wars in the Balkans, the last of which widened to become World War I.[30]

Unsurprisingly, the problem of order continues to unsettle world politics to this day. Several places have all the ingredients for trouble: an area that is strategically important to a great power but menaced by both foreign threats and internal instability and disorder. In each case, the predictable consequence has been expansion and aggression.

Take Russia. Since the Soviet Union's collapse, several of Russia's neighbors have experienced chronic domestic unrest, including "color revolutions" that replaced neutral or Russia-aligned regimes with pro-Western ones. Moscow blames Europe and the United States for the trouble, and it has responded by aggressively exploiting its neighbors' instability for its own ends. In 2008, for example, Russia intervened in Georgia to support pro-Russian separatist groups. In 2020, Moscow capitalized on mass protests in Belarus to pull the nation's embattled regime further into Russia's orbit. Two years later, Russia repeated the trick in Kazakhstan, sending in 2,500 troops following widespread popular unrest. And in Ukraine, Russia first took advantage of a pro-Western revolution in 2014 to annex Crimea and infiltrate Ukraine's south and east, laying the groundwork for a full-scale invasion of the country eight years later. One *New York Times* headline aptly summed up two decades of Russian policy: "Putin Again Seizes on Unrest to Try to Expand Influence."[31]

Or look at the example of the United States. On September 11, 2001, Americans were reminded that non-state actors like al-Qaeda can cause great harm, at least after establishing a foothold somewhere in the world. So following 9/11, the Bush administration centered its first National Security Strategy on a truism that would have been second nature to men like Theodore Roosevelt and Woodrow Wilson: "Weak states, like Afghanistan, can pose as great a danger to our national interests as strong states," and "America is now threatened less by conquering states than we are by failing ones." Given that perspective, the implications were clear: to be secure, the United States needed to deny terrorist groups like al-Qaeda and the Islamic State a base of operations, which in practice meant that Washington could no longer tolerate failing or failed states anywhere in the Muslim world. And so the War on Terror began.[32]

Other examples—including in the Middle East—abound. None can be chalked up to the problem of order alone. Russian aggression, for example, is certainly motivated by more than merely defensive concerns. Rather, the point is that whatever other motivations might enter the picture, few states can or do act any differently than the problem of order would predict.[33]

The Beaten Track of Big Powers

In mid-1973, Chinese Premier Zhou Enlai met with an American delegation. It was a heady time. Only the previous year, President Richard Nixon had gone to China to start organizing a united front against the Soviet Union. Zhou, however, was already thinking decades into the future. Calling out the youngest member of the American delegation, he asked pointedly: "Do you think China will ever become an aggressive or expansionist power?" Caught off guard, she diplomatically responded "no." But the aging premier was less sanguine: "Don't count on it. It is possible."[34]

Great powers, and especially rising powers, have long been aggressive and expansionist. Over the late nineteenth and early twentieth centuries, Americans expected to be the exception; they thought that, because of their values and their principles, they could achieve hegemony in a different way. They were wrong. Today, a new power is rising, and as the world teeters on the verge of a once-in-a-century great-power transition, Zhou's question has taken on a new urgency: can China keep rising—and even achieve regional hegemony—without turning aggressive and expansionist?

Stories about China's rise often fall between two poles, depending on how one sees its people, principles, ideas, and institutions. At one pole, China looms as a predatory power, bent on dominating its neighbors and controlling its region. Supporters of this view often invoke the purportedly boiling nationalism of the Chinese people, the Chinese Communist Party's ruthless and authoritarian nature, and Chinese president Xi Jinping's quest for global power and status. Together, these elements have allegedly created a revisionist behemoth that—in the words of the Pentagon's 2018 National Defense Strategy—"seeks Indo-Pacific regional hegemony in the near-term and displacement of the United States to achieve global preeminence in the future."[35]

On the other end of the spectrum, the story could not be more different. China, in this telling, is a new kind of great power, one dedicated by virtue of its unique culture, history, and values to a "peaceful rise," mutually beneficial economic development, and a foreign policy of "noninterference" in the affairs of others. As a Chinese Defense White Paper earnestly assured, China "stands against aggression and expansion," will never "seek any sphere of influence," and will "never follow the beaten track of big powers in seeking hegemony."[36]

Commentators have spilled much ink debating where the truth lies. But it may not ultimately matter. For the sobering lesson from the United States's own ascent is that rising powers—no matter how benign their people, principles, ideas, and institutions—can and often will be driven to expansion and aggression.

One reason why is the problem of order. States everywhere confront the problem of order in one form or another, but rising powers do so in a unique way. Not only do rising powers generally have the strength to try to resolve the problem of order forcibly, but they also tend to be rising at exactly those times when the three conditions underlying the problem are most acute.

First, rising powers face especially grave threats from their rivals. Since power in the international system is relative, one power's rise necessarily means another's decline. That imbalance puts a target on the back of a rising power, and it leads other states to try to contain or even halt that power's ascent before it becomes powerful enough to overwhelm them. Germany provoked balancing coalitions in both world wars, as did France under Napoleon. Even the United States, an ocean away, consistently prompted balancing from its European rivals. Napoleon III tried to assemble an anti-American coalition during the Civil War, and the Kaiser dreamed of doing the same in the early 1900s, when Europeans fretted publicly about the "American peril." Even in its milder forms, such balancing can lead a rising power to feel encircled and threatened, stoking the fear that motivates the problem of order.[37]

Second, rising powers see bigger slices of the world as strategically important. Some of that is subjective; small powers tend to think locally, while larger powers must think regionally, even globally. But some of it is objective. Expansion has a self-generating quality to it: as a state expands, it tends to develop new interests that require further expansion.

Once the United States annexed the West Coast, for example, it needed to protect lines of communication running across the isthmus, including an eventual canal. That in turn required the United States to guard the canal's immediate surroundings (Central America) as well as its entry points (the Caribbean and Hawai'i). Guarding those areas required a modern navy, and a modern navy demanded coaling stations (again, the Caribbean and Hawai'i).[38]

Finally, rising powers destabilize their neighborhoods. Sometimes, the rising power will intentionally embark on a revanchist or otherwise deliberately destabilizing course. Other times, destabilization is an unintended by-product of a rising power's other choices. The United States, for example, inadvertently unsettled its region through its reciprocity regimes, its changing tariff schedules, and—of course—its many interventions.

Even aside from the destabilization they themselves cause, rising powers tend to live in especially tumultuous times. Great powers rarely rise and fall solely on their own strength; instead, they surf the peaks (or fall into the troughs) of social changes, economic shifts, political overhauls, and technological transformations. These kinds of tectonic forces are deeply disruptive, and they rarely operate within one state alone. For example, the Second Industrial Revolution helped some nations, like Germany and the United States, rise to power, but it also threw many other nations—including in Latin America—into disorder and disarray. These kinds of tectonic forces will also often weaken the great powers at the top of the international system, and as those powers retrench, they will create exactly the sort of power vacuums on which the problem of order feeds.[39]

Each of these three ingredients is present in China's rise today. First, there is the keen and ever-growing sense of threat. Officials in Beijing widely believe that the great powers—particularly the United States—are bent on thwarting their nation's rightful ascent. Some of that mindset stems from historical trauma; as its leaders point out incessantly, China suffered a century of national humiliation at the hands of Europe's great powers in the wake of the Opium Wars. China's threat perceptions also reflect more recent history: the collapse of the Soviet Union, the surge in democratic values during the 1990s, the contemporaneous streak of American interventionism, and, of course, rising rhetoric in the United States and elsewhere about the threat from China. Today, Beijing fears—quite understandably—that the United States may lead the West in trying to contain it, including by co-opting China's neighbors and curbing its regional influence. From Beijing's perspective, such efforts are already well underway, including the signing of the recent "AUKUS" security pact between Australia, the United Kingdom, and the United States, as well as the strengthening of the "Quad" security dialogue between Australia, India, Japan, and the United States.[40]

Second, China is surrounded by ever-multiplying areas of strategic importance. Some of that reflects the country's vast size; China shares the world's longest land border with fourteen other countries, almost all of which have been sources of trouble at some point in the past. Other parts of China's expanding strategic perimeter reflect more modern developments. China's naval modernization requires it to seek outposts and basing facilities outside its borders, while China's economic trajectory—in particular its reliance on overseas trade—has made it extremely dependent on foreign economies. These needs have pushed China to engage more deeply with greater swaths of the world, whether it be Beijing's flagship infrastructure development program, the global Belt and Road Initiative; its concern about naval chokepoints like the Straits of Malacca and Hormuz; or its active diplomacy in places as far afield as Africa, South America, and the Caribbean.[41]

Finally, there is the potential for power vacuums to develop in many of these areas. At first glance, this factor may appear relatively muted; few of China's neighbors face the endemic instability that gripped much of the Caribbean rimlands a century ago. But appearances can be deceiving. Some of the instability on China's periphery is found within its own borders. Ethnic minorities make up about 10 percent of China's population but inhabit 60 percent of its landmass, and their long-standing resistance to central control has generated decades of simmering tension and occasional revolt in areas like Xinjiang and Tibet. Other places, like Hong Kong, pose different but equally real risks of political disorder.[42]

One can find much instability or potential instability just outside China's borders as well. In the west, China eyes insurgencies and civil war in neighbors like Afghanistan and Pakistan with concern, especially given those nations' links to China's Muslim populations. Similar concerns spring from Burma's persistent turmoil to the south. In the northeast, North Korea remains a wild card; the Kim family has ruled it for seventy-five unhappy years, but whether they can maintain their grip for another seventy-five years—or simply past tomorrow—is anyone's guess. Elsewhere, Asia is chock-full of states struggling to maintain stable governance, including Thailand, Sri Lanka, and the Solomon Islands.[43]

One should not be surprised, then, that China's foreign policy has begun to echo the policies followed by a rising United States over a century ago. To start, there is China's answer to the Monroe Doctrine, a declaration by President Xi in 2014 that "it is for the people of Asia to run the affairs of Asia, solve the problems of Asia, and uphold the security of Asia." Substitute "the Americas" for "Asia," and President Xi's slogan might just as easily have come from President Monroe's pen.[44]

Other parallels are hard to miss. For years, China said it would not develop a blue-water navy; last year, it launched its third aircraft carrier amid a soaring defense budget. For years, China said it would not acquire bases abroad; today, it has a military outpost in Tajikistan, a naval base in Djibouti, and the groundwork for additional bases in Cambodia, Pakistan, and Sri Lanka. For years, China criticized the dollar diplomacy of the United States and Western institutions; today, Beijing employs political loans habitually, refinancing its neighbors' debts, tying aid to political support, trying to internationalize its currency, and leasing or buying strategically located infrastructure. This renminbi diplomacy is tied more and more to nations that are financially unstable; one estimate suggests that countries in financial distress made up 60 percent of China's overseas lending portfolio in 2022, up from a mere 5 percent in 2010.[45]

China is also flexing its growing muscle in other ways. It has cemented control over disorderly internal areas like Xinjiang, Tibet, and Hong Kong, in effect "expanding" within its own borders. In the South China Sea, Beijing has seized contested islands and built out its possessions into military fortresses, and it has launched security operations in Afghanistan. One can even find stirrings of a Chinese Platt Amendment in a secret security agreement signed with the Solomon Islands in 2022 that gives Beijing the right to send military forces "to assist in maintaining social order." Even though that right of intervention theoretically requires the island nation's consent, political disorder is rampant in the Solomon Islands (including anti-Chinese riots), and one can easily imagine a situation where—like Cuba in 1906 or Nicaragua in 1912—the islands' government calls on Beijing to suppress its political opponents.[46]

China's principles also seem to be taking more and more of a back seat to its other interests. Even as Beijing publicly opposes "any attempt to impose one's will on others," it boycotts and sanctions nations that incur its ire. Commitments to "noninterference" have likewise been replaced by calls to respect its quasi-ally Russia's "legitimate security concerns" in the wake of the latter's invasion of Ukraine. Changes in tone are also evident, from the public chest-beating of the country's "wolf warrior" diplomats to threats uttered by Beijing's senior officials sotto voce. "China is a big country and other countries are small countries, and that's just a fact," China's foreign minister once declared, and that "fact" is increasingly shaping China's behavior.[47]

China will not follow in the United States's exact footsteps, of course. Much has changed in the intervening century, from norms to nuclear weapons, trade to technology. China also faces a trickier strategic environment than the United States ever did. Washington never had to worry about locally based competitors, which meant that it could try to stabilize and strengthen all its neighbors while exploiting its rivals' distance and relative detachment. Not so for Beijing. It must contend with several neighbors who cannot necessarily go toe to toe with China but who are strong enough to stand in the way of its bid for regional hegemony (like India and Japan). China also faces the additional challenge that its primary rival, the United States, is a regional hegemon, and can thus remain laser-focused on a distant great-power competition in a way that the United States's own distracted rivals never could.[48]

Some of these differences may dampen the risks of Chinese adventurism. So may any number of other distinctions between the China of today and the United States of a century ago. But anxiety and ambition have long ruled great-power politics, and it is not hard to imagine scenarios in which China feels compelled to defend its interests aggressively. If a Chinese military base stays or goes depending on the outcome of domestic strife in Cambodia, Pakistan, or Sri Lanka, will China look the other way? If the friendly leader of a Pacific Island nation calls for Chinese forces to put down a pro-Western revolution, will China hold back? If North Korea collapses into anarchy, will Beijing abide a unified Korean Peninsula on its border, allied with the United States and hosting American military forces?

It's possible, but don't count on it. "Man is the same in all places and in all climes," as the Count of Aranda (or Premier Zhou) might say, and history offers cold comfort that China will manage to entirely avoid "what has happened in all ages with nations that begin to rise."

The End and the Means

Observers often see international politics as a clash between good and evil. Sometimes it is. But more often than not, international politics takes place in a gray world under gray skies, where every decision requires trade-offs and difficult choices, where legitimate ends pursued rationally still lead to unsavory destinations, and where tragedy is all but inescapable. Tales pitting good against evil appeal to the human desire for moral certainty, but they are often poor vehicles for understanding the choices nations face.[49]

Over the course of the late nineteenth and early twentieth centuries, most American leaders were not hypocritical in claiming they wanted to respect the sovereignty of foreign countries, to promote democracy, or to uphold classical liberal principles. All else being equal, they did. But in the hierarchy of national priorities, those interests usually yielded to the paramount interest of national security.

So if the United States often compromised its values during this period, that reveals less about the absolute importance of those values than it does about the many conflicting and more significant demands Americans thought they faced. Washington repeatedly rode roughshod over its neighbors, its rivals, and everything else standing in the way of its security objectives. Its tactics were often "nothing less than high-handed," as Wilson and others were quick to admit. But to American leaders, high-handed tactics were the lesser evil, at least compared to letting their neighbors wallow in anarchy or, worse, be rescued by other great powers. "I do not like the argument that the end justifies the means," Wilson and others claimed, but that was exactly the argument they made, time and again, to justify disregarding the values they held dear. Sovereignty, democracy, liberalism—they were all important. They just weren't important enough.[50]

If anything, it was the strength of those values that sometimes made American policies all the more tragic. Cynics scoff at the idea of American exceptionalism, but any fair-minded look at this period's conversations, correspondence, and diary entries reveals a degree of hope, confidence, and optimism that borders on the touchingly naive. What makes Americans exceptional is not that they have ideals; it is that they never believe those ideals will have to be compromised or conceded. The United States is unique among great powers in that it will lose its innocence, again and again and again, only to rebound from each brush with great-power politics believing that this time, things will be different: that its paladins will not lose their way, that good intentions will prevail, that the mistakes of previous generations will be avoided or absolved—that it is possible for a power to be both great and good, powerful and principled.[51]

Channeled intelligently, this exceptionalism holds enormous promise. It moderates the worst impulses of American policy, and it has helped make the current period of Pax Americana the most free, peaceful, and prosperous era in world history. But it also has its perils: the belief in a beautiful dream that seems so close that Americans could hardly fail to grasp it, if tomorrow they just ran faster, stretched out their arms farther. That exceptionalism led the republic astray during its rise to hegemony, blinding Americans to what they could and could not do, and it remains a vulnerability to this day. As the world reenters a period of sustained great-power competition, American policymakers must temper their idealism with a realistic appraisal of the unprecedented challenges this century will bring, and the constraints under which even the highest ideals must labor.[52]

ACKNOWLEDGMENTS

Eight years is a long time: just long enough, I've learned, both to finish a book and to amass enough personal and professional debts to last the rest of my life.

First, I want to thank Jack Goldsmith, who sowed the seeds that eventually grew into this book. Nearly a decade ago, he observed that few scholars had compared and contrasted China's recent behavior in its near seas with the United States's behavior in the Caribbean a century ago. That observation stayed with me, and a year later I started reading histories of the Monroe Doctrine in preparation for what I naively thought would be a short article. Jack intervened again when, after hearing me recount some of what I'd learned, he asked (perhaps not so innocently), "So, you're writing a book, then?" The rest, as they say, was history.

With Jack's words rattling around in my head, I benefited from a wide variety of advice and counsel in the project's early stages. I greatly enjoyed my conversations with Gil Barndollar, Lexi Britton, Karl Chang, Mitchell Craft, Paul Cocchiaro, Matt Daniels, Rush Doshi, Madeline Lauf, David Livingston, Walter Russell Mead, Sean Merrill, Elliot Musilek, Hillel Ofek, Daniel Pessar, Kirk Redmond, Luke Rodehorst, and Ben Wittes, who all gave form, distinction, and direction to a project that had been dangerously inchoate. As always, Ashley Tellis was especially helpful, and with his usual perspicacity he cut to the heart of the book and how best to frame it.

Getting the project off the ground was also made much easier thanks to Emily Cunningham and Keith Urbahn, who helped introduce me to the often-arcane ways of the publishing industry. Alex Harris and Sam

Kleiner did likewise, in addition to spending many hours helping me whip my book proposal into something approaching coherence.

One of the project's other turning points came when the Hoover Institution named me a Visiting Scholar. Supposed to last only a year, my appointment has been cheerfully extended by the Institution so many times that I've lost count but never my deep sense of gratitude. As a Visiting Scholar, I've been able to draw on the Institute's vast network of spectacular scholars as well as the wider set of resources available to researchers at Stanford University. Case in point: Denise Elson organized a phenomenal roundtable discussion during one visit, and the feedback I received there substantially shaped the book's trajectory. Niall Ferguson and Daniel J. Sargent also gave their time freely, and I learned a great deal from my conversations with them. I'm also especially thankful for Jack and my other sponsor at the Institution, General H. R. McMaster, whose reputation for wisdom and generosity toward young scholars is, if anything, understated.

Strange as it sounds, it had not occurred to me at the outset that I could not write this book without doing a deep dive into primary sources. Once I realized my mistake, however, I incurred a great debt to the many archivists who kept me from drowning during my subsequent plunges into collections of papers, records, and microfilms scattered across the country, as well as to those like Hannah Elder at the Massachusetts Historical Society who went to epic lengths to get me copies of original documents when the pandemic made in-person visits impossible. Special thanks as well to those brave archivists who, when I could not find a microfilmed source, broke archival rules and took me back to restricted areas to see original documents firsthand. These heroes, needless to say, shall remain unnamed.

Every piece of scholarship stands on the shoulders of those that came before it, and that is particularly true in the case of this book, which seeks less to divulge new facts than to reexamine American history from a new perspective. I'm incredibly grateful to the hundreds of historians whose work has preceded and informed mine, and I hope that this book will contribute to our shared endeavor. In that regard, I'd be remiss if I did not acknowledge how much my research efforts benefited from the extensive digitization of sources in databases like HathiTrust, Google Books, and the Internet Archive. Gaps still existed, of course, but I was fortunate to have the help of the masterful librarians at the Stanford Libraries in tracking down missing sources, ranging from garden-variety books to the most esoteric early-twentieth-century pamphlets. But for their help, this book could not have happened.

As research and writing progressed, I encountered a number of thorny questions, and I was lucky to be able to call upon a community of talented specialists to answer them. I knew I was in safe hands when relying on David Boddy's help with economic figures, Dan West's military experience, Claudia Taveras's knowledge of the Dominican Republic, Cameron Kerr's insight into titles, Liz Cross's understanding of academic scholarship, and Lucia Harper and Christina Martinez's flair for languages. I also knew my son was in safe hands when he was in the care of Jin Fung, Arden Smith, and especially Gina Stone, and it was only with their help that I was able to finish the drafting process.

Once the manuscript came together, I had world-class help in revising it. I am thankful to my research assistant, Khushmita Dhabhai, who helped put the finishing touches on the draft, as well as to Chelsea Burris Berkey for connecting us. I also could not be more thankful to Tara Chandra, Aroop Mukharji, Rahul Rekhi, Eden Schiffman, and Don Stone for their review of multiple chapters and their willingness to continue sharing their thoughts and expertise even in the face of my never-ending questions. I was even more bowled over by Amy Bond, Paolo Cocchiaro, Ben Daus, and Mark Jia, who not only read the entire manuscript from start to finish, but who also gave detailed comments and feedback and then patiently endured the steady string of follow-up questions and redrafted sections that fast became my calling card. Lastly, I would like to single out Nick Harper, Andrew O'Shaughnessy, and Varun Sivaram. Each supported the project from the very beginning, and each spent literally dozens and dozens of hours line editing the proposal and then the manuscript, as well as workshopping every other aspect of the book. I am so proud to call each of you my friends, and words cannot express how much I owe you.

Even with this tremendous help, my manuscript was fated to molder on a hard drive but for the assistance of a talented group of publishing industry professionals. I am deeply grateful to my superb agent, Gail Ross, and her wonderful team at Ross Yoon (including Dara Kaye and Jennifer Manguera), for their sage guidance throughout the process. Gail is the best in the business, and I had the pleasure of discovering why again and again. I was also extremely lucky to find a home for the book at PublicAffairs and Hachette. Few people deserve thanks as much as my editor, Clive Priddle, whose incisive feedback improved the book in every possible way, and who tirelessly advocated for the book in every forum. Thank you, as well, to Anu Roy-Chaudhury and Kiyo Saso, for repeatedly walking a first-time author through the intricacies of the publication process, and to Miguel Cervantes, Brooke Parsons, and Olivia Hicks, for their peerless promotional efforts. I owe much as well to my exceptional production team—Katie Carruthers-Busser, Pete Garceau, Olivia Loperfido, Duncan McHenry, Melissa Raymond, and Jeff Williams—who took a confused and error-ridden Word document and turned it into a beautifully designed volume.

Finally, I owe the greatest debt of all to my family, whose support (and suffering) far exceeded their fair share. No one bore the brunt of this project more than my wife, Courtney, who was *always* there for me, and who gave me endless amounts of time, compassion, and wise counsel over many long years. Few things reveal the depth of a partner's love quite like writing a book, and that process reinforced that I was the luckiest and most-loved person in the world. Courtney's patience, support, and immeasurable sacrifices mean more to me than she will ever know. I am also grateful for the "support" provided by my young son, Alexander, whose disregard for the book could be described as absolute, but who will, I hope, someday read it and be proud of his "da da." I am certainly proud of my own father, who went to Herculean lengths to help this book come together, and whose fingerprints can be found on every page. I am likewise grateful to my brother, Michael, who joined the rest of the family in reviewing countless drafts and injecting some much-needed levity into my life. Last but not least, there is my mother. Nothing has made me as grateful for my parents as becoming a parent myself, and the last few years have reminded me just how much I owe her in particular. She made everything possible, and it is to her that I dedicate this book.

NOTE ON QUOTATIONS AND VOCABULARY

We May Dominate the World reprints quotations word for word, with four exceptions. First, I have altered the capitalization of words within quotations whenever doing so enhances readability and does not change the speaker's substantive meaning. Second, for similar reasons, I have omitted ellipses at the start and end of partial quotations. Third, on rare occasions I have altered the punctuation or typeface of quotations for the sake of readability; when doing so, I have acknowledged the alteration in the endnotes. Finally, I have used brackets to denote any other change from a quotation's original words as they are rendered in the cited source.

Careful readers will note that I use the word "American" to refer to people and things from the United States. Some scholars and advocates object to that usage, arguing the term "American" properly describes people and things from the Americas as a whole. Unfortunately, however, the English language offers no other accepted demonym for people from the United States, and so for reasons of both readability and familiarity I have stuck to the conventional usage.

Careful readers will also note that *We May Dominate the World* avoids using the word "empire" or its derivatives except where actors chose to use those words themselves (for example, the "anti-imperialists" or the British Empire). For a long time, American diplomatic historians avoided using those terms as part of a regrettable unwillingness to come to terms with the conduct of the United States in the region. A long overdue correction began in the 1950s and 1960s, and historians became more comfortable describing the actions of the United States as "imperialism" and comparing the conduct of the republic to its great-power brethren. Over time, however, the term "empire" and its derivatives have become, as an attorney might say, more prejudicial than probative—no one can agree on what precisely they mean, and they are instead used primarily as a vehicle for conveying an author's generalized disapproval. Rather than leave my intended meaning unclear, I try to rely on more objective and precise language to describe American conduct in the region. In so doing, I of course do not intend to whitewash the United States's conduct or to diminish its consequences.

IMAGE CAPTION CREDITS

P 20   Emperor Napoleon III of France: Victor Hugo, *Napoleon the Little* (Boston: Little, Brown, 1909), 2–3.

P 23   Emperor Maximilian I of Mexico: Metternich to Rechberg, December 2, 1861, quoted in Egon Caesar, Conte Corti, *Maximilian and Charlotte of Mexico* (New York: Alfred A. Knopf, 1929), 1:123.

P 25   Secretary of State William Henry Seward: William Howard Russell, *My Diary: North and South* (Boston: T. O. H. P. Burnham, 1863), 34.

P 29   General Philip Sheridan: Sherman to Ewing, October 26, 1864, in M. A. De-Wolfe Howe, *Home Letters of General Sherman* (New York: Charles Scribner's Sons, 1909), 314.

P 45   Secretary of State James G. Blaine: George F. Hoar, *Autobiography of Seventy Years* (New York: Charles Scribner's Sons, 1903), 1:200.

P 63   Senator Henry Cabot Lodge: Wendell to Curtis, January 18, 1920, in M. A. DeWolfe Howe, *Barrett Wendell and His Letters* (Boston: Atlantic Monthly, 1924), 320–21.

P 65   Secretary of State Richard Olney: "Thumbnail Sketch No. 14. Richard Olney.," *New York Journal*, March 5, 1896.

P 77   Captain Alfred Thayer Mahan: White, Diary Entry, July 29, 1899, in *Autobiography of Andrew Dickson White* (New York: Century, 1905), 2:347.

P 85   Queen Lydia Kamakaʻeha Dominis Liliʻuokalani: Liliuokalani, *Hawaii's Story by Hawaii's Queen* (Boston: Lothrop, Lee & Shepard, 1898), 282.

P 106   Assistant Secretary of the Navy Theodore Roosevelt: Long Diary Entry, May 5, 1898, in *America of Yesterday as Reflected in the Journal of John Davis Long*, ed. Lawrence Shaw May (Boston: Atlantic Monthly, 1923), 188.

P 115   Soldiers Learn of Santiago's Surrender: Richard Harding Davis, *The Cuban and Porto Rican Campaigns* (New York: Charles Scribner's Sons, 1898), 98–99.

P 123   Secretary of War Elihu Root: Root, n.d., quoted in Philip C. Jessup, *Elihu Root*, vol. 1, *1845–1909* (New York: Dodd, Mead, 1938), 133.

P 135   Philippe-Jean Bunau-Varilla: McCullough, Conversation with Alice Roosevelt Longworth, quoted in David McCullough, *The Path Between the Seas: The Creation of the Panama Canal 1870–1914* (New York: Simon and Schuster Paperbacks, 1977), 278.

P 158   The Panama Canal: A. T. Mahan, *The Influence of Sea Power Upon History, 1660–1783* (Boston: Little, Brown, 1890), 33.

P 162   Kaiser Wilhelm II of Germany: Roosevelt to White, August 14, 1906, in Morison 5:359.

P 173   The Great White Fleet Enters the Straits of Magellan: "Splendid Show of Naval Power," *Morning Oregonian*, December 17, 1907.

P 210   Secretary of State Philander Knox: Oswald Garrison Villard, "Philander C. Knox—Dark Horse," *The Nation*, May 22, 1920, 678.

P 211   First Assistant Secretary of State Francis M. Huntington Wilson: F. M. Huntington Wilson, *Memoirs of an Ex-Diplomat* (Boston: Bruce Humphries, 1945), 47–48.

P 224   Major Smedley Darlington Butler: Butler to Thomas S. Butler, July 14, 1910, in *General Smedley Darlington Butler: The Letters of A Leatherneck, 1898–1931*, ed. Anne Cipriano Venzon (New York: Praeger, 1992), 88.

P 238   President Woodrow Wilson: Raymond B. Fosdick, "Personal Recollections of Woodrow Wilson," in *The Philosophy and Policies of Woodrow Wilson*, ed. Earl Latham (Chicago: University of Chicago Press, 1958), 30.

P 240   Secretary of State William Jennings Bryan: F. M. Huntington Wilson, *Memoirs of an Ex-Diplomat* (Boston: Bruce Humphries, 1945), 130.

P 257   Secretary of State Robert Lansing: Josephus Daniels, *The Wilson Era: Years of Peace—1910–1917* (Chapel Hill: University of North Carolina Press, 1946), 441.

P 278   U.S. Marines on Patrol in Haiti: Carleton Beals, *Banana Gold* (Philadelphia: J. B. Lippincott, 1932), 295.

P 292   Chief of the Latin American Division Sumner Welles: Harold Ickes, Diary Entry, April 2, 1938, in *The Secret Diary of Harold I. Ickes*, vol. 2, *The Inside Struggle 1936–1939* (New York: Simon and Schuster, 1954), 351.

P 298   General Augusto César Sandino: Sandino, Manifesto to Nicaraguan Compatriots, circa July 14, 1927, in *Sandino: The Testimony of a Nicaraguan Patriot 1921–1934*, comp. and ed. Sergio Ramírez, ed. and trans. Robert Edgar Conrad (Princeton, NJ: Princeton University Press, 1990), 81.

P 305   President Franklin D. Roosevelt: Winston Churchill, n.d., in *Churchill by Himself: In His Own Words*, ed. Richard Langworth (RosettaBooks, 2008), chap. 20.

NOTES

Bartlett MSS	Willard Bartlett Papers, Rare Book & Manuscript Library, Columbia University, New York, NY
Bigelow MSS	John Bigelow Papers, New York Public Library, New York, NY
Caperton MSS	William Banks Caperton Papers, Library of Congress, Washington, DC
Cleveland MSS	Grover Cleveland Papers, Library of Congress, Washington, DC
Cortelyou MSS	George B. Cortelyou Papers, Library of Congress, Washington, DC
Daniels MSS	Josephus Daniels Papers, Library of Congress, Washington, DC
FDRL	Franklin D. Roosevelt Presidential Library and Museum, Hyde Park, NY
FRUS	*Foreign Relations of the United States*. 450+ vols. Washington, DC: Government Printing Office, 1861–present.
Hay MSS	John Hay Papers, Library of Congress, Washington, DC
Hugh Gibson MSS	Hugh Gibson Papers, Hoover Institution Archives, Stanford, CA
Huntington Wilson MSS	Francis Mairs Huntington Wilson Papers, Ursinus College, Collegeville, PA
Jessup MSS	Philip C. Jessup Papers, Library of Congress, Washington, DC
Knox MSS	Philander C. Knox Papers, Library of Congress, Washington, DC
Lane MSS	Arthur Bliss Lane Papers, Yale University, New Haven, CT

Lansing MSS	Robert Lansing Papers, Library of Congress, Washington, DC
Lincoln MSS	Abraham Lincoln Papers, Library of Congress, Washington, DC
Lodge MSS	Henry Cabot Lodge Papers, Massachusetts Historical Society, Boston, MA
Loomis MSS	Francis B. Loomis Papers, Stanford University, Stanford, CA
Moore MSS	James Bassett Moore Papers, Library of Congress, Washington, DC
Morison	Morison, Elting E., ed. *The Letters of Theodore Roosevelt.* 8 vols. Cambridge, MA: Harvard University Press, 1951–54.
NA	U.S. National Archives and Records Administration
Olney MSS	Richard Olney Papers, Library of Congress, Washington, DC
PPA	*The Public Papers and Addresses of Franklin D. Roosevelt.* 13 vols. New York: Random House, 1938–50.
PPP	*Public Papers of the Presidents of the United States.* Washington, DC: U.S. Government Printing Office, 1974–present.
PWW	Link, Arthur S., ed. *The Papers of Woodrow Wilson.* 69 vols. Princeton, NJ: Princeton University Press, 1967–94.
RG	Record Group
Richardson	Richardson, James D., ed. *A Compilation of the Messages and Papers of the Presidents, 1789–1897.* 11 vols. Washington, DC: Government Printing Office, 1897–1902.
Richardson Supp.	*A Compilation of the Messages and Papers of the Presidents.* 20 vols. New York: Bureau of National Literature, 1917.
Robert Lee Bullard MSS	Robert Lee Bullard Papers, Library of Congress, Washington, DC
Roosevelt MSS	Theodore Roosevelt Papers, Library of Congress, Washington, DC
Root MSS	Elihu Root Papers, Library of Congress, Washington, DC
Taft MSS	William H. Taft Papers, Library of Congress, Washington, DC

Wilson MSS	Woodrow Wilson Papers, Library of Congress, Washington, DC
Wood MSS	Leonard Wood Papers, Library of Congress, Washington, DC

Epigraph Sources

1. Adams to Lodge, October 26, 1901, in Reel 15, Lodge MSS.
2. Gabriel García Márquez, *One Hundred Years of Solitude*, trans. Gregory Rabassa (New York: Harper & Row, 1970), 341.

Introduction

1. *See* William B. Caperton, "History of Flag Career of Rear Admiral W. B. Caperton, U. S. Navy Commencing January 5, 1915," in Subject File ZN (Personnel), 1911–1927, RG45, NA, 46–47; *Inquiry into Occupation and Administration of Haiti and Santo Domingo: Hearings Before a S. Select Comm. on Haiti and Santo Domingo*, vol. 1, 67th Cong. 306 (1922); *see also* David Healy, *Gunboat Diplomacy in the Wilson Era: The U.S. Navy in Haiti, 1915–1916* (Madison: University of Wisconsin Press, 1976), 7–8, 16, 53.

2. Caperton, "History of Flag Career," 45; R. B. Coffey, "Notes on the Intervention in Haiti, with Some of Its Political and Strategical Aspects," February 1, 1916, in Folder 7, Box 3, Caperton MSS; *see* Healy, *Gunboat Diplomacy*, 43–52. For Washington's concern about French forces, *see* Healy, *Gunboat Diplomacy*, 43–44; Donald A. Yerxa, *Admirals and Empire: The United States Navy and the Caribbean, 1898–1945* (Columbia: University of South Carolina Press, 1991), 40–41.

3. Edward L. Beach, "Admiral Caperton in Haiti," January 7, 1920, in Subject File ZWA-7, "Haiti," RG 45, NA, 30; Davis to Lansing, January 12, 1916, in FRUS 1916, 311; *see* Lester D. Langley, *The Banana Wars: United States Intervention in the Caribbean, 1898–1934* (Chicago: Dorsey, 1988), 124–25; Healy, *Gunboat Diplomacy*, 36–41.

4. John Houston Craige, *Cannibal Cousins* (London: Stanley Paul, 1935), 42; *see* Davis to Lansing, January 12, 1916, in FRUS 1916, 313; Healy, *Gunboat Diplomacy*, 19–20, 36–41, 45, 53–54.

5. *See* Healy, *Gunboat Diplomacy*, 54–56.

6. Davis to Lansing, July 27, 1915, in FRUS 1915, 475; *see* Davis to Lansing, January 12, 1916, in FRUS 1916, 315; *see also* Healy, *Gunboat Diplomacy*, 56–57.

7. *See* Caperton, "History of Flag Career," 46; *Inquiry into Occupation and Administration of Haiti and Santo Domingo*, 1:307; *see also* Healy, *Gunboat Diplomacy*, 57–58.

8. *See* Davis to Lansing, January 12, 1916, in FRUS 1916, 316–17; *Inquiry into Occupation and Administration of Haiti and Santo Domingo*, 1:307.

9. Caperton, "History of Flag Career," 46–47; *see Inquiry into Occupation and Administration of Haiti and Santo Domingo*, 1:306; Coffey, "Notes on the Intervention."

10. Faustin Wirkus and Taney Dudley, *The White King of La Gonave* (Garden City, NY: Doubleday, Doran, 1931), 15, 17–18; *see* Beach, "Admiral Caperton in Haiti," 2; Coffey, "Notes on the Intervention"; *see also* Ivan Musicant, *The Banana Wars: A History of United States Military Intervention in Latin America from the Spanish-American War to the Invasion of Panama* (New York: Macmillan, 1990), 168–71.

11. U.S. Marine Corps, *Small Wars Manual* (Washington, DC: Government Printing Office, 1940), 4.

12. *See* John J. Mearsheimer, *The Tragedy of Great Power Politics* (New York: W. W. Norton, 2003), 41.

13. For the definition of "great power," *see* Mearsheimer, *Tragedy*, 5; Paul Kennedy, *The Rise and Fall of the Great Powers: Economic Change and Military Conflict from 1500 to 2000* (New York:

Vintage Books, 1989), 539. For a broader discussion, *see* J. Dana Stuster, "Who Are You Calling a Great Power?" *Lawfare,* January 15, 2023, https://www.lawfareblog.com/who-are-you-calling -great-power. For the definition of "regional hegemon," *see* Mearsheimer, *Tragedy,* 40.

14. *See* Mearsheimer, *Tragedy,* 40–41, 141.

15. For samples of this new scholarship, *see, e.g.,* Raphael Dalleo, *American Imperialism's Undead: The Occupation of Haiti and the Rise of Caribbean Anticolonialism* (Charlottesville: University of Virginia Press, 2016); Julie Greene, *The Canal Builders: Making America's Empire at the Panama Canal* (New York: Penguin Books, 2010); Marixa Lasso, *Erased: The Untold Story of the Panama Canal* (Cambridge, MA: Harvard University Press, 2019); Alan McPherson, *The Invaded: How Latin Americans and Their Allies Fought and Ended U.S. Occupations* (Oxford: Oxford University Press, 2016); Mary A. Renda, *Taking Haiti: Military Occupation and the Culture of U.S. Imperialism, 1915–1940* (Chapel Hill: University of North Carolina Press, 2001); Noenoe K. Silva, *Aloha Betrayed: Native Hawaiian Resistance to American Colonialism* (Durham: Duke University Press, 2004); Ellen D. Tillman, *Dollar Diplomacy by Force: Nation-Building and Resistance in the Dominican Republic* (Chapel Hill: University of North Carolina Press, 2016).

16. Scholars steeped in this field will note that this thesis aligns with several other studies about this region and period, including most notably Tony Smith's *The Pattern of Imperialism: The United States, Great Britain, and the Late-Industrializing World Since 1815* (Cambridge, UK: Cambridge University Press, 1981) and the idea of "protective imperialism" in Samuel Flagg Bemis's *The Latin American Policy of the United States: An Historical Interpretation* (New York: Harcourt, Brace, 1943), as well as (to a lesser extent) Dana G. Munro's *Intervention and Dollar Diplomacy in the Caribbean 1900–1921* (Princeton, NJ: Princeton University Press, 1964), and David Healy's *Drive to Hegemony: The United States in the Caribbean 1898–1917* (Madison: University of Wisconsin Press, 1988). Of course, numerous studies of specific events or individuals in this broader period also emphasize the importance of perceived foreign threats as a driver of U.S. foreign policy. *See, e.g.,* Hans Schmidt, *The United States Occupation of Haiti, 1915–1934* (New Brunswick, NJ: Rutgers University Press, 1995). Other works, like Robert H. Wiebe, *The Search for Order 1877–1920* (New York: Hill and Wang, 1967), and Joseph A. Fry, "In Search of an Orderly World: U.S. Imperialism, 1898-1912," in *Modern American Diplomacy,* eds. John M. Carroll and George C. Herring (Wilmington, DE: Scholarly Resources, 1986), also draw attention to the search for order in American foreign policy.

17. Jefferson to Rutledge, July 4, 1790, in *The Writings of Thomas Jefferson,* ed. Paul Leicester Ford, vol. 5, *1788–1792* (New York: G. P. Putnam's Sons, 1895), 197; George Washington, Farewell Address, September 17, 1796, in Richardson 1:222 (emphasis omitted); *see* Thomas Jefferson, First Inaugural Address, March 4, 1801, in Richardson 1:323; *Federalist,* no. 8 (Alexander Hamilton), in *The Federalist Papers,* ed. Clinton Rossiter (New York: New American Library of World Literature, 1961), 71; Jefferson to Crawford, January 2, 1812, in *The Works of Thomas Jefferson,* ed. H. A. Washington, vol. 6 (New York: Townsend MacCoun, 1884), 33; *Federalist,* no. 41 (James Madison), 258; *see also* Charles A. Kupchan, *Isolationism: A History of America's Efforts to Shield Itself from the World* (Oxford: Oxford University Press, 2020), 35–38.

18. *See* Jay Sexton, *The Monroe Doctrine: Empire and Nation in Nineteenth-Century America* (New York: Hill and Wang, 2011), 28–37; Nicholas John Spykman, *America's Strategy in World Politics: The United States and the Balance of Power* (New York: Harcourt, Brace, 1942), 66–67; John Lewis Gaddis, *Surprise, Security, and the American Experience* (Cambridge, MA: Harvard University Press, 2004), 10–16.

19. *See* Martin Sicker, *The Geopolitics of Security in the Americas: Hemispheric Denial from Monroe to Clinton* (Westport, CT: Praeger, 2002), 12–13; Spykman, *America's Strategy,* 67–68.

20. Jefferson to Claiborne, October 29, 1808, in *Writings of Thomas Jefferson* 9:212–13; *see* John A. Logan, Jr., *No Transfer: An American Security Principle* (New Haven, CT: Yale University Press, 1962), 103–04.

21. *See* Sexton, *Monroe Doctrine,* 49–50; *see generally* Dexter Perkins, *The Monroe Doctrine 1823–1826* (Gloucester, MA: Peter Smith, 1965). For fears of how Latin America's weakness could lead to an expansion of European influence, *see* James E. Lewis, Jr., *The American Union and the Problem of Neighborhood: The United States and the Collapse of the Spanish Empire, 1783–1829* (Chapel Hill: University of North Carolina Press, 1998), 164–67; Lars Schoultz, *Beneath the United States: A History of U.S. Policy Toward Latin America* (Cambridge, MA: Harvard University Press, 2003), 10; Sexton, *Monroe Doctrine,* 37–38.

22. James Monroe, Seventh Annual Message, December 2, 1823, in *The Writings of James Monroe*, ed. Stanislaus Murray Hamilton, vol. VI, *1817–1823* (New York: G. P. Putnam's Sons, 1902), 328, 340; *see ibid.*, 6:340–41. For the domestic roots of the Doctrine, *see generally* Ernest R. May, *The Making of the Monroe Doctrine* (Cambridge, MA: Belknap Press, 1975).

23. *See* Perkins, *The Monroe Doctrine 1823–1826*, 27–30, 104–43, 223–58; Sicker, *Geopolitics of Security*, 22; Spykman, *America's Strategy*, 71–73.

24. For Europe's regular violations of the Monroe Doctrine, *see* Sicker, *Geopolitics of Security*, 23, 31–42. For the sectional conflict and its impact on foreign policy, *see* Robert Kagan, *Dangerous Nation* (New York: Alfred A. Knopf, 2006), 210, 232–34; Sexton, *Monroe Doctrine*, 85–121.

25. For Canada being a weak point for the British Empire, *see* Kenneth Bourne, *Britain and the Balance of Power in North America 1815–1908* (Berkeley: University of California Press, 1967), 4, 223–24, 285–86, 408–09; Spykman, *America's Strategy*, 59–60.

26. *See* Fareed Zakaria, *From Wealth to Power: The Unusual Origins of America's World Role* (Princeton, NJ: Princeton University Press, 1998), 3.

27. Graham Allison, *Destined for War: Can America and China Escape Thucydides's Trap?* (Boston: Mariner Books, 2018); *see* A. F. K. Organski and Jacek Kugler, *The War Ledger* (Chicago: University of Chicago Press, 1980).

Chapter 1: Weakness Offers Temptation

1. *See* Sheridan to Rawlins, June 4, 1865, in *The War of the Rebellion: A Compilation of the Official Records of the Union and Confederate Armies* (Washington, DC: Government Printing Office, 1896), 48:767; Sheridan to Grant, June 28, 1865, in *War of the Rebellion*, 48:1015; *see also* William Lee Richter, "The Army in Texas During Reconstruction, 1865–1870" (PhD diss., Louisiana State University, 1970), 57, 64 n.11.

2. *See* J. David Hacker, "A Census-Based Count of the Civil War Dead," *Civil War History* 57, no. 4 (December 2011), 311, 341; Amanda Foreman, *A World on Fire: Britain's Crucial Role in the American Civil War* (New York: Random House, 2010), plates 82, 83; Doris Kearns Goodwin, *Team of Rivals: The Political Genius of Lincoln* (New York: Simon & Schuster, 2005), 346. For the standard (and lower) estimate of Civil War deaths, *see* James M. McPherson, *Battle Cry of Freedom: The Civil War Era* (New York: Ballantine Books, 1988), 854; for the differences in methodology, *see* Guy Gugliotta, "New Estimate Raises Civil War Death Toll," *New York Times*, April 2, 2012.

3. *See Personal Memoirs of P. H. Sheridan* (New York: Charles L. Webster, 1888), 2:206–210.

4. Sheridan, *Memoirs*, 2:210; *see ibid.*, 2:228; *Personal Memoirs of U. S. Grant* (New York: Charles L. Webster, 1886), 2:545–46.

5. Levasseur to the Tuileries, January 1, 1855, quoted in Dexter Perkins, *The Monroe Doctrine: 1826–1867* (Gloucester, MA: Peter Smith, 1965), 329; *see* Perkins, *The Monroe Doctrine: 1826–1867*, 328–29. For the size of the Mexican cession, *see* Franklin K. Van Zandt, *Boundaries of the United States and the Several States* (Washington, DC: Government Printing Office, 1976), 168.

6. *See* Perkins, *The Monroe Doctrine: 1826–1867*, 193–254, 323; Lester D. Langley, *Struggle for the American Mediterranean: United States-European Rivalry in the Gulf-Caribbean, 1776–1904* (Athens: University of Georgia Press, 1976), 81–106. For filibusters, *see generally* Robert E. May, *The Southern Dream of a Caribbean Empire, 1854–1861* (Gainesville: University Press of Florida, 2002); Robert E. May, *Manifest Destiny's Underworld: Filibustering in Antebellum America* (Chapel Hill: University of North Carolina Press, 2002); Robert E. May, *Slavery, Race, and Conquest in the Tropics: Lincoln, Douglas, and the Future of Latin America* (New York: Cambridge University Press, 2013).

7. *See* Charles C. Hauch, "Attitudes of Foreign Governments Towards the Spanish Reoccupation of the Dominican Republic," *Hispanic American Historical Review* 27, no. 2 (May 1947), 247–68; James W. Cortada, "A Case of International Rivalry in Latin America: Spain's Occupation of Santo Domingo, 1853–1865," *Revista de Historia de América*, no. 82 (July–December 1976), 53–69; J. Fred Rippy, "The Initiation of the Customs Receivership in the Dominican Republic," *Hispanic American Historical Review* 17, no. 4 (November 1937), 438–39.

8. "Important from Paris," *New York Times*, March 29, 1861 (emphasis omitted); *see* "Astounding Intelligence," *New York Times*, March 30, 1861; "Important from St. Domingo," *New*

York Times, March 30, 1861; "FROM FRANCE," *New York Times,* March 15, 1861; *see also* Cortada, "Case of International Rivalry," 53–69. Spain also involved itself in South America, seizing Peru's valuable Chincha Islands and sparking a war with Peru and eventually Chile, Ecuador, and Bolivia as well. Observers feared Spain was determined to resurrect its old empire, piece by piece, though it appears in retrospect that these moves were not planned from Madrid. *See* Perkins, *The Monroe Doctrine: 1826–1867,* 310–14; Samuel Flagg Bemis, *The Latin American Policy of the United States: An Historical Interpretation* (New York: Harcourt, Brace, 1943), 112–13.

9. "The Gathering of the Vultures," *Boston Daily Journal,* April 3, 1861; "Important from St. Domingo," *New York Times,* March 30, 1861 (punctuation altered); *see* "Highly Important News," *New York Times,* April 3, 1861.

10. Napoleon III to Forey, July 3, 1862, in S. Exec. Doc. No. 38-11 (1864), 190; *see* Alfred J. Hanna and Kathryn A. Hanna, *Napoleon III and Mexico: American Triumph over Monarchy* (Chapel Hill: University of North Carolina Press, 1971), 3–9, 58–68; Howard Jones, *Blue & Gray Diplomacy: A History of Union and Confederate Foreign Relations* (Chapel Hill: University of North Carolina, 2010), 164. For Napoleon III and his diplomats' mounting conviction that the United States had to be stopped, *see* Perkins, *The Monroe Doctrine: 1826–1867,* 346–56, 365–67, 418.

11. *See* Edward Shawcross, *The Last Emperor of Mexico: The Dramatic Story of the Habsburg Archduke Who Created a Kingdom in the New World* (New York: Basic Books, 2021), 24–29; Langley, *Struggle,* 117; M. M. McAllen, *Maximilian and Carlotta: Europe's Last Empire in Mexico* (San Antonio, TX: Trinity University Press, 2014), 38, 42–47. For a good account of the War of Reform, *see* Ralph Roeder, *Juarez and His Mexico: A Biographical History* (New York: Viking, 1947), 161–265.

12. Napoleon III to the Comte de Flahault, October 1861, in Egon Caesar, Conte Corti, *Maximilian and Charlotte of Mexico* (New York: Alfred A. Knopf, 1929), 1:361–62.

13. Napoleon III to the Comte de Flahault, October 1861, in Corti, *Maximilian and Charlotte,* 1:361–62; *see also* Corti, *Maximilian and Charlotte,* 1:100–01; Perkins, *The Monroe Doctrine: 1826–1867,* 365.

14. Napoleon III to the Comte de Flahault, October 1861, in Corti, *Maximilian and Charlotte,* 1:361–62; *see* McAllen, *Maximilian and Carlotta,* 42–47, 54; Roeder, *Juarez,* 161–265.

15. *See* Convention Between Great Britain, Spain, and France, Relative to Combined Operations Against Mexico, Oct 31, 1861, in Michele Cunningham, *Mexico and the Foreign Policy of Napoleon III* (Houndmills, UK: Palgrave, 2001), app. 1, 214; *see* Napoleon III to the Comte de Flahault, October 1861, in Corti, *Maximilian and Charlotte,* 1:361–62; *see also* McAllen, *Maximilian and Carlotta,* 60–62; Carl H. Bock, *Prelude to Tragedy: The Negotiation and Breakdown of the Tripartite Convention of London, October 31, 1861* (Philadelphia: University of Pennsylvania Press, 1966), 274. For the negotiation of the treaty, *see generally* Bock, *Prelude to Tragedy.*

16. Palmerston to Russell, June 19, 1862, quoted in Kenneth Bourne, *Britain and the Balance of Power in North America, 1815–1908* (Berkeley: University of California Press, 1967), 255; Clarendon to Cowley, November 4, 1863, quoted in Bourne, *Britain and the Balance of Power,* 255 & n.4; *see* Roeder, *Juarez,* 508–09, 511–12; McAllen, *Maximilian and Carlotta,* 65, 78, 93, 106–10; Bock, *Prelude to Tragedy,* 404–29; Percy F. Martin, *Maximilian in Mexico: The Story of the French Intervention (1861–1867)* (New York: Charles Scribner's Sons, 1914), 75–76.

17. Maximilian, Diary Entry, n.d., quoted in Montgomery H. Hyde, *Mexican Empire: The History of Maximilian and Carlota of Mexico* (London: Macmillan, 1946), 96–97, 103; *see* Hyde, *Mexican Empire,* 60–103; Martin, *Maximilian in Mexico,* 10–11, 15–16.

18. Napoleon III to Maximilian, January 14, 1862, in Corti, *Maximilian and Charlotte,* 1:365; *see* Corti, *Maximilian and Charlotte,* 1:136–45.

19. *See* Convention Concluded at Miramar, April 10, 1864, in Cunningham, *Mexico,* app. 2, 218–20; *see also* McAllen, *Maximilian and Carlotta,* 114–18; Corti, *Maximilian and Charlotte,* 1:325–26.

20. Carlota to Eugénie, June 18, 1864, in Corti, *Maximilian and Charlotte,* 2:836; *see* McAllen, *Maximilian and Carlotta,* 16–19; Corti, *Maximilian and Charlotte,* 2:421.

21. "Colonization of Discrowned Heads in America," *New York Times,* March 5, 1862.

22. Henry Adams to Charles Francis Adams, Jr., December 19, 1860, in *Letters of Henry Adams,* ed. Worthington Chauncey Ford, vol. 1, *1858–1891* (Cambridge, MA: Riverside, 1930), 62,

63; William B. Hesseltine, ed., *Three Against Lincoln: Murat Halstead Reports the Caucuses of 1860* (Baton Rouge: Louisiana State University, 1960), 119–20; Henry Adams to Charles Francis Adams, Jr., January 17, 1861, in Ford, *Letters of Henry Adams*, 1:81; *see* Henry Adams to Charles Francis Adams, Jr., December 29, 1860, in Ford, *Letters of Henry Adams*, 1:74; *see also* Glyndon G. Van Deusen, *William Henry Seward* (New York: Oxford University Press, 1967), 257–61.

23. *See* John M. Taylor, *William Henry Seward: Lincoln's Right Hand* (Washington, DC: Brassey's, 1991), 2–11; Van Deusen, *William Henry Seward*, 228–31.

24. *See* Walter Stahr, *Seward: Lincoln's Indispensable Man* (New York: Simon and Schuster, 2012), 236, 273; Taylor, *William Henry Seward*, 138–40, 150–53; Van Deusen, *William Henry Seward*, 246–54, 335–41.

25. *See* Stahr, *Seward*, 274–75; Cortada, "Case of International Rivalry," 67–68, 71. For Seward's suggestion of war with Europe in the spring of 1861, as well as competing explanations, *see* Seward, "Some Thoughts for the President's Consideration," April 1, 1861, in Reel 19, Lincoln MSS; *see also* Foreman, *World on Fire*, 76; D. P. Crook, *The North, the South and the Powers, 1861–1865* (New York: John Wiley & Sons, 1974), 57–62.

26. Bates, Diary Entry, August 27, 1861, in *The Diary of Edward Bates, 1859–1866*, ed. Howard K. Beale (Washington, DC: Government Printing Office, 1933), 190; *see* James Morton Callahan, *American Foreign Policy in Mexican Relations* (New York: Cooper Square, 1967), 281–89; Thomas David Schoonover, *Dollars Over Dominion: The Triumph of Liberalism in Mexican-United States Relations, 1861–1867* (Baton Rouge: Louisiana University Press, 1978), 55; Thomas Schoonover, "Napoleon Is Coming! Maximilian Is Coming?: The International History of the Civil War in the Caribbean Basin," in *The Union, the Confederacy, and the Atlantic Rim*, ed. Robert E. May, rev. ed. (Gainesville: University Press of Florida, 2013), 131–32.

27. Lincoln to the Senate, December 17, 1861, in S. Exec. Doc. No. 37-50 (1861), 1; *see* Schoonover, *Dollars Over Dominion*, 63–64.

28. *See* Taylor, *William Henry Seward*, 174–86.

29. *See* George C. Herring, *From Colony to Superpower: U.S. Foreign Relations Since 1776* (Oxford: Oxford University Press, 2008), 227–28; Crook, *The North, the South and the Powers*, 63–64; Gordon H. Warren, "Imperial Dreamer: William Henry Seward and American Destiny," in *Makers of American Diplomacy*, ed. Frank J. Merli and Theodore A. Wilson, vol. 1, *From Benjamin Franklin to Alfred Thayer Mahan* (New York: Charles Scribner's Sons, 1974), 204–09; Van Deusen, *William Henry Seward*, 301–17.

30. *See* Seward to Corwin, August 24, 1861, in H. Exec. Doc. No. 37-100 (1861), 19; *see also* Taylor, *William Henry Seward*, 198–99; Stahr, *Seward*, 350–51.

31. *See* Marvin Goldwert, "Matías Romero and Congressional Opposition to Seward's Policy Toward the French Intervention in Mexico," *The Americas* 22, no. 1 (July 1965), 22.

32. Seward to Adams, May 3, 1864, in FRUS 1864, 723–24.

33. Seward to Bigelow, May 21, 1864, in John Bigelow, *Retrospective of an Active Life*, vol. 2, *1863–1865* (New York: Baker & Taylor, 1909), 188–89.

34. Seward to Bigelow, May 5, 1864, in Bigelow, *Retrospections*, 2:182; Seward to Frances Seward (n.d.), in Frederick W. Seward, *Seward at Washington as Senator and Secretary of State* (New York: Derby and Miller, 1891), 192; *see* Seward to Adams, February 25, 1864, in FRUS 1864, 201; *see also* Schoonover, *Dollars Over Dominion*, 172; Crook, *The North, the South and the Powers*, 354.

35. Cong. Globe, 38th Cong., 1st Sess., 1408 (1864); Dayton to Seward, April 22, 1864, in FRUS 1864, 3:76; *see* Goldwert, "Matías Romero," 29–30.

36. "Interview with M. Harrison Strong," Ulysses S. Grant Homepage, last modified 2006, https://www.granthomepage.com/intstrong.htm; *see* Hamlin Garland, *Ulysses S. Grant: His Life and Character* (New York: Macmillan, 1920), 314; Ron Chernow, *Grant* (New York: Penguin, 2017), 514–15.

37. *See* Cortada, "Case of International Rivalry," 75–81; Wayne H. Bowen, *Spain and the American Civil War* (Columbia: University of Missouri Press, 2011), 92, 102–04.

38. *See* Shawcross, *The Last Emperor of Mexico*, 158. For the attempted assassinations, *see* Goodwin, *Team of Rivals*, 735–45; Taylor, *William Henry Seward*, 242–45, 251–52.

39. Grant, *Personal Memoirs*, 2:545–46. For Grant's strong, contemporary views, *see* Grant to Seward, July 23, 1864, in Horace Porter, *Campaigning with Grant* (New York: Century, 1897), 256; Grant to Johnson, September 1, 1865, in *War of the Rebellion*, 48:1221.

40. Sheridan, *Memoirs*, 2:210; *see ibid.*, 2:208; Grant, *Personal Memoirs*, 2:546.

41. George Templeton Strong, Diary Entry, November 11, 1867, in *The Diary of George Templeton Strong: Post-War Years 1865–1875*, ed. Allan Nevins and Milton Halsey Thomas (New York: Macmillan, 1952), 165; Benjamin P. Thomas, ed., *Three Years with Grant as Recalled by War Correspondent Sylvanus Cadwallader* (New York: Alfred A. Knopf, 1955), 305; H. C. Greiner, *General Phil Sheridan As I Knew Him* (Chicago: J. S. Hyland, 1908), 232; John Russel Young, *Around the World with General Grant* (New York: Subscription Book Department, 1879), 2:297; *see also* Joseph Wheelan, *Terrible Swift Sword: The Life of General Philip H. Sheridan* (Cambridge, MA: Da Capo, 2012), 85–86, 157.

42. Sheridan to Rawlins, June 4, 1865, in *War of the Rebellion*, 48:767; Sheridan, *Memoirs*, 2:213; *see* Richter, "The Army in Texas," 57, 64 n.11.

43. Sheridan to Grant, June 28, 1865, in *War of the Rebellion*, 48:1015; Sheridan to Rawlins, July 6, 1865, in H.R. Exec. Doc. No. 39-73 (1866), vol. 1, pt. 2, 464; Sheridan to Steele, July 7, 1865, in Box 2, Reel 1, Sheridan MSS; Sheridan to Steele, July 13, 1865, in Box 2, Reel 1, Sheridan MSS; *see* Sheridan, *Memoirs*, 2:213–14.

44. Sheridan to Rawlins, June 29, 1865, in *Papers of Ulysses S. Grant*, ed. John Y. Simon, vol. 15, *May 1–December 31, 1865* (Carbondale: Southern Illinois University Press, 1988), 259.

45. Grant to Johnson, July 12, 1865, in Simon, *Papers of Ulysses S. Grant*, 15:259; *see* Grant to Sheridan, July 25, 1865, in John M. Schofield, "The Withdrawal of the French from Mexico: A Chapter of Secret History," *Century* 54, no. 1 (May–October 1897), 129.

46. *See* Welles, Diary Entry, July 14, 1865, in *Diary of Gideon Welles*, ed. John T. Morse, vol. 2, *April 1, 1864–December 31, 1866* (Boston: Houghton Mifflin, 1911), 332–33.

47. Welles, Diary Entry, June 16, 1865, in *Diary of Gideon Welles*, 2:317; Romero, Report, June 18, 1865, in Thomas D. Schoonover, ed., *Mexican Lobby: Matías Romero in Washington, 1861–1867* (Lexington: University Press of Kentucky, 1986), 67; *see* Stahr, *Seward*, 442–43. For Grant laying the groundwork for Sheridan's letter, *see* Grant to Johnson, June 19, 1865, in *War of the Rebellion*, 48:923–24.

48. Welles, Diary Entry, July 14, 1865, in *Diary of Gideon Welles*, 2:332–33. For army support, *see* Welles, Diary Entry, August 1, 1865, in *Diary of Gideon Welles*, 2:348; Welles, Diary Entry, August 25, 1865, in *Diary of Gideon Welles*, 2:367; Welles, Diary Entry, November 23, 1866, in *Diary of Gideon Welles*, 2:624–25.

49. Johnson, Speech in Nashville, 1864, in John Savage, *The Life and Public Services of Andrew Johnson* (New York: Derby & Miller, Publishers, 1866), 293, 297.

50. *See* Grant to Johnson, July 15, 1865, in *War of the Rebellion*, 48:1080–81; Schofield, "Withdrawal of the French," 128–29; Robert Ryal Miller, "Lew Wallace and the French Intervention in Mexico," *Indiana Magazine of History* 59, no. 1 (March 1963), 38–40; Romero, Report, July 19, 1865, in Schoonover, *Mexican Lobby*, 81.

51. Romero, Report, July 19, 1865, in Schoonover, *Mexican Lobby*, 81; *see* Chernow, *Grant*, 558.

52. Schofield, "Withdrawal of the French from Mexico," 130; *see ibid.*, 129–30; *see also* Stahr, *Seward*, 444.

53. Bigelow, Diary Entry, December 10, 1896, in Vol. 62, John Bigelow MSS; *see* Schofield, "Withdrawal of the French from Mexico," 128, 130–37.

54. *See* Sheridan, *Memoirs*, 2:214–15.

55. Sheridan to Sedgwick, October 23, 1866, in Albert D. Richardson, *A Personal History of Ulysses S. Grant* (Hartford: American Publishing, 1868), 532; Sheridan to Nesmith, December 14, 1865, in Box 39, Reel 17, Sheridan MSS; *see* Sheridan to Rawlins, June 4, 1865, in *War of the Rebellion*, 48:767; Sheridan to Rawlins, November 14, 1866, in *Message from the President of the United States to the Two Houses of Congress* (Washington, DC: Government Printing Office, 1867), 509–10; Sheridan to Grant, November 5, 1865, in *War of the Rebellion*, 48:1252–53; Sheridan to Grant, November 26, 1865, in *War of the Rebellion*, 48:1258.

56. *See* Sheridan, *Memoirs*, 2:216–17, 223–26; *see also* Richter, "The Army in Texas," 66–67; McAllen, *Maximilian and Carlotta*, 233; Wheelan, *Terrible Swift Sword*, 3, 213–14. For the total sum of U.S. aid that flowed over the border, *see generally* Robert Benaway Brown, "Guns over the Border: American Aid to the Juárez Government During the French Intervention" (PhD diss., University of Michigan, 1951).

57. *See* Sheridan, *Memoirs*, 2:218–24; *see also* Richter, "The Army in Texas," 66–73; McAllen, *Maximilian and Carlotta*, 187, 229–30; Roy Morris, Jr., *Sheridan: The Life and Wars of General Phil Sheridan* (New York: Crown, 1992), 268–69; Shawcross, *The Last Emperor of Mexico*, 161.

58. Sheridan, *Memoirs*, 2:215–16.

59. *See* Corti, *Maximilian and Charlotte*, 2:537; McAllen, *Maximilian and Carlotta*, 183; Hyde, *Mexican Empire*, 181.

60. Sheridan, *Memoirs*, 2:217.

61. Seward to the Marquis de Montholon, December 6, 1865, in H.R. Exec. Doc. No. 39-73 (1866), vol. 1, pt. 2, 348; Seward to Bigelow, December 16, 1865, in H.R. Exec. Doc. No. 39-73 (1866), vol. 1, pt. 2, 496; *see* Seward to Bigelow, September 6, 1865, in H.R. Exec. Doc. No. 39-73 (1866), vol. 1, pt. 2, 477–78; Seward to Bigelow, November 6, 1865, in H.R. Exec. Doc. No. 39-73 (1866), vol. 1, pt. 2, 487.

62. Seward to Bigelow, November 23, 1865, in H.R. Exec. Doc. No. 39-73 (1866), vol. 1, pt. 2, 491; Seward to the Marquis de Montholon, December 6, 1865, in H.R. Exec. Doc. No. 39-73 (1866), vol. 1, pt. 2, 348; *see* Seward to the Marquis de Montholon, April 25, 1866, in FRUS 1866, 1:378–79.

63. *See* Maximilian to Napoleon III, December 27, 1865, in Corti, *Maximilian and Charlotte*, 2:927; *see also* McAllen, *Maximilian and Carlotta*, 183, 225–26, 232–34; Crook, *The North, the South and the Powers*, 367–69; Corti, *Maximilian and Charlotte*, 2:578–80.

64. *See* Seward to Bigelow, November 6, 1865, in H.R. Exec. Doc. No. 39-73 (1866), vol. 1, pt. 2, 487; Welles, Diary Entry, December 22, 1865, in *Diary of Gideon Welles*, 2:401; *see also* Dean B. Mahin, *One War at a Time: The International Dimensions of the American Civil War* (Washington, DC: Brassey's, 1999), 273–75.

65. Maximilian to Napoleon III, December 27, 1865, in Corti, *Maximilian and Charlotte*, 2:927; *see* Crook, *The North, the South and the Powers*, 354.

66. Napoleon III to Maximilian, January 15, 1866, in Corti, *Maximilian and Charlotte*, 2:930–31.

67. Dano to Drouyn de Lhuys, February 28, 1866, quoted in Hanna and Hanna, *Napoleon III and Mexico*, 275; *see* McAllen, *Maximilian and Carlotta*, 233.

68. For the French withdrawal, *see* Seward to the Marquis de Montholon, April 25, 1866, in FRUS 1866, 1:378–79. For the negotiations over Austrian reinforcements, *see* Stephen J. Valone, "'Weakness Offers Temptation': William H. Seward and the Reassertion of the Monroe Doctrine," *Diplomatic History* 19, no. 4 (Fall 1995), 592–94; McAllen, *Maximilian and Carlotta*, 237.

69. Sheridan to Grant, October 22, 1866, in *Papers of Ulysses S. Grant* 16:323.

70. Crompton to Russell, February 9, 1862, in Leone Levi, ed., *Annals of British Legislation* (London: Smith, Elder, 1865), 13:133.

71. *See* Richter, "The Army in Texas," 72 n.29; McAllen, *Maximilian and Carlotta*, 246–48; Brown, "Guns over the Border," 171.

72. *See* McAllen, *Maximilian and Carlotta*, 243–44, 247–48, 254, 258–59, 279, 298.

73. Sherman, *Memoirs*, 2:418; *see* Émile de Kératry, *The Rise and Fall of the Emperor Maximilian: A Narrative of the Mexican Empire, 1861–7*, trans. G. H. Venables (London: Sampson Low, Son, and Marston, 1868), 273; *see also* Corti, *Maximilian and Charlotte*, 2:753–54; Shawcross, *The Last Emperor of Mexico*, 214–26.

74. E. Masseras, *Un Essai d'Empire au Mexique* (Paris: G. Charpentier, 1879), 157; *see* McAllen, *Maximilian and Carlotta*, 321–22.

75. *See* Hyde, *Mexican Empire*, 254–62; McAllen, *Maximilian and Carlotta*, 327, 331–55, 378.

76. Corti, *Maximilian and Charlotte*, 2:825.

77. Ernst Schmit Ritter von Tavera, *Geschichte der Regierung des Kaisers Maximilian I. und die Französische Intervention in Mexiko 1861–1867* (Vienna: Wilhelm Braumuller, 1903), 2:485; *see* Hyde, *Mexican Empire*, 289–90; McAllen, *Maximilian and Carlotta*, 384–87.

78. Schmit Ritter von Tavera, *Geschichte der Regierung*, 2:485; *see* Hyde, *Mexican Empire*, 290–92.

79. *See* Hyde, *Mexican Empire*, 292.

80. *See* Seward, *Seward at Washington*, 452; Albert S. Evans, *Our Sister Republic: A Gala Trip Through Tropical Mexico in 1869–70* (Harford, CT: Columbian Book, 1870), 237–38.

81. *See* Seward, *Seward at Washington*, 452; Evans, *Our Sister Republic*, 237–38.

82. *See* Seward, *Seward at Washington*, 455–56, 460; Evans, *Our Sister Republic*, 227, 309–14; *see also* Stahr, *Seward*, 530–31, 535–36.

83. *See* Hanna and Hanna, *Napoleon III and Mexico*, 3–9, 58–68; Jones, *Blue & Gray Diplomacy*, 77. For an especially dire scenario, *see* Schoonover, *Dollars Over Dominion*, 109–10. Even after the Civil War ended, a European puppet state would have remained dangerous, requiring the United States to station a large army along the Rio Grande at a time when the republic needed to pare down its bloated defense budget. *See* Grant to Johnson, September 1, 1865, in *War of the Rebellion*, 48:1221.

84. *See* Perkins, *The Monroe Doctrine: 1826–1867*, 419, 545–46; Crook, *The North, the South and the Powers*, 84; Hanna and Hanna, *Napoleon III and Mexico*, 3–9, 58–68; McAllen, *Maximilian and Carlotta*, 211–12.

85. "The French in Mexico," *Harper's Weekly*, June 11, 1864, 371; I. A. Shestakov, n.d., quoted in Walter Lafeber, *The Cambridge History of American Foreign Relations*, vol. 2, *The American Search for Opportunity, 1865–1913* (Cambridge, UK: Cambridge University Press, 1998), 12; *see also* Dexter Perkins, *The Monroe Doctrine: 1867–1907* (Gloucester, MA: Peter Smith, 1966), 2–3; Jay Sexton, *The Monroe Doctrine: Empire and Nation in Nineteenth-Century America* (New York: Hill and Wang, 2011), 123–24, 153–54, 157–58.

86. For Seward's summary of the United States's position on foreign interventions at this time, *see* Seward to Kilpatrick, June 2, 1866, in Box 2:1, Reel 1, Cleveland MSS. For American landings, *see* Max Boot, *The Savage Wars of Peace: Small Wars and the Rise of American Power* (New York: Basic Books, 2002), 60. Such landings were practically unavoidable until the twentieth century, when American embassies and legations first received permanent guards. *Ibid.*

87. Seward to Dayton, September 26, 1863, in Instructions, France, Roll 56, M77, RG59, NA (punctuation altered).

88. *See* Seward to Dayton, September 26, 1863, in Instructions, France, Roll 56, M77, RG59, NA.

89. Seward to Corwin April 6, 1861, in FRUS 1861, 66–67.

90. *See* McAllen, *Maximilian and Carlotta*, 183; Corti, *Maximilian and Charlotte*, 1:268.

91. Seward to Corwin April 6, 1861, in FRUS 1861, 66.

Chapter 2: In Division There Is Weakness

1. *See* David Saville Muzzey, *James G. Blaine: A Political Idol of Other Days* (New York: Dodd, Mead, 1934), 465–66, 473–74, 489–90; David Healy, *James G. Blaine and Latin America* (Columbia: University of Missouri Press, 2001), 10, 227; Charles S. Campbell, *The Transformation of American Foreign Relations 1865–1900* (New York: Harper and Row, 1976), 174; Edward P. Crapol, *James G. Blaine: Architect of Empire* (Wilmington, DE: SR Books, 2000), 132.

2. *See* Muzzey, *James G. Blaine*, 33; Crapol, *Architect of Empire*, 3–4; Joyce S. Goldberg, *The Baltimore Affair* (Lincoln: University of Nebraska Press, 1986), 25.

3. Blaine to Garfield, December 10, 1880, in Gail Hamilton, *Biography of James G. Blaine* (Norwich: Henry Bill Publishing, 1895), 490; *see* Muzzey, *James G. Blaine*, 109–10, 496.

4. Mrs. Blaine to M., May 17, 1881, in Hamilton, *James G. Blaine*, 536; 8 Cong. Rec. 239 (1878) (punctuation altered); *see* Muzzey, *James G. Blaine*, 128–29, 491, 495–96; Healy, *James G. Blaine*, 7–10.

5. *See* Richard H. Collin, *Theodore Roosevelt's Caribbean: The Panama Canal, the Monroe Doctrine, and the Latin American Context* (Baton Rouge: Louisiana State University Press, 1990), 41–43. For a good overview of how Europe's other powers began reacting to Germany as early as 1870, *see* Paul Kennedy, *The Rise and Fall of the Great Powers: Economic Change and Military Conflict from 1500 to 2000* (New York: Vintage Books, 1989), 187–89.

6. *See* Hans J. Morgenthau, *Politics Among Nations: The Struggle for Power and Peace* (New York: Alfred A. Knopf, 1956), 332; Niall Ferguson, *Empire: The Rise and Demise of the British World Order and the Lessons for Global Power* (New York: Basic Books, 2004), 139–42; Kennedy,

Rise and Fall, 147–50; Lloyd C. Gardner, *Safe for Democracy: The Anglo-American Response to Revolution, 1913–1923* (New York: Oxford University Press, 1984), 12; Grover Clark, *The Balance Sheets of Imperialism: Facts and Figures on Colonies* (New York: Russell & Russell, 1967), 6.

7. See Milton Plesur, *America's Outward Thrust: Approaches to Foreign Affairs, 1865–1890* (DeKalb: Northern Illinois University Press, 1971), 130–32; Davis M. Pletcher, *The Awkward Years: American Foreign Relations Under Garfield and Arthur* (Columbia: University of Missouri Press, 1962), xii–xiii; Gardner, *Safe for Democracy*, 29–30; Thomas D. Schoonover, *The United States in Central America, 1860–1911: Episodes of Social Imperialism and Imperial Rivalry in the World System* (Durham, NC: Duke University Press, 1991), 62–76.

8. John A. Kasson, "The Monroe Doctrine in 1881," *North American Review* 133, no. 301 (December 1881), 526–27; Tilden to Hill, March 28, 1886, in *Letters and Literary Memorials of Samuel J. Tilden*, ed. John Bigelow (New York: Harper & Brothers, 1908), 2:717.

9. See James L. Abrahamson, *America Arms for a New Century: The Making of a Great Military Power* (New York: Free Press, 1981), 4–5; Charles A. Kupchan, *Isolationism: A History of America's Efforts to Shield Itself from the World* (Oxford: Oxford University Press, 2020), 132–34; Clay Risen, *The Crowded Hour: Theodore Roosevelt, the Rough Riders, and the Dawn of the American Century* (New York: Scribner, 2019), 8; Harold Sprout and Margaret Sprout, *The Rise of American Naval Power 1776–1918* (Princeton, NJ: Princeton University Press, 1944), 165–75; Max Boot, *The Savage Wars of Peace: Small Wars and the Rise of American Power* (New York: Basic Books, 2002), 56.

10. See Kenneth Wimmel, *Theodore Roosevelt and the Great White Fleet: American Seapower Comes of Age* (Washington, DC: Brassey's, 1998), 2–3, 30–38; Sprout and Sprout, *Rise of American Naval Power*, 181, 195–96; Kenneth J. Hagan, *American Gunboat Diplomacy and the Old Navy 1877–1889* (Westport, CT: Greenwood, 1973), 5–9; Abrahamson, *America Arms*, 10–14, 20–26; Robert L. Beisner, *From the Old Diplomacy to the New 1865–1900* (Arlington Heights, IL: Harlan Davidson, 1986), 57–60.

11. "Reorganization of the Navy," *Buffalo Daily Courier*, November 14, 1881; "How to Maintain the Monroe Doctrine," *Chicago Tribune*, March 12, 1880; 16 Cong. Rec. 1974 (1885); "A Prediction Verified," *Army and Navy Journal*, March 21, 1874, 504; A. T. Mahan, "The Future in Relation to American Naval Power," June 1895, in *The Interest of America in Sea Power, Present and Future* (Boston: Little, Brown, 1897), 138; Oscar Wilde, *The Canterville Ghost* (Boston: John W. Luce, 1906), 81.

12. James G. Blaine, *Twenty Years of Congress: From Lincoln to Garfield with a Review of the Events Which Led to the Political Revolution of 1860* (Norwich: Henry Bill Publishing, 1884), 1:597–98; Blaine to Logan, May 7, 1881, in FRUS 1881, 102; Blaine to Ubico, June 16, 1881, in FRUS 1881, 599; Blaine to Morgan, June 16, 1881, No. 138, in FRUS 1881, 767–68; *see* Blaine to Morgan, June 21, 1881, in FRUS 1881, 769; Blaine to Logan, May 7, 1881, in FRUS 1881, 103–04; Blaine to Morgan, June 16, 1881, No. 137, in Instructions, Mexico, Roll 116, M77, RG59, NA; *see also* Mike Sewell, "Political Rhetoric and Policy-Making: James G. Blaine and Britain," *Journal of American Studies* 24, no. 1 (April 1990), 74, 81–83; Crapol, *Architect of Empire*, 22–23.

13. See Joseph Smith, *Illusions of Conflict: Anglo-American Diplomacy Toward Latin America, 1865–1896* (Pittsburgh, PA: University of Pittsburgh Press, 1979), 32–33; Allan Peskin, "Blaine, Garfield, and Latin America: A New Look," *The Americas* 36, no. 1 (July 1979), 82.

14. James G. Blaine, "Foreign Policy of the Garfield Administration" (self-pub., n.d.), reprinted from *Chicago Weekly Magazine*, September 16, 1882, 4; *see* Blaine to Morgan, June 21, 1881, in FRUS 1881, 769; Blaine to Morgan, June 21, 1881, in FRUS 1881, 770; Logan to Blaine, June 28, 1881, in FRUS 1881, 110; *see also* Edward P. Crapol, *America for Americans: Economic Nationalism and Anglophobia in the Late Nineteenth Century* (Westport, CT: Greenwood, 1973), 75; Healy, *James G. Blaine*, 246–47.

15. See John Bigelow, *Retrospections of an Active Life*, vol. 4, *1867–1871* (Garden City, NY: Doubleday, Page, 1913), 53; Johnson, Fourth Annual Message, December 9, 1868, in Richardson 6:688–89; *see also* Charles Callan Tansill, *The Purchase of the Danish West Indies* (New York: Greenwood, 1968), 1; Glyndon G. Van Deusen, *William Henry Seward* (New York:

Oxford University Press, 1967), 511–34. For Seward masterminding the point behind Johnson's message, *see* Walter Stahr, *Seward: Lincoln's Indispensable Man* (New York: Simon and Schuster, 2012), 520.

16. Seward to Spalding, July 5, 1868, in FRUS 1894, app. II, 144; *see* Kupchan, *Isolationism*, 133–35; Eric T. L. Love, *Race over Empire: Racism and U.S. Imperialism 1865–1900* (Chapel Hill: University of North Carolina Press, 2004), 25–72. For the failure of Seward's annexationist projects, *see* Van Deusen, *William Henry Seward*, 511–34; for the failure of Grant's attempt to annex the Dominican Republic, *see* Allan Nevins, *Hamilton Fish: The Inner History of the Grant Administration* (New York: Dodd, Mead, 1936), 249–78, 309–34; Charles Callan Tansill, *The United States and Santo Domingo 1798–1873: A Chapter in Caribbean Diplomacy* (Gloucester, MA: Peter Smith, 1967), 338–464; William Javier Nelson, *Almost a Territory: America's Attempt to Annex the Dominican Republic* (Newark: University of Delaware Press, 1990), 59–116. For Blaine's opposition to annexationism, *see* Crapol, *Architect of Empire*, 34–35.

17. *See* Fish, Report, July 14, 1870, in Richardson 7:70–78; Evarts to Diplomatic Officers in Spanish-American Countries, July 13, 1877, in FRUS 1877, 2–3; *see also* Smith, *Illusions of Conflict*, 27–28. For Fish and Evarts's implementation of this approach, *see* David M. Pletcher, *The Diplomacy of Trade and Investment* (Columbia: University of Missouri, 1998), 32; Gary Alvin Pennanen, "The Foreign Policy of William Maxwell Evarts" (PhD diss., University of Wisconsin, 1969), 103–04; Plesur, *America's Outward Thrust*, 28–29.

18. Blaine, "Foreign Policy of the Garfield Administration," 1; *see* Blaine to Morgan, June 16, 1881, No. 137, in Instructions, Mexico, Roll 116, M77, RG59, NA; *see also* Crapol, *America for Americans*, 74–77.

19. Blaine, "Foreign Policy of the Garfield Administration," 4; Blaine to Morgan, June 16, 1881, No. 138, in FRUS 1881, 766.

20. Blaine to Lowell, November 19, 1881, in FRUS 1881, 555; *see* Pletcher, *The Awkward Years*, 22–33, 63–67; Kenneth Bourne, *Britain and the Balance of Power in North America, 1815–1908* (Berkeley: University of California Press, 1967), 344.

21. *See* Muzzey, *James G. Blaine*, 494; Healy, *James G. Blaine*, 246–47.

22. *See generally* Candice Millard, *Destiny of the Republic: A Tale of Madness, Medicine, and the Murder of a President* (New York: Anchor Books, 2012).

23. *See* Russell H. Bastert, "A New Approach to the Origins of Blaine's Pan American Policy," *Hispanic American Historical Review* 39, no. 3 (August 1959), 380–403.

24. *See* Pletcher, *The Awkward Years*, 60–61.

25. Blaine, "Foreign Policy of the Garfield Administration," 2, 8; Blaine to Trescot, December 1, 1881, in S. Ex. Doc. 47-79 (1882), 178; *see* Blaine to Osborn, November 29, 1881, in FRUS 1881, 13–15; *see also* Bastert, "A New Approach," 402–05, 411–12.

26. *See* Healy, *James G. Blaine*, 94–97.

27. *See* Crapol, *Architect of Empire*, 81–83; *see generally* Bastert, "A New Approach."

28. *See* Healy, *James G. Blaine*, 96; Russell H. Bastert, "Diplomatic Reversal: Frelinghuysen's Opposition to Blaine's Pan-American Policy in 1882," *Mississippi Valley Historical Review* 42, no. 4 (March 1956), 657–69.

29. Harriet Stanwood Blaine to M., January 28, 1882, in Beale, *Letters of Mrs. James G. Blaine*, ed. Harriet S. Blaine Beale (New York: Duffield, 1908), 1:295; *see* "A Protest from Mr. Blaine," *New York Tribune*, February 4, 1882; "Mr. Blaine's View of It," *Washington Post*, March 24, 1882; *see* Bastert, "Diplomatic Reversal," 662–64, 669–71.

30. Blaine, "Foreign Policy of the Garfield Administration," 4; *see* John A. S. Grenville and George Berkeley Young, *Politics, Strategy, and American Diplomacy: Studies in Foreign Policy, 1873–1917* (New Haven, CT: Yale University Press, 1969), 91–92.

31. *See* Muzzey, *James G. Blaine*, 242–51; Healy, *James G. Blaine*, 108–10.

32. Whyte to Blaine, April 24, 1882, quoted in Muzzey, *James G. Blaine*, 250; *see* Healy, *James G. Blaine*, 108–18; Bastert, "Diplomatic Reversal," 665 n.28.

33. *See* Healy, *James G. Blaine*, 117–18.

34. *See* Crapol, *America for Americans*, 120. Like Blaine, Frelinghuysen was also gravely concerned about European control of any future isthmian canal. He picked up the diplomatic correspondence on the subject where Blaine had left it, and then he went one step further and signed

a treaty with Nicaragua for rights to a canal route. But the treaty was blatantly at odds with a previous treaty the United States had made with Great Britain, and it was never ratified. *See* Pletcher, *The Awkward Years*, 103–06, 270–83, 328–31.

35. Frelinghuysen to Miller, March 26, 1884, in H.R. Exec. Doc. No. 49-50 (1886), 13.

36. Frelinghuysen to the Commissioners, August 27, 1884, in H.R. Exec. Doc. No. 49-50 (1886), 5; *see* Frelinghuysen to Miller, March 26, 1884, in H.R. Exec. Doc. No. 49-50 (1886), 13; *see also* John William Rollins, "Frederick Theodore Frelinghuysen, 1817–1885: The Politics and Diplomacy of Stewardship" (PhD diss., University of Wisconsin, 1974), 386–87; Crapol, *America for Americans*, 120–37.

37. *See* Sprout and Sprout, *Rise of American Naval Power*, 186–89.

38. *See* Muzzey, *James G. Blaine*, 286.

39. *See* Muzzey, *James G. Blaine*, 287–325.

40. *See* Tom E. Terrill, *The Tariff, Politics, and American Foreign Policy 1874–1901* (Westport, CT: Greenwood, 1973), 91–95.

41. *See* Terrill, *Tariff, Politics, and American Foreign Policy*, 90–140. Cleveland could not afford to play the same political game with a reciprocity treaty with Hawai'i, however. Whereas Frelinghuysen had designed his other treaties to combat long-term threats, he had renewed the Hawaiian treaty to prop up a government that seemed perpetually in danger of falling into European hands. Cleveland's administration was especially nervous about that possibility because of recent German aggression elsewhere in the Pacific, and it backed the treaty's renewal in Congress by explaining how its commercial costs paled in significance to its political significance. *See* Charles Callan Tansill, *The Foreign Policy of Thomas F. Bayard 1885–1897* (New York: Fordham University Press, 1940), 377–79, 387–88, 393, 396, 400–03; Crapol, *America for Americans*, 152–54.

42. *See* Sprout and Sprout, *Rise of American Naval Power*, 189.

43. *See* Frelinghuysen to the Commissioners, August 27, 1884, in H.R. Exec. Doc. No. 49-50 (1886), 11; *see also* Healy, *James G. Blaine*, 144–46; *see generally* James F. Vivian, "The Pan-American Conference Act of May 10, 1888: President Cleveland and the Historians," *The Americas* 27, no. 2 (October 1970), 185–92.

44. *See* Vivian, "The Pan-American Conference Act," 186.

45. *See* Healy, *James G. Blaine*, 36–38, 106–08; David McCullough, *The Path Between the Seas: The Creation of the Panama Canal 1870–1914* (New York: Simon and Schuster Paperbacks, 1977), 202–03.

46. Harrison to Blaine, January 17, 1889, in *The Correspondence Between Benjamin Harrison and James G. Blaine 1882–1893*, ed. Albert T. Volwiler (Philadelphia: American Philosophical Society, 1940), 44; *see* Harrison, Inaugural Address, March 4, 1889, in Richardson 9:10; Harrison, First Annual Message, December 3, 1889, in Richardson 9:32–33; *see also* Healy, *James G. Blaine*, 141, 158–59, 164–65, 205–06, 235.

47. *See International American Conference: Reports of Committees and Discussions Thereon*, S. Exec. Doc. No. 51-232 (1890), 1:7–8; *see also* Robert Kagan, *Dangerous Nation* (New York: Alfred A. Knopf, 2006), 322–23. For a good summary of the Conference, *see* Terrill, *Tariff, Politics, and American Foreign Policy*, 141–58.

48. M. Romero, "The Pan-American Conference. I," *North American Review* 151, no. 406 (September 1890), 366; *see* M. Romero, "The Pan-American Conference. II," *North American Review* 151, no. 407 (October 1890), 410–11, 421; *International American Conference*, 1:49–53; *see also* Healy, *James G. Blaine*, 146–59.

49. *See* Healy, *James G. Blaine*, 151–59.

50. *See* Romero, "The Pan-American Conference. II," 411–13; *see also* Healy, *James G. Blaine*, 152–53; Kagan, *Dangerous Nation*, 323.

51. *See* Terrill, *Tariff, Politics, and American Foreign Policy*, 159.

52. *See* Tariff Act of 1890 (McKinley Tariff), Pub. L. No. 51-1244, § 3, 26 Stat. 567, 612; *see also* Healy, *James G. Blaine*, 160–70.

53. *See* Healy, *James G. Blaine*, 171–78. Costa Rica, the last Central American republic, signed but did not ratify a reciprocity agreement with the United States. *See* Healy, *James G. Blaine*, 174.

54. *See* Healy, *James G. Blaine*, 177–79; David M. Pletcher, "Reciprocity and Latin America in the Early 1890s: A Foretaste of Dollar Diplomacy," *Pacific Historical Review* 47, no. 1 (February 1978), 84–88; Pletcher, *The Diplomacy of Trade and Investment*, 263, 275.

55. *See* Rayford W. Logan, *The Diplomatic Relations of the United States with Haiti, 1776–1891* (Chapel Hill: University of North Carolina Press, 1941), 415–17, 419–20, 434–35; Healy, *James G. Blaine*, 183–203.

56. "The Disorder in Chili," *New-York Daily Tribune*, January 22, 1891; *see* Healy, *James G. Blaine*, 208–13; Walter LaFeber, *The New Empire: An Interpretation of American Expansion 1860– 1898* (Ithaca, NY: Cornell University Press, 1967), 136.

57. *See* Healy, *James G. Blaine*, 213; Beisner, *Old Diplomacy to the New*, 102.

58. *See* Lars Schoultz, *Beneath the United States: A History of U.S. Policy Toward Latin America* (Cambridge, MA: Harvard University Press, 2003), 101–02; *see generally* Francis X. Holbrook and John Nikol, "The Chilean Crisis of 1891–1892," *American Neptune* 38, no. 4 (October 1978), 291–300; Goldberg, *The Baltimore Affair*.

59. *See generally* Goldberg, *The Baltimore Affair*.

60. Egan to Blaine, September 17, 1891, in FRUS 1891, 163; *see* LaFeber, *New Empire*, 135– 36; Beisner, *Old Diplomacy to the New*, 102; Grenville and Young, *Politics, Strategy, and American Diplomacy*, 100.

61. *See* LaFeber, *New Empire*, 135–36.

62. *See* Campbell, *The Transformation*, 171–76.

63. *See* Muzzey, *James G. Blaine*, 469–75, 489–90.

64. *See* Collin, *Theodore Roosevelt's Caribbean*, 41–42. For the Democrats' tariff reform, *see* Healy, *James G. Blaine*, 177–78.

65. Blaine to Scruggs, October 28, 1891, quoted in Healy, *James G. Blaine*, 248; *see* Healy, *James G. Blaine*, 248–49; Allan Spetter, "Harrison and Blaine: Foreign Policy, 1889–1893," *Indiana Magazine of History* 65, no. 3 (1969), 219–21. For Blaine's views on Hawai'i, *see* Chapter 4.

Chapter 3: All the Waste Places of the Earth

1. William L. Scruggs, *British Aggressions in Venezuela, or the Monroe Doctrine on Trial*, 3rd ed. (Atlanta, GA: Franklin Printing and Publishing, 1895), 5–6.

2. *See* John A. S. Grenville and George Berkeley Young, *Politics, Strategy, and American Diplomacy: Studies in Foreign Policy, 1873–1917* (New Haven, CT: Yale University Press, 1969), 127–28, 132–34.

3. *See* Grenville and Young, *Politics, Strategy, and American Diplomacy*, 133.

4. *See* Dexter Perkins, *The Monroe Doctrine: 1867–1907* (Gloucester, MA: Peter Smith, 1966), 136–37.

5. *See* Robert L. Beisner, *From the Old Diplomacy to the New 1865–1900* (Arlington Heights, IL: Harlan Davidson, 1986), 114–15.

6. *See* Beisner, *Old Diplomacy to the New*, 114–15; Robert Freeman Smith, "Latin America, the United States and the European Powers, 1830–1930," in *The Cambridge History of Latin America*, vol. 4, *C. 1870 to 1930* (Cambridge, UK: Cambridge University Press, 1986), 91.

7. *See* Thompson to Gresham, October 22, 1893, in Despatches, Brazil, Roll 57, M121, RG59, NA; Thompson to Gresham, December 13, 1893, in Despatches, Brazil, Roll 57, M121, RG59, NA; Gresham to Bayard, December 18, 1893, in Instructions, Great Britain, Roll 89, M77, RG59, NA; *see also* Steven C. Topik, *Trade and Gunboats: The United States and Brazil in the Age of Empire* (Stanford, CA: Stanford University Press, 1996), 121–77; Matilda Gresham, *Life of Walter Quintin Gresham, 1832–1895* (Chicago: Rand McNally, 1919), 2:777–81.

8. *See Annual Report of the Secretary of the Navy for the Year 1894* (Washington, DC: Government Printing Office, 1894), 23; *see also* Topik, *Trade and Gunboats*, 121–77.

9. *See* Grenville and Young, *Politics, Strategy, and American Diplomacy*, 118–19; Thomas M. Leonard, *Central America and the United States: The Search for Stability* (Athens: University of Georgia Press, 1991), 45–47; Topik, *Trade and Gunboats*, 176–77.

10. *See* Charles S. Campbell, *The Transformation of American Foreign Relations 1865–1900* (New York: Harper and Row, 1976), 202–03; Charles Callan Tansill, *The Foreign Policy of Thomas F. Bayard 1885–1897* (New York: Fordham University Press, 1940), 671–73, 677–90.

11. *See* FRUS 1895, 235–43, 397–402; *see also* Sumner Welles, *Naboth's Vineyard: The Dominican Republic 1844–1924* (Mamaroneck, NY: Paul P. Appel, 1966), 2:502–08. For a view that assigns less significance to the arrival of the American warships, *see* David Charles MacMichael, "The United States and the Dominican Republic, 1871–1940: A Cycle in Caribbean Diplomacy" (PhD diss., University of Oregon, 1964), 107–15.

12. Adee to Olney, August 12, 1895, in Reel 11, Olney MSS. For the skirmish between France and Brazil, *see* Walter LaFeber, *The New Empire: An Interpretation of American Expansion 1860–1898* (Ithaca, NY: Cornell University Press, 1967), 246–47. For the dispute between Great Britain and Brazil, *see ibid.*, 246.

13. *Annual Report of the Secretary of the Navy for the Year 1891* (Washington, DC: Government Printing Office, 1891), 30–31. For other examples of concern about the problem of order, *see* H. C. Lodge, "Our Blundering Foreign Policy," *Forum* 19 (March–August 1895), 17; A. T. Mahan, "The Future in Relation to American Naval Power," June 1895, in *The Interest of America in Sea Power, Present and Future* (Boston: Little, Brown, 1897), 165–70; A. T. Mahan, "The United States Looking Outward," August 1890, in *The Interest of America*, 7–9, 19–21. For naval officers' focus on the canal serving as an "attractive nuisance," *see* Mahan, "Looking Outward," in *The Interest of America*, 11–13, 19–21; A. T. Mahan, *The Influence of Sea Power Upon History*, 1660–1783 (Boston: Little, Brown, 1890), 33–34; A. T. Mahan, "A Twentieth-Century Outlook," May 1897, in *The Interest of America*, 260–61; *see also* James A. Field, Jr., "American Imperialism: The Worst Chapter in Almost Any Book," *American Historical Review* 83, no. 3 (June 1978), 655; James L. Abrahamson, *America Arms for a New Century: The Making of a Great Military Power* (New York: Free Press, 1981), 42–43. For concerns about colonial *lebensraum*, *see* "Sounds a War Tocsin," *Washington Post*, May 11, 1895; Henry Cabot Lodge, "England, Venezuela, and the Monroe Doctrine," *North American Review* 160, no. 463 (June 1895), 657–58.

14. *See* Gerald G. Eggert, *Richard Olney: Evolution of a Statesman* (University Park: Pennsylvania State University Press, 1974), 200–01; Ernest R. May, *Imperial Democracy: The Emergence of America as a Great Power* (New York: Harper Torchbooks, 1973), 34.

15. *See* Eggert, *Richard Olney*, 201–02.

16. *See generally* David M. Pletcher, "Rhetoric and Results: A Pragmatic View of American Economic Expansionism, 1865–98," *Diplomatic History* 5, no. 2 (Spring 1981), 93–105.

17. *See* William C. Widenor, *Henry Cabot Lodge and the Search for an American Foreign Policy* (Berkeley: University of California Press, 1983), 1; Warren Zimmermann, *First Great Triumph: How Five Americans Made Their Country a World Power* (New York: Farrar, Straus and Giroux, 2002), 164; John A. Garraty, *Henry Cabot Lodge: A Biography* (New York: Alfred A. Knopf, 1953), 40–41.

18. Owen Wister, *Roosevelt: The Story of a Friendship, 1889–1919* (New York: MacMillan, 1930), 153–54; *see* Garraty, *Henry Cabot Lodge*, 61, 72, 126; Edmund Morris, *The Rise of Theodore Roosevelt* (New York: Modern Library, 2001), 249–50.

19. *See* Garraty, *Henry Cabot Lodge*, 61–62; Grenville and Young, *Politics, Strategy, and American Diplomacy*, 208; Richard H. Immerman, *Empire for Liberty: A History of American Imperialism from Benjamin Franklin to Paul Wolfowitz* (Princeton, NJ: Princeton University Press, 2010), 134.

20. Lodge, "Our Blundering Foreign Policy," 16, 17; Henry Cabot Lodge, "The American Policy of Territorial Expansion," *The Independent*, January 13, 1898, 1; Henry Cabot Lodge, "Our Foreign Policy," in *Certain Accepted Heroes and Other Essays in Literature and Politics* (New York: Harper & Brothers, 1897), 243–44.

21. Lodge, "Territorial Expansion," 1; Lodge to Mendenhall, February 24, 1896, in Vol. 32, Letterbooks, Lodge MSS; *see* Lodge, "Our Foreign Policy," 262–63; Lodge to Sanford, December 20, 1895, in Vol. 31, Letterbooks, Lodge MSS; Lodge to Hurd, January 17, 1896, in Vol. 31, Letterbooks, Lodge MSS; Lodge to Hart, January 18, 1896, in Vol. 31, Letterbooks, Lodge MSS; Lodge to Balfour, February 1, 1896, in Vol. 32, Letterbooks, Lodge MSS; Lodge

to Adams, January 22, 1897, in Vol. 33, Letterbooks, Lodge MSS; *see also* Grenville and Young, *Politics, Strategy, and American Diplomacy*, 223–25.

22. Lodge, "England, Venezuela," 658; *see* Grenville and Young, *Politics, Strategy, and American Diplomacy*, 226. Lodge continued dwelling on this point as the crisis developed. "If Great Britain can extend her trritory [*sic*] in South America without remonstrance from us," he wrote, "every other European [power] can do the same and in a short time you will see South America parcelled out as Africa has been." Lodge to Blackwell, December 23, 1895, Vol. 31, Letterbooks, Lodge MSS; *see* Lodge to Sanford, December 20, 1895, in Vol. 31, Letterbooks, Lodge MSS; Lodge to Hart, January 18, 1896, in Vol. 31, Letterbooks, Lodge MSS; Lodge to Gaunt, January 29, 1896, in Vol. 32, Letterbooks, Lodge MSS; Lodge to Ginn, February 8, 1896, in Vol. 32, Letterbooks, Lodge MSS.

23. *See* 27 Cong. Rec. 1832 (1895); *see also* Grenville and Young, *Politics, Strategy, and American Diplomacy*, 135–55; Theodore D. Jervey, "William Lindsay Scruggs—A Forgotten Diplomat," *South Atlantic Quarterly* 27, no. 3 (July 1928), 292–309.

24. Lodge, "Our Blundering Foreign Policy," 8; *see* Nelson M. Blake, "Background of Cleveland's Venezuelan Policy," *American Historical Review* 47, no. 2 (January 1942), 261–62, 264–66.

25. *See* Lodge, "England, Venezuela," 657–58.

26. *See* Richard Henry Dana, Jr., *Speeches in Stirring Times and Letters to a Son*, ed. Richard H. Dana, III (Boston: Houston Mifflin, 1910), 336–37; *see also* J. Fred Rippy, *The Caribbean Danger Zone* (New York: G. P. Putnam's Sons, 1940), 25–26; Eggert, *Richard Olney*, 198–99.

27. "Thumbnail Sketch No. 14. Richard Olney.," *New York Journal*, March 5, 1896; *see* Henry James, *Richard Olney and His Public Service* (Boston: Houston Mifflin, 1923), 12; Eggert, *Richard Olney*, 3, 40–46.

28. *See* Eggert, *Richard Olney*, 200; Perkins, *The Monroe Doctrine: 1867–1907*, 148.

29. Olney to Knox, January 29, 1912, in Reel 41, Olney MSS; *see* Jay Sexton, *The Monroe Doctrine: Empire and Nation in Nineteenth-Century America* (New York: Hill and Wang, 2011), 204–05; Eggert, *Richard Olney*, 201–02.

30. *See* Eggert, *Richard Olney*, 207–08.

31. Cleveland to Olney, July 7, 1895, in Reel 59, Olney MSS.

32. *See* Campbell, *The Transformation*, 198.

33. Olney to Bayard, July 20, 1895, in FRUS 1895, 546; *see ibid.*, 545–52.

34. Olney to Bayard, July 20, 1895, in FRUS 1895, 555, 558.

35. Olney to Bayard, July 20, 1895, in FRUS 1895, 558.

36. Olney to Bayard, July 20, 1895, in FRUS 1895, 559.

37. Olney to Bayard, July 20, 1895, in FRUS 1895, 560; *see ibid.*, 559–62.

38. *See* Olney to Bayard, July 20, 1895, in FRUS 1895, 562.

39. "What England Is Doing," *Atlanta Constitution*, October 13, 1895; "Sir Julian Is Frank," *Washington Post*, October 6, 1895; Salisbury to Venezuelan Minister for Foreign Affairs, October 14, 1895, quoted in Campbell, *The Transformation*, 206; "Venezuela," *New York Times*, October 22, 1895; *see* Olney to Bayard, July 20, 1895, in FRUS 1895, 562; *see also* Campbell, *The Transformation*, 205–07.

40. Cleveland, Third Annual Message, December 2, 1895, in Richardson 9:632; 28 Cong. Rec. 26 (1895); *see* Campbell, *The Transformation*, 206.

41. *See* Beisner, *Old Diplomacy to the New*, 110–11; Perkins, *The Monroe Doctrine: 1867–1907*, 172–73.

42. Salisbury to Pauncefote, November 26, 1895, in FRUS 1895, 565; *see ibid.*, 564–66.

43. Grover Cleveland, "The Venezuelan Boundary Controversy," in *Presidential Problems* (New York: Century, 1904), 268; *see* Cleveland to Bayard, December 29, 1895, in Allan Nevins, *Letters of Grover Cleveland 1850–1908* (New York: De Capo, 1970), 418–19; *see also* Eggert, *Richard Olney*, 217, 219.

44. Cleveland, Message to Congress, December 17, 1895, in FRUS 1895, 542–45.

45. Lodge to Weld, December 20, 1895, in Vol. 31, Letterbooks, Lodge MSS; *see* Lodge to Sanford, December 20, 1895, in Vol. 31, Letterbooks, Lodge MSS; Lodge to Blackwell, December 23, 1895, Vol. 31, Letterbooks, Lodge MSS; Lodge to Ginn, February 8, 1896, in Vol. 32,

Letterbooks, Lodge MSS; *see also* Perkins, *The Monroe Doctrine: 1867–1907*, 186, 192–94; James, *Richard Olney*, 122.

46. "A Military Reconnoissance [*sic*]," *Washington Post*, December 19, 1895; *see* Thomas A. Bailey, *A Diplomatic History of the American People* (Englewood Cliffs, NJ: Prentice-Hall, 1980), 443–44; Eggert, *Richard Olney*, 223.

47. Salisbury to Pauncefote, November 26, 1895, in FRUS 1895, 564–65; *London Times*, January 16, 1896; *see* Kori Schake, *Safe Passage: The Transition from British to American Hegemony* (Cambridge, MA: Harvard University Press, 2017), 161; May, *Imperial Democracy*, 48.

48. *See* Eggert, *Richard Olney*, 227–28; Beisner, *Old Diplomacy to the New*, 112.

49. *See* Perkins, *The Monroe Doctrine: 1867–1907*, 194–99; Campbell, *The Transformation*, 211–13; May, *Imperial Democracy*, 56–59.

50. Cleveland, "The Venezuelan Boundary Controversy," 279–80; *see* James Ford Rhodes, "Cleveland's Administrations," *Scribner's Magazine* 50, no. 5 (November 1911), 611; *see also* Eggert, *Richard Olney*, 222–23; LaFeber, *New Empire*, 269–70.

51. Olney to Cleveland, July 16, 1896, in Reel 59, Olney MSS; *see* Eggert, *Richard Olney*, 225–47. For a take more friendly to the British, *see* Campbell, *The Transformation*, 214–17; Tansill, *Thomas F. Bayard*, 737–76.

52. *See* Campbell, *The Transformation*, 217–18.

53. *See* Campbell, *The Transformation*, 217–18; Perkins, *The Monroe Doctrine: 1867–1907*, 224; Eggert, *Richard Olney*, 248.

54. *See* Grenville and Young, *Politics, Strategy, and American Diplomacy*, 178.

55. *See* Sexton, *The Monroe Doctrine*, 204–05.

56. Olney to Knox, January 29, 1912, in Reel 41, Olney MSS; *see* Eggert, *Richard Olney*, 212–13.

57. Cleveland to Bayard, December 29, 1895, in Nevins, *Letters of Cleveland*, 417; *see* Beisner, *Old Diplomacy to the New*, 113–15; Hillel Ofek, "A Just Peace: Grover Cleveland, William McKinley, and the Moral Basis of American Foreign Policy" (PhD diss., University of Texas at Austin, 2018), 133–34; Eggert, *Richard Olney*, 222, 246; Sexton, *The Monroe Doctrine*, 205.

58. "Mr. Balfour on Foreign Affairs," *London Times*, January 16, 1896; *see* Campbell, *The Transformation*, 221; May, *Imperial Democracy*, 267–68.

59. *See* LaFeber, *New Empire*, 278; George B. Young, "Intervention Under the Monroe Doctrine: The Olney Corollary," *Political Science Quarterly* 57, no. 2 (June 1942), 260–61, 272–74, 276–78; Grenville and Young, *Politics, Strategy, and American Diplomacy*, 175–77.

60. *See* Ofek, "A Just Peace," 119–23.

61. Bayard, Memorandum, February 1896, quoted in Lars Schoultz, *Beneath the United States: A History of U.S. Policy Toward Latin America* (Cambridge, MA: Harvard University Press, 2003), 124; Bayard to Cleveland, May 11, 1895, in Box 2:322, Reel 90, Cleveland MSS; *see* Bayard to Cleveland, July 18, 1895, in Box 2:322, Reel 90, Cleveland MSS. Olney and Cleveland also thought in these terms. *See* Dana to Olney, December 23, 1909, in Reel 40, Olney MSS; Olney to Dana, December 24, 1909, in Reel 40, Olney MSS.

62. Sidney Low, "The Olney Doctrine and America's New Foreign Policy," *The Nineteenth Century* 40, no. 238 (December 1896), 854–57; *see* Perkins, *The Monroe Doctrine: 1867–1907*, 239–40.

63. *Philadelphia Press*, n.d., in *Public Opinion*, Nov. 19, 1896, 647; *see* Salisbury to Pauncefote, November 26, 1895, in FRUS 1895, 565–66; *see also* Sexton, *The Monroe Doctrine*, 208; Lester D. Langley, *Struggle for the American Mediterranean: United States-European Rivalry in the Gulf-Caribbean, 1776–1904* (Athens: University of Georgia Press, 1976), 161.

64. Olney to Bayard, July 20, 1895, in FRUS 1895, 554–55; Olney to Keet, January 15, 1897, in Reel 26, Olney MSS; *see* Olney to Peter B. Olney, December 27, 1904, in Reel 55, Olney MSS.

Chapter 4: A Jehad to Which All the Faithful Must Give Heed

1. *See* Statement of Liliuokalani to Blount, in FRUS 1894, app. II, 856, 863; Lorrin A. Thurston, *Memoirs of the Hawaiian Revolution*, ed. Andrew Farrell (Honolulu: Advertiser Publishing, 1936), 245.

2. *See* Thurston, *Memoirs*, 245; *see also* Merze Tate, *The United States and the Hawaiian Kingdom: A Political History* (New Haven, CT: Yale University Press, 1965), 111–12; William Michael Morgan, *Pacific Gibraltar: U.S.-Japanese Rivalry Over the Annexation of Hawaii, 1885–1898* (Annapolis, MD: Naval Institute Press, 2011), 59; Foster Rhea Dulles, *Prelude to World Power: American Diplomatic History, 1860–1900* (New York: Macmillan, 1968), 111.

3. Thurston, *Memoirs*, 245.

4. *See* Morgan, *Pacific Gibraltar*, 55–56; Ralph S. Kuykendall, *The Hawaiian Kingdom*, vol. 3, *1874–1893, The Kalakaua Dynasty* (Honolulu: University of Hawaii Press, 1967), 366–67 & *.

5. Thurston, *Memoirs*, 231, 246–50, 263; *see* Tate, *Political History*, 113; Morgan, *Pacific Gibraltar*, 89.

6. *See* Morgan, *Pacific Gibraltar*, 104–05; Gavan Daws, *Shoal of Time: A History of the Hawaiian Islands* (Honolulu: University of Hawaii Press, 1968), 276.

7. *See* Kuykendall, *The Hawaiian Kingdom*, 3:587–88.

8. *See* Kuykendall, *The Hawaiian Kingdom*, 3:587–88; Morgan, *Pacific Gibraltar*, 83–87, 241.

9. Citizen's Committee of Safety to Stevens, January 16, 1893, in FRUS 1894, app. II, 584; *see* Morgan, *Pacific Gibraltar*, 89–91. Lili'uokalani had meanwhile caved to the protests of her cabinet and postponed the declaration of her new constitution. *See* Morgan, *Pacific Gibraltar*, 83. But it was too late; Thurston and his Committee of Safety were already in motion.

10. *See* Morgan, *Pacific Gibraltar*, 92–95, 97, 103.

11. *See* Statement of Liliuokalani to Blount, in FRUS 1894, app. II, 866; *see also* Morgan, *Pacific Gibraltar*, 96–102.

12. Statement of Liliuokalani to Blount, in FRUS 1894, app. II, 866.

13. *See* Thurston, *Memoirs*, 283; *see also* Kuykendall, *The Hawaiian Kingdom*, 3:616–17.

14. For the influence of Mahan's arguments, *see, e.g.*, Allen Lee Hamilton, "Military Strategists and the Annexation of Hawaii," *Journal of the West* 15, no. 2 (April 1976), 82–83; William E. Livezey, *Mahan on Sea Power* (Norman: University of Oklahoma Press, 1985), 55–82.

15. Mahan to Ellen Evans Mahan, October 27, 1894, in *Letters and Papers of Alfred Thayer Mahan*, ed. Robert Seager, II, and Doris D. Maguire, vol. 2, *1890–1901* (Annapolis, MD: Naval Institute Press, 1975), 352; *see* Robert Seager, II, *Alfred Thayer Mahan: The Man and His Letters* (Annapolis, MD: Naval Institute Press, 2017), xi, 2, 14, 45–46; W. D. Puleston, *Mahan: The Life and Work of Captain Alfred Thayer Mahan, U.S.N.* (London: Jonathan Cape, 1939), 30–31.

16. A. T. Mahan, "The United States Looking Outward," August 1890, in *The Interest of America in Sea Power, Present and Future* (Boston: Little, Brown, 1897), 18; A. T. Mahan, "The Future in Relation to American Naval Power," June 1895, in *Interest of America*, 161–62; A. T. Mahan, "Why Not Disarm?," September 1913, in Seager and Maguire, *Letters and Papers*, 3:687; *see* Puleston, *Mahan*, 56, 66, 89; Warren Zimmermann, *First Great Triumph: How Five Americans Made Their Country a World Power* (New York: Farrar, Straus and Giroux, 2002), 93, 107, 110, 112.

17. Mahan to Ashe, July 26, 1884, in Seager and Maguire, *Letters and Papers*, 1:573–74; Mahan, "Looking Outward," in *Interest of America*, 8–9; *see* Seager, *Alfred Thayer Mahan*, 141, 146–47. For the centrality of the problem of order in Mahan's worldview, *see, e.g.*, Mahan, "The Future," in *Interest of America*, 165–70; Mahan, "Looking Outward," in *Interest of America*, 19–21; A. T. Mahan, *The Interest of America in International Conditions* (Boston: Little, Brown, 1910), 199–200.

18. Mahan to Ellen Evans Mahan, September 6, 1893, in Seager and Maguire, *Letters and Papers*, 2:149; *see* Seager, *Alfred Thayer Mahan*, 142–45.

19. *See* Mahan, "Looking Outward," in *Interest of America*, 26; *see also* Livezy, *Mahan on Sea Power*, 50–53; James A. Field, Jr., "American Imperialism: The Worst Chapter in Almost Any Book," *American Historical Review* 83, no. 3 (June 1978), 647–48; David Healy, *Drive to Hegemony: The United States in the Caribbean 1898–1917* (Madison: University of Wisconsin Press, 1988), 79–80.

20. Mahan to Ellen Evans Mahan, October 5, 1894, in Seager and Maguire, *Letters and Papers*, 2:341; *see* Zimmermann, *First Great Triumph*, 94; Livezy, *Mahan on Sea Power*, 51–53; Puleston, *Mahan*, 128–29; Daniel Immerwahr, *How To Hide An Empire: A Short History of the Greater United States* (London: Bodley Head, 2019), 64.

21. *See* Mahan, "Hawaii and Our Future Sea Power," in *Interest of America*, 42–43; *see also* Morgan, *Pacific Gibraltar*, 157.

22. Mahan, "Looking Outward," in *Interest of America*, 26; *see* Mahan, "Hawaii and Our Future Sea Power," in *Interest of America*, 43–45; *see also* Morgan, *Pacific Gibraltar*, 158.

23. Mahan, "Hawaii and Our Future Sea Power," in *Interest of America*, 47–49; *see* Morgan, *Pacific Gibraltar*, 159.

24. Mahan, "Hawaii and Our Future Sea Power," in *Interest of America*, 47–49; Mahan, "Looking Outward," in *Interest of America*, 26.

25. *Views of Commodore George W. Melville*, S. Doc. No. 188 (1898), 19; *see* Morgan, *Pacific Gibraltar*, 170.

26. *See* "Pearl Harbor Coaling Station," *New York Times*, January 9, 1893; John W. Foster, *Diplomatic Memoirs* (Boston: Houghton Mifflin, 1909), 2:171; *see also* Morgan, *Pacific Gibraltar*, 11–12; Milton Plesur, *America's Outward Thrust: Approaches to Foreign Affairs, 1865–1890* (DeKalb: Northern Illinois University Press, 1971), 204–10. In 1842, President Tyler declared the "Tyler Doctrine," in which he echoed the Monroe Doctrine by declaring that the United States would react to "any attempt by another power ... to take possession of the islands, colonize them, and subvert the native Government" with "dissatisfaction." Tyler to Congress, December 30, 1842, in Richardson 6:212; *see* Eric T. L. Love, *Race over Empire: Racism and U.S. Imperialism 1865–1900* (Chapel Hill: University of North Carolina Press, 2004), 82–83. Commentators sometimes debated thereafter whether Hawai'i technically fell under the Monroe Doctrine's umbrella, but for practical purposes nearly all Americans treated the islands as if they did. *See, e.g.*, *Annexation of Hawaii (Davis Report)*, S. Rep. No. 55-681 (1898), 54.

27. Mahan, "Looking Outward," in *Interest of America*, 7–8; *see* Charles S. Campbell, *The Transformation of American Foreign Relations 1865–1900* (New York: Harper and Row, 1976), 72–83; Dulles, *Prelude to World Power*, 102–07; Morgan, *Pacific Gibraltar*, 25–26.

28. 27 Cong. Rec. 1210 (1895). Lodge may have mixed up the dates and names for a few of these islands, and in a few of the cited cases the British had declared only a protectorate, not a colony.

29. 27 Cong. Rec. 3082 (1895); *see ibid.*, 3083; *see also* Morgan, *Pacific Gibraltar*, 174–75.

30. *See* Morgan, *Pacific Gibraltar*, 203.

31. *See* "Comparative Table of Nationalty [*sic*] of Population of Hawaiian Islands at Various Census Periods Since 1853," in Thos. G. Thrum, *Hawaiian Almanac and Annual for 1898* (Honolulu: Press Publishing, 1898), 45; *see also* Morgan, *Pacific Gibraltar*, 16–18; Love, *Race over Empire*, 81, 84–89; James Burke Chapin, "Hamilton Fish and American Expansion" (PhD diss., Cornell University, June 1971), 513; Tate, *Political History*, 43–48; *see generally* Noenoe K. Silva, *Aloha Betrayed: Native Hawaiian Resistance to American Colonialism* (Durham, NC: Duke University Press, 2004), 15–44. Note that the statistics given for Native Hawaiians do not include the numbers for "Part Hawaiians," a population that the census indicated had increased from 1,487 in 1872 to 6,186 in 1890.

As Love notes, the overall trend line—though genuinely believed by most American policymakers—was "a more complex phenomenon," and it thankfully underestimated Native Hawaiians' resilience. *See* Love, *Race over Empire*, 87.

32. Fish to Pierce, March 25, 1873, in FRUS 1894, app. II, 19; *see* "Secretary Fish on the Foreign Policy of the Government," *New York Herald*, January 8, 1873; *see also* John M. Dobson, *America's Ascent: The United States Becomes a Great Power, 1880–1914* (DeKalb: Northern Illinois University Press, 1978), 55–56.

33. *See* Convention Between the United States of America and His Majesty the King of the Hawaiian Islands, art. IV, January 30, 1875, in FRUS 1875, 1:xxix; *see also* Merze Tate, *Hawaii: Reciprocity or Annexation* (East Lansing: Michigan State University Press, 1968), 83, 108–09; Charles Callan Tansill, *The Foreign Policy of Thomas F. Bayard 1885–1897* (New York: Fordham University Press, 1940), 369. For the lackluster economic benefits to the United States of reciprocity, *see* Tate, *Reciprocity or Annexation*, 113, 117; Daws, *Shoal of Time*, 203; Morgan, *Pacific*

Gibraltar, 20, 23–24. For the strategic benefits to the United States of reciprocity, *see* Tate, *Reciprocity or Annexation*, 87–88, 93–94, 100–02; Ralph S. Kuykendall and A. Grove Day, *Hawaii: A History, from Polynesian Kingdom to American State* (Englewood Cliffs, NJ: Prentice-Hall, 1961), 151–52; Love, *Race over Empire*, 100–02; Barry Rigby, "The Origins of American Expansion in Hawaii and Samoa, 1865–1900," *International History Review* 10, no. 2 (May 1988), 225.

34. *See* "Comparative View of Commerce of Hawaiian Islands from 1869, Giving Totals for Each Year," in Thrum, *Hawaiian Almanac and Annual*, 25; *see also* Tate, *Reciprocity or Annexation*, 118–19.

35. *See* Morgan, *Pacific Gibraltar*, 29, 31, 39–41.

36. *See* Morgan, *Pacific Gibraltar*, 28; Tate, *Reciprocity or Annexation*, 119.

37. *See* Morgan, *Pacific Gibraltar*, 32, 51; Kuykendall, *The Hawaiian Kingdom*, 3:26–40, 54–57.

38. *See* Morgan, *Pacific Gibraltar*, 35; Tate, *Reciprocity or Annexation*, 120–21.

39. *See* Morgan, *Pacific Gibraltar*, 29–30.

40. Thurston, *Memoirs*, 129–31; "Pledge of the Hawaiian League," in Thurston, *Memoirs*, 608; *see* Kuykendall, *The Hawaiian Kingdom*, 3:347–72.

41. *See* Morgan, *Pacific Gibraltar*, 57–62.

42. Carter to Blaine, March 29, 1889, and enclosed extracts from Hawaiian minister of foreign affairs to Carter, March 8, 1889, in Notes, Hawaii, Roll 3, T160, RG59, NA; *see* Kuykendall, *The Hawaiian Kingdom*, 3:436. For a clear account of the negotiations, *see* Sylvester K. Stevens, *American Expansion in Hawaii, 1842–1898* (Harrisburg: Archives Publishing Company of Pennsylvania, 1945), 196–98.

43. Carter-Blaine Treaty of 1889, art. III, in Carter to Blaine, April 11, 1889, in Notes, Hawaii, Roll 3, T160, RG59, NA.

44. *See* Julius W. Pratt, *Expansionists of 1898: The Acquisition of Hawaii and the Spanish Islands* (Chicago: Quadrangle Books, 1964), 49. For Blaine's opposition to annexation during most of his career, *see* Love, *Race over Empire*, 93–94.

45. *See* Stevens, *American Expansion in Hawaii*, 198–99.

46. *See* Harrison, Second Annual Message, December 1, 1890, in Richardson 9:110; *see also* César J. Ayala, *American Sugar Kingdom: The Plantation Economy of the Spanish Caribbean, 1898–1934* (Chapel Hill: University of North Carolina Press, 1999), 54–55; Pratt, *Expansionists of 1898*, at 45; Tate, *Political History*, 114; Tate, *Reciprocity or Annexation*, 218–19; Kuykendall, *The Hawaiian Kingdom*, 3:466–68.

47. *See* Tate, *Political History*, 114; Dobson, *America's Ascent*, 59–60.

48. Stevens to Foster, November 20, 1892, in FRUS 1894, app. II, 379, 382; Stevens to Blaine, September 5, 1891, in FRUS 1894, app. II, 351; *see* Walter LaFeber, *The New Empire: An Interpretation of American Expansion 1860–1898* (Ithaca, NY: Cornell University Press, 1967), 143.

49. Stevens to Blaine, February 8, 1892, in FRUS 1894, app. II, 353–54; [Stevens], "America's Opportunity in the Pacific Ocean," *Daily Kennebec Journal*, November 17, 1892, reprinted in *New York Sun*, November 28, 1892.

50. Blaine to Harrison, September 16, 1891, in *The Correspondence Between Benjamin Harrison and James G. Blaine 1882–1893*, ed. Albert T. Volwiler (Philadelphia: American Philosophical Society, 1940), 187; Harrison to Blaine, September 18, 1891, in Volwiler, *Correspondence*, 190; *see* Harrison to Blaine, October 14, 1891, in Volwiler, *Correspondence*, 206.

51. *See* Blaine to Harrison, August 10, 1891, in Volwiler, *Correspondence*, 174; *see also* LaFeber, *New Empire*, 143.

52. Stevens to Blaine, February 22, 1891, in FRUS 1894, app. II, 343; *see* Tate, *Political History*, 109–10.

53. *See* Thurston, *Memoirs*, 283.

54. Harrison to Blaine, October 1, 1891, in Volwiler, *Correspondence*, 202. Over the year before the revolution, Stevens had bombarded the State Department with frantic questions about how to respond to an attempt to overthrow Lili'uokalani. *See, e.g.*, Stevens to Blaine, March 8, 1892, in FRUS 1894, app. II, 354–55. But Blaine was too sick and distracted to respond meaningfully to his minister's queries, *see* Allan Spetter, "Harrison and Blaine: Foreign Policy, 1889–1893," *Indiana Magazine of History* 65, no. 3 (1969), 219–21, and Stevens was left

completely—and, as it proved, dangerously—adrift. Some historians have nevertheless argued that there was some sort of "unspoken complicity" between the two. "In this case," writes one historian, "silence *was* consent." Edward P. Crapol, *James G. Blaine: Architect of Empire* (Wilmington, DE: SR Books, 2000), 126; *see also* Tom Coffman, *Nation Within: The Story of America's Annexation of the Nation of Hawai'i* (Kāne'ohe, HI: Epicenter, 2003), 111–14. But that seems unlikely. Stevens would not have repeatedly asked Blaine and Harrison whether to support a revolution if he had already conspired with them to do just that. Certainly, Blaine and Harrison missed an opportunity to rein in the agitated minister. But their failure to do so can easily be explained by Blaine's faltering health and other distractions. For other reasons to discount the "double conspiracy" theory, *See* Morgan, *Pacific Gibraltar*, 65–66.

Some historians have also supported the "double conspiracy" theory by pointing to Thurston's own account. Shortly before the revolution, Thurston went to Washington, where he later claimed he met both Blaine and Secretary of the Navy Benjamin F. Tracy. Thurston, *Memoirs*, 230–32. According to Thurston, Tracy brought word from the president that the administration would be sympathetic to any annexation proposal. *Ibid.*, 231–32. But even taking him at his word (always dangerous), Thurston did not claim that Harrison promised to support his revolution; in fact, Thurston had disavowed any "intention of precipitating action in Honolulu." *Ibid.* Thurston also claims in his memoirs that he received word from a source in Washington that the administration was looking to buy the throne from Lili'uokalani. *See ibid.*, 233–40. But it is hard to believe that Thurston's source—Archibald Hopkins, a clerk of the court of claims—had anywhere near the access to the administration he claimed, and in any event, the account again suggests merely that the administration favored annexation—not that it promoted revolution. *See* Morgan, *Pacific Gibraltar*, 68.

55. Harrison, Message to the Senate, February 15, 1893, in Richardson 9:348.

56. Foster, *Diplomatic Memoirs*, 2:166–68. For Foster acting on these concerns contemporaneously, *see* Pratt, *Expansionists of 1898*, 115–16. Many newspapers shared Harrison and Foster's concerns. *See ibid.*, 149–50.

57. Harrison, Message to the Senate, February 15, 1893, in Richardson 9:348–49; *see* "Treaty with Hawaii," *New York World*, February 16, 1893.

58. *See* "Treaty with Hawaii," *New York World*, February 16, 1893.

59. "Snap-Shot Diplomacy," *New York World*, February 17, 1893; *see* "An Administration Plot," *New York World*, February 16, 1893; "Taking Time," *New York Times*, March 10, 1893; *see also* Berkeley E. Tompkins, *Anti-Imperialism in the United States: The Great Debate, 1890–1920* (Philadelphia: University of Pennsylvania Press, 1970), 37–39; Pratt, *Expansionists of 1898*, 150; Merze Tate, "Hawaii: A Symbol of Anglo-American Rapprochement," *Political Science Quarterly* 79, no. 4 (December 1964), 567–68. For the treaty initially seeming like a sure thing, *see, e.g.*, "Treaty with Hawaii," *New York World*, February 16, 1893; Foster, *Diplomatic Memoirs*, 2:168.

60. *See* Tate, *Political History*, 213–14.

61. *See* Cleveland, Second Annual Message, December 6, 1886, in Richardson 8:500; *see also* Tate, *Reciprocity or Annexation*, 194–96; Hugh B. Hammett, "The Cleveland Administration and Anglo-American Naval Friction in Hawaii, 1893–1894," *Military Affairs* 40, no. 1 (February 1976), 29. For an excellent discussion of Cleveland's moral attitude toward the Hawaiian situation, *see* Hillel Ofek, "A Just Peace: Grover Cleveland, William McKinley, and the Moral Basis of American Foreign Policy" (PhD diss., University of Texas at Austin, 2018), 89–111.

62. Gresham to Blount, March 11, 1893, in H.R. Exec. Doc. No. 53-47 (1893), 2; *see* Gresham, Memorandum on Meeting with Japanese Minister, March 16, 1893, in Memoranda of Conversations, RG59, NA; Gresham, Memorandum on Meeting with Russian Minister, March 16, 1893, in Memoranda of Conversations, RG59, NA; Gresham, Memorandum on Meeting with British Minister, March 16, 1893, in Memoranda of Conversations, RG59, NA; *see also* John A. S. Grenville and George Berkeley Young, *Politics, Strategy, and American Diplomacy: Studies in Foreign Policy, 1873–1917* (New Haven, CT: Yale University Press, 1969), 109–10.

63. Blount to Gresham, July 17, 1893, in H.R. Exec. Doc. No. 53-47 (1893), 133; *see ibid.*, 128.

64. Cleveland to Congress, December 18, 1893, in FRUS 1894, app. II, 456; Dole to Willis, December 23, 1893, in FRUS 1894, app. II, 1276; *see* Willis to Gresham, December 20, 1893,

in FRUS 1894, app. II, 1270; Willis Memorandum, December 20, 1893, in FRUS 1894, app. II, 1275; *see also* Tate, *Political History*, 246; Morgan, *Pacific Gibraltar*, 132.

65. "Utopian But Not American," *New York World*, in *Literary Digest*, December 23, 1898, 146; *see* "To Restore a Monarchy," *New York Sun*, November 12, 1893; "The Policy of Infamy," *New York Sun*, November 12, 1893; Cleveland, Message to Congress, December 18, 1893, in FRUS 1894, app. II, 445–58; *see also* Tompkins, *Anti-Imperialism*, 54–55; Pratt, *Expansionists of 1898*, 172–73.

66. *See* Morgan, *Pacific Gibraltar*, 135; Grenville and Young, *Politics, Strategy, and American Diplomacy*, 115.

67. 27 Cong. Rec. 3082–84 (1895); *see* Henry Cabot Lodge, "The American Policy of Territorial Expansion," *The Independent*, January 13, 1898, 1; *see also* Richard H. Immerman, *Empire for Liberty: A History of American Imperialism from Benjamin Franklin to Paul Wolfowitz* (Princeton, NJ: Princeton University Press, 2010), 140–41.

68. Herbert to Walker, March 27, 1894, in Sen. Ex. Doc. No. 53-16 (1894), 2; *see* 26 Cong. Rec. 2001 (1894); 27 Cong. Rec. 5499 (1894); *see also* Morgan, *Pacific Gibraltar*, 139, 146; Thomas J. Osborne, *"Empire Can Wait": American Opposition to Hawaiian Annexation, 1893–1898* (Kent, OH: Kent State University Press, 1981), 81.

69. Walker to Herbert, August 17, 1894, in Sen. Ex. Doc. No. 53-16 (1894), 20–21; *see* Pratt, *Expansionists of 1898*, 187, 193.

70. *See* Pratt, *Expansionists of 1898*, 195–97. The *Philadelphia* was also withdrawn in part because of indiscretions on the part of its commander. *See* Hammett, "Anglo-American Naval Friction in Hawaii," 30.

71. For an account of the attempted revolution and its aftermath, *see* Willis to Gresham, January 11, 1895, in FRUS 1894, app. II, 1393–94; Willis to Gresham, February 6, 1895, in FRUS 1894, app. II, 1396–97; Willis to Gresham, January 30, 1895, in FRUS 1895, 818–20; *see also* Stevens, *American Expansion in Hawaii*, 274–75.

72. 27 Cong. Rec. 622 (1895); *see* Gresham to Thurston, January 20, 1895, in FRUS 1894, app. II, 1395; *see also* Pratt, *Expansionists of 1898*, 198, 200–09; Stevens, *American Expansion in Hawaii*, 277–78.

73. *See Report of the Secretary of the Navy*, H.R. Doc. No. 54-3 (1895), 137, 146; *Annual Report of the Secretary of the Navy for the Year 1896* (Washington, DC: Government Printing Office, 1896), 234, 236; *Annual Reports of the Navy Department for the Year 1897* (Washington, DC: Government Printing Office, 1897), 234, 236, 237.

74. For a good account of the Japanese immigration crisis, *see* Aroop Mukharji, "Sea Change: McKinley, Roosevelt, and the Expansion of U.S. Foreign Policy 1897–1909" (PhD diss., Harvard University, April 2020), 61–68; *see generally* Morgan, *Pacific Gibraltar*.

75. *See* Morgan, *Pacific Gibraltar*, 188–91.

76. *See* Morgan, *Pacific Gibraltar*, 44–45, 49, 190–97; "Comparative Table of Nationalty [*sic*]," in Thrum, *Hawaiian Almanac and Annual*, 45.

77. *See* "Comparative Table of Nationalty [*sic*]," in Thrum, *Hawaiian Almanac and Annual*, 45; "Estimated Population Hawaiian Islands, July 1, 1897," in Thrum, *Hawaiian Almanac and Annual*, 45. Note that the statistics given for Native Hawaiians do not include the numbers for "Part Hawaiians," a population that the census indicated had increased from 6,186 in 1890 to 8,485 in 1896. For the numbers of voting-age males, *see* Morgan, *Pacific Gibraltar*, 196.

78. *See* Morgan, *Pacific Gibraltar*, 29, 141–42, 190–91. For startling reports from the islands about Japanese pushiness, *see, e.g.*, Walker to Herbert, April 28, 1894, in Sen. Ex. Doc. No. 53-16 (1894), 6–7; Walker to Herbert, May 14, 1894, in Sen. Ex. Doc. No. 53-16 (1894), 9; *see also* Morgan, *Pacific Gibraltar*, 197. For the Republic's success in excluding the Japanese and other non-white races from the franchise, *see, e.g.*, Love, *Race over Empire*, 115–19.

79. *See* Morgan, *Pacific Gibraltar*, 200–02.

80. *See* Morgan, *Pacific Gibraltar*, 179.

81. Carl Schurz, "William McKinley," 1900–01, in *Speeches, Correspondence and Political Papers of Carl Schurz*, ed. Frederic Bancroft, vol. 6, *January 1, 1899–Apr. 8, 1906* (New York: G. P. Putnam's Sons, 1913), 270–71; *see* James Francis Burke, *Official Proceedings of the Eleventh Republican National Convention* (1896), 84; Henry S. Pritchett, "Some Recollections of President McKinley

and the Cuban Intervention," *North American Review* 189, no. 640 (March 1909), 397, 400–01; *see also* Love, *Race over Empire*, 131; Morgan, *Pacific Gibraltar*, 177. For evidence that McKinley was interested in annexing Hawaii in the long run, *see* Morgan, *Pacific Gibraltar*, 186–87.

82. Mahan to Roosevelt, May 6, 1897, in Seager and Maguire, *Letters and Papers*, 2:507; Mahan to Roosevelt, May 1, 1897, in Seager and Maguire, *Letters and Papers*, 2:506; *see ibid.*, 505–06; Roosevelt to Mahan, May 3, 1897, in Morison 1:607; Roosevelt to Hartwell, June 7, 1897, in Morison 1:622.

83. *See* Morgan, *Pacific Gibraltar*, 203–06; William Michael Morgan, "The Anti-Japanese Origins of the Hawaiian Annexation Treaty of 1897," *Diplomatic History* 6, no. 1 (Winter 1982), 37–38. For the war plans, *see* Navy Department, "Plans of Campaign Against Spain and Japan," June 30, 1897, in John A. S. Grenville, "American Naval Preparations for War with Spain, 1896–1898," *Journal of American Studies* 2, no. 1 (April 1968), 44–45.

84. *See* "Cruiser Naniwa in Port," *Evening Bulletin* (Honolulu), May 5, 1897; Fred T. Jane, *All the World's Fighting Ships* (London: Sampson Low, Marston, 1898), 147; *see also* Morgan, *Pacific Gibraltar*, 207.

85. *See* Mills to Sherman, May 22, 1897, in Despatches, Hawaii, Roll 28, T30, RG59, NA; Mills to Sherman, May 24, 1897, in Despatches, Hawaii, Roll 28, T30, RG59, NA; *see also* Morgan, *Pacific Gibraltar*, 206–07.

86. "Getting Serious," *Pacific Commercial Advertiser* (Honolulu), May 25, 1897; *see* Mukharji, "Sea Change," 65.

87. *See* Morgan, *Pacific Gibraltar*, 207.

88. *See* Morgan, *Pacific Gibraltar*, 203–05.

89. *See* Morgan, *Pacific Gibraltar*, 205–07; Hamilton, "Military Strategists," 88.

90. Pritchett, "Some Recollections," 400–01; *see* Morgan, *Pacific Gibraltar*, 206–10.

91. Long to Beardslee, June 10, 1897, quoted in Morgan, *Pacific Gibraltar*, 209.

92. *See* Morgan, *Pacific Gibraltar*, 211 & n.93.

93. Ōkuma to Hoshi, June 19, 1897, quoted in Morgan, *Pacific Gibraltar*, 212; *see* Morgan, *Pacific Gibraltar*, 209. The Japanese also responded by trying to rope the British and other powers into an anti-annexation campaign against the United States. The British declined. Having recently resolved the Venezuela boundary crisis, they knew how excitable their former colonials were; any attempt to block annexation was the surest way to spur it. Without British help, Japan's diplomatic effort soon collapsed. *See* Morgan, *Pacific Gibraltar*, 212–16.

94. *See* Morgan, *Pacific Gibraltar*, 212. For the renewed instructions to forces in Hawai'i, *see* Sherman to Cooper, July 10, 1897, in Instructions, Hawaii, Roll 100, M77, RG59, NA.

95. *See* Morgan, *Pacific Gibraltar*, 215–16.

96. *See* Morgan, *Pacific Gibraltar*, 208–09; Morgan, "Anti-Japanese Origins," 24–25. For McKinley knowing that the Senate could not act until December, *see* Schurz, "William McKinley," 272–73.

97. John R. Procter, "Hawaii and the Changing Front of the World," *Forum* 24, no. 1 (September 1897), 41; *see* "Hawaiian Debate Resumed," *New York Tribune*, January 19, 1898.

98. George F. Hoar, *Autobiography of Seventy Years* (New York: Charles Scribner's Sons, 1903), 2:307–08; *see Davis Report*, 8; *see also* Morgan, *Pacific Gibraltar*, 221.

99. Hoar, *Autobiography*, 2:307–08; *see* Morgan, *Pacific Gibraltar*, 220–21; Richard F. Hamilton, *America's New Empire: The 1890s and Beyond* (New Brunswick, NJ: Transaction Publishers, 2010), 98–99.

100. *See* Schurz, "William McKinley," 272–73; *see also* Morgan, *Pacific Gibraltar*, 222–36.

101. *See* Morgan, *Pacific Gibraltar*, 234–35; Tate, *Political History*, 305–06. Shortly afterward, the administration strong-armed Hawai'i into settling the immigration dispute with Japan. Conceding the issue no longer mattered to the United States; Hawai'i was, at long last, secure. *See* William Adam Russ, Jr., *The Hawaiian Republic (1894–98) and Its Struggle to Win Annexation* (Selinsgrove, PA: Susquehanna University Press, 1961), 361–63.

102. Miller to Long, August 14, 1898, in *Annual Reports of the Navy Department for the Year 1898* (Washington, DC: Government Printing Office, 1898), 145–46, 148.

103. Miller to Long, August 14, 1898, in *Annual Reports 1898*, 146; *see* Coffman, *Nation Within*, 314–18.

104. "Last Princess of Hawaii to Leave Her Island Home," *San Francisco Chronicle*, July 28, 1898; *see* Clifford Gessler, *Tropic Landfall: The Port of Honolulu* (Garden City, NY: Doubleday, Doran, 1942), 221; Tate, *Political History*, 307; Coffman, *Nation Within*, 215.

105. 31 Cong. Record 6258 (1898).

106. 31 Cong. Record 6306 (1898).

107. *See* Silva, *Aloha Betrayed*, 145–59; Tate, *Political History*, 284; Coffman, *Nation Within*, 273–87. A second petition garnered over 17,000 signatures, though many likely overlapped with the larger petition. *See* Silva, *Aloha Betrayed*, 151.

108. *See, e.g.*, Pratt, *Expansionists of 1898*.

109. *See* discussion *supra* n.54.

110. For a good summary, *see Davis Report*, 28, 39, 61–62.

111. *Davis Report*, 29, 52, 61 (emphasis omitted); *St. James's Gazette*, 1898, in *Literary Digest*, February 26, 1898, 261; *see Davis Report*, 27, 53 (emphasis omitted); *see also* Livezy, *Mahan on Sea Power*, 189.

112. *Davis Report*, 31; *see ibid.*, 56; *Annexation of Hawaii (Hitt Report)*, H.R. Rep. No. 55-1355 (1898), 13–14; 31 Cong. Rec. 5830 (1898); Schofield to Morgan, January 12, 1898, in *Davis Report*, 105; Sherman, Report Accompanying Annexation Treaty of 1897, June 15, 1897, in *Davis Report*, 75.

113. 31 Cong. Record 6663 (1898); *Davis Report*, 29; *see* Lodge, "American Policy," 1; *see also* Love, *Race over Empire*, 155. For Senator Hoar's introduction of the native petition opposing annexation, *see* 31 Cong. Rec. 45 (1897); *see also* Silva, *Aloha Betrayed*, 158–59. The consensus that Native Hawaiians were going extinct was partially rooted in census results—the population had shrunk some 90 percent from its size in 1778—but also in racist views about the supposed "degeneracy" of the Native Hawaiian people. *See* Love, *Race over Empire*, 85–88.

114. "A Plea for Taking Hawaii," *New York Times*, May 31, 1898; 31 Cong. Rec. 5829 (1898).

115. 31 Cong. Rec. 6660, 6663 (1898); *see* Hoar, *Autobiography*, 2:308–09. Other examples abound. Even President Harrison—who submitted the first annexation treaty to the Senate—would ultimately come out against the annexation of the Philippines. *See* Robert L. Beisner, *Twelve Against Empire: The Anti-Imperialists, 1898–1900* (New York: McGraw-Hill Book, 1968), 187–93.

116. *See* 31 Cong. Rec. 6661–62 (1898). Notably, many anti-annexationists seemed to believe the islands would have to be annexed at some point; the question was only when. *See* Osborne, *"Empire Can Wait,"* 135.

117. *See* Schurz, "William McKinley," 272–73; *see also* Morgan, *Pacific Gibraltar*, 186–87, 225–27; Thomas J. Osborne, "Trade or War?: America's Annexation of Hawaii Reconsidered," *Pacific Historical Review* 50, no. 3 (August 1981), 287; Mukharji, "Sea Change," 75–78.

118. *See* Morgan, *Pacific Gibraltar*, 231–33. For a contrary view, *see generally* Osborne, *"Empire Can Wait"*; Osborne, "Trade or War?". Contrary to Osborne's suggestion that commercial factors were central during the congressional debates, Morgan identifies strategic considerations as "most important." Morgan, *Pacific Gibraltar*, 229.

119. 31 Cong. Rec. 6357 (1898); 31 Cong. Rec. 6189 (1898); 31 Cong. Rec. 5790 (1898). For an excellent account of the role that race played in the debates over Hawai'i's annexation, *see* Love, *Race over Empire*, 73–158. Given the strategic concerns, however, Love likely overemphasizes the degree to which it mattered for annexationists that Hawai'i's oligarchy was white. For the "yellow peril" narrative, *see* Rubin Francis Weston, *Racism in U.S. Imperialism: The Influence of Racial Assumptions on American Foreign Policy, 1893–1946* (Columbia: University of South Carolina Press, 1972), 50–51, 53–54, 58.

120. *See* Field, "The Worst Chapter," 653 n.27; Kenneth Wimmel, *Theodore Roosevelt and the Great White Fleet: American Seapower Comes of Age* (Washington, DC: Brassey's, 1998), 236. For Congress's belated authorization, *see* An Act Making Appropriations for the Naval Service for the Fiscal Year Ending June Thirtieth, Nineteen Hundred and Nine, and for Other Purposes, Pub. L. No. 60-115, 35 Stat. 127, 141 (May 13, 1908). General John M. Schofield, one of the nation's foremost experts on the subject, advised Congress during the annexation debates that although owning Pearl Harbor would have many direct benefits, the "greatest value" would come

from "the fact that its position and adequate defense by us prevents the possibility of an enemy using it." Schofield to Morgan, January 12, 1898, in *Davis Report*, 105.

121. *See, e.g.*, Nicholas John Spykman, *America's Strategy in World Politics: The United States and the Balance of Power* (New York: Harcourt, Brace, 1942), 415–17; David Vergun, "Remembering the Battle of Okinawa," DOD News, US Department of Defense, last modified April 1, 2020, https://www.defense.gov/News/Feature-Stories/story/Article/2130718/remembering-the -battle-of-okinawa.

122. Sherman to Powell, January 11, 1898, in Instructions, Haiti, Roll 97, M77, RG59, NA.

Chapter 5: The Conquest of the United States by Spain

1. Andrew Carnegie, *Triumphant Democracy, or Fifty Years' March of the Republic* (London: Sampson Low, Marston, Searle, & Rivington, 1886), 1; *see* Paul Kennedy, *The Rise and Fall of the Great Powers: Economic Change and Military Conflict from 1500 to 2000* (New York: Vintage Books, 1989), 199–203, 242–49; Walter LaFeber, *The Cambridge History of American Foreign Relations*, vol. 2, *The American Search for Opportunity, 1865–1913* (Cambridge, UK: Cambridge University Press, 1998), 26–27. For American GDP growth, *see* Bureau of the Census, U.S. Department of Commerce, "Gross and Net National Product, by Major Type of Product, in 1929 Prices: 1869 to 1931," in *Historical Statistics of the United States: Colonial Times to 1970, Bicentennial Edition* (Washington, DC: Government Printing Office, 1975), 1:231. For American export growth, *see* Bureau of the Census, "International Transactions and Foreign Commerce," in *Historical Statistics*, 2:889, 890. "Manufactured goods" includes manufactured food and semi-manufactures in addition to finished manufactures. Relative increase in exports is adjusted for inflation using the Consumer Price Index. *See* Federal Reserve Bank of Minneapolis, "Consumer Price Index, 1800–," last modified 2022, https://www.minneapolisfed.org/about-us/monetary-policy/inflation-calculator/consumer -price-index-1800-. I thank David Boddy for his assistance with some of these calculations. For the American demographic jump, *see* Bureau of the Census, "Population," in *Historical Statistics*, 1:8.

2. *See* Ernest R. May, *Imperial Democracy: The Emergence of America as a Great Power* (New York: Harper Torchbooks, 1973), 6.

3. *See* May, *Imperial Democracy*, 220–21, 263–64.

4. James to Forbes, June 11, 1907, in *The Letters of William James*, ed. Henry James (Boston: Atlantic Monthly, 1920), 2:289; George F. Hoar, "The Opinion of Massachusetts on Imperialism," Speech to the Massachusetts Club, July 29, 1898, in Anti-Imperialist League, "Save the Republic," Anti-Imperialist Leaflet No. 13 (1899).

5. *Theodore Roosevelt: An Autobiography* (New York: Charles Scribner's Sons, 1922), 13; *see* Edmund Morris, *The Rise of Theodore Roosevelt* (New York: Modern Library, 2001), 3–5; Warren Zimmermann, *First Great Triumph: How Five Americans Made Their Country a World Power* (New York: Farrar, Straus and Giroux, 2002), 190.

6. Corinne Roosevelt Robinson, *My Brother Theodore Roosevelt* (New York: Charles Scribner's Sons, 1921), 50; *see* Zimmermann, *First Great Triumph*, 190.

7. Roosevelt, *Autobiography*, 27–28; Hermann Hagedorn, *The Boy's Life of Theodore Roosevelt* (New York: Harper & Brothers, 1918), 64; *see* Roosevelt, *Autobiography*, 29–31; *see also* Morris, *The Rise*, 33, 41, 129–30.

8. *See* Morris, *The Rise*, 17–19, 33, 36–40, 45, 86–87, 95, 108, 116–19, 123–26, 130–35.

9. William Roscoe Thayer, *Theodore Roosevelt: An Intimate Biography* (Boston: Houghton Mifflin, 1919), 21; Martha Bulloch Roosevelt to Anna Louisa Bulloch, July 28, 1872, in Carleton Putnam, *Theodore Roosevelt*, vol. 1, *The Formative Years 1858–1886* (New York: Charles Scribner's Son, 1958), 78; *see* Zimmermann, *First Great Triumph*, 195; Morris, *The Rise*, xxi, xxv–xxvi, xxx, 4–5.

10. *See* Morris, *The Rise*, 143–80, 221.

11. Roosevelt to Theodore Roosevelt, Jr., October 20, 1903, in Morison 3:635; Roosevelt to Anna Roosevelt, February 25, 1895, in Morison 1:428; *see* David Healy, *US Expansionism: The Imperialist Urge in the 1890s* (Madison: University of Wisconsin Press, 1970), 111–12; Zimmermann, *First Great Triumph*, 241; Morris, *The Rise*, 560. For Roosevelt's prodigious authorship, *see*

generally The Works of Theodore Roosevelt, ed. Hermann Hagedorn, vol. 1–24 (New York: Charles Scribner's Sons, 1923–26).

12. Burroughs to Putnam, 1919, in *Theodore Roosevelt Memorial Addresses* (New York: Century Association, 1919), 58; William Bayard Hale, *A Week in the White House with Theodore Roosevelt: A Study of the President at the Nation's Business* (New York: G. P. Putnam's Sons, 1908), 116–17; *The Education of Henry Adams: An Autobiography* (Boston: Houghton Mifflin, 1918), 417; *see also* Morris, *The Rise*, xxix n.96, 106.

13. *See* John A. S. Grenville and George Berkeley Young, *Politics, Strategy, and American Diplomacy: Studies in Foreign Policy, 1873–1917* (New Haven, CT: Yale University Press, 1969), 212–13; Zimmermann, *First Great Triumph*, 170–71.

14. *What Me Befell: The Reminiscences of J. J. Jusserand* (Boston: Houghton Mifflin, 1933), 330; *see* Morris, *The Rise*, 249–50; William C. Widenor, *Henry Cabot Lodge and the Search for an American Foreign Policy* (Berkeley: University of California Press, 1983), 87–88.

15. Joseph Hodges Choate to Caroline Dutcher Sterling Choate, January 25, 1896, in Edward Sandford Martin, *The Life of Joseph Hodges Choate as Gathered Chiefly from His Letters* (New York: Charles Scribner's Sons, 1902), 2:34; *see* Morris, *The Rise*, 560–61, 577–84.

16. Bellamy Storer, "How Theodore Roosevelt Was Appointed Assistant Secretary of the Navy," *Harper's Weekly*, June 1, 1912, 9; Lodge to Roosevelt, December 2, 1896, in *Selections from the Correspondence of Theodore Roosevelt and Henry Cabot Lodge 1884–1918* (New York: Charles Scribner's, 1925), 1:241; *see* Roosevelt to Lodge, December 4, 1896, in Morison 1:567.

17. Roosevelt to Lodge, April 6, 1897, in *Selections* 1:266.

18. Ferdinand Cowle Iglehart, *Theodore Roosevelt: The Man as I Knew Him* (New York: Christian Herald, 1919), 122.

19. *See* Ivan Musicant, *Empire by Default: The Spanish-American War and the Dawn of the American Century* (New York: Henry Holt, 1998), 38–40.

20. *See* Musicant, *Empire by Default*, 40–50.

21. *See* David F. Healy, *The United States in Cuba 1898–1902: Generals, Politicians, and the Search for Policy* (Madison: University of Wisconsin Press, 1963), 8; John M. Dobson, *America's Ascent: The United States Becomes a Great Power, 1880–1914* (DeKalb: Northern Illinois University Press, 1978), 96; Musicant, *Empire by Default*, 45–48.

22. *See* Musicant, *Empire by Default*, 48–50.

23. Gomez to Moreno, February 6, 1897, in Máximo Gómez, *Recuerdos y Revisiones: Publicaciones de la Secretaría de Educación, Dirección de Cultura* (Havana: Talleres de Cultural, 1935), 133; Emilio Roig de Leuchsenring, *Cuba no Debe su Independencia a los Estados Unidos* (Havana: Sociedad Cubana de Estudios Históricos e Internacionales, 1950), 24; *see* Philip S. Foner, *The Spanish-Cuban-American War and the Birth of American Imperialism 1895–1902*, vol. 1, *1895–1898* (New York: Monthly Review, 1972), 20–21; John L. Offner, "McKinley and the Spanish-American War," *Presidential Studies Quarterly* 34, no. 1 (March 2004), 50–51.

24. Martí to de Quesada, October 19, 1889, in José Martí, *Obras Completas*, ed. M. Isidro Mendez (Havana: Editorial Lex, 1946), 1:656; *see* May, *Imperial Democracy*, 71. For the Junta's work, *see* Foner, *The Spanish-Cuban-American War*, 1:163–76. For Cuban rebels' opposition to American intervention, *see* Foner, *The Spanish-Cuban-American War*, 1:xxx, 143–47; Louis A. Pérez, Jr., *The War of 1898: The United States and Cuba in History and Historiography* (Chapel Hill: University of North Carolina Press, 1998), 55.

25. "Famine and Flames," *New York World*, May 17, 1896; *see* Thomas A. Bailey, *A Diplomatic History of the American People* (Englewood Cliffs, NJ: Prentice-Hall, 1980), 454; Kenneth Wimmel, *Theodore Roosevelt and the Great White Fleet: American Seapower Comes of Age* (Washington, DC: Brassey's, 1998), 98; Musicant, *Empire by Default*, 66–67; Offner, "McKinley," 51. For the horrific death count as McKinley likely understood it in spring 1898—600,000 dead out of a population of 1.6 million—*see* Woodford to McKinley, March 9, 1898, in FRUS 1898, 683; Woodford to McKinley, March 18, 1898, in FRUS 1898, 690.

26. Gómez to Cleveland, February 9, 1897, in S. Exec. Doc. No. 55-75 (1897), 7; 28 Cong. Rec. 3123 (1896); *see* Robert Kagan, *Dangerous Nation* (New York: Alfred A. Knopf, 2006), 384–85, 407–08. Historians have generally downplayed the importance of the Monroe Doctrine as a

direct cause of the Spanish-American War, and rightly so—the Doctrine pledged noninterference with existing European colonies in the hemisphere, and as a result it was rarely mentioned in the debates over Cuba. *See, e.g.*, Dexter Perkins, *The Monroe Doctrine: 1867–1907* (Gloucester, MA: Peter Smith, 1966), 264–76. But the Doctrine nonetheless played an important and under-appreciated role in establishing the necessary context for war. Americans would not have cared nearly as much about the human rights abuses in Cuba if those abuses were not being meted out by European hands.

27. *See* Foner, *The Spanish-Cuban-American War*, 1:19–20. Some authors have argued that Cubans were on the verge of victory in 1898 (or at least perceived to be so). *See ibid.*, 1:136–43; Pérez, *The War of 1898*, 10–13; Louis A. Pérez, Jr., *Cuba Under the Platt Amendment, 1902–1934* (Pittsburgh, PA: University of Pittsburgh Press, 1986), 144–69. But that view conflicts with the evidence, and more importantly, it does not represent the perspective that Americans had on the situation. *See* Navy Department, "Plan of Operations Against Spain," December 17, 1896, in John A. S. Grenville, "American Naval Preparations for War with Spain, 1896–1898," *Journal of American Studies* 2, no. 1 (April 1968), 38; *see also* Aroop Mukharji, "Sea Change: McKinley, Roosevelt, and the Expansion of U.S. Foreign Policy 1897–1909" (PhD diss., Harvard University, April 2020), 105–08.

28. Roosevelt, *Autobiography*, 208; Roosevelt to White, April 30, 1897, in Morison 1:606; Roosevelt, "Washington's Forgotten Maxim," Address Before the Naval War College, June 2, 1897, in *The Works of Theodore Roosevelt in Fourteen Volumes*, vol. 1, *American Ideals and Administration—Civil Service* (New York: P. F. Collier & Son, 1897), 269; *see* Roosevelt to Hall, November 29, 1899, in Morison 2:1100; *see also* Healy, *US Expansionism*, 115–22; H. W. Brands, *The Reckless Decade: America in the 1890s* (Chicago: University of Chicago Press, 1995), 292.

29. Roosevelt to Lodge, December 4, 1896, in Morison 1:567; Roosevelt to Moore, February 9, 1898, in Morison 1:771; Roosevelt to Chanler, December 23, 1897, in Morison 1:746. Roosevelt was remarkably consistent during this period about his central foreign policy objective, repeating it almost word for word year after year. *See, e.g.*, Roosevelt to Clarkson, April 22, 1893, in Morison 1:313; Roosevelt to Cowles, April 5, 1896, in Morison 1:524; Roosevelt to Kimball, November 19, 1897, in Morison 1:716–17; Roosevelt to Adams, March 21, 1898, in Morison 1:798; *see also* Morris, *The Rise*, 473, 624.

30. Roosevelt to Kimball, November 19, 1897, in Morison 1:717; Roosevelt to Mahan, May 3, 1897, in Morison 1:607; *see* Roosevelt to Kimball, December 17, 1897, in Morison 1:743. Echoing this basic logic, Roosevelt had also emphatically favored the annexation of Hawai'i. "We cannot help Hawaii's being either a strong defence to us or a perpetual menace," he argued. "We can only decide whether we will now take the islands when offered to us as a gift, or by force try to conquer them from the first powerful nation with which we may become embroiled." "Dined on Lincoln Day," *New York Sun*, February 13, 1898; *see also* Robert L. Beisner, *From the Old Diplomacy to the New 1865–1900* (Arlington Heights, IL: Harlan Davidson, 1986), 51.

31. Olney to Cleveland, September 25, 1895, in Reel 59, Olney MSS; *Affairs in Cuba*, S. Rep. No. 55-885 (1898), xx; *see* Olney, Drafts of Cuba Portion of Cleveland's 1896 State of the Union Address, November 9, 1896, in Reel 23, Olney MSS; Cleveland, Fourth Annual Message, December 7, 1896, in Richardson 9:721; Lodge to Pickman, March 12, 1896, in Reel 9, Lodge MSS; Lodge to Bigelow, December 31, 1896, in Vol. 33, Letterbooks, Lodge MSS; Lodge to Adams, January 22, 1897, in Vol. 33, Letterbooks, Lodge MSS; *see also* May, *Imperial Democracy*, 85–87; Grenville and Young, *Politics, Strategy, and American Diplomacy*, 230, 236.

32. Roosevelt to Bacon, April 8, 1898, in Morison 2:814; Roosevelt to Anna Roosevelt Cowles, January 2, 1897, in Morison 1:573–74; *see* Roosevelt to Root, April 5, 1898, in Morison 2:813; Lodge to Pickman, March 12, 1896, in Reel 9, Lodge MSS; Lodge to Lyman, March 17, 1896, in Vol. 32, Letterbooks, Lodge MSS; Lodge to Adams, January 22, 1897, in Vol. 33, Letterbooks, Lodge MSS; Lodge to Higginson, March 9, 1898, in Vol. 37, Letterbooks, Lodge MSS; Lodge to Bigelow, March 25, 1898, in Vol. 38, Letterbooks, Lodge MSS; *see also* Grenville and Young, *Politics, Strategy, and American Diplomacy*, 230–31.

33. Roosevelt to Spring Rice, April 28, 1897, in Morison 1:604; *see* Musicant, *Empire by Default*, 98; Morris, *The Rise*, 605–07.

34. Roosevelt to Storer, September 26, 1897, in Morison 1:691; Roosevelt to Davis, August 13, 1897, in Morison 1:649; Roosevelt to Storer, August 19, 1897, in Morison 1:655; *see* Morris, *The Rise*, 605–07, 610–15. For Roosevelt's work as assistant secretary, *see* Henry J. Hendrix, *Theodore Roosevelt's Naval Diplomacy: The U.S. Navy and the Birth of the American Century* (Annapolis, MD: Naval Institute Press, 2009), 12–22.

35. *See* McKinley, First Message to Congress, December 6, 1897, in FRUS 1897, xx; Roosevelt to Kimball, December 17, 1897, in Morison 1:743; *see also* Wayne H. Morgan, *America's Road to Empire: The War with Spain and Overseas Expansion* (New York: McGraw-Hill, 1965), 29–35.

36. de Lome to Canalejas, December 1897, in FRUS 1898, 1007, 1008; *see* Morgan, *America's Road to Empire*, 38–44.

37. Thomas Beer, *Hanna, Crane, and the Mauve Decade* (New York: Alfred A. Knopf, 1941), 548; *see* G. J. A. O'Toole, *The Spanish War: An American Epic—1898* (New York: W. W. Norton, 1994), 99–120; Musicant, *Empire by Default*, 137–41.

38. William Randolph Hearst, "In the News," *San Francisco Examiner*, July 1, 1940; Roosevelt to Adams, March 21, 1898, in Morison 1:798; *Appleton Post*, March 10, 1898; *see* Musicant, *Empire by Default*, 143–47, 151–52, 168; Charles S. Campbell, *The Transformation of American Foreign Relations 1865–1900* (New York: Harper and Row, 1976), 256–57. For the naval commission's report, *see* S. Doc. No. 55-207 (1898).

Richard Hamilton provides an important corrective to the traditional emphasis on popular opinion and, to a lesser extent, on the "yellow press" as causes for war. *See* Richard F. Hamilton, *President McKinley, War and Empire*, vol. 1, *President McKinley and the Coming of War* (New Brunswick, NJ: Transaction Publishers, 2006), 149–238. Hamilton makes a persuasive case that the "yellow press" played little direct role in starting the war, but he ultimately understates how much contemporary observers saw (especially from their perches in the capital) a widespread national movement in favor of war.

39. 31 Cong. Rec. 2917 (1898); *see* Campbell, *The Transformation*, 257; Musicant, *Empire by Default*, 164–66.

40. Hermann Hagedorn, *Leonard Wood: A Biography* (New York: Harper and Brothers, 1931), 1:141; Long, Diary Entry, April 2, 1898, in *America of Yesterday as Reflected in the Journal of John Davis Long*, ed. Lawrence Shaw Mayo (Boston: Atlantic Monthly, 1923), 175; Long, Diary Entry, April 4, 1898, in Mayo, *America of Yesterday*, 176; Long, Diary Entry, February 17, 1898, in Mayo, *America of Yesterday*, 165; *see* H. H. Kohlsaat, *From McKinley to Harding: Personal Recollections of Our Presidents* (New York: Charles Scribner's Sons, 1923), 66–67; Garret A. Hobart, *Memories* (self-pub., 1930), 62; *see also* Robert W. Merry, *Architect of the American Century: President McKinley* (New York: Simon & Schuster, 2017), 25–27; Mukharji, "Sea Change," 135.

41. Long to Roosevelt, February 25, 1898, in Joseph Bucklin Bishop, *Theodore Roosevelt and His Time* (New York: Charles Scribner's Sons, 1920), 86; *see* Long, Diary Entry, February 25, 1898, in Mayo, *America of Yesterday*, 168–69; Long, Diary Entry, February 26, 1898, in Mayo, *America of Yesterday*, 169–70; Long, Diary Entry, May 5, 1898, in Mayo, *America of Yesterday*, 188; *see also* Musicant, *Empire by Default*, 153–54.

42. Long, Diary Entry, February 26, 1898, in Mayo, *America of Yesterday*, 169; Roosevelt to Dewey, February 25, 1898, in *Annual Reports of the Navy Department for the Year 1898* (Washington, DC: Government Printing Office, 1898), 23; *see* Evan Thomas, *The War Lovers: Roosevelt, Lodge, Hearst, and the Rush to Empire, 1898* (New York: Little, Brown, 2010), 178; Morris, *The Rise*, 629–30. For the long-standing war plans against Spain, *see* Navy Department, "Plans of Campaign Against Spain and Japan," June 30, 1897, in Grenville, "American Naval Preparations," 43; *see also* Grenville, "American Naval Preparations," 34. Contrary to some early dramatizations, Roosevelt's actions at this juncture had little to no appreciable effect on the course of the Spanish-American War. *See* Richard H. Collin, *Theodore Roosevelt, Culture, Diplomacy, and Expansion* (Baton Rouge: Louisiana State University Press, 1985), 104–34.

43. "Grumbling at Washington," *New York Times*, April 7, 1898; *see* Hobart, *Memories*, 60–61; Long, Diary Entry, April 6, 1898, in Mayo, *America of Yesterday*, 177; *see also* Morgan, *America's Road to Empire*, 53, 59–60; Musicant, *Empire by Default*, 172–75, 178.

44. For a balanced summary, *see* Joseph A. Fry, "William McKinley and the Coming of the Spanish-American War: A Study of the Besmirching and Redemption of an Historical Image," *Diplomatic History* 3, no. 1 (Winter 1979), 96–97; Morgan, *America's Road to Empire*, 37–63. For good (if conflicting) discussions of how other factors, especially commercial ones, were not significant causal factors in starting the Spanish-American War, *see* Mukharji, "Sea Change," 139–71; Hamilton, *War and Empire*, 1:119–35; Kristin L. Hoganson, *Fighting for American Manhood: How Gender Politics Provoked the Spanish-American and Philippine-American Wars* (New Haven, CT: Yale University Press, 1998), 210–14 n.14.

45. McKinley, Message to Congress, April 11, 1898, in FRUS 1898, 759–60; Joint Resolution for the Recognition of the Independence of the People of Cuba, 30 Stat. 738 (April 20, 1898). For McKinley's focus on reestablishing order in Cuba, *see* Mukharji, "Sea Change," 123–32. For the political compromises leading to the Teller Amendment and the authorization to use force, *see* Paul S. Holbo, "Presidential Leadership in Foreign Affairs: William McKinley and the Turpie-Foraker Amendment," *American Historical Review* 72, no. 4 (July 1967), 1321–35.

46. *See* Musicant, *Empire by Default*, 187–90; Merry, *Architect*, 276. For the declaration of war, *see* An Act Declaring that War Exists Between the United States of America and the Kingdom of Spain, 30 Stat. 364 (April 25, 1898). For McKinley's signature of the declaration of war, *see* Margaret Leech, *In the Days of McKinley* (New York: Harper & Brothers, 1959), 192–93; Merry, *Architect*, 276.

47. "Rough Riders Home Again," *Philadelphia Inquirer*, August 16, 1898; *see* Thomas, *War Lovers*, 357–58; Zimmermann, *First Great Triumph*, 299.

48. "Rough Riders Home Again," *Philadelphia Inquirer*, August 16, 1898; *see* Adams to Cunliffe, January 25, 1900, in *Letters of Henry Adams*, ed. Worthington Chauncey Ford, vol. 2, *1892–1918* (Boston: Houghton Mifflin, 1938), 254–55.

49. *See* Musicant, *Empire by Default*, 191–234, 432–66; Zimmermann, *First Great Triumph*, 270.

50. Roosevelt to Kimball, November 19, 1897, in Morison 1:717; Theodore Roosevelt, *The Rough Riders* (New York: Review of Reviews, 1904), 124; *see* Musicant, *Empire by Default*, 352–431, 467–504; Frank Freidel, *The Splendid Little War* (Boston: Burford Books, 2002), 27–33, 47–75. For an excellent overview of Roosevelt, the Rough Riders, and the war, *see* Clay Risen, *The Crowded Hour: Theodore Roosevelt, the Rough Riders, and the Dawn of the American Century* (New York: Scribner, 2019).

51. Richard Harding Davis, *The Cuban and Porto Rican Campaigns* (New York: Charles Scribner's Sons, 1898), 96–97; *see* Morgan, *America's Road to Empire*, 65.

52. Mahan to Roosevelt, n.d., quoted in W. D. Puleston, *Mahan: The Life and Work of Captain Alfred Thayer Mahan, U.S.N.* (London: Jonathan Cape, 1939), 198; Lodge to White, August 12, 1898, in Reel 13, Lodge MSS.

53. [Finley Peter Dunne], *Mr. DOOLEY In Peace and in War* (Boston: Small, Maynard, 1899), 9.

54. Tom Hall, *The Fun and Fighting of the Rough Riders* (New York: Frederick A. Stokes, 1899), 114; John H. Parker, *History of the Gatling Gun Detachment* (Kansas City, MO: Hudson-Kimberly, 1898), 77; *see The War Dispatches of Stephen Crane*, ed. R. W. Stallman and E. R. Hagemann (New York: New York University Press, 1964), 182; George Kennan, *Campaigning in Cuba* (New York: Century, 1899), 92; Roosevelt, *Rough Riders*, 75; H. Irving Hancock, *What One Man Saw: Being the Personal Impressions of a War Correspondent in Cuba* (New York: Street & Smith, 1900), 31; *see also* David Healy, *Drive to Hegemony: The United States in the Caribbean 1898–1917* (Madison: University of Wisconsin Press, 1988), 46.

55. Parker, *History*, 78; Stallman and Hagemann, *War Dispatches*, 181; *see* James L. Abrahamson, *America Arms for a New Century: The Making of a Great Military Power* (New York: Free Press, 1981), 79; George C. Herring, *From Colony to Superpower: U.S. Foreign Relations Since 1776* (Oxford: Oxford University Press, 2008), 320–21. For Cubans' invaluable contributions to the war effort, *see* Foner, *The Spanish-Cuban-American War*, 2:339–378; Pérez, *The War of 1898*, 86–94.

56. *See Autobiography of George Dewey, Admiral of the Navy* (New York: Charles Scribner's Sons, 1913), 254; *see also* Musicant, *Empire by Default*, 556–58.

57. For Germany's attempt to organize a prewar coalition against the United States, *see* May, *Imperial Democracy*, 196–219; Samuel Flagg Bemis, *The Latin American Policy of the United States: An Historical Interpretation* (New York: Harcourt, Brace, 1943), 134–36. For Germany's behavior at Manila, *see* Dewey, *Autobiography*, 255, 558, 262–64, 267; *see also* Musicant, *Empire by Default*, 557, 559–63; Thomas A. Bailey, "Dewey and the Germans at Manila Bay," *American Historical Review* 45, no. 1 (October 1939), 67–71 & n.50; Nathan Sargent, *Admiral Dewey and the Manila Campaign* (Washington, DC: Naval Historical Foundation, 1947), 72–73. For Germany's serious interest in acquiring territory as a result of the war, *see* Bailey, "Dewey and the Germans," 61; Holger H. Herwig, *Politics of Frustration: The United States in German Naval Planning, 1889–1941* (Boston: Little, Brown, 1976), 24–36; Nancy Mitchell, *The Danger of Dreams: German and American Imperialism in Latin America* (Chapel Hill: University of North Carolina Press, 1999), 26–32.

58. Sargent, *Admiral Dewey*, 76.

59. Lodge to Roosevelt, May 24, 1898, in *Selections* 1:300; A. T. Mahan, *The Problem of Asia and Its Effect upon International Policies* (Boston: Little, Brown 1900), 6–7; *see* Roosevelt to Lodge, May 19, 1898, in *Selections* 1:299; Roosevelt to Lodge, May 25, 1898, in *Selections* 1:301. In 1897, Mahan had outlined many of these points in an influential article titled "The Strategic Features of the Gulf of Mexico and the Caribbean Sea." *See* A. T. Mahan, "The Strategic Features of the Gulf of Mexico and the Caribbean Sea," *Harper's New Monthly Magazine*, October 1897, in *The Interest of America in Sea Power, Present and Future* (Boston: Little, Brown, 1897), 271–314; *see generally* James A. Field, Jr., "American Imperialism: The Worst Chapter in Almost Any Book," *American Historical Review* 83, no. 3 (June 1978), 644–68.

60. Mahan to Sterling, December 23, 1898, in *Letters and Papers of Alfred Thayer Mahan*, ed. Robert Seager, II, and Doris D. Maguire, vol. 2, *1890–1901* (Annapolis, MD: Naval Institute Press, 1975), 619; Dunne, *Mr. DOOLEY in Peace*, 43; Moore, "Moore's Memoirs," ed. Edwin Borchard, n.d., in Box 217, Moore MSS, 183; *see* Healy, *US Expansionism*, 56–57. Lodge likewise stated in January 1898 that "we seek no possessions and no control beyond our own hemisphere." Henry Cabot Lodge, "The American Policy of Territorial Expansion," *The Independent*, January 13, 1898, 1.

61. Lodge to Roosevelt, June 24, 1898, in *Selections* 1:313; Mahan to Lodge, July 27, 1898, in Seager and Maguire, *Letters and Papers*, 2:569; Lodge to Day, August 11, 1898, in Reel 12, Lodge MSS; *see* Lodge to Fall, May 5, 1898, in Vol. 38, Letterbooks, Lodge MSS; Lodge to Wright, May 6, 1898, in Vol. 38, Letterbooks, Lodge MSS; Lodge to Lyman, May 19, 1898, in Vol. 38, Letterbooks, Lodge MSS; Lodge to Lyman, June 13, 1898, in Vol. 39, Letterbooks, Lodge MSS; *see also* Grenville and Young, *Politics, Strategy, and American Diplomacy*, 292–94. For Mahan's hesitancy in particular, *see* Mahan to Clarke, August 17, 1898, in Seager and Maguire, *Letters and Papers*, 2:579–80; Mahan, "The Navy and the Philippines," Remarks to the Associate Alumni of the College of the City of New York at the Savoy Hotel, February 24, 1900, in Seager and Maguire, *Letters and Papers*, 3:603; *see also* Suzanne Geissler, *God and Sea Power: The Influence of Religion on Alfred Thayer Mahan* (Annapolis, MD: Naval Institute Press, 2015), 134–35; Robert Seager, II, *Alfred Thayer Mahan: The Man and His Letters* (Annapolis, MD: Naval Institute Press, 2017), 394.

62. James F. Rusling, "Interview with President McKinley," *Christian Advocate*, January 22, 1903, 137; *see* Chandler P. Anderson, Memorandum, "Re Bering Seas Arbitration," November 19, 1898, in Ephraim K. Smith, "'A Question from Which We Could Not Escape': William McKinley and the Decision to Acquire the Philippine Islands," *Diplomatic History* 9, no. 4 (Fall 1985), 369; Adams to Cameron, January 22, 1899, in Ford, *Letters of Henry Adams*, 2:208; Henry S. Pritchett, "Some Recollections of President McKinley and the Cuban Intervention," *North American Review* 189, no. 640 (March 1909), 400–01; Jacob Gould Schurman, *Philippine Affairs: A Retrospect and Outlook* (New York: Charles Scribner's Sons, 1902), 2–3. For an excellent overview of McKinley as "reluctant" expansionist, *see* Ephraim K. Smith, "William McKinley's Enduring Legacy: The Historiographical Debate on the Taking of the Philippine Islands," in *Crucible of Empire: The Spanish-American War & Its Aftermath*, ed. James C. Bradford (Annapolis, MD: Naval Institute Press, 1993), 205–49; Mukharji, "Sea Change," 177–84; Hamilton, *War and Empire*, 2:84; *see generally* Philip Zelikow, "Why Did America Cross the Pacific?: Reconstructing the U.S. Decision to Take the Philippines, 1898–99," *Texas National Security Review* 1, no. 1

(December 2017), 36–66. For the Methodist delegation myth, *see* Mukharji, "Sea Change," 180 n.28, and the sources cited therein.

63. Rusling, "Interview," 137; Olcott, *William McKinley*, 2:61–63; Anderson, "Bering Seas Arbitration," 369; *see* Hay to Day, October 28, 1898, in FRUS 1898, 937; McKinley, Speech at Banquet of Board of Trade and Associated Citizens in Savannah, Georgia, December 17, 1898, in *Speeches and Addresses of William McKinley* (New York: Doubleday & McClure, 1900), 174–75; McKinley, Speech at Dinner of the Home Market Club, Boston, February 16, 1899, in *Speeches and Addresses of William McKinley*, 187–88.

64. "Future Work in the Philippines," *New York Times*, February 7, 1899; *see* McKinley, Message to Congress, December 5, 1899, in Richardson Supp. 14:6397–98; F. V. Greene, Memoranda Concerning the Situation in the Philippines on August 30, 1898, September 30, 1898, in S. Doc. No. 55-62 (1899), 424–25; McKinley to Day, September 28, 1898, in FRUS 1898, 915; *see also* Healy, *US Expansionism*, 65–66; Richard E. Welch, Jr., *Response to Imperialism: The United States and the Philippine-American War, 1899–1902* (Chapel Hill: University of North Carolina Press, 1979), 7–8; Zelikow, "Why Did America Cross the Pacific?," 50, 58–59. For Aguinaldo and his relationship with the United States during the war, *see* David F. Trask, *The War with Spain in 1898* (Lincoln: University of Nebraska Press, 1996), 391–410.

65. White to Day, June 18, 1898, in Box 185, Moore MSS; *see* Dobson, *America's Ascent*, 117; Musicant, *Empire by Default*, 600–01; Healy, *US Expansionism*, 65–66; Zimmermann, *First Great Triumph*, 318; Mukharji, "Sea Change," 203–14; James K. Eyre, Jr., "Japan and the American Annexation of the Philippines," *Pacific Historical Review* 11, no. 1 (March 1942), 63–64; Robert L. Beisner, *Twelve Against Empire: The Anti-Imperialists, 1898–1900* (New York: McGraw-Hill Book, 1968), 230–31; Beisner, *Old Diplomacy to the New*, 136–37. For Germany's simultaneous annexation of the Carolines, the Marshalls, and the Marianas (with the exception of Guam), *see* Tristram E. Farmer, "Too Little, Too Late: The Fight for the Carolines, 1898," *Naval History* 3, no. 1 (Winter 1989), 20–25; Don A. Farrell, "The Partition of the Marianas: A Diplomatic History, 1898–1919," *Journal of Micronesian Studies* 2, no. 2 (Dry Season 1994), 273–301. Of course, Germany reciprocally objected to Great Britain or France grabbing the islands. *See* Healy, *US Expansionism*, 65–66. Even France may have had interest in annexing the islands. *See* "Europe and the Philippines," *New York Times*, May 29, 1898; *see also* Love, *Race over Empire*, 168.

66. McKinley, Message to Congress, December 5, 1899, in Richardson Supp. 14:6397–98; Schurman, *Philippine Affairs*, 2–3 (punctuation omitted); *see* McKinley, Home Market Speech, in *Speeches and Addresses of William McKinley*, 187–88; *see also* Hillel Ofek, "A Just Peace: Grover Cleveland, William McKinley, and the Moral Basis of American Foreign Policy" (PhD diss., University of Texas at Austin, 2018), 232–41.

67. Treaty of Peace Between the United States of America and the Kingdom of Spain, December 10, 1898, in FRUS 1898, 831–40. For the annexation of Guam, *see* Farrell, "Partition of the Marianas," 273–301. For the annexation of Puerto Rico, *see* Trask, *War with Spain*, 338–40, 342–43. Besides the Treaty of Paris annexations, the United States also annexed uninhabited Wake Island in early 1899 for use as a cable relay station. *See* Dirk H. R. Spennemann, "The United States Annexation of Wake Atoll, Central Pacific Ocean," *Journal of Pacific History* 33, no. 2 (September 1998), 239–47. The same year, the United States also annexed a portion of the Samoas in a settlement with Germany and Great Britain. *See* Campbell, *The Transformation*, 311–13.

68. Kohlsaat, *McKinley to Harding*, 68; *see* Anderson, "Bering Seas Arbitration," 370; "President Schurman on the Philippine Situation: The Immediate Duty of the United States," *Outlook*, November 4, 1899, 534; Schurman, *Philippine Affairs*, 2–3; *see also* Leech, *Days of McKinley*, 484.

69. 32 Cong. Rec. 959 (1899); *see* Richard Hofstadter, "Cuba, the Philippines, and Manifest Destiny," in *The Paranoid Style in American Politics and Other Essays* (Chicago: University of Chicago Press, 1965), 145, 169.

70. *See* Berkeley E. Tompkins, *Anti-Imperialism in the United States: The Great Debate, 1890–1920* (Philadelphia: University of Pennsylvania Press, 1970), 123–39, 184–85; Beisner, *Twelve Against Empire*, 32. For a description of anti-imperialists, their motivations, and their ranks, *see* Healy, *US Expansionism*, 213–31; *see generally* Tompkins, *Anti-Imperialism*; Beisner, *Twelve*

Against Empire. For how much anti-imperialists relied on racism in their arguments, *see, e.g.,* Love, *Race over Empire*, 159–95.

71. 32 Cong. Rec. 498 (1899); Roosevelt to Wood, April 17, 1901, in Morison 3:60; *see* Tompkins, *Anti-Imperialism*, 161–95.

72. Cortelyou, Diary Entry, February 4, 1899, in Box 52, Cortelyou MSS; *see* Zimmermann, *First Great Triumph*, 325; Brian McAllister Linn, *The Philippine War 1899–1902* (Lawrence: University Press of Kansas, 2000), 42, 45–55.

73. *See* Lodge to Roosevelt, February 9, 1899, in *Selections* 1:391–92; *see also* Tompkins, *Anti-Imperialism*, 192. Devastated after the Treaty of Paris failure, the anti-imperialists regrouped to try to pass an amendment promising the Philippines early independence. This time, the vote was even closer—an outright tie that the anti-imperialists lost only after the vice president cast his ballot against it. *See* Healy, *US Expansionism*, 229; Beisner, *Twelve Against Empire*, 156–58.

74. *See* Zimmermann, *First Great Triumph*, 327, 386–87; Welch, *Response to Imperialism*, 24–25. For good general overviews of the Philippine-American War, *see* Welch, *Response to Imperialism*; Linn, *The Philippine War*.

75. Anti-Imperialist League, *Soldier's Letters* (Boston: Rockwell and Churchill, 1899), 3; "The Campaign in Samar," *New York Tribune*, May 1, 1902; Root to Roosevelt, July 12, 1902, in "President Retires Gen. Jacob H. Smith," *New York Times*, July 17, 1902; *see* Zimmermann, *First Great Triumph*, 406–13; *see generally* Paul A. Kramer, "Race-Making and Colonial Violence in the U.S. Empire: The Philippine-American War as Race War," *Diplomatic History* 30, no. 2 (April 2006), 169–210.

76. *See* Zimmermann, *First Great Triumph*, 407.

77. James to Schiller, August 6, 1902, quoted in Beisner, *Twelve Against Empire*, 44; Dunne, *Mr. DOOLEY in Peace*, 46–47; F. P. Dunne, *Mr. DOOLEY in the Hearts of His Countrymen* (London: Grant Richards, 1899), 267.

78. Roosevelt to Speck von Sternberg, July 19, 1902, in Morison 3:297–98; *see* Zimmermann, *First Great Triumph*, 409–10.

79. Roosevelt to Capen, July 3, 1901, in Morison 3:105; Roosevelt to Taft, August 21, 1907, in Morison 5:762; *see* Roosevelt to Eliot, November 14, 1900, in Morison 2:1415; *Autobiography of Andrew Carnegie* (Boston: Houghton Mifflin, 1920), 365; *see also* Edmund Morris, *Theodore Rex* (London: HarperCollins, 2002), 117; Tompkins, *Anti-Imperialism*, 274–75; Love, *Race over Empire*, 196–97; Richard H. Immerman, *Empire for Liberty: A History of American Imperialism from Benjamin Franklin to Paul Wolfowitz* (Princeton, NJ: Princeton University Press, 2010), 156.

80. *See* Zimmermann, *First Great Triumph*, 413; Herring, *From Colony to Superpower*, 329; Welch, *Response to Imperialism*, 42; Ralph Eldin Minger, *William Howard Taft and United States Foreign Policy: The Apprenticeship Years, 1900–1908* (Urbana: University of Illinois Press, 1975), 56–57. For the many different estimates of the Filipino casualties of the war, *see* John M. Gates, "War-Related Deaths in the Philippines, 1898–1902," *Pacific Historical Review* 53, no. 3 (August 1984), 367–78.

81. *See* Welch, *Response to Imperialism*, 146.

82. Lodge to Meyer, May 6, 1903, quoted in John A. Garraty, *Henry Cabot Lodge: A Biography* (New York: Alfred A. Knopf, 1953), 210; *see* Ernest R. May, *American Imperialism: A Speculative Essay* (New York: Atheneum, 1968), 14–15, 212–23; Tompkins, *Anti-Imperialism*, 272–73; Emily S. Rosenberg, *Spreading the American Dream: American Economic and Cultural Expansion, 1890–1945* (New York: Hill and Wang, 1989), 44–45.

83. "Mr. Root Studying Cuba," *New York Times*, November 21, 1900; *see* Zimmermann, *First Great Triumph*, 278.

84. Root, "The Lawyer of Today," Address Before the New York Country Lawyers Association, March 13, 1915, in *Addresses on Government and Citizenship by Elihu Root*, ed. Robert Bacon and James Brown Scott (Cambridge, MA: Harvard University Press, 1916), 503–04; *see* Leech, *Days of McKinley*, 378.

85. Philip C. Jessup, *Elihu Root*, vol. 1, *1845–1909* (New York: Dodd, Mead, 1938), 3, 4–15, 17, 47–48.

86. "Y.M.C.A. Regular Monthly Meeting—Essay by Mr. Elihu Root on 'Christianized Ambition'—A Lively Discussion," *Brooklyn Union*, February 13, 1867; *see* Jessup, *Elihu Root*, 1:56, 62, 82–87, 134–35, 164–87, 190–95; Zimmermann, *First Great Triumph*, 146.

87. Hay to White, June 15, 1900, in William Roscoe Thayer, *The Life and Letters of John Hay* (Boston: Houghton Mifflin, 1915), 2:342; *see* Zimmermann, *First Great Triumph*, 124–25, 142; Jessup, *Elihu Root*, 1:111; Healy, *US Expansionism*, 147.

88. Root, "The Lawyer of Today," in *Addresses on Government and Citizenship*, 504.

89. Root, "The Lawyer of Today," in *Addresses on Government and Citizenship*, 504.

90. *See* Jessup, *Elihu Root*, 1:285–86.

91. *See* Root to McKinley, November 29, 1899, in *Annual Reports of the War Department for the Fiscal Year Ended June 30, 1899* (Washington, DC: Government Printing Office, 1899), 12–17; *see also* Foner, *The Spanish-Cuban-American War*, 2:379–82; Jessup, *Elihu Root*, 1:285–86.

92. Wood to McKinley, February 6, 1900, in Box 28, Wood MSS; *see* Wood to Root, January 13, 1900, in Box 28, Wood MSS; Root to McKinley, November 29, 1899, in *Annual Reports of the War Department 1899*, 12–17; *see also* Healy, *United States in Cuba*, 63–64.

93. "Shafter's Idea of the Cubans," *New York Tribune*, December 19, 1898; *see* Stanhope Sams, "Cubans Not Fit to Govern," *New York Times*, July 29, 1898; O. H. Platt, "The Pacification of Cuba," *The Independent*, June 27, 1901, 1468; Lodge to White, August 12, 1898, in Reel 13, Lodge MSS.

94. "Our Duty in Cuba," *Chicago Inter-Ocean*, November 20, 1899; Sams, "Cubans Not Fit"; 34 Cong. Rec. 3042 (1901); *see* Foner, *The Spanish-Cuban-American War*, 2:516. Strangely, Senator Morgan thought that independence was still the correct course, since the opportunity for the Cubans to "fight their way out" would be "the best way" for them to learn "to have respect for the liberties and rights of each other." 34 Cong. Rec. 3042 (1901).

95. Root to Dana, January 16, 1900, in Root MSS; McKinley, Message to Congress, December 5, 1899, in Richardson Supp. 14:6377. For senior officials' obsession with preventing Cuba from turning into another "Hayti" or "San Domingo," *see, e.g.*, Reid to McKinley, April 19, 1898, in Royal Cortissoz, *The Life of Whitelaw Reid*, vol. 2, *Politics–Diplomacy* (New York: Charles Scribner's Sons, 1921), 2:222–23; Wood to Root, February 16, 1900, in Box 28, Wood MSS; Root to Wood, June 20, 1900, in Box 28, Wood MSS; Wood to Roosevelt, October 28, 1901, in Box 29/30, Wood MSS; *see also* Jessup, *Elihu Root*, 1:287–88. Congressional leaders shared these concerns. *See, e.g.*, Albert J. Beveridge, "Cuba and Congress," *North American Review* 172, no. 533 (April 1901), 546; Platt, "The Pacification of Cuba," 1468.

96. *See* Pérez, *The War of 1898*, 31–32. For these concerns among military officers, *see* Abrahamson, *America Arms*, 80–82.

97. Jessup, Interview with Root, January 11, 1930, in Box I:244/245, Jessup MSS; Jessup, Conversation with Root, October 28, 1935, in Box I:244/245, Jessup MSS.

98. Robert P. Porter, *Industrial Cuba* (New York: G. P. Putnam's Sons, 1899), 44; Roosevelt to Lodge, July 21, 1899, in Morison 2:1038; 32 Cong. Rec. 326–27 (1898); *see* Lodge to Ward, June 13, 1898, in Vol. 39, Letterbooks, Lodge MSS; Lodge to White, August 12, 1898, in Reel 13, Lodge MSS; Adams to Cameron, January 22, 1899, in Ford, *Letters of Henry Adams*, 2:206; *see also* Healy, *United States in Cuba*, 120–21; Foner, *The Spanish-Cuban-American War*, 2:514–19.

99. Joint Resolution for the Recognition of the Independence of the People of Cuba, 30 Stat. 738, 739 (April 20, 1898); "Spanish for Soldiers," *Indianapolis News*, May 12, 1898; *see* Platt to Wood, June 1, 1900, in Box 28, Wood MSS; *see also* Foner, *The Spanish-Cuban-American War*, 2:292–93.

100. *See* Foner, *The Spanish-Cuban-American War*, 2:531–32. Americans were also not keen to annex another predominantly non-white island. *See* Rubin Francis Weston, *Racism in U.S. Imperialism: The Influence of Racial Assumptions on American Foreign Policy, 1893–1946* (Columbia: University of South Carolina Press, 1972), 160.

101. *Nomination of Leonard Wood to Be Major-General: Hearings before the S. Comm. on Military Affairs*, 58th Cong. (1904), 868; Root to Bartlett, December 31, 1899, in Box 16/17, Bartlett MSS; *see* Adams to Cameron, February 26, 1899, in Ford, *Letters of Henry Adams*, 2:220; *see also* Healy, *United States in Cuba*, 71–72, 95–96, 120, 208–09.

102. Lodge to Wood, January 15, 1901, in Box 29/30, Wood MSS.

103. "Mr. Root Studying Cuba," *New York Times*, November 21, 1900.

104. For Root's views on suffrage, *see* Root to Dana, January 16, 1900, in Root MSS; Root to Wood, June 20, 1900, in Box 28, Wood MSS; *see also* Pérez, *Cuba Under the Platt Amendment*,

33–34; Lars Schoultz, *Beneath the United States: A History of U.S. Policy Toward Latin America* (Cambridge, MA: Harvard University Press, 2003), 145–48.

105. Root to Wood, February 9, 1901, in Box 29/30, Wood MSS; *see* Wood to Root, January 4, 1901, in Root MSS; Root to Hay, January 11, 1901, in Box 30, Wood MSS. For Root's claim to primary authorship of the resulting Platt Amendment, *see generally* Lejeune Cummins, "The Formulation of the 'Platt' Amendment," *The Americas* 23, no. 4 (April 1967), 370–89.

106. Root to Wood, February 9, 1901, in Box 29/30, Wood MSS; *see* Root to Hay, January 11, 1901, in Box 30, Wood MSS; Jessup, Interview with Root, November 19, 1929, in Box I:244, Jessup MSS.

107. Root to Wood, February 9, 1901, in Box 29/30, Wood MSS. This safeguard was originally devised by Republican senators during an early February meeting and then communicated to Root. *See* Chandler, Recollection of February 3, 1901 Meeting, in Louis A. Coolidge, *An Old-Fashioned Senator: Orville H. Platt of Connecticut* (New York: G. P. Putnam's Sons, 1910), 339–40; *see also* Healy, *United States in Cuba*, 156–57.

108. Root to Wood, February 9, 1901, in Box 29/30, Wood MSS; *see* Root to Hay, January 11, 1901, in Box 30, Wood MSS; Jessup, Interview with Root, November 19, 1929, in Box I:244, Jessup MSS; Jessup, Interview with Root, January 11, 1930, in Box I:244/245, Jessup MSS; Elihu Root, "External Policies in 1904," Address as Temporary Chairman of the Republican National Convention in Chicago, June 21, 1904, in *The Military and Colonial Policy of the United States: Addresses and Reports by Elihu Root*, ed. Robert Bacon and James Brown Scott (Cambridge, MA: Harvard University Press, 1916), 100; *see also* Healy, *US Expansionism*, 154. Of course, to give the right to intervene real bite, Root wanted the Cubans to also hand over land for American naval bases. *See* Root to Wood, June 20, 1900, in Box 28, Wood MSS.

109. *See* Carter-Blaine Treaty of 1889, art. III, in Carter to Blaine, April 11, 1889, in Notes, Hawaii, Roll 3, T160, RG59, NA.

110. Jessup, Interview with Root, November 19, 1929, in Box I:244, Jessup MSS; *see* Zimmermann, *First Great Triumph*, 377.

111. *See* Root to Shaw, February 23, 1901, in Box 29/30, Wood MSS; "At the White House," *Washington Evening Star*, June 1, 1901.

112. *See* Root to Wood, January 9, 1901, in Box 29/30, Wood MSS; Root to Shaw, February 23, 1901, in Box 29/30, Wood MSS. For a good summary of the back-and-forth between Root, Congress, and the Cuban Constitutional Convention, *see* Healy, *United States in Cuba*, 153–67; Jessup, *Elihu Root*, 1:311–12.

113. For accounts of the development of the Platt Amendment from the congressional side, *see* Coolidge, *An Old-Fashioned Senator*, 338–44; Leon Burr Richardson, *William E. Chandler, Republican* (New York: Dodd, Mead, 1940), 604–06.

114. An Act Making Appropriation for the Support of the Army for the Fiscal Year Ending June Thirtieth, Nineteen Hundred and Two, Pub. L. No. 56-803, 31 Stat. 895, 897–98 (March 2, 1901). Article IV of the Platt Amendment "ratified and validated" "all Acts of the United States in Cuba during its military occupancy thereof." Article V required Havana to continue implementing Wood's sanitation measures. Article VI left title of the Isle of Pines "to future adjustment by treaty" with the United States. Article VIII required Cuba's government, "by way of future assurance," to "embody the foregoing provisions in a permanent treaty with the United States."

115. Root to Wood, March 2, 1901, in Box 29/30, Wood MSS; 34 Cong. Rec. 3145 (1901); *see* Platt to Root, February 25, 1901, in Root MSS; Coolidge, *An Old-Fashioned Senator*, 341; Richardson, *William E. Chandler*, 606.

116. Wood to Root, April 2, 1901, in Box 29/30, Wood MSS; Wood to Root, March 23, 1901, in Box 29/30, Wood MSS; *see* Wood to Root, February 19, 1901, in Box 29/30, Wood MSS. For Cubans' public hostility to the draft Amendment, *see* Foner, *The Spanish-Cuban-American War*, 2:568–70.

117. Root to Wood, March 29, 1901, in Box 29/30, Wood MSS; *see* Wood to Root, March 23, 1901, in Box 29/30, Wood MSS; Root to Wood, April 2, 1901, in Box 29/30, Wood MSS.

118. Root to Wood, March 2, 1901, in Box 29/30, Wood MSS; Root to Wood, March 2, 1901, in Box 29/30, Wood MSS; *see* Root to Wood, March 20, 1901, in Box 29/30, Wood MSS.

119. Root to Hay, February 25, 1901, in Root MSS; *see* Wood to Root, February 24, 1901, in Box 29/30, Wood MSS.

120. *Report of the Committee Appointed to Confer with the Government of the United States, Giving an Account of the Result of Its Labors,* May 6, 1901, in Root MSS, 6–9, 12; Platt to Root, April 26, 1901, in Root MSS; *see Report of the Committee,* 5–6; Wood to Root, April 15, 1901, in Box 29/30, Wood MSS; *see also* Foner, *The Spanish-Cuban-American War,* 2:618.

121. Wood to Root, May 23, 1901, in Box 29/30, Wood MSS; *see* Wood to Root, May 26, 1901, in Box 29/30, Wood MSS; Root to Roosevelt, June 4, 1901, in Reel 15, Roosevelt MSS; *see also* Healy, *United States in Cuba,* 178.

122. Root to Wood, May 28, 1901, in Box 29/30, Wood MSS; *see* Root to Wood, May 31, 1901, in Box 29/30, Wood MSS; Root to Roosevelt, June 4, 1901, in Reel 15, Roosevelt MSS; "At the White House," *Washington Evening Star,* June 1, 1901.

123. *See* Healy, *United States in Cuba,* 178, 207. Four delegates did not vote. *See ibid.*

124. William G. Sumner, *The Conquest of the United States by Spain* (Boston: Dana Estes, 1899); *see* Ernest R. May, *From Imperialism to Isolationism 1898–1919* (New York: Macmillan, 1964), 10; Love, *Race under Empire,* 196–97.

125. For the first half of the explanation, *see* May, *From Imperialism to Isolationism,* 31–32.

126. Senator Platt, for example, expressly believed that only "two solutions" were available in Cuba—"one, the annexation of the island by the United States; the other, the establishment of an independent republic there in which the vital and just interests, both of Cuba and the United States, shall be defined and maintained." Like many others, he favored the latter. O. H. Platt, "The Solution of the Cuban Problem," *World's Work* 2 (May 1901), 730.

127. Root to Jessup, December 20, 1934, quoted in Jessup, *Elihu Root,* 1:314; Jessup, Interview with Root, November 19, 1929, in Box I:244, Jessup MSS.

128. Jessup, Interview with Root, January 11, 1930, in Box I:244/245, Jessup MSS; Root to Platt, May 9, 1901, in Box 179, Root MSS; 34 Cong. Rec. 3146 (1901); Platt, "The Solution of the Cuban Problem," 734; Wood to Roosevelt, October 28, 1901, in Box 29/30, Wood MSS; *see* Wood to Root, March 23, 1901, in Box 29/30, Wood MSS; Platt, "The Pacification of Cuba," 1467. For the administration's willingness to let Cuba draft its own constitution, *see* Healy, *United States in Cuba,* 151. Some historians cite Wood's remark as evidence of the United States's hidden domineering purpose. But that interpretation ignores the rest of the military governor's letter. Wood wanted the United States to reduce its tariff on Cuban goods. He argued that the United States had a moral obligation to do so because it had made it impossible for Cuba to form a special commercial relationship with any other power. Wood was certainly given to exuberant language—in the same letter, he referenced Cuba being "a practical dependency of the United States" and "absolutely in our hands"—but those flights of rhetoric were calculated to exaggerate the deep responsibility which Wood felt the United States owed Cuba. *See* Wood to Roosevelt, October 28, 1901, in Box 29/30, Wood MSS.

129. 34 Cong. Rec. 3151 (1901).

130. *See* 34 Cong. Rec. 3151–52 (1901).

Chapter 6: The Homicidal Corruptionists of Bogotá

1. Victor Hugo, *Les Misérables,* trans. Isabel F. Hapgood, vol. IV, *St. Denis,* bk. 10 (New York: Thomas Y. Crowell, 1887), 212.

2. *See* Thomas Schoonover, "Max Farrand's Memorandum on the U.S. Role in the Panamanian Revolution of 1903," *Diplomatic History* 12, no. 4 (Fall 1988), 504; *see also* Ovidio Diaz Espino, *How Wall Street Created a Nation: J. P. Morgan, Teddy Roosevelt, and the Panama Canal* (New York: Four Walls Eight Windows, 2001), 18–20; David McCullough, *The Path Between the Seas: The Creation of the Panama Canal 1870–1914* (New York: Simon and Schuster Paperbacks, 1977), 162, 276–78.

3. *See* Philippe Bunau-Varilla, *Panama: The Creation, Destruction, and Resurrection* (New York: McBride, Nast, 1914), 35; *see also* McCullough, *The Path,* 128–30, 162.

4. *See* Bunau-Varilla, *Panama,* 48; *see also* McCullough, *The Path,* 162, 171–74, 179–80.

5. *See* McCullough, *The Path*, 203–41.

6. *See* McCullough, *The Path*, 288–89.

7. *See* Bunau-Varilla, *Panama*, 281; Loomis to Roosevelt, January 5, 1904, in Reel 40, Roosevelt MSS; *see also* Dwight Carroll Miner, *The Fight for the Panama Route: The Story of the Spooner Act and the Hay-Herran Treaty* (New York: Octagon Books, 1966), 77.

8. Bunau-Varilla, *Panama*, 331. Bunau-Varilla's account of events is undoubtedly puffed up and self-centered, and in certain places misleading or even fabricated. For the most part, however, historians have judged his account to be mostly credible, if handled with caution. *See* Edmund Morris, *Theodore Rex* (London: HarperCollins, 2002), 666 n.275.

9. Bunau-Varilla, *Panama*, 332, 333.

10. Pablo Neruda, "United Fruit Co.," in *Canto General*, trans. Jack Schmitt (Berkeley: University of California Press, 1991), 179; *see* Gerstle Mack, *The Land Divided: A History of the Panama Canal and Other Isthmian Canal Projects* (New York: Alfred A. Knopf, 1944), 53–60; Lester D. Langley, *Struggle for the American Mediterranean: United States-European Rivalry in the Gulf-Caribbean, 1776–1904* (Athens: University of Georgia Press, 1976), 71–106.

11. *See* Mack, *The Land Divided*, 104–05, 246–49.

12. A General Treaty of Peace, Amity, Navigation, and Commerce Between the United States of America and the Republic of New Granada (Bidlack-Mallarino Treaty), art. 35 (December 12, 1846), in Miles P. DuVal, Jr., *Cadiz to Cathay: The Story of the Long Diplomatic Struggle for the Panama Canal* (Stanford, CA: Stanford University Press, 1947), app. A, 451–52; *see* Report by Manuel María Mallarino, Minister of Foreign Affairs of Colombia, Upon the Reasons that Make the Stipulations of the Treaty Proposed, Useful and Acceptable to the United States of America (December 10, 1846), in William R. Manning, ed., *Diplomatic Correspondence of the United States: Inter-American Affairs 1831–1860*, vol. 5, *Chile and Colombia* (Washington, DC: Carnegie Endowment for International Peace, 1935), 630–31; *see also* Langley, *Struggle*, 81–89. For an overview of the Bidlack-Mallarino Treaty, *see* Richard H. Collin, *Theodore Roosevelt's Caribbean: The Panama Canal, the Monroe Doctrine, and the Latin American Context* (Baton Rouge: Louisiana State University Press, 1990), 132–35.

13. *See* Gustave Anguizola, *Philippe Bunau-Varilla: The Man Behind the Panama Canal* (Chicago: Nelson-Hall, 1980), 8–9. Great Britain and the United States had also divided the Oregon Territory between themselves earlier that year. *See ibid.*

14. Convention Between the United States of America and Great Britain for Facilitating and Protecting the Construction of a Ship Canal Connecting the Atlantic and Pacific Oceans, art. I (Clayton-Bulwer Treaty) (April 19, 1850), in DuVal, *Cadiz to Cathay*, app. B, 455; *see* Walter LaFeber, *The Panama Canal: The Crisis in Historical Perspective* (New York: Oxford University Press, 1989), 9–10.

15. *See* "The Darien Canal and the Monroe Doctrine," *New York Herald*, July 3, 1879; *see also* Harold Sprout and Margaret Sprout, *The Rise of American Naval Power 1776–1918* (Princeton, NJ: Princeton University Press, 1944), 241, 250–51; Aroop Mukharji, "Sea Change: McKinley, Roosevelt, and the Expansion of U.S. Foreign Policy 1897–1909" (PhD diss., Harvard University, April 2020), 246. For details on the Panama railroad and its success, *see* McCullough, *The Path*, 35–36.

16. *See* David Healy, *Drive to Hegemony: The United States in the Caribbean 1898–1917* (Madison: University of Wisconsin Press, 1988), 27–28; Daniel H. Wicks, "Dress Rehearsal: United States Intervention on the Isthmus of Panama, 1885," *Pacific Historical Review* 49, no. 4 (November 1980), 584. For a history of the American interpretation and these landings, *see* Howard C. Hill, *Roosevelt and the Caribbean* (Chicago: University of Chicago Press, 1927), 41–46. Everyone who counts the number of revolutionary events comes up with a different number, although they are all uniformly high. *See* Roosevelt, Third Annual Message, December 7, 1903, in Richardson Supp. 15:6810–12; LaFeber, *Panama Canal*, 20; G. A. Mellander, *The United States in Panamanian Politics: The Intriguing Formative Years* (Danville, IL: Interstate Printers & Publishers, 1971), 10; Miner, *The Fight*, 168.

17. Hayes, Message to Senate, March 8, 1880, in Richardson 7:585–86; *see* Dexter Perkins, *The Monroe Doctrine: 1867–1907* (Gloucester, MA: Peter Smith, 1966), 64; Edward P. Crapol, *James G. Blaine: Architect of Empire* (Wilmington, DE: SR Books, 2000), 74–76; William

Whatley Pierson, Jr., "The Political Influences of an Interoceanic Canal, 1826–1926," *Hispanic American Historical Review* 6, no. 4 (November 1926), 217–22.

18. *See* Miner, *The Fight*, 24; McCullough, *The Path*, 203–41. For American opposition to a French rescue of de Lesseps's Compagnie, *see* DuVal, *Cadiz to Cathay*, 108–09; Joseph Smith, *Illusions of Conflict: Anglo-American Diplomacy Toward Latin America, 1865–1896* (Pittsburgh, PA: University of Pittsburgh Press, 1979), 113–14; Lars Schoultz, *Beneath the United States: A History of U.S. Policy Toward Latin America* (Cambridge, MA: Harvard University Press, 2003), 157.

19. *See* Sprout and Sprout, *Rise of American Naval Power*, 233–34, 263; McCullough, *The Path*, 254–55; Ivan Musicant, *Empire by Default: The Spanish-American War and the Dawn of the American Century* (New York: Henry Holt, 1998), 329–35.

20. 32 Cong. Rec. 180 (1898); *see* Alexander Missal, *Seaway to the Future: American Social Visions and the Construction of the Panama Canal* (Madison: University of Wisconsin Press, 2008), 28–29 & n.19; McCullough, *The Path*, 254–55; Sprout and Sprout, *Rise of American Naval Power*, 241, 250–51; Musicant, *Empire by Default*, 329–35. For a more skeptical view, *see* Mukharji, "Sea Change," 273–74. Mukharji is correct that key decision-makers like McKinley were already persuaded by the merits of a canal. But popular opinion still mattered in terms of moving the canal up the priority list (both in the Executive Branch and, more importantly, in Congress).

21. *See* Aaron L. Friedberg, *The Weary Titan: Britain and the Experience of Relative Decline, 1895–1905* (Princeton, NJ: Princeton University Press, 1988), 171–72; Kenneth Bourne, *Britain and the Balance of Power in North America 1815–1908* (Berkeley: University of California Press, 1967), 340–42, 346–50; Charles S. Campbell, Jr., *Anglo-American Understanding, 1898–1903* (Baltimore, MD: Johns Hopkins Press, 1957), 23–24, 120–23; McCullough, *The Path*, 259. For the overall British withdrawal from the hemisphere, *see* Samuel F. Wells, Jr., "British Strategic Withdrawal from the Western Hemisphere, 1904–1906," *Canadian Historical Review* 49, no. 4 (December 1968), 335–56.

22. Richard Harding Davis, "The Isthmus of Panama," *Harper's Weekly*, January 11, 1896, 34; "Extent of Opposition to the Canal Bill," *New York Times*, December 8, 1901; *see* Miner, *The Fight*, 29; McCullough, *The Path*, 261–65.

23. H. H. Kohlsaat, *From McKinley to Harding: Personal Recollections of Our Presidents* (New York: Charles Scribner's Sons, 1923), 101; *see* Edmund Morris, *The Rise of Theodore Roosevelt* (New York: Modern Library, 2001), 777–78.

24. Roosevelt to Lee, November 23, 1900, in Morison 2:1439–40; Roosevelt to Lodge, September 23, 1901, in Morison 3:150; *see* Morris, *The Rise*, 754–68.

25. *See* McCullough, *The Path*, 266–67. Roosevelt may have favored the Panama route even before these conversations. *See* Allan Nevins, *Henry White: Thirty Years of American Diplomacy* (New York: Harper and Brothers, 1930), 156.

26. An Act to Provide for the Construction of a Canal Connecting the Waters of the Atlantic and Pacific Oceans, Pub. L. No. 57-183, § 4, 32 Stat. 481, 482 (June 28, 1902); *see generally* Charles D. Ameringer, "The Panama Canal Lobby of Philippe Bunau-Varilla and William Nelson Cromwell," *American Historical Review* 68, no. 2 (January 1963), 346–63; McCullough, *The Path*, 305–28. Senator Marcus Alonzo Hanna of Ohio, who more than any other senator helped swing the vote to Panama, finished his two-day-long peroration on the subject by raising the concern that if the United States built a Nicaraguan canal, it risked seeing a great-power rival pick up the spade and finish the work at Panama. *See* 35 Cong. Rec. 6387 (1902).

27. *See* Miner, *The Fight*, 191.

28. *See* Miner, *The Fight*, 202–04, 229–30; Noel Maurer and Carlos Yu, *The Big Ditch: How America Took, Built, Ran, and Ultimately Gave Away the Panama Canal* (Princeton, NJ: Princeton University Press, 2011), 76–77; Mack, *The Land Divided*, 436–37. For the contrary view that Marroquín did not actually want the United States to build a canal in Colombia at all, *see* Collin, *Theodore Roosevelt's Caribbean*, 311–15.

29. Roosevelt to Thayer, July 2, 1915, in Morison 8:945; *see* McCullough, *The Path*, 329–32; Alfred L. P. Dennis, *Adventures in American Diplomacy 1896–1906* (New York: E. P. Dutton, 1928), 314; Miner, *The Fight*, 202–04, 229–30; Mack, *The Land Divided*, 436–37.

30. *See* McCullough, *The Path*, 336–38; Miner, *The Fight*, 133–36, 210–16.

31. "Says Panama Crisis Was Peril to Peace," *New York Times*, December 16, 1903; *see* DuVal, *Cadiz to Cathay*, 142; McCullough, *The Path*, 336–38. Loomis prepared this speech ahead of time, presumably with Roosevelt's approval. *See* "Mr. Loomis' Speech," letter to the editor, *New York Times*, December 20, 1903. If not, Roosevelt gave his approval soon afterward, telling the assistant secretary that he had "brought out the points in excellent shape." Roosevelt to Loomis, December 17, 1903, in Reel 332, Roosevelt MSS; *see* "President Thanked Loomis," *New York Times*, December 20, 1903. Roosevelt also raised this concern in his autobiography, writing: "If we had sat supine, ... France would have interfered to protect the company, and we should then have had on the Isthmus, not the company, but France; and the gravest international complications might have ensued." *Theodore Roosevelt: An Autobiography* (New York: Charles Scribner's Sons, 1922), 523–24. Root made a similar point as well. *See* Root, "The Ethics of the Panama Question," Address Before the Union League Club of Chicago, February 22, 1904, in Elihu Root, *Addresses on International Subjects*, ed. Robert Bacon and James Brown Scott (Cambridge, MA: Harvard University Press, 1916), 189. Loomis, Roosevelt, and Root were referring to the threat of total expropriation of the Compagnie Nouvelle's assets, rather than a partial payoff, but the fundamental logic of the problem they saw was the same regardless of its scale and timing. For a more skeptical view that emphasizes the lack of any concrete intelligence and France's stated disinterest in the Compagnie's fate, *see* Thomas D. Schoonover, *The United States in Central America, 1860–1911: Episodes of Social Imperialism and Imperial Rivalry in the World System* (Durham, NC: Duke University Press, 1991), 109–10. Schoonover overlooks, however, the considerable evidence of nonpublic concerns about foreign intervention discussed in the next endnote.

32. *See* Theodore Roosevelt, *Fear God and Take Your Own Part* (New York: George H. Doran, 1916), 324; *see also* Miner, *The Fight*, 192; DuVal, *Cadiz to Cathay*, 221; Mack, *The Land Divided*, 452; Ivan Musicant, *The Banana Wars: A History of United States Military Intervention in Latin America from the Spanish-American War to the Invasion of Panama* (New York: Macmillan, 1990), 116; Henry J. Hendrix, *Theodore Roosevelt's Naval Diplomacy: The U.S. Navy and the Birth of the American Century* (Annapolis, MD: Naval Institute Press, 2009), 57, 59. For the Naval College War Game, *see* Richard W. Turk, "The United States Navy and the 'Taking' of Panama, 1901–1903," *Military Affairs* 38, no. 3 (October 1974), 92. Subsequently, the U.S. Navy took steps to survey the canal route and the military approaches to it; it also asked the State Department to begin discussions with Colombia for either American naval bases or a non-alienation agreement. *Ibid.*; *see* Dewey to Moody, General Board No. 284, October 7, 1902, attached to Moody to Hay, November 21, 1902, in Misc. Letters, Roll 1154, M179, RG59, NA.

33. Convention Between the United States of America and the Republic of Colombia (Hay-Herrán Treaty), art. VI, January 22, 1903, in DuVal, *Cadiz to Cathay*, app. D, 465; *see ibid.*, arts. II, III, XXV; *see* McCullough, *The Path*, 332. For the reasoning behind the non-alienation provision, *see* Dewey to Moody, General Board No. 284, October 7, 1902, attached to Moody to Hay, November 21, 1902, in Misc. Letters, Roll 1154, M179, RG59, NA; *see also* "Warning to Germany in Canal Treaty?," *New York Herald*, January 31, 1903.

34. Roosevelt to Hay, March 12, 1903, in Morison 3:445; *see* DuVal, *Cadiz to Cathay*, 208–12.

35. Beaupré to Hay, March 30, 1903, in FRUS 1903, 133; Beaupré to Hay, April 15, 1903, in FRUS 1903, 134; Beaupré to Hay, May 4, 1903, in FRUS 1903, 142.

36. Beaupré to Hay, July 21, 1903, in FRUS 1903, 166; Beaupré to Hay, June 27, 1903, in FRUS 1903, 155; *see* Hay to Beaupré, June 2, 1903, in FRUS 1903, 146; "New Republic May Arise to Grant Canal," *New York World*, June 14, 1903; *see also* Hill, *Roosevelt and the Caribbean*, 49–50. For concerns about German and other foreign influence, *see* "New Republic May Arise to Grant Canal," *New York World*, June 14, 1903; *see also* Miner, *The Fight*, 312–14.

37. Hay to Beaupré, June 9, 1903, in FRUS 1903, 146; *see* "New Republic May Arise to Grant Canal," *New York World*, June 14, 1903; Roosevelt to Hay, July 14, 1903, in Reel 331, Roosevelt MSS; *see also* McCullough, *The Path*, 334–39.

38. *See* McCullough, *The Path*, 339; Collin, *Theodore Roosevelt's Caribbean*, 233.

39. Rudyard Kipling, *Something of Myself: For My Friends Known and Unknown* (London, Macmillan, 1937), 124; Roosevelt to Kermit Roosevelt, November 4, 1903, in Morison 3:644; Roosevelt to Hay, July 14, 1903, in Reel 331, Roosevelt MSS; Roosevelt to Hanna, October 5,

1903, in Morison 3:625; Roosevelt to Hay, August 17, 1903, in Reel 331, Roosevelt MSS; Roosevelt to Hay, August 19, 1903, in Morison 3:566.

40. Hay to Roosevelt, August 16, 1903, in Reel 36, Roosevelt MSS; Roosevelt to Shaw, October 10, 1903, in Morison 3:628; *see* Roosevelt to Hay, August 19, 1903, in Morison 3:566; "New Republic May Arise to Grant Canal," *New York World*, June 14, 1903; *see also* Turk, "The United States Navy," 95.

41. John Bassett Moore, Memorandum, August 2, 1903, in Miner, *The Fight*, app. D, 431; Roosevelt to Hay, September 15, 1903, in Morison 3:599; Roosevelt to Shaw, October 7, 1903, in Morison 3:626; *see* Roosevelt to Hay, August 19, 1903, in Morison 3:566; Roosevelt to Hanna, October 5, 1903, in Morison 3:625.

42. Roosevelt to Shaw, October 10, 1903, in Morison 3:628; *see* Roosevelt to Schurman, September 10, 1903, in Morison 3:595–96; Adee to Hay, August 18, 1903, in Reel 6, Hay MSS.

43. Hay to Roosevelt, September 13, 1903, in Reel 37, Roosevelt MSS; *see* Hay to Adee, September 20, 1903, in William Roscoe Thayer, *The Life and Letters of John Hay* (Boston: Houghton Mifflin, 1915), 2:312.

44. Roosevelt to Hay, September 15, 1903, in Morison 3:599; Roosevelt to Spring Rice, November 9, 1903, in Morison 3:651; *see* Roosevelt to Shaw, October 7, 1903, in Morison 3:625–26; *see also* Healy, *Drive to Hegemony*, 84; DuVal, *Cadiz to Cathay*, 232–33, 240–41, 430–31.

45. Adee to Hay, August 20, 1903, in Reel 6, Hay MSS; *see* Theodore Roosevelt, "Columbia: The Proposed Message to Congress," in Roosevelt, *Autobiography*, 530.

46. *See The Story of Panama: Hearings on the Rainey Resolution Before the Comm. on Foreign Affairs*, 62nd Cong. 357, 359 (1913); *see also* McCullough, *The Path*, 341–42.

47. *Story of Panama*, 349; *see ibid.*, 357, 359; McCullough, *The Path*, 341–42.

48. *See Story of Panama*, 360–62; Mellander, *Panamanian Politics*, 13–14; McCullough, *The Path*, 345–47.

49. *Story of Panama*, 365; *see* Mack, *The Land Divided*, 458.

50. Bigelow, Diary Entry, September 1903, in Margaret Clapp, *Forgotten First Citizen: John Bigelow* (Boston: Little, Brown, 1947), 311; *see* Bunau-Varilla, *Panama*, 288–89.

51. *See* Bunau-Varilla, *Panama*, 289–90, 320.

52. *See* Bunau-Varilla, *Panama*, 292.

53. *See* Bunau-Varilla, *Panama*, 292–93.

54. Roosevelt to Moore, January 6, 1904, in Morison 3:691; Bunau-Varilla, *Panama*, 311–12. For the Americans' recollections of this meeting, *see* Loomis to Roosevelt, January 5, 1904, in Reel 40, Roosevelt MSS; Roosevelt to Bigelow, January 6, 1904, in Morison 3:689; Roosevelt to Lodge, January 6, 1904, in Morison 3:690; Roosevelt to Thayer, March 1, 1917, in Reel 416, Roosevelt MSS. For Roosevelt's later claims that Bunau-Varilla did not tell him any revolutionary plans, *see* Roosevelt to Shaw, November 6, 1903, in Morison 3:649; Roosevelt to Schurman, November 12, 1903, in Morison 3:651; Roosevelt to Abbott, November 12, 1903, in Reel 332, Roosevelt MSS; Roosevelt, Message to Congress, January 4, 1904, in Richardson Supp. 15:6845.

John Bigelow recorded in his diary that Bunau-Varilla had gone much further and actually informed Roosevelt of his revolutionary plans. *See* Bigelow, Diary Entry, October 16, 1903, in Clapp, *Forgotten First Citizen*, 313; *see also* McCullough, *The Path*, 352. Bigelow, however, was not present at the meeting, and Bunau-Varilla later said that Bigelow had misunderstood his summary of it. *See* Clapp, *Forgotten First Citizen*, 312; *see also* Morris, *Theodore Rex*, 665 n.275.

55. Loomis to Roosevelt, January 5, 1904, in Reel 40, Roosevelt MSS; *see* Schoonover, "Max Farrand's Memorandum," 505.

56. Schoonover, "Max Farrand's Memorandum," 505 n.5; *see* Bunau-Varilla, *Panama*, 312; Roosevelt to Thayer, March 1, 1917, in Reel 416, Roosevelt MSS.

57. *See* Bunau-Varilla, *Panama*, 312–20.

58. *See* Collin, *Theodore Roosevelt's Caribbean*, 254.

59. Bunau-Varilla, *Panama*, 321; *see ibid.*, 320–23.

60. Bunau-Varilla, *Panama*, 321; *see* Mellander, *Panamanian Politics*, 18–19.

61. Bunau-Varilla, *Panama*, 327.

62. Bunau-Varilla, *Panama*, 328.

63. *See* Bunau-Varilla, *Panama*, 328–29.

64. *See* McCullough, *The Path*, 361–62; Mellander, *Panamanian Politics*, 19–20.

65. *See* McCullough, *The Path*, 363.

66. Bunau-Varilla, *Panama*, 329–30. Bunau-Varilla may have developed this plan based on an earlier "assurance" from Hay that "if safety of the R.R. [railroad] is threatened a sufficient naval force will be at both extremities of the RR to protect it." Bigelow, Diary Entry, October 19, 1903, in Clapp, *Forgotten First Citizen*, 313.

67. Bunau-Varilla, *Panama*, 331. Loomis also later reported that he had not expressly confirmed to Bunau-Varilla that the United States would be sending forces. *See* Loomis to Roosevelt, January 5, 1904, in Reel 40, Roosevelt MSS. Still, it was not a hard guess to make, as Hay had previously told Bunau-Varilla that "orders have been given to naval forces on the Pacific to sail towards the Isthmus." Bunau-Varilla, *Panama*, 318.

68. *See* Bunau-Varilla, *Panama*, 331.

69. Bunau-Varilla, *Panama*, 331. Later that day, Bunau-Varilla sent a second telegram informing his co-conspirators that he expected additional U.S. warships to arrive in Panama City four days later. *See* Bunau-Varilla, *Panama*, 332. He was far less accurate in this second estimate; the first U.S. warship did not arrive off Panama City until November 7. *See* DuVal, *Cadiz to Cathay*, 356.

70. "Nashville Off—For Colombia?," *New York Times*, November 1, 1903; *see* McCullough, *The Path*, 360.

71. *See* McCullough, *The Path*, 362, 364–65; Mukharji, "Sea Change," 255. For the *Nashville's* orders and the thinking behind them, *see* Darling to U.S.S. Nashville, November 2, 1903, in Richardson Supp. 15:6765–66; Roosevelt to Kermit Roosevelt, November 4, 1903, in Morison 3:644.

72. *See Story of Panama*, 387; *see also* Mellander, *Panamanian Politics*, 25.

73. *See Story of Panama*, 388.

74. *See Story of Panama*, 388.

75. *See Story of Panama*, 393–94; *see also* McCullough, *The Path*, 370–71.

76. *Story of Panama*, 446, 447; *see ibid.*, 446–47.

77. *See Story of Panama*, 440–42.

78. *See Story of Panama*, 441–42.

79. *See* Log Book of the U.S.S. *Nashville*, November 4, 1903, in *Story of Panama*, 430, 430; *Story of Panama*, 442–43.

80. *Story of Panama*, 443; *see ibid.*, 443–44.

81. *See Story of Panama*, 454–58.

82. *See* Ehrman to Hay, November 6, 1903, in Richardson Supp. 15:6750; Hay to Ehrman, November 6, 1903, in Richardson Supp. 15:6750; *see also* Maurer and Yu, *The Big Ditch*, 84; William Reynolds Braisted, *The United States Navy in the Pacific, 1897–1909* (Austin: University of Texas Press, 1958), 148.

83. Bidlack-Mallarino Treaty, art. 35, in DuVal, app. A, 451–52. If Bogotá had attempted to force the issue, Roosevelt planned to not simply repulse the attack but actually invade Colombia and occupy Cartagena, among other cities. *See* Hendrix, *Theodore Roosevelt's Naval Diplomacy*, 72–79. For the total displacement of the ten ships, *see Annual Reports of the Navy Department for the Year 1901* (Washington, DC: Government Printing Office, 1901), 2:672–79, 961.

84. *See* Schoonover, "Max Farrand's Memorandum," 504; *see also* Anguizola, *Philippe Bunau-Varilla*, 141–42.

85. *See* Bunau-Varilla, *Panama*, 357–58, 367.

86. Bunau-Varilla to Hay, November 17, 1903, in Bunau-Varilla, *Panama*, 370, 370; *see* Bunau-Varilla, *Panama*, 368–69. For Hay's substantial role in the revisions, *see generally* John Major, "Who Wrote the Hay–Bunau-Varilla Convention?," *Diplomatic History* 8, no. 2 (Spring 1984), 115–23; John Major, *Prize Possession: The United States and the Panama Canal, 1903–1979* (Cambridge, UK: Cambridge University Press, 1993), 43–49.

87. *See* Bunau-Varilla, *Panama*, 372.

88. Jorge E. Boyd, *Refutation of Bunau-Varilla's Book: Open Letter of Dr. George E. Boyd to President Porras* (Panama: 1913), 3.

89. Bunau-Varilla, *Panama*, 378.

90. *See* Bunau-Varilla, *Panama*, 378; Boyd, *Refutation*, 3; *see also* McCullough, *The Path*, 395.

91. Bunau-Varilla, *Panama*, 381; Convention Between the United States of America and the Republic of Panama (Hay–Bunau-Varilla Treaty), art. XXIII, November 18, 1903, in DuVal, *Cadiz to Cathay*, app. E, 485; *see* Hay–Bunau-Varilla Treaty, arts. I, II, III, XIV.

92. Hay to Spooner, January 20, 1904, in Reel 4, Hay MSS; *see* Hay to Cullom, January 20, 1904, in Reel 4, Hay MSS.

93. Bunau-Varilla, *Panama*, 368. Bunau-Varilla and Hay accomplished their objective by combing through the congressional debates on the earlier Hay-Herrán Treaty, noting every criticism made, and addressing as many of those criticisms as possible in the new treaty. *See* Major, "Who Wrote the Hay–Bunau-Varilla Convention?," 117; Richard H. Collin, "Symbiosis Versus Hegemony: New Directions in the Foreign Relations Historiography of Theodore Roosevelt and William Howard Taft," *Diplomatic History* 19, no. 3 (Summer 1995), 478.

94. 38 Cong. Rec. 2133 (1904); *see* McCullough, *The Path*, 397.

95. *See* Bunau-Varilla, *Panama*, 383–85.

96. *See* Mellander, *Panamanian Politics*, 42–43.

97. *See* Mellander, *Panamanian Politics*, 42–43.

98. "Elephants to Uplift Touched Upon by Former President in Address in Outdoor Theatre," *San Francisco Examiner*, March 24, 1911; *see* McCullough, *The Path*, 383–84. For a slightly different account of his remarks, *see* "Roosevelt Boasts of Canal," *New York Times*, March 24, 1911. For the debate about what, exactly, Roosevelt said, *see* James F. Vivian, "The 'Taking' of the Panama Canal Zone: Myth and Reality," *Diplomatic History* 4, no. 1 (Winter 1980), 95–100. Roosevelt may have misspoken or been misquoted: in his prepared remarks, Roosevelt wrote that he "took a trip to the Isthmus" rather than "took the isthmus." *See ibid.* Whether the fault lay with him or the press, however, the more aggressive version of the statement seized the public's attention.

99. Roosevelt, *Autobiography*, 512; Theodore Roosevelt, "How the United States Acquired the Right to Dig the Panama Canal," *The Outlook*, October 7, 1911, 315; 38 Cong. Rec. 801 (1904); "The Panama Dishonor," *The Nation*, November 12, 1903, 375; Olney to Peter B. Olney, November 11, 1903, in Reel 54, Olney MSS. For a selection of public opinion in the immediate wake of the affair, *see Public Opinion*, November 19, 1903, 644–45.

100. *See Public Opinion*, November 19, 1903, 643; *see also* John M. Thompson, *Great Power Rising: Theodore Roosevelt and the Politics of U.S. Foreign Policy* (Oxford: Oxford University Press, 2019), 59–70, 74–76; LaFeber, *Panama Canal*, 32; Berkeley E. Tompkins, *Anti-Imperialism in the United States: The Great Debate, 1890–1920* (Philadelphia: University of Pennsylvania Press, 1970), 260–61.

101. "Canalimony," *Post-Intelligencer*, n.d., in *The American Review of Reviews* 49, no. 5 (May 1914), 556; *see* Thomas A. Bailey, *A Diplomatic History of the American People* (Englewood Cliffs, NJ: Prentice-Hall, 1980), 497.

102. Schoonover, "Max Farrand's Memorandum," 505–06. For historians' near-universal criticism of Roosevelt's course, *see* Collin, "Symbiosis Versus Hegemony," 477. For defenses of Roosevelt's actions, *see* Frederick W. Marks, III, *Velvet on Iron: The Diplomacy of Theodore Roosevelt* (Lincoln: University of Nebraska Press, 1979), 89–105; Robert A. Friedlander, "A Reassessment of Roosevelt's Role in the Panamanian Revolution of 1903," *Western Political Quarterly* 14, no. 2 (June 1961), 535–43; Collin, *Theodore Roosevelt's Caribbean*, 306–38.

103. For a contrary view, *see* Friedlander, "A Reassessment."

104. For weak attempts by Roosevelt to claim otherwise, *see* Roosevelt to Cannon, September 12, 1904, in Morison 4:922; Roosevelt, "How the United States Acquired," 316.

Critics have long debated the extent to which Roosevelt incited revolution in Panama. His administration was clearly more involved than he let on publicly; Bunau-Varilla was able to predict the administration's every move with uncanny accuracy. Of course, it's true that, as Roosevelt argued, Bunau-Varilla "would have been a very dull man had he been unable to make such guess[es]" about the administration's conduct. Roosevelt to Bigelow, January 6, 1904, in Morison 3:689. Bunau-Varilla was many things, but dull was not one of them, and it did not take a self-proclaimed French genius to see that the president was hopping mad at the Colombians and eager to get moving on a Panama canal. Still, some of Bunau-Varilla's moves do smack of insider information. Later in life, Roosevelt acknowledged that Hay might have leaked information about naval movements to the Frenchman, though the president continued to deny having coordinated with Bunau-Varilla's revolutionary plans. *See* Roosevelt to Thayer, July 2, 1915, in Morison 8:944. Regardless of Roosevelt's particular involvement in Bunau-Varilla's specific conspiracy, it is likely that events would have turned out similarly even if he had never met Bunau-Varilla. Roosevelt correctly observed that "there were a dozen different trains of powder laid" on the isthmus. *Ibid.* One was sure to go off sooner rather than later regardless of whether the president proactively lit the match or merely, as he claimed, "ceased to stamp out the ... fuses that were already burning." Roosevelt, *Autobiography*, 525.

105. *See* McCullough, *The Path*, 400–01.

106. James Bryce, *South America: Observations and Impressions* (Detroit: Macmillan, 1912), 36; *see* McCullough, *The Path*, 11, 400, 610.

Chapter 7: An International Police Power

1. *See* "Landings of Marines at La Guayra Begun," *New York Times*, December 11, 1902; "Venezuelan Ships Sunk," *London Times*, December 12, 1902; *see also* Wayne Lee Guthrie, "The Anglo-German Intervention in Venezuela, 1902–03" (PhD diss., University of California, San Diego, 1983), 123.

2. *See* Haggard to the Marquess of Lansdowne, December 10, 1902, in Richard W. Brant and Willoughby Maycock, eds., *British and Foreign State Papers 1901–1902* (London: Harrison and Sons, 1905), 95:1110; "The Captured Fleet," *New York Times*, December 14, 1902; *see also* Guthrie, "Anglo-German Intervention," 121–22.

3. "Venezuelan Ships Sunk," *London Times*, December 12, 1902; *see* "President Castro's Appeal," *New York Times*, December 11, 1902; *see also* Guthrie, "Anglo-German Intervention," 122–23.

4. Quoted in Andrew Graham-Yooll, *Imperial Skirmishes: War and Gunboat Diplomacy in Latin America* (Oxford: Signal Books, 2002), 153; *see* "President Castro's Appeal," *New York Times*, December 11, 1902; *see also* Guthrie, "Anglo-German Intervention," 122–23.

5. *See* Haggard to the Marquess of Lansdowne, December 10, 1902, in Brant and Maycock, *British and Foreign State Papers*, 95: 1110; "The Captured Fleet," *New York Times*, December 14, 1902; *see also* Guthrie, "Anglo-German Intervention," 123.

6. Roosevelt to Meyer, April 12, 1901, in Morison 3:52; *see* Roosevelt to Oliver, July 22, 1915, in Morison 8:956; *see also* Aaron L. Friedberg, *The Weary Titan: Britain and the Experience of Relative Decline, 1895–1905* (Princeton, NJ: Princeton University Press, 1988), 162–65, 67, 169–73, 184–90, 198; Kori Schake, *Safe Passage: The Transition from British to American Hegemony* (Cambridge, MA: Harvard University Press, 2017), 163–64; Kenneth Bourne, *Britain and the Balance of Power in North America 1815–1908* (Berkeley: University of California Press, 1967), 350–51.

7. *The Education of Henry Adams: An Autobiography* (Boston: Houghton Mifflin, 1918), 363.

8. *See* Holger H. Herwig, *Politics of Frustration: The United States in German Naval Planning, 1889–1941* (Boston: Little, Brown, 1976), 13; Nancy Mitchell, *The Danger of Dreams: German and American Imperialism in Latin America* (Chapel Hill: University of North Carolina Press, 1999), 10–21.

9. *See* Mitchell, *Danger of Dreams*, 23–24; Edmund Morris, *Theodore Rex* (London: Harper-Collins, 2002), 179.

10. *See* George C. Herring, *From Colony to Superpower: U.S. Foreign Relations Since 1776* (Oxford: Oxford University Press, 2008), 338–39; Morris, *Theodore Rex*, 179. "Kiauchau" was one of many anglicized terms for the area around Jiaozhou Bay in northern China.

11. Holleben to Bülow, February 12, 1900, quoted in Herwig, *Politics of Frustration*, 68; Bülow to Wilhelm II, February 24, 1900, quoted in Herwig, *Politics of Frustration*, 68; Holleben to Bülow, February 9, 1902, quoted in Herwig, *Politics of Frustration*, 69; Holstein to Rath, January 2, 1908, quoted in Alfred Vagts, *Deutschland und die Vereinigten Staaten in der Weltpolitik* (New York: Macmillan, 1935), 2:1475; *see* Herwig, *Politics of Frustration*, 68–69; Holger H.

Herwig, *Germany's Vision of Empire in Venezuela 1871–1914* (Princeton, NJ: Princeton University Press, 1986), 191–92. For Operations Plan III and its explicit challenge to the Monroe Doctrine, *see* Donald A. Yerxa, *Admirals and Empire: The United States Navy and the Caribbean, 1898–1945* (Columbia: University of South Carolina Press, 1991), 13–14; Herwig, *Politics of Frustration*, 85–90; John A. S. Grenville and George Berkeley Young, *Politics, Strategy, and American Diplomacy: Studies in Foreign Policy, 1873–1917* (New Haven, CT: Yale University Press, 1969), 305–07.

12. "Assail Monroe Doctrine," *New York Times*, March 4, 1903; Wolf von Schierbrand, *Germany: The Welding of a World Power* (New York: Doubleday, Page, 1907), 284; Bülow, Notes, November 24, 1988, quoted in Herwig, *Politics of Frustration*, 39; Baron von Lüttwitz, "German Naval Policy and Strategy," *Journal of the Royal United Service Institution* 41, no. 229 (March 1897), 328; *see* Guthrie, "Anglo-German Intervention," 19; *see generally* Herwig, *Germany's Vision*, 175–208.

For Germany's interest in naval bases in the region, *see* Herwig, *Politics of Frustration*, 67–76; Yerxa, *Admirals and Empire*, 10–13; Serge Ricard, "Monroe Revisited: The Roosevelt Doctrine, 1901–1909," in *Impressions of a Gilded Age: The American Fin de Siecle*, ed. Marc Chenetier and Rob Kroes (Amsterdam: Amerika Instituut, 1983), 237; *see generally* Herwig, *Germany's Vision*, 141–74.

13. *See* Frederick W. Marks, III, *Velvet on Iron: The Diplomacy of Theodore Roosevelt* (Lincoln: University of Nebraska Press, 1979), 6–7; Herwig, *Germany's Vision*, 110–40; Richard D. Challener, *Admirals, Generals, and American Foreign Policy 1898–1914* (Princeton, NJ: Princeton University Press, 1979), 111–13; Barbara W. Tuchman, *The Zimmermann Telegram* (New York: Ballantine, 1985), 27–28; Friedrich Katz, *The Secret War in Mexico: Europe, the United States and the Mexican Revolution* (Chicago: University of Chicago Press, 1981), 63; Ernest R. May, *Imperial Democracy: The Emergence of America as a Great Power* (New York: Harper Torchbooks, 1973), 128. For the expectations of the German political and military class, *see* Herwig, *Politics of Frustration*, 13–39, 86–87. For the best assessment of Germany's motivations during this time period, *see generally* Herwig, *Germany's Vision*.

14. "Venezuela Situation," *Army and Navy Journal*, January 24, 1903, 503; Dewey to Bonaparte, September 28, 1906, quoted in Challener, *Admirals, Generals, and American Foreign Policy*, 28; *see* Asa Walker, "Notes on Cuban Ports," *Proceedings of the United States Naval Institute* 26, no. 2 (June 1900), 339.

15. Root, Speech at Grant Monument Association Dinner, April 27, 1900, in "Standard Oil Plot Foreshadowed War," *New York Times*, May 1, 1900; Hay to Lodge, July 27, 1898, quoted in Schake, *Safe Passage*, 181. Senator Lodge called two weeks after Root's speech for greater naval preparations against that European power "whose navy is just now receiving such a rapid increase." "I am not conjuring up imaginary dangers," he told the Senate. "I think that they exist and are very real." 33 Cong. Rec. 5403 (1900); *see* Lodge to Roosevelt, June 10, 1905, in *Selections from the Correspondence of Theodore Roosevelt and Henry Cabot Lodge 1884–1918* (New York: Charles Scribner's, 1925), 2:135–36.

16. Roosevelt to Lodge, June 19, 1901, in Morison 3:98; Roosevelt to Lodge, March 27, 1901, in Morison 3:32; Roosevelt to Meyer, April 12, 1901, in Morison 3:52; *see* Roosevelt to Moore, February 5, 1898, in Morison 1:768–69; Roosevelt to Spring Rice, August 13, 1897, in Morison 1:644–45; Roosevelt to Spring Rice, April 14, 1889, in Morison 1:156–57; Roosevelt to Mahan, May 3, 1897, in Morison 1:607–08; Roosevelt to McCalla, August 3, 1897, in Morison 1:636; Roosevelt to Kimball, December 17, 1897, in Morison 1:743; Roosevelt to Moore, February 9, 1898, in Morison 1:771–72; Roosevelt to Strachey, January 27, 1900, in Morison 2:1145; Roosevelt to Cowles, March 2, 1900, in Morison 2:1208; Roosevelt to Spring Rice, July 3, 1901, in Morison 3:109; Roosevelt, "National Duties," Address at Minnesota State Fair, September 2, 1901, in Theodore Roosevelt, *The Strenuous Life: Essays and Addresses* (New York: Century, 1905), 290.

For Roosevelt's liking of and connection to Germany, *see* Roosevelt to Speck von Sternburg, March 6, 1902, in Morison 3:239; *see also* Morris, *Theodore Rex*, 178. For Roosevelt's toleration of—even enthusiasm for—German commercial influence and its stabilizing effects, *see* Richard H. Collin, *Theodore Roosevelt's Caribbean: The Panama Canal, the Monroe Doctrine, and the Latin*

American Context (Baton Rouge: Louisiana State University Press, 1990), 121; Howard K. Beale, *Theodore Roosevelt and the Rise of America to World Power* (Baltimore, MD: Johns Hopkins University Press, 1984), 392–93. German reports suggest that Roosevelt may have even suggested he would not oppose a German-speaking independent state (though not colony) in Brazil, *see ibid.*, though it is nearly impossible to take such a statement at face value, as it is flatly inconsistent with the president's frequent and vehement concern about German political expansion into the hemisphere.

17. *See* Sigsbee, Memorandum of Information, Office of Naval Intelligence, March 22, 1902, in Reel 25, Roosevelt MSS; *see* Ronald Spector, "Roosevelt, the Navy, and the Venezuelan Controversy, 1902–1903," *American Neptune* 32, no. 4 (October 1972), 257–63; Morris, *Theodore Rex*, 180; Mitchell, *Danger of Dreams*, 43–46. For American awareness of the limited restraining effects of the European balance of power, *see, e.g.*, Lodge to Roosevelt, March 30, 1901, in *Selections*, 1:487; Roosevelt to Spring Rice, August 13, 1897, in Morison 1:645; *see also* James L. Abrahamson, *America Arms for a New Century: The Making of a Great Military Power* (New York: Free Press, 1981), 51–54. Notably, Operations Plan III assumed a situation in Europe that allowed Germany to go to war with the United States without having to worry about challenges on the continent. *See* Yerxa, *Admirals and Empire*, 13.

For American concerns about the structural forces underlying German expansion, *see, e.g.*, Lodge to Roosevelt, March 30, 1901, in *Selections*, 1:487; *see also* Challener, *Admirals, Generals, and American Foreign Policy*, 16–17; Beale, *Rise of America to World Power*, 392. German analysts often agreed with their American counterparts about the existence of a historical riptide pulling them into the world. *See, e.g.*, Ian L. D. Forbes, "German Informal Imperialism in South America Before 1914," *Economic History Review* 31, no. 3 (August 1978), 384–85. Many saw the same trends pulling the United States into conflict with them. *See, e.g.*, Herwig, *Politics of Frustration*, 18–24.

18. *See Army and Navy Journal*, March 21, 1903, 703; *see also* George T. Davis, *A Navy Second to None: The Development of Modern American Naval Policy* (New York: Harcourt, Brace, 1940), 124.

19. Roosevelt to Speck von Sternburg, July 12, 1901, in Morison 3:116; *see* David Healy, *Drive to Hegemony: The United States in the Caribbean 1898–1917* (Madison: University of Wisconsin Press, 1988), 59–61.

20. Roosevelt to Hay, April 2, 1905, in Morison 4:1156; *London Daily News*, December 11, 1902, quoted in Mitchell, *Danger of Dreams*, 89; *see* Dana G. Munro, *Intervention and Dollar Diplomacy in the Caribbean 1900–1921* (Princeton, NJ: Princeton University Press, 1964), 66–69; Herwig, *Germany's Vision*, 81, 86–90. For an account of foreign claims against Venezuela, *see* P. F. Fenton, "Diplomatic Relations of the United States and Venezuela, 1880–1915," *Hispanic American Historical Review* 8, no. 3 (August 1928), 332–43.

21. *See* Dexter Perkins, *The Monroe Doctrine: 1867–1907* (Gloucester, MA: Peter Smith, 1966), 324; Edmund Morris, "'A Few Pregnant Days': Theodore Roosevelt and the Venezuelan Crisis of 1902," *Theodore Roosevelt Association Journal* 15, no. 1 (Winter 1989), 3, 6–7.

22. Roosevelt, First Annual Message, December 3, 1901, in Richardson Supp. 15:6665; Imperial German Embassy, Promemoria, December 11, 1901, in FRUS 1901, 194. For timing, *see* Hay to von Holleben, December 16, 1901, in FRUS 1901, 195.

23. Imperial German Embassy, Promemoria, December 11, 1901, in FRUS 1901, 194; Haggard to Landsdowne, September 21, 1901, quoted in Mitchell, *Danger of Dreams*, 98; *see* Collin, *Theodore Roosevelt's Caribbean*, 92–93; Challener, *Admirals, Generals, and American Foreign Policy*, 111–13; Guthrie, "Anglo-German Intervention," 19.

24. State Department, Memorandum for Ambassador Holleben, December 16, 1901, in FRUS 1901, 195; *see* John M. Thompson, *Great Power Rising: Theodore Roosevelt and the Politics of U.S. Foreign Policy* (Oxford: Oxford University Press, 2019), 35–36. Roosevelt confided to a friend the day after granting Germany permission that "in South America it is positively difficult to know just how far it is best to leave the nations alone and how far there must be interference, and also how far we can with justice prevent interference by others." Roosevelt to Hale, December 17, 1901, in Morison 3:209.

25. Dewey to Long, August 28, 1901, quoted in Seward W. Livermore, "Theodore Roosevelt, the American Navy, and the Venezuelan Crisis of 1902–1903," *American Historical Review* 51, no. 3 (April 1946), 458 n. 24; *see* Roosevelt to Dewey, June 14, 1902, in Morison 3:275; *see also* Marks, *Velvet on Iron*, 40–41; Beale, *Rise of America to World Power*, 416–17; Livermore, "Theodore Roosevelt," 459–60. For the construction of the Culebra base, *see* Henry J. Hendrix, *Theodore Roosevelt's Naval Diplomacy: The U.S. Navy and the Birth of the American Century* (Annapolis, MD: Naval Institute Press, 2009), 33. For Dewey's reputation and use as "a diplomatic weapon," *see generally* John Garry Clifford, "Admiral Dewey and the Germans, 1903: A New Perspective," *Mid-America* 49, no. 3 (July 1967), 214–20.

26. *See* Howard C. Hill, *Roosevelt and the Caribbean* (Chicago: University of Chicago Press, 1927), 117; Guthrie, "Anglo-German Intervention," 46–107.

27. Roosevelt to Thayer, August 21, 1916, in Morison 8:1102; Roosevelt to Reid, June 27, 1906, in Morison 5:319.

28. Taylor to Roosevelt, late November 1902, quoted in Alfred L. P. Dennis, *Adventures in American Diplomacy 1896–1906* (New York: E. P. Dutton, 1928), 291–92. For a similar argument, *see* Collin, *Theodore Roosevelt's Caribbean*, 96–97.

29. *See* Edmund Morris, "'A Matter of Extreme Urgency': Theodore Roosevelt, Wilhelm II, and the Venezuela Crisis of 1902," *Naval War College Review* 55, no. 2 (Spring 2002), 79; Hendrix, *Theodore Roosevelt's Naval Diplomacy*, 41.

30. *See* Hendrix, *Theodore Roosevelt's Naval Diplomacy*, 39, 46.

31. Morris, "'A Matter of Extreme Urgency,'" 79.

32. Roosevelt to White, August 14, 1906, in Morison 5:358–59; *see* Morris, *Theodore Rex*, 185–87.

33. Roosevelt to Thayer, August 21, 1916, in Morison 8:1102.

34. Roosevelt to Thayer, August 21, 1916, in Morison 8:1102–03.

35. Roosevelt to Thayer, August 21, 1916, in Morison 8:1103; *see* Collin, *Theodore Roosevelt's Caribbean*, 101–02.

36. Reconstructing Roosevelt's ultimatum to von Holleben is no easy task. Generations of historians have disagreed virulently over its timing, scope, and tone, as well as whether it was even delivered. Most historians now agree, however, that the conversation did happen substantially as Roosevelt remembered it. Edmund Morris, Roosevelt's preeminent biographer, concludes that "TR's memory is 'amazingly correct.'" Morris, "'A Few Pregnant Days,'" 2; *see* Collin, *Theodore Roosevelt's Caribbean*, 98; William N. Tilchin, *Theodore Roosevelt and the British Empire: A Study in Presidential Statecraft* (London: Macmillan, 1997), 32. For the most completely reconstructed timeline of the ultimatum, *see* Morris, "'A Few Pregnant Days,'" 8–11.

37. *See* Montgomerie to Admiralty, December 16, 1902, in Brant and Maycock, *British and Foreign State Papers*, 95:1120–21; "German Cruisers Sail," *New York Times*, December 16, 1902; *see also* Hill, *Roosevelt and the Caribbean*, 118, 120; Hendrix, *Theodore Roosevelt's Naval Diplomacy*, 43–44.

38. *See* Collin, *Theodore Roosevelt's Caribbean*, 96–97. For a sample of the British press recognizing their country's dilemma, *see* Robert Giffen, letter to the editor, "The Venezuelan Mess," *London Times*, December 18, 1902; *see also* Mitchell, *Danger of Dreams*, 90–91.

39. *See* Guthrie, "Anglo-German Intervention," 138; Mitchell, *Danger of Dreams*, 89–97.

40. *See* Mitchell, *Danger of Dreams*, 87–89, 97–98.

41. *See* Morris, *Theodore Rex*, 187–90.

42. *See* Morris, *Theodore Rex*, 188–89; Morris, "'A Few Pregnant Days,'" 10.

43. Roosevelt to Thayer, August 21, 1916, in Morison 8:1103.

44. Roosevelt to Thayer, August 21, 1916, in Morison 8:1103; *see* Morris, *Theodore Rex*, 189. For contemporaneous naval operations, *see* Hendrix, *Theodore Roosevelt's Naval Diplomacy*, 47.

45. Roosevelt to Thayer, August 21, 1916, in Morison 8:1103–04; *see* Morris, *Theodore Rex*, 189.

46. *See* Morris, "'A Matter of Extreme Urgency,'" 83–84; Mitchell, *Danger of Dreams*, 87–89, 97–98.

47. *See* Morris, "'A Matter of Extreme Urgency,'" 83–84; Morris, "'A Few Pregnant Days,'" 11.

48. Roosevelt to Cleveland, December 26, 1902, in Morison 3:398.

49. See "Italy Joins the Allies," *New York Times*, December 16, 1902; *see also* Beale, *Rise of America to World Power*, 397; Charles S. Campbell, Jr., *Anglo-American Understanding, 1898–1903* (Baltimore, MD: Johns Hopkins Press, 1957), 285–86. Roosevelt's decision not to arbitrate the dispute may also have reflected domestic considerations. *See* Thompson, *Great Power Rising*, 41–42. For a good overview of the negotiations, *see* Guthrie, "Anglo-German Intervention," 193–301.

50. "Mr. Balfour in Liverpool," *London Times*, February 14, 1903.

51. "Germany Recognizes Monroe Doctrine, Says New Envoy," *New York Herald*, January 31, 1903; *see* Morris, "'A Matter of Extreme Urgency,'" 84; Edward B. Parsons, "The German-American Crisis of 1902–1903," *Historian* 33, no. 3 (May 1971), 445; Campbell, *Anglo-American Understanding*, 291–92.

52. See Hill, *Roosevelt and the Caribbean*, 142–43.

53. Roosevelt to Shaw, December 26, 1902, in Morison 3:397; *see* Roosevelt to Schurz, December 26, 1902, in Morison 3:397; *see also* Hill, *Roosevelt and the Caribbean*, 141 n.3; Collin, *Theodore Roosevelt's Caribbean*, 115.

54. See Munro, *Intervention and Dollar Diplomacy*, 74; Marks, *Velvet on Iron*, 44–47; Morris, *Theodore Rex*, 210. One of the historical ironies involved in the final protocols is that they awarded control of Venezuela's two biggest customhouses (La Guaira and Puerto Cabello) to Belgium in the event that Venezuela failed to live up to its agreed-upon responsibilities. *See* Munro, *Intervention and Dollar Diplomacy*, 74. Roosevelt understandably did not see Belgium as a threat to the Monroe Doctrine in the same way as Germany, but in less than two years' time he would draw the line at *any* European control of customhouses on the continent. His approval of the protocols thus reflects how far away he still was from claiming an "international police power" at this time.

55. Roosevelt to White, August 14, 1906, in Morison 5:358–59.

56. See, e.g., Mitchell, *Danger of Dreams*, 98–101. For the contrary view, *see* Morris, *Theodore Rex*, 177–81, 185–86; Morris, "'A Few Pregnant Days,'" 3, 6–7; Marks, *Velvet on Iron*, 5–10.

57. See Hill, *Roosevelt and the Caribbean*, 148–49.

58. Roosevelt, Speech in Chicago, April 2, 1903, in Theodore Roosevelt, *Presidential Addresses and State Papers* (New York: Review of Reviews, 1910), 1:266; *see* Morris, *Theodore Rex*, 215–16.

59. "Jingoes Discover 'A Lesson,'" *Boston Journal*, n.d., in *Public Opinion*, December 25, 1902, 805–06; *see* "Congress May Increase Navy," *New York Times*, December 20, 1902; *see also* Morris, *Theodore Rex*, 216; Campbell, *Anglo-American Understanding*, 289.

60. See Yerxa, *Admirals and Empire*, 8–9; *see generally* Samuel F. Wells, Jr., "British Strategic Withdrawal from the Western Hemisphere, 1904–1906," *Canadian Historical Review* 49, no. 4 (December 1968), 335–56. Roosevelt and the navalists factored the Panama Canal into their calculations as well. Once the canal opened, the United States would no longer need to smear its navy across two oceans. But the canal would also draw Europe into the region. Europe's powers did not have enough trade there today to justify significant political or naval involvement; tomorrow, however, the canal would bring online what Mahan called "one of the greatest of the nerve centres of the whole body of European civilization." A. T. Mahan, "A Twentieth-Century Outlook," May 1897, in *The Interest of America in Sea Power, Present and Future* (Boston: Little, Brown, 1897), 260–61. If the American navy did not prepare in the meantime, Roosevelt warned, "the building of the canal would be merely giving a hostage to any power of superior strength." Roosevelt, Second Annual Message, December 2, 1902, in Richardson Supp. 14:6722; *see* Dewey to Moody, General Board No. 284, October 7, 1902, attached to Moody to Hay, November 21, 1902, in Misc. Letters, Roll 1154, M179, RG59, NA; *see also* Harold Sprout and Margaret Sprout, *The Rise of American Naval Power 1776–1918* (Princeton, NJ: Princeton University Press, 1944), 251.

61. For the naval buildup, *see Navy Yearbook: Compilation of Annual Naval Appropriation Laws from 1883 to 1912*, S. Doc. No. 955 (1912); *see also* Bourne, *Britain and the Balance*, 338; Sprout and Sprout, *Rise of American Naval Power*, 259–70; Kenneth Wimmel, *Theodore Roosevelt and the Great White Fleet: American Seapower Comes of Age* (Washington, DC: Brassey's, 1998), 194–97. The Navy Yearbook counts two more "Dreadnought type" vessels in construction as

Roosevelt left office—the *Michigan* and *South Carolina*—but both are best considered as transitional vessels rather than full *Dreadnought* battleships. *See* Wimmel, *Great White Fleet*, 194–97.

62. "Splendid Show of Naval Power," *Morning Oregonian*, December 17, 1907; *see* Wimmel, *Great White Fleet*, xi–xvi.

63. *See* Dana G. Munro, *The United States and the Caribbean Republics 1921–1933* (Princeton, NJ: Princeton University Press, 1974), 11–12; Healy, *Drive to Hegemony*, 61, 110; Walter H. Posner, "American Marines in Haiti, 1915–1922," *The Americas* 20, no. 3 (January 1964), 236. For the British financial takeover of Egypt, *see* William H. Wynne, *State Insolvency and Foreign Bondholders*, vol. 2, *Selected Case Histories of Governmental Foreign Bond Defaults and Debt Readjustments* (Washington, DC: BeardBooks, 2000), 577–617.

64. *Theodore Roosevelt: An Autobiography* (New York: Charles Scribner's Sons, 1922), 507–08.

65. Drago to Mérou, December 29, 1902, in FRUS 1903, 3, 4.

66. Indeed, despite its reputation as a "bondholders' war," the Venezuelan intervention was itself primarily about injuries to foreign nationals and their property rather than contract disputes. *See generally* Guthrie, "Anglo-German Intervention"; D. C. M. Platt, "The Allied Coercion of Venezuela, 1902–3—A Reassessment," *Inter-American Economic Affairs* 15, no. 4 (Spring 1962), 3–28. One other potential downside to the Drago Doctrine was that it might disincentivize states from paying their debts regularly, injuring these states' credit ratings and thereby making it harder for them to develop over the long run into stable neighbors.

67. *See generally* Amos S. Hershey, "The Calvo and Drago Doctrines," *American Journal of International Law* 1, no. 1 (January 1907), 26–45.

68. Roosevelt to Theodore Roosevelt, Jr., February 1, 1903, in Morison 3:415; Roosevelt to Hay, March 13, 1903, in Morison 3:446.

69. Roosevelt to Hay, March 13, 1903, in Morison 3:446. For Speck von Sternburg's account of the conversation, *see* Speck von Sternburg to Wilhelmstrasse, March 13, 1903, quoted in Perkins, *The Monroe Doctrine: 1867–1907*, 408.

70. "Mr. Balfour in Liverpool," *London Times*, February 14, 1903; *see* Healy, *Drive to Hegemony*, 106; Perkins, *The Monroe Doctrine: 1867–1907*, 361–64. It is worth noting that neither Great Britain nor any other European power was eager to turn over *all* its interests to American supervision. *See* Warren G. Kneer, *Great Britain and the Caribbean, 1901–1913: A Study in Anglo-American Relations* (East Lansing, MI: Michigan State University Press, 1975), 214. Instead, London was looking for a policy that yoked American power to the creation of a regional order in which British commercial interests could thrive unmolested.

71. Roosevelt, indeed, recognized the second point even before the Venezuelan intervention. He assured German Consul General Karl Bünz that he "did not want any exclusive trade privileges as against Germany with South America save as they might come legitimately by reciprocity treaties." Roosevelt to Lodge, June 19, 1901, in Morison 3:97–98. Shortly after becoming president, he told Speck von Sternburg that he regarded "the Monroe Doctrine as being equivalent to the open door in South America." Roosevelt to Speck von Sternburg, October 11, 1901, in Morison 3:172; *see* Beale, *Rise of America to World Power*, 392–93.

72. Roosevelt, Second Annual Message, December 2, 1902, in Richardson Supp. 14:6718; *see* Munro, *Intervention and Dollar Diplomacy*, 66; Frank Ninkovich, "Theodore Roosevelt: Civilization as Ideology," *Diplomatic History* 10, no. 3 (Summer 1986), 221–45. For other signals of Roosevelt's early interest in the British proposal, *see* Speck von Sternburg to Wilhelmstrasse, March 13, 1903, in Perkins, *The Monroe Doctrine: 1867–1907*, 408.

Concerns about the moral hazard problem created by the Monroe Doctrine were rampant. The American minister to Venezuela, for example, argued that "[t]he fear of losing territory and sovereignty is, and has always been, a wholesome fear to every nation. We, by our Monroe Doctrine, relieve Venezuela of that fear.... It is useless for us to answer that can not intervene, for we do intervene to the extent of relieving them of fear." Bowen to Hay, June 25, 1904, in Despatches, Venezuela, Roll 58, M79, RG59, NA. Frederick Palmer, a prominent journalist, likewise observed later in Roosevelt's term that "we put a fence around corruption, rapine, assassination, confiscation and execution without trial." Palmer to Roosevelt, December 1, 1908, 10859/25-26, in Roll 746, M862, RG59, NA. Palmer urged the administration to reform its neighbors and particularly Central America, but as the second assistant secretary of state wondered (and foreshadowed), "how could we carry out Mr. Palmer's recommendation without the acquiescence of the Cent. American Countries—except by assuming and enforcing a dictatorial authority toward them"? Adee to Bacon, December 5, 1908, 847/83, in Roll 122, M862, RG59, NA.

73. Speck von Sternburg to Wilhelmstrasse, March 13, 1903, quoted in Perkins, *The Monroe Doctrine: 1867–1907*, 408; *see* Roosevelt to Spring Rice, December 27, 1904, in Morison 4:1084. For Roosevelt's opposition to helping out investors generally, *see* David H. Burton, *Theodore Roosevelt: Confident Imperialist* (Philadelphia, PA: University of Pennsylvania Press, 1968), 118.

74. A. T. Mahan, "The Monroe Doctrine," in *Naval Administration and Warfare: Some General Principles* (Boston: Little, Brown 1908), 395–96.

75. *See* J. Fred Rippy, "The Initiation of the Customs Receivership in the Dominican Republic," *Hispanic American Historical Review* 17, no. 4 (November 1937), 438–39; Munro, *Intervention and Dollar Diplomacy*, 78–79; Cyrus Veeser, *A World Safe for Capitalism: Dollar Diplomacy and America's Rise to Global Power* (New York: Columbia University Press, 2002), 51–52.

76. *See* Munro, *Intervention and Dollar Diplomacy*, 79–81; Hill, *Roosevelt and the Caribbean*, 150–51; Frank Moya Pons, *The Dominican Republic: A National History* (Princeton, NJ: Markus Wiener, 2010), 248–54, 262–78; Cyrus Veeser, "Inventing Dollar Diplomacy: The Gilded-Age Origins of the Roosevelt Corollary to the Monroe Doctrine," *Diplomatic History* 27, no. 3 (June 2003), 304–05; Collin, *Theodore Roosevelt's Caribbean*, 352.

77. *See* Rippy, "The Initiation," 428; Veeser, *A World*, 13, 23, 26–28, 41–43; Richard H. Collin, "The 1904 *Detroit* Compact: U.S. Naval Diplomacy and Dominican Revolutions," *Historian* 52, no. 3 (May 1990), 433–34; Perkins, *The Monroe Doctrine: 1867–1907*, 412–18; Munro, *Intervention and Dollar Diplomacy*, 87–88; Healy, *Drive to Hegemony*, 114; David Charles MacMichael, "The United States and the Dominican Republic, 1871–1940: A Cycle in Caribbean Diplomacy" (PhD diss., University of Oregon, 1964), 146–70.

78. General Board Letter #87, December 10, 1900, quoted in Challener, *Admirals, Generals, and American Foreign Policy*, 124; *see* Powell to Hay, September 12, 1903, in Despatches, Dominican Republic, Roll 8, M93, RG59, NA; *see also* Challener, *Admirals, Generals, and American Foreign Policy*, 19–21, 43–44, 121, 124–26; Rippy, "The Initiation," 429–38.

79. *See* [Adee ?], Memorandum, January 1904, in Despatches, Dominican Republic, Roll 10, M93, RG59, NA; Powell to Hay, January 9, 1904, in Despatches, Dominican Republic, Roll 9, M93, RG59, NA; Powell to Hay, December 17, 1903, in Despatches, Dominican Republic, Roll 9, M93, RG59, NA; *see also* Rippy, "The Initiation," 440–41; Hill, *Roosevelt and the Caribbean*, 154–55. One reason why Morales may have been so well disposed toward American involvement is because he had already enjoyed its benefits. Contrary to instructions from Washington, Commander A. C. Dillingham of the USS *Detroit* had decided to involve himself in the ongoing Dominican civil war, and in January 1904, he arranged his forces in a way that helped Morales emerge victorious from a decisive battle with his enemies. *See* Ellen D. Tillman, *Dollar Diplomacy by Force: Nation-Building and Resistance in the Dominican Republic* (Chapel Hill: University of North Carolina Press, 2016), 33–34; Rippy, "The Initiation," 443–44. Some scholars suggest that Morales was obliged after Dillingham's intervention to request greater American involvement, but that gets the chronology backward: Dillingham supported Morales in large part because Morales had already begun courting the Americans. *See* Powell to Hay, December 17, 1903, in Despatches, Dominican Republic, Roll 9, M93, RG59, NA; *see also* Collin, "The 1904 *Detroit* Compact," 437–38.

80. Roosevelt to Theodore Roosevelt, Jr., February 10, 1904, in Morison 4:724; Roosevelt to Bishop, February 23, 1904, in Morison 4:734–35. Hay delivered Roosevelt's unwelcome rejection to Morales's representative in late March. In Hay's words, Morales's representative "bore his doom like a soldier and a gentleman. He rose and said: 'When I came here my hope was in the generous good will of the American people. Now my only hope is in God.'" Hay quipped that "he seemed to regard [that] as an inadequate compensation." Hay to Roosevelt, March 30, 1904, in Reel 43, Roosevelt MSS.

81. *See* Perkins, *The Monroe Doctrine: 1867–1907*, 419–21.

82. "Decision Regretted," *New York Times*, February 23, 1904; *see* "The Hague Court's 'Premium on Violence,'" *Literary Digest* (March 5, 1904), 318; Penfield to Hay, May 15, 1904, in FRUS 1904, 512. For the considerable impact that the tribunal's ruling had on the development of the Roosevelt Corollary, *see generally* Matthias Maass, "Catalyst for the Roosevelt Corollary:

Arbitrating the 1902–1903 Venezuela Crisis and Its Impact on the Development of the Roosevelt Corollary to the Monroe Doctrine," *Diplomacy & Statecraft* 20, no. 3 (Fall 2009), 383–402.

83. Powell to Hay, April 14, 1904, in Despatches, Dominican Republic, Roll 11, M93, RG59, NA; *see* Powell to Hay, April 13, 1904, in Despatches, Dominican Republic, Roll 11, M93, RG59, NA.

84. Roosevelt to Hale, February 26, 1904, in Morison 4:740; Roosevelt to Eliot, April 4, 1904, in Morison 4:770; Hay to Loomis, March 28, 1904, in Notes from the Dominican Legation, Roll 3, T801, RG59, NA; Adee to Combs, August 29, 1904, in Instructions, Central America, Roll 34, M77, RG59, NA; *see* Roosevelt to Hay, March 30, 1904, in Reel 416, Roosevelt MSS; *see also* Munro, *Intervention and Dollar Diplomacy*, 93–94. For Morales's offer, *see* Powell to Hay, April 16, 1904, in Despatches, Dominican Republic, Roll 11, M93, RG59, NA; Powell to Hay, April 18, 1904, 3:10pm Cable, in Despatches, Dominican Republic, Roll 11, M93, RG59, NA; Powell to Hay, April 18, 1904, No. 841, in Despatches, Dominican Republic, Roll 11, M93, RG59, NA.

Exactly who first proposed the idea of a Dominican customs receivership is unclear. As early as mid-December 1903, Morales told the American minister he wanted "the United States to be given a controlling influence over the fiscal affairs of the Government as a guarantee for full payment of its Foreign creditors." Powell to Hay, December 17, 1903, in Despatches, Dominican Republic, Roll 9, M93, RG59, NA; *see* Powell to Hay, January 26, 1904, in Despatches, Dominican Republic, Roll 10, M93, RG59, NA. One month later, the State Department was evaluating the idea in advance of the visit of Morales's agent. *See* [Adee ?], Memorandum, January 1904, in Despatches, Dominican Republic, Roll 10, M93, RG59, NA. But it is likely that both the Dominicans and the Americans already had the idea in their heads long before talks began. Given their experience with the San Domingo Improvement Company, the Dominicans knew that third-party administration of their customhouses was an option. And the State Department had toyed with the idea of a consensual custom receivership since at least the time of Secretaries Fish and Blaine, albeit with Venezuela rather than the Dominican Republic. *See* J. Fred Rippy, "Antecedents of the Roosevelt Corollary of the Monroe Doctrine," *Pacific Historical Review* 9, no. 3 (September 1940), 271–75; Lars Schoultz, *Beneath the United States: A History of U.S. Policy Toward Latin America* (Cambridge, MA: Harvard University Press, 2003), 178. Of course, there were also European examples in Turkey, Greece, and Egypt. *See* Wynne, *State Insolvency*, 2:283–347, 393–454, 577–617; Emily S. Rosenberg, *Financial Missionaries to the World: The Politics and Culture of Dollar Diplomacy, 1900–1930* (Durham, NC: Duke University Press, 2003), 52–56.

85. Adams to Cameron, April 10, 1904, in *The Letters of Henry Adams*, ed. J. C. Levenson et al., vol. 5, *1899–1905* (Cambridge, MA: Belknap Press, 1988), 270; Roosevelt to Eliot, April 4, 1904, in Morison 4:770; *see* Roosevelt to Hay, March 30, 1904, in Reel 416, Roosevelt MSS; *see also* Thompson, *Great Power Rising*, 82.

86. Roosevelt to Root, May 20, 1904, in Morison 4:801; *see* Morison 4:801 n.801–02.

87. Roosevelt to Root, May 20, 1904, in Morison 4:801 n.801–02; Roosevelt to Root, June 7, 1904, in Morison 4:821–22; *see* Roosevelt to Schurman, July 25, 1904, in Morison 4:865; Root to Roosevelt, June 9, 1904, in Reel 45, Roosevelt MSS; *see also* Thompson, *Great Power Rising*, 81. For a survey of press reactions, *see* John W. Blassingame, "The Press and American Intervention in Haiti and the Dominican Republic, 1904–1920," *Caribbean Studies* 9, no. 2 (July 1969), 27–43.

88. Corinne Roosevelt Robinson, *My Brother Theodore Roosevelt* (New York: Charles Scribner's Sons, 1921), 217; *see* Morris, *Rex Theodore*, 693 n.364.

89. Roosevelt, Fourth Annual Message, December 6, 1904, in Richardson Supp. 16:6923–24.

90. For the criticisms, *see, e.g.*, Mark T. Gilderhus, "The Monroe Doctrine: Meaning and Implications," *Presidential Studies Quarterly* 36, no. 1 (March 2006), 11; Perkins, *The Monroe Doctrine: 1867–1907*, 396–97, 433; Gerald G. Eggert, *Richard Olney: Evolution of a Statesman* (University Park: Pennsylvania State University Press, 1974), 304–05. For many (though not all) of the Corollary's antecedents, *see* Rippy, "Antecedents."

91. Sheridan to Rawlins, June 29, 1865, in *The Papers of Ulysses S. Grant*, ed. John Y. Simon, vol. 15, *May 1–December 31, 1865* (Carbondale: Southern Illinois University Press, 1988), 259; Olney, Drafts of Cuba Portion of Cleveland's 1896 State of the Union Address, November 9, 1896, in Reel 23, Olney MSS; *see* Seward to Bruce, August 15, 1865, in FRUS 1865, 2:191; Cong. Globe App., 41st Cong., 3rd sess. 33 (1871).

92. Roosevelt, Fourth Annual Message, December 6, 1904, in Richardson Supp. 16:6923–24; Root, "The Monroe Doctrine," Address at the Ninety-Ninth Annual Banquet of the New England Society of New York, December 22, 1904, in *Miscellaneous Addresses by Elihu Root*, ed. Robert Bacon and James Brown Scott (Cambridge, MA: Harvard University Press, 1917), 271–72.

93. Speck von Sternburg to Wilhelmstrasse, March 13, 1903, quoted in Perkins, *The Monroe Doctrine: 1867–1907*, 408; Roosevelt to Hale, February 26, 1904, in Morison 4:740; *see* Roosevelt to Spring Rice, July 24, 1905, in Morison 4:1286; Roosevelt to Root, September 14, 1905, in Morison 5:26; Roosevelt to Theodore Roosevelt, Jr., February 10, 1904, in Morison 4:724; Roosevelt to Bishop, February 23, 1904, in Morison 4:734–35.

94. Hay to Dawson, December 30, 1904, in FRUS 1905, 298; *see* Rippy, "The Initiation," 436–37; Veeser, "Inventing Dollar Diplomacy," 313–14 & n.47. For the administration's concern about Germany, *see* Jessup, Interview with Root, January 11, 1930, in Box I:244/245, Jessup MSS; Jessup, Conversation with Root, October 28, 1935, in Box I:244/245, Jessup MSS; *see also* Sumner Welles, *Naboth's Vineyard: The Dominican Republic 1844–1924* (Mamaroneck, NY: Paul P. Appel, 1966), 2:620–21. Europe's frustration partially stemmed from the fact that, pursuant to an arbitral award issued earlier that year, the Dominican Republic was repaying the claims of the San Domingo Improvement Company over the claims of others. The basic problem, however, was simply that there was not enough money to go around, and no matter how it was divvied up, some creditors were always going to get left out in the cold. *See* Veeser, "Inventing Dollar Diplomacy," 305–14.

95. Roosevelt to Bishop, March 23, 1905, in Morison 4:1444–45; Dawson to Hay, January 21, 1905, in Despatches, Dominican Republic, Roll 13, M93, RG59, NA; *see* Hay to Dawson, December 30, 1904, in FRUS 1905, 298; Hay to Dillingham, January 5, 1905, in FRUS 1905, 300; Dawson to Hay, February 13, 1905, in Despatches, Dominican Republic, Roll 13, M93, RG59, NA; *see also* Healy, *Drive to Hegemony*, 119–20. For a good history of the negotiations over the initial agreements and later modus vivendi, *see* MacMichael, "A Cycle in Caribbean Diplomacy," 170–91. For a financial history of the treaty, *see* Wynne, *State Insolvency*, 2:199–280.

It is difficult to determine exactly how popular or unpopular Morales's request was among Dominicans. Several scholars suggest that it was imposed on the country, but several of Morales's political opponents, including the leader of the primary rebellion against him, Juan Isidro Jimenes, also supported American intervention at various times. *See* Loomis, Memorandum for the Secretary of State on the Dominican Republic, March 19, 1904, in Folder 37, No. 96, Box 6, Loomis MSS; *see also* Rippy, "The Initiation," 444–48. On the other hand, the American minister opined in mid-February 1905 that "the rash and ignorant elements" opposing the treaty were "in the majority." Dawson to Hay, February 13, 1905, in Despatches, Dominican Republic, Roll 13, M93, RG59, NA.

96. *See* Protocol of an Agreement Signed Between the United States and the Dominican Republic (February 4, 1905), in FRUS 1905, 342–43; *see also* Healy, *Drive to Hegemony*, 116.

97. Message from the President of the United States, February 15, 1905, in FRUS 1905, 337, 339, 341; *see ibid.*, 334–35.

98. *See* Collin, *Theodore Roosevelt's Caribbean*, 413, 426–29. Press reaction to the president's course was also generally negative. *See* Blassingame, "The Press and American Intervention," 28.

99. Roosevelt to Bonaparte, September 4, 1905, in Morison 5:10; *see* Veeser, "Inventing Dollar Diplomacy," 319–25; Collin, *Theodore Roosevelt's Caribbean*, 433; Hill, *Roosevelt and the Caribbean*, 160–62.

100. *See* Rosenberg, *Financial Missionaries*, 46. For the differences between the modus vivendi and the final treaty, *see* Hill, *Roosevelt and the Caribbean*, 166–68.

101. *See* Ernest R. May, *From Imperialism to Isolationism 1898–1919* (New York: Macmillan, 1964), 27–28. For the contemplated French intervention in Venezuela, *see* Embert J. Hendrickson, "Roosevelt's Second Venezuelan Controversy," *Hispanic American Historical Review* 50, no. 3 (August 1970), 489–91; Philip C. Jessup, *Elihu Root*, vol. 1, *1845–1909* (New York: Dodd, Mead, 1938), 495–97; Collin, *Theodore Roosevelt's Caribbean*, 446–47. For the contemplated British intervention in Uruguay, *see* Kneer, *Great Britain and the Caribbean*, 116–17. For the contemplated Dutch intervention in Venezuela, *see* Hendrickson, "Roosevelt's Second Venezuelan Controversy," 495–96.

102. Roosevelt to Lodge, April 30, 1906, in Morison 5:256–57.

103. Roosevelt to Lodge, April 30, 1906, in Morison 5:256–57; *see* Message from the President of the United States, February 15, 1905, in FRUS 1905, 339; *see also* Healy, *Drive to Hegemony*, 115–119, 123–24; Noel Maurer, *The Empire Trap: The Rise and Fall of U.S. Intervention to Protect American Property Overseas, 1893–2013* (Princeton, NJ: Princeton University Press, 2013), 66–67.

104. *See* Hill, *Roosevelt and the Caribbean*, 168; Pons, *The Dominican Republic*, 296–99; Collin, *Theodore Roosevelt's Caribbean*, 452, 455.

105. Roosevelt to Carnegie, February 26, 1909, in Morison 6:1539; Roosevelt, *Autobiography*, 507; *see* Roosevelt to Watson, August 18, 1906, in Morison 5:374; Roosevelt to Grey, February 28, 1907, in Morison 5:602; Roosevelt to Hale, December 3, 1908, in Morison 6:1407; *see also* Healy, *Drive to Hegemony*, 124–25.

106. For Great Britain's exploitation of this dynamic, *see* Chapters 4 and 5.

107. Roosevelt to Spring Rice, July 24, 1905, in Morison 4:1286; Roosevelt to Hale, December 3, 1908, in Morison 6:1407; *see* Roosevelt to Johnson, December 4, 1908, in "Roosevelt Desired to Spank the Venezuelans," *Duluth Evening Herald*, March 8, 1909; Roosevelt to Robinson, August 31, 1905, in Morison 4:1328; Roosevelt to Hay, January 14, 1905, in Reel 337, Roosevelt MSS.

108. *See* Robert James Neymeyer, "The Establishment and Operation of the Dominican Republic Customs Receivership, 1905–1916" (PhD diss., University of Iowa, 1990), 139–41; Rosenberg, *Financial Missionaries*, 58; Tillman, *Dollar Diplomacy by Force*, 39–47.

109. *See* MacMichael, "A Cycle of Caribbean Diplomacy," 295, 303.

110. *See* MacMichael, "A Cycle of Caribbean Diplomacy," 193–96; Tillman, *Dollar Diplomacy by Force*, 44–46.

Chapter 8: The Creation of a Revolutionary Habit

1. Wood, Diary Entry, May 20, 1902, in Box 3, Wood MSS; *see* "'Cuba Libre' at Last," *Boston Daily Globe*, May 21, 1902; *see also* Lester D. Langley, *The Banana Wars: United States Intervention in the Caribbean, 1898–1934* (Chicago: Dorsey, 1988), 1–2.

2. *See* 34 Cong. Rec. 3151 (1901).

3. Roosevelt to White, September 13, 1906, in Reel 343, Roosevelt MSS.

4. *See* Edmund Morris, *Theodore Rex* (London: HarperCollins, 2002), 395, 701.

5. Stewart Notes, 1905, quoted in Morris, *Theodore Rex*, 395.

6. Morris, *Theodore Rex*, 395.

7. *See* Dexter Perkins, *The Monroe Doctrine: 1867–1907* (Gloucester, MA: Peter Smith, 1966), 451–58; Frederick W. Marks, III, *Velvet on Iron: The Diplomacy of Theodore Roosevelt* (Lincoln: University of Nebraska Press, 1979), 180–90; *see generally* John Patterson, "Latin-American Reactions to the Panama Revolution of 1903," *Hispanic American Historical Review*, 24, no. 2 (May 1944), 342–51.

8. Roosevelt to Hay, October 8, 1901, in Morison 3:166; *see* Moody, Order, October 4, 1902, in File 420-1, General Board, NA; *see also* Marks, *Velvet on Iron*, 185–86.

9. Root to Tillman, December 13, 1905, in Box 186, Root MSS; *see* Philip C. Jessup, *Elihu Root*, vol. 1, *1845–1909* (New York: Dodd, Mead, 1938), 468–92.

10. Root to Flagler, January 3, 1905, in Box 185, Root MSS; Root to Shaw, January 3, 1908, in Box 188, Root MSS; Jessup, Interview with Root, November 19, 1929, in Box I:244, Jessup MSS; *see* Root to Buchanan, March 20, 1909, in Box 58, Root MSS; *see also* Jessup, *Elihu Root*, 1:513–14, 554–55, 559–60. Like his chief, Root believed firmly in the Roosevelt Corollary. He considered it a core "truth" that "the obligation to do within the limits of the Monroe Doctrine what that doctrine prevents a concert of powers from doing, is correlative to the right of prevention." Root to Roosevelt, June 9, 1904, in Reel 45, Roosevelt MSS.

11. *See* Jessup, *Elihu Root*, 1:471–75.

12. *See* J. Lloyd Mecham, *The United States and Inter-American Security, 1889–1960* (Austin: University of Texas Press, 1962), 58–62.

13. *See* Jessup, *Elihu Root*, 1:482–83; John M. Dobson, *America's Ascent: The United States Becomes a Great Power, 1880–1914* (DeKalb: Northern Illinois University Press, 1978), 165–66. Several authors claim that no previous secretary of state had left the United States while in office, but that is incorrect: Secretary William Henry Seward toured several islands in the Caribbean during his tenure.

14. Root, Speech at an Extraordinary Session of the Third Conference of American Republics held in Rio de Janeiro, July 31, 1906, in *Speeches Incident to the Visit of Secretary Root to South America* (Washington, DC: Government Printing Office, 1906), 12. Roosevelt found Root's words so important that he quoted them in full in his December State of the Union Message. *See* Roosevelt, Sixth Annual Message, December 3, 1906, in Richardson Supp. 16:7059.

15. *Jorno do Brazil*, n.d., quoted in Jessup, *Elihu Root*, 1:482; *see* Perkins, *The Monroe Doctrine: 1867–1907*, 458–59.

16. Root to Roosevelt, August 2, 1906, in Reel 66, Roosevelt MSS; Root to Shaw, October 8, 1906, in Box 186, Root MSS.

17. Root, Reply to Drago Speech at the Banquet Given by the Committee of Reception to Mr. Root at the Opera House in Buenos Aires, August 17, 1906, in *Speeches Incident*, 158; *see* Richard W. Leopold, *Elihu Root and the Conservative Tradition* (Boston: Little, Brown, 1954), 66.

18. Root to Wallace, June 22, 1906, in Box 186, Root MSS; *see* Jessup, *Elihu Root*, 1:478–88.

19. *See* Richard H. Collin, *Theodore Roosevelt's Caribbean: The Panama Canal, the Monroe Doctrine, and the Latin American Context* (Baton Rouge: Louisiana State University Press, 1990), 490.

20. Root to Roosevelt, August 2, 1906, in Reel 66, Roosevelt MSS; *Report of the Delegates of the United States to the Third International Conference of the American States Held at Rio de Janeiro* (Washington, DC: Government Printing Office, 1907), 23. Roosevelt was overjoyed as well, bragging to Andrew Carnegie "how well the Pan-American Conference has gone off" and how "Root's going there was a great stroke." He thought Root's tour would help "insure [*sic*] permanent peace in the Western Hemisphere." Roosevelt to Carnegie, August 6, 1906, in Morison 5:346.

21. *See* Jessup, *Elihu Root*, 1:531.

22. *See* Ralph Eldin Minger, *William Howard Taft and United States Foreign Policy: The Apprenticeship Years, 1900–1908* (Urbana: University of Illinois Press, 1975), 85; Richard L. Millett, *Searching for Stability: The U.S. Development of Constabulary Forces in Latin America and the Philippines* (Fort Leavenworth, KS: Combat Studies Institute Press, 2010), 18–19. For Cuba's growth, *see* Table 15 of the online Appendix for Marianne Ward and John Devereux, "The Road Not Taken: Pre-Revolutionary Cuban Living Standards in Comparative Perspective," *Journal of Economic History* 72, no. 1 (March 2012): 104–33, https://static.cambridge.org/content/id/urn:cambridge.org:id:article:S0022050711002452/resource/name/S0022050711002452sup001.pdf.

23. Roosevelt, Message on "Trade Relations with Cuba," June 13, 1902, in 35 Cong. Rec. 6720 (1902); *see* Roosevelt, First Annual Message, December 3, 1901, in Richardson Supp. 15:6660–61; Roosevelt to Butler, February 4, 1902, in Morison 3:228; Roosevelt, Speech at the Charleston Exposition, April 9, 1902, in *Addresses and Presidential Messages of Theodore Roosevelt 1902–1904* (New York: G. P. Putnam's Sons, 1903), 7–8; Roosevelt, Second Annual Message, December 2, 1902, in Richardson Supp. 15:6717; *see also* Howard C. Hill, *Roosevelt and the Caribbean* (Chicago: University of Chicago Press, 1927), 78–82; David F. Healy, *The United States in Cuba 1898–1902: Generals, Politicians, and the Search for Policy* (Madison: University of Wisconsin Press, 1963), 195, 214–15; Mary Speck, "Closed-Door Imperialism: The Politics of Cuban-U.S. Trade, 1902–1933," *Hispanic American Historical Review* 85, no. 3 (Aug. 2005), 449–61. Speck notes that, if anything, Cubans were disappointed that the treaty did not tie them closer to the United States economically. *Ibid.*

Roosevelt's chief Cuban advisors, Root and Wood, were equally enthusiastic and committed to helping Cuba through reciprocity. For Wood, *see, e.g.*, Wood to Root, January 4, 1901, in Root MSS; Wood to Lodge, January 12, 1901, in Box 29/30, Wood MSS; Wood to Root, October 22, 1901, in Root MSS; Wood to Roosevelt, October 28, 1901, in Box 29/30, Wood MSS; "Gen. Wood Explains," *New York Times*, June 13, 1902. For Root, *see* Root to Wood, January 9, 1901, in Box 29/30, Wood MSS; Roosevelt to Wood, November 11, 1901, in Morison 3:195–96; *see also* Jessup, *Elihu Root*, 1:326–28.

For the treaty's imbalance in Cuba's favor, *see* Alfred E. Eckes, Jr., *Opening America's Market: U.S. Foreign Trade Policy Since 1776* (Chapel Hill: University of North Carolina Press, 1995),

79–80. Neither the Americans nor the Cubans yet realized the extent to which reciprocity could lead Cuba to become economically dependent on the United States. *See* Dana G. Munro, *Intervention and Dollar Diplomacy in the Caribbean 1900–1921* (Princeton, NJ: Princeton University Press, 1964), 32–33.

24. *Report of the Committee Appointed to Confer with the Government of the United States, Giving an Account of the Result of Its Labors*, May 6, 1901, in Root MSS, 12; Roosevelt to Lodge April 30, 1906, in Morison 5:256; *see* David Healy, *Drive to Hegemony: The United States in the Caribbean 1898–1917* (Madison: University of Wisconsin Press, 1988), 214; Charles E. Chapman, "New Corollaries of the Monroe Doctrine," *University of California Chronicle* 33, no. 2 (April 1931), 173; David H. Burton, *Theodore Roosevelt: Confident Imperialist* (Philadelphia, PA: University of Pennsylvania Press, 1968), 105–06; Richard D. Challener, *Admirals, Generals, and American Foreign Policy 1898–1914* (Princeton, NJ: Princeton University Press, 1979), 94–98.

For the wrangling around the Cuban-British reciprocity treaty, *see* Adee to Squiers, March 20, 1905, in Instructions, Cuba, Roll 49, M77, RG59, NA; Loomis to Squiers, June 12, 1905, in Despatches, Cuba, Roll 49, M77, RG59, NA; Loomis to Squiers, June 21, 1905, in Instructions, Cuba, Roll 49, M77, RG59, NA; Root to Morgan, April 23, 1906, in Instructions, Cuba, Roll 49, M77, RG59, NA; *see also* Warren G. Kneer, *Great Britain and the Caribbean, 1901–1913: A Study in Anglo-American Relations* (East Lansing, MI: Michigan State University Press, 1975), 82–95.

25. *See* Allan Reed Millett, *The Politics of Intervention: The Military Occupation of Cuba, 1906–1909* (Columbus: Ohio State University Press, 1968), 259–60; Louis A. Pérez, Jr., *Cuba Under the Platt Amendment, 1902–1934* (Pittsburgh, PA: University of Pittsburgh Press, 1986), 60–65, 70–74, 82; Hugh Thomas, *Cuba: The Pursuit of Freedom* (New York: Harper and Row, 1971), 415–28, 434, 458; *see also* Chapter 5. Pérez and some other scholars are critical of American reconstruction policies in Cuba, which they accurately note produced significant long-term problems for the island. But it is not clear that any alternative reconstruction policy would have fared any better, and all came with significant downsides. *See* Richard H. Collin, "Symbiosis Versus Hegemony: New Directions in the Foreign Relations Historiography of Theodore Roosevelt and William Howard Taft," *Diplomatic History* 19, no. 3 (Summer 1995), 481–82.

26. *See* Magoon to Roosevelt, April 16, 1908, in Box 82, Roosevelt MSS; *see also* Millett, *Politics of Intervention*, 24–25; Healy, *United States in Cuba*, 195, 214–15; Collin, *Theodore Roosevelt's Caribbean*, 527–28; Munro, *Intervention and Dollar Diplomacy*, 32–33. Among others, Root had warned Cubans about the importance of diversifying their economy, but that sound advice was lost amid the din of independence and the allure of sky-high short-term profits. *See* Jessup, *Elihu Root*, 1:527–29. For the point that Cuba's sugar monoculture long predated reciprocity, *see* Speck, "Closed-Door Imperialism," 470–72.

27. *See* Millett, *Politics of Intervention*, 46–48.

28. *See* Millett, *Politics of Intervention*, 49–51; David A. Lockmiller, *Magoon in Cuba: A History of the Second Intervention, 1906–1909* (Chapel Hill: University of North Carolina Press, 1938), 27–31.

29. *See* Millett, *Politics of Intervention*, 50–52.

30. *See* Millett, *Politics of Intervention*, 52–53; Langley, *Banana Wars*, 36.

31. *Diario de la Marina*, October 4, 1905, quoted in Thomas, *Cuba*, 474; *see* Millett, *Politics of Intervention*, 52.

32. Roosevelt, Fourth Annual Message, December 6, 1904, in Richardson Supp. 16:6923–24; Root to Eliot, June 18, 1906, in Box 186, Root MSS; *see* Roosevelt to Lodge, April 30, 1906, in Morison 5:256.

33. *See* Millett, *Politics of Intervention*, 59–60.

34. *See* Ivan Musicant, *The Banana Wars: A History of United States Military Intervention in Latin America from the Spanish-American War to the Invasion of Panama* (New York: Macmillan, 1990), 55; Millett, *Politics of Intervention*, 63–65.

35. Steinhart to Root, September 8, 1906, in *Annual Reports of the War Department for the Fiscal Year Ended June 30, 1906* (Washington, DC: Government Printing Office, 1906), 444–45.

36. Roosevelt to Trevelyan, September 9, 1906, in Morison 5:401. Roosevelt later added that if the United States did not restore order, he feared that "various European nations" would. Roosevelt, Sixth Annual Message, December 3, 1906, in Richardson Supp. 16:7056–57. But there is little evidence that Roosevelt had any imminent threat in mind during the crisis.

37. Roosevelt to Trevelyan, September 9, 1906, in Morison 5:401; *see* Millett, *Politics of Intervention*, 65–67, 80, 90–91; Collin, *Theodore Roosevelt's Caribbean*, 532–33.

38. Roosevelt to Trevelyan, September 9, 1906, in Morison 5:401; Roosevelt to Bacon, September 10, 1906, in Morison 5:402; Bacon to Steinhart, September 11, 1906, in *War Department Annual Reports 1906*, 445; *see* Bacon to Steinhart, September 10, 1906, in *War Department Annual Reports 1906*, 445.

39. Roosevelt to Trevelyan, September 9, 1906, in Morison 5:401.

40. Roosevelt to Eliot, September 13, 1906, in Morison 5:410–11; Roosevelt to White, September 13, 1906, in Box 343, Roosevelt MSS. Lodge was also perplexed. "Disgust with the Cubans is very general," he reported to Roosevelt. "Nobody wants to annex them, but the general feeling is that they ought to be taken by the neck and shaken until they behave themselves." Lodge to Roosevelt, September 16, 1906, in *Selections from the Correspondence of Theodore Roosevelt and Henry Cabot Lodge 1884–1918* (New York: Charles Scribner's, 1925), 2:233.

41. Steinhart to Bacon, September 14, 1906, in *War Department Annual Reports 1906*, 446–47.

42. Roosevelt to de Quesada, September 14, 1906, in Morison 5:411–12; *see* Roosevelt to Bacon, September 14, 1906, in Morison 5:411.

43. *See* Lockmiller, *Magoon in Cuba*, 43, 46; Munro, *Intervention and Dollar Diplomacy*, 130.

44. Taft to Roosevelt, September 16, 1906, in Reel 68, Roosevelt MSS; Taft to Root, September 15, 1908, in Box 166, Root MSS.

45. *See* William Inglis, "The Collapse of the Cuban House of Cards," *Harper's Weekly*, October 20, 1906, 1488–89; *War Department Annual Reports 1906*, 449–50, 457; Taft to Roosevelt, September 20, 1906, in *War Department Annual Reports 1906*, 469; *see also* Pérez, *Cuba Under the Platt Amendment*, 96.

46. Taft to Roosevelt, September 21, 1906, in *War Department Annual Reports 1906*, 470; *see* Taft to Roosevelt, September 20, 1906, in *War Department Annual Reports 1906*, 469; Taft to Roosevelt, September 21, 1906, in *War Department Annual Reports 1906*, 469; *War Department Annual Reports 1906*, 454–56; Taft to Roosevelt, September 22, 1906, in Reel 68, Roosevelt MSS; *see also* Musicant, *Banana Wars*, 53–54.

47. *War Department Annual Reports 1906*, 456; Taft to Roosevelt, September 26, 1906, in *War Department Annual Reports 1906*, 477; *see* Taft to Roosevelt, September 22, 1906, in Reel 68, Roosevelt MSS.

48. Taft to Roosevelt, September 26, 1906, in *War Department Annual Reports 1906*, 476; Taft to Helen Taft, September 23, 1906, in Reel 25, Taft MSS; *see War Department Annual Reports 1906*, 461; Taft to Root, October 4, 1906, in Box 166, Root MSS; *see also* Millett, *Politics of Intervention*, 96–97.

49. Taft to Roosevelt, September 21, 1906, in *War Department Annual Reports 1906*, 470; *see* Taft to Charles P. Taft, October 4, 1906, in Reel 603, Taft MSS.

50. "The Cuban Insurrection," *London Times*, September 7, 1906; *see* Interview with Col. Ernesto Asbert, August 29, 1906, in FRUS 1906, 466; *see also* Millett, *The Politics of Intervention*, 68; Pérez, *Cuba Under the Platt Amendment*, 94–95.

51. William Inglis, "The Disappointed Rebels in Wait About Havana," *Harper's Weekly*, October 13, 1906, 1454; *see* Taft to Helen Taft, September 30, 1906, in Reel 25, Taft MSS.

52. Roosevelt to Taft, September 26, 1906, in Morison 5:426; Roosevelt to Taft, September 25, 1906, in Morison 5:423; Roosevelt to Lodge, September 27, 1906, in Morison 5:427–28; Roosevelt to Foraker, September 28, 1906, in Morison 5:431; Roosevelt to Foraker, September 28, 1906, in Morison 5:430; Roosevelt to Taft, September 26, 1906, in Morison 5:424; *see* Roosevelt to Taft, September 28, 1906, in Morison 5:432–33; Taft to Helen Taft, September 28, 1906, in Reel 25, Taft MSS; *see also* Millett, *Politics of Intervention*, 91–92, 97–101.

53. Taft to Roosevelt, September 28, 1906, in *War Department Annual Reports 1906*, 482; Roosevelt to Taft, September 28, 1906, in Morison 5:434.

54. *See* "Taft Governor of Cuba To-Day," *New York Times*, September 29, 1906; *see also* Millett, *Politics of Intervention*, 101–02.

55. Roosevelt to Taft, October 2, 1906, in Morison 5:437–38; *see* Millett, *Politics of Intervention*, 104–07, 120–22. Historians generally agree that once the rebellion began in mid-August, it would have been difficult if not impossible for Roosevelt to avoid reoccupying the island. Two

of the crisis's keenest scholars, however, argue that Roosevelt missed an off-ramp, although they disagree as to what that off-ramp was. David Lockmiller argues that if Roosevelt had stood by Palma from the beginning, the United States could have ended the rebellion with a show of force and minimum bloodshed and thereby avoided intervention. *See* Lockmiller, *Magoon in Cuba*, 60–61. But that argument hinges on the Liberal rebels not fighting back against the United States, an assumption that runs counter to the Liberal attitude at the time and the universal assessment of the Roosevelt administration. *See, e.g., War Department Annual Reports 1906*, 457–58. Lockmiller defends the assumption by noting that several Liberal generals were emphatic after the fact that they would not have fought against American forces. But those statements are contradicted by others, *see* "What Are We Doing in Cuba?," *New York Times*, October 1, 1906, and in any event they count for little because once the occupation began, the Liberals had every incentive to appear cooperative and pro-American, and to claim that they had been bluffing all along.

For his part, Allan Reed Millett argues that Roosevelt erred in sending naval vessels in response to Palma's request for military support. *See* Millett, *Politics of Intervention*, 73–82. Once the vessels arrived, Millett argues, both Palma and the Liberals hardened their positions and became determined to provoke an American intervention that could otherwise have been avoided. *See ibid.* But Millett ascribes too much importance to the dispatch of the warships. First, as he admits, both Palma and the Liberals were clamoring for an American intervention even before Roosevelt sent vessels to monitor the situation, so at most the vessels' arrival confirmed their preexisting strategies. Furthermore, there was almost no chance of either Palma or the Liberals compromising from the beginning, in large part because Palma's only shot at survival was American intervention. Millett never fully explains how or why the Liberals would have compromised with Palma if Roosevelt had held back.

56. *See* Buchanan to Russell, February 1, 1904, in Despatches, Panama, Roll 1, T726, RG59, NA; Buchanan to Hay, January 30, 1904, in Despatches, Panama, Roll 1, T726, RG59, NA; *see also* G. A. Mellander, *The United States in Panamanian Politics: The Intriguing Formative Years* (Danville, IL: Interstate Printers & Publishers, 1971), 53–54; Harold F. Peterson, *Diplomat of the Americas: A Biography of William I. Buchanan (1852–1909)* (Albany, NY: State University of New York Press, 1977), 247.

57. Adee to Hay, January 18, 1904, in Instructions, Panama, Roll 126, M77, RG59, NA; Adee to Loomis, January 20, 1904, in Despatches, Panama, Roll 1, T726, RG59, NA; *see* Hay to Adee, January 18, 1904, in Instructions, Panama, Roll 126, M77, RG59, NA; Hay to Buchanan, January 19, 1904, in Instructions, Panama, Roll 126, M77, RG59, NA; *see also* Mellander, *Panamanian Politics*, 49–54, 192.

58. Buchanan to Hay, January 28, 1904, in Despatches, Panama, Roll 1, T726, RG59, NA; Buchanan to Hay, January 30, 1904, in Despatches, Panama, Roll 1, T726, RG59, NA; Buchanan to Russell, February 1, 1904, in Despatches, Panama, Roll 1, T726, RG59, NA; Constitution of the Republic of Panama, art. 136, in FRUS 1904, 578. Buchanan claimed responsibility for the less-objectionable portion of Article 136 that granted the United States the right to intervene to preserve Panama's independence, but—apart from his sparse initial cable—he consistently maintained that the remainder of the article was "purely the wish and good sense of the Panama People and has not had its origin with us." Buchanan to Russell, February 1, 1904, in Despatches, Panama, Roll 1, T726, RG59, NA.

59. Amador's bargain paid off, at least at first. In late 1904, the head of Panama's army planned a coup with Liberal opposition leaders against Amador's Conservative government. Amador called on his guardian angel for help, and the United States was only too happy to answer. Backed by a buildup of American forces, Amador requested and received the army chief's resignation. Shortly afterward, the Panamanian president ordered the remainder of the army dismantled. Like Cuba, Panama would henceforth have only one custodian: the U.S. military. *See* Mellander, *Panamanian Politics*, 64–67; William D. McCain, *The United States and the Republic of Panama* (Durham, NC: Duke University Press: 1937), 48–60.

60. *See* Mellander, *Panamanian Politics*, 80–81.

61. Root to Magoon, December 4, 1905, in Instructions, Panama, Roll 126, M77, RG59, NA; Belisario Porras, "Una Lección de Civismo que debe Permanecer Eternamente Fresca en la

Memoria de los Panameños," June 13, 1924, in *Revista Lotería*, Nos. 346–47 (January–February 1985), 124; *see also* McCain, *United States and Panama*, 68–70; Mellander, *Panamanian Politics*, 81–89.

62. Porras, "Una Lección de Civismo," in *Revista Lotería*, 124.

63. *See* Mellander, *Panamanian Politics*, 105–13, 134, 144. Some of the Liberal loss stemmed from a strategic decision not to vote, but that strategy in turn reflected rampant Conservative electoral manipulation. *See ibid.*, 105–13.

64. Taft to Root, October 4, 1906, in Box 166, Root MSS; Root to Wilson, October 24, 1906, in Box 187, Root MSS; James Brown Scott, *Robert Bacon: Life and Letters* (Garden City, NY: Doubleday, Page, 1923), 118; *see* Taft to Charles P. Taft, October 4, 1906, in Reel 603, Taft MSS; Taft to Helen Taft, September 27, 1906, in Reel 25, Taft MSS. For a comparison of the situation in Panama to the events leading up to the second occupation of Cuba, *see* Squiers to Root, May 19, 1908, 847/59.69, in Roll 122, M862, RG59, NA; *see also* Mellander, *Panamanian Politics*, 123–25, 146.

65. Blackburn to Taft, May 7, 1908, quoted in Mellander, *Panamanian Politics*, 144; *see* Mellander, *Panamanian Politics*, 129–31, 134, 144–47, 153–54.

66. *See* Taft to Amador, May 12, 1908, 847/61, in Roll 122, M862, RG59, NA; *see also* Mellander, *Panamanian Politics*, 135–38, 154, 178, 180.

67. Taft to Amador, May 12, 1908, 847/61, in Roll 122, M862, RG59, NA; *see* Roosevelt to Taft, May 11, 1908, in Morison 6:1028–29; *see also* Mellander, *Panamanian Politics*, 147–53.

68. Arias to Members of the National Directorate of the Constitutional Party, July 4, 1908, in "Señor Arias' Renunciation," *Panama Star & Herald*, July 6, 1908; *see* Mellander, *Panamanian Politics*, 151–53, 165–67, 178–79.

69. Taft to Wright, July 14, 1908, in Reel 473, Taft MSS. Even Taft, however, admitted that the pressure he had applied "detracts from the independence of the Republic." But "the Republic has not shown itself competent in this regard," and "the thing of all others which must be avoided … is disturbance of any kind in Panama and Colon, and nothing is more certain to engender this than the bitterness of a party defeated by fraud at the polls." Taft to Roosevelt, May 16, 1908, in Reel 83, Roosevelt MSS.

70. Denby to Root, June 16, 1908, quoted in Jessup, *Elihu Root*, 1:525–26.

71. Obaldía to Taft, July 4, 1908, 847/83, in Roll 122, M862, RG59, NA; Adee to Bacon, July 7, 1908, 847/83, in Roll 122, M862, RG59, NA.

72. *See* Mellander, *Panamanian Politics*, 180.

73. Root to Watterson, March 5, 1908, in Box 188, Root MSS.

74. Roosevelt to Root, July 20, 1908, in Morison 6:1138; *see* Millett, *Politics of Intervention*, 146–48.

75. Roosevelt, Address at the Harvard Union, February 23, 1907, in Theodore Roosevelt, *Presidential Addresses and State Papers* (New York: Review of Reviews, 1910), 6:1178–79; Roosevelt to Taft, January 22, 1907, in Morison 5:560; *see* Root to Wilson, October 24, 1906, in Box 187, Root MSS; *see also* Millett, *Politics of Intervention*, 246.

76. Roosevelt to Lane, April 15, 1907, in Morison 5:648; Root, "South American Commerce," Address at the National Convention for the Extension of the Foreign Commerce of the United States in Washington, D.C., January 14, 1907, in *Latin America and the United States: Addresses by Elihu Root*, ed. Robert Bacon and James Brown Scott (Cambridge, MA: Harvard University Press, 1917), 275; *see* Roosevelt to Taft, January 22, 1907, in Morison 5:560; Root to Wilson, October 24, 1906, in Box 187, Root MSS; *see also* Wilfrid Hardy Callcott, *The Caribbean Policy of the United States 1890–1920* (New York: Octagon, 1977), 237–38; Lockmiller, *Magoon in Cuba*, 70.

77. *See* Millett, *Politics of Intervention*, 171–72, 178–85, 261–67.

78. Robert Lee Bullard, Diary Entry, February 13, 1909, in Box 1, Diary Book #4, Bullard MSS; *see* Musicant, *Banana Wars*, 67.

79. *Havana Post*, January 29, 1909, quoted in Millett, *Politics of Intervention*, 258; *see* Charles E. Magoon, "Supplemental Report of Provisional Governor," February 1, 1909, in S. Doc. No. 80 (1909), 8; "Fair Waters Mark Cuba's Launching," *Chicago Daily Tribune*, January 28, 1909;

"Festivities in Havana," *New York Times*, January 28, 1909; "Gomez Installed, Magoon Quits Cuba," *New York Times*, January 29, 1909.

80. Hirshinger to Adj. Gen., ACP, June 28, 1908, quoted in Millett, *Politics of Intervention*, 268; *see* Millett, *Politics of Intervention*, 243–45, 254–56.

81. *See* Magoon, "Supplemental Report," 7–8; "Cuba Once Again Pilots Own Ship," *Chicago Daily Tribune*, January 29, 1909.

82. O. H. Platt, "The Pacification of Cuba," *The Independent*, June 27, 1901, 1468; Elihu Root, "External Policies in 1904," Address as Temporary Chairman of the Republican National Convention in Chicago, June 21, 1904, in *The Military and Colonial Policy of the United States: Addresses and Reports by Elihu Root*, ed. Robert Bacon and James Brown Scott (Cambridge, MA: Harvard University Press, 1916), 100; *see Report of the Committee*, 10, 19.

83. *See* Healy, *Drive to Hegemony*, 132–33; Pérez, *Cuba Under the Platt Amendment*, 101–02; Whitney T. Perkins, *Constraint of Empire: The United States and Caribbean Interventions* (Westport, CT: Greenwood, 1981), 13.

84. Roosevelt to Taft, September 26, 1906, in Morison 5:424; Roosevelt to Kermit Roosevelt, October 23, 1906, in Morison 5:465; *see* Archibald Butt to Lewis F. Butt, February 3, 1909, in *The Letters of Archie Butt: Personal Aide to President Roosevelt*, ed. Lawrence F. Abbott (Garden City, NY: Doubleday, Page, 1924), 325; Lodge to Roosevelt, September 16, 1906, in *Selections* 2:232–33; Magoon to Roosevelt, April 16, 1908, in Reel 82, Roosevelt MSS; *see also* Lars Schoultz, *That Infernal Little Cuban Republic: The United States and the Cuban Revolution* (Chapel Hill: University of North Carolina Press, 2009), 26.

85. Root to Buchanan, March 20, 1909, in Box 58, Root MSS (punctuation altered). Of the relevant senior officials, only Governor Magoon began to grasp the problem. He warned Roosevelt that "the authority granted by the Platt Amendment should not be perverted into a menace to the object it was intended to conserve." Magoon to Roosevelt, April 16, 1908, in Reel 82, Roosevelt MSS. But that warning was ignored.

86. *See* Pérez, *Cuba Under the Platt Amendment*, 102.

87. *See* Healy, *Drive to Hegemony*, 137–44; Collin, *Theodore Roosevelt's Caribbean*, 496–99.

Chapter 9: Dollar Diplomacy

1. Roosevelt to Carnegie, February 26, 1909, in Morison 6:1538.

2. *See* Philip C. Jessup, *Elihu Root*, vol. 2, *1905–1937* (New York: Dodd, Mead, 1938), 123–26; Walter V. Scholes and Marie V. Scholes, *The Foreign Policies of the Taft Administration* (Columbia: University of Missouri Press, 1970), 2.

3. *See* Dana G. Munro, *Intervention and Dollar Diplomacy in the Caribbean 1900–1921* (Princeton, NJ: Princeton University Press, 1964), 160–61.

4. Henry Adams to Brooks Adams, February 17, 1909, in *Henry Adams and His Friends: A Collection of His Unpublished Letters*, ed. Harold Dean Cater (Boston: Houghton Mifflin, 1947), 640; *see* Richard H. Immerman, *Empire for Liberty: A History of American Imperialism from Benjamin Franklin to Paul Wolfowitz* (Princeton, NJ: Princeton University Press, 2010), 156; Scholes and Scholes, *Foreign Policies*, 6, 13.

5. Thomas Schoonover, "Max Farrand's Memorandum on the U.S. Role in the Panamanian Revolution of 1903," *Diplomatic History* 12, no. 4 (Fall 1988), 505; *see* Scholes and Scholes, *Foreign Policies*, 6–7.

6. Oswald Garrison Villard, "Philander C. Knox—Dark Horse," *The Nation*, May 22, 1920, 676, 678; Root to Jessup, September 15, 1930, quoted in Scholes and Scholes, *Foreign Policies*, 13; *see ibid.*, 8–14.

7. *See* F. M. Huntington Wilson, *Memoirs of an Ex-Diplomat* (Boston: Bruce Humphries, 1945), 13, 46–47, 143; Scholes and Scholes, *Foreign Policies*, 15.

8. *See* Jessup, *Elihu Root*, 1:457; Scholes and Scholes, *Foreign Policies*, 15–17.

9. *See* Huntington Wilson, *Memoirs*, 173–77; Scholes and Scholes, *Foreign Policies*, 15–16.

10. *The Autobiography of John Hays Hammond* (Murray Hill, NY: Farrar & Rinehart, 1935), 2:545; *see* Huntington Wilson, *Memoirs*, 175, 180.

11. Huntington Wilson, *Memoirs*, 55; *see ibid.*, 180.

12. *See generally* Scholes and Scholes, *Foreign Policies.*

13. Huntington Wilson, *Memoirs*, 183.

14. Taft to Storer, March 23, 1903, in Reel 38, Taft MSS; Meyer, Diary Entry, June 1, 1909, in M. A. DeWolfe Howe, *George von Lengerke Meyer: His Life and Public Services* (New York: Dodd, Mead, 1919), 433–34; Taft, First Annual Message, December 9, 1909, in Richardson Supp. 17:7795–96; *see* Holger H. Herwig, *Politics of Frustration: The United States in German Naval Planning, 1889–1941* (Boston: Little, Brown, 1976), 90–92. Taft admitted in making his comment about Pomeranian grenadiers that he "had not studied the question carefully." Taft to Storer, March 23, 1903, in Reel 38, Taft MSS.

15. *See* Herwig, *Politics of Frustration*, 101–04. By the time Taft left office, he was burning with the passion of the convert. *See* William H. Taft, "The Monroe Doctrine: Its Limitations and Implications," in *The United States and Peace* (New York: Charles Scribner's Sons, 1914), 6–7, 16–17.

16. Huntington Wilson, *Memoirs*, 196; *see* Friedrich E. Schuler, *Secret Wars and Secret Policies in the Americas, 1842–1929* (Albuquerque: University of New Mexico Press, 2010), 43–45; Friedrich Katz, *The Secret War in Mexico: Europe, the United States and the Mexican Revolution* (Chicago: University of Chicago Press, 1981), 412–13.

17. U.S. Navy General Board to Daniels, War Plan Black, July 1913, quoted in Herwig, *Politics of Frustration*, 105; *Hearing Before the H. Committee on Naval Affairs*, 63d Cong. 580 (1914). Of course, not everyone agreed. For the debate, *see* Donald A. Yerxa, *Admirals and Empire: The United States Navy and the Caribbean, 1898–1945* (Columbia: University of South Carolina Press, 1991), 30.

18. 48 Cong. Rec. 10045 (1912); *see ibid.*, 10046; *see also* Thomas A. Bailey, "The Lodge Corollary to the Monroe Doctrine," *Political Science Quarterly* 48, no. 2 (June 1933), 220–39; Richard D. Challener, *Admirals, Generals, and American Foreign Policy 1898–1914* (Princeton, NJ: Princeton University Press, 1979), 272–75; Eugene Keither Chamberlin, "The Japanese Scare at Magdalena Bay," *Pacific Historical Review* 24, no. 4 (November 1955), 345–59; David H. Grover, "Maneuvering for Magdalena Bay: International Intrigue at a Baja California Anchorage," *Southern California Quarterly* 83, no. 3 (Fall 2001), 261–84.

19. Meyer to Knox, June 21, 1910, 838.802/1, in Roll 94, M610, RG59, NA; *see* Huntington Wilson, *Memoirs*, 195–96; *see also* Challener, *Admirals, Generals, and American Foreign Policy*, 328–31; E. Taylor Parks and J. Fred Rippy, "The Galápagos Islands, A Neglected Phase of American Strategy Diplomacy," *Pacific Historical Review* 9, no. 1 (March 1940), 44.

20. Huntington Wilson, *Memoirs*, 196; *see* Huntington Wilson, "The Relation of Government to Foreign Investment," *Annals of the American Academy of Political and Social Science* 68 (November 1916), 305.

21. *See* Economic Commission for Latin America, UN Department of Economic and Social Affairs, *External Financing in Latin America* (New York: United Nations, 1965), 14, Table 12; *see also* J. Fred Rippy, *The Caribbean Danger Zone* (New York: G. P. Putnam's Sons, 1940), 224–25; Lester D. Langley and Thomas Schoonover, *The Banana Men: American Mercenaries and Entrepreneurs in Central America, 1880–1930* (Lexington: University Press of Kentucky, 1995), 167; Lloyd C. Gardner, *Imperial America: American Foreign Policy Since 1898* (New York: Harcourt Brace Jovanovich, 1976), 52–53. For the rise and overseas expansion of banks in particular, *see* Peter James Hudson, *Bankers and Empire: How Wall Street Colonized the Caribbean* (Chicago: University of Chicago Press, 2017).

22. *See* Rich Cohen, *The Fish That Ate the Whale: The Life and Times of America's Banana King* (New York: Picador, 2012), 34–37.

23. *See* Langley and Schoonover, *Banana Men*, 33–35; Cohen, *Fish That Ate the Whale*, 38–50; Steve Striffler and Mark Moberg, "Introduction," in *Banana Wars: Power, Production, and History in the Americas* (Durham, NC: Duke University Press, 2003), 10.

24. William H. Taft, Address at the Banquet Given in His Honor by the Americus Club, Pittsburgh, Pennsylvania, May 2, 1910 (self-pub., 1910), 13; Taft, Fourth Annual Message, December 3, 1912, in Richardson Supp. 18:8152–53. For the Taft administration's lack of concern about the Southern Cone, *see* Taft, "The Monroe Doctrine," 10–11.

25. Knox, "The Monroe Doctrine and Some Incidental Obligations in the Zone of the Caribbean," Address Before the New York State Bar Association, January 19, 1912, in FRUS 1912, 1092; *see* Knox, Statement Before the S. Comm. on Foreign Relations, May 24, 1911, in FRUS 1912, 588.

26. *See* Knox to Taft, September 28, 1909, in Reel 326, Taft MSS.

27. Knox, "The Spirit and Purpose of American Diplomacy," Address at the Commencement Exercises of the University of Pennsylvania, June 15, 1910 (self-pub., 1910), 45–46; Huntington Wilson, Address at the Third National Peace Congress, May 4, 1911, in *Bulletin of the Pan American Union* 32, no. 1 (January 1911), 893; Huntington Wilson, *Memoirs*, 216; *see* Division of Latin-American Affairs, Memorandum on the "Altruistic Policy of the United States Toward Latin American Countries," May 28, 1910, 710.11/379, in Roll 3, M1276, RG59, NA; An American Diplomat [Huntington Wilson], "Honduras Finances," *Washington Star*, February 26, 1911, in Folder 1-13, Doc. 7, Huntington Wilson MSS; Huntington Wilson, "Relation of Government," 305.

28. Knox, Address Before the National Civic Federation, December 11, 1911 (self-pub., 1911), 39–41; Taft, Fourth Annual Message, December 3, 1912, in Richardson Supp. 18:8152–53; *see* Huntington Wilson, *Memoirs*, 216; Huntington Wilson, Notes on Foreign Trade and Dollar Diplomacy, January 2, 1912, in Folder 1-15, Doc. 9, Huntington Wilson MSS.

29. Huntington Wilson, Notes on Dollar Diplomacy and the Monroe Doctrine, July 17, 1911, in Folder 1-13, Doc. 12, Huntington Wilson MSS; *see* Knox, "The Monroe Doctrine," in FRUS 1912, 1088; Knox, Statement, in FRUS 1912, 588; [Huntington Wilson], Draft, "Dollars vs. Bullets," *Washington Post*, January 25, 1911, in Folder 1-13, Doc. 6, Huntington Wilson MSS; Huntington Wilson to Taft, February 26, 1911, in Reel 385, Taft MSS; Knox to Taft, January 23, 1911, in Reel 385, Taft MSS. For the trauma from the second occupation of Cuba, *see* Allan Reed Millett, *The Politics of Intervention: The Military Occupation of Cuba, 1906–1909* (Columbus: Ohio State University Press, 1968), 265–66.

30. Huntington Wilson to Baldwin, January 19, 1910, in Folder 1-9, Doc. 2, Huntington Wilson MSS; *see* Knox, Address Before the National Civic Federation, 39–41.

31. Huntington Wilson, Address at the Third National Peace Congress, in *Bulletin*, 892; Taft, Address at the Americus Club Banquet, 16–17; *see* "Latin America," Memorandum, October 6, 1909, in Knox MSS; Knox, Address Before the National Civic Federation, 23–24.

32. *See* Huntington Wilson, Address at the Third National Peace Congress, in *Bulletin*, 893; Huntington Wilson, Notes on Foreign Trade and Dollar Diplomacy; Taft, Fourth Annual Message, December 3, 1912, in Richardson Supp. 18:8150–51, 153; Knox, "The Achievements of Dollar Diplomacy," *Saturday Evening Post*, March 9, 1912, 4; Knox to Certain Members of the Senate Committee on Foreign Relations, May 3, 1911, in FRUS 1912, 581; *see also* Scholes and Scholes, *Foreign Policies*, 35–36.

33. "Central American Treaties," *Newark Evening News*, August 17, 1911, quoted in Walter LaFeber, *Inevitable Revolutions: The United States in Central America*, 2nd ed. (New York: W. W. Norton, 1993), 49; Knox to Speyer, February 24, 1910, 814.51/55A, in Roll 20, M655, RG59, NA; *see* Huntington Wilson, "Honduras Finances"; *see also* Emily S. Rosenberg, *Financial Missionaries to the World: The Politics and Culture of Dollar Diplomacy, 1900–1930* (Durham, NC: Duke University Press, 2003), 56; Cyrus Veeser, *A World Safe for Capitalism: Dollar Diplomacy and America's Rise to Global Power* (New York: Columbia University Press, 2002), 4–5, 140–41, 156. For examples of the State Department's due diligence, *see* Huntington Wilson to Knox, Sept. 1, 1910, in Folder 1-9, Doc. 19, Huntington Wilson MSS; Knox to Taft, January 23, 1911, in Reel 385, Taft MSS; Huntington Wilson to Hoster, June 24, 1911, in Folder 1-13, Doc. 21, Huntington Wilson MSS; *see also* Munro, *Intervention and Dollar Diplomacy*, 223, 235, 537–38.

34. Huntington Wilson, *Memoirs*, 216; Huntington Wilson, Memorandum, July 10, 1911, 817.51/168, in Roll 71, M632, RG59, NA; *see* David Charles MacMichael, "The United States and the Dominican Republic, 1871–1940: A Cycle in Caribbean Diplomacy" (PhD diss., University of Oregon, 1964), 241. For the primacy of political objectives over commercial ones, *see* Huntington Wilson, Notes on Dollar Diplomacy; *see also* Munro, *Intervention and Dollar Diplomacy*, 162–63.

35. Huntington Wilson, *Memoirs*, 215.

36. *See* Munro, *Intervention and Dollar Diplomacy*, 161–62; Samuel Flagg Bemis, *The Latin American Policy of the United States: An Historical Interpretation* (New York: Harcourt, Brace, 1943), 164–65.

37. Taft to Horace D. Taft, July 3, 1904, in Reel 20, Taft MSS; Knox to Taft, March 14, 1911, in Reel 359, Taft MSS; Huntington Wilson, *Memoirs*, 166, 172, 208; *see* Taft to Storer, March 23, 1903, in Reel 38, Taft MSS; *see also* Warren G. Kneer, *Great Britain and the Caribbean, 1901–1913: A Study in Anglo-American Relations* (East Lansing, MI: Michigan State University Press, 1975), 146–47.

38. Huntington Wilson, Address at the Third National Peace Congress, in *Bulletin*, 894.

39. Knox, Notes Relative to Central American Countries, n.d., quoted in D. H. Dinwoodie, "Dollar Diplomacy in the Light of the Guatemalan Loan Project, 1909–1913," *The Americas* 26, no. 3 (January 1970), 237. Besides the policies discussed below, dollar diplomacy also hoped to reform the region's monetary systems by "introducing into strategic countries a stable, gold-based currency regulated by a central bank with reserves safely deposited in New York." Rosenberg, *Financial Missionaries*, 61. The United States also engaged in "battleship diplomacy"—selling battleships and other war material to "countries affected by the Monroe Doctrine," in part because the Bureau of Ordnance calculated that doing so "would result in increasing our available resources in time of war, or threatened war." Chambers, First Endorsement, May 14, 1909, 1070/55-59, in Roll 139, M862, RG59, NA; *see* Seward W. Livermore, "Battleship Diplomacy in South America: 1905–1925," *Journal of Modern History* 16, no. 1 (March 1944), 34–45. Finally, dollar diplomacy also called for continuing to build up the U.S. Navy, as well as keeping a weather eye out for attempts by other powers to take control of naval bases in the region. Although the U.S. Navy did not need additional naval bases, the United States nevertheless actively tried to acquire them in places as far-flung as the Galapagos Islands. It was the old problem of order: the Navy Department regarded "the acquisition of the islands as necessary only as a means of preventing the acquiring of influence at that point by a foreign power." Knox to Dickinson, April 19, 1911, 822.014/176a, in Roll 7, M1468, RG59, NA.

40. *See* Huntington Wilson, "Relation of Government," 302; *see also* Munro, *Intervention and Dollar Diplomacy*, 162.

41. Root to Hay, January 7, 1905, in Box 185, Root MSS; *see* Roosevelt to Hay, January 14, 1905, in Reel 337, Roosevelt MSS. Secretary Seward wanted the United States to refinance Mexico's debt rather than a private bank. In that respect, he was ahead of even the Taft administration. Roosevelt had also expressed interest in refinancing Venezuela's debt prior to the infamous Anglo-German blockade in late 1902, but nothing came of the project. *See* Kneer, *Great Britain and the Caribbean*, 67 n.72. For the State Department's desire to flush European influence out of Haiti, *see* Hudson, *Bankers and Empire*, 92–94; Munro, *Intervention and Dollar Diplomacy*, 245–55; out of Nicaragua, *see ibid.*, 193–204, 211–15; out of Honduras, *see ibid.*, 217–25, 231–35; out of Costa Rica, *see ibid.*, 235–38; and out of Guatemala, *see ibid.*, 238–45, Dinwoodie, "Dollar Diplomacy," 237–53. For the administration's policies in East Asia, *see* Scholes and Scholes, *Foreign Policies*, 109–248.

42. Knox, "The Spirit and Purpose of American Diplomacy," 48–50; Knox, "The Monroe Doctrine," in FRUS 1912, 1089; Huntington Wilson to Taft, February 26, 1911, in Reel 385, Taft MSS; *see* Huntington Wilson, "Honduras Finances"; Huntington Wilson, "Dollars vs. Bullets."

43. *See* Huntington Wilson, "Dollars vs. Bullets"; *see also* Scholes and Scholes, *Foreign Policies*, 37–38.

44. Knox to Taft, March 14, 1911, in Reel 359, Taft MSS.

45. "Cuban Government Matters," *The Cuba Review* 10, no. 4 (March 1912), 7; *see* Huntington Wilson to Taft, March 9, 1912, 837.0/777a, in Roll 6, M488, RG59, NA.

46. Knox, Address Before the National Civic Federation, 39–41; Knox to American Minister to Cuba, May 6, 1911, quoted in Scholes and Scholes, *Foreign Policies*, 35 n.2; *see* Munro, *Intervention and Dollar Diplomacy*, 469–84. For a similarly hands-on approach in Panama, *see* John Major, *Prize Possession: The United States and the Panama Canal, 1903–1979* (Cambridge, UK: Cambridge University Press, 1993), 124–29; William D. McCain, *The United States and*

the Republic of Panama (Durham, NC: Duke University Press: 1937), 72–73; Noel Maurer and Carlos Yu, *The Big Ditch: How America Took, Built, Ran, and Ultimately Gave Away the Panama Canal* (Princeton, NJ: Princeton University Press, 2011), 202–03.

47. For the administration making Nicaragua a priority early on, *see* Meyer, Diary Entry, March 12, 1909, in Howe, *George von Lengerke Meyer*, 426; Meyer, Diary Entry, March 16, 1909, in Howe, *George von Lengerke Meyer*, 426; Knox to Leon de la Barra, March 26, 1909, in Knox MSS; *see also* Dana G. Munro, "Dollar Diplomacy in Nicaragua, 1909–1913," *Hispanic American Historical Review* 38, no. 2 (May 1958), 210–11.

48. *See* Michael Gobat, *Confronting the American Dream: Nicaragua Under U.S. Imperial Rule* (Durham, NC: Duke University Press, 2005), 67–68; Munro, *Intervention and Dollar Diplomacy*, 167–69; Jürgen Buchenau, "Counter-Intervention Against Uncle Sam: Mexico's Support for Nicaraguan Nationalism, 1903–1910," *The Americas* 50, no. 2 (October 1993), 212–14.

49. Taft, Address at the Americus Club Banquet, 14–15; Knox, "The Spirit and Purpose of American Diplomacy," 44–45; Bryce to Grey, May 30, 1909, quoted in Kneer, *Great Britain and the Caribbean*, 152; Huntington Wilson to Reid, July 1, 1910, 817.00/1147, in Roll 6, M632, RG59, NA.

50. Knox to American Embassy in Paris, May 27, 1909, 5691/20, in Roll 466, M862, RG59, NA; *see* Taft, First Annual Message, December 9, 1909, in Richardson Supp. 17:7797; Taft, Address at the Americus Club Banquet, 14–15; Huntington Wilson, *Memoirs*, 209; *see also* Munro, *Intervention and Dollar Diplomacy*, 169–70.

51. *See* "Nicaragua Shows Hostility to Us," *New York Times*, May 18, 1909; George T. Weitzel, "American Policy in Nicaragua," in S. Doc. No. 64-334 (1916), 9–10; *see also* Thomas D. Schoonover, *The United States in Central America, 1860–1911: Episodes of Social Imperialism and Imperial Rivalry in the World System* (Durham, NC: Duke University Press, 1991), 130. Schoonover suggests that American officials feared Nicaragua securing "a better economic position ... outside the U.S. economic subsystem," but there is little evidence to support that concern.

52. *See* LaFeber, *Inevitable Revolutions*, 48.

53. *See* Moffat to Knox, October 12, 1909, in FRUS 1909, 452; Langley and Schoonover, *Banana Men*, 93; David Healy, "A Hinterland in Search of a Metropolis: The Mosquito Coast, 1894–1910," *International History Review* 3, no. 1 (January 1981), 38–39.

54. *See* Adee to Moffat, October 13, 1909, in FRUS 1909, 453; *see also* Munro, *Intervention and Dollar Diplomacy*, 173–75, Munro, "Dollar Diplomacy in Nicaragua," 214, Langley and Schoonover, *Banana Men*, 82–89. The American consul was subsequently forced out for violating Department instructions. *See* Lars Schoultz, *Beneath the United States: A History of U.S. Policy Toward Latin America* (Cambridge, MA: Harvard University Press, 2003), 212.

55. José Joaquín Morales, *De la Historia de Nicaragua de 1889–1913* (Granada, Nicaragua: MAGYS, 1963), 323; *see* Caldera to Knox, November 20, 1909, in FRUS 1909, 449; *see also* Langley and Schoonover, *Banana Men*, 85–90.

56. Huntington Wilson, Notes, November 26, 1909, 6369/334, in Roll 507, M862, RG59, NA; *see* Scholes and Scholes, *Foreign Policies*, 52–54.

57. Knox to the Nicaraguan Chargé, December 1, 1909, in FRUS 1909, 455; *see* Challener, *Admirals, Generals, and American Foreign Policy*, 294–95; Munro, *Intervention and Dollar Diplomacy*, 176–79.

58. *See* Stephen Kinzer, *Overthrow: America's Century of Regime Change from Hawaii to Iraq* (New York: Henry Holt and Company, 2006), 70.

59. Huntington Wilson, Notes, November 26, 1909, 6369/334, in Roll 507, M862, RG59, NA; *see* Scholes and Scholes, *Foreign Policies*, 56–57.

60. Huntington Wilson to Dawson, February 24, 1910, 817.00/1373, in Roll 7, M632, RG59, NA; Taft to Knox, December 22, 1909, in Reel 499, Taft MSS; *see* Munro, "Dollar Diplomacy in Nicaragua," 216.

61. *See* Lowell Thomas, *Old Gimlet Eye: The Adventures of Smedley D Butler* (New York: Farrar & Rinehart, 1933), 127; *see also* Munro, *Intervention and Dollar Diplomacy*, 180–81, 183. For Butler's primary authorship of *Old Gimlet Eye*, *see* Mark Strecker, *Smedley D. Butler, USMC: A Biography* (Jefferson, NC: McFarland, 2011), 146.

62. Thomas, *Old Gimlet Eye*, 125; *see* Hans Schmidt, *Maverick Marine: General Smedley D. Butler and the Contradictions of American Military History* (Lexington: University Press of Kentucky, 1998), 1, 6–37.

63. Thomas, *Old Gimlet Eye*, 3, 40; Butler to Ethel C. P. Butler, February 9, 1910, in *General Smedley Darlington Butler: The Letters of A Leatherneck, 1898–1931*, ed. Anne Cipriano Venzon (New York: Praeger, 1992), 75; *see* Thomas, *Old Gimlet Eye*, 73; Schmidt, *Maverick Marine*, 23, 33–34.

64. Butler to Maud D. Butler and Thomas S. Butler, January 2, 1910, in Venzon, *General Smedley Darlington Butler*, 65; Butler to Maud D. Butler and Thomas S. Butler, March 1, 1910, in Venzon, *General Smedley Darlington Butler*, 75–78.

65. *See* Butler to Maud D. Butler, June 4, 1910, in Venzon, *General Smedley Darlington Butler*, 82 & n.7; Thomas, *Old Gimlet Eye*, 127.

66. Butler, "America's Armed Forces 3. 'Happy Days Are Here Again': The Navy," *Common Sense* 4, no. 12 (November 1935), 13; *see* Thomas, *Old Gimlet Eye*, 127–28.

67. Thomas, *Old Gimlet Eye*, 128.

68. Thomas, *Old Gimlet Eye*, 128.

69. Butler, "America's Armed Forces 3," 13–14; *see* Thomas, *Old Gimlet Eye*, 128. One should treat Butler's account with some caution, as contemporary letters indicate that far from supporting the rebels, he planned to "remain absolutely neutral." Butler to Maud D. Butler, June 4, 1910, in Venzon, *General Smedley Darlington Butler*, 84–85. In later years, Butler may have exaggerated his involvement as he increasingly came to oppose American interventionism. Regardless, he and the rest of the American military were critical to Estrada's success. *See* Challener, *Admirals, Generals, and American Foreign Policy*, 300–01; Munro, *Intervention and Dollar Diplomacy*, 183–85.

70. *See* Lester D. Langley, *The Banana Wars: United States Intervention in the Caribbean, 1898–1934* (Chicago: Dorsey, 1988), 64; Munro, "Dollar Diplomacy in Nicaragua," 219.

71. *See* Scholes and Scholes, *Foreign Policies*, 59–60.

72. *See* Scholes and Scholes, *Foreign Policies*, 59–60; Munro, "Dollar Diplomacy in Nicaragua," 219.

73. Knox, "The Monroe Doctrine," in FRUS 1912, 1089–90.

74. *See* Malcolm D. McLean, "O. Henry in Honduras," *American Literary Realism, 1870–1910* 1, no. 3 (Summer 1968), 39; Cohen, *Fish That Ate the Whale*, 60; Alison Acker, *Honduras: The Making of A Banana Republic* (Boston: South End, 1988), 69; Scholes and Scholes, *Foreign Policies*, 68.

75. Huntington Wilson to Hoster, June 24, 1911, in Folder 1-13, Doc. 21, Huntington Wilson MSS; *see* Knox, "The Monroe Doctrine," in FRUS 1912, 1089–90; *see also* Scholes and Scholes, *Foreign Policies*, 68.

76. Knox to Leon de la Barra, March 26, 1909, in Knox MSS; Knox, "The Monroe Doctrine," in FRUS 1912, 1090–91; *see* Knox to Taft, September 28, 1909, in Reel 326, Taft MSS; Huntington Wilson, Draft of Memorandum to the Mexican Embassy, November 26, 1909, 6369/334, in Roll 507, M862, RG59, NA; Knox, "The Spirit and Purpose of American Diplomacy," 46–47; Knox to Cullom, June 17, 1911, 817.51/154A, in Roll 70, M632, RG59, NA; Huntington Wilson, "Honduras Finances"; Taft, Message Transmitting a Loan Convention Between the United States and Honduras to the Senate, January 26, 1911, in FRUS 1912, 558.

77. *See* Adee to Huntington Wilson, March 22, 1909, 17624/8, in Roll 1008, M862, RG59, NA; State Department, Memorandum, September 1909, in FRUS 1912, 550; Huntington Wilson, "Honduras Finances"; Huntington Wilson to Hoster, June 24, 1911, in Folder 1-13, Doc. 21, Huntington Wilson MSS.

78. Huntington Wilson to Hoster, June 24, 1911, in Folder 1-13, Doc. 21, Huntington Wilson MSS; *see* Munro, *Intervention and Dollar Diplomacy*, 217–21.

79. *See* Munro, *Intervention and Dollar Diplomacy*, 221–23.

80. *See* Henry F. Pringle, "A Jonah Who Swallowed the Whale," *American Magazine* 116 (September 1933), 114; *see also* Cohen, *Fish That Ate the Whale*, 11–12, 17–29, 117–20, 137–44; David Healy, *Drive to Hegemony: The United States in the Caribbean 1898–1917* (Madison: University of Wisconsin Press, 1988), 255.

81. Ernest Hamlin Baker, "United Fruit II: The Conquest of Honduras," *Fortune* 7, no. 3 (March 1933), 31; Pringle, "A Jonah," 115; *see* Thomas P. McCann, *An American Company: The Tragedy of United Fruit* (New York: Crown, 1976), 19; Cohen, *Fish That Ate the Whale*, 67–69, 72–74.

82. *See* Baker, "United Fruit II," 31; *see also* Cohen, *Fish That Ate the Whale*, 76–77.

83. *See* Baker, "United Fruit II," 31; *see also* Cohen, *Fish That Ate the Whale*, 77–79.

84. *See* Cohen, *Fish That Ate the Whale*, 78–79.

85. *See* Cohen, *Fish That Ate the Whale*, 79–80.

86. Christmas, "Autobiography" (unpublished manuscript), quoted in Herman Deutsch, *Incredible Yanqui: The Career of Lee Christmas* (Gretna, LA: Pelican, 2012), 8–9; *see* Deutsch, *Incredible Yanqui*, 4–10, 15–22.

87. *See* Langley and Schoonover, *Banana Men*, 49–51; Deutsch, *Incredible Yanqui*, 10–13; LaFeber, *Inevitable Revolutions*, 45.

88. Baker, "United Fruit II," 31–32; *see* Deutsch, *Incredible Yanqui*, 112–15; Cohen, *Fish That Ate the Whale*, 3–5. Sources differ on details, including the number of Secret Service agents, when they turned in, and exactly what was said.

89. Deutsch, *Incredible Yanqui*, 115; *see* Baker, "United Fruit II," 32; *see also* Langley and Schoonover, *Banana Men*, 127.

90. Deutsch, *Incredible Yanqui*, 118.

91. *See* Langley and Schoonover, *Banana Men*, 129–131; Cohen, *Fish That Ate the Whale*, 91–92.

92. *See* Langley and Schoonover, *Banana Men*, 132, 135–40, 144–45.

93. *See* Cohen, *Fish That Ate the Whale*, 92; Munro, *Intervention and Dollar Diplomacy*, 226–28. Some historians have suggested that the United States purposefully allowed Bonilla's revolution to gather a head of steam in order to pressure Dávila into ratifying the customs receivership treaty. But a thorough search of the documentary record has revealed little to support this theory. *See ibid.*, 231. On the contrary, Knox supported Dávila however he could, and Bonilla himself did not think that the Americans were aiding him. *See ibid.*, 226–28.

94. Rómulo E. Durón, Recollection, in Deutsch, *Incredible Yanqui*, app. 10, 231–32; *see* Dávila to Taft, January 28, 1911, in FRUS 1911, 297; *see also* Deutsch, *Incredible Yanqui*, 141.

95. Hitt to Knox, January 25, 1911, 815.00/1092, in Roll 4, M647, RG59, NA; *see* Langley and Schoonover, *Banana Men*, 133, 142–43.

96. Adee to Huntington Wilson, July 29, 1909, 19475/86, in Roll 1066, M862, RG59, NA.

97. *See* Munro, *Intervention and Dollar Diplomacy*, 229–30; Deutsch, *Incredible Yanqui*, 167.

98. *See* Munro, *Intervention and Dollar Diplomacy*, 231–34; Langley and Schoonover, *Banana Men*, 147–49.

99. Adee to Knox, April 4, 1911, 815.00/1316, in Roll 6, M647, RG59, NA.

100. *See* Knox, "Achievements of Dollar Diplomacy," 43; Knox, "The Monroe Doctrine," in FRUS 1912, 1091.

101. Huntington Wilson to Adee, January 13, 1911, 815.51/207, in Roll 35, M647, RG59, NA; *see* Munro, *Intervention and Dollar Diplomacy*, 193–94, 199, 203–04; Rosenberg, *Financial Missionaries*, 65–69. For the treaties' importance to the State Department, *see* Huntington Wilson, Notes on Foreign Trade and Dollar Diplomacy; Huntington Wilson, "Dollars vs. Bullets"; Huntington Wilson to Taft, February 26, 1911, in Reel 385, Taft MSS; Knox to Taft, January 23, 1911, in Reel 385, Taft MSS.

Europe also began pushing back on dollar diplomacy. Roosevelt had premised his Corollary on an evenhanded, "open door" policy in Latin America, in which Washington would protect European commercial interests in exchange for Europe's political and military forbearance. But dollar diplomacy upended that logic by privileging American commercial interests. Europe's great powers could not seriously challenge that reversal just then—the lamps were going out all over Europe as the darkness of the Great War crept closer—but some of the continent's diplomats nonetheless started asking why they should respect the Corollary if it meant Europe's total elimination from the hemisphere. *See* Kneer, *Great Britain and the Caribbean*, 187–88, 206. Even Great Britain—desperate for American friendship as the boots of the Kaiser clunked closer—adopted an increasingly sharp tone in its interactions with the Knox State Department. *See ibid.*, 188–207.

102. *See* Howard F. Cline, *The United States and Mexico* (New York: Atheneum, 1968), 54–56; Katz, *Secret War in Mexico*, 3–35; Charles H. Harris, III, and Louis R. Sadler, *The Border and the Revolution: Clandestine Activities of the Mexican Revolution 1910–1920* (Silver City, NM: High-Lonesome, 1988), vii–viii; Alan Knight, *The Mexican Revolution*, vol. 1, *Porfirians, Liberals and Peasants* (Lincoln: University of Nebraska Press, 1990), 78–115.

103. Evaristo Madero to Madero, November 22, 1909, in José C. Valadés, *Imaginación y Realidad de Francisco I. Madero* (Mexico City: Antigua Librería Robredo, 1960), 1:273; *see* Knight, *The Mexican Revolution*, 2:101; Scholes and Scholes, *Foreign Policies*, 84–89. For Taft's mobilization, *see* "Europe Made United States Guard Mexico," *Washington Herald*, March 10, 1911; "U.S. Troops to Aid in Crushing Revolt," *Washington Post*, March 10, 1911; "Germany's Note of Defiance," *Washington Post*, March 11, 1911; "Mexican Invasion Only a Last Resort," *New York Tribune*, March 14, 1911.

104. Taft to Farquhar, September 11, 1912, in Reel 514, Taft MSS; Taft to Knox, December 14, 1912, 812.00/5697, in Roll 1, M274, RG59, NA; *see* Scholes and Scholes, *Foreign Policies*, 89–95.

105. *See generally* Louis A. Pérez, Jr., "Politics, Peasants, and People of Color: The 1912 'Race War' in Cuba Reconsidered," *Hispanic American Historical Review* 66, no. 3 (August 1986), 509–39. For the interest in American intervention, *see* Beaupré to Knox, May 29, 1912, in FRUS 1912, 250–51; Commanding Officer of the U.S.S. Petrel to the Secretary of the Navy, July 17, 1912, 837.00/908, in Roll 7, M488, RG59, NA; *see also* Healy, *Drive to Hegemony*, 214–16.

106. Ham to Holaday, June 25, 1912, 837.00/877, in Roll 7, M488, RG59, NA; *see* Commanding Officer of the U.S.S. Petrel to the Secretary of the Navy, July 17, 1912, 837.00/908, in Roll 7, M488, RG59, NA; Bayliss to Beaupré, June 15, 1912, 837.00/827, in Roll 7, M488, RG59, NA; Goodrich to Lewis, July 20, 1912, 837.00/911, in Roll 7, M488, RG59, NA; *see also* Ivan Musicant, *The Banana Wars: A History of United States Military Intervention in Latin America from the Spanish-American War to the Invasion of Panama* (New York: Macmillan, 1990), 67–71.

107. *See* Scholes and Scholes, *Foreign Policies*, 60; Munro, "Dollar Diplomacy in Nicaragua," 219–21.

108. Northcott to Taft, February 25, 1911, in FRUS 1911, 655; Gunther to Knox, January 6, 1912, in FRUS 1912, 1013; *see* Weitzel to Knox, August 2, 1912, 817.00/1811, in Roll 12, M632, RG59, NA; Huntington Wilson, Memorandum, July 10, 1911, 817.51/168, in Roll 71, M632, RG59, NA; *see also* Whitney T. Perkins, *Constraint of Empire: The United States and Caribbean Interventions* (Westport, CT: Greenwood, 1981), 29–32; Rosenberg, *Financial Missionaries*, 77. For a good account of the bankers' involvement, *see* Zachary Karabell, *Inside Money: Brown Brothers Harriman and the American Way of Power* (New York: Penguin Press, 2021), 183–210. Díaz, like so many of his regional predecessors, floated the idea of establishing a Platt Amendment–like protectorate to secure Nicaragua (and his regime) against revolution. But the State Department did not run with the idea. *See* Munro, "Dollar Diplomacy in Nicaragua," 233.

109. *See* Gobat, *Confronting the American Dream*, 84–88, 94–98. The American minister in Managua reported that Mena had been egged on by "certain influential European subjects." Weitzel to Knox, July 31, 1912, in FRUS 1912, 1027.

110. Huntington Wilson to Taft, August 30, 1912, 817.00/1940a, in Roll 12, M632, RG59, NA; Huntington Wilson to Taft, Enc. 2, August 30, 1912, 817.00/1940A, in Roll 12, M632, RG59, NA.

111. Germany was rumored to be backing Mena's revolution. *See* Gobat, *Confronting the American Dream*, 111.

112. Thomas, *Old Gimlet Eye*, 139; *see ibid.*, 151–52, 157–58; *see also* Musicant, *Banana Wars*, 145–52.

113. *See* Munro, *Intervention and Dollar Diplomacy*, 215. Casualties were much higher in battles between rival Nicaraguan forces. *See* Gobat, *Confronting the American Dream*, 120–21.

114. Butler to Ethel C. P. Butler, September 30, 1912, in Venzon, *General Smedley Darlington Butler*, 116, 118–19; Thomas, *Old Gimlet Eye*, 138; *see ibid.*, 162.

115. *See* Munro, *Intervention and Dollar Diplomacy*, 209–10; Healy, *Drive to Hegemony*, 159–60. Many of the rank-and-file rebels wanted to continue fighting, but most of their leaders decided to follow Mena's lead. *See* Gobat, *Confronting the American Dream*, 112–20.

116. *See* Munro, *Intervention and Dollar Diplomacy*, 210, 216.

117. *See* Scholes and Scholes, *Foreign Policies*, 40; Healy, *Drive to Hegemony*, 160; MacMichael, "A Cycle of Caribbean Diplomacy," 257–58, 268–69.

118. *See* "Santo Domingan President Slain," *New York Times*, November 21, 1911; *see also* Healy, *Drive to Hegemony*, 160–61; Ellen D. Tillman, *Dollar Diplomacy by Force: Nation-Building and Resistance in the Dominican Republic* (Chapel Hill: University of North Carolina Press, 2016), 54–58.

119. Russell to Knox, September 16, 1912, in FRUS 1912, 366; Russell to Knox, September 19, 1912, in FRUS 1912, 366; *see* Russell to Knox, August 3, 1912, in FRUS 1912, 363; *see also* Scholes and Scholes, *Foreign Policies*, 41; Healy, *Drive to Hegemony*, 160–61; MacMichael, "A Cycle of Caribbean Diplomacy," 274–75, 285–86, 296.

120. Huntington Wilson to Taft, September 19, 1912, 839.00/659d, in Roll 5, M626, RG59, NA.

121. *See* Healy, *Drive to Hegemony*, 161–62.

122. *See* Munro, *Intervention and Dollar Diplomacy*, 266; MacMichael, "A Cycle of Caribbean Diplomacy," 267–68.

Chapter 10: God Save Us from the Worst

1. *See* Patricia O'Toole, *The Moralist: Woodrow Wilson and the World He Made* (New York: Simon & Schuster, 2018), 62.

2. "Rift in Clouds as Wilson Rises and Takes Oath," *New York World*, March 5, 1913; *see* Arthur S. Link, *Wilson*, vol. 2, *The New Freedom* (Princeton, NJ: Princeton University Press, 1956), 57–58; George C. Herring, *From Colony to Superpower: U.S. Foreign Relations Since 1776* (Oxford: Oxford University Press, 2008), 379.

3. *See* Wilson, "An Address on Latin American Policy in Mobile, Alabama," October 27, 1913, in PWW 28:452; *see also* Arthur S. Link, *Woodrow Wilson: Revolution, War, and Peace* (Arlington Heights, IL: Harlan Davidson, 1979), 4–5; Ross Gregory, "To Do Good in the World: Woodrow Wilson and America's Mission," in *Makers of American Diplomacy*, eds. Frank J. Merli and Theodore A. Wilson, vol. 2, *From Theodore Roosevelt to Henry Kissinger* (New York: Charles Scribner's Sons, 1974), 56.

4. *See* O'Toole, *The Moralist*, xvi, 8–11, 14–23.

5. *See* O'Toole, *The Moralist*, 11, 16–25, 30–31, 58–59; Herring, *From Colony to Superpower*, 379.

6. *See* Charles T. Thompson, *The Peace Conference Day by Day: A Presidential Pilgrimage Leading to the Discovery of Europe* (New York: Brentano's, 1920), 190–91; *see also* Howard F. Cline, *The United States and Mexico* (New York: Atheneum, 1968), 139–40; Herring, *From Colony to Superpower*, 379; O'Toole, *The Moralist*, 165.

7. Frederick Palmer, *Bliss, Peacemaker: The Life and Letters of General Tasker Howard Bliss* (New York: Dodd, Mead, 1934), 400 (emphasis omitted); Spring Rice to Tyrrell, February 7, 1914, in *The Letters and Friendships of Sir Cecil Spring Rice: A Record*, ed. Stephen Gwynn (Boston: Houghton Mifflin, 1929), 2:202; Raymond B. Fosdick, "Before Wilson Died," *The Survey*, February 15, 1924, 495.

8. *See* Mark T. Gilderhus, *Pan American Visions: Woodrow Wilson in the Western Hemisphere 1913–1921* (Tucson: University of Arizona Press, 1986), 11. For similar jubilation in the Philippines at Wilson's election, *see* Jonathan M. Katz, *Gangsters of Capitalism: Smedley Butler, the Marines, and the Making and Breaking of America's Empire* (New York: St. Martin's, 2022), 181–82.

9. *Official Proceedings of the Democratic National Convention* (Chicago: McLellan, 1900), 115–16; Bryan, "America's Mission," Speech in Washington, D.C., February 22, 1899, in *Speeches of William Jennings Bryan* (New York: Funk & Wagnalls, 1913), 2:11; Bryan, "Imperialism," Speech in Indianapolis, August 8, 1900, in *Speeches of William Jennings Bryan*, 2:44; Bryan, "Naboth's

Vineyard," Speech in Denver, Winter 1898–99, in *Speeches of William Jennings Bryan*, 2:7; *see* Bryan, "A Black Spot," *The Commoner*, November 20, 1903, 1; "Conscience in Diplomacy and Business," *The Commoner*, May 2, 1913, 2; *see also* Selig Adler, "Bryan and Wilsonian Caribbean Penetration," *Hispanic American Historical Review* 20, no. 2 (May 1940), 201–02; Dana G. Munro, *Intervention and Dollar Diplomacy in the Caribbean 1900–1921* (Princeton, NJ: Princeton University Press, 1964), 269.

10. Edward House, Diary Entry, November 25, 1914, in PWW 31:354–55; *see generally* Lee A. Craig, *Josephus Daniels: His Life and Times* (Chapel Hill: University of North Carolina Press, 2013).

11. Wilson, "A Statement on Relations with Latin America," March 12, 1913, in PWW 27:172; David F. Houston, *Eight Years with Wilson's Cabinet: 1913 to 1920* (Garden City, NY: Doubleday, Page 1926), 1:43–44; "Conscience in Diplomacy and Business," *The Commoner*, May 2, 1913, 2. Over the first few months, the administration seemed to be living up to its promise. Days after entering the White House, the president pulled the United States out of a six-power banking consortium in China that had been the centerpiece of Taft's dollar diplomacy in Asia. *See* Munro, *Intervention and Dollar Diplomacy*, 271; Emily S. Rosenberg, *Financial Missionaries to the World: The Politics and Culture of Dollar Diplomacy, 1900–1930* (Durham, NC: Duke University Press, 2003), 79. Closer to home, the administration moved to repair relations with Colombia on generous terms, including the payment of $25 million in reparations. Republican Senators predictably blocked the resulting treaty—Roosevelt called it "the payment of belated blackmail"—but the handsome gesture was nonetheless appreciated across the region. Roosevelt to Stone, July 11, 1914, in Morison 7:778; *see* Link, *New Freedom*, 320–24.

12. Wilson, "An Address on Latin American Policy," in PWW 28:448.

13. Cary T. Grayson, *Woodrow Wilson: An Intimate Memoir* (New York: Holt, Rinehart and Winston, 1960), 2.

14. Tyrrell to Grey, November 14, 1913, in PWW 28:543–44; *see* Oswald Garrison Villard, Diary Entry, August 14, 1912, in PWW 25:24–25; *see also* Gilderhus, *Pan American Visions*, 9–10.

15. *See* Paul W. Drake, "From Good Men to Good Neighbors: 1912–1932," in *Exporting Democracy: The United States and Latin America*, ed. Abraham F. Lowenthal (Baltimore: Johns Hopkins University Press, 1991), 10.

16. William H. Taft, "The Monroe Doctrine: Its Limitations and Implications," in *The United States and Peace* (New York: Charles Scribner's Sons, 1914), 33; Taft to Karger, July 22, 1913, in Reel 519, Taft MSS.

17. Wilson, "A Statement on Relations with Latin America," in PWW 27:172; Bryan to O'Shaughnessy, November 24, 1913, in FRUS 1914, 443; *see* Wilson, First Annual Message, December 2, 1913, in PWW 29:4–5; Wilson, A Draft of an Address to Congress, October 31, 1913, in PWW 28:479–80; *see also* Lloyd Gardner, "Woodrow Wilson and the Mexican Revolution," in *Woodrow Wilson and a Revolutionary World 1913–1921*, ed. Arthur S. Link (Chapel Hill: University of North Carolina Press, 1982), 14; Frederick S. Calhoun, *Power and Principle: Armed Intervention in Wilsonian Foreign Policy* (Kent, OH: Kent State University Press, 1986), 24.

18. Wilson, "A Statement on Relations with Latin America," in PWW 27:172; *see* Cline, *The United States and Mexico*, 141–42. For the Taft administration's own instrumental and ad hoc policy of nonrecognition, *see* Munro, *Intervention and Dollar Diplomacy*, 426. For Wilson's departures from his own nonrecognition policy, *see* Drake, "From Good Men to Good Neighbors," 13.

19. Woodrow Wilson, *The State: Elements of Historical and Practical Politics* (Boston: D. C. Heath, 1901), 639; Woodrow Wilson, "Bryce's American Commonwealth," *Political Science Quarterly* 4, no. 1 (March 1889), 168–69; Wilson, Remarks to the New York Press Club, June 30, 1916, in PWW 37:334; *see* Woodrow Wilson, *Constitutional Government in the United States* (New York: Columbia University Press, 1908), 182; *see also* Mark Benbow, *Leading Them to the Promised Land: Woodrow Wilson, Covenant Theology, and the Mexican Revolution, 1913–1915* (Kent, OH: Kent State University Press, 2010), 8–9. For Wilson's belief in every people's fitness for self-government, *see* Link, *Revolution, War, and Peace*, 5–6.

20. For example, see Wilson's determination to eradicate the influence of foreign corporations, as well as the dictators those corporations held in office. *See infra.*

21. Wilson, Interview with Samuel G. Blythe, April 27, 1914, in PWW 29:521–22.

22. Burton J. Hendrick, *The Life and Letters of Walter H. Page* (Garden City, NY: Doubleday, Page, 1922), 1:204.

23. Edward G. Lowry, "What the President Is Trying to Do for Mexico," January 1914, in PWW 29:92, 92–95, 97–98; *see* Wilson, A Draft of an Address to Congress, in PWW 28:480–81; *see also* PWW 29:92 n.1. For Wilson and Bryan's belief that nations could naturally take care of themselves in the absence of foreign interference, *see* Wilson and Bryan, Draft of a Circular Note to the Powers, October 24, 1913, in PWW 28:431–32.

24. Lowry, "What the President Is Trying to Do," in PWW 29:93, 94–95; *see* "Wilson Sums Up Campaign Issues," *New York Times*, November 3, 1912; Wilson, A Draft of an Address to Congress, in PWW 28:481; Wilson, A Fourth of July Address, July 4, 1914, in PWW 30:251–52.

25. Wilson, "An Address on Latin American Policy," in PWW 28:450; *see* Edward House, Diary Entry, October 30, 1913, in PWW 28:476–77.

26. Bryan to Wilson, October 28, 1913, in PWW 28:455–56.

27. Lowry, "What the President Is Trying to Do," in PWW 29:93–94; Wilson, "An Address on Latin American Policy," in PWW 28:450; *see* Wilson, A Draft of an Address to Congress, in PWW 28:480–81.

28. Bryan to Wilson, August 6, 1913, in PWW 28:124–25; Bryan to Wilson, August 16, 1913, in PWW 28:177.

29. *See* Pierrepont, Memorandum of the Latin-American Division of the Department of State for the Information of the Secretary on Nicaraguan Finances and the Mixed Claims Commission, May 22, 1913, in FRUS 1913, 1041–42; *see also* Whitney T. Perkins, *Constraint of Empire: The United States and Caribbean Interventions* (Westport, CT: Greenwood, 1981), 36–37; Link, *New Freedom*, 335.

30. Weitzel to Huntington Wilson, December 22, 1911, note to 817.00/1745, in Roll 11, M632, RG59, NA; *see* Convention Between the United States and the Republic of Nicaragua, February 8, 1913, in Confidential S. Exec. Doc. No. 62-D (1913); *see also* Thomas A. Bailey, "Interest in a Nicaragua Canal, 1903–1931," *Hispanic American Historical Review* 16, no. 1 (February 1936), 3.

31. *See* Bryan to Wilson, June 12, 1914, in PWW 30:174–75; Bryan to Wilson, June 16, 1913, in PWW 27:526; Draft Convention Between the United States and Nicaragua, June 1913, in PWW 27:529; Bryan to Wilson, May 24, 1913, in PWW 27:470. Bryan saw the new right to intervene as little more than a statement of the obvious. "It will give us the right to do that which we might be called upon to do anyhow," he remarked to Wilson. "We cannot escape the responsibilities of our position." Bryan to Wilson, June 12, 1914, in PWW 30:174–75. That was an especially stunning turnaround for Bryan, who had once called the Platt Amendment "a scheme of injustice" and a "wholesale surrender of independence." Bryan, "Deceiving the Cubans," *The Commoner*, May 17, 1901, 3; Bryan, "Justice to Cuba," *The Commoner*, March 15, 1901, 6.

32. Wilson to Bryan, June 19, 1913, in PWW 27:552.

33. "Dollar Diplomacy Outdone," *New York Times*, July 21, 1913; *see* "Distortion of the Monroe Doctrine," *New York World*, August 3, 1913; "No Protectorate over Nicaragua; Treaty Rejected," *New York World*, August 3, 1913; *see also* George W. Baker, Jr., "The Wilson Administration and Nicaragua, 1913–1921," *The Americas* 22, no. 4 (April 1966), 344–45.

34. *See* Bryan, Memorandum, July 20, 1913, in PWW 28:48; Bryan to Wilson, August 6, 1913, in PWW 28:124–25; Bryan to Wilson, October 28, 1913, in PWW 28:456.

35. Bryan to Wilson, August 6, 1913, in PWW 28:124–25; Bryan to Wilson, August 16, 1913, in PWW 28:176; Bryan, Memorandum, July 20, 1913, in PWW 28:48; Bryan to Wilson, October 28, 1913, in PWW 28:456.

36. Bryan, Memorandum, July 20, 1913, in PWW 28:48.

37. Bryan to Wilson, October 28, 1913, in PWW 28:456; *see* Bryan, Memorandum, July 20, 1913, in PWW 28:48; Bryan to Wilson, August 6, 1913, in PWW 28:124–25; Bryan to Wilson, August 16, 1913, in PWW 28:176–77. For the basic problem with Bryan's plan, *see* Wilfrid Hardy Callcott, *The Caribbean Policy of the United States 1890–1920* (New York: Octagon, 1977), 335–37.

38. Wilson to Bryan, March 20, 1914, in PWW 29:360.

39. *See* Baker, "The Wilson Administration and Nicaragua," 349.

40. *See* Chamorro to Bryan, October 7, 1913, in FRUS 1913, 1057; Chamorro to Bryan, October 31, 1913, in FRUS 1913, 1064; *see also* Paolo E. Coletta, *William Jennings Bryan*, vol. 2, *Progressive Politician and Moral Statesman 1909–1915* (Lincoln: University of Nebraska Press, 1969), 190, 193–94.

41. For an excellent overview of Madero's short rule, *see* Alan Knight, *The Mexican Revolution*, vol. 1, *Porfirians, Liberals and Peasants* (Lincoln: University of Nebraska Press, 1990), 247–487.

42. *See* John S. D. Eisenhower, *Intervention!: The United States and the Mexican Revolution, 1913–1917* (New York: W. W. Norton, 1993), 12–16.

43. *See* Eisenhower, *Intervention!*, 17–25.

44. Knox to Taft, January 27, 1913, 812.00/7229A, in Roll 25, M274, RG59, NA; *see* Knox to Wilson, January 21, 1913, 812.00/5912B, in Roll 22, M274, RG59, NA; *see also* Knight, *The Mexican Revolution*, 1:486–88; Eisenhower, *Intervention!*, 18–26. Under the Pact of the Embassy, Díaz was supposed to win a national election later that year and take over from Huerta. But over the summer, Huerta would sideline his co-conspirator by exiling him to Japan. *See* Eisenhower, *Intervention!*, 26.

45. Wilson to Knox, February 19, 1913, in FRUS 1913, 724; *see* Knox to Wilson, February 20, 1913, in FRUS 1913, 725–26; Knox to Wilson, February 21, 1913, in FRUS 1913, 728–29.

46. *See* Eisenhower, *Intervention!*, 7–9. José María Pino Suárez, the former vice president, was assassinated alongside Madero. *See ibid.*

47. Josephus Daniels, Diary Entry, April 18, 1913, in *The Cabinet Diaries of Josephus Daniels, 1913–1921*, ed. E. David Cronon (Lincoln: University of Nebraska Press, 1963), 42–44.

48. Wilson to Hale, April 19, 1913, in PWW 27:335; Thompson to Bull, May 22, 1913, in PWW 27:465; Knight, *The Mexican Revolution*, 2:11–33, 67–69, 103–29.

49. Instructions to John Lind, August 4, 1913, in PWW 28:110–11; S. Doc. No. 66-285 (1920), 1:1743; *see* Nancy Mitchell, *The Danger of Dreams: German and American Imperialism in Latin America* (Chapel Hill: University of North Carolina Press, 1999), 177–79.

50. *See* Gamboa to Lind, August 16, 1913, in PWW 28:174–75.

51. Wilson to Hulbert, August 24, 1913, in PWW 28:217–18; Wilson to Ellen Axson Wilson, August 19, 1913, in PWW 28:190–91; *see* Edward House, Diary Entry, August 10, 1913, in PWW 28:139; *see also* Kenneth J. Grieb, *The United States and Huerta* (Lincoln: University of Nebraska Press, 1969), 97. Wilson's opposition to intervention in Mexico was widely shared. "I dread intervention and war there beyond words," wrote Lodge. "Everything must be done that can be done in honor to avoid it." Lodge to Shattuck, August 26, 1913, in Reel 39, Lodge MSS.

52. Wilson, An Address on Mexican Affairs to a Joint Session of Congress, August 27, 1913, in PWW 28:227–29, 330. The Taft administration had previously placed an arms embargo on the country, but American officials understood that it was so riddled with exceptions to be a virtually nonexistent obstacle for Huerta's government. *See* Benbow, *Leading Them to the Promised Land*, 27–28, Mitchell, *Danger of Dreams*, 180–81. Despite Wilson's protestations of neutrality, he had already begun to secretly favor the Constitutionalists. *See* Benbow, *Leading Them to the Promised Land*, 38.

53. Wilson, An Address on Mexican Affairs to a Joint Session of Congress, August 27, 1913, in PWW 28:228.

54. Wilson, First Annual Message, December 2, 1913, in PWW 29:4–5; *see* O'Toole, *The Moralist*, 101; Grieb, *The United States and Huerta*, 106–07.

55. Huntington Wilson to Reid, July 1, 1910, 817.00/1147, in Roll 6, M632, RG59, NA; *see* Lloyd C. Gardner, *Safe for Democracy: The Anglo-American Response to Revolution, 1913–1923* (New York: Oxford University Press, 1984), 54–55; Grieb, *The United States and Huerta*, 113–14, 130–33.

56. Edward House, Diary Entry, October 30, 1913, in PWW 28:477; *see* Wilson, Outline of a Circular Note to the Powers, October 24, 1913, in PWW 28:434; *see also* Link, *New Freedom*, 369–73.

57. Wilson and Bryan, Draft of a Circular Note to the Powers, October 24, 1913, in PWW 28:431–32.

58. Wilson and Bryan, Draft of a Circular Note to the Powers, October 24, 1913, in PWW 28:431–32. One other likely factor in the administration's thinking was that American diplomats in Mexico were raising the alarm about Germany's concern for the lives of its nationals in the country. *See* O'Shaughnessy to Bryan, October 18, 1913, 812.00/9275, in Roll 30, M274, RG59, NA.

59. Lind to Bryan, March 12, 1914, in PWW 29:338.

60. Wilson, Outline of a Circular Note to the Powers, October 24, 1913, in PWW 28:434; Wilson, "An Address on Latin American Policy," in PWW 28:450; Bryan, A Note to the Powers, November 7, 1913, in PWW 28:504; *see* Bryan to Page, November 19, 1913, 812.00/9817a, in Roll 31, M274, RG59, NA; Moore to Wilson, October 28, 1913, in PWW 28:463; *see also* Link, *New Freedom*, 373–75.

61. Wilson to Hulbert, November 2, 1913, in PWW 28:483–84; Edward House, Diary Entry, October 30, 1913, in PWW 28:478; *see* Edward House, Diary Entry, October 30, 1913, in PWW 28:477–78; Wilson, A Draft of a Joint Resolution, October 31, 1913, in PWW 28:478; Wilson, A Draft of an Address to Congress, October 31, 1913, in PWW 28:479; Bryan to Page, November 19, 1913, 812.00/9817a, in Roll 31, M274, RG59, NA.

62. *See* Knight, *The Mexican Revolution*, 2:62–103; Grieb, *The United States and Huerta*, 134–37; Mitchell, *Danger of Dreams*, 189–94.

63. *See* Grieb, *The United States and Huerta*, 134–37; Mitchell, *Danger of Dreams*, 189–94.

64. Lind to Bryan, November 15, 1913, 812.00/9760, in Roll 31, M274, RG59, NA; *see* Bryan to Page, November 19, 1913, 812.00/9817a, in Roll 31, M274, RG59, NA.

65. "A New Mexican Crisis," *New York Times*, January 14, 1914; Wilson to Hulbert, February 1, 1914, in PWW 29:211–12; *see* Mitchell, *Danger of Dreams*, 193.

66. Spring Rice to Grey, February 7, 1914, in PWW 29:229–30; *see* A Press Release, February 3, 1914, in PWW 29:216; Spring Rice to Tyrrell, February 7, 1914, in Gwynn, *The Letters and Friendships*, 2:202; *see also* Knight, *The Mexican Revolution*, 2:138–39.

67. Gerard to Bryan, March 6, 1914, 812.00/11206, in Roll 35, M274, RG59, NA; "Lifting the Lid from the Mexican Kettle," *The Literary Digest*, March 21, 1914, 602; *see* Gardner, "Woodrow Wilson and the Mexican Revolution," 23; Friedrich Katz, *The Secret War in Mexico: Europe, the United States and the Mexican Revolution* (Chicago: University of Chicago Press, 1981), 189–90.

68. *See* Hans Schmidt, *Maverick Marine: General Smedley D. Butler and the Contradictions of American Military History* (Lexington: University Press of Kentucky, 1998), 61–68.

69. *See* Robert E. Quirk, *An Affair of Honor: Woodrow Wilson and the Occupation of Veracruz* (New York: W. W. Norton, 1962), 8, 13–14.

70. *See* Quirk, *An Affair of Honor*, 19–26; O'Toole, *The Moralist*, 101.

71. *See* Wilson, Interview with Samuel G. Blythe, April 27, 1914, in PWW 29:521; *see also* Link, *New Freedom*, 395–99.

72. Joseph P. Tumulty, *Woodrow Wilson as I Know Him* (Garden City, NY: Doubleday, Page, 1921), 151–52; *see* Lodge, Memorandum, April 20, 1914, in Henry Cabot Lodge, *The Senate and the League of Nations* (New York: Charles Scribner's Sons, 1925), 13–14; *see also* O'Toole, *The Moralist*, 104–05; Quirk, *An Affair of Honor*, 67–77. For the *Ypiranga*'s journey and cargo, *see* Michael C. Meyer, "The Arms of the *Ypiranga*," *Hispanic American Historical Review* 50, no. 3 (January 1970), 543–56. For the German side of the story, *see* Thomas Baecker, "The Arms of the *Ypiranga*: The German Side," *The Americas* 30, no. 1 (July 1973), 1–17.

73. Tumulty, *Woodrow Wilson*, 152; *see* Quirk, *An Affair of Honor*, 77; Gardner, *Safe for Democracy*, 61.

74. *See* Quirk, *An Affair of Honor*, 85–103. Some sources list slightly different casualty counts. *See, e.g.*, O'Toole, *The Moralist*, 105.

75. "Mexico City Ablaze for War; Japs Cheer Crisis," *New York World*, April 25, 1914; Canada to Bryan, April 25, 1914, 812.00/10720, in Roll 36, M274, RG59, NA; *see* Canada to Bryan, April 23, 1914, 812.00/11652, in Roll 36, M274, RG59, NA; *see also* Quirk, *An Affair of Honor*, 107–10; Link, *New Freedom*, 400; Knight, *The Mexican Revolution*, 2:161.

76. Ray Stannard Baker, *Woodrow Wilson: Life and Letters*, vol. 4, *President, 1913–1914* (London: William Heinemann, 1932), 330; Arthur Walworth, *Woodrow Wilson*, vol. 1, *American*

Prophet (New York: Longmans, Green, 1958), 373; Wilson to Jacobus, April 29, 1914, in Reel 137, Vol. 13, Wilson MSS; *see* Wilson to Van Dyke, April 27, 1914, in Reel 137, Vol. 13, Wilson MSS; *see also* Quirk, *An Affair of Honor*, 109–10, 151. One further reason why Wilson may not have acted on the *Ypiranga*'s visit to Puerto México is because the administration had learned to its considerable embarrassment that the arms on board had been brought from the United States, not Europe. *See* Quirk, *An Affair of Honor*, 98.

77. *See* Knight, *The Mexican Revolution*, 2:170.

78. Wilson to Garrison, August 8, 1914, in PWW 30:362.

79. Josef Kohler, ed., *Der Prozess gegen die Attentäter von Sarajewo: Nach dem amtlichen Stenogramm der Gerichtsverhandlung Aktenmässig Dargestellt* (Berlin, R. v. Decker's Verlag, 1918), 159; *see* Christopher Clark, *The Sleepwalkers: How Europe Went to War in 1914* (New York: HarperCollins, 2013), 367–76.

80. For an excellent account of the July Crisis, *see generally* Clark, *The Sleepwalkers*.

81. Edward House, Diary Entry, November 25, 1914, in PWW 31:355.

82. *See* Barbara W. Tuchman, *The Zimmermann Telegram* (New York: Ballantine, 1985), 76; Charles H. Harris, III, and Louis R. Sadler, *The Border and the Revolution: Clandestine Activities of the Mexican Revolution 1910–1920* (Silver City, NM: High-Lonesome, 1988), 116–17; Thomas Boghardt, *The Zimmermann Telegram: Intelligence, Diplomacy, and America's Entry into World War I* (Annapolis, MD: Naval Institute Press, 2012), 221.

83. Wilson, An Address in Pittsburgh on Preparedness, January 29, 1916, in PWW 36:32; *see War Memoirs of Robert Lansing* (Indianapolis: Bobbs-Merrill, 1935), 310; *see also* Donald A. Yerxa, *Admirals and Empire: The United States Navy and the Caribbean, 1898–1945* (Columbia: University of South Carolina Press, 1991), 35–36.

84. For a lucid example of this concern, *see Universal Military Training: Hearing Before the S. Subcommittee of the Committee on Military Affairs*, 64th Cong. 97 (1917).

85. *See* U.S. Navy General Board Executive Committee Memorandum, August 6, 1915, in Reel 36, Microfilm Shelf No. 19815, Daniels MSS; Charles A. Bennett, "From Harbor Defense to Coast Defense," *Journal of the United States Artillery* 44, no. 2 (September–October 1915), 159; *see also* George T. Davis, *A Navy Second to None: The Development of Modern American Naval Policy* (New York: Harcourt, Brace, 1940), 222; James L. Abrahamson, *America Arms for a New Century: The Making of a Great Military Power* (New York: Free Press, 1981), 162–67; John A. S. Grenville, "Diplomacy and War Plans in the United States, 1890–1917," *Transactions of the Royal Historical Society* 11 (1961), 18–20.

86. Huse to Commander-in-Chief Atlantic Fleet, February 10, 1915, in Reel 36, Microfilm Shelf No. 19815, Daniels MSS; Page to House, September 22, 1914, in Hendrick, *The Life and Letters*, 1:334; *see* General Board to Secretary of the Navy, August 1, 1914, in *Naval Investigation: Hearings Before the S. Subcommittee of the Comm. on Naval Affairs*, 66th Cong. 736 (1921); *see also* Abrahamson, *America Arms*, 162–67; Yerxa, *Admirals and Empire*, 55.

87. Huse to Commander-in-Chief Atlantic Fleet, February 10, 1915, in Reel 36, Microfilm Shelf No. 19815, Daniels MSS; *see* George Louis Beer, "America's International Responsibilities and Foreign Policy," *Annals of the American Academy of Political and Social Science* 66 (July 1916), 84; *see also* Holger H. Herwig, *Politics of Frustration: The United States in German Naval Planning, 1889–1941* (Boston: Little, Brown, 1976), 156–59. Such fears gripped the public as well. Several popular books warned grimly about the need to prepare for a postwar attack on the nation or hemisphere. One author underlined that "whichever side wins, the United States will likely have to fight the winner within a short time." Hudson Maxim, *Defenseless America* (New York: Hearst's International Library, 1915), 71–72; *see* Abrahamson, *America Arms*, 166–67.

88. "Our Haitian Responsibility," *Chicago Daily Tribune*, July 30, 1915; *see* U.S. Navy General Board Executive Committee Memorandum, August 6, 1915, in Reel 36, Microfilm Shelf No. 19815, Daniels MSS; Caperton to Benson, October 30, 1916, in Folder 5, Box 1, Caperton MSS; *see also* Martin Sicker, *The Geopolitics of Security in the Americas: Hemispheric Denial from Monroe to Clinton* (Westport, CT: Praeger, 2002), 67; David Healy, *Drive to Hegemony: The United States in the Caribbean 1898–1917* (Madison: University of Wisconsin Press, 1988), 174–75.

89. *See* O'Toole, *The Moralist*, 130–31, 164–65; Arthur S. Link, *Wilson*, vol. 3, *The Struggle for Neutrality, 1914–1915* (Princeton, NJ: Princeton University Press, 1960), 45.

90. Josephus Daniels, *The Wilson Era: Years of Peace—1910–1917* (Chapel Hill: University of North Carolina Press, 1946), 441; *see* Coletta, *William Jennings Bryan*, 2:112; O'Toole, *The Moralist*, 130–31.

91. *See* O'Toole, *The Moralist*, 131, 166; David Glaser, *Robert Lansing: A Study in Statecraft* (Xlibris, 2015), 15–17; Link, *Struggle for Neutrality*, 45.

92. Lansing, Memorandum on the "Present Nature and Extent of the Monroe Doctrine, and Its Need of Restatement," June 11, 1914, in FRUS–Lansing, 2:463; *see* Lansing, "Consideration and Outline of Policies," July 11, 1915, in Lansing, *War Memoirs*, 19.

93. Wilson, An Address in New York on Preparedness, January 27, 1916, in PWW 36:10–11; Lansing, "Consideration and Outline of Policies," in Lansing, *War Memoirs*, 20.

94. Edward House, Diary Entry, December 16, 1914, in PWW 31:469–70; *see* Edward House, Diary Entry, December 16, 1914, in PWW 31:470; Lansing to the Chilean Ambassador, April 29, 1915, in FRUS–Lansing, 2:484; Wilson, Address to the Pan American Scientific Congress, January 6, 1916, in PWW 35:444–45; *see also* Link, *New Freedom*, 324–27. For the administration's efforts on the Pan-American Pact, *see generally* Gilderhus, *Pan American Visions*, 49–56, 65–68, 74–77. For the first full draft of the treaty, *see* A Draft of a Pan-American Treaty, December 16, 1914, in PWW 31:471.

95. Lansing to Bryan, June 16, 1914, in FRUS–Lansing, 2:459; Enclosure, Lansing to Wilson, November 24, 1915, in PWW 35:252.

96. Enclosure, Lansing to Wilson, November 24, 1915, in PWW 35:249–50.

97. Lansing to Wilson, November 24, 1915, in PWW 35:246–47.

98. Wilson to Lansing, November 29, 1915, in PWW 35:263.

99. Root to Borah, January 7, 1915, in 68 Cong. Rec. 1557 (1927); *see* Link, *New Freedom*, 339–40. For the rumor of a German bid and its impact, *see* "Germany Bids High on Nicaragua Route," *New York Times*, February 15, 1916; *see also* Link, *New Freedom*, 340; Joseph O. Baylen, "American Intervention in Nicaragua, 1909–33: An Appraisal of Objectives and Results," *Southwestern Social Science Quarterly* 35, no. 2 (September 1954), 150–51.

100. Lansing to Wilson, December 4, 1915, in FRUS–Lansing, 2:503; Wilson to Lansing, December 5, 1915, in PWW 35:290; *see* Wilson to Lansing, June 16, 1915, in FRUS–Lansing, 2:501; Lansing, Memorandum of Conversation with Danish Minister, November 15, 1915, in PWW 35:202; *see also* Arthur S. Link, *Wilson*, vol. 5, *Campaigns for Progressivism and Peace, 1916–1917* (Princeton, NJ: Princeton University Press, 1965), 80–83; Hans Schmidt, *The United States Occupation of Haiti, 1915–1934* (New Brunswick, NJ: Rutgers University Press, 1995), 9, 57. For fears about Germany motivating the purchase, *see* Lansing, "Consideration and Outline of Policies," in Lansing, *War Memoirs*, 20; Lansing, "Drama of the Virgin Islands Purchase," *New York Times Magazine*, July 19, 1931.

101. Lansing, "Consideration and Outline of Policies," in Lansing, *War Memoirs*, 19; *see* General Board to the Secretary of the Navy, November 14, 1914, in *Naval Investigation*, 1155; *see also* Yerxa, *Admirals and Empire*, 37.

102. *See* Davis to Lansing, January 12, 1916, in FRUS 1916, 311; *see also* Perkins, *Constraint of Empire*, 62–63; Schmidt, *The United States Occupation of Haiti*, 42.

103. *See* Schmidt, *The United States Occupation of Haiti*, 42–43.

104. *See* Stabler to Bryan, May 13, 1914, 838.00/1667, in Roll 8, M610, RG59, NA; *see also* Munro, *Intervention and Dollar Diplomacy*, 326–27.

105. Bryan to Wilson, June 14, 1913, in PWW 27:519; *see* Munro, *Intervention and Dollar Diplomacy*, 327.

106. *See* Bryan to Smith, February 26, 1914, in FRUS 1914, 340; Bryan to Blanchard, November 12, 1914, in FRUS 1914, 359; Bryan to Wilson, April 3, 1915, in PWW 32:472; Bryan to Fuller, May 6, 1915, in PWW 33:117.

107. Bryan to von Bernstorff, September 16, 1914, in PWW 31:35; *see* Stabler to Bryan, May 13, 1914, 838.00/1667, in Roll 8, M610, RG59, NA; J. H. Stabler, Memorandum, May 14, 1914, 838.00/1668, in Roll 8, M610, RG59, NA; *see also* Link, *Struggle for Neutrality*, 520–21; Healy, *Drive to Hegemony*, 188–89; Walter H. Posner, "American Marines in Haiti, 1915–1922," *The Americas* 20, no. 3 (January 1964), 238–39.

108. Bryan to Blanchard, December 19, 1914, in FRUS 1914, 370–71; *see* Wilson to Bryan, June 25, 1914, in PWW 30:213; Bryan to Blanchard, November 12, 1914, in FRUS 1914, 359;

Blanchard to Bryan, December 2, 1914, in FRUS 1914, 363; Bryan to Blanchard, December 12, 1914, in FRUS 1914, 367; Bryan to Wilson, December 18, 1914, in PWW 31:482.

109. *See* Bryan to Wilson, January 7, 1915, in PWW 32:27–28; Wilson to Bryan, January 13, 1915, in PWW 32:62; Bryan to Wilson, April 3, 1915, in PWW 32:472–73; *see also* Link, *Struggle for Neutrality*, 527–29.

110. Bryan to Wilson, March 27, 1915, in PWW 32:439; *see* Peter James Hudson, *Bankers and Empire: How Wall Street Colonized the Caribbean* (Chicago: University of Chicago Press, 2017), 100–08; Schmidt, *The United States Occupation of Haiti*, 53; Schmidt, *Maverick Marine*, 82.

111. Wilson to Bryan, March 31, 1915, in PWW 32:458; Wilson to Bryan, April 6, 1915, in PWW 32:487; *see* Bryan to Wilson, April 3, 1915, in PWW 32:472–73.

112. *See* Bryan to Fuller, May 6, 1915, in PWW 33:116–17.

113. *See* Wilson to Lansing, July 2, 1915, and Fuller, Report Summary, in PWW 33:467.

114. *See* William B. Caperton, "History of Flag Career of Rear Admiral W. B. Caperton, U.S. Navy Commencing January 5, 1915," in Subject File ZN (Personnel), 1911–1927, RG45, NA, 49.

115. Lansing to Wilson, August 3, 1915, in PWW 34:69; Wilson to Lansing, August 4, 1915, in PWW 34:78; Wilson to Fort, August 2, 1915, in Reel 142, Vol. 23, Wilson MSS; *see* Wilson to Galt, August 9, 1915, in PWW 34:139.

116. Lansing to Wilson, August 7, 1915, in FRUS–Lansing, 2:523; Wilson to Lansing, August 4, 1915, in PWW 34:78; *see also* Daniels to FDR, July 15, 1933, in Reel 59, Microfilm Shelf 18416, Daniels MSS; Lansing to McCormick, May 4, 1922, in S. Rep. No. 67-794 (1922), 31. For a survey of generally positive press reactions, *see* John W. Blassingame, "The Press and American Intervention in Haiti and the Dominican Republic, 1904–1920," *Caribbean Studies* 9, no. 2 (July 1969), 37, 39.

Some historians have suggested that the European threat was a justification contrived after the occupation began. *See* Perkins, *Constraint of Empire*, 69. For support, they cite a letter written by Sumner Welles in advance of Lansing's testimony to Congress about the cause of the occupation, in which Welles called it "desir[able]" that Lansing "lay stress upon the position assumed by the German Government just prior to our intervention." Welles to Hughes, April 17, 1922, 838.00/2006, in Roll 13, M610, RG59, NA. Of course, emphasizing one particular reason for the occupation is hardly the same as fabricating that reason out of whole cloth. In any event, there is overwhelming evidence of the administration's concern about Germany and the European threat more broadly in the run-up to and during the intervention. Besides the sources already cited, *see*, *e.g.*, Wilson to Daniels, July 31, 1915, in Reel 65, Microfilm Shelf 18416, Daniels MSS.

117. Benson to Caperton, August 10, 1915, in *Inquiry into Occupation and Administration of Haiti and Santo Domingo: Hearings Before a S. Select Comm. on Haiti and Santo Domingo*, vol. 1, 67th Cong. 315 (1922); Josephus Daniels, "The Problem of Haiti," *Saturday Evening Post*, July 12, 1930, 34; *see* Daniels to FDR, July 15, 1933, in Reel 59, Microfilm Shelf 18416, Daniels MSS; *see also* Schmidt, *The United States Occupation of Haiti*, 73–74.

118. Caperton, "History of Flag Career," 87; Lowell Thomas, *Old Gimlet Eye: The Adventures of Smedley D Butler* (New York: Farrar & Rinehart, 1933), 182; *see* Ivan Musicant, *The Banana Wars: A History of United States Military Intervention in Latin America from the Spanish-American War to the Invasion of Panama* (New York: Macmillan, 1990), 179.

119. Lansing to Wilson, August 13, 1915, in PWW 34:183; Lansing to McCormick, May 4, 1922, in S. Rep. No. 67-794 (1922), 31; *see also* David Healy, *Gunboat Diplomacy in the Wilson Era: The U.S. Navy in Haiti, 1915–1916* (Madison: University of Wisconsin Press, 1976), 133–34.

120. Lansing to Wilson, August 13, 1915, in PWW 34:183–84.

121. Wilson to Galt, August 15, 1915, in PWW 34:208–09; Wilson to Galt, August 24, 1915, in PWW 34:311. Secretary of the Navy Daniels was also "far from happy" with the decisions the United States was making. *See* Daniels, "The Problem of Haiti," 34. Like the others, however, Daniels believed the United States's actions were necessary under the circumstances; "the danger of that pivotal country, so near our shores, falling into the control of some European nation, added to the business of assassinating presidents, made it imperative for us to take the course followed." Daniels to FDR, July 15, 1933, in Reel 59, Microfilm Shelf 18416, Daniels MSS; *see* Daniels, "The Problem of Haiti," 32.

122. *See* Max Boot, *The Savage Wars of Peace: Small Wars and the Rise of American Power* (New York: Basic Books, 2002), 161–62; Healy, *Gunboat Diplomacy*, 139–58. For the final treaty, *see* Draft of Treaty Between the United States and Haiti Concerning the Finances, Economic Development and Tranquillity of Haiti, September 16, 1915, in FRUS 1915, 449–51.

123. Sullivan to Bryan, December 4, 1913, quoted in Sumner Welles, *Naboth's Vineyard: The Dominican Republic 1844–1924* (Mamaroneck, NY: Paul P. Appel, 1966), 2:722; *see* Calhoun, *Power and Principle*, 76–80.

124. Wilson to Various Dominican Leaders, July 27, 1914, in PWW 30:307–09; *see* Calhoun, *Power and Principle*, 80–86; Link, *Struggle for Neutrality*, 506–16.

125. Sullivan to Bryan, January 10, 1914, 839.51/1204, in Roll 52, M626, RG59, NA; Johnston to Long, September 9, 1915, quoted in David Charles MacMichael, "The United States and the Dominican Republic, 1871–1940: A Cycle in Caribbean Diplomacy" (PhD diss., University of Oregon, 1964), 397; *see* Link, *Struggle for Neutrality*, 539–43; Ellen D. Tillman, *Dollar Diplomacy by Force: Nation-Building and Resistance in the Dominican Republic* (Chapel Hill: University of North Carolina Press, 2016), 63–65.

126. *See* Link, *Struggle for Neutrality*, 540–43; Tillman, *Dollar Diplomacy by Force*, 65, 71; Eric Paul Roorda, *The Dictator Next Door: The Good Neighbor Policy and the Trujillo Regime in the Dominican Republic, 1930–1945* (Durham, NC: Duke University Press, 2006), 16.

127. *See* Musicant, *Banana Wars*, 237, 244–46; Munro, *Intervention and Dollar Diplomacy*, 311–12.

128. Frederic M. Wise and Meigs O. Frost, *A Marine Tells It To You* (New York: J. H. Sears, 1929), 143.

129. *See* Calhoun, *Power and Principle*, 110.

130. *See* Frederick S. Calhoun, *Uses of Force and Wilsonian Foreign Policy* (Kent, OH: Kent State University Press, 1993), 31; Stephen M. Fuller and Graham A. Cosmas, *Marines in the Dominican Republic 1916–1924* (Washington, DC: History and Museum Division, 1974), 9–22.

131. *See* Link, *Struggle for Neutrality*, 545–47; Bruce J. Calder, *The Impact of Intervention: The Dominican Republic During the U.S. Occupation of 1916–1924* (Austin: University of Texas Press, 1988), 11–12.

132. Caperton to Benson, June 15, 1916, in Folder 1, Box 1, Caperton MSS; *see* Caperton to Benson, May 18, 1916, in Folder 1, Box 1, Caperton MSS; *see also* Healy, *Drive to Hegemony*, 197; Musicant, *Banana Wars*, 265.

133. Wilson to Lansing, November 26, 1916, in FRUS 1916, 242; *see* Lansing to Wilson, November 22, 1916, 839.00/2013, in Roll 14, M626, RG59, NA; J. H. Stabler, "Re Dominican Situation: Conference with Mr. Polk," October 31, 1916, 839.00/2013, in Roll 14, M626, RG59, NA; *see also* Tillman, *Dollar Diplomacy by Force*, 83; Munro, *Intervention and Dollar Diplomacy*, 312–14; Frank Moya Pons, *The Dominican Republic: A National History* (Princeton, NJ: Markus Wiener, 2010), 319; MacMichael, "A Caribbean Cycle of Diplomacy," 433–34 & n.35.

134. Harry S. Knapp, Proclamation of Occupation and Military Government, November 29, 1916, in FRUS 1916, 247.

135. Wilson to House, July 7, 1915, in PWW 33:479–80; Lansing, Private Memorandum, "The Conference in Regard to Mexico," October 10, 1915, in Box 64, Reel 1, Lansing MSS (punctuation altered); *see* Tumulty, *Woodrow Wilson*, 159–60; *see also* Benbow, *Leading Them to the Promised Land*, 117; Knight, *The Mexican Revolution*, 2:345–46.

136. *See* Knight, *The Mexican Revolution*, 2:263–328.

137. *See* Knight, *The Mexican Revolution*, 2:285–86, 302–28; John Mason Hart, *Revolutionary Mexico: The Coming and Process of the Mexican Revolution* (Berkeley: University of California Press, 1989), 14–15, 280–81, 291–94, 298–300; Benbow, *Leading Them to the Promised Land*, 97–98.

138. *See* Katz, *Secret War in Mexico*, 328–30, 557–61.

139. *See* Tuchman, *The Zimmermann Telegram*, 66–83; Friedrich E. Schuler, *Secret Wars and Secret Policies in the Americas, 1842–1929* (Albuquerque: University of New Mexico Press, 2010), 111–13.

140. *See* Lansing, Private Memorandum, "The Conference in Regard to Mexico," October 10, 1915, in Box 64, Reel 1, Lansing MSS; *see also* Katz, *Secret War in Mexico*, 329–44; Tuchman, *The Zimmermann Telegram*, 95–96.

141. Lansing, Private Memorandum, "The Conference in Regard to Mexico," October 10, 1915, in Box 64, Reel 1, Lansing MSS; *see* Lansing, "Consideration and Outline of Policies," in Lansing, *War Memoirs*, 20; *see also* Katz, *Secret War in Mexico*, 298–302. Earlier that summer, Lansing had suggested that Villa be given "an opportunity to obtain funds" because "we do not wish the Carranza faction to be the only one to deal with in Mexico," and "an appearance, at least, of opposition to him will give us an opportunity to invite a compromise of factions." Lansing to Wilson, August 9, 1915, in Reel 72, Wilson MSS. But by October, Lansing had committed to making Carranza's faction "dominant" because of his fears of Germany.

Like Lansing, Wilson was "determin[ed] not to allow Germany to force him into intervention in Mexico." Edward House, Diary Entry, March 17, 1916, in PWW 36:335; *see* Edward House, Diary Entry, March 29, 1916, in PWW 36:379; House to Wilson, April 7, 1916, in PWW 36:434.

142. Wilson, An After-Luncheon Talk at the White House to the Members of the Democratic National Committee, December 8, 1915, in PWW 35:314–15.

143. *See* Eisenhower, *Intervention!*, 217–32, 244; Arthur S. Link, *Wilson*, vol. 4, *Confusions and Crises, 1915–1916* (Princeton, NJ: Princeton University Press, 1964), 205–09; Russell Crandall, *America's Dirty Wars: Irregular Warfare from 1776 to the War on Terror* (Cambridge, UK: Cambridge University Press, 2014), 95; Katz, *Secret War in Mexico*, 303, 308.

144. Wilson to House, June 22, 1916, in PWW 37:281; *see* Wilson, Draft of an Address of a Joint Session of Congress, June 26, 1916, in PWW 37:298; *see also* Knight, *The Mexican Revolution*, 2:345–46, 351–52; Michael Clodfelter, *Warfare and Armed Conflicts: A Statistical Encyclopedia of Casualty and Other Figures, 1492–2015*, 4th ed. (Jefferson, MO: McFarland, 2017), 424–25; Katz, *Secret War in Mexico*, 310–11. For German involvement with Villa, *see* Katz, *Secret War in Mexico*, 334–39; Michael C. Meyer, "Felix Sommerfeld and the Columbus Raid of 1916," *Arizona and the West* 25, no. 3 (Autumn 1983), 213–28; Francis J. Munch, "Villa's Columbus Raid: Practical Politics or German Design?," *New Mexico Historical Review* 44, no. 3 (July 1969), 189–214; James A. Sandos, "German Involvement in Northern Mexico, 1915–1916: A New Look at the Columbus Raid," *Hispanic American Historical Review* 50, no. 1 (February 1970), 70–88.

145. *See* Lansing to Smith, March 3, 1917, in Box 25, Lansing MSS; *see also* Knight, *The Mexican Revolution*, 2:352; Eisenhower, *Intervention!*, 307.

146. *See* Knight, *The Mexican Revolution*, 2:347–48. For Wilson's advisors' concerns about the impact on American credibility abroad if the United States failed to respond to Villa, *see* Lane to Wilson, March 13, 1916, in PWW 36:301; Edward House, Diary Entry, March 17, 1916, in PWW 36:335; House to Wilson, April 7, 1916, in PWW 36:434.

147. *See* Knight, *The Mexican Revolution*, 2:343–46; Katz, *Secret War in Mexico*, 308–09.

148. *See* Katz, *Secret War in Mexico*, 344–50.

149. *See* Katz, *Secret War in Mexico*, 349–50; Boghardt, *The Zimmermann Telegram*, 59–63; Herwig, *Politics of Frustration*, 121–26.

150. "Text of Germany's Proposal to Form an Alliance With Mexico and Japan Against the United States," *New York Times*, March 1, 1917; *see* Michael C. Desch, *When the Third World Matters: Latin America and United States Grand Strategy* (Baltimore, MD: Johns Hopkins University Press, 1993), 32–33; Katz, *Secret War in Mexico*, 352–53. Boghardt argues that the original German text has been "subtly" mistranslated; rather than reading "it is understood that Mexico is to reconquer the lost territory in New Mexico, Texas, and Arizona" (or similar variations), the relevant portion of the telegram is better translated as "consent on our part for Mexico to reconquer." Boghardt, *The Zimmermann Telegram*, 74. I use the classic translation here because it was the one circulated to the public by the administration and thus the basis for the country's subsequent actions.

151. Spring Rice to Balfour, February 23, 1917, in Gwynn, *The Letters and Friendships*, 2:381; *see* Boghardt, *The Zimmermann Telegram*, 2, 96–104.

152. *See* Tuchman, *The Zimmermann Telegram*, 168–69, 174–87, 198–200; Boghardt, *The Zimmermann Telegram*, 2, 135, 138–40, 189–90; Desch, *When the Third World Matters*, 39–44.

153. Wilson, An Address to the Senate, January 22, 1917, in PWW 40:536, 539.

154. Josephus Daniels, Diary Entry, February 27, 1917, in PWW 41:298. For Cuba, *see* Musicant, *Banana Wars*, 71–78; Healy, *Drive to Hegemony*, 198–99; Munro, *Intervention and Dollar Diplomacy*, 489–99. For Haiti, *see* Schmidt, *The United States Occupation of Haiti*, 82–86, 97–98. For the Dominican Republic, *see generally* Calder, *Impact of Intervention*.

155. Wicker to Lansing, February 29, 1916, 817.00/2440, in Roll 15, M632, RG59, NA. For Panama, *see* Walter LaFeber, *The Panama Canal: The Crisis in Historical Perspective* (New York: Oxford University Press, 1989), 55–58; Noel Maurer and Carlos Yu, *The Big Ditch: How America Took, Built, Ran, and Ultimately Gave Away the Panama Canal* (Princeton, NJ: Princeton University Press, 2011), 202–03; Richard L. Millett, *Searching for Stability: The U.S. Development of Constabulary Forces in Latin America and the Philippines* (Fort Leavenworth, KS: Combat Studies Institute Press, 2010), 35–36. For Nicaragua, *see* Healy, *Drive to Hegemony*, 234–36; Baker, "The Wilson Administration and Nicaragua," 357–58.

156. Edith O'Shaughnessy, *Intimate Pages of Mexican History* (New York: George H. Doran, 1920), 307.

Chapter 11: All the Nuisance of Empire

1. For this ladder of interventionism in the Dominican Republic, *see* Abraham F. Lowenthal, "The United States and the Dominican Republic to 1965: Background to Intervention," *Caribbean Studies* 10, no. 2 (July 1970), 32–33.

2. *See* Richard Millett and G. Dale Gaddy, "Administering the Protectorates: The U.S. Occupation of Haiti and the Dominican Republic," *Revista/Review Interamericana* 6, no. 3 (Fall 1976), 399. For an example from Nicaragua, *see* Michael Gobat, *Confronting the American Dream: Nicaragua Under U.S. Imperial Rule* (Durham, NC: Duke University Press, 2005), 76–77.

3. Taft to Helen Taft, September 20, 1906, in Reel 25, Taft MSS; *see* Chapter 8. For prejudices, *see* David Healy, *Drive to Hegemony: The United States in the Caribbean 1898–1917* (Madison: University of Wisconsin Press, 1988), 58–76, 288; for race in particular, *see generally* Eric T. L. Love, *Race over Empire: Racism and U.S. Imperialism 1865–1900* (Chapel Hill: University of North Carolina Press, 2004); Rubin Francis Weston, *Racism in U.S. Imperialism: The Influence of Racial Assumptions on American Foreign Policy, 1893–1946* (Columbia: University of South Carolina Press, 1972).

4. *See* Healy, *Drive to Hegemony*, 58–76, 238–54, 288; *see generally* William E. Leuchtenburg, "Progressivism and Imperialism: The Progressive Movement and American Foreign Policy, 1898–1916," *Mississippi Valley Historical Review* 39, no. 3 (December 1952), 483–504. For a skeptical view and the debate Leuchtenburg spawned, *see* Joseph M. Siracusa, "Progressivism, Imperialism, and the Leuchtenburg Thesis, 1952–1974: An Historiographical Appraisal," *Australian Journal of Politics & History* 20, no. 3 (1974), 312–25, and the sources cited therein.

5. Carleton Beals, *Banana Gold* (Philadelphia: J. B. Lippincott, 1932), 294–95; *see* Aroop Mukharji, "Sea Change: McKinley, Roosevelt, and the Expansion of U.S. Foreign Policy 1897–1909" (PhD diss., Harvard University, April 2020), 131 n.187; Bruce J. Calder, *The Impact of Intervention: The Dominican Republic During the U.S. Occupation of 1916–1924* (Austin: University of Texas Press, 1988), xxi.

6. Roosevelt to Bishop, February 23, 1904, in Morison 4:734–35; *see* David Charles MacMichael, "The United States and the Dominican Republic, 1871–1940: A Cycle in Caribbean Diplomacy" (PhD diss., University of Oregon, 1964), 257–58, 268–69.

7. *See* Dana G. Munro, *Intervention and Dollar Diplomacy in the Caribbean 1900–1921* (Princeton, NJ: Princeton University Press, 1964), 542–43; Dana G. Munro, *The United States and the Caribbean Republics 1921–1933* (Princeton, NJ: Princeton University Press, 1974), 12.

8. *See* discussion in Chapter 10.

9. *See* Calder, *Impact of Intervention*, xxii; Healy, *Drive to Hegemony*, 280–86.

10. *See* Healy, *Drive to Hegemony*, 132–33; Louis A. Pérez, Jr., *Cuba Under the Platt Amendment, 1902–1934* (Pittsburgh, PA: University of Pittsburgh Press, 1986), 101–02; Whitney T. Perkins,

Constraint of Empire: The United States and Caribbean Interventions (Westport, CT: Greenwood, 1981), 13.

11. *See* Ashley J. Tellis, "Pakistan's Political Development: Will the Future Be Like the Past?," in *Development Challenges Confronting Pakistan*, ed. Anita M. Weiss and Saba Gul Khattak (Sterling, VA: Kumarian, 2012), 225–29; Alan McPherson, *The Invaded: How Latin Americans and Their Allies Fought and Ended U.S. Occupations* (Oxford: Oxford University Press, 2016), 14.

12. *See* Calder, *Impact of Intervention*, xxii. For a variation of this argument in the context of military interventions specifically, *see* Ellen D. Tillman, *Dollar Diplomacy by Force: Nation-Building and Resistance in the Dominican Republic* (Chapel Hill: University of North Carolina Press, 2016). For this argument in the modern-day context, *see* Philip H. Gordon, *Losing the Long Game: The False Promise of Regime Change in the Middle East* (New York: St. Martin's, 2020), 260–63.

13. *See* Munro, *Intervention and Dollar Diplomacy*, 542; Andrew J. Bacevich, "The American Electoral Mission in Nicaragua, 1927–28," *Diplomatic History* 4, no. 3 (Summer 1980), 241.

14. *See* Munro, *The United States and the Caribbean Republics*, 373. Of course, direct American governance was especially unconducive to the development of democratic institutions. One Democratic official noted bitterly that the occupation of the Dominican Republic had not given the Dominicans "the slightest instruction in self-government"; "on the contrary, they have had a very strong lesson in government by force, something they were already well schooled in, from a people who they thought were the champions of freedom throughout the world." Vance to Wilson, October 25, 1920, 839.00/2353, in Roll 21, M626, RG59, NA.

15. *See* Healy, *Drive to Hegemony*, 236, 287; Paul W. Drake, "From Good Men to Good Neighbors: 1912–1932," in *Exporting Democracy: The United States and Latin America*, ed. Abraham F. Lowenthal (Baltimore: Johns Hopkins University Press, 1991), 36.

16. John F. Kennedy, Address on the First Anniversary of the Alliance for Progress, March 13, 1962, in PPP 1962, 223. For perceptive appreciations of this problem, *see* White to Grew, "Our Central American Policy," November 7, 1924, 711.13/65, in M673, RG59, NA; Wicker to Lansing, February 29, 1916, 817.00/2440, in Roll 15, M632, RG59, NA; *see also* William Kamman, *A Search For Stability: United States Diplomacy Toward Nicaragua 1925–1933* (Notre Dame, IN: University of Notre Dame Press, 1968), 232.

17. *See* Healy, *Drive to Hegemony*, 228, 236–37; Drake, "From Good Men to Good Neighbors," 35. For a perceptive appreciation of this problem, *see* White to Grew, "Our Central American Policy," November 7, 1924, 711.13/65, in Roll 1, M673, RG59, NA.

18. *See* McPherson, *The Invaded*, 38–39; Drake, "From Good Men to Good Neighbors," 36; Jules Robert Benjamin, *The United States and Cuba: Hegemony and Dependent Development, 1880–1934* (Pittsburgh, PA: University of Pittsburgh Press, 1977), 6. For the United States continuing to make this mistake to this day, *see* Gordon, *Losing the Long Game*, 249–51.

19. Walter Lippmann, "Second Thoughts on Havana," *Foreign Affairs* 6, no. 4 (July 1928), 550. For the trade-off between stability and democracy, *see* Theodore P. Wright, Jr., "Honduras: A Case Study of United States Support of Free Elections in Central America," *Hispanic American Historical Review* 40, no. 2 (May 1960), 213.

20. *See, e.g.*, discussion *supra* Chapter 10 n.146.

21. Huntington Wilson to Taft, September 19, 1912, 839.00/659d, in Roll 5, M626, RG59, NA; Wright to Lansing, January 24, 1916, 839.00/1781, in Roll 13, M626, RG59, NA; *see* Huntington Wilson to Meyer, February 16, 1911, 839.00/326e, in Roll 3, M626, RG59, NA.

22. Churchill almost certainly did not come up with the quip. *See* Scott Horsley, "A Churchill 'Quote' that U.S. Politicians Will Never Surrender," NPR, October 28, 2013, https://www.npr.org/sections/itsallpolitics/2013/10/28/241295755/a-churchill-quote-that-u-s-politicians-will-never-surrender.

Chapter 12: At the Point of Bayonets

1. John Quincy Adams, *An Address Delivered at the Request of a Committee of the Citizens of Washington; on the Occasion of Reading the Declaration of Independence, on the Fourth of July, 1821* (Washington, DC: Davis and Force, 1821), 28–29.

2. Adams, *An Address*, 28–29 (punctuation altered).

3. *See* Congressional Research Service, *Instances of Use of United States Armed Forces Abroad, 1798–2022* (March 8, 2022), 7–9; Walter LaFeber, *The Panama Canal: The Crisis in Historical Perspective* (New York: Oxford University Press, 1989), 42.

4. *See* John Steele Gordon, *An Empire of Wealth: The Epic History of American Economic Power* (New York: Harper Perennial, 2004), 293–94; George C. Herring, *From Colony to Superpower: U.S. Foreign Relations Since 1776* (Oxford: Oxford University Press, 2008), 437. For a good overview of the personal and material costs of the war for Europe, *see* Paul Kennedy, *The Rise and Fall of the Great Powers: Economic Change and Military Conflict from 1500 to 2000* (New York: Vintage Books, 1989), 278–91. Only Japan still presented a possible military challenge to the United States, but in early 1922, the United States neutered the threat at the Washington Naval Conference, where attendees fixed the ratio of battleship tonnage at 5:5:3 for the United States, Great Britain, and Japan, respectively; Italy and France were doled out rations of 1.67 each. *See* Adam Tooze, *The Deluge: The Great War, America and the Remaking of the Global Order, 1916–1931* (New York: Viking, 2014), 11–12, 396–401.

5. Lord Riddell, Diary Entry, May 26, 1919, in *Lord Riddell's Intimate Diary of the Peace Conference and After 1918–1923* (London: Victor Gollancz, 1933), 78; Wilson, An Address in Convention Hall in Kansas City, September 6, 1919, in PWW 63:74; *see* Wilson, An Address in the Auditorium in Omaha, September 8, 1919, in PWW 63:106; *see also* Gordon, *Empire of Wealth*, 293; Kennedy, *Rise and Fall*, 199.

6. *See* Kennedy, *Rise and Fall*, 243–44; Gordon, *Empire of Wealth*, 288–89, 293.

7. *See* J. Fred Rippy, *The Caribbean Danger Zone* (New York: G. P. Putnam's Sons, 1940), 226–27; Michael L. Krenn, *U.S. Policy Toward Economic Nationalism in Latin America, 1917–1929* (Wilmington, DE: Scholarly Resources, 1990), xiii–xiv; Mark T. Gilderhus, *Pan American Visions: Woodrow Wilson in the Western Hemisphere 1913–1921* (Tucson: University of Arizona Press, 1986), 37–45.

8. *See* Krenn, *Economic Nationalism in Latin America*, 9, 21; Gilderhus, *Pan American Visions*, 133; Warren I. Cohen, *Empire Without Tears: America's Foreign Relations 1921–1933* (New York: Alfred A. Knopf, 1987), 12; Alan McPherson, *The Invaded: How Latin Americans and Their Allies Fought and Ended U.S. Occupations* (Oxford: Oxford University Press, 2016), 195; Emily S. Rosenberg, *Spreading the American Dream: American Economic and Cultural Expansion, 1890–1945* (New York: Hill and Wang, 1989), 89–97. Over the next decade, American companies would begin establishing their own monopolies in cable, radio, and news services, along with areas like commercial aviation. *See* Rosenberg, *Spreading the American Dream*, 87–107; Walter LaFeber, *Inevitable Revolutions: The United States in Central America*, 2nd ed. (New York: W. W. Norton, 1993), 61–62.

9. The League of Nations Covenant, April 28, 1919, in PWW 58:195; Wilson, An Address in the Auditorium in Omaha, September 8, 1919, in PWW 63:103. For the debate over the League and the Doctrine, *see* John A. Garraty, *Henry Cabot Lodge: A Biography* (New York: Alfred A. Knopf, 1953), 357–82; William C. Widenor, *Henry Cabot Lodge and the Search for an American Foreign Policy* (Berkeley: University of California Press, 1983), 300–48; Dexter Perkins, *A History of the Monroe Doctrine* (Boston: Little, Brown, 1963), 276–313.

10. *See* Tooze, *The Deluge*, 248–49, 440–61.

11. Craigie to Foreign Office, "Outstanding Problems Affecting Anglo-American Relations," November 12, 1928, in *Documents on British Foreign Policy 1919–1939*, ed. W. N. Medlicott, Douglas Dakin, and M. E. Lambert, series IA, vol. 5 (London: Her Majesty's Stationery Office, 1973), 861–62.

12. *See* John A. Logan, Jr., *No Transfer: An American Security Principle* (New Haven, CT: Yale University Press, 1962), 275–76. One official observed that "if there was ever a time in the history of the world when Europe was not thinking of interfering in the Western Hemisphere,

it is the present." John T. Vance, "A Good Word for Santo Domingo," *Current History* 16, no. 5 (August 1922), 852.

13. *See* Frederick W. Marks, III, *Velvet on Iron: The Diplomacy of Theodore Roosevelt* (Lincoln: University of Nebraska Press, 1979), 180–90.

14. *The Nation,* February 23, 1921, 278; *see* Hans Schmidt, *Maverick Marine: General Smedley D. Butler and the Contradictions of American Military History* (Lexington: University Press of Kentucky, 1998), 54.

15. *See* David Healy, *Drive to Hegemony: The United States in the Caribbean 1898–1917* (Madison: University of Wisconsin Press, 1988), 283. For abuses in Haiti and the Dominican Republic, *see generally* Hans Schmidt, *The United States Occupation of Haiti, 1915–1934* (New Brunswick, NJ: Rutgers University Press, 1995); Bruce J. Calder, *The Impact of Intervention: The Dominican Republic During the U.S. Occupation of 1916–1924* (Austin: University of Texas Press, 1988).

16. *See* Editor, Response to Medill McCormick, "Our Failure in Haiti," *The Nation,* December 1, 1920, 616; John Kenneth Turner, "Nicaragua," *The Nation,* May 13, 1922, 648; *see also* John W. Blassingame, "The Press and American Intervention in Haiti and the Dominican Republic, 1904–1920," *Caribbean Studies* 9, no. 2 (July 1969), 37, 39–43; Cohen, *Empire Without Tears,* 69–70; Emily S. Rosenberg, *Financial Missionaries to the World: The Politics and Culture of Dollar Diplomacy, 1900–1930* (Durham, NC: Duke University Press, 2003), 124; Dana G. Munro, *The United States and the Caribbean Republics 1921–1933* (Princeton, NJ: Princeton University Press, 1974), 13–15.

17. "Says America Has 12 League Votes," *New York Times,* August 19, 1920.

18. "Favors Body with 'Teeth,'" *New York Times,* August 29, 1920; "Constitution or League—Harding," *New York Times,* September 18, 1920.

19. Anonymous, *The Mirrors of Washington* (New York: G.P. Putnam's Sons, 1921), 5; *see* Joseph Robert Juárez, "United States Withdrawal from Santo Domingo," *Hispanic American Historical Review* 42, no. 2 (May 1, 1962), 170; Rosenberg, *Financial Missionaries,* 124–31; *see generally* McPherson, *The Invaded.*

20. Samuel Guy Inman, "Imperialistic America," *Atlantic Monthly* 134, no. 1, July 1924, 107; *see* Richard V. Salisbury, "Mexico, the United States, and the 1926–1927 Nicaraguan Crisis," *Hispanic American Historical Review* 66, no. 2 (January 1986), 323; Richard V. Salisbury, *Anti-Imperialism and International Competition in Central America 1920–1929* (Wilmington, DE: Scholarly Resources, 1989), 77–81; Juárez, "United States Withdrawal," 167–68. For outreach by occupied countries to the rest of the region, *see generally* McPherson, *The Invaded.* For an account that sees a longer history of counter-American balancing, *see generally* Max Paul Friedman and Tom Long, "Soft Balancing in the Americas: Latin American Opposition to U.S. Intervention, 1898–1936," *International Security* 40, no. 1 (Summer 2015), 120–56.

21. Vance, "A Good Word," 851; *see* Stephen Solarz, foreword to Schmidt, *United States Occupation of Haiti,* xi; *see generally* Calder, *Impact of Intervention.*

22. *See* Juárez, "United States Withdrawal," 183–86.

23. Samuel Guy Inman, "The Monroe Doctrine and Hispanic America," *Hispanic American Historical Review* 4, no. 4 (November 1921), 670–71; Inman, "Imperialistic America," 115; Horace G. Knowles, "Santo Domingo to Be Free," *Current History* 14, no. 5 (August 1921), 734–35; *see also* Paul W. Drake, "From Good Men to Good Neighbors: 1912–1932," in *Exporting Democracy: The United States and Latin America,* ed. Abraham F. Lowenthal (Baltimore: Johns Hopkins University Press, 1991), 23. Such concerns only grew through the 1920s. *See* Kellogg to American Diplomatic Officers in Latin America, February 28, 1929, in FRUS 1929, 1:711, 713–16.

24. Wiseman, A Memorandum, October 16, 1918, in PWW 51:350; Colby to Daniels, November 27, 1920, in FRUS 1920, 2:136; *see* Munro, *The United States and the Caribbean Republics,* 17–22, 45, 118; Joseph S. Tulchin, *The Aftermath of War: World War I and U.S. Policy Toward Latin America* (New York: New York University Press, 1971), 66, 72–78. For Wilson's conversion to anti-interventionism, *see generally* Daniel M. Smith, "Bainbridge Colby and the Good Neighbor Policy, 1920–1921," *Mississippi Valley Historical Review* 50, no. 1 (June 1963), 56–78.

25. Cummings, A Memorandum, December 23, 1920, in PWW 66:194; *see* Wilson to Colby, November 5, 1920, in PWW 66:321–22; Josephus Daniels, Diary Entry, December 4, 1919, in

PWW 64:122. For the pressures on Wilson to intervene in Mexico after the end of World War I, *see* Lloyd C. Gardner, "Woodrow Wilson and the Mexican Revolution," in *Woodrow Wilson and a Revolutionary World, 1913–1921*, ed. Arthur S. Link (Chapel Hill: University of North Carolina Press, 1982), 29–41; Clifford W. Trow, "Woodrow Wilson and the Mexican Interventionist Movement of 1919," *Journal of American History* 58, no. 1 (June 1971), 46–72.

26. Quoted in Tooze, *The Deluge*, 372; Hughes, "Observations on the Monroe Doctrine," Address Delivered Before the American Bar Association at Minneapolis, Minnesota, August 30, 1923, in *The Pathway of Peace: Representative Addresses Delivered During His Term as Secretary of State (1921–1925)* (New York: Harper & Brothers, 1925), 126–27; *see* Hughes, Address at the Dedication of the Site for the American Centennial Monument at Rio de Janeiro, September 8, 1922, in *Addresses in Brazil Delivered by the Hon. Charles Evans Hughes* (Washington, DC: Pan American Union, 1922), 3; Hughes, "The Monroe Doctrine—A Review: Its Relation to American Foreign Policy in the Twentieth Century," Reading at a Meeting Held Under the Auspices of the American Academy of Political and Social Science and the Philadelphia Forum at Philadelphia, November 30, 1923, in *The Pathway of Peace*, 158; Hughes, "Latin-American Relations," Radio Address, January 20, 1925, in *The Pathway of Peace*, 166.

27. For the overall orientation of the Harding administration toward the region, *see generally* Kenneth J. Grieb, *The Latin American Policy of Warren G. Harding* (Fort Worth, TX: Texas Christian University Press, 1977); *see also* Lars Schoultz, *Beneath the United States: A History of U.S. Policy Toward Latin America* (Cambridge, MA: Harvard University Press, 2003), 257–58. Colombian-American reconciliation was helped by the fact that the Rough Rider was dead while Colombia's oil industry was very much alive. *See* Krenn, *Economic Nationalism in Latin America*, 84.

28. Harold Ickes, Diary Entry, April 2, 1938, in *The Secret Diary of Harold I. Ickes*, vol. 2, *The Inside Struggle 1936–1939* (New York: Simon and Schuster, 1954), 351; Alexander Cadogan, Diary Entry, August 10, 1941, in *The Diaries of Sir Alexander Cadogan O.M., 1938–1945*, ed. David Dilks (New York: G. P. Putnam's Sons, 1972), 398–99; *see* Benjamin Welles, *Sumner Welles: FDR's Global Strategist* (New York: St. Martin's, 1997), 1, 7–8, 10, 29, 65, 81.

29. "FOREIGN RELATIONS: Diplomat's Diplomat," *Time*, August 11, 1941, 11, 12; Wheeler to Welles, May 11, 1932, quoted in Welles, *Sumner Welles*, 69; "THE PRESIDENCY: When the War Ends," *Time*, February 19, 1940, 15; *see* Michael Fullilove, *Rendezvous with Destiny: How Franklin D. Roosevelt and Five Extraordinary Men Took America into the War and into the World* (New York: Penguin, 2013), 24–26.

30. *See* Welles, *Sumner Welles*, 1–3, 29, 35, 82–83, 117, 184, 341–50, 357–58, 373, 379; Fullilove, *Rendezvous with Destiny*, 20–23.

31. *See* Welles, *Sumner Welles*, 64.

32. *See* Congressional Research Service, *Instances of Use*, 9.

33. For the dilemma American policymakers faced, *see* Calder, *Impact of Intervention*, xxii.

34. *See* Frank Moya Pons, *The Dominican Republic: A National History* (Princeton, NJ: Markus Wiener, 2010), 335–36. For an account of the negotiations, *see* Munro, *The United States and the Caribbean Republics*, 44–70; Welles, *Sumner Welles*, 80–101. For a good discussion of the reasons behind the withdrawal from the Dominican Republic, *see* Juárez, "United States Withdrawal," 186, 190.

35. *See* Convention Between the United States of America and the Dominican Republic, December 27, 1924, in FRUS 1924, 1:663–65; *see also* Abraham F. Lowenthal, "The United States and the Dominican Republic to 1965: Background to Intervention," *Caribbean Studies* 10, no. 2 (July 1970), 33–34.

36. Mayer to Hughes, July 30, 1921, 839.00/2451, in Roll 22, M626, RG59, NA; *see* Munro, *The United States and the Caribbean Republics*, 76; Schoultz, *Beneath the United States*, 256–57, 293; *see generally* Stephen Pampinella, "'The Way of Progress and Civilization': Racial Hierarchy and US State Building in Haiti and the Dominican Republic (1915–1922)," *Journal of Global Security Studies* 6, no. 3 (2020), 1–17. For other reasons why Haiti presented a special case, *see* Juárez, "United States Withdrawal," 186–88; McPherson, *The Invaded*, 159–93.

37. *See* Welles to Hughes, June 2, 1924, 815.00/3185, in Roll 16, M647, RG59, NA; *see also* Grieb, *The Latin American Policy*, 51–55; LaFeber, *Inevitable Revolutions*, 63–64; Tulchin, *The*

Aftermath of War, 246–47. Continuing the long tradition of eyeing American companies' regional involvement with skepticism, Welles blamed "certain important American interests" for "the disasters which have lately overwhelmed the Republic of Honduras." Welles to Hughes, June 2, 1924, 815.00/3185, in Roll 16, M647, RG59, NA.

38. *See* Rosenberg, *Financial Missionaries*, 101–05; Tulchin, *The Aftermath of War*, 104–07.

39. *See* Rosenberg, *Financial Missionaries*, 120–21, 148–49; Tulchin, *The Aftermath of War*, 107–10, 152, 203–05; John Braeman, "The New Left and American Foreign Policy During the Age of Normalcy: A Re-Examination," *Business History Review* 57, no. 1 (Spring 1983), 89–91, 94–96.

40. *See* Rosenberg, *Financial Missionaries*, 148–49, 151, 156–60, 164–65, 197–98. For the money doctors, *see generally* Paul W. Drake, ed., *Money Doctors, Foreign Debts, and Economic Reforms in Latin America from the 1890s to the Present* (Wilmington, DE: Scholarly Resources, 1994); Paul W. Drake, *The Money Doctor in the Andes: The Kemmerer Missions, 1923–1933* (Durham, NC: Duke University Press, 1989).

41. *See* Rosenberg, *Financial Missionaries*, 111, 120–50, 155–56, 257; Herbert Feis, *The Diplomacy of the Dollar: 1919–1932* (New York: Norton Library, 1966), 12–13.

42. Sumner Welles, "Is America Imperialistic?," *Atlantic Monthly* 134, no. 3 (September 1924), 418; White to Grew, "Our Central American Policy," November 7, 1924, 711.13/65, in Roll 1, M673, RG59, NA; *see* Kellogg to Summerlin, December 22, 1925, 815.00/3913, in Roll 19, M647, RG59, NA; *see also* Tulchin, *The Aftermath of War*, 102–03, 107–10, 152, 203–05.

43. *See* Munro, *The United States and the Caribbean Republics*, 162–65, 185; Drake, "From Good Men to Good Neighbors," 26; *see generally* Virginia L. Greer, "State Department Policy in Regard to the Nicaraguan Election of 1924," *Hispanic American Historical Review* 34, no. 4 (November 1954), 445–67.

44. *See* Munro, *The United States and the Caribbean Republics*, 168–69, 175–76.

45. *See* William Kamman, *A Search For Stability: United States Diplomacy Toward Nicaragua 1925–1933* (Notre Dame, IN: University of Notre Dame Press, 1968), 24–27; Whitney T. Perkins, *Constraint of Empire: The United States and Caribbean Interventions* (Westport, CT: Greenwood, 1981), 106; Munro, *The United States and the Caribbean Republics*, 172–73, 177–78; Gobat, *Confronting the American Dream*, 135.

46. *See* Munro, *The United States and the Caribbean Republics*, 180; Perkins, *Constraint of Empire*, 106–08; Kamman, *A Search For Stability*, 31–35.

47. *See* Kamman, *A Search For Stability*, 38; Ivan Musicant, *The Banana Wars: A History of United States Military Intervention in Latin America from the Spanish-American War to the Invasion of Panama* (New York: Macmillan, 1990), 288–89.

48. Kellogg to Eberhardt, December 21, 1925, in FRUS 1925, 2:645; *see* Grew to Eberhardt, December 14, 1925, in FRUS 1925, 2:643; *see also* Munro, *The United States and the Caribbean Republics*, 189–200.

49. *See* Kamman, *A Search For Stability*, 62, 70.

50. *See* Kellogg to Ellis, October 22, 1926, in FRUS 1926, 2:800; Stokely W. Morgan, "Mexican Activities in Central America," December 2, 1926, 817.00/4170, in Roll 29, M632, RG59, NA; *see also* Munro, *The United States and the Caribbean Republics*, 205–06; Robert Freeman Smith, "Latin America, The United States and the European Powers, 1830–1930," in *The Cambridge History of Latin America*, vol. 4, *C. 1870 to 1930* (Cambridge, UK: Cambridge University Press, 1986), 117; *see generally* James J. Horn, "U. S. Diplomacy and 'the Specter of Bolshevism' in Mexico (1924–1927)," *The Americas* 32, no. 1 (July 1975), 31–45. For Mexico's support for the rebels in exchange for an anti-American alliance, *see* Salisbury, "The 1926–1927 Nicaraguan Crisis," 329, 333.

51. *See* Kamman, *A Search For Stability*, 71–74, 83–86. For the reconciliation between Mexico and the United States, *see* Bryce Wood, *The Making of the Good Neighbor Policy* (New York: Columbia University Press, 1962), 15–21.

52. Coolidge, Message to Congress, January 10, 1927, in FRUS 1927, 3:297–98. Left unsaid was the credibility factor. Having recognized Diáz, Washington could not let his government fall without losing prestige. *See* Wood, *The Making*, 16–17.

53. Claude M. Fuess, "Calvin Coolidge—Twenty Years After," *Proceedings of the American Antiquarian Society* 63, no. 2 (October 1953), 363; Henry L. Stimson's *American Policy in Nicaragua: The Lasting Legacy* (New York: Markus Wiener, 1991), 18; *see* Munro, *The United States and the Caribbean Republics*, 217–18; Kamman, *A Search For Stability*, 96.

54. *See* Munro, *The United States and the Caribbean Republics*, 222–31; *see generally* Charles E. Frazier, "Colonel Henry L. Stimson's Peace Mission to Nicaragua, April–May, 1927," *Journal of the West* 2 (January 1963), 66–84. Stimson's settlement mirrored earlier plans that Washington had suggested or used in Haiti, the Dominican Republic, and especially Cuba. For example, like the deal brokered to stop Cuba's civil war in 1906, Stimson's plan required American forces to disarm Liberal rebels that had nearly reached the gates of the capital and to preside over a temporary truce until Washington could supervise free and fair elections.

55. *See* Kamman, *A Search For Stability*, 113–15.

56. *See* Gobat, *Confronting the American Dream*, 234, 236–38.

57. *Report of the Delegates of the United States of America to the Sixth International Conference of American States* (Washington, DC: Government Printing Office, 1928), 14–15; *see* Dexter Perkins, *Charles Evans Hughes and American Democratic Statesmanship* (Boston: Little, Brown, 1956), 134–36. "Butchered in the jungle" was modified in the official text of the speech to "killed." *See* Merlo J. Pusey, *Charles Evans Hughes* (New York: Macmillan, 1951), 2:559 n.15. For the depth of Latin American antipathy, *see* Kamman, *A Search For Stability*, 83; McPherson, *The Invaded*, 194–212, 217–25, 231.

58. 69 Cong. Rec. 6974 (1928); *see* Musicant, *Banana Wars*, 327–28; Kamman, *A Search For Stability*, 136; Schoultz, *Beneath the United States*, 265–69; Rosenberg, *Financial Missionaries*, 123–24, 130–31, 144–47; Richard Grossman, "Solidarity with Sandino: The Anti-Intervention and Solidarity Movements in the United States, 1927–1933," *Latin American Perspectives* 36, no. 6 (November 2009), 67–79.

59. Kellogg to McCoy, March 3, 1928, 817.00/5444a, in Roll 38, M632, RG59, NA.

60. *See* Kamman, *A Search For Stability*, 167, 170–71.

61. Duggan to Wilson, January 27, 1933, in FRUS 1932, 5:832; Acting Secretary of State to Curtis, February 26, 1930, in FRUS 1930, 2:704; *see* Drake, "From Good Men to Good Neighbors," 28–29; Andrew J. Bacevich, "The American Electoral Mission in Nicaragua, 1927–28," *Diplomatic History* 4, no. 3 (Summer 1980), 255–56; Gobat, *Confronting the American Dream*, 208.

62. Muller to Munro, Nov. 8, 1930, quoted in McPherson, *The Invaded*, 233; Stimson, Diary Entry, April 15, 1931, in Henry L. Stimson and McGeorge Bundy, *On Active Service in Peace and War* (New York: Harper & Brothers, 1948), 182; *see* Wood, *The Making*, 41–44; Musicant, *Banana Wars*, 355.

63. Stimson, Diary Entry, March 7, 1932, in Stimson and Bundy, *On Active Service*, 182; *see* Kamman, *A Search For Stability*, 217; Wood, *The Making*, 13.

64. Hoover, Address at the Custom House of Amapala, November 26, 1928, in *Addresses Delivered During the Visit of Herbert Hoover, President-Elect of the United States, to Central and South America, November–December 1928* (Washington, DC: Pan American Union, 1929), 3; *see The Memoirs of Herbert Hoover: The Cabinet and the Presidency, 1920–1933* (New York: Macmillan, 1952), 210–11; "The Hoover Idea on Argentina," *Review of the River Plate*, December 21, 1928, 13; *see also* Alexander DeConde, *Herbert Hoover's Latin-American Policy* (Stanford, CA: Stanford University Press, 1951), 13–24; Brian Loveman, *No Higher Law: American Foreign Policy and the Western Hemisphere Since 1776* (Chapel Hill: University of North Carolina Press, 2010), 239–40. After returning from the tour, Hoover gave several speeches reiterating his commitment to an anti-interventionist policy. *See* Hoover, Inaugural Address, March 4, 1929, in PPP 1929, 8–9; Hoover, Address to the Gridiron Club, April 13, 1929, in PPP 1929, 70; Hoover, First Annual Message, December 3, 1929, in PPP 1929, 406.

65. *See* J. Lloyd Mecham, *The United States and Inter-American Security, 1889–1960* (Austin: University of Texas Press, 1962), 113. For Hoover's reluctance to intervene, *see* "Our Intervention Limited by Hoover," *New York Times*, April 16, 1931; *see also* Loveman, *No Higher Law*, 241–42; Donald A. Yerxa, *Admirals and Empire: The United States Navy and the Caribbean, 1898–1945* (Columbia: University of South Carolina Press, 1991), 79, 85–86. For the end of official support for the money doctors, *see* Rosenberg, *Financial Missionaries*, 229–31. For the return

to the traditional recognition policy, *see* Munro, *The United States and the Caribbean Republics*, 280; Kamman, *A Search For Stability*, 232; DeConde, *Herbert Hoover's Latin-American Policy*, 58. For the beginning of the end of the Haitian occupation, *see generally* Donald B. Cooper, "The Withdrawal of the United States from Haiti, 1928–1934," *Journal of Inter-American Studies* 5, no. 1 (January 1963), 83–101; Alan McPherson, "Herbert Hoover, Occupation Withdrawal, and the Good Neighbor Policy," *Presidential Studies Quarterly* 44, no. 4 (December 2014), 623–39. Finally, the State Department signaled the end of the customs receivership experiment in 1932 when it refused to allow bankers to take over El Salvador's customhouses after the nation defaulted on a loan. *See* "Doubts Contract on Salvador Loan," *New York Times*, August 16, 1932; *see also* Munro, *The United States and the Caribbean Republics*, 286–87; Noel Maurer, *The Empire Trap: The Rise and Fall of U.S. Intervention to Protect American Property Overseas, 1893–2013* (Princeton, NJ: Princeton University Press, 2013), 203–10.

66. Smedley D. Butler, "America's Armed Forces: 2. 'In Time of Peace': The Army," *Common Sense* 4, no. 11 (November 1935), 8; *see* Smedley D. Butler, *War Is a Racket* (New York: Round Table, 1935), 1; *see also* Rosenberg, *Financial Missionaries*, 252; Schmidt, *Maverick Marine*, 204–05, 237–38, 249; Max Boot, *The Savage Wars of Peace: Small Wars and the Rise of American Power* (New York: Basic Books, 2002), 269–70.

67. J. Reuben Clark, *Memorandum on the Monroe Doctrine* (Washington, DC: Government Printing Office, 1928), xix; *see* Munro, *The United States and the Caribbean Republics*, 377–78; *see generally* Gene A. Sessions, "The Clark Memorandum Myth," *The Americas* 34, no. 1 (July 1977), 40–58.

68. Munro, *The United States and the Caribbean Republics*, 379; *see ibid.*, 382–83; *see also* Schmidt, *United States Occupation of Haiti*, 232; Schoultz, *Beneath the United States*, 290.

69. Stimson, Diary Entry, November 11, 1932, in Stimson and Bundy, *On Active Service*, 185; *see* Norman H. Davis, "Wanted: A Consistent Latin America Policy," *Foreign Affairs* 9, no. 4 (July 1931), 547; *see also* DeConde, *Herbert Hoover's Latin-American Policy*, 90, 93; Irwin F. Gellman, *Good Neighbor Diplomacy: United States Policies in Latin America, 1933–1945* (Baltimore, MD: Johns Hopkins University Press, 1979), 8–9.

70. *See* Welles, *Sumner Welles*, 70–71.

Chapter 13: The Colossus

1. Henry R. Luce, "The American Century," *Life*, February 17, 1941, in *Diplomatic History* 23, no. 2 (Spring 1999), 167; *see ibid.*, 165; *see also* Donald W. White, "The 'American Century' in World History," *Journal of World History* 3, no. 1 (1992), 106.

2. Luce, "The American Century," 166.

3. Luce, "The American Century," 169–71.

4. FDR, Inaugural Address, March 4, 1933, in PPA 2:14; *see* FDR, Address Before the Special Session of the Governing Board of the Pan-American Union on the Occasion of the Celebration of "Pan-American Day," April 12, 1933, in PPA 2:130; *see also* Eric Paul Roorda, *The Dictator Next Door: The Good Neighbor Policy and the Trujillo Regime in the Dominican Republic, 1930–1945* (Durham, NC: Duke University Press, 2006), 88.

5. Reed to Stimson, September 29, 1932, in FRUS 1932, 5:557; *see* Luis E. Aguilar, *Cuba 1933: Prologue to Revolution* (Ithaca, NY: Cornell University Press, 1972), 98–127; Samuel Flagg Bemis, *The Latin American Policy of the United States: An Historical Interpretation* (New York: Harcourt, Brace, 1943), 279; Louis A. Pérez, Jr., *Cuba Under the Platt Amendment, 1902–1934* (Pittsburgh, PA: University of Pittsburgh Press, 1986), 277–82, 292.

6. *See* Bryce Wood, *The Making of the Good Neighbor Policy* (New York: Columbia University Press, 1962), 52–58. In 1930, Stimson had officially returned the country to Secretary Elihu Root's original, narrower interpretation of the Platt Amendment. *See* Memorandum of Conference by the Secretary of State with the Press, October 2, 1930, in FRUS 1930, 2:662–63.

7. Norman H. Davis, "Wanted: A Consistent Latin America Policy," *Foreign Affairs* 9, no. 4 (July 1931), 557–58; Sumner Welles, *Naboth's Vineyard: The Dominican Republic 1844–1924* (Mamaroneck, NY: Paul P. Appel, 1966), 2:925–26; Hull to Welles, May 1, 1933, in FRUS 1933,

5:283–84; *see* Benjamin Welles, *Sumner Welles: FDR's Global Strategist* (New York: St. Martin's, 1997), 158; Jules Robert Benjamin, *The United States and Cuba: Hegemony and Dependent Development, 1880–1934* (Pittsburgh, PA: University of Pittsburgh Press, 1977), 74–80. Welles ghostwrote the Norman Davis article. *See* Welles, *Sumner Welles*, 135–36.

8. *See* Welles to Hull, May 22, 1933, in FRUS 1933, 5:571; *see also* Noel Maurer, *The Empire Trap: The Rise and Fall of U.S. Intervention to Protect American Property Overseas, 1893–2013* (Princeton, NJ: Princeton University Press, 2013), 230–32; Philip Dur and Christoper Gilcrease, "US Diplomacy and the Downfall of a Cuban Dictator: Machado in 1933," *Journal of Latin American Studies* 34, no. 2 (May 2002), 255–56, 259–79; Pérez, *Cuba Under the Platt Amendment*, 306–15; Hugh Thomas, *Cuba: The Pursuit of Freedom* (New York: Harper and Row, 1971), 615–25; Welles, *Sumner Welles*, 166.

9. *See* Thomas, *Cuba*, 625; Welles, *Sumner Welles*, 166.

10. *See* Benjamin, *The United States and Cuba*, 109–11, 130–32.

11. *See* Irwin F. Gellman, *Good Neighbor Diplomacy: United States Policies in Latin America, 1933–1945* (Baltimore, MD: Johns Hopkins University Press, 1979), 19–20; Aguilar, *Cuba 1933*, 159–62, 172.

12. Welles to Hull, September 5, 1933, in FRUS 1933, 5:382; Memorandum of Telephone Conversation Between Hull and Welles, September 5, 1933, in FRUS 1933, 5:380; Welles to Hull, September 5, 1933, in FRUS 1933, 5:379; *see* Memorandum of Telephone Conversations Between Hull and Welles and Between Caffery and Welles, September 5, 1933, in FRUS 1933, 5:385–86.

13. Welles to Hull, September 7, 1933, in FRUS 1933, 5:398; Welles to Hull, September 8, 1933, in FRUS 1933, 5:407; *see* Welles to Gibson, October 10, 1933, in Box 64, Hugh Gibson MSS; *see also* Wood, *The Making*, 96–97; Irwin F. Gellman, *Roosevelt and Batista: Good Neighbor Diplomacy in Cuba, 1933–1945* (Albuquerque: University of New Mexico, 1973), 52–53. Welles also thought that the right of intervention under the Platt Amendment imposed responsibilities on the United States as well as rights; if Washington failed to intervene, it would tacitly bless the revolutionary government. *See* Welles to Hull, August 8, 1933, in FRUS 1933, 5:342.

14. Memorandum of Telephone Conversation Between Hull and Welles, September 6, 1933, in FRUS 1933, 5:389; *see* Wood, *The Making*, 71–75.

15. Welles to Hull, September 10, 1933, in FRUS 1933, 5:417; *see* Wood, *The Making*, 82–83. For Welles's tactics, *see* Gellman, *Roosevelt and Batista*, 77–98; Benjamin, *The United States and Cuba*, 152–55.

16. *See* Welles to Hull, September 10, 1933, in FRUS 1933, 5:416; *see also* Aguilar, *Cuba 1933*, 187–99; Gellman, *Roosevelt and Batista*, 55–56.

17. Welles to Hull, October 4, 1933, in FRUS 1933, 5:471–72; *see* Wood, *The Making*, 88–89; Aguilar, *Cuba 1933*, 199; Benjamin, *The United States and Cuba*, 160–61.

18. "In Today's News," *Miami Herald*, January 17, 1934; *see* Gellman, *Roosevelt and Batista*, 85; Aguilar, *Cuba 1933*, 226–28.

19. Hubert Herring, "Another Chance for Cuba," *Current History* 39, no. 6 (March 1934), 657.

20. *See* Gellman, *Roosevelt and Batista*, 54; E. David Cronon, "Interpreting the New Good Neighbor Policy: The Cuban Crisis of 1933," *Hispanic American Historical Review* 39, no. 4 (November 1959), 564–65.

21. *Many Battles: The Autobiography of Ernest Gruening* (New York: Liveright, 1973), 162; *see* Gellman, *Good Neighbor Diplomacy*, 22–26.

22. Hull to Phillips, December 19, 1933, in FRUS 1933, 4:201; FDR, "From Now on, War by Governments Shall Be Changed to Peace by Peoples," Address Before the Woodrow Wilson Foundation, December 28, 1933, in PPA 2:545. Hull left a loophole for interventions permitted by international law, but the administration agreed to close it three years later. *See* Hull to Phillips, December 19, 1933, in FRUS 1933, 4:202; Additional Protocol Relative to Non-Intervention, art. 1, December 23, 1936, in *Report of the Delegation of the United States of America to the Inter-American Conference for the Maintenance of Peace: Buenos Aires, Argentina, December 1–23, 1936* (Washington, DC: Government Printing Office, 1937), 127.

23. *See* Gellman, *Good Neighbor Diplomacy*, 70. For Cuba, *see* Treaty of Relations Between the United States and Cuba, May 29, 1934, in FRUS 1934, 5:183. For Haiti, *see* Agreement Between

the United States of America and Haiti for the Haitianization of the Garde and Withdrawal of Military Forces from Haiti and Financial Arrangement, August 7, 1933, in FRUS 1933, 5:756; *see also* Gellman, *Good Neighbor Diplomacy*, 33–36. For Panama, *see* General Treaty of Friendship and Cooperation Between the United States and Panama, March 2, 1936, in 53 Stat. 1807; *see also* Welles, *Sumner Welles*, 183–85; *see generally* Lester D. Langley, "Negotiating New Treaties with Panama: 1936," *Hispanic American Historical Review* 48, no. 2 (May 1968), 220–33; Lester D. Langley, "The World Crisis and the Good Neighbor Policy in Panama, 1936–41," *The Americas* 24, no. 2 (October 1967), 137–52. For the Dominican Republic, *see* Convention Between the United States of America and the Dominican Republic Modifying the Convention of December 27, 1924 Respecting the Collection and Application of the Customs Revenue of the Dominican Republic, September 14, 1940, in 55 Stat. 1104; *see also* Roorda, *The Dictator Next Door*, 210–19. In 1937, the United States also abrogated Article 8 of the Gadsden Treaty, which had given the United States the right (never exercised) to move forces across the Mexican isthmus. *See* Treaty Between the United States of America and Mexico Terminating Article VIII of the Treaty of December 30, 1853 (Gadsen Treaty), April 13, 1937, in 52 Stat. 1457; *see also* Lars Schoultz, *Beneath the United States: A History of U.S. Policy Toward Latin America* (Cambridge, MA: Harvard University Press, 2003), 306.

24. Corrigan to Hull, January 21, 1936, in FRUS 1936, 5:126–27; *see* Corrigan to Hull, May 14, 1936, 817.00/8416, in Roll 8, M1273, RG59, NA.

25. Welles to Duggan, Memorandum, March 26, 1936, in FRUS 1936, 5:130–31; *see* Corrigan to Hull, May 14, 1936, 817.00/8416, in Roll 8, M1273, RG59, NA; *see also* Wood, *The Making*, 143–49.

26. Welles to FDR, 1933, in Charles C. Griffin, "Welles to Roosevelt: A Memorandum on Inter-American Relations, 1933," *Hispanic American Historical Review* 34, no. 2 (May 1954), 192. For the collapse in world trade, *see* Dick Steward, *Trade and Hemisphere: The Good Neighbor Policy and Reciprocal Trade* (Columbia: University of Missouri Press, 1975), 1–2. For the reciprocity treaties, *see* Bemis, *Latin American Policy*, 304; Gellman, *Good Neighbor Diplomacy*, 48; Fredrick B. Pike, *FDR's Good Neighbor Policy: Sixty Years of Generally Gentle Chaos* (Austin: University of Texas Press, 1995), 208.

Other than trade, the FDR administration also had to navigate a wave of regional defaults. In the run-up to the Great Depression, Latin American states had splurged on loans (often on the advice of American "money doctors") and could no longer pay. For the president, the defaults mattered less than the stiffed American creditors, who he worried would sabotage his policies through their constant whining. FDR solved that problem by creating the quasi-private "Foreign Bondholders Protective Council," which not only assumed responsibility for the creditors' cases but—far more importantly—also prevented debt issues from getting in the way of the Good Neighbor Policy. As one advisor explained, the Council acted as "a step away from dollar diplomacy, and not toward it." Feis to Hull, March 28, 1933, in Herbert Feis, *1933: Characters in Crisis* (Boston: Little, Brown, 1966), 274 (emphasis omitted); *see* FDR to Rayburn, May 20, 1933, in *Franklin D. Roosevelt and Foreign Affairs*, ed. Edgar B. Nixon (Cambridge, MA: Belknap, 1969), 1:152; FDR to Steiwer, November 6, 1933, in Nixon, *Roosevelt and Foreign Affairs*, 1:463; *see also* Roorda, *The Dictator Next Door*, 72–76, 194, 218–19.

27. *See* Alan McPherson, *The Invaded: How Latin Americans and Their Allies Fought and Ended U.S. Occupations* (Oxford: Oxford University Press, 2016), 259; Roorda, *The Dictator Next Door*, 88–89. For a more skeptical view of the Policy, *see* Frederick W. Marks III, *Wind Over Sand: The Diplomacy of Franklin Roosevelt* (Athens: University of Georgia Press, 1988), 217–50.

28. *See* Richard L. Millett, *Searching for Stability: The U.S. Development of Constabulary Forces in Latin America and the Philippines* (Fort Leavenworth, KS: Combat Studies Institute Press, 2010), 3; Dana G. Munro, *The United States and the Caribbean Republics 1921–1933* (Princeton, NJ: Princeton University Press, 1974), 381–82. Theodore Roosevelt helped establish a constabulary during Cuba's second occupation, but the practice did not become routinized until the 1910s.

29. *See generally* Millett, *Searching for Stability*; Marvin Goldwert, *The Constabulary in the Dominican Republic and Nicaragua: Progeny and Legacy of United States Intervention* (Gainesville: University of Florida Press, 1962).

30. *See* Millett, *Searching for Stability*, 124–27.

31. Benis M. Frank, Interview of Graves B. Erskine, "Oral History Transcript" (Washington, DC: History and Museum Division, 1975), 95.

32. *See* Richard Millett, *Guardians of the Dynasty* (Maryknoll, NY: Orbis Books, 1977), 145–58; Lester D. Langley, *The Banana Wars: United States Intervention in the Caribbean, 1898–1934* (Chicago: Dorsey, 1988), 218–19; McPherson, *The Invaded*, 236–37. Simultaneously, Somoza's *Guardia Nacional* raided Sandino's compound and massacred hundreds of Sandino's followers. *See ibid.*

33. Munro, *The United States and the Caribbean Republics*, 382; *see ibid.*, 300, 381–82.

34. *See* Whitney T. Perkins, *Constraint of Empire: The United States and Caribbean Interventions* (Westport, CT: Greenwood, 1981), 158; Roorda, *The Dictator Next Door*, 61; Millett, *Guardians of the Dynasty*, 173.

35. *See* David F. Schmitz, *Thank God They're On Our Side: The United States and Right-Wing Dictatorships, 1921–1965* (Chapel Hill: University of North Carolina Press, 1999), 48; Goldwert, *The Constabulary*, vi–vii; *see generally* Millett, *Searching for Stability*.

36. Lane to Beaulac, July 27, 1935, in Folder 1102, Box 61, Lane MSS; *see* Perkins, *Constraint of Empire*, 183; Roorda, *The Dictator Next Door*, 223–24.

37. Laurence Duggan, "Our Relations with the Other American Republics," *Annals of the American Academy of Political and Social Science* 198 (July 1938), 129. Even the major exception—reciprocity—was mostly about rolling back recently enacted trade barriers.

38. *See* Gellman, *Good Neighbor Diplomacy*, 38; Martin Sicker, *The Geopolitics of Security in the Americas: Hemispheric Denial from Monroe to Clinton* (Westport, CT: Praeger, 2002), 92.

39. *See* Welles, *Sumner Welles*, 70–71. For Welles's desire to Pan-Americanize the Monroe Doctrine, *see* FDR, "Our Foreign Policy: A Democratic View," *Foreign Affairs* 6, no. 4 (July 1928), 584–85; Welles, *Naboth's Vineyard*, 2:931–32; Davis, "Wanted," 564; Welles to FDR, March 17, 1941, 710.11/2669½, in Roll 19, M1276, RG59, NA.

40. *See* Tooze, *The Deluge*, 512–14. For Hitler's global objectives, *see* Holger H. Herwig, *Politics of Frustration: The United States in German Naval Planning, 1889–1941* (Boston: Little, Brown, 1976), 175–234; Michael C. Desch, *When the Third World Matters: Latin America and United States Grand Strategy* (Baltimore, MD: Johns Hopkins University Press, 1993), 58–60; *see generally* Milan Hauner, "Did Hitler Want a World Dominion?," *Journal of Contemporary History* 13, no. 1 (January 1978), 15–32; Norman J. W. Goda, *Tomorrow the World: Hitler, Northwest Africa, and the Path Toward America* (College Station, TX: Texas A&M University Press, 1998).

41. Henry Morgenthau, Jr., Notes on Cabinet Meeting, November 14, 1938, in the Morgenthau Diaries, FDRL, 150:338; *see* Henry Morgenthau, Jr. to Roosevelt, October 17, 1938, in the Morgenthau Diaries, FDRL, 146:104; *The Memoirs of Cordell Hull* (New York: Macmillan, 1948), 1:496; *see also* David G. Haglund, *Latin America and the Transformation of U.S. Strategic Thought, 1936–1940* (Albuquerque: University of New Mexico Press, 1984), 92–97. For German trade with Latin America, *see* Frederick C. Adams, *Economic Diplomacy: The Export-Import Bank and American Foreign Policy, 1934–1939* (Columbia: University of Missouri Press, 1976), 197–98; Steward, *Trade and Hemisphere*, 86–88, 249–50, 256–57. For FDR's concerns about German economic strangulation of South America, *see* Conference with the Senate Military Affairs Committee in the White House, January 31, 1939, in *Franklin D. Roosevelt and Foreign Affairs*, ed. Donald B. Schewe, vol. 8, *Dec. 1938–Feb. 1939* (New York: Garland, 1979), 9–10; FDR, Annual Press Conference with Editors of Trade Publications 557-A, June 23, 1939, in Press Conferences, FDRL, 13:462–63.

42. Conference with the Senate Military Affairs Committee in the White House, January 31, 1939, in Schewe, *Roosevelt and Foreign Affairs*, 8:10; Hull, *Memoirs*, 1:602; *see ibid.*, 1:495, 813–14; *see also* Donald A. Yerxa, *Admirals and Empire: The United States Navy and the Caribbean, 1898–1945* (Columbia: University of South Carolina Press, 1991), 111–12; Haglund, *The Transformation of U.S. Strategic Thought*, 16–17, 55–56; Gellman, *Good Neighbor Diplomacy*, 106–08.

43. For the best overview of these plots and how they were perceived, *see* Haglund, *The Transformation of U.S. Strategic Thought*, 82–83, 87–89, 116–18, 172–80. For related concerns throughout the public sphere, *see* Max Paul Friedman, *Nazis and Good Neighbors: The United*

States Campaign Against the Germans of Latin America in World War II (Cambridge, UK: Cambridge University Press, 2003), 52–57.

44. Adolf Berle, Diary Entry, May 26, 1939, in *Navigating the Rapids 1917–1971*, ed. Beatrice Bishop Berle and Travis Beal Jacobs (New York: Harcourt Brace Jovanovich, 1973), 223; Livingston Hartley, *Is America Afraid?: A New Foreign Policy for the United States* (New York: Prentice Hall, 1937), 74; *see* Bemis, *Latin American Policy*, 363.

45. Brian Connell, *Knight Errant: A Biography of Douglas Fairbanks Jr.* (Garden City, NY: Doubleday, 1955), 122; *see generally* Haglund, *The Transformation of U.S. Strategic Thought*, especially 3–9.

46. FDR, Press Conference with the American Society of Newspaper Editors 636-A, April 18, 1940, in Press Conferences, FDRL, 15:277; FDR, Address at Chicago, October 5, 1937, in PPA 6:408, 410. For other warnings, *see* FDR, Press Conference with the Associated Church Press 452-A, April 20, 1938, in Press Conferences, FDRL, 11:331–32; FDR, Press Conference 500, November 15, 1938, in Press Conferences, FDRL, 12:230–31; Conference with the Senate Military Affairs Committee in the White House, January 31, 1939, in Schewe, *Roosevelt and Foreign Affairs*, 8:10–11; Franklin D. Roosevelt, Annual Message to Congress, January 4, 1939, in PPA 8:1, 2–3; Franklin D. Roosevelt, Press Conference to the American Society of Newspaper Editors 540-A, April 20, 1939, in Press Conferences, FDRL, 13:313; *see generally* Haglund, *The Transformation of U.S. Strategic Thought*.

47. FDR, Fireside Chat, September 3, 1939, in PPA 8:463.

48. *See* Haglund, *The Transformation of U.S. Strategic Thought*, 146–49; John A. Logan, Jr., *No Transfer: An American Security Principle* (New Haven, CT: Yale University Press, 1962), 287; Walter LaFeber, *Inevitable Revolutions: The United States in Central America*, 2nd ed. (New York: W. W. Norton, 1993), 84. Of course, the neutrality zone was neutral in neither theory nor practice, and it helped the Allies significantly. *See* Gellman, *Good Neighbor Diplomacy*, 91–92. For Welles's wartime attempts to multilateralize hemispheric security, *see* J. Lloyd Mecham, *The United States and Inter-American Security, 1889–1960* (Austin: University of Texas Press, 1962), 112–245; Sicker, *Geopolitics of Security*, 92–103.

49. *See* American Association for Public Opinion Research, "Gallup and Fortune Polls," *The Public Opinion Quarterly* 4, no. 1 (March 1940), 108, 112. For subsequent public opinion on this question, *see* American Association for Public Opinion Research, "Gallup and Fortune Polls," *The Public Opinion Quarterly* 4, no. 3 (September 1940), 553; American Association for Public Opinion Research, "Gallup and Fortune Polls," *The Public Opinion Quarterly* 4, no. 4 (December 1940), 715; American Association for Public Opinion Research, "Gallup and Fortune Polls," *The Public Opinion Quarterly* 5, no. 2 (June 1941), 333; American Association for Public Opinion Research, "Gallup and Fortune Polls," *The Public Opinion Quarterly* 5, no. 4 (Winter 1941), 686–87. Americans also increasingly believed that Hitler had designs on the region; by August 1941, 72.2 percent thought he would try to conquer the region. *See* American Association for Public Opinion Research, "Gallup and Fortune Polls," 677.

50. *See* Haglund, *The Transformation of U.S. Strategic Thought*, 141–45, 151.

51. FDR, Fireside Chat on National Security, December 29, 1940, in PPA 9:635; *see* Haglund, *The Transformation of U.S. Strategic Thought*, 184–202.

52. FDR, Annual Message to Congress, January 6, 1941, in PPA 9:664, 665–66.

53. *See* Haglund, *The Transformation of U.S. Strategic Thought*, 203–08, 213–16, 220; Logan, *No Transfer*, 6, 388–90.

54. *See* Desch, *When the Third World Matters*, 73; Haglund, *The Transformation of U.S. Strategic Thought*, 203–22.

55. FDR, Radio Address, May 27, 1941, in PPA 10:181; FDR, Fireside Chat to the Nation, September 11, 1941, in PPA 10:388; *see* FDR, Fireside Chat on National Security, December 29, 1940, in PPA 9:635, 637; FDR, Annual Message to Congress, January 6, 1941, in PPA 9:666; FDR, Radio Address, May 27, 1941, in PPA 10:181, 185, 190; *see also* Susan Dunn, *A Blueprint for War: FDR and the Hundred Days that Mobilized America* (New Haven, CT: Yale University Press, 2018), 40. FDR had no second Zimmermann Telegram to help his case, but that did not stop him. Citing flimsy discoveries of "a secret map" and "secret air-landing fields," the president insisted that "conspiracy has followed conspiracy" in Hitler's efforts to seize "footholds and

bridgeheads in the New World." FDR, Navy and Total Defense Day Address, October 27, 1941, in PPA 10:439; FDR, Fireside Chat to the Nation, September 11, 1941, in PPA 10:387; *see* FDR, Radio Address, May 27, 1941, in PPA 10:189; *see also* Desch, *When the Third World Matters*, 51–53; *see generally* Francis Macdonnell, "The Search for a Second Zimmermann Telegram: FDR, BSC, and the Latin American Front," *International Journal of Intelligence and CounterIntelligence* 4, no. 4 (1990), 487–505; John F. Bratzel and Leslie B. Rout Jr., "FDR and the 'Secret Map,'" *Wilson Quarterly* 9, no. 1 (New Year's 1985), 167–73.

56. *See* Bemis, *Latin American Policy*, 367–68.

57. *See* Joint Resolution Affirming and Approving Nonrecognition of the Transfer of Any Geographic Region in this Hemisphere from One Non-American Power to Another Non-American Power, and Providing for Consultation with Other American Republics in the Event that Such Transfer Should Appear Likely, Pub. L. 32, 55 Stat. 133 (April 10, 1941); 86 Cong. Rec. 8353, 8360–61, 8394 (1940); 86 Cong. Rec. 8455, 8556, 8859 (1940); *see also* Mecham, *Inter-American Security*, 187–88; Haglund, *The Transformation of U.S. Strategic Thought*, 216–20. For the long-standing rule, *see generally* Logan, *No Transfer*.

58. *See* Yerxa, *Admirals and Empire*, 122–30, 143–48; Logan, *No Transfer*, 348–53, 368–74.

59. Wilson to Bryan, March 20, 1914, in PWW 29:360; *see* LaFeber, *Inevitable Revolutions*, 83–84; Steward, *Trade and Hemisphere*, 266. For the earliest glimpses of this policy in Cuba, *see* Benjamin, *The United States and Cuba*, 171–72.

60. *See* Franklin D. Roosevelt, Address to the Governing Board of the Pan American Union, April 14, 1939, in PPA 8:198; *see also* Adams, *Economic Diplomacy*, 66, 70–72, 188–225, 250–58; Steward, *Trade and Hemisphere*, 267–68; Lloyd C. Gardner, *Economic Aspects of New Deal Diplomacy* (Boston: Beacon, 1971), 129, 194–95, 198–99. For the intent to use these direct loans and other measures to stabilize the region in the face of the German threat, *see* Adolf A. Berle, "The Economic Interests of the United States in Inter-American Relations," Address at the Fourth Conference on Canadian-American Affairs at Queen's University in Kingston, Ontario, June 24, 1941, in *The Department of State Bulletin*, June 28, 1941, 760; *see also* Wood, *The Making*, 354–55; David Green, *The Containment of Latin America: A History of the Myths and Realities of the Good Neighbor Policy* (Chicago: Quadrangle Books, 1971), 42, 91–92; Eric Helleiner, *Forgotten Foundations of Bretton Woods: International Development and the Making of the Postwar Order* (Ithaca, NY: Cornell University Press, 2014), 12–13, 29, 40, 43–51, 133–34, 136, 172–82.

For stabilizing aid outside the bank, *see* U.S. Office of Inter-American Affairs, *History of the Office of the Coordinator of Inter-American Affairs* (Washington, DC: Government Printing Office, 1947), 115–16; *see also* Alfred E. Eckes, Jr., *Opening America's Market: U.S. Foreign Trade Policy Since 1776* (Chapel Hill: University of North Carolina Press, 1995), 156; *see generally* Gerald K. Haines, "Under the Eagle's Wing: The Franklin Roosevelt Administration Forges an American Hemisphere," *Diplomatic History* 1, no. 4 (1977), 373–88.

61. *See* FDR, Press Conference 614-A, January 12, 1940, in Press Conferences, FDRL, 15:75–76, 78; *see also* Gellman, *Good Neighbor Diplomacy*, 49–55; Wood, *The Making*, 168–259; Pike, *FDR's Good Neighbor Policy*, 194–95. Secretary of the Treasury Henry Morgenthau, Jr., was aghast at the idea of cold-shouldering Mexico: "And give the Japs and Germans and Italians a chance to go in there?" Transcript of Group Meeting, December 16, 1937, in the Morgenthau Diaries, FDRL, 102:177; *see* Conference with the Senate Military Affairs Committee in the White House, January 31, 1939, in Schewe, *Roosevelt and Foreign Affairs*, 8:25. For the State Department strong-arming creditors into resolving debt disputes, *see* Roorda, *The Dictator Next Door*, 200–02; Gellman, *Good Neighbor Diplomacy*, 161.

62. FDR, Press Conference with the Associated Church Press 452-A, April 20, 1938, in Press Conferences, FDRL, 11:330–31.

63. For the "Proclaimed List," *see* Friedman, *Nazis and Good Neighbors*, 88–101; Schoultz, *Beneath the United States*, 311, 322–23. For the return of dollar diplomacy's interference, *see* Adams, *Economic Diplomacy*, 203–25.

64. For plans for preemptive occupation, *see* Mark Skinner Watson, *Chief of Staff: Prewar Plans and Preparations* (Washington, DC: Center of Military History, 1991), 95–96, 106–07; Stetson Conn and Byron Fairchild, *The Framework of Hemisphere Defense* (Washington, DC: Center of Military History, 1989), 33–34; John Child, "From 'Color' to 'Rainbow': U.S. Strategic

Planning for Latin America, 1919–1945," *Journal of Interamerican Studies and World Affairs* 21, no. 2 (May 1979), 233, 248–52, 256; Yerxa, *Admirals and Empire*, 129. Operation Pot of Gold nominally required "consultation" with Brazil, but it is doubtful that Washington would have hesitated to implement it if the Brazilian government failed to give its permission in an emergency. For the cartel plan, *see* Haglund, *The Transformation of U.S. Strategic Thought*, 210–13.

65. Shockingly, even two months after Germany's invasion of the Soviet Union, one out of every three Americans polled thought that it would be a "good idea" for the United States to take over Mexico, Central America, and the top of South America "before any other power can get it." American Association for Public Opinion Research, "Gallup and Fortune Polls," *The Public Opinion Quarterly* 5, no. 4 (Winter 1941), 687. Even Welles, who would soon criticize the country's interventionist turn, was never willing to give up the power to intervene entirely. Rather, if a neighbor ever became "subservient to Nazi or Fascist influence," Welles preferred to remove the "danger spot" through "joint inter-American action" rather than unilateral intervention. Welles to FDR, March 17, 1941, 710.11/2669½, in Roll 19, M1276, RG59, NA.

66. For the "Asian Monroe Doctrine," *see* John R. Murnane, "Japan's Monroe Doctrine?: Re-Framing the Story of Pearl Harbor," *The History Teacher* 40, no. 4 (August 2007), 511; *see also* George H. Blakeslee, "The Japanese Monroe Doctrine," *Foreign Affairs* 11, no. 4 (July 1933), 671–81; Gaddis Smith, *The Last Years of the Monroe Doctrine, 1945–1993* (New York: Hill and Wang, 1994), 35.

67. Adolf Berle, Diary Entry, December 10, 1941, in Berle and Jacobs, *Navigating the Rapids*, 384; *see* Adolf Berle, Diary Entry, December 18, 1941, in Berle and Jacobs, *Navigating the Rapids*, 387; *see also* Welles, *Sumner Welles*, 314; Gellman, *Good Neighbor Diplomacy*, 125.

68. *See* Paul Kennedy, *The Rise and Fall of the Great Powers: Economic Change and Military Conflict from 1500 to 2000* (New York: Vintage Books, 1989), 357–58; Desch, *When the Third World Matters*, 47. "Mostly on foreign soil" because besides Pearl Harbor, the Philippines was still formally part of the United States during this time. *See* Daniel Immerwahr, *How To Hide An Empire: A Short History of the Greater United States* (London: Bodley Head, 2019), 212. The United States, however, had already begun the ten-year transition period to independence mandated under the Tydings-McDuffie Act, Pub. L. No. 73-127, 48 Stat. 456, 463 (March 24, 1934).

69. For the detention and confiscation program, *see generally* Friedman, *Nazis and Good Neighbors*. For pressure on Chile, Bolivia, and Argentina, *see* Mecham, *Inter-American Security*, 229–31; Green, *The Containment of Latin America*, 147; Gellman, *Good Neighbor Diplomacy*, 191–94; Bryce Wood, *The Dismantling of the Good Neighbor Policy* (Austin: University of Texas Press, 1985), 14–121.

70. Sumner Welles, "Intervention and Interventions," *Foreign Affairs* 26, no. 1 (October 1947), 116; *see* Wood, *The Making*, 349–50; Welles, *Sumner Welles*, 1–3, 341–54; Yerxa, *Admirals and Empire*, 157.

71. *See* John Steele Gordon, *An Empire of Wealth: The Epic History of American Economic Power* (New York: Harper Perennial, 2004), 361–62; Kennedy, *Rise and Fall*, 257–58; G. John Ikenberry, *Liberal Leviathan: The Origins, Crisis, and Transformation of the American World Order* (Princeton, NJ: Princeton University Press, 2011), 162–63; G. John Ikenberry, *After Victory: Institutions, Strategic Restraint, and the Rebuilding of Order After Major Wars* (Princeton, NJ: Princeton University Press, 2001), 167–70.

72. Harold J. Laski, "America—1947," *The Nation*, December 13, 1947, 641.

73. Dean Acheson, "Peace Through Strength: A Foreign Policy Objective," Address before the Civil Federation of Dallas and the Community Course of Southern Methodist University (June 13, 1950), in *The Department of State Bulletin*, June 26, 1950, 1038; *see* Logan, *No Transfer*, 6, 385–95. For other contemporary recognitions of this reality, *see* FDA, Annual Message to Congress, January 7, 1943, in PPA 12:32; Harry S. Truman, Address on Foreign Economic Policy Delivered Baylor University, March 6, 1947, in PPP 1947, 167.

74. LaVerre to Welles, November 9, 1942, 710.11/2905½, in Roll 21, M1276, RG59, NA; Embassy Dispatch, April 25, 1943, in H. G. Nicholas, ed., *Washington Despatches, 1941–1945: Weekly Political Reports from the British Embassy* (London: Weidenfeld and Nicolson, 1981), 181; *see* FDR to Norris, September 21, 1943, in *F.D.R.: His Personal Letters*, ed. Elliott Roosevelt, vol. II, *1928–1945* (New York: Duell, Sloan and Pearce, 1950), 1445; Sumner Welles, *The Time for*

Decision (London: Hamish Hamilton, 1944), 187–88; Forrest Davis, "Roosevelt's World Blueprint," *Saturday Evening Post*, April 10, 1943, 109–10; *see also* Warren F. Kimball, *The Juggler: Franklin Roosevelt as Wartime Statesman* (Princeton, NJ: Princeton University Press, 1991), 107–26. President Harry S. Truman echoed the point as well. Harry S. Truman, Address in Mexico City, March 3, 1947, in PPP 1947, 165.

75. *See* Sumner Welles, *Seven Decisions That Shaped History* (New York: Harper & Brothers, 1951), 189; *see also* Helleiner, *Forgotten Foundations*, 2–3, 9–10, 24–25, 51–52, 76–77, 99–100, 120, 128; Welles, *Sumner Welles*, 300–09; Steward, *Trade and Hemisphere*, 268, 284–85; Marks, *Wind Over Sand*, 242; Emily S. Rosenberg, *Financial Missionaries to the World: The Politics and Culture of Dollar Diplomacy, 1900–1930* (Durham, NC: Duke University Press, 2003), 254–56; *see generally* Christopher D. O'Sullivan, *Sumner Welles, Postwar Planning, and the Quest for a New World Order, 1937–1943* (New York: Columbia University Press, 2008).

76. Welles, Memorial Day Address at the Arlington National Amphitheater, May 25, 1942, in *The Department of State Bulletin*, May 30, 1942, 487. FDR, too, wanted a "transition period" during which the United States and its most powerful allies would "polic[e] the world," though he had somewhat contradictory impulses about how long this transition period would last. FDR to Norris, September 21, 1943, in Roosevelt, *F.D.R.: His Personal Letters*, 2:1446–47; William D. Hassett, Diary Entry, April 5, 1943, in William D. Hassett, *Off the Record with F.D.R., 1942–1945* (New Brunswick, NJ: Rutgers University Press, 1958), 166–67; *see* Davis, "Roosevelt's World Blueprint," 109; Welles, *Seven Decisions*, 189.

77. *See* Central Intelligence Agency, "Review of the World Situation as It Relates to the Security of the United States," September 26, 1947, https://www.cia.gov/readingroom/docs/CIA -RDP67-00059A000500060004-6.pdf.

78. *See* Central Intelligence Agency, "Review of the World Situation."

79. Harry S. Truman, Special Message to the Congress on Greece and Turkey, March 12, 1947, in PPP 1947, 178–79; X [George F. Kennan], "The Sources of Soviet Conduct," *Foreign Affairs* 25, no. 4 (July 1947), 575–76.

80. James Monroe, Seventh Annual Message, December 2, 1823, in *The Writings of James Monroe*, ed. Stanislaus Murray Hamilton, vol. VI, *1817–1823* (New York: G. P. Putnam's Sons, 1902), 340; *see* Logan, *No Transfer*, 6, 385–95.

81. *Angola: Hearings Before the Subcomm. on African Affairs of the S. Comm. on Foreign Relations on U.S. Involvement in Civil War in Angola*, 94th Cong. 45 (1976); *see* Brian Loveman, *No Higher Law: American Foreign Policy and the Western Hemisphere Since 1776* (Chapel Hill: University of North Carolina Press, 2010), 263–64; Smith, *The Last Years*, 56–57.

82. Central Intelligence Agency, "Review of the World Situation"; *see* Cyrus Veeser, *A World Safe for Capitalism: Dollar Diplomacy and America's Rise to Global Power* (New York: Columbia University Press, 2002), 140.

83. *See* Gardner, *Economic Aspects*, 204; Sicker, *Geopolitics of Security*, 107–08.

84. Kennan to Lyon, October 13, 1947, quoted in Ikenberry, *After Victory*, 181; Dean Acheson, "Peace Through Strength: A Foreign Policy Objective," Address before the Civil Federation of Dallas and the Community Course of Southern Methodist University, June 13, 1950, in *The Department of State Bulletin*, June 26, 1950, 1039; Dean Rusk, News Conference, May 4, 1961, in *The Department of State Bulletin*, May 22, 1961, 763; *see* Dean Acheson, Address Before the Alfred E. Smith Memorial Foundation in New York, New York, October 20, 1949, in *The Department of State Bulletin*, October 31, 1949, 668; Central Intelligence Agency, "Review of the World Situation."

85. Luce, "The American Century," 169–70; *see* Eckes, *Opening America's Market*, 157–59; Michael H. Hunt, *Ideology and U.S. Foreign Policy* (New Haven, CT: Yale University Press, 1987), 159–60, 164–66; Schoultz, *Beneath the United States*, 356–57.

86. Luce, "The American Century," 171; Army Intelligence Report, n.d., quoted in Smith, *The Last Years*, 63; Arthur M. Schlesinger, Jr., *A Thousand Days: John F. Kennedy in the White House* (New York: Fawcett Crest, 1967), 704–05 (punctuation altered); *see* Tony Smith, *The Pattern of Imperialism: The United States, Great Britain, and the Late-Industrializing World Since 1815* (Cambridge, UK: Cambridge University Press, 1981), 242–43; Schmitz, *The United States and Right-Wing Dictatorships*, 3–8, 126–27.

87. Kennan to Byrnes, February 22, 1946, in FRUS 1946, 6:702; Luce, "The American Century," 171. For decolonization, *see* Kennedy, *Rise and Fall*, 381–82; Smith, *Pattern of Imperialism*, 158–65, 195–97. For dictatorships, *see* Schmitz, *The United States and Right-Wing Dictatorships*, 125–77.

88. For how the destabilization of the world provided opportunities for communist expansions, *see* Greg Grandin, *Empire's Workshop: Latin America, the United States, and the Rise of the New Imperialism* (New York: Metropolitan Books, 2006), 46; Hunt, *Ideology and U.S. Foreign Policy*, 159. For how the problem of order drew Americans into new interventions from Korea to Vietnam, *see* Smith, *Pattern of Imperialism*, 182–86.

89. "Transcript of Khrushchev's News Conference on U. S. Plane and Other Issues," *New York Times*, July 13, 1960; *see* Smith, *The Last Years*, 91–112.

90. For a good overview of this history as it relates to the Monroe Doctrine, *see* Smith, *The Last Years*, 65–230.

91. Zbigniew Brzezinski, *Power and Principle: Memoirs of the National Security Adviser, 1977–1981* (New York: Farrar Straus Giroux, 1985), 136; *see* Noel Maurer and Carlos Yu, *The Big Ditch: How America Took, Built, Ran, and Ultimately Gave Away the Panama Canal* (Princeton, NJ: Princeton University Press, 2011), 259–62.

92. Dean Acheson, Address Before the Alfred E. Smith Memorial Foundation, in *The Department of State Bulletin*, October 31, 1949, 669.

Conclusion

1. *See* Charles Sumner, "Prophetic Voices About America," *The Atlantic Monthly* 20, no. 119 (September 1867), 296–97; Lester D. Langley, *Struggle for the American Mediterranean: United States-European Rivalry in the Gulf-Caribbean, 1776–1904* (Athens: University of Georgia Press, 1976), 2–3.

2. Conde de Aranda, "Dictamen Reservado que el Excmo. Señor Conde de Aranda dió al Rey Sobre la Independencia de las Colonias Inglesas Después de Haber Hecho el Tratado de Paz Ajustado en París el Año de 1783," in *Boletín del Instituto de Estudios Americanistas de Sevilla*, año 1, no. 2 (June 1913), 53–54.

3. Conde de Aranda, "Dictamen Reservado," 55.

4. *Federalist*, no. 11 (Alexander Hamilton), in *The Federalist Papers*, ed. Clinton Rossiter (New York: New American Library of World Literature, 1961), 90; *see* John A. Logan, Jr., *No Transfer: An American Security Principle* (New Haven, CT: Yale University Press, 1962), 386–88.

5. Root to Shaw, January 3, 1908, in Box 188, Root MSS; *see generally* Jeffrey W. Meiser, *Power and Restraint: The Rise of the United States, 1898–1941* (Washington, DC: Georgetown University Press, 2015). In Nicaragua, for example, the United States turned down multiple invitations to impose a Platt Amendment–style protectorate, including in 1911 (twice), in 1914, and in 1927. *See* Dana G. Munro, "Dollar Diplomacy in Nicaragua, 1909–1913," *Hispanic American Historical Review* 38, no. 2 (May 1958), 233; Paolo E. Coletta, *William Jennings Bryan*, vol. 2, *Progressive Politician and Moral Statesman 1909–1915* (Lincoln: University of Nebraska Press, 1969), 189, 191–93; Dana G. Munro, *The United States and the Caribbean Republics 1921–1933* (Princeton, NJ: Princeton University Press, 1974), 218–19; Whitney T. Perkins, *Constraint of Empire: The United States and Caribbean Interventions* (Westport, CT: Greenwood, 1981), 116.

A similar story can be told about the Dominican Republic. *See* David Charles MacMichael, "The United States and the Dominican Republic, 1871–1940: A Cycle in Caribbean Diplomacy" (PhD diss., University of Oregon, 1964), 7, 9, 11, 63–64, 126–28, 130, 161. In April 1898, for example, President Ulises Heureaux wanted to avoid the domestic unrest that would result from selling the strategic harbor of Samaná Bay, so he instead encouraged Washington to seize the harbor outright in exchange for secret concessions. If the United States was truly a great power, he observed, it should treat weaker states the same way its peers did. "Come and take it," he prodded. "You understand me." Grimké to Day, April 7, 1898, quoted in MacMichael, "A Cycle of Caribbean Diplomacy," 127. Washington ignored this inducement as well as several subsequent ones. *See* MacMichael, "A Cycle of Caribbean Diplomacy," 126–28.

6. For the dizzying array of contemporary ideologies, *see, e.g.*, Robert Seager, II, *Alfred Thayer Mahan: The Man and His Letters* (Annapolis, MD: Naval Institute Press, 2017), 438–39.

7. *See* Charles E. Chapman, "New Corollaries of the Monroe Doctrine," *University of California Chronicle* 33, no. 2 (April 1931), 170–71.

8. Roosevelt to Speck von Sternburg, July 12, 1901, in Morison 3:116; Roosevelt to Bishop, February 23, 1904, in Morison 4:734–35; Roosevelt to Trevelyan, September 9, 1906, in Morison 5:401; Taft to Root, October 4, 1906, in Box 166, Root MSS; Root to Wilson, October 24, 1906, in Box 187, Root MSS; Wilson to Ellen Axson Wilson, August 19, 1913, in PWW 28:190–91; Wilson to Lansing, November 26, 1916, in FRUS 1916, 242; *see* Abraham F. Lowenthal, "The United States and the Dominican Republic to 1965: Background to Intervention," *Caribbean Studies* 10, no. 2 (July 1970), 41–42. Other times, interventions were launched with atavistic glee, including Roosevelt's taking of the isthmus and the Taft administration's toppling of Zelaya. But these counterexamples underscore the influence of personal pique, not overarching ideology, and strategic considerations still played a significant role in both cases.

9. *See* Walter LaFeber, *The New Empire: An Interpretation of American Expansion 1860–1898* (Ithaca, NY: Cornell University Press, 1967), 63–72. For criticism of Turner's influence, *see* Richard F. Hamilton, *America's New Empire: The 1890s and Beyond* (New Brunswick, NJ: Transaction Publishers, 2010), 123–24. Or consider Social Darwinism, which is often associated with war and aggression. In the United States, however, the country's leading Social Darwinists all lined up *against* the Spanish-American War and its spoils. *See* James A. Field, Jr., "American Imperialism: The Worst Chapter in Almost Any Book," *American Historical Review* 83, no. 3 (June 1978), 650; Paul S. Holbo, "Economics, Emotion, and Expansion: An Emerging Foreign Policy," in H. Wayne Morgan, ed., *The Gilded Age* (Syracuse, NY: Syracuse University Press, 1970), 214–15; Walter LaFeber, Comment on "American Imperialism: The Worst Chapter in Almost Any Book," *American Historical Review* 83, no. 3 (June 1978), 669. Furthermore, there is little evidence suggesting that these ideologies actually influenced policymakers' decisions. *See* Field, "The Worst Chapter," 646–47, 649.

10. *See generally* Rubin Francis Weston, *Racism in U.S. Imperialism: The Influence of Racial Assumptions on American Foreign Policy, 1893–1946* (Columbia: University of South Carolina Press, 1972); Eric T. L. Love, *Race over Empire: Racism and U.S. Imperialism 1865–1900* (Chapel Hill: University of North Carolina Press, 2004).

11. *See generally* Love, *Race over Empire*.

12. *See* Weston, *Racism in U.S. Imperialism*, 137–62, 258, 261–62. For Cuba and the Platt Amendment, *see also* Chapter 5.

13. For a contemporary view of race as a destabilizing but not dispositive force, *see, e.g.*, O.H. Platt, "The Pacification of Cuba," *The Independent*, June 27, 1901, 1468.

14. *See* Love, *Race over Empire*, 24–25; Weston, *Racism in U.S. Imperialism*, 261; David Healy, *Drive to Hegemony: The United States in the Caribbean 1898–1917* (Madison: University of Wisconsin Press, 1988), 65–66. Love suggests that while racism hindered annexation, it may have had less of a restraining effect on other forms of intervention by the United States. *See* Love, *Race over Empire*, 200. That is likely true to some extent, but many concerns about annexation—including the moral and physical degradation that whites allegedly suffered from prolonged exposure to "the tropics"—also applied to other forms of American involvement in Latin America. *See ibid.*, 24–25.

15. Smedley D. Butler, "America's Armed Forces: 2. 'In Time of Peace': The Army," *Common Sense* 4, no. 11 (November 1935), 8.

16. *See* Munro, *The United States and the Caribbean Republics*, 379–81; Max Boot, *The Savage Wars of Peace: Small Wars and the Rise of American Power* (New York: Basic Books, 2002), 138–40. For a case study in the Mexican context, *see* N. Stephen Kane, "American Businessmen and Foreign Policy: The Recognition of Mexico, 1920–1923," *Political Science Quarterly* 90, no. 2 (Summer 1975), 293–313. For some recent notable exceptions, *see* Jonathan M. Katz, *Gangsters of Capitalism: Smedley Butler, the Marines, and the Making and Breaking of America's Empire* (New York: St. Martin's, 2022); Noel Maurer, *The Empire Trap: The Rise and Fall of U.S. Intervention to Protect American Property Overseas, 1893–2013* (Princeton, NJ: Princeton University Press, 2013).

17. David A. Wells, *Freer Trade Essential to Future National Prosperity and Development* (New York: WM. C. Martin's Steam Printing House, 1882), 28. For the "New Empire" thesis's foundational works, *see* William Appleman Williams, *The Tragedy of American Diplomacy* (New York: W. W. Norton, 1972); William Appleman Williams, *The Roots of the Modern American Empire: A Study of the Growth and Shaping of Social Consciousness in a Marketplace Society* (New York: Random House, 1969); LaFeber, *New Empire*.

18. *See* Robert L. Beisner, *From the Old Diplomacy to the New 1865–1900* (Arlington Heights, IL: Harlan Davidson, 1986), 14–24; Holbo, "Economics, Emotion, and Expansion," 202–11; Milton Plesur, *America's Outward Thrust: Approaches to Foreign Affairs, 1865–1890* (DeKalb: Northern Illinois University Press, 1971), 16–19; John Braeman, "The New Left and American Foreign Policy During the Age of Normalcy: A Re-Examination," *Business History Review* 57, no. 1 (Spring 1983), 91–92, 94–97; David M. Pletcher, *The Diplomacy of Trade and Investment* (Columbia: University of Missouri, 1998), 3–4, 45; John A. S. Grenville and George Berkeley Young, *Politics, Strategy, and American Diplomacy: Studies in Foreign Policy, 1873–1917* (New Haven, CT: Yale University Press, 1969), 55–56; *see generally* David M. Pletcher, "Rhetoric and Results: A Pragmatic View of American Economic Expansionism, 1865–98," *Diplomatic History* 5, no. 2 (Spring 1981), 93–105; Richard F. Hamilton, *President McKinley, War and Empire*, vol. 2, *President McKinley and America's "New Empire"* (New Brunswick, NJ: Transaction Publishers, 2007).

19. *See* Kristin L. Hoganson, *Fighting for American Manhood: How Gender Politics Provoked the Spanish-American and Philippine-American Wars* (New Haven, CT: Yale University Press, 1998), 210–11 n.4.

20. *See* J. A. Thompson, "William Appleman Williams and the 'American Empire,'" *Journal of American Studies* 7, no. 1 (April 1973), 99, 103–04; Gerald G. Eggert, *Richard Olney: Evolution of a Statesman* (University Park: Pennsylvania State University Press, 1974), 180–81.

21. Examples of overstated threats include the Roosevelt administration's use of the threat from France to justify its course in Panama, as well as Roosevelt's reference to the threat from Europe in explaining the reoccupation of Cuba in 1906. *See* discussion *supra* Chapters 6 and 8. In both cases, however, the foreign threat was still a minor part of the administration's account of its actions.

22. *See* Nancy Mitchell, *The Danger of Dreams: German and American Imperialism in Latin America* (Chapel Hill: University of North Carolina Press, 1999), 220–22.

23. *See* Hans J. Morgenthau, *Politics Among Nations: The Struggle for Power and Peace* (New York: Alfred A. Knopf, 1956), 332. Counting on European leaders to rationally assess Europe's balance of power, moreover, was a dicey proposition. Rationality often lies in the eye of the beholder, and it would have been foolish for Americans to ignore the Kaiser's stated hostility to the Monroe Doctrine simply because those views did not align with what Americans thought Germany's policies should be.

24. Roosevelt exemplified some of this long-term thinking when he explained who the United States was fortifying the Panama Canal against. "It is not a present enemy," he told his brother-in-law, "it is against a possible future enemy." Citing the examples of Japan and Germany, he added presciently: "No human being can be certain that there never will be a war between us … [and if we] had not fortified the canal, our people might have cause to rue it for generations." Roosevelt to Cowles, October 27, 1911, in Morison 7:423. Root made a similar point when he explained why the Monroe Doctrine continued to apply to South America despite its relative stability and strength. "That South American states have become too strong for colonization or occupation is cause for satisfaction. That Europe has no purpose or wish to colonize American territory is most gratifying. These facts may make it improbable that it will be necessary to apply the Monroe Doctrine in the southern parts of South America; but they furnish no reason whatever for retracting or denying or abandoning a declaration of public policy, just and reasonable when it was made, and which, if occasion for its application shall arise in the future, will still be just and reasonable." Root, "The Real Monroe Doctrine," Presidential Address at the Eighth Annual Meeting of the American Society of International Law in Washington, DC, April 22, 1914, in Elihu Root, *Addresses on International Subjects*, ed. Robert Bacon and James Brown Scott (Cambridge, MA: Harvard University Press, 1916), 122–23.

25. *See* Dana G. Munro, *Intervention and Dollar Diplomacy in the Caribbean 1900–1921* (Princeton, NJ: Princeton University Press, 1964), 5–6; Barry Rigby, "The Origins of American

Expansion in Hawaii and Samoa, 1865–1900," *International History Review* 10, no. 2 (May 1988), 221–22. For this point in the context of the British Empire's expansion, *see generally* Niall Ferguson, *Empire: The Rise and Demise of the British World Order and the Lessons for Global Power* (New York: Basic Books, 2004).

26. "As regards Germany," Captain Mahan explained in 1909, "it made no difference to us what object she had in view…Her navy was a big fact, that called on us to sit up and take notice." Mahan to Clark, July 23, 1909, in *Letters and Papers of Alfred Thayer Mahan*, ed. Robert Seager, II, and Doris D. Maguire, vol. 3, *1902–1914* (Annapolis, MD: Naval Institute Press, 1975), 307–08; *see* Mahan, "Germany's Naval Ambition," *Collier's Weekly*, April 24, 1909, 13; *see also* John J. Mearsheimer, *The Tragedy of Great Power Politics* (New York: W. W. Norton, 2003), 31–36.

27. *See* Chapman, "New Corollaries of the Monroe Doctrine," 165–68. For the figures used in the calculation, *see* Grover Clark, *The Balance Sheets of Imperialism: Facts and Figures on Colonies* (New York: Russell & Russell, 1967), 23–28, Table 1. I added up and compared the amount of "independent" territory in Asia, Africa, and Oceania for 1878 and 1913, subtracting out the non-dependency territory of Japan and Russia from both years' totals and the territory of China from the 1913 total (by which point China's loss of sovereignty at the hands of foreign powers was manifest).

28. *See generally* Mearsheimer, *The Tragedy of Great Power Politics*.

29. H. C. Lodge, "Our Blundering Foreign Policy," *Forum* 19 (March–August 1895), 17; William L. Langer, "Farewell to Empire," *Foreign Affairs* 41, no. 1 (October 1862), 120; *see* R. E. Robinson and J. Gallagher, "The Partition of Africa," in *The New Cambridge Modern History*, ed. F. H. Hinsley, vol. 11, *Material Progress and World-Wide Problems, 1870–1898* (Cambridge, UK: Cambridge University Press, 1962), 593–640; Tony Smith, *The Pattern of Imperialism: The United States, Great Britain, and the Late-Industrializing World Since 1815* (Cambridge, UK: Cambridge University Press, 1981), 16–17, 47–49; Morgenthau, *Politics Among Nations*, 51. For the point about the Philippines, *see* John L. Offner, "Imperialism by International Consensus: The United States and the Philippine Islands," in *From Theodore Roosevelt to FDR: Internationalism and Isolationism in American Foreign Policy*, ed. Daniela Rossini (Staffordshire: Keele University Press, 1995), 45–54.

30. *See* Smith, *Pattern of Imperialism*, 21–22, 48; Morgenthau, *Politics Among Nations*, 332–33. Some of the parallels between European policy toward the Ottoman Empire and American policy toward the Western Hemisphere are quite close. Decades before the Dominican customs receivership, for example, there was the Ottoman Public Debt Administration, a European-run organization that collected the Empire's internal revenue to pay off its external debts. *See* William H. Wynne, *State Insolvency and Foreign Bondholders*, vol. 2, *Selected Case Histories of Governmental Foreign Bond Defaults and Debt Readjustments* (Washington, DC: BeardBooks, 2000), 417–81.

31. Andrew Higgins, "In Kazakhstan, Putin Again Seizes on Unrest to Try to Expand Influence," *New York Times*, January 6, 2022.

32. White House, *The National Security Strategy of the United States of America* (Washington, DC: September 2002), ii, 1.

33. For the Middle East, *see, e.g.*, Michael Stephens and Thomas Juneau, "Saudi Arabia: Why We Need This Flawed Ally," *Lawfare*, September 15, 2016, https://www.lawfareblog.com/saudi-arabia-why-we-need-flawed-ally.

34. Harold K. Jacobson and Michel Oksenberg, *China's Participation in the IMF, the World Bank, and GATT: Toward a Global Economic Order* (Ann Arbor: University of Michigan Press, 1990), 139.

35. U.S. Department of Defense, *Summary of the National Defense Strategy of the United States of America* (2018), 2, https://dod.defense.gov/Portals/1/Documents/pubs/2018-National-Defense-Strategy-Summary.pdf.

36. Wen Jiabao, "Turning Your Eyes to China," Remarks at Harvard University, December 11, 2003, https://news.harvard.edu/gazette/story/2003/12/harvard-gazette-remarks-of-chinese-premier-wen-jiabao; Wen Jiabao, "Carrying Forward the Five Principles of Peaceful Coexistence in the Promotion of Peace and Development," Speech at Rally Commemorating the 50th Anniversary of the Five Principles of Peaceful Coexistence, June 28, 2004, http://id.china-embassy.gov.cn/eng/xntjgk/200406/t20040628_2114572.htm; State Council Information Office of the People's Republic of China, *China's National Defense in the New Era* (July 24, 2019), 8,

available at https://english.www.gov.cn/archive/whitepaper/201907/24/content_WS5d3941ddc 6d08408f502283d.html.

37. *See* Ernest R. May, *Imperial Democracy: The Emergence of America as a Great Power* (New York: Harper Torchbooks, 1973), 263. For the logic behind countering rising powers, *see generally* Mearsheimer, *The Tragedy of Great Power Politics*.

38. *Cf.* Fareed Zakaria, *From Wealth to Power: The Unusual Origins of America's World Role* (Princeton, NJ: Princeton University Press, 1998), 5, 130. For the specific example, *see* Eric Paul Roorda, *The Dictator Next Door: The Good Neighbor Policy and the Trujillo Regime in the Dominican Republic, 1930–1945* (Durham, NC: Duke University Press, 2006), 10–11.

39. *See generally* Paul Kennedy, *The Rise and Fall of the Great Powers: Economic Change and Military Conflict from 1500 to 2000* (New York: Vintage Books, 1989). For the Second Industrial Revolution example in the context of sugar specifically, *see generally* César J. Ayala, *American Sugar Kingdom: The Plantation Economy of the Spanish Caribbean, 1898–1934* (Chapel Hill: University of North Carolina Press, 1999), including 25–26.

40. *See* Sulmaan Wasif Khan, *Haunted By Chaos: China's Grand Strategy from Mao Zedong to Xi Jinping* (Cambridge, MA: Harvard University Press, 2018), 217–18, 232–33, 241, 243–44; Robert Kagan, *The World America Made* (New York: Alfred A. Knopf, 2012), 63–64; Iain Marlow, "Why the Aukus, Quad and Five Eyes Pacts Anger China," *Bloomberg*, September 23, 2021; *see generally* Rush Doshi, *The Long Game: China's Grand Strategy to Displace American Order* (New York: Oxford University Press, 2021).

41. *See generally* U.S.-China Economic and Security Review Commission, *2020 Report to Congress* (Washington, DC: Government Publishing Office, 2020).

42. *See* Tony Saich, *From Rebel to Ruler: One Hundred Years of the Chinese Communist Party* (Cambridge, MA: Belknap, 2021), 24; Khan, *Haunted by Chaos*, 233–34.

43. *See* Steven Lee Myers, "China Criticized the Afghan War. Now It Worries About the Withdrawal," *New York Times*, July 15, 2021; USIP Senior Study Group, *China's Role in Myanmar's Internal Conflicts* (Washington, DC: U.S. Institute of Peace, 2018); Eleanor Albert, "The China–North Korea Relationship," Council on Foreign Relations, June 25, 2019, https://www .cfr.org/backgrounder/china-north-korea-relationship; "War, Conflict and Fragile States in Asia and the Pacific: 12 Things to Know," Asian Development Bank, June 13, 2013, https://www.adb .org/features/handle-care-fragility-and-conflict-asia-and-pacific.

44. Xi Jinping, "New Asian Security Concept for New Progress in Security Cooperation," Remarks at the Fourth Summit of the Conference on Interaction and Confidence Building Measures in Asia at the Shanghai Expo Center, May 21, 2014, https://www.mfa.gov.cn/ce /ceindo//eng/gdxw/t1160962.htm (punctuation altered); *see* Doshi, *The Long Game*, 208–34. For how concerns about the problem of order have been driving Chinese foreign policy since the creation of the People's Republic of China, *see generally* Khan, *Haunted by Chaos*.

45. *See* Alexandra Stevenson, "China Launches Third Aircraft Carrier in Major Milestone for Xi Jinping," *New York Times*, June 17, 2022; Gerry Shih, "In Central Asia's Forbidding Highlands, a Quiet Newcomer: Chinese Troops," *Washington Post*, February 18, 2019; Ellen Nakashima and Cate Cadell, "China Secretly Building Naval Facility in Cambodia, Western Officials Say," *Washington Post*, June 6, 2022; Sebastian Horn, Carmen M. Reinhart, and Christoph Trebesch, "China's Overseas Lending and the War in Ukraine," VoxEU Centre for Economic Policy Research, April 11, 2022, https://cepr.org/voxeu/columns/chinas-overseas-lending-and -war-ukraine; Doshi, *The Long Game*, 119, 184–85, 235–58, 293–96, 307–08.

46. Draft Framework Agreement Between the Government of the People's Republic of China and the Government of Solomon Islands on Security Cooperation, art. I, 2022, posted at https://twitter.com/Anne_MarieBrady/status/1506993807421853702; *see* Kate Lyons, "Solomons PM Could Use Chinese Police to Stay in Power, Key Provincial Adviser Fears," *The Guardian*, April 27, 2022; Damien Cave, "Why a Chinese Security Deal in the Pacific Could Ripple Through the World," *New York Times*, April 20, 2022; Shih, "A Quiet Newcomer"; Doshi, *The Long Game*, 261–98.

47. State Council Information Office, *China's National Defense*, 8; Zoe Jordan, "How Beijing Squares Its Noninterference Circle," *Asia Unbound*, March 7, 2022, https://www.cfr.org/blog

/how-beijing-squares-its-noninterference-circle; John Pomfret, "U.S. Takes a Tougher Stance with China," *Washington Post*, July 30, 2010; *see* Doshi, *The Long Game*, 277–78, 291.

48. *See* Kagan, *The World America Made*, 126–27. For the best assessment of China's strategic situation, *see* Ashley J. Tellis, *Balancing Without Containment: An American Strategy for Managing China* (Washington, DC: Carnegie Endowment for International Peace, 2014).

49. For a forceful statement of this point, *see* Robert Kagan, *The Jungle Grows Back: America and Our Imperiled World* (New York: Alfred A. Knopf, 2018), 77–78.

50. Wilson to Edith Bolling Galt, August 15, 1915, in PWW 34:208–209; *see* Samuel Flagg Bemis, *The Latin American Policy of the United States: An Historical Interpretation* (New York: Harcourt, Brace, 1943), 384.

51. *See* Kagan, *The Jungle Grows Back*, 160; Rich Cohen, *The Fish That Ate the Whale: The Life and Times of America's Banana King* (New York: Picador, 2012), xii–xiii.

52. *Cf.* F. Scott Fitzgerald, *The Great Gatsby* (New York: Charles Scribner's Sons, 1925), 218.

BIBLIOGRAPHY OF SELECTED SECONDARY SOURCES

Books

Abrahamson, James L. *America Arms for a New Century: The Making of a Great Military Power*. New York: Free Press, 1981.

Acker, Alison. *Honduras: The Making of A Banana Republic*. Boston: South End, 1988.

Adams, Frederick C. *Economic Diplomacy: The Export-Import Bank and American Foreign Policy, 1934–1939*. Columbia: University of Missouri Press, 1976.

Aguilar, Luis E. *Cuba 1933: Prologue to Revolution*. Ithaca, NY: Cornell University Press, 1972.

Allen, Helena G. *The Betrayal of Liliuokalani: Last Queen of Hawaii 1838–1917*. Honolulu: Mutual, 1982.

Allison, Graham. *Destined for War: Can America and China Escape Thucydides's Trap?* Boston: Mariner Books, 2018.

Anguizola, Gustave. *Philippe Bunau-Varilla: The Man Behind the Panama Canal*. Chicago: Nelson-Hall, 1980.

Ayala, César J. *American Sugar Kingdom: The Plantation Economy of the Spanish Caribbean, 1898–1934*. Chapel Hill: University of North Carolina Press, 1999.

Bailey, Thomas A. *A Diplomatic History of the American People*. Englewood Cliffs, NJ: Prentice-Hall, 1980.

Barrows, Chester L. *William M. Evarts: Lawyer, Diplomat, Statesman*. Chapel Hill: University of North Carolina Press, 1941.

Beale, Howard K. *Theodore Roosevelt and the Rise of America to World Power*. Baltimore, MD: Johns Hopkins University Press, 1984.

Beisner, Robert L. *From the Old Diplomacy to the New 1865–1900*. Arlington Heights, IL: Harlan Davidson, 1986.

———. *Twelve Against Empire: The Anti-Imperialists, 1898–1900*. New York: McGraw-Hill Book, 1968.

Bemis, Samuel Flagg. *The Latin American Policy of the United States: An Historical Interpretation*. New York: Harcourt, Brace, 1943.

Benbow, Mark. *Leading Them to the Promised Land: Woodrow Wilson, Covenant Theology, and the Mexican Revolution, 1913–1915*. Kent, OH: Kent State University Press, 2010.

Benjamin, Jules Robert. *The United States and Cuba: Hegemony and Dependent Development, 1880–1934*. Pittsburgh, PA: University of Pittsburgh Press, 1977.

Bermann, Karl. *Under the Big Stick: Nicaragua and the United States Since 1848*. Boston: South End Press, 1986.

Black, George. *The Good Neighbor: How the United States Wrote the History of Central America and the Caribbean*. New York: Pantheon Books, 1988.

Blasier, Cole. *The Hovering Giant: U.S. Responses to Revolutionary Change in Latin America 1910–1985*. Pittsburgh, PA: University of Pittsburgh Press, 1985.

Bock, Carl H. *Prelude to Tragedy: The Negotiation and Breakdown of the Tripartite Convention of London, October 31, 1861*. Philadelphia: University of Pennsylvania Press, 1966.

Boghardt, Thomas. *The Zimmermann Telegram: Intelligence, Diplomacy, and America's Entry into World War I*. Annapolis, MD: Naval Institute Press, 2012.

Boot, Max. *The Savage Wars of Peace: Small Wars and the Rise of American Power*. New York: Basic Books, 2002.

Borchard, Edwin. *State Insolvency and Foreign Bondholders*. Vol. 1, *General Principles*. Washington, DC: BeardBooks, 2000.

Bourne, Kenneth. *Britain and the Balance of Power in North America 1815–1908*. Berkeley: University of California Press, 1967.

Bowen, Wayne H. *Spain and the American Civil War*. Columbia: University of Missouri Press, 2011.

Braisted, William Reynolds. *The United States Navy in the Pacific, 1897–1909*. Austin: University of Texas Press, 1958.

Brands, H. W. *American Colossus: The Triumph of Capitalism, 1865–1900*. New York: Doubleday, 2010.

———. *The Reckless Decade: America in the 1890s*. Chicago: University of Chicago Press, 1995.

———. *TR: The Last Romantic*. New York: Basic Books, 1997.

Buchenau, Jürgen. *In the Shadow of the Giant: The Making of Mexico's Central America Policy, 1876–1930*. Tuscaloosa: University of Alabama Press, 1996.

Burton, David H. *Theodore Roosevelt: Confident Imperialist*. Philadelphia: University of Pennsylvania Press, 1968.

Caesar, Conte Corti, Egon. *Maximilian and Charlotte of Mexico*. 2 vols. New York: Alfred A. Knopf, 1929.

Calder, Bruce J. *The Impact of Intervention: The Dominican Republic During the U.S. Occupation of 1916–1924*. Austin: University of Texas Press, 1988.

Calhoun, Frederick S. *Power and Principle: Armed Intervention in Wilsonian Foreign Policy*. Kent, OH: Kent State University Press, 1986.

———. *Uses of Force and Wilsonian Foreign Policy*. Kent, OH: Kent State University Press, 1993.

Callahan, James Morton. *American Foreign Policy in Mexican Relations*. New York: Cooper Square, 1967.

Callcott, Wilfrid Hardy. *The Caribbean Policy of the United States 1890–1920*. New York: Octagon, 1977.

Campbell, Charles S., Jr. *Anglo-American Understanding, 1898–1903*. Baltimore, MD: Johns Hopkins Press, 1957.

———. *The Transformation of American Foreign Relations 1865–1900*. New York: Harper and Row, 1976.

Challener, Richard D. *Admirals, Generals, and American Foreign Policy 1898–1914.* Princeton, NJ: Princeton University Press, 1979.

Chernow, Ron. *Grant.* New York: Penguin, 2017.

———. *The House of Morgan: An American Banking Dynasty and the Rise of Modern Finance.* New York: Atlantic Monthly, 1990.

Cherny, Robert W. *A Righteous Cause: The Life of William Jennings Bryan.* Boston: Little, Brown, 1985.

Clapp, Margaret. *Forgotten First Citizen: John Bigelow.* Boston: Little, Brown, 1947.

Clark, Christopher. *The Sleepwalkers: How Europe Went to War in 1914.* New York: HarperCollins, 2013.

Clark, Grover. *The Balance Sheets of Imperialism: Facts and Figures on Colonies.* New York: Russell & Russell, 1967.

Cline, Howard F. *The United States and Mexico.* New York: Atheneum, 1968.

Clodfelter, Michael. *Warfare and Armed Conflicts: A Statistical Encyclopedia of Casualty and Other Figures, 1492–2015.* 4th ed. Jefferson, MO: McFarland, 2017.

Coffman, Tom. *Nation Within: The Story of America's Annexation of the Nation of Hawai'i.* Kāne'ohe, HI: Epicenter, 2003.

Cohen, Rich. *The Fish That Ate the Whale: The Life and Times of America's Banana King.* New York: Picador, 2012.

Cohen, Warren I. *Empire Without Tears: America's Foreign Relations 1921–1933.* New York: Alfred A. Knopf, 1987.

Colby, Jason M. *The Business of Empire: United Fruit, Race, and U.S. Expansion in Central America.* Ithaca, NY: Cornell University Press, 2011.

Coletta, Paolo E. *William Jennings Bryan.* Vol. 2, *Progressive Politician and Moral Statesman 1909–1915.* Lincoln: University of Nebraska Press, 1969.

Collin, Richard H. *Theodore Roosevelt, Culture, Diplomacy, and Expansion: A New View of American Imperialism.* Baton Rouge: Louisiana State University Press, 1985.

———. *Theodore Roosevelt's Caribbean: The Panama Canal, the Monroe Doctrine, and the Latin American Context.* Baton Rouge: Louisiana State University Press, 1990.

Conn, Stetson, and Byron Fairchild. *The Framework of Hemisphere Defense.* Washington, DC: Center of Military History, 1989.

Cooper, John Milton, Jr. *The Warrior and the Priest: Woodrow Wilson and Theodore Roosevelt.* Cambridge, MA: Belknap Press, 1983.

———. *Woodrow Wilson: A Biography.* New York: Alfred A. Knopf, 2009.

Craig, Lee A. *Josephus Daniels: His Life and Times.* Chapel Hill: University of North Carolina Press, 2013.

Crandall, Russell. *America's Dirty Wars: Irregular Warfare from 1776 to the War on Terror.* Cambridge, UK: Cambridge University Press, 2014.

Crapol, Edward P. *America for Americans: Economic Nationalism and Anglophobia in the Late Nineteen Century.* Westport, CT: Greenwood, 1973.

———. *James G. Blaine: Architect of Empire.* Wilmington, DE: SR Books, 2000.

Crook, D. P. *The North, the South and the Powers, 1861–1865.* New York: John Wiley & Sons, 1974.

Cullinane, Michael Patrick. "Imperial 'Character': How Race and Civilization Shaped Theodore Roosevelt's Imperialism." In *America's Transatlantic Turn: Theodore Roosevelt and the "Discovery" of Europe,* edited by Hans Krabbendam and John M. Thompson, 31–47. New York: Palgrave Macmillan, 2012.

————. *Liberty and American Anti-Imperialism, 1898–1909*. New York: Palgrave Macmillan, 2012.

Cunningham, Michele. *Mexico and the Foreign Policy of Napoleon III*. Houndmills, UK: Palgrave, 2001.

Curry, E. R. *Hoover's Dominican Diplomacy and the Origins of the Good Neighbor Policy*. New York: Garland, 1979.

Dalleo, Raphael. *American Imperialism's Undead: The Occupation of Haiti and the Rise of Caribbean Anticolonialism*. Charlottesville: University of Virginia Press, 2016.

Davis, George T. *A Navy Second to None: The Development of Modern American Naval Policy*. New York: Harcourt, Brace, 1940.

Daws, Gavan. *Shoal of Time: A History of the Hawaiian Islands*. Honolulu: University of Hawaii Press, 1968.

DeConde, Alexander. *Herbert Hoover's Latin-American Policy*. Stanford, CA: Stanford University Press, 1951.

Dennis, Alfred L. P. *Adventures in American Diplomacy 1896–1906*. New York: E. P. Dutton, 1928.

Desch, Michael C. *When the Third World Matters: Latin America and United States Grand Strategy*. Baltimore, MD: Johns Hopkins University Press, 1993.

Deutsch, Herman. *Incredible Yanqui: The Career of Lee Christmas*. Gretna, LA: Pelican, 2012.

Dobson, John M. *America's Ascent: The United States Becomes a Great Power, 1880–1914*. DeKalb: Northern Illinois University Press, 1978.

Doshi, Rush. *The Long Game: China's Grand Strategy to Displace American Order*. New York: Oxford University Press, 2021.

Dozer, Donald Marquand. *The Monroe Doctrine: Its Modern Significance*. New York: Alfred A. Knopf, 1965.

Drake, Paul W. "From Good Men to Good Neighbors: 1912–1932." In *Exporting Democracy: The United States and Latin America*, edited by Abraham F. Lowenthal, 3–40. Baltimore: Johns Hopkins University Press, 1991.

————. *The Money Doctor in the Andes: The Kemmerer Missions, 1923–1933*. Durham, NC: Duke University Press, 1989.

————, ed. *Money Doctors, Foreign Debts, and Economic Reforms in Latin America from the 1890s to the Present*. Wilmington, DE: Scholarly Resources, 1994.

Dulles, Foster Rhea. *The Imperial Years*. New York: Thomas Y. Crowell, 1966.

————. *Prelude to World Power: American Diplomatic History, 1860–1900*. New York: Macmillan, 1968.

Dunn, Susan. *A Blueprint for War: FDR and the Hundred Days that Mobilized America*. New Haven, CT: Yale University Press, 2018.

DuVal, Miles P., Jr. *Cadiz to Cathay: The Story of the Long Diplomatic Struggle for the Panama Canal*. Stanford, CA: Stanford University Press, 1947.

Eckes, Alfred E., Jr. *Opening America's Market: U.S. Foreign Trade Policy Since 1776*. Chapel Hill: University of North Carolina Press, 1995.

Eggert, Gerald G. *Richard Olney: Evolution of a Statesman*. University Park: Pennsylvania State University Press, 1974.

Eisenhower, John S. D. *Intervention!: The United States and the Mexican Revolution, 1913–1917*. New York: W. W. Norton, 1993.

Espino, Ovidio Diaz. *How Wall Street Created a Nation: J. P. Morgan, Teddy Roosevelt, and the Panama Canal*. New York: Four Walls Eight Windows, 2001.

Ewell, Judith. *Venezuela and the United States: From Monroe's Hemisphere to Petroleum's Empire*. Athens: University of Georgia Press, 1996.

Feis, Herbert. *The Diplomacy of the Dollar: 1919–1932*. New York: Norton Library, 1966.

Ferguson, Niall. *Colossus: The Rise and Fall of America's Empire*. New York: Penguin Books, 2005.

———. *Empire: The Rise and Demise of the British World Order and the Lessons for Global Power*. New York: Basic Books, 2004.

Ferrell, Robert H. *American Diplomacy in the Great Depression: Hoover-Stimson Foreign Policy, 1929–1933*. New Haven, CT: Yale University Press, 1957.

Fieldhouse, D. K. *The Colonial Empires: A Comparative Survey from the Eighteenth Century*. 2nd ed. London: Macmillan, 1982.

Foner, Philip S. *The Spanish-Cuban-American War and the Birth of American Imperialism 1895–1902*. 2 vols. New York: Monthly Review, 1972.

Foreman, Amanda. *A World on Fire: Britain's Crucial Role in the American Civil War*. New York: Random House, 2010.

Freidel, Frank. *The Splendid Little War*. Boston: Burford Books, 2002.

Friedberg, Aaron L. *The Weary Titan: Britain and the Experience of Relative Decline, 1895–1905*. Princeton, NJ: Princeton University Press, 1988.

Friedman, Max Paul. *Nazis and Good Neighbors: The United States Campaign Against the Germans of Latin America in World War II*. Cambridge, UK: Cambridge University Press, 2003.

Fry, Joseph A. "In Search of an Orderly World: U.S. Imperialism, 1898-1912." In *Modern American Diplomacy*, edited by John M. Carroll and George C. Herring, 1–20. Wilmington, DE: Scholarly Resources, 1986.

Frye, Alton. *Nazi Germany and the American Hemisphere 1933–1941*. New Haven, CT: Yale University Press, 1967.

Fuller, Stephen M., and Graham A. Cosmas. *Marines in the Dominican Republic 1916–1924*. Washington, DC: History and Museum Division, 1974.

Fullilove, Michael. *Rendezvous with Destiny: How Franklin D. Roosevelt and Five Extraordinary Men Took America into the War and into the World*. New York: Penguin, 2013.

Gaddis, John Lewis. *Surprise, Security, and the American Experience*. Cambridge, MA: Harvard University Press, 2004.

Gardner, Lloyd C. *Economic Aspects of New Deal Diplomacy*. Boston: Beacon, 1971.

———. *Imperial America: American Foreign Policy Since 1898*. New York: Harcourt Brace Jovanovich, 1976.

———. *Safe for Democracy: The Anglo-American Response to Revolution, 1913–1923*. New York: Oxford University Press, 1984.

———. "Woodrow Wilson and the Mexican Revolution." In *Woodrow Wilson and a Revolutionary World 1913–1921*, edited by Arthur S. Link, 3–48. Chapel Hill: University of North Carolina Press, 1982.

Gardner, Lloyd C., Walter F. LaFeber, and Thomas J. McCormick. *Creation of the American Empire: U.S. Diplomatic History*. Chicago: Rand McNally, 1973.

Garraty, John A. *Henry Cabot Lodge: A Biography*. New York: Alfred A. Knopf, 1953.

———. *The New Commonwealth 1877–1890*. New York: Harper and Row, 1968.

Geissler, Suzanne. *God and Sea Power: The Influence of Religion on Alfred Thayer Mahan*. Annapolis, MD: Naval Institute Press, 2015.

Gellman, Irwin F. *Good Neighbor Diplomacy: United States Policies in Latin America, 1933–1945*. Baltimore, MD: Johns Hopkins University Press, 1979.

———. *Roosevelt and Batista: Good Neighbor Diplomacy in Cuba, 1933–1945*. Albuquerque: University of New Mexico, 1973.

———. *Secret Affairs: Franklin Roosevelt, Cordell Hull, and Sumner Welles*. Baltimore, MD: Johns Hopkins University Press, 1995.

Gilderhus, Mark T. *Pan American Visions: Woodrow Wilson in the Western Hemisphere 1913–1921*. Tucson: University of Arizona Press, 1986.

Glaser, David. *Robert Lansing: A Study in Statecraft*. Xlibris, 2015.

Gobat, Michael. *Confronting the American Dream: Nicaragua Under U.S. Imperial Rule*. Durham, NC: Duke University Press, 2005.

Goda, Norman J. W. *Tomorrow the World: Hitler, Northwest Africa, and the Path Toward America*. College Station: Texas A&M University Press, 1998.

Goldberg, Joyce S. *The Baltimore Affair*. Lincoln: University of Nebraska Press, 1986.

Goldwert, Marvin. *The Constabulary in the Dominican Republic and Nicaragua: Progeny and Legacy of United States Intervention*. Gainesville: University of Florida Press, 1962.

Goodwin, Doris Kearns. *Team of Rivals: The Political Genius of Lincoln*. New York: Simon & Schuster, 2005.

Gordon, John Steele. *An Empire of Wealth: The Epic History of American Economic Power*. New York: Harper Perennial, 2004.

Gordon, Philip H. *Losing the Long Game: The False Promise of Regime Change in the Middle East*. New York: St. Martin's, 2020.

Gould, Lewis L. *The Presidency of William McKinley*. Lawrence: University Press of Kansas, 1980.

———. *The Spanish-American War and President McKinley*. Lawrence: University Press of Kansas, 1982.

Graham-Yooll, Andrew. *Imperial Skirmishes: War and Gunboat Diplomacy in Latin America*. Oxford, UK: Signal Books, 2002.

Grandin, Greg. *Empire's Workshop: Latin America, the United States, and the Rise of the New Imperialism*. New York: Metropolitan Books, 2006.

Green, David. *The Containment of Latin America: A History of the Myths and Realities of the Good Neighbor Policy*. Chicago: Quadrangle Books, 1971.

Greene, Julie. *The Canal Builders: Making America's Empire at the Panama Canal*. New York: Penguin Books, 2010.

Grenville, John A. S., and George Berkeley Young. *Politics, Strategy, and American Diplomacy: Studies in Foreign Policy, 1873–1917*. New Haven, CT: Yale University Press, 1969.

Grieb, Kenneth J. *The Latin American Policy of Warren G. Harding*. Fort Worth: Texas Christian University Press, 1977.

———. *The United States and Huerta*. Lincoln: University of Nebraska Press, 1969.

Hagan, Kenneth J. *American Gunboat Diplomacy and the Old Navy 1877–1889*. Westport, CT: Greenwood, 1973.

Haglund, David G. *Latin America and the Transformation of U.S. Strategic Thought, 1936–1940*. Albuquerque: University of New Mexico Press, 1984.

Hahn, Steven. *A Nation Without Borders: The United States and Its World in an Age of Civil Wars, 1830–1910*. New York: Penguin Books, 2017.

Haley, James I. *Captive Paradise: A History of Hawai'i*. New York: St. Martin's Press, 2014.

Hall, Linda B. *Oil, Banks, and Politics: The United States and Postrevolutionary Mexico, 1917–1924.* Austin: University of Texas Press, 1995.

Hamilton, Richard F. *America's New Empire: The 1890s and Beyond.* New Brunswick, NJ: Transaction Publishers, 2010.

———. *President McKinley, War and Empire.* 2 vols. New Brunswick, NJ: Transaction Publishers, 2006–07.

Hanna, Alfred J., and Kathryn A. Hanna. *Napoleon III and Mexico: American Triumph over Monarchy.* Chapel Hill: University of North Carolina Press, 1971.

Hannigan, Robert E. *The New World Power: American Foreign Policy, 1898–1917.* Philadelphia: University of Pennsylvania Press, 2002.

Harris, Charles H., III, and Louis R. Sadler. *The Border and the Revolution: Clandestine Activities of the Mexican Revolution 1910–1920.* Silver City, NM: High-Lonesome, 1988.

Hart, John Mason. *Revolutionary Mexico: The Coming and Process of the Mexican Revolution.* Berkeley: University of California Press, 1989.

Haslip, Joan. *The Crown of Mexico: Maximilian and His Empress Carlota.* New York: Holt, Rinehart and Winston, 1971.

Healy, David. *Drive to Hegemony: The United States in the Caribbean 1898–1917.* Madison: University of Wisconsin Press, 1988.

———. *Gunboat Diplomacy in the Wilson Era: The U.S. Navy in Haiti, 1915–1916.* Madison: University of Wisconsin Press, 1976.

———. *James G. Blaine and Latin America.* Columbia: University of Missouri Press, 2001.

———. *The United States in Cuba 1898–1902: Generals, Politicians, and the Search for Policy.* Madison: University of Wisconsin Press, 1963.

———. *US Expansionism: The Imperialist Urge in the 1890s.* Madison: University of Wisconsin Press, 1970.

Helleiner, Eric. *Forgotten Foundations of Bretton Woods: International Development and the Making of the Postwar Order.* Ithaca, NY: Cornell University Press, 2014.

Hendrix, Henry J. *Theodore Roosevelt's Naval Diplomacy: The U.S. Navy and the Birth of the American Century.* Annapolis, MD: Naval Institute Press, 2009.

Herring, George C. *From Colony to Superpower: U.S. Foreign Relations Since 1776.* Oxford, UK: Oxford University Press, 2008.

Herwig, Holger H. *Germany's Vision of Empire in Venezuela 1871–1914.* Princeton, NJ: Princeton University Press, 1986.

———. *Politics of Frustration: The United States in German Naval Planning, 1889–1941.* Boston: Little, Brown, 1976.

Hill, Howard C. *Roosevelt and the Caribbean.* Chicago: University of Chicago Press, 1927.

Hofstadter, Richard. *The Paranoid Style in American Politics and Other Essays.* Chicago: University of Chicago Press, 1965.

Hoganson, Kristin L. *Fighting for American Manhood: How Gender Politics Provoked the Spanish-American and Philippine-American Wars.* New Haven, CT: Yale University Press, 1998.

Holmes, James R. *Theodore Roosevelt and World Order: Police Power in International Relations.* Washington, DC: Potomac Books, 2006.

Hood, Miriam. *Gunboat Diplomacy, 1895–1905: Great Power Pressure in Venezuela.* London: George Allen & Unwin, 1983.

Hopkins, A. G. *American Empire: A Global History.* Princeton, NJ: Princeton University Press, 2018.

Hudson, Peter James. *Bankers and Empire: How Wall Street Colonized the Caribbean*. Chicago: University of Chicago Press, 2017.

Hunt, Michael H. *Ideology and U.S. Foreign Policy*. New Haven, CT: Yale University Press, 1987.

Hyde, Montgomery H. *Mexican Empire: The History of Maximilian and Carlota of Mexico*. London: Macmillan, 1946.

Ikenberry, G. John. *After Victory: Institutions, Strategic Restraint, and the Rebuilding of Order After Major Wars*. Princeton, NJ: Princeton University Press, 2001.

———. *Liberal Leviathan: The Origins, Crisis, and Transformation of the American World Order*. Princeton, NJ: Princeton University Press, 2011.

Immerman, Richard H. *Empire for Liberty: A History of American Imperialism from Benjamin Franklin to Paul Wolfowitz*. Princeton, NJ: Princeton University Press, 2010.

Immerwahr, Daniel. *How To Hide An Empire: A Short History of the Greater United States*. London: Bodley Head, 2019.

James, Henry. *Richard Olney and His Public Service*. Boston: Houston Mifflin, 1923.

Jessup, Philip C. *Elihu Root*. 2 vols. New York: Dodd, Mead, 1938.

Jones, Howard. *Blue & Gray Diplomacy: A History of Union and Confederate Foreign Relations*. Chapel Hill: University of North Carolina, 2010.

Kagan, Robert. *Dangerous Nation*. New York: Alfred A. Knopf, 2006.

———. *The Jungle Grows Back: America and Our Imperiled World*. New York: Alfred A. Knopf, 2018.

———. *The World America Made*. New York: Alfred A. Knopf, 2012.

Kamman, William. *A Search For Stability: United States Diplomacy Toward Nicaragua 1925–1933*. Notre Dame, IN: University of Notre Dame Press, 1968.

Kaplan, Amy. "'Left Alone with America': The Absence of Empire in the Study of American Culture." In *Cultures of United States Imperialism*, edited by Amy Kaplan and Donald E. Pease, 3–21. Durham, NC: Duke University, 1993.

Karabell, Zachary. *Inside Money: Brown Brothers Harriman and the American Way of Power*. New York: Penguin Press, 2021.

Karp, Walter. *The Politics of War: The Story of Two Wars Which Altered Forever the Political Life of the American Republic (1890–1920)*. New York: Harper Colophon Books, 1979.

Katz, Friedrich. *The Secret War in Mexico: Europe, the United States and the Mexican Revolution*. Chicago: University of Chicago Press, 1981.

Katz, Jonathan M. *Gangsters of Capitalism: Smedley Butler, the Marines, and the Making and Breaking of America's Empire*. New York: St. Martin's, 2022.

Kazin, Michael. *A Godly Hero: The Life of William Jennings Bryan*. New York: Alfred A. Knopf, 2006.

Kennedy, Paul. *The Rise and Fall of the Great Powers: Economic Change and Military Conflict from 1500 to 2000*. New York: Vintage Books, 1989.

Khan, Sulmaan Wasif. *Haunted By Chaos: China's Grand Strategy from Mao Zedong to Xi Jinping*. Cambridge, MA: Harvard University Press, 2018.

Kimball, Warren F. *The Juggler: Franklin Roosevelt as Wartime Statesman*. Princeton, NJ: Princeton University Press, 1991.

Kinzer, Stephen. *Overthrow: America's Century of Regime Change from Hawaii to Iraq*. New York: Henry Holt and Company, 2006.

Kirkwood, Burton. *The History of Mexico*. Westport, CT: Greenwood Press, 2000.

Kneer, Warren G. *Great Britain and the Caribbean, 1901–1913: A Study in Anglo-American Relations*. East Lansing: Michigan State University Press, 1975.

Knight, Alan. *The Mexican Revolution*. 2 vols. Lincoln: University of Nebraska Press, 1990.

Krenn, Michael L. *The Color of Empire: Race and American Foreign Relations*. Washington, DC: Potomac Books, 2006.

———. *U.S. Policy Toward Economic Nationalism in Latin America, 1917–1929*. Wilmington, DE: Scholarly Resources, 1990.

Kupchan, Charles A. *Isolationism: A History of America's Efforts to Shield Itself from the World*. Oxford, UK: Oxford University Press, 2020.

Kuykendall, Ralph S. *The Hawaiian Kingdom*. Vol. 3, *1874–1893, The Kalakaua Dynasty*. Honolulu: University of Hawaii Press, 1967.

Kuykendall, Ralph S., and A. Grove Day. *Hawaii: A History, from Polynesian Kingdom to American State*. Englewood Cliffs, NJ: Prentice-Hall, 1961.

Laderman, Charlie. "Civilization, Empire, and Humanity: Theodore Roosevelt's Second Corollary to the Monroe Doctrine." In *Rhetorics of Empire: Languages of Colonial Conflict After 1900*, edited by Martin Thomas and Richard Toye, 58–74. Manchester, UK: Manchester University Press, 2017.

LaFeber, Walter. *The American Age: United States Foreign Policy at Home and Abroad Since 1750*. New York: W. W. Norton, 1989.

———. *The Cambridge History of American Foreign Relations*. Vol. 2, *The American Search for Opportunity, 1865–1913*. Cambridge, UK: Cambridge University Press, 1998.

———. *Inevitable Revolutions: The United States in Central America*. 2nd ed. New York: W. W. Norton, 1993.

———. *The New Empire: An Interpretation of American Expansion 1860–1898*. Ithaca, NY: Cornell University Press, 1967.

———. *The Panama Canal: The Crisis in Historical Perspective*. New York: Oxford University Press, 1989.

Langley, Lester D. *America and the Americas: The United States in the Western Hemisphere*. Athens: University of Georgia Press, 2010.

———. *The Banana Wars: United States Intervention in the Caribbean, 1898–1934*. Chicago: Dorsey, 1988.

———. *Struggle for the American Mediterranean: United States-European Rivalry in the Gulf-Caribbean, 1776–1904*. Athens: University of Georgia Press, 1976.

Langley, Lester D., and Thomas Schoonover. *The Banana Men: American Mercenaries and Entrepreneurs in Central America, 1880–1930*. Lexington: University Press of Kentucky, 1995.

Lasso, Marixa. *Erased: The Untold Story of the Panama Canal*. Cambridge, MA: Harvard University Press, 2019.

Leech, Margaret. *In the Days of McKinley*. New York: Harper & Brothers, 1959.

Leonard, Thomas M. *Central America and the United States: The Search for Stability*. Athens: University of Georgia Press, 1991.

Leopold, Richard W. *Elihu Root and the Conservative Tradition*. Boston: Little, Brown, 1954.

Leuchsenring, Emilio Roig de. *Cuba no Debe Su Independencia a los Estados Unidos*. Habana: Sociedad Cubana de Estudios Históricos e Internacionales, 1950.

Lewis, James E., Jr. *The American Union and the Problem of Neighborhood: The United States and the Collapse of the Spanish Empire, 1783–1829*. Chapel Hill: University of North Carolina Press, 1998.

Link, Arthur S. *Wilson.* 5 vols. Princeton, NJ: Princeton University Press, 1947–65.

———. *Woodrow Wilson: Revolution, War, and Peace.* Arlington Heights, IL: Harlan Davidson, 1979.

Linn, Brian McAllister. *The Philippine War 1899–1902.* Lawrence: University Press of Kansas, 2000.

Livezey, William E. *Mahan on Sea Power.* Norman: University of Oklahoma Press, 1985.

Lockmiller, David A. *Magoon in Cuba: A History of the Second Intervention, 1906–1909.* Chapel Hill: University of North Carolina Press, 1938.

Logan, John A., Jr. *No Transfer: An American Security Principle.* New Haven, CT: Yale University Press, 1962.

Logan, Rayford W. *The Diplomatic Relations of the United States with Haiti, 1776–1891.* Chapel Hill: University of North Carolina Press, 1941.

Love, Eric T. L. *Race over Empire: Racism and U.S. Imperialism 1865–1900.* Chapel Hill: University of North Carolina Press, 2004.

Loveman, Brian. *No Higher Law: American Foreign Policy and the Western Hemisphere Since 1776.* Chapel Hill: University of North Carolina Press, 2010.

Macaulay, Neill. *The Sandino Affair.* Durham, NC: Duke University Press, 1985.

Mack, Gerstle *The Land Divided: A History of the Panama Canal and Other Isthmian Canal Projects.* New York: Alfred A. Knopf, 1944.

Mahin, Dean B. *One War at a Time: The International Dimensions of the American Civil War.* Washington, DC: Brassey's, 1999.

Major, John. *Prize Possession: The United States and the Panama Canal, 1903–1979.* Cambridge, UK: Cambridge University Press, 1993.

Marks, Frederick W., III. *Velvet on Iron: The Diplomacy of Theodore Roosevelt.* Lincoln: University of Nebraska Press, 1979.

———. *Wind Over Sand: The Diplomacy of Franklin Roosevelt.* Athens: University of Georgia Press, 1988.

Martin, Percy F. *Maximilian in Mexico: The Story of the French Intervention (1861–1867).* New York: Charles Scribner's Sons, 1914.

Maurer, Noel, and Carlos Yu. *The Big Ditch: How America Took, Built, Ran, and Ultimately Gave Away the Panama Canal.* Princeton, NJ: Princeton University Press, 2011.

Maurer, Noel. *The Empire Trap: The Rise and Fall of U.S. Intervention to Protect American Property Overseas, 1893–2013.* Princeton, NJ: Princeton University Press, 2013.

May, Ernest R. *American Imperialism: A Speculative Essay.* New York: Atheneum, 1968.

———. *From Imperialism to Isolationism 1898–1919.* New York: Macmillan, 1964.

———. *Imperial Democracy: The Emergence of America as a Great Power.* New York: Harper Torchbooks, 1973.

———. *The Making of the Monroe Doctrine.* Cambridge, MA: Belknap Press, 1975.

May, Robert E. *Manifest Destiny's Underworld: Filibustering in Antebellum America.* Chapel Hill: University of North Carolina Press, 2002.

———. *Slavery, Race, and Conquest in the Tropics: Lincoln, Douglas, and the Future of Latin America.* New York: Cambridge University Press, 2013.

———. *The Southern Dream of a Caribbean Empire, 1854–1861.* Gainesville: University Press of Florida, 2002.

McAllen, M. M. *Maximilian and Carlotta: Europe's Last Empire in Mexico.* San Antonio, TX: Trinity University Press, 2014.

McBeth, Brian S. *Gunboats, Corruption, and Claims: Foreign Intervention in Venezuela, 1899–1908.* Westport, CT: Greenwood, 2001.

McCain, William D. *The United States and the Republic of Panama*. Durham, NC: Duke University Press: 1937.

McCallum, Jack. *Leonard Wood: Rough Rider, Surgeon, Architect of American Imperialism*. New York: New York University Press, 2006.

McCann, Thomas P. *An American Company: The Tragedy of United Fruit*. New York: Crown, 1976.

McConahay, Mary Jo. *The Tango War: The Struggle for the Hearts, Minds and Riches of Latin America During World War II*. New York: St. Martin's Press, 2018.

McCormick, Thomas J. *China Market: America's Quest for Informal Empire 1893–1901*. Chicago: Quadrangle Books, 1967.

McCormick, Thomas J., and Walter LaFeber, eds. *Behind the Throne: Servants of Power to Imperial Presidents, 1898–1968*. Madison: University of Wisconsin Press, 1993.

McCullough, David. *The Path Between the Seas: The Creation of the Panama Canal 1870–1914*. New York: Simon and Schuster Paperbacks, 1977.

McPherson, Alan, ed. *Anti-Americanism in Latin America and the Caribbean*. Oxford, UK: Berghahn, 2008.

———. *The Invaded: How Latin Americans and Their Allies Fought and Ended U.S. Occupations*. Oxford, UK: Oxford University Press, 2016.

———. *A Short History of U.S. Interventions in Latin America and the Caribbean*. Chichester, UK: Wiley Blackwell, 2016.

McPherson, James M. *Battle Cry of Freedom: The Civil War Era*. New York: Ballantine Books, 1988.

Mearsheimer, John J. *The Tragedy of Great Power Politics*. New York: W. W. Norton, 2003.

Mecham, J. Lloyd. *The United States and Inter-American Security, 1889–1960*. Austin: University of Texas Press, 1962.

Meiser, Jeffrey W. *Power and Restraint: The Rise of the United States, 1898–1941*. Washington, DC: Georgetown University Press, 2015.

Mellander, Gustavo A. *The United States in Panamanian Politics: The Intriguing Formative Years*. Danville, IL: Interstate Printers & Publishers, 1971.

Mellander, Gustavo A., and Nelly Maldonado Mellander. *Charles Edward Magoon: The Panama Years*. Rio Piedras, PR: Editorial Plaza Mayor, 1999.

Merli, Frank J., and Theodore A. Wilson, eds. *Makers of American Diplomacy*. 2 vols. New York: Charles Scribner's Sons, 1974.

Merry, Robert W. *Architect of the American Century: President McKinley*. New York: Simon & Schuster, 2017.

Millard, Candice. *Destiny of the Republic: A Tale of Madness, Medicine, and the Murder of a President*. New York: Anchor Books, 2012.

Millett, Allan Reed. *The Politics of Intervention: The Military Occupation of Cuba, 1906–1909*. Columbus: Ohio State University Press, 1968.

Millett, Richard L. *Guardians of the Dynasty*. Maryknoll, NY: Orbis Books, 1977.

———. *Searching for Stability: The U.S. Development of Constabulary Forces in Latin America and the Philippines*. Fort Leavenworth, KS: Combat Studies Institute Press, 2010.

Miner, Dwight Carroll. *The Fight for the Panama Route: The Story of the Spooner Act and the Hay-Herran Treaty*. New York: Octagon Books, 1966.

Minger, Ralph Eldin. *William Howard Taft and United States Foreign Policy: The Apprenticeship Years, 1900–1908*. Urbana: University of Illinois Press, 1975.

Missal, Alexander. *Seaway to the Future: American Social Visions and the Construction of the Panama Canal*. Madison: University of Wisconsin Press, 2008.

Mitchell, Nancy. *The Danger of Dreams: German and American Imperialism in Latin America*. Chapel Hill: University of North Carolina Press, 1999.

Moore, Colin D. *American Imperialism and the State, 1893–1921*. Cambridge, UK: Cambridge University Press, 2017.

Morgan, H. Wayne. *America's Road to Empire: The War with Spain and Overseas Expansion*. New York: McGraw-Hill, 1965.

———, ed. *The Gilded Age*. Syracuse, NY: Syracuse University Press, 1970.

———. *William McKinley and His America*. Rev. ed. Kent, OH: Kent State University Press, 2003.

Morgan, William Michael. *Pacific Gibraltar: U.S.-Japanese Rivalry Over the Annexation of Hawaii, 1885–1898*. Annapolis, MD: Naval Institute Press, 2011.

Morgenthau, Hans J. *Politics Among Nations: The Struggle for Power and Peace*. New York: Alfred A. Knopf, 1956.

Morris, Edmund. *The Rise of Theodore Roosevelt*. New York: Modern Library, 2001.

———. *Theodore Rex*. London: HarperCollins, 2002.

Morris, Roy, Jr. *Sheridan: The Life and Wars of General Phil Sheridan*. New York: Crown, 1992.

Munro, Dana G. *Intervention and Dollar Diplomacy in the Caribbean 1900–1921*. Princeton, NJ: Princeton University Press, 1964.

———. *The United States and the Caribbean Republics 1921–1933*. Princeton, NJ: Princeton University Press, 1974.

Musicant, Ivan. *The Banana Wars: A History of United States Military Intervention in Latin America from the Spanish-American War to the Invasion of Panama*. New York: Macmillan, 1990.

———. *Empire by Default: The Spanish-American War and the Dawn of the American Century*. New York: Henry Holt, 1998.

Muzzey, David Saville. *James G. Blaine: A Political Idol of Other Days*. New York: Dodd, Mead, 1934.

Nelson, William Javier. *Almost a Territory: America's Attempt to Annex the Dominican Republic*. Newark: University of Delaware Press, 1990.

Nevins, Allan. *Hamilton Fish: The Inner History of the Grant Administration*. New York: Dodd, Mead, 1936.

———. *Henry White: Thirty Years of American Diplomacy*. New York: Harper and Brothers, 1930.

Ninkovich, Frank. *The United States and Imperialism*. Malden, MA: Blackwell, 2007.

O'Sullivan, Christopher D. *Sumner Welles, Postwar Planning, and the Quest for a New World Order, 1937–1943*. New York: Columbia University Press, 2008.

O'Toole, G. J. A. *The Spanish War: An American Epic–1898*. New York: W. W. Norton, 1994.

O'Toole, Patricia. *The Moralist: Woodrow Wilson and the World He Made*. New York: Simon & Schuster, 2018.

Offner, John L. "Imperialism by International Consensus: The United States and the Philippine Islands." In *From Theodore Roosevelt to FDR: Internationalism and Isolationism in American Foreign Policy*, edited by Daniela Rossini, 45–54. Staffordshire: Keele University Press, 1995.

———. *An Unwanted War: The Diplomacy of the United States and Spain over Cuba, 1895–1898*. Chapel Hill: University of North Carolina Press, 1992.

Organski, A. F. K., and Jacek Kugler. *The War Ledger*. Chicago: University of Chicago Press, 1980.

Osborne, Thomas J. *"Empire Can Wait": American Opposition to Hawaiian Annexation, 1893–1898*. Kent, OH: Kent State University Press, 1981.

Paolino, Ernest N. *The Foundations of the American Empire: William Henry Seward and U.S. Foreign Policy*. Ithaca, NY: Cornell University Press, 1973.

Parks, Taylor E. *Colombia and the United States 1765–1934*. Durham, NC: Duke University Press, 1935.

Pastor, Robert A. *Exiting the Whirlpool: U.S. Foreign Policy Toward Latin America and the Caribbean*. Boulder, CO: Westview Press, 2001.

Peraino, Kevin. *Lincoln in the World: The Making of a Statesman and the Dawn of American Power*. New York: Crown, 2013.

Pérez, Louis A., Jr. *Cuba Between Empires 1878–1902*. Pittsburgh, PA: University of Pittsburgh Press, 1983.

———. *Cuba Under the Platt Amendment, 1902–1934*. Pittsburgh, PA: University of Pittsburgh Press, 1986.

———. *The War of 1898: The United States and Cuba in History and Historiography*. Chapel Hill: University of North Carolina Press, 1998.

Perkins, Bradford. *The Great Rapprochement: England and the United States, 1895–1914*. New York: Atheneum, 1968.

Perkins, Dexter. *Charles Evans Hughes and American Democratic Statesmanship*. Boston: Little, Brown, 1956.

———. *A History of the Monroe Doctrine*. Boston: Little, Brown, 1963.

———. *The Monroe Doctrine 1823–1826*. Gloucester, MA: Peter Smith, 1965.

———. *The Monroe Doctrine: 1826–1867*. Gloucester, MA: Peter Smith, 1965.

———. *The Monroe Doctrine: 1867–1907*. Gloucester, MA: Peter Smith, 1966.

Perkins, Whitney T. *Constraint of Empire: The United States and Caribbean Interventions*. Westport, CT: Greenwood, 1981.

Peterson, Harold F. *Diplomat of the Americas: A Biography of William I. Buchanan (1852–1909)*. Albany: State University of New York Press, 1977.

Pike, Fredrick B. *Chile and the United States, 1880–1962: The Emergence of Chile's Social Crisis and the Challenge to United States Diplomacy*. Notre Dame, IN: University of Notre Dame Press, 1963.

———. *FDR's Good Neighbor Policy: Sixty Years of Generally Gentle Chaos*. Austin: University of Texas Press, 1995.

Plesur, Milton. *America's Outward Thrust: Approaches to Foreign Affairs, 1865–1890*. DeKalb: Northern Illinois University Press, 1971.

Pletcher, Davis M. *The Awkward Years: American Foreign Relations Under Garfield and Arthur*. Columbia: University of Missouri Press, 1962.

———. *The Diplomacy of Trade and Investment*. Columbia: University of Missouri, 1998.

Plummer, Brenda Gayle. *Haiti and the Great Powers, 1902–1915*. Baton Rouge: Louisiana State University Press, 1988.

Pons, Frank Moya. *The Dominican Republic: A National History*. Princeton, NJ: Markus Wiener, 2010.

Pratt, Julius W. *America's Colonial Experiment: How the United States Gained, Governed, and in Part Gave Away a Colonial Empire*. New York: Prentice-Hall, 1950.

———. *Expansionists of 1898: The Acquisition of Hawaii and the Spanish Islands*. Chicago: Quadrangle Books, 1964.

Puleston, W. D. *Mahan: The Life and Work of Captain Alfred Thayer Mahan, U.S.N.* London: Jonathan Cape, 1939.

Pusey, Merlo J. *Charles Evans Hughes.* 2 vols. New York: Macmillan, 1951.

Quirk, Robert E. *An Affair of Honor: Woodrow Wilson and the Occupation of Veracruz.* New York: W. W. Norton, 1962.

Renda, Mary A. *Taking Haiti: Military Occupation and the Culture of U.S. Imperialism, 1915–1940.* Chapel Hill: University of North Carolina Press, 2001.

Ricard, Serge. "The Anglo-German Intervention in Venezuela and Theodore Roosevelt's Ultimatum to the Kaiser: Taking a Fresh Look at an Old Enigma." In *Anglo-Saxonism in U.S. Foreign Policy: The Diplomacy of Imperialism, 1899–1919*, edited by Serge Ricard and Hélène Christol, 65–77. Aix-en-Provence: Université de Provence, 1991.

———. "Monroe Revisited: The Roosevelt Doctrine, 1901–1909." In *Impressions of a Gilded Age: The American Fin de Siecle*, edited by Marc Chenetier and Rob Kroes, 228–41. Amsterdam: Amerika Instituut, 1983.

Richardson, Leon Burr. *William E. Chandler, Republican.* New York: Dodd, Mead, 1940.

Rippy, J. Fred. *The Caribbean Danger Zone.* New York: G. P. Putnam's Sons, 1940.

Risen, Clay. *The Crowded Hour: Theodore Roosevelt, the Rough Riders, and the Dawn of the American Century.* New York: Scribner, 2019.

Rister, Carl Coke. *Border Command: General Phil Sheridan in the West.* Norman: University of Oklahoma Press, 1944.

Robert Dallek, *Franklin D. Roosevelt and American Foreign Policy, 1932–1945.* Oxford, UK: Oxford University Press, 1981.

Robertson, William Spence. *Hispanic-American Relations with the United States.* New York: Oxford University Press, 1923.

Robinson, R. E., and J. Gallagher. "The Partition of Africa." In *The New Cambridge Modern History*, Vol. 11, *Material Progress and World-Wide Problems, 1870–1898*, edited by F. H. Hinsley, 593–640. Cambridge, UK: Cambridge University Press, 1962.

Roeder, Ralph. *Juarez and His Mexico: A Biographical History.* New York: Viking, 1947.

Rolde, Neil. *Continental Liar From the State of Maine: James G Blaine.* Gardiner, ME: Tilbury House, 2007.

Roorda, Eric Paul. *The Dictator Next Door: The Good Neighbor Policy and the Trujillo Regime in the Dominican Republic, 1930–1945.* Durham, NC: Duke University Press, 2006.

Rosenberg, Emily S. *Financial Missionaries to the World: The Politics and Culture of Dollar Diplomacy, 1900–1930.* Durham, NC: Duke University Press, 2003.

———. *Spreading the American Dream: American Economic and Cultural Expansion, 1890–1945.* New York: Hill and Wang, 1989.

Russ, William Adam, Jr. *The Hawaiian Republic (1894–98) and Its Struggle to Win Annexation.* Selinsgrove, PA: Susquehanna University Press, 1961.

Saich, Tony. *From Rebel to Ruler: One Hundred Years of the Chinese Communist Party.* Cambridge, MA: Belknap, 2021.

Salisbury, Richard V. *Anti-Imperialism and International Competition in Central America 1920–1929.* Wilmington, DE: Scholarly Resources, 1989.

———. "Good Neighbors?: The United States and Latin America in the Twentieth Century." In *American Foreign Relations: A Historiographical Review*, edited by Gerald K. Haines and J. Samuel Walker, 311–33. Westport, CT: Greenwood: 1981.

Sánchez, Peter M. *Panama Lost? U.S. Hegemony, Democracy, and the Canal.* Gainesville: University Press of Florida, 2008.

Sargent, Nathan. *Admiral Dewey and the Manila Campaign.* Washington, DC: Naval Historical Foundation, 1947.

Schake, Kori. *Safe Passage: The Transition from British to American Hegemony.* Cambridge, MA: Harvard University Press, 2017.

Schmidt, Hans. *Maverick Marine: General Smedley D. Butler and the Contradictions of American Military History.* Lexington: University Press of Kentucky, 1998.

———. *The United States Occupation of Haiti, 1915–1934.* New Brunswick, NJ: Rutgers University Press, 1995.

Schmitz, David F. *Thank God They're On Our Side: The United States and Right-Wing Dictatorships, 1921–1965.* Chapel Hill: University of North Carolina Press, 1999.

Scholes, Walter V., and Marie V. Scholes. *The Foreign Policies of the Taft Administration.* Columbia: University of Missouri Press, 1970.

Schoonover, Thomas David. *Dollars Over Dominion: The Triumph of Liberalism in Mexican-United States Relations, 1861–1867.* Baton Rouge: Louisiana University Press, 1978.

———. "Napoleon Is Coming! Maximilian Is Coming?: The International History of the Civil War in the Caribbean Basin." In *The Union, the Confederacy, and the Atlantic Rim*, revised edition, edited by Robert E. May, 115–44. Gainesville: University Press of Florida, 2013.

———. *Uncle Sam's War of 1898 and the Origins of Globalization.* Lexington: University Press of Kentucky, 2005.

———. *The United States in Central America, 1860–1911: Episodes of Social Imperialism and Imperial Rivalry in the World System.* Durham, NC: Duke University Press, 1991.

Schoultz, Lars. *Beneath the United States: A History of U.S. Policy Toward Latin America.* Cambridge, MA: Harvard University Press, 2003.

———. *In Their Own Best Interest: A History of the U.S. Effort to Improve Latin Americans.* Cambridge, UK: Cambridge University Press, 2018.

———. *That Infernal Little Cuban Republic: The United States and the Cuban Revolution.* Chapel Hill: University of North Carolina Press, 2009.

Schriftgiesser, Karl. *The Gentleman from Massachusetts: Henry Cabot Lodge.* Boston: Little, Brown, 1944.

Schuler, Friedrich E. *Secret Wars and Secret Policies in the Americas, 1842–1929.* Albuquerque: University of New Mexico Press, 2010.

Seager, Robert, II. *Alfred Thayer Mahan: The Man and His Letters.* Annapolis, MD: Naval Institute Press, 2017.

Sexton, Jay. *The Monroe Doctrine: Empire and Nation in Nineteenth-Century America.* New York: Hill and Wang, 2011.

Shawcross, Edward. *The Last Emperor of Mexico: The Dramatic Story of the Habsburg Archduke Who Created a Kingdom in the New World.* New York: Basic Books, 2021.

Sicker, Martin. *The Geopolitics of Security in the Americas: Hemispheric Denial from Monroe to Clinton.* Westport, CT: Praeger, 2002.

Silva, Noenoe K. *Aloha Betrayed: Native Hawaiian Resistance to American Colonialism.* Durham, NC: Duke University Press, 2004.

Smith, Ephraim K. "William McKinley's Enduring Legacy: The Historiographical Debate on the Taking of the Philippine Islands." In *Crucible of Empire: The*

Spanish-American War & Its Aftermath, edited by James C. Bradford, 205–49. Annapolis, MD: Naval Institute Press, 1993.

Smith, Gaddis. *The Last Years of the Monroe Doctrine, 1945–1993.* New York: Hill and Wang, 1994.

Smith, Joseph. *Illusions of Conflict: Anglo-American Diplomacy Toward Latin America, 1865–1896.* Pittsburgh, PA: University of Pittsburgh Press, 1979.

Smith, Peter H. *Talons of the Eagle: Latin America, the United States, and the World.* New York: Oxford University Press, 2008.

Smith, Robert Freeman. "Latin America, the United States and the European Powers, 1830–1930." In *The Cambridge History of Latin America*, Vol. 4, *C. 1870 to 1930*, edited by Leslie Bethell, 83–119. Cambridge, UK: Cambridge University Press, 1986.

———. *The United States and Revolutionary Nationalism in Mexico, 1916–1932.* Chicago: University of Chicago Press, 1972.

Smith, Tony. *America's Mission: The United States and the Worldwide Struggle for Democracy in the Twentieth Century.* Princeton, NJ: Princeton University Press, 1994.

———. *The Pattern of Imperialism: The United States, Great Britain, and the Late-Industrializing World Since 1815.* Cambridge, UK: Cambridge University Press, 1981.

Sprout, Harold, and Margaret Sprout. *The Rise of American Naval Power 1776–1918.* Princeton, NJ: Princeton University Press, 1944.

Spykman, Nicholas John. *America's Strategy in World Politics: The United States and the Balance of Power.* New York: Harcourt, Brace, 1942.

Stahr, Walter. *Seward: Lincoln's Indispensable Man.* New York: Simon and Schuster, 2012.

Stephanson, Anders. *Manifest Destiny: American Expansionism and the Empire of Right.* New York: Hill and Wang, 1996.

Stevens, Sylvester K. *American Expansion in Hawaii, 1842–1898.* Harrisburg: Archives Publishing Company of Pennsylvania, 1945.

Steward, Dick. *Trade and Hemisphere: The Good Neighbor Policy and Reciprocal Trade.* Columbia: University of Missouri Press, 1975.

Strecker, Mark. *Smedley D. Butler, USMC: A Biography.* Jefferson, NC: McFarland, 2011.

Striffler, Steve, and Mark Moberg, eds. *Banana Wars: Power, Production, and History in the Americas.* Durham, NC: Duke University Press, 2003.

Stuart, Graham H. *The Department of State: A History of Its Organization, Procedure, and Personnel.* New York: Macmillan, 1949.

Suri, Jeremi. "The Limits of American Empire: Democracy and Militarism in the Twentieth and Twenty-first Centuries." In *Colonial Crucible: Empire in the Making of the Modern American State*, edited by Alfred W. McCoy and Francisco A. Scarano, 523–31. Madison: University of Wisconsin Press, 2009.

Tansill, Charles Callan. *The Foreign Policy of Thomas F. Bayard 1885–1897.* New York: Fordham University Press, 1940.

———. *The Purchase of the Danish West Indies.* New York: Greenwood, 1968.

———. *The United States and Santo Domingo 1798–1873: A Chapter in Caribbean Diplomacy.* Gloucester, MA: Peter Smith, 1967.

Tate, Merze. *Hawaii: Reciprocity or Annexation.* East Lansing: Michigan State University Press, 1968.

———. *The United States and the Hawaiian Kingdom: A Political History.* New Haven, CT: Yale University Press, 1965.

Taylor, John M. *William Henry Seward: Lincoln's Right Hand.* Washington, DC: Brassey's, 1991.

Tellis, Ashley J. *Balancing Without Containment: An American Strategy for Managing China*. Washington, DC: Carnegie Endowment for International Peace, 2014.

———. "Pakistan's Political Development: Will the Future Be Like the Past?" In *Development Challenges Confronting Pakistan*, edited by Anita M. Weiss and Saba Gul Khattak, 225–37. Sterling, VA: Kumarian, 2012.

Terrill, Tom E. *The Tariff, Politics, and American Foreign Policy 1874–1901*. Westport, CT: Greenwood, 1973.

Thomas, Evan. *The War Lovers: Roosevelt, Lodge, Hearst, and the Rush to Empire, 1898*. New York: Little, Brown, 2010.

Thomas, Hugh. *Cuba: The Pursuit of Freedom*. New York: Harper and Row, 1971.

Thompson, John A. *A Sense of Power: The Roots of America's Global Role*. Ithaca, NY: Cornell University Press, 2015.

Thompson, John M. *Great Power Rising: Theodore Roosevelt and the Politics of U.S. Foreign Policy*. Oxford, UK: Oxford University Press, 2019.

Tilchin, William N. *Theodore Roosevelt and the British Empire: A Study in Presidential Statecraft*. London: Macmillan, 1997.

Tillman, Ellen D. *Dollar Diplomacy by Force: Nation-Building and Resistance in the Dominican Republic*. Chapel Hill: University of North Carolina Press, 2016.

Tompkins, Berkeley E. *Anti-Imperialism in the United States: The Great Debate, 1890–1920*. Philadelphia: University of Pennsylvania Press, 1970.

Tooze, Adam. *The Deluge: The Great War, America and the Remaking of the Global Order, 1916–1931*. New York: Viking, 2014.

Topik, Steven C. *Trade and Gunboats: The United States and Brazil in the Age of Empire*. Stanford, CA: Stanford University Press, 1996.

Trask, David F. *The War with Spain in 1898*. Lincoln: University of Nebraska Press, 1996.

Tuchman, Barbara W. *The Zimmermann Telegram*. New York: Ballantine, 1985.

Tulchin, Joseph S. *The Aftermath of War: World War I and U.S. Policy Toward Latin America*. New York: New York University Press, 1971.

Tyrner-Tyrnauer, A. R. *Lincoln and the Emperors*. New York: Harcourt, Brace & World, 1962.

Vagts, Alfred. *Deutschland und die Vereinigten Staaten in der Weltpolitik*. 2 vols. New York: Macmillan, 1935.

Van Alestyne, Richard W. *The Rising American Empire*. Oxford, UK: Basil Blackwell, 1960.

Van Deusen, Glyndon G. *William Henry Seward*. New York: Oxford University Press, 1967.

Veeser, Cyrus. *A World Safe for Capitalism: Dollar Diplomacy and America's Rise to Global Power*. New York: Columbia University Press, 2002.

Wakukawa, Ernest K. *A History of the Japanese People in Hawaii*. Honolulu: Toyo Shoin, 1938.

Walworth, Arthur. *Woodrow Wilson*. 2 vols. New York: Longmans, Green, 1958.

Watson, Mark Skinner. *Chief of Staff: Prewar Plans and Preparations*. Washington, DC: Center of Military History, 1991.

Welch, Richard E., Jr. *Response to Imperialism: The United States and the Philippine-American War, 1899–1902*. Chapel Hill: University of North Carolina Press, 1979.

Welles, Benjamin *Sumner Welles: FDR's Global Strategist*. New York: St. Martin's, 1997.

Weston, Rubin Francis. *Racism in U.S. Imperialism: The Influence of Racial Assumptions on American Foreign Policy, 1893–1946*. Columbia: University of South Carolina Press, 1972.

Wheelan, Joseph. *Terrible Swift Sword: The Life of General Philip H. Sheridan*. Cambridge, MA: Da Capo, 2012.

Wiarda, Howard I., and Michael J. Kryzanek. *The Dominican Republic: A Caribbean Crucible*. Boulder, CO: Westview Press, 1982.

Widenor, William C. *Henry Cabot Lodge and the Search for an American Foreign Policy*. Berkeley: University of California Press, 1983.

Wiebe, Robert H. *The Search for Order 1877–1920*. New York: Hill and Wang, 1967.

Williams, William Appleman. *The Roots of the Modern American Empire: A Study of the Growth and Shaping of Social Consciousness in a Marketplace Society*. New York: Random House, 1969.

———. *The Tragedy of American Diplomacy*. New York: W. W. Norton, 1972.

Wimmel, Kenneth. *Theodore Roosevelt and the Great White Fleet: American Seapower Comes of Age*. Washington, DC: Brassey's, 1998.

Wood, Bryce. *The Dismantling of the Good Neighbor Policy*. Austin: University of Texas Press, 1985.

———. *The Making of the Good Neighbor Policy*. New York: Columbia University Press, 1962.

Wynne, William H. *State Insolvency and Foreign Bondholders*. Vol. 2, *Selected Case Histories of Governmental Foreign Bond Defaults and Debt Readjustments*. Washington, DC: BeardBooks, 2000.

Yerxa, Donald A. *Admirals and Empire: The United States Navy and the Caribbean, 1898–1945*. Columbia: University of South Carolina Press, 1991.

Zakaria, Fareed. *From Wealth to Power: The Unusual Origins of America's World Role*. Princeton, NJ: Princeton University Press, 1998.

Zimmermann, Warren. *First Great Triumph: How Five Americans Made Their Country a World Power*. New York: Farrar, Straus and Giroux, 2002.

Articles

Abrams, Richard M. "United States Intervention Abroad: The First Quarter Century." *American Historical Review* 79, no. 1 (February 1974): 72–102.

Adler, Selig. "Bryan and Wilsonian Caribbean Penetration." *Hispanic American Historical Review* 20, no. 2 (May 1940): 198–226.

Ahmed, Faisal Z., Laura Alfaro, and Noel Maurer. "Lawsuits and Empire: On the Enforcement of Sovereign Debt in Latin America." *Law and Contemporary Problems* 73, no. 4 (Fall 2010): 39–46.

Ambrosius, Lloyd E. "The Orthodoxy of Revisionism: Woodrow Wilson and the New Left." *Diplomatic History* 1, no. 3 (Summer 1977): 199–214.

Ameringer, Charles D. "The Panama Canal Lobby of Philippe Bunau-Varilla and William Nelson Cromwell." *American Historical Review* 68, no. 2 (January 1963): 346–63.

———. "Philippe Bunau-Varilla: New Light on the Panama Canal Treaty." *Hispanic American Historical Review* 46, no. 1 (February 1966): 28–52.

Atkins, George Pope, and Larry V. Thompson. "German Military Influence in Argentina, 1921–1940." *Journal of Latin American Studies* 4, no. 2 (November 1972): 257–74.

Bacevich, Andrew J. "The American Electoral Mission in Nicaragua, 1927–28." *Diplomatic History* 4, no. 3 (Summer 1980): 241–61.

Baecker, Thomas. "The Arms of the *Ypiranga*: The German Side." *The Americas* 30, no. 1 (July 1973): 1–17.

Bailey, Thomas A. "America's Emergence as a World Power: The Myth and the Verity." *Pacific Historical Review* 30, no. 1 (February 1961): 1–16.

———. "Dewey and the Germans at Manila Bay." *American Historical Review* 45, no. 1 (October 1939): 59–81.

———. "Interest in a Nicaragua Canal, 1903–1931." *Hispanic American Historical Review* 16, no. 1 (February 1936): 2–28.

———. "Japan's Protest Against the Annexation of Hawaii." *Journal of Modern History* 3, no. 1 (March 1931): 46–61.

———. "The Lodge Corollary to the Monroe Doctrine." *Political Science Quarterly* 48, no. 2 (June 1933): 220–39.

———. "The United States and Hawaii During the Spanish-American War." *American Historical Review* 36, no. 3 (April 1931): 552–60.

Baker, George W., Jr. "Benjamin Harrison and Hawaiian Annexation: A Reinterpretation." *Pacific Historical Review* 33, no. 3 (August 1964): 295–309.

———. "Ideals and Realities in the Wilson Administration's Relations with Honduras." *The Americas* 21, no. 1 (July 1964): 3–19.

———. "The Wilson Administration and Cuba, 1913–1921." *Mid-America* 46, no. 1 (January 1964): 48–63.

———. "The Wilson Administration and Nicaragua, 1913–1921." *The Americas* 22, no. 4 (April 1966): 339–76.

———. "The Wilson Administration and Panama, 1913–1921." *Journal of Inter-American Studies* 8, no. 2 (April 1966): 279–93.

———. "The Woodrow Wilson Administration and Guatemalan Relations." *The Historian* 27, no. 2 (February 1965): 155–69.

———. "Woodrow Wilson's Use of the Non-Recognition Policy in Costa Rica." *The Americas* 22, no. 1 (July 1965): 3–21.

Bastert, Russell H. "Diplomatic Reversal: Frelinghuysen's Opposition to Blaine's Pan-American Policy in 1882." *Mississippi Valley Historical Review* 42, no. 4 (March 1956): 653–71.

———. "A New Approach to the Origins of Blaine's Pan American Policy." *Hispanic American Historical Review* 39, no. 3 (August 1959): 375–412.

Baylen, Joseph O. "American Intervention in Nicaragua, 1909–33: An Appraisal of Objectives and Results." *Southwestern Social Science Quarterly* 35, no. 2 (September 1954): 128–54.

Benjamin, Jules R. "The New Deal, Cuba, and the Rise of a Global Foreign Economic Policy." *Business History Review* 51, no. 1 (Spring 1977): 57–78.

Blake, Nelson M. "Background of Cleveland's Venezuelan Policy." *American Historical Review* 47, no. 2 (January 1942): 259–77.

Blasier, Cole. "The United States, Germany, and the Bolivian Revolutionaries (1941–1946)." *Hispanic American Historical Review* 52, no. 1 (February 1972): 26–54.

Blassingame, John W. "The Press and American Intervention in Haiti and the Dominican Republic, 1904–1920." *Caribbean Studies* 9, no. 2 (July 1969): 27–43.

Blumberg, Arnold. "The Diplomacy of the Mexican Empire, 1863–1867." *Transactions of the American Philosophical Society* 61, no. 8 (1971): 1–152.

Bourne, Kenneth. "British Preparations for War with the North, 1861–1862." *English Historical Review* 76, no. 301 (October 1961): 600–32.

Braeman, John. "The New Left and American Foreign Policy During the Age of Normalcy: A Re-Examination." *Business History Review* 57, no. 1 (Spring 1983): 73–104.

Bratzel, John F., and Leslie B. Rout Jr. "FDR and the 'Secret Map.'" *Wilson Quarterly* 9, no. 1 (New Year's 1985): 167–73.

Buchenau, Jürgen. "Counter-Intervention Against Uncle Sam: Mexico's Support for Nicaraguan Nationalism, 1903–1910." *The Americas* 50, no. 2 (October 1993): 207–32.

Burnett, Christina Duffy. "The Edge of Empire and the Limits of Sovereignty: American Guano Islands." *American Quarterly* 57, no. 3 (September 2005): 779–803.

Burton, David H. "Theodore Roosevelt's Social Darwinism and Views on Imperialism." *Journal of the History of Ideas* 26, no. 1 (January–March 1965): 103–18.

Calvert, Peter. "The Last Occasion on Which Britain Used Coercion to Settle a Dispute with a Non-colonial Territory in the Caribbean: Guatemala and the Powers, 1909–1913." *Inter-American Economic Affairs* 25, no. 3 (Winter 1971): 57–75.

Chamberlin, Eugene Keither. "The Japanese Scare at Magdalena Bay." *Pacific Historical Review* 24, no. 4 (November 1955): 345–59.

Chapman, Charles E. "New Corollaries of the Monroe Doctrine." *University of California Chronicle* 33, no. 2 (April 1931): 161–89.

Child, John. "From 'Color' to 'Rainbow': U.S. Strategic Planning for Latin America, 1919–1945." *Journal of Interamerican Studies and World Affairs* 21, no. 2 (May 1979): 233–59.

Clifford, John Garry. "Admiral Dewey and the Germans, 1903: A New Perspective." *Mid-America* 49, no. 3 (July 1967): 214–20.

Collin, Richard H. "The 1904 *Detroit* Compact: U.S. Naval Diplomacy and Dominican Revolutions." *The Historian* 52, no. 3 (May 1990): 432–52.

————. "The Caribbean Theater Transformed: Britain, France, Germany, and the U.S., 1900–1906." *American Neptune* 52, no. 2 (Spring 1992): 102–12.

————. "Symbiosis Versus Hegemony: New Directions in the Foreign Relations Historiography of Theodore Roosevelt and William Howard Taft." *Diplomatic History* 19, no. 3 (Summer 1995): 473–97.

Cooper, Donald B. "The Withdrawal of the United States from Haiti, 1928–1934." *Journal of Inter-American Studies* 5, no. 1 (January 1963): 83–101.

Cooper, John Milton, Jr. "'An Irony of Fate': Woodrow Wilson's Pre-World War I Diplomacy." *Diplomatic History* 3, no. 4 (Fall 1979): 425–37.

Cortada, James W. "A Case of International Rivalry in Latin America: Spain's Occupation of Santo Domingo, 1853–1865." *Revista de Historia de América*, no. 82 (July–December 1976): 53–82.

Crapol, Edward P. "Coming to Terms with Empire: The Historiography of Late-Nineteenth-Century American Foreign Relations." *Diplomatic History* 16, no. 4 (Fall 1992): 573–97.

Cronon, E. David. "Interpreting the New Good Neighbor Policy: The Cuban Crisis of 1933." *Hispanic American Historical Review* 39, no. 4 (November 1959): 538–67.

Cummins, Lejeune. "The Formulation of the 'Platt' Amendment." *The Americas* 23, no. 4 (April 1967): 370–89.

Da Gama, Luize Philippe Saldanha, A. E. K. Benham, and Michael B. McCloskey. "The United States and the Brazilian Naval Revolt, 1893–1894." *The Americas* 2, no. 3 (January 1946): 296–321.

Devine, Michael J. "John W. Foster and the Struggle for the Annexation of Hawaii." *Pacific Historical Review* 46, no. 1 (February 1977): 29–50.

Dinwoodie, D. H. "Dollar Diplomacy in the Light of the Guatemalan Loan Project, 1909–1913." *The Americas* 26, no. 3 (January 1970): 237–53.

Dozer, Donald Marquand. "The Opposition to Hawaiian Reciprocity, 1876–1888." *Pacific Historical Review* 14, no. 2 (June 1945): 157–83.

Duniway, Clyde Augustus. "Reasons for the Withdrawal of the French from Mexico." *Annual Report of the American Historical Society for the Year 1902* (1903): 1:315–28.

Dur, Philip, and Christoper Gilcrease. "US Diplomacy and the Downfall of a Cuban Dictator: Machado in 1933." *Journal of Latin American Studies* 34, no. 2 (May 2002): 255–82.

Eyre, James K., Jr. "Japan and the American Annexation of the Philippines." *Pacific Historical Review* 11, no. 1 (March 1942): 55–71.

Farmer, Tristram E. "Too Little, Too Late: The Fight for the Carolines, 1898." *Naval History* 3, no. 1 (Winter 1989): 20–25.

Farrell, Don A. "The Partition of the Marianas: A Diplomatic History, 1898–1919." *Journal of Micronesian Studies* 2, no. 2 (Dry Season 1994): 273–301.

Fenton, P. F. "Diplomatic Relations of the United States and Venezuela, 1880–1915." *Hispanic American Historical Review* 8, no. 3 (August 1928): 330–56.

Ferguson, Niall, and Moritz Schularick. "The Empire Effect: The Determinants of Country Risk in the First Age of Globalization, 1880–1913." *Journal of Economic History* 66, no. 2 (June 2006): 283–312.

Field, James A., Jr. "American Imperialism: The Worst Chapter in Almost Any Book." *American Historical Review* 83, no. 3 (June 1978): 644–68.

Forbes, Ian L. D. "German Informal Imperialism in South America Before 1914." *Economic History Review* 31, no. 3 (August 1978): 384–98.

Frazier, Charles E. "Colonel Henry L. Stimson's Peace Mission to Nicaragua, April–May 1927." *Journal of the West* 2 (January 1963): 66–84.

Friedlander, Robert A. "A Reassessment of Roosevelt's Role in the Panamanian Revolution of 1903." *Western Political Quarterly* 14, no. 2 (June 1961): 535–43.

Friedman, Max Paul, and Tom Long. "Soft Balancing in the Americas: Latin American Opposition to U.S. Intervention, 1898–1936." *International Security* 40, no. 1 (Summer 2015): 120–56.

Fry, Joseph A. "From Open Door to World Systems: Economic Interpretations of Late Nineteenth Century American Foreign Relations." *Pacific Historical Review* 65, no. 2 (May 1996): 277–303.

———. "William McKinley and the Coming of the Spanish-American War: A Study of the Besmirching and Redemption of an Historical Image." *Diplomatic History* 3, no. 1 (Winter 1979): 77–97.

Gatell, Frank Otto. "The Canal in Retrospect—Some Panamanian and Colombian Views." *The Americas* 15, no. 1 (July 1958): 23–36.

Gates, John M. "War-Related Deaths in the Philippines, 1898–1902." *Pacific Historical Review* 53, no. 3 (August 1984): 367–78.

Gilderhus, Mark T. "The Monroe Doctrine: Meaning and Implications." *Presidential Studies Quarterly* 36, no. 1 (March 2006): 5–16.

Gismondi, Michael, and Jeremy Mouat. "Merchants, Mining and Concessions on Nicaragua's Mosquito Coast: Reassessing the American Presence, 1895–1912." *Journal of Latin American Studies* 34, no. 4 (November 2002): 845–79.

Goldwert, Marvin. "Matías Romero and Congressional Opposition to Seward's Policy Toward the French Intervention in Mexico." *The Americas* 22, no. 1 (July 1965): 22–40.

Gould, Lewis L. "The Reick Telegram and the Spanish-American War: A Reappraisal." *Diplomatic History* 3, no. 2 (Spring 1979): 193–99.

Gow, Douglas R. "How Did the Roosevelt Corollary Become Linked to the Dominican Republic?" *Mid-America* 58, no. 3 (October 1976): 159–65.

Greer, Virginia L. "State Department Policy in Regard to the Nicaraguan Election of 1924." *Hispanic American Historical Review* 34, no. 4 (November 1954): 445–67.

Grenville, John A. S. "Diplomacy and War Plans in the United States, 1890–1917." *Transactions of the Royal Historical Society* 11 (1961): 1–21.

———. "American Naval Preparations for War with Spain, 1896–1898." *Journal of American Studies* 2, no. 1 (April 1968): 33–47.

Grieb, Kenneth J. "Warren G. Harding and the Dominican Republic U.S. Withdrawal, 1921–1923." *Journal of Inter-American Studies* 11, no. 3 (July 1969): 425–40.

Grossman, Richard. "Solidarity with Sandino: The Anti-Intervention and Solidarity Movements in the United States, 1927–1933." *Latin American Perspectives* 36, no. 6 (November 2009): 67–79.

Grover, David H. "Maneuvering for Magdalena Bay: International Intrigue at a Baja California Anchorage." *Southern California Quarterly* 83, no. 3 (Fall 2001): 261–84.

Hacker, J. David. "A Census-Based Count of the Civil War Dead." *Civil War History* 57, no. 4 (December 2011): 307–48.

Haines, Gerald K. "Under the Eagle's Wing: The Franklin Roosevelt Administration Forges an American Hemisphere." *Diplomatic History* 1, no. 4 (1977): 373–88.

Hamilton, Allen Lee. "Military Strategists and the Annexation of Hawaii." *Journal of the West* 15, no. 2 (April 1976): 81–91.

Hammett, Hugh B. "The Cleveland Administration and Anglo-American Naval Friction in Hawaii, 1893–1894." *Military Affairs* 40, no. 1 (Feb. 1976): 27–32.

Hanson, Gail. "Ordered Liberty: Sumner Welles and the Crowder-Welles Connection in the Caribbean." *Diplomatic History* 18, no. 3 (Summer 1994): 311–32.

Harrington, Fred H. "The Anti-Imperialist Movement in the United States, 1898–1900." *Mississippi Valley Historical Review* 22, no. 2 (September 1935): 211–30.

Harrison, Benjamin. "The United States and the 1909 Nicaragua Revolution." *Caribbean Quarterly* 41, no. 3/4 (September–December 1995): 45–63.

Hauch, Charles C. "Attitudes of Foreign Governments Towards the Spanish Reoccupation of the Dominican Republic." *Hispanic American Historical Review* 27, no. 2 (May 1947): 247–68.

Hauner, Milan. "Did Hitler Want a World Dominion?" *Journal of Contemporary History* 13, no. 1 (January 1978): 15–32.

Healy, David. "A Hinterland in Search of a Metropolis: The Mosquito Coast, 1894–1910." *International History Review* 3, no. 1 (January 1981): 20–43.

Hendrickson, Embert J. "Roosevelt's Second Venezuelan Controversy." *Hispanic American Historical Review* 50, no. 3 (August 1970): 482–98.

Hershey, Amos S. "The Calvo and Drago Doctrines." *American Journal of International Law* 1, no. 1 (January 1907): 26–45.

Hodge, Carl Cavanagh. "A Whiff of Cordite: Theodore Roosevelt and the Transoceanic Naval Arms Race, 1897–1909." *Diplomacy & Statecraft* 19, no. 4 (2008): 712–31.

Holbo, Paul S. "Perilous Obscurity: Public Diplomacy and the Press in the Venezuelan Crisis, 1902–1903." *The Historian* 32, no. 3 (May 1970): 428–48.

———. "Presidential Leadership in Foreign Affairs: William McKinley and the Turpie-Foraker Amendment." *American Historical Review* 72, no. 4 (July 1967): 1321–35.

Holbrook, Francis X., and John Nikol. "The Chilean Crisis of 1891–1892." *American Neptune* 38, no. 4 (October 1978): 291–300.

Horn, James J. "U. S. Diplomacy and 'the Specter of Bolshevism' in Mexico (1924–1927)." *The Americas* 32, no. 1 (July 1975): 31–45.

Hudson, Manley O. "The Central American Court of Justice." *American Journal of International Law* 26, no. 4 (October 1932): 759–86.

Jervey, Theodore D. "William Lindsay Scruggs—A Forgotten Diplomat." *South Atlantic Quarterly* 27, no. 3 (July 1928): 292–309.

Juárez, Joseph Robert. "United States Withdrawal from Santo Domingo." *Hispanic American Historical Review* 42, no. 2 (May 1, 1962): 152–90.

Kane, N. Stephen. "American Businessmen and Foreign Policy: The Recognition of Mexico, 1920–1923." *Political Science Quarterly* 90, no. 2 (Summer 1975): 293–313.

———. "Bankers and Diplomats: The Diplomacy of the Dollar in Mexico, 1921–1924." *Business History Review* 47, no. 3 (Autumn 1973): 335–52.

———. "Corporate Power and Foreign Policy: Efforts of American Oil Companies to Influence United States Relations with Mexico, 1921–1928." *Diplomatic History* 1, no. 2 (Spring 1977): 170–98.

Kapur, Nick. "William McKinley's Values and the Origins of the Spanish-American War: A Reinterpretation." *Presidential Studies Quarterly* 41, no. 1 (March 2011): 18–38.

Karsten, Peter. "The Nature of 'Influence': Roosevelt, Mahan, and the Concept of Sea Power." *American Quarterly* 23, no. 4 (October 1971): 585–600.

Katz, Friedrich. "Pancho Villa and the Attack on Columbus, New Mexico." *American Historical Review* 83, no. 1 (February 1978): 101–30.

Kaufman, Burton I. "United States Trade and Latin America: The Wilson Years." *Journal of American History* 58, no. 2 (September 1971): 342–63.

Kennedy, Philip W. "Race and American Expansion in Cuba and Puerto Rico, 1895–1905." *Journal of Black Studies* 1, no. 3 (March 1971): 306–16.

Kiernan, V. G. "Foreign Interests in the War of the Pacific." *Hispanic American Historical Review* 35, no. 1 (February 1955): 14–36.

Kramer, Paul A. "Empires, Exceptions, and Anglo-Saxons: Race and Rule Between the British and U.S. Empires, 1880–1910." *Journal of American History* 88, no. 4 (March 2002): 1315–53.

———. "How Not to Write the History of U.S. Empire." *Diplomatic History* 42, no. 5 (2018): 911–31.

———. "Power and Connection: Imperial Histories of the United States in the World." *American Historical Review* 116, no. 5 (December 2011): 1348–91.

LaFeber, Walter, and Robert L. Beisner. Comments on "American Imperialism: The Worst Chapter in Almost Any Book." *American Historical Review* 83, no. 3 (June 1978): 669–78.

LaFeber, Walter. "The American Business Community and Cleveland's Venezuelan Message." *Business History Review* 34, no. 4 (Winter 1960): 393–402.

———. "The Background of Cleveland's Venezuelan Policy: A Reinterpretation." *American Historical Review* 66, no. 4 (July 1961): 947–67.

———. "United States Depression Diplomacy and the Brazilian Revolution, 1893–1894." *Hispanic American Historical Review* 40, no. 1 (February 1960): 107–18.

Langer, William L. "Farewell to Empire." *Foreign Affairs* 41, no. 1 (October 1962): 115–30.

Langley, Lester D. "Negotiating New Treaties with Panama: 1936." *Hispanic American Historical Review* 48, no. 2 (May 1968): 220–33.

———. "The World Crisis and the Good Neighbor Policy in Panama, 1936–41." *The Americas* 24, no. 2 (October 1967): 137–52.

Leuchtenburg, William E. "Progressivism and Imperialism: The Progressive Movement and American Foreign Policy, 1898–1916." *Mississippi Valley Historical Review* 39, no. 3 (December 1952): 483–504.

Livermore, Seward W. "Battleship Diplomacy in South America: 1905–1925." *Journal of Modern History* 16, no. 1 (March 1944): 31–48.

———. "Theodore Roosevelt, the American Navy, and the Venezuelan Crisis of 1902–1903." *American Historical Review* 51, no. 3 (April 1946): 452–71.

Lowenthal, Abraham F. "The United States and the Dominican Republic to 1965: Background to Intervention." *Caribbean Studies* 10, no. 2 (July 1970): 30–55.

Luthin, Reinhard H. "St. Bartholomew: Sweden's Colonial and Diplomatic Adventure in the Caribbean." *Hispanic American Historical Review* 14, no. 3 (August 1934): 307–24.

Maass, Matthias. "Catalyst for the Roosevelt Corollary: Arbitrating the 1902–1903 Venezuela Crisis and Its Impact on the Development of the Roosevelt Corollary to the Monroe Doctrine." *Diplomacy & Statecraft* 20, no. 3 (Fall 2009): 383–402.

Macdonnell, Francis. "The Search for a Second Zimmermann Telegram: FDR, BSC, and the Latin American Front." *International Journal of Intelligence and CounterIntelligence* 4, no. 4 (1990): 487–505.

Major, John. "Who Wrote the Hay–Bunau-Varilla Convention?" *Diplomatic History* 8, no. 2 (Spring 1984): 115–23.

Markowitz, Gerald E. "Progressivism and Imperialism: A Return to First Principles." *The Historian* 37, no. 2 (February 1975): 257–75.

Martínez-Fernández, Luis. "Caudillos, Annexationism, and the Rivalry Between Empires in the Dominican Republic, 1844–1874." *Diplomatic History* 17, no. 4 (Fall 1993): 571–97.

Maurer, Noel, and Carlos Yu. "What T. R. Took: The Economic Impact of the Panama Canal, 1903–1937." *Journal of Economic History* 68, no. 3 (September 2008): 686–721.

McLean, Malcolm D. "O. Henry in Honduras." *American Literary Realism, 1870–1910* 1, no. 3 (Summer 1968): 39–46.

McPherson, Alan. "Herbert Hoover, Occupation Withdrawal, and the Good Neighbor Policy." *Presidential Studies Quarterly* 44, no. 4 (December 2014): 623–39.

Meyer, Michael C. "The Arms of the *Ypiranga*." *Hispanic American Historical Review* 50, no. 3 (January 1970): 543–56.

———. "Felix Sommerfeld and the Columbus Raid of 1916." *Arizona and the West* 25, no. 3 (Autumn 1983): 213–28.

———. "The Mexican-German Conspiracy of 1915." *The Americas* 23, no. 1 (July 1966): 76–89.

Miller, Robert Ryal. "Arms Across the Border: United States Aid to Juárez During the French Intervention in Mexico." *Transactions of the American Philosophical Society* 63, no. 6 (1973): 1–68.

————. "Lew Wallace and the French Intervention in Mexico." *Indiana Magazine of History* 59, no. 1 (March 1963): 31–50.

Millett, Allan R. "U.S. Interventions Abroad, 1798–1999." *Strategic Review* 28, no. 2 (Spring 2000): 28–38.

Millett, Richard, and G. Dale Gaddy. "Administering the Protectorates: The U.S. Occupation of Haiti and the Dominican Republic." *Revista/Review Interamericana* 6, no. 3 (Fall 1976): 383–402.

Minger, Ralph Eldin. "William H. Taft and the United States Intervention in Cuba in 1906." *Hispanic American Historical Review* 41, no. 1 (February 1961): 75–89.

Mitchener, Kris James, and Marc Weidenmier. "Empire, Public Goods, and the Roosevelt Corollary." *Journal of Economic History* 65, no. 3 (September 2005): 658–92.

Morgan, William Michael. "The Anti-Japanese Origins of the Hawaiian Annexation Treaty of 1897." *Diplomatic History* 6, no. 1 (Winter 1982): 23–44.

Morris, Edmund. "'A Few Pregnant Days': Theodore Roosevelt and the Venezuelan Crisis of 1902." *Theodore Roosevelt Association Journal* 15, no. 1 (Winter 1989): 3–13.

————. "'A Matter of Extreme Urgency': Theodore Roosevelt, Wilhelm II, and the Venezuela Crisis of 1902." *Naval War College Review* 55, no. 2 (Spring 2002): 73–85.

Munch, Francis J. "Villa's Columbus Raid: Practical Politics or German Design?" *New Mexico Historical Review* 44, no. 3 (July 1969): 189–214.

Munro, Dana G. "Dollar Diplomacy in Nicaragua, 1909–1913." *Hispanic American Historical Review* 38, no. 2 (May 1958): 209–34.

Murnane, John R. "Japan's Monroe Doctrine?: Re-Framing the Story of Pearl Harbor." *The History Teacher* 40, no. 4 (August 2007): 503–20.

Nelson, William Javier. "The Haitian Political Situation and Its Effect on the Dominican Republic: 1849–1877." *The Americas* 45, no. 2 (October 1988): 227–35.

Ninkovich, Frank. "Theodore Roosevelt: Civilization as Ideology." *Diplomatic History* 10, no. 3 (Summer 1986): 221–45.

Offner, John L. "McKinley and the Spanish-American War." *Presidential Studies Quarterly* 34, no. 1 (March 2004): 50–61.

Osborne, Thomas J. "Trade or War?: America's Annexation of Hawaii Reconsidered." *Pacific Historical Review* 50, no. 3 (August 1981): 285–307.

Palen, Marc-William. "The Imperialism of Economic Nationalism, 1890–1913." *Diplomatic History* 39, no. 1 (January 2015): 157–85.

Pampinella, Stephen. "'The Way of Progress and Civilization': Racial Hierarchy and US State Building in Haiti and the Dominican Republic (1915–1922)." *Journal of Global Security Studies* 6, no. 3 (2020): 1–17.

Pani, Erika. "Dreaming of a Mexican Empire: The Political Projects of the 'Imperialistas.'" *Hispanic American Historical Review* 82, no. 1 (February 2002): 1–31.

Parks, E. Taylor, and J. Fred Rippy. "The Galápagos Islands, A Neglected Phase of American Strategy Diplomacy." *Pacific Historical Review* 9, no. 1 (March 1940): 37–45.

Parsons, Edward B. "The German-American Crisis of 1902–1903." *Historian* 33, no. 3 (May 1971): 436–52.

Patterson, John. "Latin-American Reactions to the Panama Revolution of 1903." *Hispanic American Historical Review*, 24, no. 2 (May 1944): 342–51.

Pérez, Louis A., Jr. "Armies of the Caribbean: Historical Perspectives, Historiographical Trends." *Latin American Perspectives* 14, no. 4 (Autumn 1987): 490–507.

————. "Intervention, Hegemony, and Dependency: The United States in the Circum-Caribbean, 1898–1980." *Pacific Historical Review* 51, no. 2 (May 1982): 165–94.

————. "The Meaning of the *Maine*: Causation and the Historiography of the Spanish-American War." *Pacific Historical Review* 58, no. 3 (August 1989): 293–322.

————. "Politics, Peasants, and People of Color: The 1912 'Race War' in Cuba Reconsidered." *Hispanic American Historical Review* 66, no. 3 (August 1986): 509–39.

————. "Supervision of a Protectorate: The United States and the Cuban Army, 1898–1908." *Hispanic American Historical Review* 52, no. 2 (May 1972): 250–71.

Peskin, Allan. "Blaine, Garfield, and Latin America: A New Look." *The Americas* 36, no. 1 (July 1979): 79–89.

Pierson, William Whatley, Jr. "The Political Influences of an Interoceanic Canal, 1826–1926." *Hispanic American Historical Review* 6, no. 4 (November 1926): 205–31.

Platt, D. C. M. "The Allied Coercion of Venezuela, 1902–3—A Reassessment." *Inter-American Economic Affairs* 15, no. 4 (Spring 1962): 3–28.

Pletcher, David M. "Inter-American Trade in the Early 1870s—A State Department Survey." *The Americas* 33, no. 4 (April 1977): 593–612.

————. "Reciprocity and Latin America in the Early 1890s: A Foretaste of Dollar Diplomacy." *Pacific Historical Review* 47, no. 1 (February 1978): 53–89.

————. "Rhetoric and Results: A Pragmatic View of American Economic Expansionism, 1865–98." *Diplomatic History* 5, no. 2 (Spring 1981): 93–105.

Posner, Walter H. "American Marines in Haiti, 1915–1922." *The Americas* 20, no. 3 (January 1964): 231–66.

Powell, Anna I. "Relations Between the United States and Nicaragua, 1898–1916." *Hispanic American Historical Review* 8, no. 1 (February 1928): 43–64.

Pratt, Julius W. "The 'Large Policy' of 1898." *Mississippi Valley Historical Review* 19, no. 2 (September 1932): 219–42.

Prisco, Salvatore. "Vampire Diplomacy: Nazi Economic Nationalism in Latin America, 1934–40." *Diplomacy & Statecraft* 2, no. 1 (1991): 173–81.

Pulley, Raymond H. "The United States and the Trujillo Dictatorship, 1933–1940: The High Price of Caribbean Stability." *Caribbean Studies* 5, no. 3 (October 1965): 22–31.

Rabe, Stephen G. "Inter-American Military Cooperation, 1944–1951." *World Affairs* 137, no. 2 (Fall 1974): 132–49.

Rausch, George J., Jr. "The Exile and Death of Victoriano Huerta." *Hispanic American Historical Review* 42, no. 2 (May 1962): 133–51.

Ricard, Serge. "The Roosevelt Corollary." *Presidential Studies Quarterly* 36, no. 1 (March 2006): 17–26.

Rigby, Barry. "The Origins of American Expansion in Hawaii and Samoa, 1865–1900." *International History Review* 10, no. 2 (May 1988): 221–37.

Rippy, J. Fred. "Antecedents of the Roosevelt Corollary of the Monroe Doctrine." *Pacific Historical Review* 9, no. 3 (September 1940): 267–79.

————. "The British Bondholders and the Roosevelt Corollary of the Monroe Doctrine." *Political Science Quarterly* 49, no. 2 (June 1934): 195–206.

————. "The Initiation of the Customs Receivership in the Dominican Republic." *Hispanic American Historical Review* 17, no. 4 (November 1937): 419–57.

Robertson, William Spence. "The Tripartite Treaty of London." *Hispanic American Historical Review* 20, no. 2 (May 1940): 167–89.

Rofe, J. Simon. "'Under the Influence of Mahan': Theodore and Franklin Roosevelt and Their Understanding of the National Interest." *Diplomacy & Statecraft* 19, no. 4 (2008): 732–45.

Rosenberg, Emily S. "'The Empire' Strikes Back." *Reviews in American History.* 16, no. 4 (December 1988): 585–90.

———. "Revisiting Dollar Diplomacy: Narratives of Money and Manliness." *Diplomatic History* 22, no. 2 (Spring 1998): 155–76.

Russ, William A., Jr. "Hawaiian Labor and Immigration Problems Before Annexation." *Journal of Modern History* 15, no. 3 (September 1943): 207–22.

Salisbury, Richard V. "Mexico, the United States, and the 1926–1927 Nicaraguan Crisis." *Hispanic American Historical Review* 66, no. 2 (January 1986): 319–39.

———. "Revolution and Recognition: A British Perspective on Isthmian Affairs During the 1920s." *The Americas* 48, no. 3 (January 1992): 331–49.

Sandos, James A. "German Involvement in Northern Mexico, 1915–1916: A New Look at the Columbus Raid." *Hispanic American Historical Review* 50, no. 1 (February 1970): 70–88.

Schiff, Warren. "German Military Penetration into Mexico During the Late Díaz Period." *Hispanic American Historical Review* 39, no. 4 (November 1959): 568–79.

Seager, Robert, II. "Ten Years Before Mahan: The Unofficial Case for the New Navy, 1880–1890." *Mississippi Valley Historical Review* 40, no. 3 (December 1953): 491–512.

Sensabaugh, Leon F. "The Attitude of the United States Toward the Colombia–Costa Rica Arbitral Proceedings." *Hispanic American Historical Review* 19, no. 1 (February 1939): 16–30.

Sessions, Gene A. "The Clark Memorandum Myth." *The Americas* 34, no. 1 (July 1977): 40–58.

Sewell, Mike. "Political Rhetoric and Policy-Making: James G. Blaine and Britain." *Journal of American Studies* 24, no. 1 (April 1990): 61–84.

Shi, David E. "Seward's Attempt to Annex British Colombia, 1865–1869." *Pacific Historical Review* 47, no. 2 (May 1978): 217–38.

Siracusa, Joseph M. "Progressivism, Imperialism, and the Leuchtenburg Thesis, 1952–1974: An Historiographical Appraisal." *Australian Journal of Politics & History* 20, no. 3 (1974): 312–25.

Sloan, Jennie A. "Anglo-American Relations and the Venezuelan Boundary Dispute." *Hispanic American Historical Review* 18, no. 4 (November 1938): 486–506.

Small, Melvin. "The United States and the German 'Threat' to the Hemisphere, 1905–1914." *The Americas* 28, no. 3 (January 1972): 252–70.

Smith, Daniel M. "Bainbridge Colby and the Good Neighbor Policy, 1920–1921." *Mississippi Valley Historical Review* 50, no. 1 (June 1963): 56–78.

Smith, Ephraim K. "'A Question from Which We Could Not Escape': William McKinley and the Decision to Acquire the Philippine Islands." *Diplomatic History* 9, no. 4 (Fall 1985): 363–75.

Smith, Joseph. "Britain and the Brazilian Naval Revolt of 1893–4." *Journal of Latin American Studies* 2, no. 2 (November 1970): 175–98.

Smith, Robert Freeman. "Cuba: Laboratory for Dollar Diplomacy, 1898–1917." *The Historian* 28, no. 4 (August 1966): 586–609.

Snowbarger, Willis E. "Pearl Harbor in Pacific Strategy, 1898–1908." *The Historian* 19, no. 4 (August 1957): 361–84.

Speck, Mary. "Closed-Door Imperialism: The Politics of Cuban-U.S. Trade, 1902–1933." *Hispanic American Historical Review* 85, no. 3 (August 2005): 449–83.

Spector, Ronald. "Roosevelt, the Navy, and the Venezuelan Controversy, 1902–1903." *American Neptune* 32, no. 4 (October 1972): 257–63.

Spence, Richard B. "K. A. Jahnke and the German Sabotage Campaign in the United States and Mexico, 1914–1918." *The Historian* 59, no. 1 (Fall 1996): 89–112.

Spennemann, Dirk H. R. "The United States Annexation of Wake Atoll, Central Pacific Ocean." *Journal of Pacific History* 33, no. 2 (September 1998): 239–47.

Spetter, Allan. "Harrison and Blaine: Foreign Policy, 1889–1893." *Indiana Magazine of History* 65, no. 3 (1969): 215–27.

Steigerwald, David. "The Reclamation of Woodrow Wilson?" *Diplomatic History* 23, no. 1 (Winter 1999): 79–99.

Tate, Merze. "Hawaii: A Symbol of Anglo-American Rapprochement." *Political Science Quarterly* 79, no. 4 (December 1964): 555–75.

Taylor, Lawrence D. "Gunboat Diplomacy's Last Fling in the New World: The British Seizure of San Quintin, April 1911." *The Americas* 52, no. 4 (April 1996): 521–43.

Thomas, David Y. "The Monroe Doctrine from Roosevelt to Roosevelt." *South Atlantic Quarterly* 34, no. 2 (April 1935): 117–36.

Thompson, J. A. "William Appleman Williams and the 'American Empire.'" *Journal of American Studies* 7, no. 1 (April 1973): 91–104.

Thompson, John A. "The Exaggeration of American Vulnerability: The Anatomy of a Tradition." *Diplomatic History* 16, no. 1 (Winter 1992): 23–43.

Tillman, Ellen D. "Militarizing Dollar Diplomacy in the Early Twentieth-Century Dominican Republic: Centralization and Resistance." *Hispanic American Historical Review* 95, no. 2 (May 2015): 269–97.

Trask, Roger R. "George F. Kennan's Report on Latin America." *Diplomatic History* 2, no. 3 (Summer 1978): 307–11.

Trow, Clifford W. "Woodrow Wilson and the Mexican Interventionist Movement of 1919." *Journal of American History* 58, no. 1 (June 1971): 46–72.

Turk, Richard W. "The United States Navy and the 'Taking' of Panama, 1901–1903." *Military Affairs* 38, no. 3 (October 1974): 92–96.

Turner, Frederick C. "Anti-Americanism in Mexico, 1910–1913." *Hispanic American Historical Review* 47, no. 4 (November 1967): 502–18.

Vagts, Alfred. "Hopes and Fears of an American-German War, 1870–1915 I." *Political Science Quarterly* 54, no. 4 (December 1939): 514–35.

———. "Hopes and Fears of an American-German War, 1870–1915 II." *Political Science Quarterly* 55, no. 1 (March 1940): 53–76.

Valone, Stephen J. "'Weakness Offers Temptation': William H. Seward and the Reassertion of the Monroe Doctrine." *Diplomatic History* 19, no. 4 (Fall 1995): 583–99.

Veeser, Cyrus. "Inventing Dollar Diplomacy: The Gilded-Age Origins of the Roosevelt Corollary to the Monroe Doctrine." *Diplomatic History* 27, no. 3 (June 2003): 301–26.

Vivian, James F. "The Pan-American Conference Act of May 10, 1888: President Cleveland and the Historians." *The Americas* 27, no. 2 (October 1970): 185–92.

———. "The 'Taking' of the Panama Canal Zone: Myth and Reality." *Diplomatic History* 4, no. 1 (Winter 1980): 95–100.

Volwiler, A. T. "Harrison, Blaine, and American Foreign Policy, 1889–1893." *Proceedings of the American Philosophical Society* 79, no. 4 (November 1938): 637–48.

Ward, Marianne, and John Devereux. "The Road Not Taken: Pre-Revolutionary Cuban Living Standards in Comparative Perspective." *Journal of Economic History* 72, no. 1 (March 2012): 104–33.

Weisberger, Bernard A. "The Strange Affair of the Taking of the Panama Canal Zone." *American Heritage* 27, no. 6 (October 1976): 6–11, 68–77.

Wells, Samuel F., Jr. "British Strategic Withdrawal from the Western Hemisphere, 1904–1906." *Canadian Historical Review* 49, no. 4 (December 1968): 335–56.

White, Donald W. "The 'American Century' in World History." *Journal of World History* 3, no. 1 (1992): 105–27.

Whitfield, Stephen J. "Strange Fruit: The Career of Samuel Zemurray." *American Jewish History* 73, no. 3 (March 1984): 307–23.

Wicks, Daniel H. "Dress Rehearsal: United States Intervention on the Isthmus of Panama, 1885." *Pacific Historical Review* 49, no. 4 (November 1980): 581–605.

Wright, Theodore P., Jr. "Free Elections in the Latin American Policy of the United States." *Political Science Quarterly* 74, no. 1 (March 1959): 89–112.

———. "Honduras: A Case Study of United States Support of Free Elections in Central America." *Hispanic American Historical Review* 40, no. 2 (May 1960): 212–23.

———. "United States Electoral Intervention in Cuba." *Inter-American Economic Affairs* 8, no. 3 (Winter 1959): 50–71.

Young, George B. "Intervention Under the Monroe Doctrine: The Olney Corollary." *Political Science Quarterly* 57, no. 2 (June 1942): 247–80.

Zelikow, Philip. "Why Did America Cross the Pacific?: Reconstructing the U.S. Decision to Take the Philippines, 1898–99." *Texas National Security Review* 1, no. 1 (December 2017): 36–67.

Zevin, Robert. "An Interpretation of American Imperialism." *Journal of Economic History* 32, no. 1 (March 1972): 316–60.

Theses and Dissertations

Brown, Robert Benaway. "Guns over the Border: American Aid to the Juárez Government During the French Intervention." PhD diss., University of Michigan, 1951.

Chapin, James Burke. "Hamilton Fish and American Expansion." PhD diss., Cornell University, 1971.

Crabbe, Irene E. "John L. Stevens and American Expansion in Hawaii." PhD diss., University of South Carolina, 1957.

Griffin, Albert Joseph, Jr. "Intelligence Versus Impulse: William H. Seward and the Threat of War with France over Mexico, 1861–1867." PhD diss., University of New Hampshire, 2003.

Guthrie, Wayne Lee. "The Anglo-German Intervention in Venezuela, 1902–03." PhD diss., University of California, San Diego, 1983.

MacMichael, David Charles. "The United States and the Dominican Republic, 1871–1940: A Cycle in Caribbean Diplomacy." PhD diss., University of Oregon, 1964.

McCoy, Mary Ellene Chenevey. "Guantánamo Bay: The United States Naval Base and Its Relationship with Cuba." PhD diss., University of Akron, 1995.

Mukharji, Aroop. "Sea Change: McKinley, Roosevelt, and the Expansion of U.S. Foreign Policy 1897–1909." PhD diss., Harvard University, April 2020.

Neymeyer, Robert James. "The Establishment and Operation of the Dominican Republic Customs Receivership, 1905–1916." PhD diss., University of Iowa, 1990.

Ofek, Hillel. "A Just Peace: Grover Cleveland, William McKinley, and the Moral Basis of American Foreign Policy." PhD diss., University of Texas at Austin, 2018.

Pennanen, Gary Alvin. "The Foreign Policy of William Maxwell Evarts." PhD diss., University of Wisconsin, 1969.

Reynolds, Bradley Michael. "Guantanamo Bay, Cuba: The History of an American Naval Base and Its Relationship to the Formulation of United States Foreign Policy and Military Strategy Toward the Caribbean, 1895–1910." PhD diss., University of South Carolina, 1982.

Richter, William Lee. "The Army in Texas During Reconstruction, 1865–1870." PhD diss., Louisiana State University, 1970.

Rigby, Barry Russ. "American Expansion in the Pacific and Caribbean Islands 1865–1877." PhD diss., Duke University, 1978.

Rollins, John William. "Frederick Theodore Frelinghuysen, 1817–1885: The Politics and Diplomacy of Stewardship." PhD diss., University of Wisconsin, 1974.

Vivian, James Floyd. "The South American Commission to the Three Americas Movement: The Politics of Pan Americanism, 1884–1890." PhD diss., American University, 1971.

Winchester, Richard Carlyle. "James G. Blaine and the Ideology of American Expansionism." PhD diss., University of Rochester, 1966.

INDEX

Gilbert Horst

Sean A. Mirski is a lawyer and U.S. foreign policy scholar who has worked on national security issues across multiple U.S. presidential administrations. A term member of the Council on Foreign Relations, he currently practices national security, foreign relations, and appellate law at Arnold & Porter Kaye Scholer LLP, and is also a Visiting Scholar at the Hoover Institution at Stanford University. He previously served in the U.S. Department of Defense under both Republican and Democratic administrations as Special Counsel to the General Counsel, where he earned the Office of the Secretary of Defense's Award for Outstanding Achievement. He has written extensively on American history, international relations, law, and politics, including as editor of the book *Crux of Asia: China, India, and the Emerging Global Order* (CEIP 2013). Earlier in his career, he clerked for two U.S. Supreme Court justices and served as a fellow at the Carnegie Endowment for International Peace. Named one of *Forbes* magazine's "30 Under 30," he graduated *magna cum laude* from Harvard Law School and holds a master's degree in international relations with honors from the University of Chicago.

PublicAffairs is a publishing house founded in 1997. It is a tribute to the standards, values, and flair of three persons who have served as mentors to countless reporters, writers, editors, and book people of all kinds, including me.

I. F. STONE, proprietor of *I. F. Stone's Weekly*, combined a commitment to the First Amendment with entrepreneurial zeal and reporting skill and became one of the great independent journalists in American history. At the age of eighty, Izzy published *The Trial of Socrates*, which was a national bestseller. He wrote the book after he taught himself ancient Greek.

BENJAMIN C. BRADLEE was for nearly thirty years the charismatic editorial leader of *The Washington Post*. It was Ben who gave the *Post* the range and courage to pursue such historic issues as Watergate. He supported his reporters with a tenacity that made them fearless and it is no accident that so many became authors of influential, best-selling books.

ROBERT L. BERNSTEIN, the chief executive of Random House for more than a quarter century, guided one of the nation's premier publishing houses. Bob was personally responsible for many books of political dissent and argument that challenged tyranny around the globe. He is also the founder and longtime chair of Human Rights Watch, one of the most respected human rights organizations in the world.

· · ·

For fifty years, the banner of Public Affairs Press was carried by its owner Morris B. Schnapper, who published Gandhi, Nasser, Toynbee, Truman, and about 1,500 other authors. In 1983, Schnapper was described by *The Washington Post* as "a redoubtable gadfly." His legacy will endure in the books to come.

Peter Osnos, *Founder*